dBASE — FROM THE DOT PROMPT

An Introduction to Structured Programming Using dBASE IV

dBASE — FROM THE DOT PROMPT

An Introduction to Structured
Programming Using dBASE IV

By

Warren M. Littlefield

STATE UNIVERSITY OF NEW YORK PRESS

Cover photo: courtesy Library of Congress, Washington, DC. Used by permission. The Library of Congress is the largest database in the world.

Published by
State University of New York Press, Albany

© 1993 State University of New York

All rights reserved

Printed in the United States of America

No part of this book may be used or reproduced in any manner whatsoever without written permission except in the case of brief quotations embodied in critical articles and reviews.

For information, address State University of New York Press, State University Plaza, Albany, N.Y., 12246

Production by Marilyn P. Semerad
Marketing by Fran Keneston

Library of Congress Cataloging-in-Publication Data

Littlefield, Warren M., 1942-
    dBASE, from the dot prompt : an introduction to structured programming using dBASE IV / by Warren M. Littlefield.
       p.   cm.
    Includes index.
    ISBN 0-7914-1780-8 (pbk. : alk. paper)
    1. Data base management. 2. dBASE IV (Computer file)
  3. Structured programming. I. Title.
  QA76.76.063F644   1993
    005.75' 65—dc20   93-18937
                                                                              CIP

10 9 8 7 6 5 4

This book is dedicated to Gurumayi Chidvilasananda,
the source of inspiration in my life.

CONTENTS

Preface	xvii
Acknowledgments	xxiii
Introduction	1

Chapter 1 Creating Your First Database   5

1.1	Preparing Your Diskette	6
1.2	Getting Into dBASE4	7
1.3	Creating a Database	10
1.4	Appending Records to a Database	15
1.5	Editing the Database	17
1.6	Browsing the Database	19
1.7	Appending to Your Database While in EDIT	22
1.8	Listing Your Database	26
1.9	Quitting from dBASE4	28
1.10	Example II: A Checkbook/Budget Account	29
1.11	Summary	30
1.12	Review	31
1.13	Laboratory Work	31
1.14	Exercises	32

Chapter 2 Editing Your Database   35

2.1	Modifying your Database	36
2.2	Deleting Fields from the Database Structure	39
2.3	DISPLAYing your Database One Page at a Time	39
2.4	Deleting Records from your Database	41
2.5	Inserting a Record into a Database	47

2.6	Useful Features of the BROWSE Mode	50
2.6.1	Appending new data in BROWSE	50
2.6.2	Entering Data into a Database by Field	51
2.6.3	Browse Menu Options	54
2.7	Example II: Expanding the ACCOUNTS database	59
2.7.1	Navigating Around the Database in BROWSE Mode	61
2.8	Summary	67
2.9	Review	68
2.10	Laboratory Work	68
2.11	Exercises	68

Chapter 3 Ordering a Database   71

3.1	Sorting a Database	72
3.2	Erasing a Database	78
3.3	Indexing a Database	80
3.3.1	Creating Individual (.NDX) Indexes	80
3.3.2	Indexing on Two Character Fields	81
3.4	Use of a Multiple or Production (.MDX) Index	83
3.4.1	Making a Multiple Index on LASTNAME + FIRSTNAME	84
3.4.2	Indexing on a Date Field and Character Field	85
3.4.3	Indexing on Numeric and Character Fields	87
3.4.4	Indexing on a Logical Field	88
3.4.5	Indexing in Descending Order	89
3.5	Selecting the Master Index in a Production (.MDX) Index	91
3.5.1	Selecting Individual (.NDX) Indexes	94
3.6	Deleting Indexes	95
3.7	Example II: Use of INDEXing Options in ACCOUNTS Database	96
3.7.1	Use of the UNIQUE Option	97
3.7.2	Use of the FOR Option	98
3.8	Summary	100
3.9	Review	101
3.10	Laboratory Work	101
3.11	Exercises	102

Chapter 4 Columnar Reports   103

4.1	The Report Form Generator	104
4.1.1	Creating a Columnar Report	106
4.1.2	Modifying Report Forms	118
4.2	Example II: Quick Layout for ACCOUNTS Database	122
4.2.1	Using Group Bands with Subtotals	133
4.2.2	Printing a Group Report	139
4.3	Example II: Use of the Calculated Field in a Report Form	141
4.3.1	Use of a Running Sum of a Field in the Detail Line	149
4.4	Summary	153
4.5	Review	153
4.6	Laboratory Work	153
4.7	Exercises	154

Chapter 5 Conditional Reports & Searches   157

5.1	Selecting Records in a Database	158
5.2	Conditional Reports	158
5.2.1	The HEADING Clause	159
5.2.2	Relational Operators	160
5.2.3	Use of the SET FILTER Command	162
5.2.4	Conditional Report Using a Date Function	163
5.2.5	Conditional Report Using the Substring Relational Operator	165
5.2.6	Use of the Logical Function LIKE(,) in a Filter	166
5.3	Calculations	168
5.3.1	The **COUNT** Command	168
5.3.2	Logical Operators	170
5.3.3	The **SUM** Command	170
5.3.4	Arithmetic Operators	171
5.3.5	The **AVERAGE** Command	172
5.3.6	Use of the **CALCULATE** Command	172
5.4	Searches	174
5.4.1	Searching Using the **LOCATE** Instruction	174
5.4.2	Searching Using the **FIND** and **SEEK** Commands	176
5.4.3	LOCATE Search versus INDEX Search	180

5.5	Summary	180
5.6	Review	181
5.7	Laboratory Work	181
5.8	Exercises	182

Chapter 6 Labels, Mailmerge Reports and Forms 183

6.1	Label Form Generator	184
6.1.1	Creating a Label Form	184
6.1.2	Printing Sample Labels	192
6.2	Mailmerge Report Form	194
6.2.1	Importing a Text File Letter into the Mailmerge Layout	204
6.3	The Screen Generator	205
6.3.1	The Format File	219
6.4	Summary	220
6.5	Review	221
6.6	Laboratory Work	221
6.7	Exercises	221

Chapter 7 Command Files & Memory Variables 225

7.1	Introduction to Command Files	226
7.1.1	Creating an "Add Records" Command File	226
7.1.2	Use of the WAIT Command in the COMPPACK Command File	230
7.2	Memory Variables	232
7.2.1	Use of System Memory Variables	233
7.2.2	Design of the Print Report Command File: COMPREPO.PRG	235
7.2.3	Design of the Label and Mailmerge Command Files	235
7.3	Design of a Search/Edit Command File	238
7.3.1	The @ and SAY Display Instructions	238
7.3.2	The **GET** and **READ** Instructions	241
7.3.3	The Design of COMPEDIT.PRG	242
7.4	Design of a Menu Driving Command File	249
7.5	Summary	254

7.6	Review	255
7.7	Laboratory Work	256
7.8	Exercises	257
7.9	Term Project	258

Chapter 8 Selection   261

8.1	Structured Programming	262
8.2	Flow Charts	264
8.3	Binary Selection	265
8.4	Example of Binary Selection, COM_EDIT.prg	268
8.5	Multiple Selection—The DO CASE Structure	273
8.6	Alternative Data Entry Commands	276
8.6.1	The **INPUT** Command	278
8.6.2	The **ACCEPT** Command	279
8.6.3	The **WAIT** Command Revisited	280
8.7	Saving, Restoring and Releasing Memory Variables	280
8.8	The **REPLACE** Command	282
8.8.1	Example Using the **REPLACE** Command for Block Replacements	283
8.8.2	The **REPLACE ALL** Command	285
8.9	Program Example Using **ACCEPT, INPUT, WAIT** and **REPLACE**	286
8.10	Summary	288
8.11	Review	291
8.12	Laboratory Work	292
8.13	Exercises	292
8.14	Term Project	293

Chapter 9 Iteration   295

9.1	Introduction to The Loop	296
9.1.1	The **DO WHILE** Command	297
9.1.2	Example of Use of **DO WHILE** Loop	298
9.2	Design of a Delay Loop	299
9.3	Use of **DO WHILE** Loop with EOF() Function	303
9.4	The Deletion Program—COM_DELE.prg	309
9.5	Design of a Fast Indexed Search Program	313

9.5.1	The **LOCATE WHILE** Instruction	315
9.5.2	Use of the **FOUND()** Function	316
9.5.3	An Example of Indexed Search—COM_EVAL.prg	316
9.6	Use of the **SCAN—ENDSCAN** Instruction	321
9.6.1	The Design of a Range Search Program	322
9.6.2	Example: The Design of COM_GRAD.prg	323
9.6.3	Use of the **SCAN—ENDSCAN** Loop for a LOCATE Search	324
9.6.4	Use of the **SCAN FOR ...** Loop	328
9.7	Remarks on the use of the **WHILE** Clause	330
9.8	Summary	331
9.9	Review	331
9.10	Laboratory Work	332
9.11	Exercises	332
9.12	Term Project	333

Chapter 10 System Organization   335

10.1	Bottom Up Systems Design	336
10.2	The Systems Structure Chart	337
10.3	Menu Driver Program with Pop-Up Windows	339
10.3.1	Design of Menu Sub-Modules	344
10.4	Use of Windows in Sub-Menus	347
10.5	Program Structure Chart	350
10.6	Use of Procedures in dBASE	352
10.6.1	Appending Programs Together to Form COM_PROC.prg	355
10.6.2	Design of a Procedure Driver Program	357
10.7	Comments About Compiled Code in dBASE IV	360
10.8	Summary	362
10.9	Review	363
10.10	Laboratory Work	364
10.11	Exercises	364
10.12	Term Project	365

Chapter 11 Controlling Your Environment   367

11.1	The **SET** Command	368
11.1.1	The **SET** Mode	370
11.1.2	The **SET FUNCTION TO** Command	372
11.1.3	Setting a Color Display	373
11.2	The CONFIG.DB File	374
11.2.1	DBSETUP Routine	380
11.3	Password Protection	386
11.4	Backing Up Your System	389
11.4.1	Backing Up a Floppy Diskette	389
11.4.2	Backing Up Between Different Types of Media	390
11.5	Running DOS Commands While in dBASE	391
11.5.1	Macros	394
11.6	Modification of COMPCLAS System to Include BACKUP.prg	396
11.7	Summary	399
11.8	Review	399
11.9	Laboratory Work	400
11.10	Exercises	400
11.11	Term Project	401

Chapter 12 Debugging & Documentation   403

12.1	Debugging	404
12.1.1	Using the **Debugger**	404
12.1.2	Use of **SET TRAP** Command to Locate Errors	411
12.1.3	Obtaining a Printed Trace of Your Program Execution	411
12.1.4	Use Modular Programming to Minimize Errors	413
12.2	Creating Help and Reference Screens	414
12.2.1	Creating Help Screens	415
12.2.2	Creating Reference/Help Screens	419
12.3	Documentation	427
12.3.1	Brief Narrative of System Function	428
12.3.2	User Instruction Guide	430
12.3.3	Sample Reports	430
12.3.4	Program Structure Diagram	430
12.3.5	System Structure Chart Diagram	439

12.3.6	Database Contents List	441
12.3.7	List of all Indexes & their Keys	443
12.3.8	Fully Documented Program Listings	443
12.3.9	Optional Documentation	444
12.4	Summary	444
12.5	Review	448
12.6	Laboratory Work	448
12.7	Exercises	448
12.8	Term Project	449

Chapter 13 Accounts System—Multiple Files   451

13.1	Top Down Systems Design	452
13.1.1	The Budget Database	453
13.1.2	System Structure Chart for ACCOUNTS System	454
13.1.3	The Database ACCOUNTS.DBF	455
13.2	Use of Saved Memory Variables to Select Multiple Databases	458
13.3	Use of Stubs in Top Down Implementation	460
13.4	Design of the Update Accounts Sub-Modules	463
13.4.1	Design of BROWSIT.prg	463
13.4.2	Design of CATHELP.prg— Use of Multiple Databases	464
13.4.3	Design of REBALANC.prg	466
13.4.4	Design of RECONCIL.prg	472
13.5	Powerful Commands— The Design of SPREADIT.prg	473
13.5.1	Use of the **TOTAL** Command	474
13.5.2	Use of the **SET RELATION TO** Command	476
13.5.3	Design of BROWBUDG.prg	478
13.6	Design of the SETUP Module	480
13.6.1	The Use of a "Do Until" Loop	482
13.6.2	The Design of CHANGEYR.prg	487
13.7	Use of **FUNCTION** and **PICTURE** in Design of SEARCAT.prg	493
13.8	The Budget Report	496
13.9	Summary	501

13.10	Review	503
13.11	Laboratory Work	503
13.12	Exercises	503
13.13	Term Project	505

Chapter 14 Functions, Arrays & Queries   507

14.1	User Defined Functions	508
14.1.1	Elements of User-Defined Functions	508
14.1.2	Function Example: **CDATE()**	509
14.2	Use of Arrays in dBASE	511
14.3	PUBLIC & PRIVATE Memory Variables	515
14.4	Inserting Memory Variables Into a Customized Screen Form	519
14.5	Design of the Re-Calculation Function: **RETOTAL()**	524
14.5.1	Attaching a Function to a Screen Entry	524
14.5.2	The Program BUDGEDIT.prg	528
14.6	Query Generator	528
14.6.1	Creating a QUERY of Two Databases Linked Together on a Single Common Key	530
14.6.2	Creating a QUERY of Multiple Databases Using Multiple Keys	539
14.6.3	Creating a Composite Database	549
14.7	Use of the **JOIN** Command	551
14.8	Use of the **UPDATE** Command	554
14.8.1	Design of an Updating Program for the COMPCLAS System	555
14.9	Summary	557
14.10	Review	558
14.11	Laboratory Work	558
14.12	Exercises	559
14.13	Term Project	562

Appendix A Setting Up the Proper Pathways and Directories 563

A.1	Accessing an Already Installed Copy of dBASE IV on Your Hard Drive	563
A.2	Creating an AUTOEXEC.BAT file that Establishes the Proper Pathway	564
A.3	Creating a CONFIG.SYS file that Establishes the Proper System Config	566
A.4	Creating the Proper Directories	567

Appendix B Free Form Reports 569

B.1	The Free Form Report	569

Appendix C Query By Example 575

C.1	Creation of Simple Queries	575
C.2	Queries With More than One Condition in an AND Relationship	581
C.3	Queries With More Than One Condition in an OR Relationship	581
C.3.1	Queries with Inclusive OR Conditions Existing in the Same Field	581
C.3.2	Queries With Inclusive OR Conditions Existing in Different Fields	584

Index 587

PREFACE

There are at least two ways one can learn to speak a foreign language. One is to stay at home and learn it from a textbook, memorizing a lot of words. Another is to take your classes in a foreign country where you will actually be speaking the language, and learn your vocabulary as it naturally arises. I've had four years of French by the first method, and I've had two years of Spanish by the second method. I still speak Spanish fluently, but I'm afraid I can't even order from a French menu[1] without help.

One of the main things that makes this book different from others that I have seen is that no topic is introduced until it arises naturally. Hence, the order in which topics are presented is not necessarily the order you will see in most texts. I have always found it difficult, in my classes, to present a topic that seemed to be totally out of context simply because the author: 1) decided that it should be mentioned at that time, or 2) for completeness.

Most of the books out on the market are written around the dBASE ASSIST or "Control Center", which makes most of the commands menu driven. This is fine if you do not desire to do any programming work in dBASE. However, I teach dBASE from the point of view of its being a full fledged programming language. If you want to learn a language, you have to learn to use the vocabulary, not consult a menu.

This book teaches dBASE IV as a first programming language. The approach is a structured one as dBASE is a structured language. Even though I also teach BASIC and Pascal as

---

[1] When I was learning French, I would always carry an English-French, French-English dictionary around with me. Whenever my teacher saw me with one, she would take it from me. However, I would always buy another. Rather than making the language my own, I would always rely on looking up the French word I wanted from the English. After confiscating my seventh dictionary my teacher finally gave up and left me with my dictionary to assist me. Even after four years of French classes, I still don't speak or understand French.

In Chapter 12 debugging and documentation are discussed. SNAP[2] is presented as a documentation tool. In Chapter 13, using a *top-down* approach, a complete checkbook/budget system using multiple databases is designed. Chapter 14 introduces advanced topics including user-defined functions, arrays, and query view files linking multiple databases.

This book was specifically written using dBASE IV, Version 1.1. However, all the figures and information found in the text applies to dBASE IV Version 1.5 also. The chapters are each intended to represent the material covered in one week of a normal three hour per week course. The text was intended for use by either undergraduate students or by part-time adult students wishing to learn something about computers. The text assumes no prior knowledge of computers. It is written, however, for IBM PC, IBM PC System 2 or IBM compatible computers.

The progression of these chapters reflects the order in which the author teaches this material. The instructor is encouraged to request the student to do a term project. Enough material is presented in the first seven weeks that the student can create a system on his or her own based simply on what he or she has learned to that point. I often allow students to pair up on a project so that they can reinforce each other. By the end of the seventh week the student should be deciding what his or her term project is going to be.

By the end of the twelfth week, debugging and documentation should be on the mind of the student. Chapters 13 and 14 are intended to broaden the view of the students, but the material may not be timely enough to be incorporated into the term projects. The author usually stops assigning homework after the eleventh or twelfth week in order to give the students time to work

---

[2]**SNAP** is an XBASE documentation program written by Walter J. Kennamer and is in the public domain. Version **5.02**, may be downloaded from **COMPUSERVE** by specifying **GO FOXFORUM**, and requesting the file **SNP502.EXE** in library 6.

first languages, I prefer dBASE as a first language for two reasons: 1) The commands are higher level, hence more powerful (think what you have to go through to do a simple sort in either BASIC or Pascal), and 2) I know of no other third generation language that allows one to get an application up and running faster than in dBASE.

Three examples are carried along throughout most of the text. The first example is a computer class grade database which contains within it the seeds of most of the concepts we have to learn. The second example is a checkbook/budget database which allows the user to see how he or she is doing against their budget. The reader is assigned the task of applying the steps learned in the text to a mailing list database.

Although this is an introductory structured programming text for dBASE IV, the first six chapters involve no programming at all. Rather, elementary database creation and maintenance, indexing, report generation, customized screen forms, and searches are introduced in these chapters. The purpose here is to ensure that the reader is firmly established in the basics, as well as to accustom the reader to the dBASE language as executed in the "Interpretive" mode. Chapter 7 introduces command files written as simple sequences. If the instructor wishes to teach only a 4 — 7 week course on dBASE, he or she may cover the first 4 — 7 chapters (depending on whether or not they wish to talk about command files) without ever even reading the word "programming".

By the end of Chapter 7 the student will know how to create a small customized menu driven file handling system for two of the example databases. Selection and Looping are covered in Chapters 8 and 9. By the end of Chapter 9 the systems will have blossomed into fancier, more user friendly, file handling systems. In Chapter 10 the reader is introduced to the "System Structure Chart" and begins looking at what he or she is creating from a systems point of view. Chapter 11 shows the student how the environment may be controlled and customized by means of the CONFIG.DB file.

on their projects. However, exercises have been developed for each of the chapters in the book, including thirteen and fourteen, and the instructor is by no means bound by the author's ordering of the text material.

It is recommended, but not mandatory, that the student complete every step covered in the text on the computer itself. The appropriate command to enter is shown in **BOLD UPPER CASE** print just to the right of a dot on the page. Each screen that appears as a result of entering a command is shown as a figure, so that the student can examine the consequences of executing the commands or keystrokes.

The text is intended as a didactic aid. It allows the student to spend "efficient" time at the computer without always needing an instructor about to answer questions. In the past, my students used to complain of the hours they have wasted alone trying to figure out some step in a textbook where the author had taken a quantum leap leaving the student behind. If any student finds such gaps in this text, I would appreciate him or her bringing them to my attention. It is my intention that all steps presented in the text be small enough that anyone having the desire to understand dBASE can negotiate them simply by reading the material.

Although the book can be used as a self teaching manual, it was not intended to replace the instructor altogether, but rather to allow him or her to teach large numbers of students simultaneously without overburdening the teacher.

I find that students learn far more doing a project of their own choice than by simply taking exams. Some students get so carried away by their projects that they continue work on them long after the semester is over. There is something very satisfying in generating a system that does exactly what you want it to do. In addition, one's self confidence with computers is enhanced by the successful completion of such a project. The last week consists of a "show and tell" session in which the students present their projects to the rest of the class.

The book makes no pretext at trying to be complete. dBASE IV is too vast a subject to be easily contained in one volume. By design, the Control Center, Applications Generator, and Catalogue files are omitted. Query files are discussed only insofar as they may be of interest to the programmer. Multi-User systems were considered to be beyond the scope of this text. Only those topics that a dBASE programmer would actually use on a single user system are discussed. As such, it is assumed that the system has been configured for "Exclusive" use only [EXCLUSIVE = ON in the CONFIG.DB file (see Chapter 11)].

If the reader finds the text worth the study time spent in its reading, and learns what he or she desires to know about programming in general and dBASE IV in particular, the author will be pleased. Enjoy!

ACKNOWLEDGMENTS

I would like to thank all those students who have made comments and corrections on the earlier drafts of this work, and encouraged me to publish it. I appreciate the patience they showed as we struggled to get it right. I particularly wish to acknowledge Mary Lu Drobysh, who painstakingly proofread and typeset this book. I am also indebted to Bill Eastman of SUNY Press, whose faith in the project never faltered. Finally, I am extremely grateful to my wife, Shyamala, for her support. It was because of her never ending encouragement that it finally did happen.

INTRODUCTION

Welcome to the world of dBASE IV. This is a rich environment in which to manipulate information and to write programs.

The first three questions that should arise for those new to dBASE and databases in general are: 1) What is a Database, 2) What is a Database Management System, and 3) Why dBASE IV in particular?

A database is defined as a collection of interrelated files stored together with minimum redundancy. Basically it is a file, or a group of integrated files that together form the aggregate of all the information contained on a particular subject. For example, a database might be the personnel records for a company, its inventory, its mailing list, its accounts payable and receivable, the credit history of all its clients, etc.

A Database Management System (DBMS) is a set of programs that create, manage, protect, and provide access to a database. dBASE IV, which is software originally written by Ashton-Tate Corporation (version 1.1), more recently having been improved by Borland (version 1.5), can be considered a generalized DBMS for databases created in its environment. However, it is more than just a DBMS. It is also a full fledged, high level programming language.

One can use dBASE in the ASSIST mode through the "Control Center", which is entirely run by use of menus and popup windows. These windows ask you to fill in the blanks (this is referred to as "Menu-Driven"). For many purposes, this is an entirely sufficient means of managing a database. There is even an applications generator available, which enables the user to generate commonly used applications in a menu-driven fashion.

However, for those of you: 1) who want to make your own customized systems; 2) who would like to be able to answer "Yes" to the question, "Would it be possible to ..."; 3) who just like to program, then you will want to make use of the powerful XBASE[3] family of programming languages. This family includes:

>Borland's dBASE IV
>Microsoft's FoxPro2
>Nantucket's Clipper

just to mention a few. It is for those of you in this category that this book is written.

FoxPro is a faster executing language than dBASE IV. Clipper creates fully executable files that will run independently of Clipper. Nevertheless, dBASE IV, versions 1.1, 1.5, and 2.0 well represent the current generation of XBASE languages, and since dBASE IV accounts for a major part of the XBASE market, dBASE IV pretty well sets the standard of what an XBASE language should look like. It is for this reason that this book is written around dBASE IV.

dBASE builds up its database file out of a collection of individual records. A record consists of a group of related fields. A field might be a person's name, an address, an account number, a zip code, a phone number, a quantity, an item description, a price, a date of birth, a person's gender, whether a person smokes or not, a pay rate, etc. By putting together a group of related fields to form a record (e.g. an individual employee's payroll record), and then combining a group of similar records (e.g. all the employees in a company), a database is created.

dBASE allows a user to do the normal things that a DBMS should do: structure data, enter data, order it in any fashion, search for any information contained in the database, select data from the database, create reports, delete information, update it, and alter the structure of the database with ease. In addition, the dBASE programming language facilitates you're creating systems that allow

---

XBASE is the generic name that refers to the family of languages that have grown up around the generations of dBASE (dBASE II, dBASE III, dBASE III Plus, and dBASE IV).

users, with no programming experience, to do their work in a customized "user friendly" environment.

I have created dozens of these systems, many for my own use as well as for others who know nothing about dBASE. It is my view that although nearly every computer user may learn how to operate a word processing program, not every user has the patience nor desire to learn how to use a DBMS. Even the dBASE IV "Control Center" can seem daunting to the uninitiated. For this reason I believe that it will continue to be necessary for developers to create customized systems for the use of those people who neither have the time nor desire to master the use of a DBMS.

In addition, there are companies that have developed enormously complex systems, selling for tens of thousands of dollars, written in an XBASE language. Multi-user hotel reservations systems, using millions of bytes of compiled code, are examples of such applications.

Whether it is for small applications, or large, for personal or for corporate use, or for simply learning how to program in a modern high level structured programming language, that this book has been designed.

CHAPTER 1

CREATING YOUR FIRST DATABASE

1.0   Topics Covered in Chapter 1

Getting into dBASE.

Creating a database.

Entering data into a database.

Looking at a database in the EDIT mode.

Looking at a database in the BROWSE mode.

Placing Memo fields in a database.

Appending new data to a database.

Printing out a listing of a Database Structure.

Printing out a listing of the contents of a database.

6   CREATING YOUR FIRST DATABASE

1.1   Preparing Your Diskette

Depending on just what type of system you have, you may enter dBASE4 in one of many ways. In this text, it will be assumed that the pathway (PATH, MAP or APPEND) has been defined to include the directory containing DBASE4. If this step is unclear to you, consult Appendix A. We will assume that you will be keeping your databases on drive A, throughout this text. If this is not the case in your situation, you may substitute whatever drive letter and directory you wish for the **A:\>** which will be used to represent the DOS[4] prompt.

Turn on your machine, and insert your diskette into Drive A: (if that is the drive you are using for your data). If the DOS prompt is not already addressing the drive you wish to use, change the logged disk drive to **A:\>** (or the one you will be using). For example, if you are currently logged into drive **C:** (if so you will see a prompt that begins with the letter C such as **C:\>**), then type **A:** at the DOS prompt and strike the enter key.

C:\> **A:**   <Enter>

Your screen should now have your DOS prompt with the blinking cursor next to it. It should look like the following:

A:\>_

The dash represents the blinking cursor.

In order to keep everything orderly in your work, we are going to create individual directories for the various systems that you will be creating in the course of this book. If you think of your diskette as a file cabinet in which you store your files, then a directory is a drawer of the file cabinet. The topmost directory (that which already exists after you have newly formatted your diskette)

---

[4]DOS refers to the Disk Operating System. It is assumed throughout the text that the user is utilizing either MS-DOS (written by Microsoft Corporation) or one of its DOS looks-alike.

CREATING YOUR FIRST DATABASE

is referred to as the "root" directory. You may think of the root directory as being the top drawer of your filing cabinet. We will not be using that drawer as DOS uses it for its own purposes.

Appendix A also tells you how to create the various subdirectories that we will be using in this course. If you have not already done so, go to Appendix A and follow the steps to create the directories[5] as well as to create a DOS prompt indicating what directory you are in.

We will now go to the COMPCLAS directory where we will be doing the bulk of the work in this text. This is done by typing CD\COMPCLAS at the DOS prompt. "CD" stands for change directory. Executing this command:

A:\> **CD\COMPCLAS**   <Enter>

note the DOS prompt changes to reflect the fact that we are now in a new directory. (From now on the word <Enter>, which refers to striking the Enter key will not be used. It will be assumed that a command is always executed by striking this key.)

A:\COMPCLAS>

1.2 Getting Into dBASE4

We are now ready to enter the dBASE4 environment. dBASE4 is an applications program just like a word processor or a spreadsheet or any other program that you have been using to do some application. We enter dBASE4 by typing **DBASE** at the DOS prompt as shown:

A:\COMPCLAS> **DBASE**

---

[5]You may Make a new Directory called **COMPCLAS** by typing **MD\COMPCLAS** at the DOS prompt.
    A:\> **MD\COMPCLAS**
You must make this directory before you can Change Directory to it.

8 CREATING YOUR FIRST DATABASE

Now your environment will change drastically. After the initial screen is shown, you will see one of two things depending on how your version of dBASE4 is configured. Either you will see a solitary dot in the lower left hand corner of the screen (see Fig. 1.1) or you will see the control center[6] with all its options (see Fig. 1.2). If what you get is the control center, strike the Escape key immediately. That is the key labeled: **Esc** . When it asks you, "Are you sure you want to abandon operation?", select "Yes" by hitting the left arrow key and then press the Enter key. (see Fig. 1.3) This will return you to the dot prompt which will be our home (Fig. 1.1).

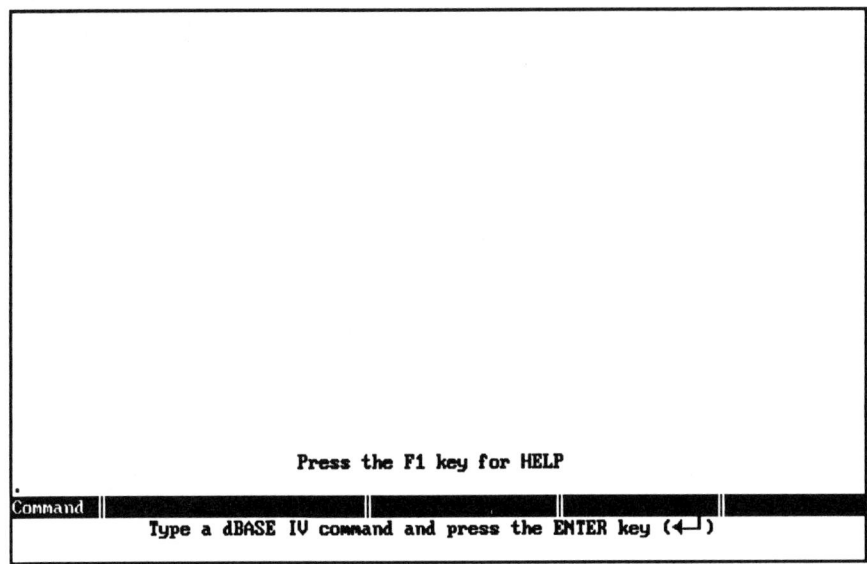

Figure 1.1 The opening screen of dBASE IV at the Dot Prompt.

The Control Center is helpful to the person who is interested in using the standard functions offered in dBASE4. However, for the person interested in going beyond and actually doing some programming in dBASE4, the Control Center can become a hindrance to learning the rich dBASE4 language. It is for this reason that we will stay away from the Control Center. Hence,

---

[6]The Control Center may be reached by typing **ASSIST** at the dot prompt.

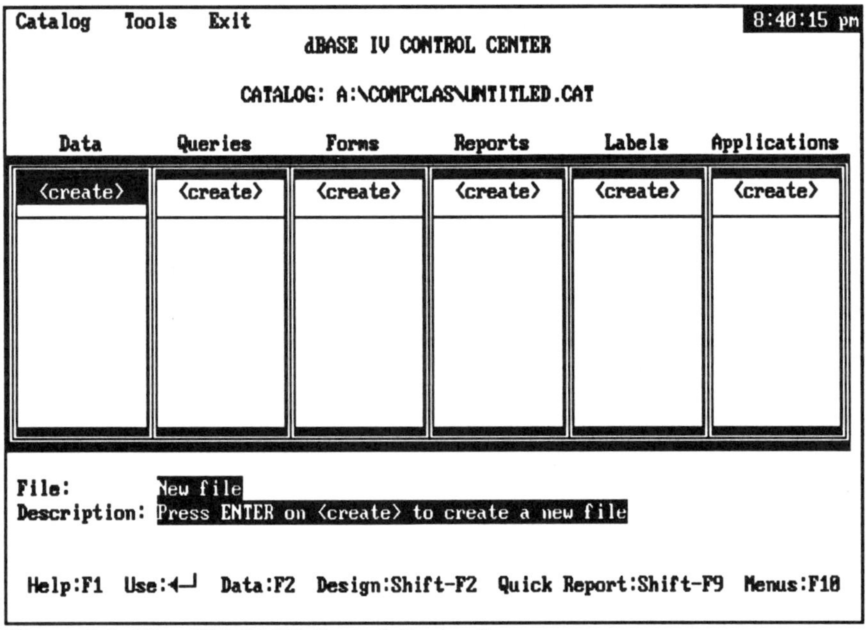

CREATING YOUR FIRST DATABASE

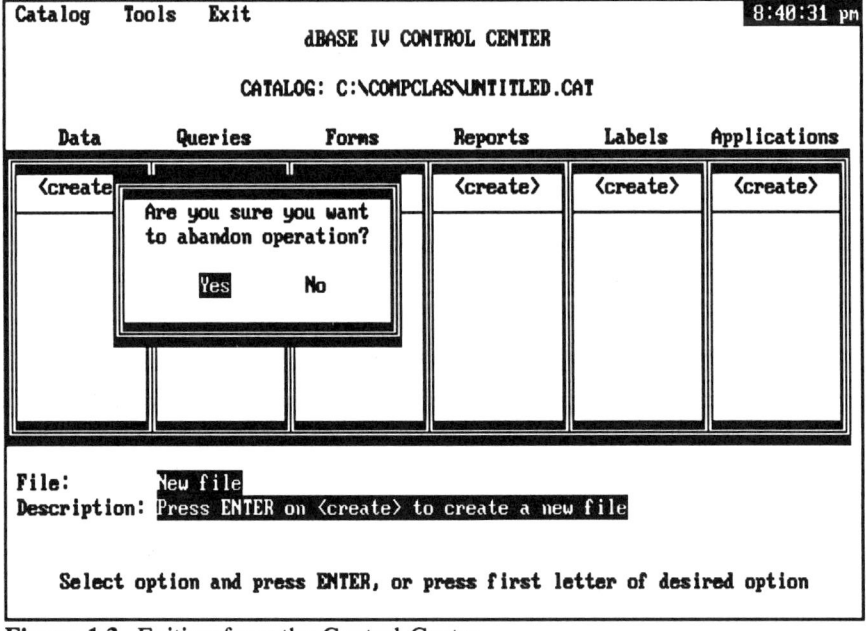

Figure 1.2 The dBASE IV Control Center Screen.

Figure 1.3 Exiting from the Control Center.

10   CREATING YOUR FIRST DATABASE

whenever you enter dBASE4 from now on, be sure that you go directly to the dot prompt.

1.3   Creating a Database

Let us begin by creating our first database. Since this is a computer course, the name of the database will be **COMPCLAS**, which stands for Computer Class. As we are only allowed 8 characters in a database or file name, we abbreviate our database name in this way. We create a database by typing the word: **CREATE** followed by the name of the database, that we wish to create, at the dot prompt.

. CREATE COMPCLAS

Figure 1.4 shows the screen that will appear. The Field Name refers to the name of the data field that you wish to tabulate in your database. If you examine the structure of the database COMPCLAS.dbf shown in Table 1.1, you'll notice that there are several different types of fields that a database can have. To be precise, there are six: 1) Character fields, 2) Logical fields, 3) Date fields, 4) Numeric fields, 5) Memo fields, and 6) Floating point numeric fields.

1. Names are clearly good candidates for being **Character** fields, as they consist of strings of characters. We must specify the width of the field (or the number of characters that the field will reserve for the name). A width of 15 is chosen as most first and last names will not exceed 15 characters.

2. The **Logical** field takes on the value of **True** or **False** (or a **Yes** or a **No**). In the computer course, a student has an option to take a final exam or to do a term project instead. The field **TERM_PROJ** indicates the student's choice. Needless to say, a field that takes either a **T** or an **F** need only be 1 character wide.

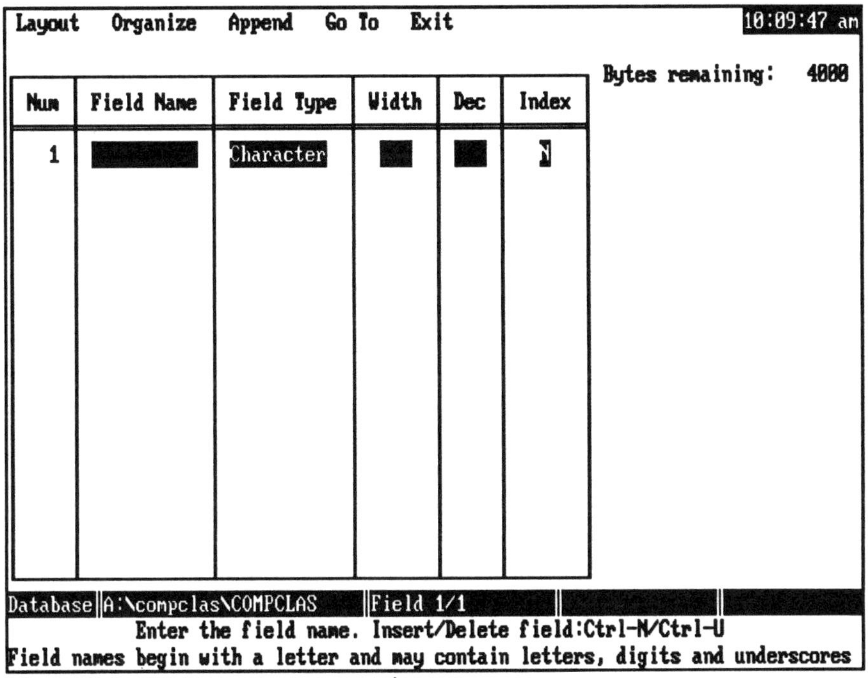

CREATING YOUR FIRST DATABASE 11

Figure 1.4 Database structure creation screen.

Table 1.1 Structure of COMPCLAS.DBF

Field	Field Name	Type	Width	Dec
1	FIRSTNAME	Character	15	
2	LASTNAME	Character	15	
3	TERM_PROJ	Logical	1	
4	EVALUATION	Date	8	
5	PROJ_GRADE	Numeric	3	0
6	COMMENTS	Memo	10	

3. The field labeled **EVALUATION** refers to the date on which the student must come and demonstrate his or her project to the professor. Note that we have here another kind of field known as a **Date** field. A **Date** field is always 8 characters wide. If you count the number of characters in a date, 12-31-1992, it should be clear why a date field reserves 8 characters for its width.

4. The field labeled **PROJ_GRADE** is a fixed point **Numeric** field and is used whenever you think you might be doing arithmetic with the numbers contained in the field. Since we'll probably be using the grade received on the project to compute the student's average, a **Numeric** field is a good choice. Since the grade we could give might be anywhere from 0 to 100, we need to allow 3 characters for the width (just in case someone gets 100). The column labeled **Dec** refers to the number of places needed after a decimal point. Since we're not interested in grading someone to one-tenth or one-hundredth of a point, we'll make this column zero width.[7] Obviously, the **Dec** column only has significance for a **Numeric** field, and is ignored in all other cases.

5. The **COMMENTS** field is a **Memo** field. This field allows you to type in memos up to 524,288 characters in length. Since this is the size of a large novel, dBASE4 uses a separate file for this purpose.[8] Memos are entered using the built-in text editor or may be entered using a word processor.

6. There is one more type of field that is available in dBASE4 and that is the **Floating** point numeric field. The problem with the fixed point Numeric field is that it only allows

---

[7] If, on the other hand, we had a numeric field which held the hourly wage rate, given in dollars and cents, then we would want two decimal places after the decimal point. Thus we would choose the value in the **Dec** column to be 2.

[8] This file has the extension **.DBT** rather than the **.DBF** extension that is given to the database file containing all the other fields. In our case, the name of this file is **COMPCLAS.DBT**. The "T" at the end of the extension **.DBT** stands for Text file. All other database fields are contained in the **.DBF** file.

numbers up to 10 quadrillion (10^{16}) which is approximately 2 thousand times the size of the United States National debt. Numbers that go beyond 10 quadrillion (that's a 1 with 16 zeroes following it) or its inverse, are too large or too small to be handled by the fixed point **Numeric** field. For numbers of this sort, they are handled using **Floating** point numeric fields which are ordinarily represented in scientific notation. However, unless you are a scientist or engineer, it is unlikely that you will have much need of the **Floating** point numeric field. We will not be using them in this text.

Now you may begin typing in the structure of the Computer Class Database. When you finish typing in **FIRSTNAME**, simply strike the Enter Key. All you need to do to specify the type of field is to strike the first letter of the field type. For example, all you would need to do to specify a Logical field is to type the letter "**L**". If you type nothing, a Character field will be assumed. In each case, striking the Enter key will move you on to the next item to enter. You may ignore the Index column for now. Simply strike the Enter key when the cursor goes to that column. Use the cursor movement keys (the four keys with arrows on them pointing in four different directions) to move the cursor around the database structure that you've entered. This is done for editing purposes.

Once you have entered all the data, and it looks identical to that shown in Table 1.1, then we need to access the menu at the top of the screen (see Figure 1.5). This is done by holding down the key labeled **Alt** and then striking the first letter of the word in the menu that you desire. For example, to Exit, all we need do is depress the **Alt** key and then strike: **E**. When that occurs, a window drops down below the "Exit" as shown in Figure 1.6. As the menu item already selected by default is: "Save changes and exit", strike the Enter key.

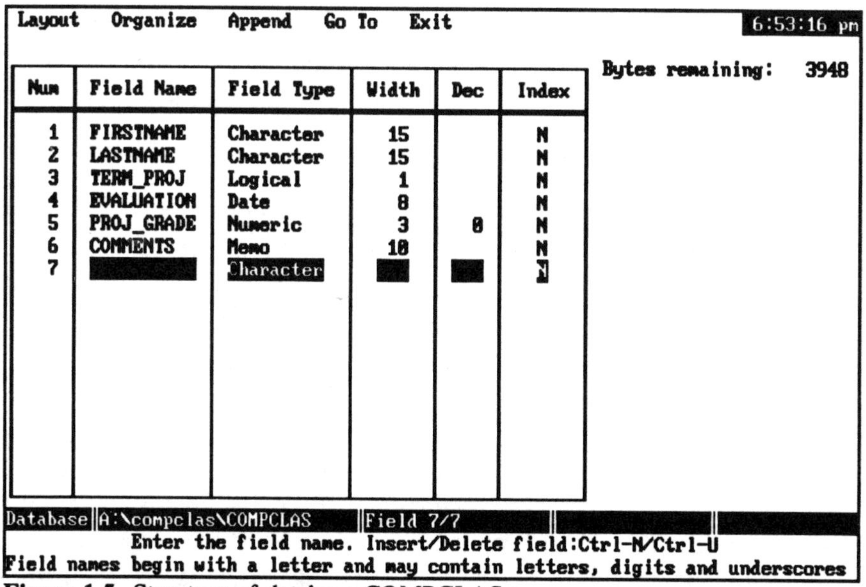

14 CREATING YOUR FIRST DATABASE

Figure 1.5 Structure of database COMPCLAS.

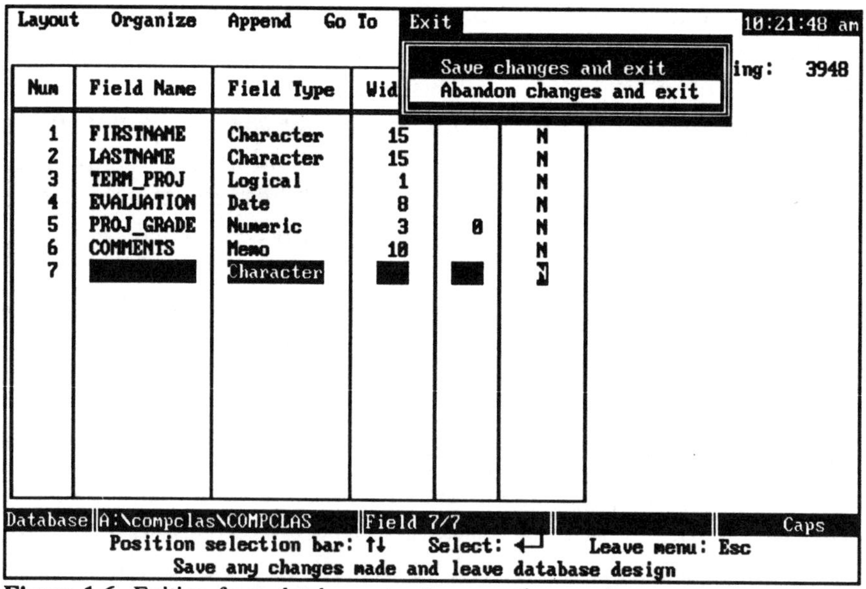

Figure 1.6 Exiting from database structure creation mode.

CREATING YOUR FIRST DATABASE 15

1.4 Appending Records to a Database

We have now completed creating the structure for the database, COMPCLAS, and we find ourselves back at the dot prompt. However, we have yet to enter any data into the database. The adding of new records into a database is done by means of the **APPEND** command. Typing **APPEND** at the dot prompt:

. **APPEND**

we get the data entry screen shown in Figure 1.7. You may now proceed to enter the data shown in Table 1.2.

Table 1.2 Contents of Database COMPCLAS.DBF

FIRSTNAME	LASTNAME	TERM PROJ	EVALUATION	PROJ GRADE
Gladys	Naboa	T	12/15/92	93
Consuelo	Naboa	T	12/16/92	89
Derek	Caruthers	F	/ /	
Wendel	Little	T	12/17/92	87
Jeremy	Witherspoon	T	12/19/92	82
Nancy	Hardwick	F	/ /	
Jonathan	Samuels	T	12/14/92	76
Raquel	Ransworth	F	/ /	
Matts	Engleberg	T	12/13/92	62
Mary Beth	Swazey	T	12/14/92	52

16 CREATING YOUR FIRST DATABASE

Once again you can use your cursor movement keys to move about. When necessary, strike the Enter key to move on to the next field (Note that when you type in the last space on the right in a field, the cursor automatically moves on to the next field). For now we can skip entering data in the **Memo** field, so simply strike the Enter key when you get to that field. Immediately a new blank record will appear. When you have entered all the data for the final record, Figure 1.8 shows what should appear on your screen.

Just as in the Database Structure Design, we left the mode by pressing the **Alt E** key combination and then struck Enter, to leave the Data Entry mode, we do the same thing.

Now for completion, let's close our database. If you think of a database file as a file folder that we have taken out of a file cabinet and spread out on our desk, then before we leave it to go take a coffee break, we want to close it and put it away. Suppose we don't and the window were left open. When we open the door, some of the file papers might blow out the window, and we'd lose them. In the same way, we should close our database whenever we

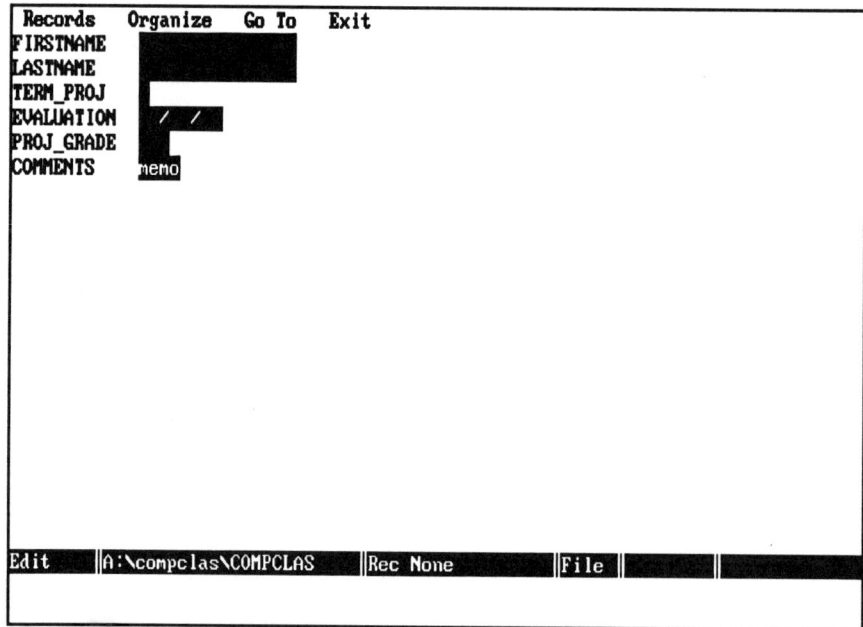

Figure 1.7 Blank data entry screen for database COMPCLAS.

CREATING YOUR FIRST DATABASE   17

leave it even for a few minutes. To do this type the word **USE** at the dot prompt. Paradoxically, the command **USE**, all by itself, closes the database thus preserving its integrity.

. USE

1.5 Editing the Database

Suppose you did not finish entering all the data, and you now wish to continue entering the data from Table 1.2. The first thing that we must do is to re-open our database, **COMPCLAS**. This is done by simply typing at the dot prompt, **USE COMPCLAS**.

. USE COMPCLAS

Now our database is opened, however, nothing seems changed. Where is that data entry screen that we had before? We'll get to that in a second. Now it's time to learn about the Status Line. At the bottom of your screen there should be a bar going across

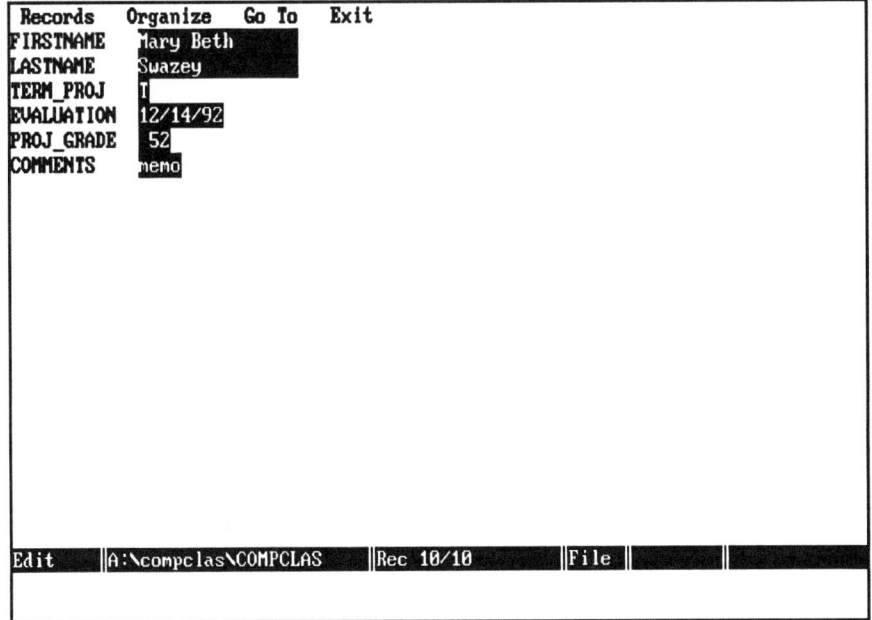

Figure 1.8 Data entry screen for last record in COMPCLAS database.

which looks like that shown in Figure 1.1. If there is no such bar displayed on the screen, you can type:

. SET STATUS ON

This will cause the Status Line to go on.

Examining the status line you will notice that the name of our database is now prominently displayed on the line. This is a clear indication that the database, **COMPCLAS,** is indeed open. Other things to notice about the status line are the fact that **A:** is prominently displayed (unless you are using some other logged disk drive). This means that the drive all data will be read from and written to is the one indicated on the Status Line.

Finally, note that it says: **Rec: 1/10** over on the right hand side. This means that there have been 10 records of data entered into the database, but that we're currently positioned at record number 1. Now what does that mean? We still have only a blank screen in front of us.

If we type the word **EDIT**, we will see that we are indeed looking at record 1 (see Figure 1.9).

. EDIT

Note that we are looking at the same type of screen that we were looking at earlier, except that we are looking at the first record rather than at a blank screen. Looking at the Status Line we notice the word **EDIT** clearly written in the lower left hand corner. Both APPEND and EDIT modes have EDIT written in the lower left.

We are now free to use our cursor movement keys to move around and make whatever changes in the data as we deem necessary. To move onto the next record, simply strike the **PgDn** (Page Down) key. Note the change in the status line to **Rec: 2/10,** thus indicating that we are looking at Record 2. If we now choose to go back to Record 1, we need only strike the **PgUp** (Page Up) key. If we wish to continue stepping through the rest of the

CREATING YOUR FIRST DATABASE   19

database, a record at a time, we need only continue striking the **PgDn** key.

1.6 Browsing the Database

In the **EDIT** mode, we see the fields of the database listed vertically for each individual record. There is another way of looking at the database. If we list the fields across horizontally on the screen, and then list each record vertically, one line per record, we are able to see 17 records at one time. This is referred to as the **BROWSE** mode. We can enter the **BROWSE** mode very easily from the **EDIT** mode, by merely striking the **F2** function key. We may also enter the **BROWSE** mode from the dot prompt by typing **BROWSE**. If you are currently in the **EDIT** mode, strike the **F2** key, otherwise type at the dot prompt:

. BROWSE

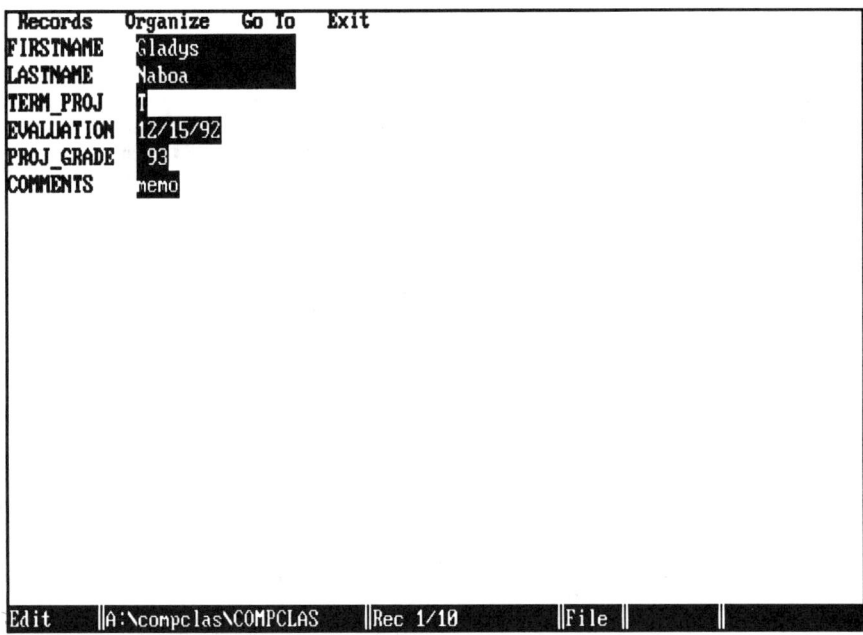

Figure 1.9 Examining the first record in the Edit Mode.

CREATING YOUR FIRST DATABASE

Figure 1.10 shows what you should see when you have entered the **BROWSE** mode. Notice that since we only have 10 records currently in the database, we are able to look at its contents all at once. This broad view of a database makes the **BROWSE** a very popular means of examining as well as editing data in a database.

Using the cursor movement keys, notice how you can move around in each field and from record to record. Strike the Enter key several times, and note that you move from field to field. Note that striking the Enter key when you are positioned in the last field takes you automatically to the first field of the next record in sequence. You can move backwards in the same way by holding down the Shift key and striking the Tab key (This is the key directly below the "1" key on your keyboard. Note that it has arrows going in both directions).

Using the **PgUp** and **PgDn** keys we can move backward and forward through our database 16 records at a time. Of course with this short database, striking the **PgDn** key takes us immediately to

FIRSTNAME	LASTNAME	TERM_PROJ	EVALUATION	PROJ_GRADE	COMMENTS
Gladys	Naboa	T	12/15/92	93	memo
Consuelo	Naboa	T	12/16/92	89	memo
Derek	Caruthers	F	/ /		memo
Wendel	Little	T	12/17/92	87	memo
Jeremy	Witherspoon	T	12/19/92	82	memo
Nancy	Hardwick	F	/ /		memo
Jonathan	Samuels	T	12/14/92	76	memo
Raquel	Ransworth	F	/ /		memo
Matts	Engleberg	T	12/13/92	62	memo
Mary Beth	Swazey	T	12/14/92	52	memo

Figure 1.10 COMPCLAS examined in the BROWSE Mode.

CREATING YOUR FIRST DATABASE

the last record. Likewise striking **PgUp** takes us back to the first record again.

Although we could enter the **COMMENTS** into the **MEMO** fields directly in the **EDIT** mode, it is even easier to do it in the **BROWSE** mode. Begin by putting your cursor in the **memo** field of Gladys Naboa (use the cursor movement keys, Enter key, or Shift Tab to move to this field). Now strike the **F9** key to take you into the **MEMO** field text editor. Note the ruler at the top of the screen. This type of ruler is typical of text editors and word processors in general. Now you may type in the comment we wish to make about Gladys (see Table 1.3 below). The result should appear as shown in Figure 1.11.

Note that the text automatically wraps to the next line as you type (there is no need to strike the Enter key). When you have finished typing in the first comment, you may leave the **Memo** text editor in the usual way, by depressing the **Alt** key and striking **E** for Exit, and then striking the Enter key.

Table 1.3 Contents of the MEMO field COMMENTS for COMPCLAS.DBF

Record	
1.	Gladys does superior work. She seems to be very highly motivated.
3.	Derek elected to take the Final instead.
5.	Jeremy is bright, but he's just a little sloppy in his work. If he would take more time to be precise, he would do "A" work.
6.	Nancy elected to take the Final.
8.	Raquel elected to take the Final.
10.	Mary Beth clearly did not put any effort into her project. Her attendance has been very spotty also.

22 CREATING YOUR FIRST DATABASE

This takes us back to the **BROWSE** mode, right where we left it. Use the Down Arrow key to move directly to the **MEMO** field of the next record. Repeat the procedure adding in the second comment. Continue doing this till all records that should have comments have been entered. When you get done, the result should look like that shown in Figure 1.12.

Notice that all the records to which you added a comment now have the word **MEMO** capitalized, while those to which you didn't add comments, have **memo** in small letters. This is a way of telling, at a glance, which records have comments added in their **memo** fields, and which don't.

1.7 Appending to Your Database While in EDIT

Suppose you had not entered all the data contained in Table 1.2 before you quit the session, and now you have returned and want to continue entering data. Or suppose, you have some additional students you want to add to our database. If you have just restarted

Figure 1.11 Memo Field Text editor with comment for first record.

CREATING YOUR FIRST DATABASE

dBASE4 and there is no file open, remember you must first open the database.

. USE COMPCLAS

You may, of course, simply add new records using the **APPEND** command as before. Another possibility is that you may be in the **EDIT** mode, and you may wish to add a record while you are there. Let's go into **EDIT** right now.

. EDIT

Having just opened the database, COMPCLAS, again, the screen that we would see is shown in Figure 1.13. Note that we are looking at the very first record in our database once more.

FIRSTNAME	LASTNAME	TERM_PROJ	EVALUATION	PROJ_GRADE	COMMENTS
Gladys	Naboa	T	12/15/92	93	MEMO
Consuelo	Naboa	T	12/16/92	89	memo
Derek	Caruthers	F	/ /		MEMO
Wendel	Little	T	12/17/92	87	memo
Jeremy	Witherspoon	T	12/19/92	82	MEMO
Nancy	Hardwick	F	/ /		MEMO
Jonathan	Samuels	T	12/14/92	76	memo
Raquel	Ransworth	F	/ /		MEMO
Matts	Engleberg	T	12/13/92	62	memo
Mary Beth	Swazey	T	12/14/92	52	MEMO

Browse A:\compclas\COMPCLAS Rec 10/10 File

Figure 1.12 Browse of COMPCLAS after having entered MEMO fields.

24 CREATING YOUR FIRST DATABASE

To switch into the **APPEND** mode from this point, we need to access the Menu option "Records" by depressing the **Alt** key and striking the **R** key. This brings down the window menu shown in Figure 1.14. Note that the menu item selected in the window is "Add new records". Striking the Enter key at this point gives you the screen in Figure 1.15, which is basically the same as the data entry screen we had in Figure 1.7.

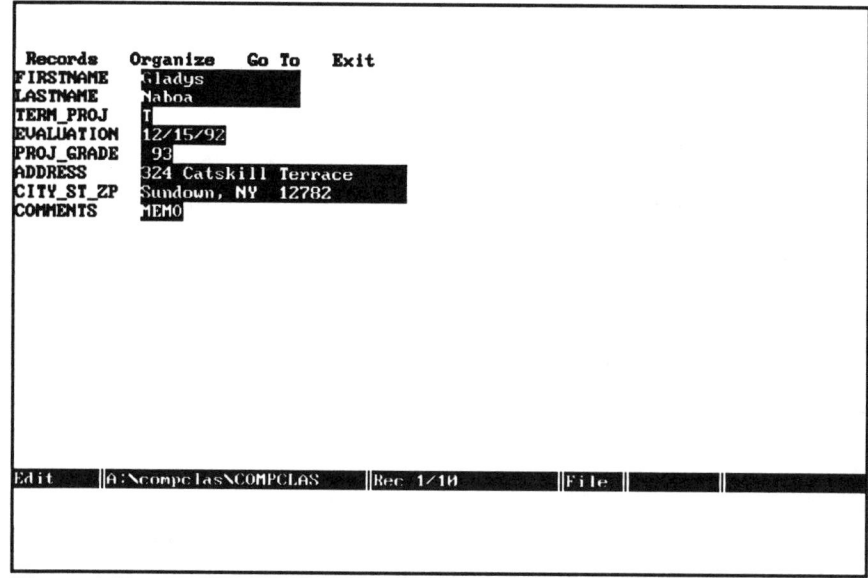

Figure 1.13 EDIT Mode showing Record Number 1.

Note that on the bottom right of the status line there appears: **Rec: EOF/10** . The number 10 indicates the number of records you have already entered. The word **EOF** stands for End Of File. This means that any new records that are added will be appended to the end of the file, which is exactly where you would expect to have them added.

We shall now add a new record to our database. Mary Wong, who had only been auditing our class is now interested in taking it for credit. Let's add Mary to our list. When you get done appending Mary, your screen should look like that shown in Figure 1.16.

CREATING YOUR FIRST DATABASE 25

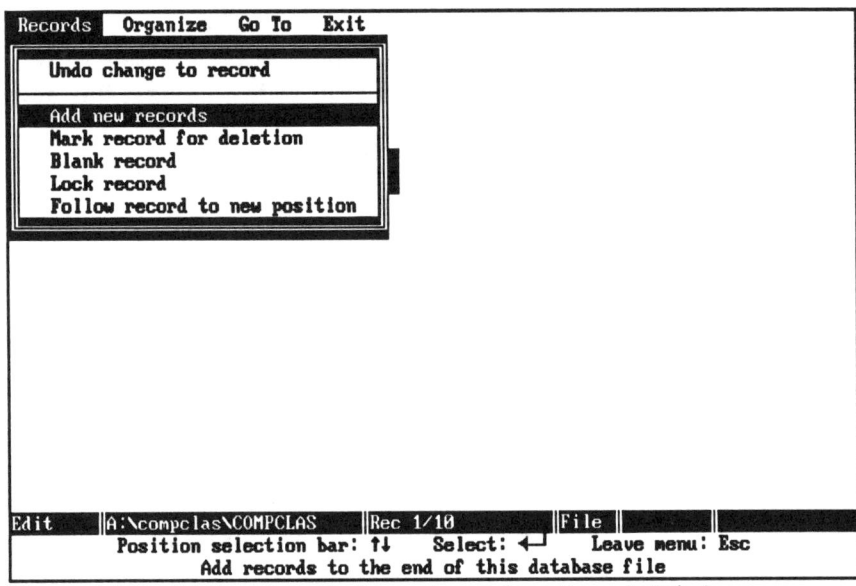

Figure 1.14 Add New Records item selected from Records Window.

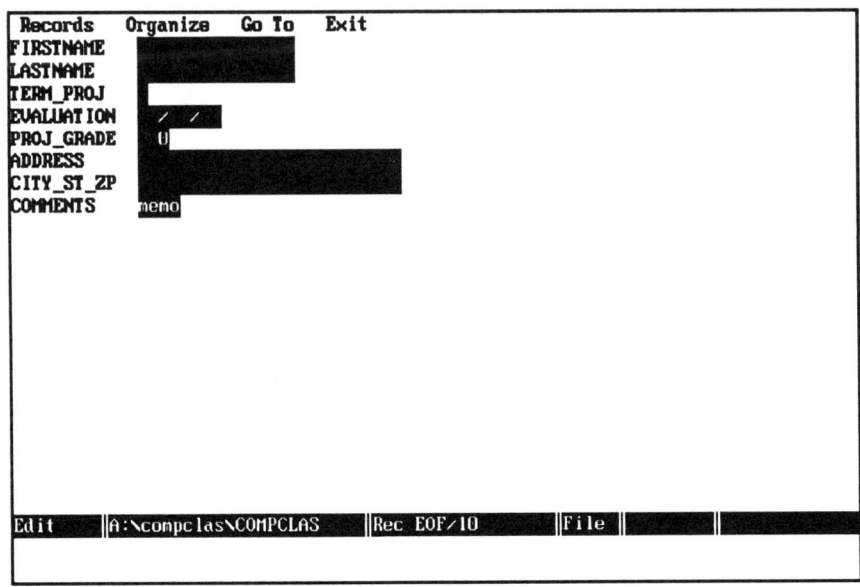

Figure 1.15 Blank record Appended within EDIT mode

26 CREATING YOUR FIRST DATABASE

If for any reason we do not want to save the record that we have just entered in the **APPEND**, we can abort the creation of this new record simply by striking the **Escape** key. In so doing, this new record will not be added. If the **Esc** key is struck in the **EDIT** mode, then any changes to the current record will also be ignored. Except as a means of error recovery, the **Esc** key should not be used.

Now we may exit from the **APPEND** mode in the usual way by selecting the **EXIT** menu option (depress **Alt E**) and then striking the Enter key.

1.8   Listing Your Database

If you would like to quickly list the contents of your database in one fell swoop, the **LIST** command is available. Unlike the **BROWSE** mode, you will simply see a listing with no ability to edit the contents of the database. With your database already open (it's name should appear on the Status Line), simply type **LIST** at the dot prompt.

. LIST

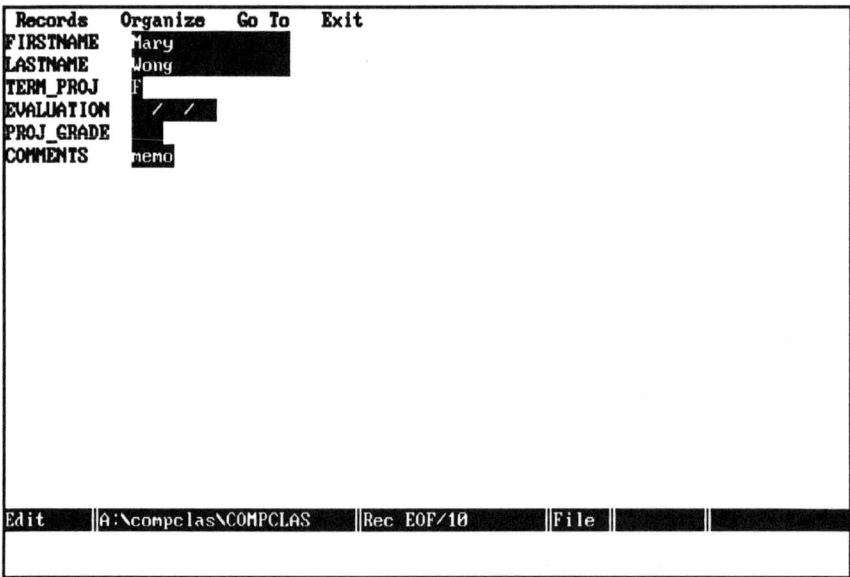

Figure 1.16 Appending a new record to the COMPCLAS database

CREATING YOUR FIRST DATABASE

Listing 1.1 shows what will appear on the screen using our database **COMPCLAS**. Note that the "S" in the field heading COMMENTS is wrapped around on the screen and appears in the first column on the second line.

We can make more space for the last field by doing away with the record numbers at the beginning. This can be accomplished by following the word **LIST** with the word **OFF**. Listing 1.2 results from executing the following command:

. **LIST OFF**

Record#s	FIRSTNAME	LASTNAME	TERM_PROJ	EVALUATION	PROJ_GRADE	COMMENT
1	Gladys	Naboa	.T.	12/15/92	93	MEMO
2	Consuelo	Naboa	.T.	12/16/92	89	MEMO
3	Derek	Caruthers	.F.	/ /		memo
4	Wendel	Little	.T.	12/17/92	87	memo
5	Jeremy	Witherspoon	.T.	12/19/92	82	MEMO
6	Nancy	Hardwick	.F.	/ /		MEMO
7	Jonathan	Samuels	.T.	12/14/92	76	memo
8	Raquel	Ransworth	.F.	/ /		MEMO
9	Matts	Engleberg	.T.	12/13/92	62	memo
10	Mary Beth	Swazey	.T.	12/14/92	52	Memo
11	Mary	Wong	.F.	/ /		memo

Listing 1.1 LIST of the database COMPCLAS.

FIRSTNAME	LASTNAME	TERM_PROJ	EVALUATION	PROJ_GRADE	COMMENTS
Gladys	Naboa	.T.	12/15/92	93	MEMO
Consuelo	Naboa	.T.	12/16/92	89	MEMO
Derek	Caruthers	.F.	/ /		memo
Wendel	Little	.T.	12/17/92	87	memo
Jeremy	Witherspoon	.T.	12/19/92	82	MEMO
Nancy	Hardwick	.F.	/ /		MEMO
Jonathan	Samuels	.T.	12/14/92	76	memo
Raquel	Ransworth	.F.	/ /		MEMO
Matts	Engleberg	.T.	12/13/92	62	memo
Mary Beth	Swazey	.T.	12/14/92	52	MEMO
Mary	Wong	.F.	/ /		memo

Listing 1.2 LIST OFF of the database COMPCLAS.

28 CREATING YOUR FIRST DATABASE

We can also **LIST** our database structure with the **LIST STRUCTURE** command. Executing this command results in the display shown in Listing 1.3.

. LIST STRUCTURE

```
Structure for database: A:\COMPCLAS\COMPCLAS.DBF
Number of data records:      11
Date of last update   : 01/07/92
Field  Field Name  Type       Width    Dec    Index
    1  FIRSTNAME   Character    15                N
    2  LASTNAME    Character    15                N
    3  TERM_PROJ   Logical       1                N
    4  EVALUATION  Date          8                N
    5  PROJ_GRADE  Numeric       3                N
    6  COMMENTS    Memo         10                N
** Total **                     53
```

Listing 1.3 LIST STRUCTURE of database COMPCLAS

To obtain printed output from your printer, you need only add the words: **TO PRINT** at the end of the command. If you wish to send the listings of **COMPCLAS** and its structure to the printer, simply type the following:

. LIST OFF TO PRINT

. LIST STRUCTURE TO PRINT

We will refer to this printed output as "Hard Copy" from now on.

1.9 Quitting from dBASE4

Never exit from dBASE4 *without* doing a **QUIT** first. Unless you have closed all open files and databases, there might be some data still in memory which has not been written onto your disk. You can even render your file unreadable (meaning you would have

CREATING YOUR FIRST DATABASE 29

to resort to using some utilities and expertise beyond the scope of this book to doctor up the file) if you do not exit without using **QUIT**. This is done by simply typing **QUIT** at the dot prompt.

. **QUIT**

Now the DOS prompt should be displaying itself on your screen as shown below.

A:\COMPCLAS>

This means that you are now free to turn off your computer or do something else if you desire.

1.10 Example II: A Checkbook/Budget Account

As a second example of a database, we will also be carrying a checkbook/budget account database throughout this text.

We don't want to mix up this database with the unrelated COMPCLAS database, so let's move to the ACCOUNTS directory to keep these two databases separate from each other[9]. This is done by typing **CD\ACCOUNTS** at the DOS prompt.

A:\COMPCLAS> CD\ACCOUNTS

A:\ACCOUNTS>

Now we should see the above DOS prompt on our screen, so we can begin. As you recall, to enter dBASE, type it at the DOS prompt.

A:\ACCOUNTS> DBASE

---

[9]If you have not already done so, you may **M**ake a new **D**irectory called **ACCOUNTS** by typing **MD\ACCOUNTS** at the DOS prompt.

A:\> MD\ACCOUNTS

You must make this directory before you can **C**hange **D**irectory to it.

Listing 1.4 shows the structure of the database ACCOUNTS.DBF, while Listing 1.5 shows the **LIST** of the data contained in the database for the month of January. Note that since we're dealing with money in the **DEBITS** and **RECEIPTS** fields, we are specifying 2 decimal places for each of these fields.

Note also that a logical field, **CASHED**, has been included which is used for check reconciliation purposes at the end of the month. As you can see, all the deposits, but only a few checks were returned this month in the monthly bank statement. The entries marked **.F.** are still outstanding.

Create the ACCOUNTS database using the structure shown in Listing 1.4. Enter the data shown in Listing 1.5. We will be referring to this database in future chapters so it is good to have it on your disk.

```
Structure for database: A:\ACCOUNTS\ACCOUNTS.DBF
Number of data records:     12
Date of last update    : 01/07/91
Field  Field Name  Type         Width     Dec     Index
    1  DATE        Date             8                 N
    2  CHECK       Character        3                 N
    3  DESCRIPT    Character       32                 N
    4  DEBITS      Numeric          8       2         N
    5  RECEIPTS    Numeric          8       2         N
    6  CASHED      Logical          1                 N
** Total **                        61
```

Listing 1.4 Structure of database ACCOUNTS.

1.11 Summary

In this chapter we have learned how to **CREATE** a database, **APPEND** new data to it, **EDIT** the data that has been entered into it, as well as **BROWSE** the data. In addition, we have learned not only how to **LIST** the data on the screen, but also how to print it out on the printer. Also, we have learned how to LIST the STRUCTURE of the database on the printer too.

CREATING YOUR FIRST DATABASE   31

```
DATE       CHECK  DESCRIPT                      DEBITS  RECEIPTS  CASHED
01/01/92          Jan. 1 Balance                  0.00   100.00   .T.
01/05/92          Deposit: Salary                 0.00   750.00   .T.
01/09/92   401    Cash: January Allowance       100.00     0.00   .T.
01/09/92   402    Sullivan Co. Cablevision       20.00     0.00   .F.
01/09/92   403    N.Y. Telephone: Dec. bill      50.00     0.00   .F.
01/12/92   404    Dr. John McIntyre, D.D.S.      75.00     0.00   .F.
01/13/92   405    Sierra Club: Donation          10.00     0.00   .F.
01/14/92   406    Shoprite: Groceries            18.60     0.00   .T.
01/14/92   407    Farmer's Market: Groceries      4.20     0.00   .T.
01/14/92   408    Feed-n-things: Pet Food         8.50     0.00   .T.
01/15/92   409    State Farm Mutual:Insurance   232.94     0.00   .F.
01/15/92   410    Sherman's: Auto repairs        10.00     0.00   .F.
```

Listing 1.5 Checkbook data for ACCOUNTS database

This gives the reader not only the ability to start putting data into the computer in any form he or she would like, but also the ability to present hard copy of the data that has been entered.

1.12 Review

In Chapter 1 we have covered the following commands:

> **APPEND**   **LIST STRUCTURE**
> **BROWSE**   **LIST TO PRINT**
> **CREATE**   **QUIT**
> **EDIT**   **USE** *filename*
> **LIST**   **USE**

These are your most commonly used dBASE4 commands. If you haven't already done so, you'll want to write them down prominently in your glossary of dBASE4 commands. We will be entering a number of commands to this glossary, so set aside a couple of pages in your notebook just for this glossary. These are commands that you will be using over and over.

1.13 Laboratory Work

Following all the steps outlined in this chapter, enter the database **COMPCLAS** onto your disk and obtain the printed copy

32 CREATING YOUR FIRST DATABASE

similar to that shown in Listings 1.1 and 1.2. In addition create the database **ACCOUNTS** and obtain printed copies of the structure as well as the data of this database as shown in Listings 1.4 and 1.5.

1.14 Exercises

In the course of learning dBASE4, we will concurrently be creating a mailing list program as homework for our own use. The Logical Field Card refers to whether or not we intend to send the individual a Christmas, or Hanukkah, or New Year's card this year. (I usually make such decisions by looking at who sent me cards last year.) Following is the record structure that we will be using for this mailing list.

Field #	Field Name	Type	Width
1	First	Character	12
2	Last	Character	12
3	Mail_Addr	Character	22
4	City	Character	11
5	State	Character	2
6	Zip	Character	6
7	Card	Logical	1

1. Move to the directory **\MAILIST** by using the DOS command: **CD\MAILIST** at the DOS prompt[10].

2. Create a new database called MAILIST.dbf that has the structure shown above.

---

[10]If you have not already done so, you may Make a new Directory called **MAILIST** by typing **MD\MAILIST** at the DOS prompt.

A:\> MD\MAILIST

You must make this directory before you can Change Directory to it.

CREATING YOUR FIRST DATABASE 33

3. Enter the eleven records shown in Listing 1.6 into your mailing list.

FIRST	LAST	MAIL_ADDR	CITY	STATE	ZIP	CARD
Donald	Duck	Disney World	Orlando	FL	31560	.T.
Hewey	Duck	Disney World	Orlando	FL	31560	.F.
Dewey	Duck	Disney World	Orlando	FL	31560	.F.
Louie	Duck	Disney World	Orlando	FL	31560	.F.
Mickey	Mouse	Disney World	Orlando	FL	31560	.T.
Bugs	Bunny	Warner Bros. Studios	Hollywood	CA	91223	.T.
Elmer	Fudd	Warner Bros. Studios	Hollywood	CA	91223	.T.
Yosemite	Sam	Warner Bros. Studios	Hollywood	CA	91223	.T.
Daffy	Duck	Warner Bros. Studios	Hollywood	CA	91223	.T.
Road	Runner	Warner Bros. Studios	Hollywood	CA	91223	.F.
Woody	Woodpecker	Walter Lanz Studios	Burbank	CA	91325	.T.

Listing 1.6 Contents of the database MAILIST.dbf

4. If necessary, edit your file so that it is exactly as you want it to be.

5. Print out a hard copy of your database.

6. Print out a copy of the structure of your database.

7. Hand in the printed output generated in problems 5 and 6.

CHAPTER 2

EDITING YOUR DATABASE

2.0   Topics Covered in Chapter 2

Modifying the structure of a database.

Use of the DISPLAY instruction.

Deleting records from a database.

Inserting records into a database.

Using BROWSE mode for editing data.

Using BROWSE for appending new records to a database.

Using Lock fields and Freeze fields from the BROWSE "Fields" menu.

Using the BROWSE "Go To" menu option to navigate around in a database.

Doing Forward and Backward searches while in the BROWSE mode.

2.1 Modifying your Database

I spent years writing programs in other high level languages to do specific database applications. It all worked pretty well until I wanted to change something in the structure of the database. If I wanted to add a field, or widen a field, it would be such a headache that I would use every bit of reasoning I could muster to justify why I shouldn't change what I already had. One of the joys of dBASE is the facility with which you can modify the very structure of the database with almost the same ease with which you can modify the data contained in the database.

Suppose we want to modify our database **COMPCLAS** to include some fields that we do not already have. Suppose, for instance, we decide that we want to include an address, a city-state-zip field, and a phone number for each student. To modify our database, first open the database (If you don't remember how to do this, consult Chapter 1. You never want to forget how to **USE** a database). Then type: **MODIFY STRUCTURE** at the dot prompt.

. **MODIFY STRUCTURE**

Figure 2.1 shows a screen similar to the one we obtained when we first created **COMPCLAS**.

Now we will change the structure so that it conforms to the structure shown in Figure 2.2. Note that we have added three new fields to the structure, and that we have inserted them right before the **COMMENTS** field. The way that this is done is to move the cursor (the selected field name is shown highlighted in reverse video) down to the field just below where we want the insertion to occur. In our case this would be the field labeled **COMMENTS**.

Now, looking down at the line just below the Status Line, shown in Figure 2.1, we see what is called the **Navigation Line**. This line describes any instructions or special keys we need to know. Note that it says, "Insert/Delete field: Ctrl-N/Ctrl-U". This means to insert a field, we merely depress the key labeled **Ctrl**[11] and strike **N**. Doing this once, we create a blank field name, as shown in Figure 2.3. On that blank field name line we can type in the first of our inserts, **ADDRESS** , a **Character** field, with a Width of **25**.

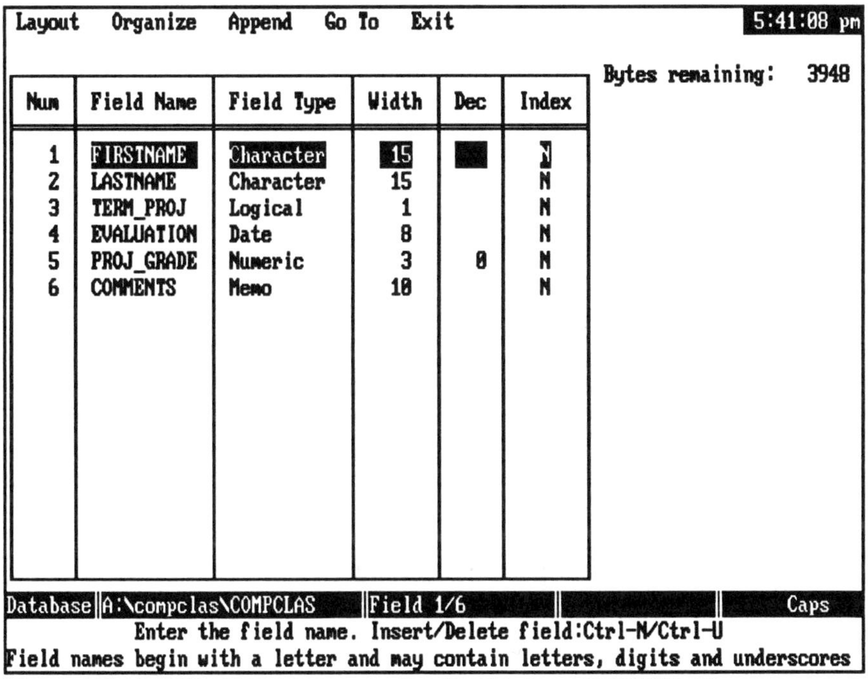
Layout Organize Append Go To Exit 5:41:08 pm
Bytes remaining: 3948
Num Field Name Field Type Width Dec Index
1 FIRSTNAME Character 15 N
2 LASTNAME Character 15 N
3 TERM_PROJ Logical 1 N
4 EVALUATION Date 8 N
5 PROJ_GRADE Numeric 3 0 N
6 COMMENTS Memo 10 N
Database A:\compclas\COMPCLAS Field 1/6 Caps
Enter the field name. Insert/Delete field:Ctrl-N/Ctrl-U
Field names begin with a letter and may contain letters, digits and underscores

Figure 2.1 Modify Structure screen for the database COMPCLAS

To insert the two additional fields, **CITY_ST_ZP** and **PHONE**, simply repeat the process of moving the cursor down to the field **COMMENTS** each time before striking **^N**. Type in these last two fields so that the result looks exactly like that shown in Figure 2.2.

Now return to the dot prompt, once again we may use the menu at the top and do our usual **Alt E** keystroke combination,

---

[11]The upward carat key, ^, is often used to denote the **Ctrl** key. In this way the keystroke pair, **Ctrl-N**, would be represented by: **^N**.

EDITING YOUR DATABASE

Num	Field Name	Field Type	Width	Dec	Index
1	FIRSTNAME	Character	15		N
2	LASTNAME	Character	15		N
3	TERM_PROJ	Logical	1		N
4	EVALUATION	Date	8		N
5	PROJ_GRADE	Numeric	3	0	N
6	ADDRESS	Character	25		N
7	CITY_ST_ZP	Character	25		N
8	PHONE	Character	12		N
9	COMMENTS	Memo	10		N

Figure 2.2 COMPCLAS structure with all the new fields inserted

Num	Field Name	Field Type	Width	Dec	Index
1	FIRSTNAME	Character	15		N
2	LASTNAME	Character	15		N
3	TERM_PROJ	Logical	1		N
4	EVALUATION	Date	8		N
5	PROJ_GRADE	Numeric	3	0	N
6		Character			N
7	COMMENTS	Memo	10		N

Figure 2.3 Using Ctrl-N to insert a new blank field in COMPCLAS

EDITING YOUR DATABASE

followed by striking the Enter key[12]. As usual it will ask you to confirm this choice by striking the Enter key.

2.2 Deleting Fields from the Database Structure

After we added the new **PHONE** field to the database, we came to realize that most of the students didn't have a phone number at which we could readily find them. So it was decided that all notifications would be done through the mail. Hence it is no longer necessary to have a field for the phone number. Since we want our database to be as tight as possible, wasting as little storage space as necessary, we opt to delete this field from the database structure.

To do this we simply do our **MODIFY STRUCTURE** command once more, and move our cursor down to the field name labeled **PHONE**. Looking down at the **Navigation Line** we see that to delete a field we need only use the keystroke pair ^U. So we depress the **Ctrl** key and strike **U** . Voila! The field labeled **PHONE** disappears, and we end up with the structure shown in Figure 2.4.

Once more we complete our operation by exiting in the usual manner (**Alt-E** followed by Enter).

2.3 DISPLAYing your Database One Page at a Time

If we were to **LIST** our database now, we would find that the first record rolls off the screen at the top. If our database were even longer, we would find that the database would zip past so fast that we would not be able to see anything but the last ten records of the file. A way of displaying the database so that it lists one screen page at a time is to use the **DISPLAY ALL** command.

. **DISPLAY ALL**

---

[12]There is a faster way to exit from the Database Structure mode, or the Edit, Browse and Memo editor modes, and that is simply to type the keystroke pair: ^ **End** (depress the **Ctrl** key and strike the key labeled **End**).

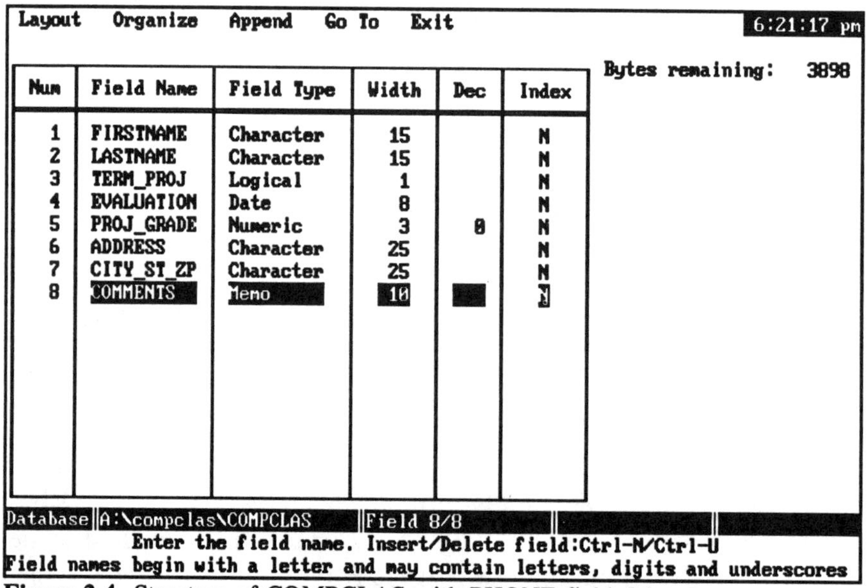

40   EDITING YOUR DATABASE

```
Layout   Organize   Append   Go To   Exit                6:21:17 pm
                                              Bytes remaining:  3898
┌─────┬────────────┬───────────┬───────┬─────┬───────┐
│ Num │ Field Name │ Field Type│ Width │ Dec │ Index │
├─────┼────────────┼───────────┼───────┼─────┼───────┤
│  1  │ FIRSTNAME  │ Character │  15   │     │   N   │
│  2  │ LASTNAME   │ Character │  15   │     │   N   │
│  3  │ TERM_PROJ  │ Logical   │   1   │     │   N   │
│  4  │ EVALUATION │ Date      │   8   │     │   N   │
│  5  │ PROJ_GRADE │ Numeric   │   3   │  0  │   N   │
│  6  │ ADDRESS    │ Character │  25   │     │   N   │
│  7  │ CITY_ST_ZP │ Character │  25   │     │   N   │
│  8  │ COMMENTS   │ Memo      │  10   │     │   N   │
└─────┴────────────┴───────────┴───────┴─────┴───────┘
Database A:\compclas\COMPCLAS     Field 8/8
          Enter the field name. Insert/Delete field:Ctrl-N/Ctrl-U
Field names begin with a letter and may contain letters, digits and underscores
```

Figure 2.4 Structure of COMPCLAS with PHONE field deleted

Doing this, we see displayed the result shown in Figure 2.5. Striking any key, the next page (and last page in this case) gets displayed.

Note that our database records are now so long that they no longer fit on one line of the screen but rather wrap around to the very next line. This is a formatting problem that can be partially remedied if we are willing to omit fields from our database display. For example, we can fit the contents of each record on one line rather than two, if we were to omit the two new fields: **ADDRESS** and **CITY_ST_ZIP** . This can be done by simply listing the fields that we do want displayed. Executing the following **DISPLAY ALL** command will result in what is shown in Figure 2.6.

. DISPLAY ALL FIELD FIRSTNAME,LASTNAME,
    TERM_PROJ,EVALUATION,PROJ_GRADE

Note that the **LIST TO PRINT** command is appropriate for printing out the contents of databases on hard copy while **DISPLAY ALL** is more appropriate for displaying a database on the screen. If we wished to print out only selected fields as we did

```
Record# FIRSTNAME        LASTNAME       TERM_PROJ EVALUATION PROJ_GRADE ADDRESS
                 CITY_ST_ZP                      COMMENTS
     1  Gladys           Naboa             .T.    12/15/92      93
                                                   MEMO
     2  Consuelo         Naboa             .T.    12/16/92      89
                                                   memo
     3  Derek            Caruthers         .F.      / /          0
                                                   MEMO
     4  Wendel           Little            .T.    12/17/92      87
                                                   memo
     5  Jeremy           Witherspoon       .T.    12/19/92      82
                                                   MEMO
     6  Nancy            Hardwick          .F.      / /          0
                                                   MEMO
     7  Jonathan         Samuels           .T.    12/14/92      76
                                                   memo
     8  Raquel           Ransworth         .F.      / /          0
                                                   MEMO
     9  Matts            Engleberg         .T.    12/13/92      62
                                                   memo
    10  Mary Beth        Swazey            .T.    12/14/92      52
Press any key to continue...
Command  A:\compclas\COMPCLAS    Rec 1/11       File
         Type a dBASE IV command and press the ENTER key (⏎)
```

Figure 2.5 Use of the DISPLAY ALL instruction on COMPCLAS

with the **DISPLAY ALL FIELD** command used above, we can do the same with the **LIST** command. The following will generate a hard copy of what was displayed in Figure 2.6.

. **LIST FIELD FIRSTNAME,LASTNAME,
   TERM_PROJ,EVALUATION,PROJ_GRADE TO PRINT**

2.4 Deleting Records from your Database

Raquel withdrew from the course so we no longer need to keep her in our database. Deleting records from a database occurs often and there are several ways one can accomplish this. The simplest way (and the *least* recommended) is to remember the fact that Raquel was Record Number 8. Then you can simply use the **DELETE RECORD** command.

. **DELETE RECORD 8**

The problem with this is suppose you did not remember the record number correctly. You might end up deleting the wrong record by

```
. DISPLAY ALL FIELD FIRSTNAME,LASTNAME,TERM_PROJ,EVALUATION,PROJ_GRADE
Record#  FIRSTNAME    LASTNAME      TERM_PROJ  EVALUATION  PROJ_GRADE
      1  Gladys       Naboa         .T.        12/15/92    93
      2  Consuelo     Naboa         .T.        12/16/92    89
      3  Derek        Caruthers     .F.          /  /       0
      4  Wendel       Little        .T.        12/17/92    87
      5  Jeremy       Witherspoon   .T.        12/19/92    82
      6  Nancy        Hardwick      .F.          /  /       0
      7  Jonathan     Samuels       .T.        12/14/92    76
      8  Raquel       Ransworth     .F.          /  /       0
      9  Matts        Engleberg     .T.        12/13/92    62
     10  Mary Beth    Swazey        .T.        12/14/92    52
     11  Mary         Wong          .F.          /  /       0
.
Command  A:\compclas\COMPCLAS   Rec EOF/11    File              Caps
```

Figure 2.6 Use of DISPLAY ALL FIELD instruction to limit display

mistake, and in this case that would be a serious error. For this reason it is strongly recommended that you *not* use this command!

The preferred way to delete records is to view the record you want to delete first, then delete it. This way you see exactly what you're getting rid of, much reducing the chance of accidental error. To do this, you can use the **EDIT** command. If you are reasonably certain that the record you want to delete is Record 8, then you can type **EDIT 8** at the dot prompt. Even if you miss the record by 1 or 2, it will get you into the area where the record exists quickly, thus minimizing the number of Page Ups and Page Downs you have to do. Typing:

. EDIT 8

we see the record shown in Figure 2.7.

To delete this record we look at the menu at the top and choose the option **Records**. This is done by depressing the **Alt** key and then striking **R** for Records. Choose the menu item "Mark record for deletion" shown in the window (see Figure 2.8). Strike

EDITING YOUR DATABASE 43

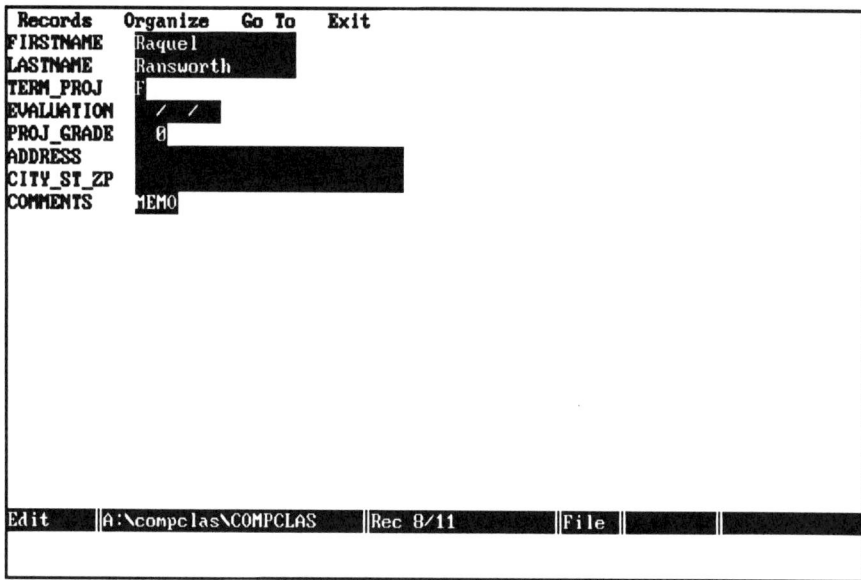

Figure 2.7 Edit screen resulting from EDIT 8 command

the Enter key[13]. Notice in Figure 2.9 that on the Status Line in the lower right hand corner the word "Del" has appeared (see Figure 2.9). This means that the record has been marked for deletion. It has *not* been deleted yet. Deletion is a two step process.

Now let's exit from **EDIT** and return to the dot prompt. You can do this in the usual way or do **^End**. Do not use **Esc** to exit from **EDIT** as that will cause the deletion to be abandoned.

Now do a **DISPLAY ALL** and notice that Record 8 has an asterisk next to it (see Figure 2.10). This asterisk indicates that Record 8 is now marked for deletion. Just as a marked man's days are numbered, in the same way Record 8's minutes are numbered.

We may also give Record 8 a reprieve, in one of two ways. First, we may go back into **EDIT** and un-delete the record in the same way that we deleted it. This time though, we choose the menu

---

[13]There is a simpler keystroke pair that will delete a record, and that is to use the combination **Ctrl-U** which we used to delete a field in the structure of the COMPCLAS database.

44   EDITING YOUR DATABASE

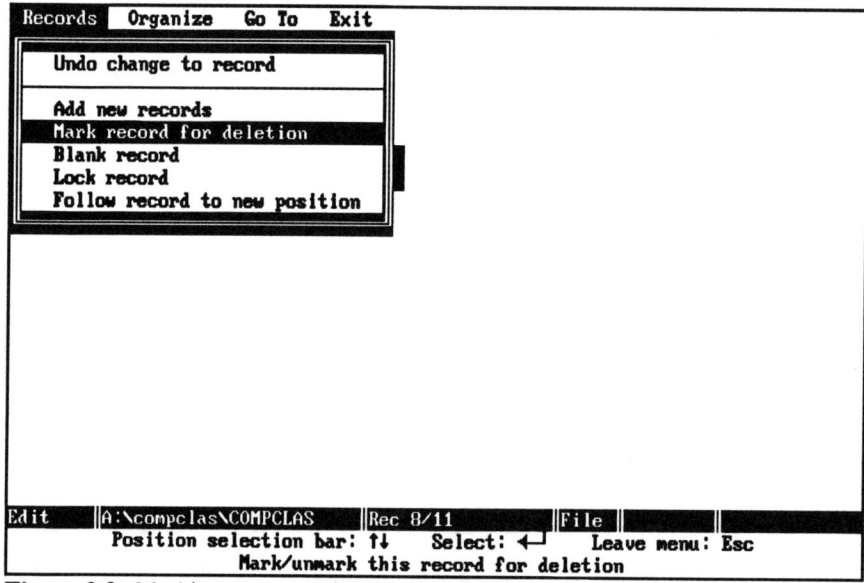

Figure 2.8 Marking a record for deletion using a menu option

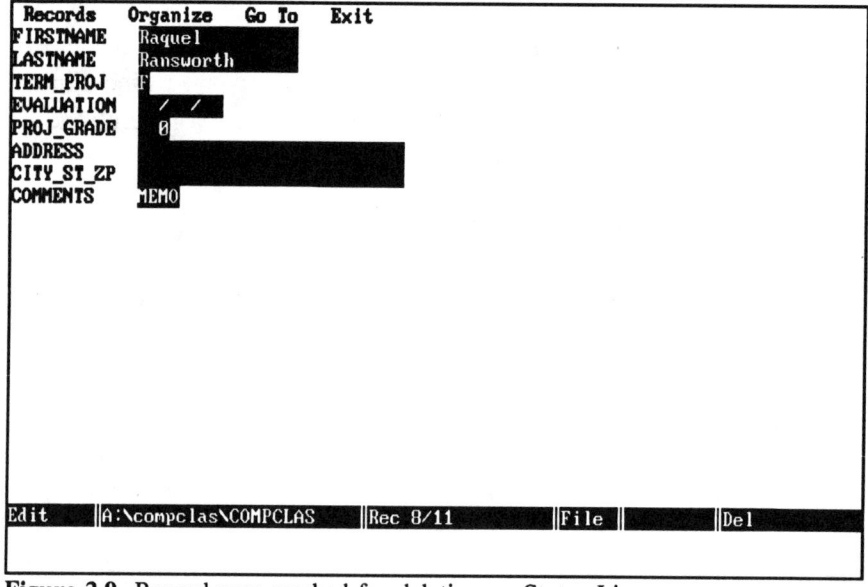

Figure 2.9 Record now marked for deletion on Status Line

EDITING YOUR DATABASE   45

```
Record# FIRSTNAME        LASTNAME         TERM_PROJ EVALUATION PROJ_GRADE ADDRESS
                CITY_ST_ZP                          COMMENTS
     1  Gladys           Naboa            .T.       12/15/92      93
                                                    MEMO
     2  Consuelo         Naboa            .T.       12/16/92      89
                                                    memo
     3  Derek            Caruthers        .F.          /  /        0
                                                    MEMO
     4  Wendel           Little           .T.       12/17/92      87
                                                    memo
     5  Jeremy           Witherspoon      .T.       12/19/92      82
                                                    MEMO
     6  Nancy            Hardwick         .F.          /  /        0
                                                    MEMO
     7  Jonathan         Samuels          .T.       12/14/92      76
                                                    memo
     8 *Raquel           Ransworth        .F.          /  /        0
                                                    MEMO
     9  Matts            Engleberg        .T.       12/13/92      62
                                                    memo
    10  Mary Beth        Swazey           .T.       12/14/92      52
Press any key to continue...
Command  A:\compclas\COMPCLAS       Rec 1/11        File
```

Figure 2.10 DISPLAY ALL showing record marked for deletion with *

item "Clear deletion mark" as shown in Figure 2.11, and then strike the Enter key[14]. The result of doing this un-deletion is to get the screen that we saw originally in Figure 2.7 once more.

Another way of un-deleting Record 8 is to use the **RECALL RECORD** command. This is done at the dot prompt by typing:

. **RECALL RECORD 8**

Now if we do a **DISPLAY ALL** you will notice that Record 8 is no longer flagged for deletion (i.e. the asterisk is no longer present as shown in Figure 2.5).

If we had several records deleted, we could grant general amnesty by using the **RECALL ALL** command.

. **RECALL ALL**

---

[14]We can also un-delete (or RECALL) a record by striking the **Ctrl-U** keystroke pair once more. This keystroke pair is a toggle which alternately deletes and recalls a deleted record.

46   EDITING YOUR DATABASE

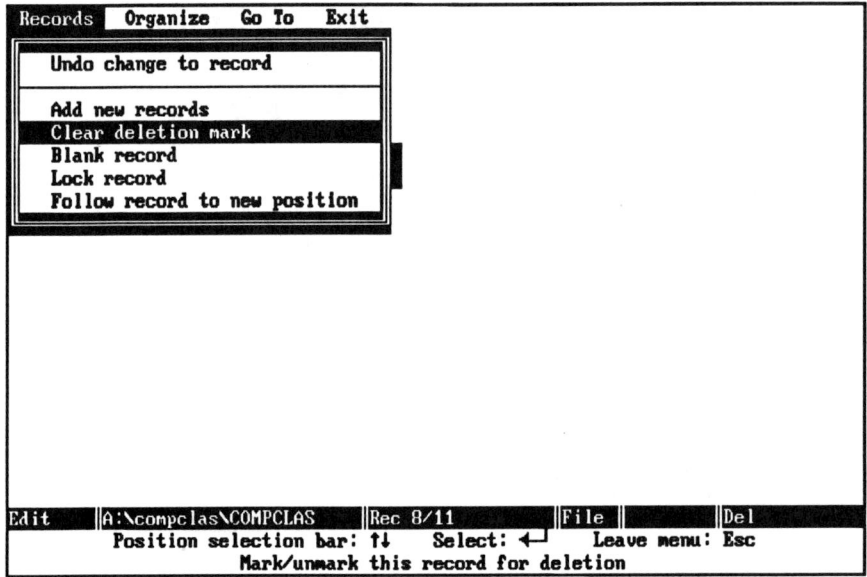

Figure 2.11 Choosing menu item to un-delete a record marked for deletion

RECALL ALL recalls any deleted records. If there were none deleted, obviously none will be recalled, and you will get a message to that effect.

We are now ready to terminate Record 8's existence, as well as any other records that have been marked for deletion. So, let us do a **DELETE RECORD 8** one last time to mark it for deletion. (At this point we should have enough confidence that Record 8 is indeed the one we want to delete that we need not look at it to be certain.) So once more:

. **DELETE RECORD 8**

Now to permanently delete records marked for deletion, we use the command **PACK**.

. **PACK**

Now type **DISPLAY ALL** and notice that Raquel's record is indeed missing (see Figure 2.12), but Matts Engleberg's record has taken its place and is now Record Number 8. Likewise, all records

EDITING YOUR DATABASE 47

above Record 8 have been renumbered one lower than before, thus filling up the gap left by Raquel's deletion. Our deletion has been completed.

2.5 Inserting a Record into a Database

It seems that Raquel Ransworth changed her mind again and decided to return to class. To be consistent with our original records, we would like to insert her record back in exactly the same position that we had her before (i.e. Record 8). Since when we APPEND a record to a database it always goes to the end of the database, this is not the command that we wish to use. In order to insert a record into a particular position in a database, we must use the **INSERT** command.

The way that we do this is to first go to Record Number 7, the record just preceding where we want to insert our new record. We go to this record by using the **GOTO** command followed by the number **7** at the dot prompt (followed by striking Enter, of course):

. GOTO 7

Record#	FIRSTNAME	LASTNAME	TERM_PROJ	EVALUATION	PROJ_GRADE	ADDRESS
		CITY_ST_ZP		COMMENTS		
1	Gladys	Naboa	.T.	12/15/92	93	
				MEMO		
2	Consuelo	Naboa	.T.	12/16/92	89	
				memo		
3	Derek	Caruthers	.F.	/ /	0	
				MEMO		
4	Wendel	Little	.T.	12/17/92	87	
				memo		
5	Jeremy	Witherspoon	.T.	12/19/92	82	
				MEMO		
6	Nancy	Hardwick	.F.	/ /	0	
				MEMO		
7	Jonathan	Samuels	.T.	12/14/92	76	
				memo		
8	Matts	Engleberg	.T.	12/13/92	62	
				memo		
9	Mary Beth	Swazey	.T.	12/14/92	52	
				MEMO		
10	Mary	Wong	.F.	/ /	0	

Press any key to continue...
Command A:\compclas\COMPCLAS   Rec 1/10   File

Figure 2.12 DISPLAY of COMPCLAS after executing a PACK

Just to be sure that we are indeed at the record preceding the one we want to **INSERT** (the record belonging to Jonathan Samuels), we need only type **DISPLAY** (or **DISPLAY OFF**) at the dot prompt. This will display the record that we are currently addressing.

. **DISPLAY**

FIRSTNAME   LASTNAME   TERM_PROJ EVALUATION
PROJ_GRADE ADDRESS   CITY_ST_ZP
COMMENTS
Jonathan   Samuels   .T.   12/14/92
76

Now we are ready to make our insertion. We do this by typing the command: **INSERT** at the dot prompt:

. **INSERT**

The screen that we see is shown in Figure 2.13 and looks exactly like the blank record we see when we do an APPEND. The only difference is that instead of seeing **EOF** on the bottom right hand part of the Status Line, we see: **8/10**, meaning that this will now be the eighth of ten records presently in the database.

We enter Raquel Ransworth into our new blank record just as we would do if we were appending a new person. We then Exit as we usually do (**Alt-E** and Enter), and then doing one of our **DISPLAY ALL** commands results in the screen shown in Figure 2.5 once more. Note that Raquel is indeed now Record 8, and that all other records below her have been pushed down by one.

A moment of reflection will tell us that this system of inserting will work fine for every case except when we wish to **INSERT** a record preceding Record 1. The way in which this is accomplished is by executing an: **INSERT BEFORE** command. It operates in exactly the same way as an **INSERT** command except that it inserts a record immediately before the current record rather than immediately after.

EDITING YOUR DATABASE

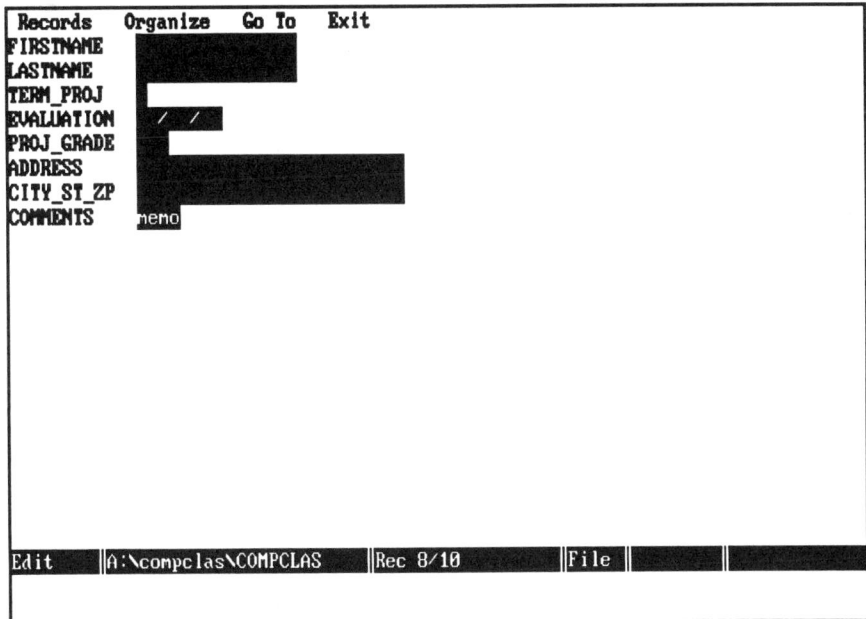

Figure 2.13 Result of INSERT command when positioned at Record 7

Let us **INSERT** a record **BEFORE** Record 1. As before, let's go to the record that we wish to **INSERT BEFORE**, which in this case is Record 1.
. **GOTO 1**

Now, typing: **INSERT BEFORE** at the dot prompt we get the screen shown in Figure 2.14. Note that we get the same blank **INSERT** screen as before, but this time the Status Line on the bottom right displays: **Rec: 1/11**, indicating that we are entering what will be Record 1 and that we presently have 11 records in the database.

Let's change our minds and decide *not* to **INSERT** a record at this time. We can do this by striking the **Esc** key, which returns us to the dot prompt without a new record having been inserted.

Raquel Ransworth split once again. As an exercise left to the reader, delete Raquel once more using the BROWSE mode and **Ctrl-U** to do the deleting. PACK your database to make this deletion permanent.

50 EDITING YOUR DATABASE

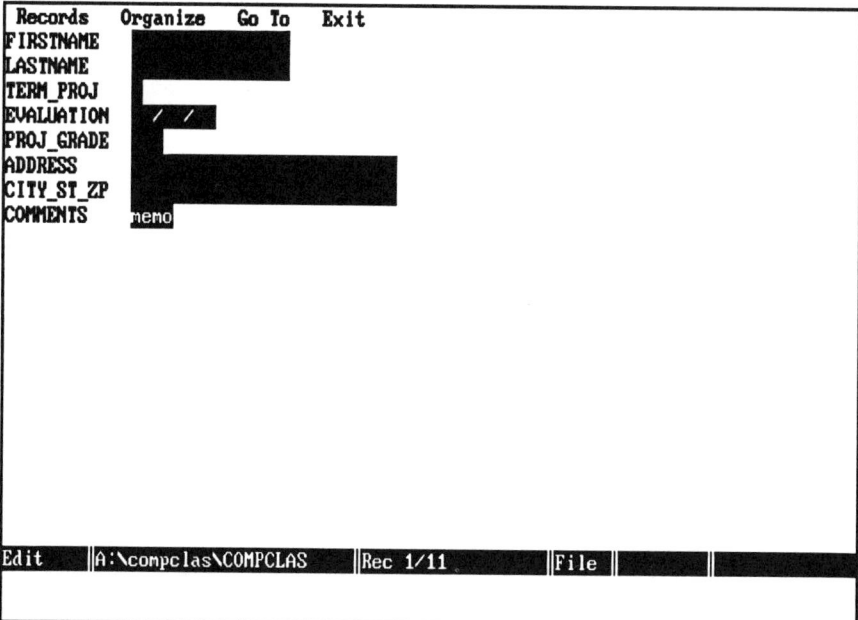

Figure 2.14 Screen resulting from INSERT BEFORE command when positioned at Record 1

2.6 Useful Features of the BROWSE Mode

2.6.1 Appending new data in BROWSE

There are some features to the BROWSE mode that are extremely useful. One of the principal ones is the ability to append new records without ever leaving the BROWSE mode. This is such a useful feature that often data entry as well as editing is done within BROWSE, and the EDIT/APPEND modes are completely bypassed.

With our COMPCLAS database open, let's go into the BROWSE mode once more.

. BROWSE

EDITING YOUR DATABASE 51

Now arrow down (strike the down arrow key 9 times) to the final record, that of Mary Wong. Next, strike the down arrow key one more time, Figure 2.15 shows us a message that we will see at the bottom of the screen: **Add new records? (Y/N)**. Answer **Y** to this question. Now you see the screen of Figure 2.16. We now have a blank record available to us to fill in as we like. Now strike the up arrow key once more. Note that we have returned to our original database of ten records (Figure 2.15) without having appended a blank record. This ability to change our minds without adding extra blank records is a very useful feature.

FIRSTNAME	LASTNAME	TERM_PROJ	EVALUATION	PROJ_GRADE	ADDRESS
Gladys	Naboa	T	12/15/92	93	
Consuelo	Naboa	T	12/16/92	89	
Derek	Caruthers	F	/ /	0	
Wendel	Little	T	12/17/92	87	
Jeremy	Witherspoon	T	12/19/92	82	
Nancy	Hardwick	F	/ /	0	
Jonathan	Samuels	T	12/14/92	76	
Matts	Engleberg	T	12/13/92	62	
Mary Beth	Swazey	T	12/14/92	52	
Mary	Wong	F	/ /	0	

Browse | A:\compclas\COMPCLAS | Rec 10/10 | File
===> Add new records? (Y/N)

Figure 2.15 Appending a new record while in the BROWSE Mode

2.6.2 Entering Data into a Database by Field

At the beginning of this chapter we added some new fields to COMPCLAS, but we didn't add any data to these fields. In addition, the newly added fields, **ADDRESS** and **CITY_ST_ZP** as well as our memo field, **COMMENTS**, are missing from view when we initially enter the **BROWSE** mode. The missing fields may be thought of as currently lying just off screen to the right.

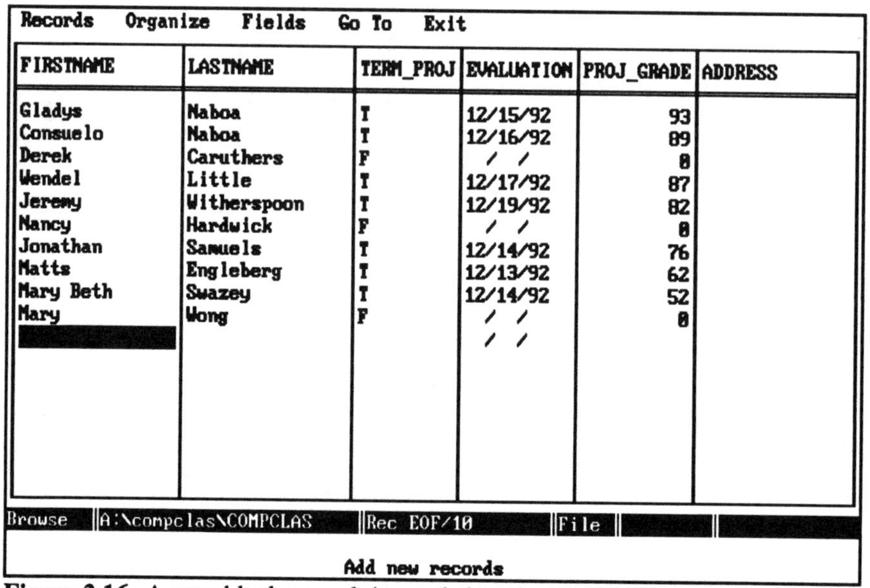

```
Records    Organize   Fields   Go To    Exit
FIRSTNAME  LASTNAME          TERM_PROJ EVALUATION PROJ_GRADE ADDRESS
Gladys     Naboa             T         12/15/92   93
Consuelo   Naboa             T         12/16/92   89
Derek      Caruthers         F         /  /       0
Wendel     Little            T         12/17/92   87
Jeremy     Witherspoon       T         12/19/92   82
Nancy      Hardwick          F         /  /       0
Jonathan   Samuels           T         12/14/92   76
Matts      Engleberg         T         12/13/92   62
Mary Beth  Swazey            T         12/14/92   52
Mary       Wong              F         /  /       0
                                       /  /
Browse  A:\compclas\COMPCLAS   Rec EOF/10   File
                      Add new records
```

Figure 2.16 A new blank record Appended to the BROWSE screen

We can bring them into view by striking the Enter key six times (if the cursor was originally in FIRSTNAME field). However, note that the **FIRSTNAME, LASTNAME,** and **TERM_PROJ** fields are now no longer in view (see Figure 2.17). We may think of those fields lying just off screen to the left. Hence, the **BROWSE** screen is like a window that can look at only 80 characters of any one record at a time. On the other hand, we can view up to 17 records simultaneously.

We would now like to add our additional address data to complete our database. The data is shown in Table 2.1.

Here is where the **BROWSE** command really comes in handy. We can type in one column of this data at a time without having to use the Up and Down arrows repeatedly to position ourselves in the appropriate field entry slot as would have to be done in the **EDIT** mode. This is done by using the **BROWSE FIELD** command, just as we did with **LIST** and **DISPLAY**. Figure 2.18 shows the results of limiting our **BROWSE** screen to three fields:

. BROWSE FIELD FIRSTNAME, LASTNAME, ADDRESS

EDITING YOUR DATABASE 53

```
Records  Organize  Fields  Go To  Exit
┌──────────┬──────────┬─────────┬──────────────────────┬─────┐
│EVALUATION│PROJ_GRADE│ADDRESS  │CITY_ST_ZP            │COMM │
├──────────┼──────────┼─────────┼──────────────────────┼─────┤
│12/15/92  │    93    │         │██████████████████████│MEMO │
│12/16/92  │    89    │         │                      │memo │
│  /  /    │     0    │         │                      │MEMO │
│12/17/92  │    87    │         │                      │memo │
│12/19/92  │    82    │         │                      │MEMO │
│  /  /    │     0    │         │                      │MEMO │
│12/14/92  │    76    │         │                      │memo │
│12/13/92  │    62    │         │                      │memo │
│12/14/92  │    52    │         │                      │MEMO │
│  /  /    │     0    │         │                      │memo │
└──────────┴──────────┴─────────┴──────────────────────┴─────┘
Browse  A:\compclas\COMPCLAS    Rec 1/10    File
```

Figure 2.17 BROWSE of COMPCLAS after striking Enter 6 times

Table 2.1 Data for new ADDRESS and CITY_ST_ZP fields in COMPCLAS

LASTNAME	ADDRESS	CITY ST ZP
Naboa	324 Catskill Terrace	Sundown, NY 12782
Naboa	324 Catskill Terrace	Sundown, NY 12782
Caruthers	21 Spring Glen Road	Cooks Falls, NY 12728
Little	1021 Cochecton Street	Jeffersonville, NY 12748
Witherspoon	821 Kiamesha Circle	Glen Spey, NY 12737
Hardwick	512 Delaware Overlook	Callicoon, NY 12723
Samuels	96 Rainbow's End	Roscoe, NY 12776
Engleberg	2021 Mountain View	Mountaindale, NY 12758
Swazey	86 Cider Mill Lane	North Branch, NY 12766
Wong	321 Lakeside Avenue	Swan Lake, NY 12783

```
Records   Organize   Fields   Go To   Exit
FIRSTNAME      LASTNAME       ADDRESS
Gladys         Naboa          ███████████████
Consuelo       Naboa
Derek          Caruthers
Wendel         Little
Jeremy         Witherspoon
Nancy          Hardwick
Jonathan       Samuels
Matts          Engleberg
Mary Beth      Swazey
Mary           Wong



Browse  A:\compclas\COMPCLAS   Rec 1/10    File
```

Figure 2.18   Using BROWSE FIELD command to enter column data in ADDRESS field

Now we simply type in all the data for the **ADDRESS** field at the same time, striking the Down Arrow key at the end of each line. When we do that, it goes to the **ADDRESS** field of the very next record. When we get done entering all the data for the **ADDRESS** field, we get the result shown in Figure 2.19

2.6.3 Browse Menu Options

We could do one more **BROWSE FIELD** command, choosing our fields judiciously, in order to enter the final **CITY_ST_ZP** data. However, there is another way of entering field data using the Menu, which doesn't require us to make such a complicated **BROWSE** command. After having exited **BROWSE (Ctrl-End)**, go back into **BROWSE** the normal way.

. **BROWSE**

Now choose the "Fields" menu option at the top by depressing the **Alt** key and striking the **F** key. The result is shown

EDITING YOUR DATABASE

```
Records   Organize   Fields   Go To   Exit
FIRSTNAME     LASTNAME      ADDRESS
Gladys        Naboa         324 Catskill Terrace
Consuelo      Naboa         324 Catskill Terrace
Derek         Caruthers     21 Spring Glen Road
Wendel        Little        1821 Cochecton Street
Jeremy        Witherspoon   821 Kianesha Circle
Nancy         Hardwick      512 Delaware Overlook
Jonathan      Samuels       96 Rainbow's End
Matts         Engleberg     2821 Mountain View
Mary Beth     Swazey        85 Cider Mill Lane
Mary          Wong          321 Lakeside Avenue

Browse  A:\compclas\COMPCLAS   Rec 10/10   File
```

Figure 2.19 ADDRESS field data entered using BROWSE FIELD command

```
Records   Organize   Fields   Go To   Exit
FIRSTNAME     LAST    Lock fields on left  {0}      GRADE  ADDRESS
                      Blank field
Gladys        Nabo    Freeze field          {}       93    324 Catskill T
Consuelo      Nabo    Size field                     89    324 Catskill T
Derek         Caru                                    0    21 Spring Glen
Wendel        Little       T       12/17/92          87    1821 Cochecton
Jeremy        Witherspoon  T       12/19/92          82    821 Kianesha C
Nancy         Hardwick     F         / /              0    512 Delaware O
Jonathan      Samuels      T       12/14/92          76    96 Rainbow's E
Matts         Engleberg    T       12/13/92          62    2821 Mountain
Mary Beth     Swazey       T       12/14/92          52    85 Cider Mill
Mary          Wong         F         / /              0    321 Lakeside A

Browse  A:\compclas\COMPCLAS   Rec 1/10   File
         Position selection bar: ↑↓   Select: ↵   Leave menu: Esc
    Enter the number of fields to remain stationary on the left when scrolling
```

Figure 2.20 Choosing the "Lock Field" item of the "Field" menu option in BROWSE

in Figure 2.20. Note that the highlighted menu option is, "Lock fields on left". Select this option by striking the Enter key. Next a new window drops down saying, "Enter number of fields to remain stationary: " (see Figure 2.21). Type 2 in response to this question. Now strike the Enter key six times and watch what happens. In Figure 2.22 we see that the fields: TERM_PROJ, EVALUATION, PROJ_GRADE, and ADDRESS have disappeared to the left, but the two fields we "Locked", FIRSTNAME and LASTNAME, have remained in place.

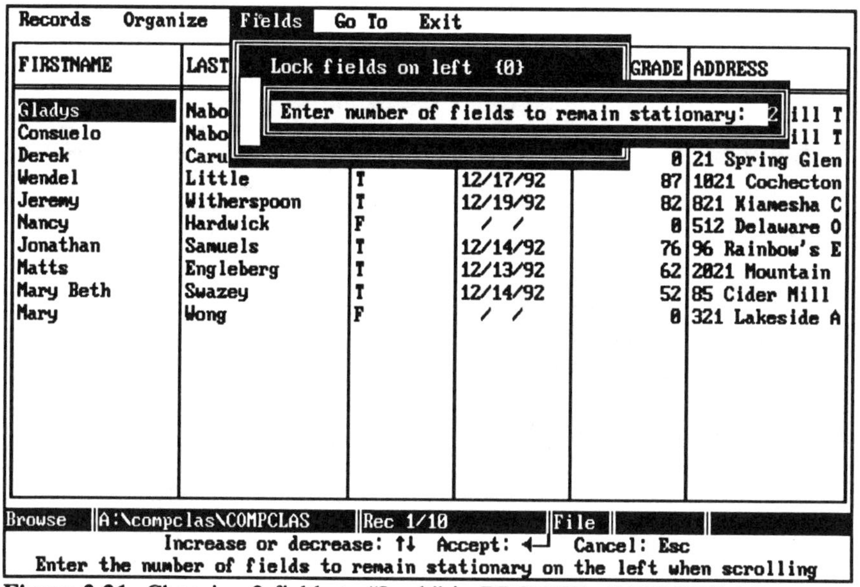

Figure 2.21 Choosing 2 fields to "Lock" in BROWSE of COMPCLAS

This "Locking" feature allows us to keep the **key** fields in view so we can identify to which record the data we are entering, for CITY_ST_ZP, belongs. If it were not for this feature, there would be no way, short of the **BROWSE FIELD** command, for us to see the three fields: FIRSTNAME, LASTNAME, and CITY_ST_ZP, on the screen at the same time.

Now there is one more feature which allows us to use the Enter key rather than the Down Arrow key to enter the field data in for CITY_ST_ZP. Choose the "Fields" menu option once more

EDITING YOUR DATABASE 57

```
Records   Organize   Fields   Go To   Exit
FIRSTNAME      LASTNAME       CITY_ST_ZP              COMMENTS
Gladys         Naboa                                  MEMO
Consuelo       Naboa                                  memo
Derek          Caruthers                              MEMO
Wendel         Little                                 memo
Jeremy         Witherspoon                            MEMO
Nancy          Hardwick                               MEMO
Jonathan       Samuels                                memo
Matts          Engleberg                              memo
Mary Beth      Swazey                                 MEMO
Mary           Wong                                   memo




Browse   A:\compclas\COMPCLAS      Rec 1/10      File
```

Figure 2.22 BROWSE of COMPCLAS with first two fields "Locked" and CITY_ST_ZP field panned into view

```
Records   Organize   Fields   Go To   Exit
FIRSTNAME      LAST     Lock fields on left  {2}     COMMENTS
                        Blank field
Gladys         Nabo     Freeze field         { }     MEMO
Consuelo       Nabo     Size field                   memo
Derek          Caru                                  MEMO
Wendel         Little                                memo
Jeremy         Witherspoon                           MEMO
Nancy          Hardwick                              MEMO
Jonathan       Samuels                               memo
Matts          Engleberg                             memo
Mary Beth      Swazey                                MEMO
Mary           Wong                                  memo




Browse   A:\compclas\COMPCLAS      Rec 1/10      File
         Position selection bar: ↑↓   Select: ↵    Leave menu: Esc
                Limit editing to the specified field
```

Figure 2.23 Choosing "Freeze Field" item of "Field" menu option

(**Alt-F**). Now choose the menu item, "Freeze field" (see Figure 2.23). Striking the Enter key, a window opens and asks the question, "Enter field name: ". Type in the field name, CITY_ST_ZP, at this time (See Figure 2.24). Now the cursor is "Frozen" in the CITY_ST_ZP field. No matter how many times you strike the Enter key, or any of the arrow keys, the cursor remains "Frozen" in the CITY_ST_ZP field.

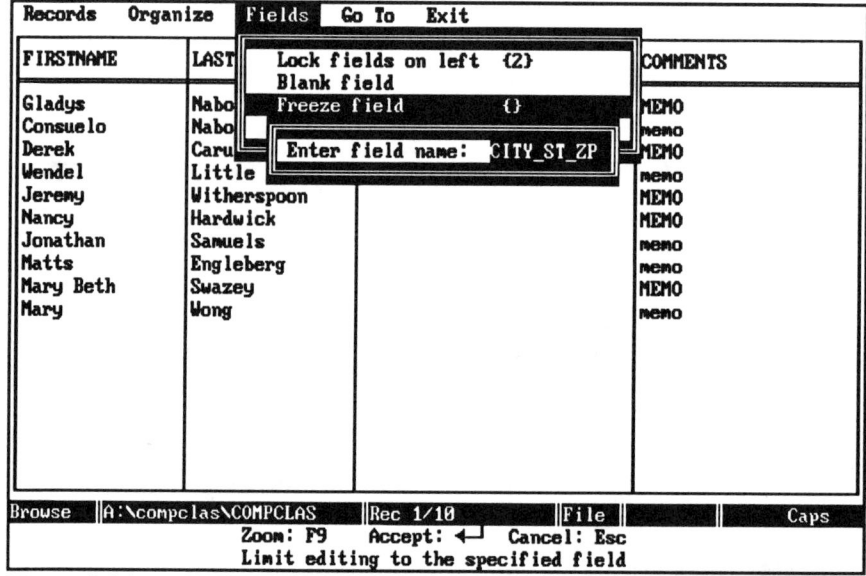

Figure 2.24 Freezing field CITY_ST_ZP in BROWSE of COMPCLAS

Now we can input the CITY_ST_ZP data from Table 2.1.

The final result is shown in Figure 2.25.

To undo the effect of **Lock** and **Freeze** it is only necessary to select the one that you want turned off, and instead of entering any value, clear the value that was entered before. In the case of "Freeze", simply backspace out the CITY_ST_ZP field. In the case of "Lock", simply type in **0** in answer to the question, "Enter number of fields to remain stationary: ". Of course exiting from **BROWSE** will accomplish the same task.

EDITING YOUR DATABASE

```
Records   Organize   Fields   Go To   Exit
┌──────────────┬──────────────┬─────────────────────────┬──────────┐
│FIRSTNAME     │LASTNAME      │CITY_ST_ZP               │COMMENTS  │
├──────────────┼──────────────┼─────────────────────────┼──────────┤
│Gladys        │Naboa         │Sundown, NY    12782     │MEMO      │
│Consuelo      │Naboa         │Sundown, NY    12782     │memo      │
│Derek         │Caruthers     │Cooks Falls, NY   12728  │MEMO      │
│Wendel        │Little        │Jeffersonville,  NY 12748│memo      │
│Jeremy        │Witherspoon   │Glen Spey, NY   12737    │MEMO      │
│Nancy         │Hardwick      │Callicoon, NY   12723    │MEMO      │
│Jonathan      │Samuels       │Roscoe, NY   12776       │memo      │
│Matts         │Engleberg     │Mountaindale, NY   12758 │memo      │
│Mary Beth     │Swazey        │North Branch, NY   12766 │MEMO      │
│Mary          │Wong          │Swan Lake, NY    12783   │memo      │
└──────────────┴──────────────┴─────────────────────────┴──────────┘
 Browse  ‖A:\compclas\COMPCLAS‖ Rec 10/10 ‖    ‖File‖
```

Figure 2.25 Data input with first 2 fields Locked, CITY_ST_ZP frozen

2.7 Example II: Expanding the ACCOUNTS database

So far, the ACCOUNTS database has no more information in it than an ordinary checkbook. We would like to expand its capability so that we can also keep totals of how we are doing in various budget categories that we will set up. In order to do this, we must add a new field that we will call **CAT**egory. The various budget categories that we will allow are shown in Table 2.2.

Open your database, ACCOUNTS.dbf, and MODIFY the STRUCTURE so that it has the structure shown in Listing 2.1.

Now enter the **CAT**egory data shown in Figure 2.26 using the BROWSE FIELD command. Note that the CASHED field has also changed. Using the BROWSE mode, freezing the CASHED field, make the changes indicated. Finally, appending records in the BROWSE mode, add the additional records shown in Figure 2.27.

60 EDITING YOUR DATABASE

Table 2.2 List of CATegories and their Definitions for ACCOUNTS

	CATegory	Description
1.	CAB	Cablevision
2.	CAR	Automobile expenses
3.	DOC	Medical and Dental Care
4.	DON	Donation
5.	ENT	Entertainment
6.	GIF	Gifts
7.	GRO	Groceries
8.	HOU	Household items
9.	INS	Insurance
10.	MAI	Maintenance
11.	PER	Personal expenses
12.	PET	expenses
13.	REI	Reimbursements
14.	SAL	Salary deposit
15.	TAX	Taxes
16.	TEL	Telephone
17.	UTI	Utilities

```
Structure for database: A:\ACCOUNTS\ACCOUNTS.DBF
Number of data records:     12
Date of last update   : 01/13/91
Field  Field Name  Type        Width      Dec    Index
    1  DATE        Date            8                 N
    2  CHECK       Character       3                 N
    3  DESCRIPT    Character      32                 N
    4  CAT         Character       3                 N
    5  DEBITS      Numeric         8         2       N
    6  RECEIPTS    Numeric         8         2       N
    7  CASHED      Logical         1                 N
** Total **                       64
```

Listing 2.1 LIST STRUCTURE of modified ACCOUNTS.dbf with field CAT

2.7.1 Navigating Around the Database in BROWSE Mode

Suppose we want to move quickly around the database ACCOUNTS. We can always Page Down and Page Up using the PgDn and PgUp keys. This moves us through the database 16 records at a time. I routinely move through databases of more that 10,000 records. You can grow quite a callous on your finger paging up and down through databases of that size, not to mention the time involved.

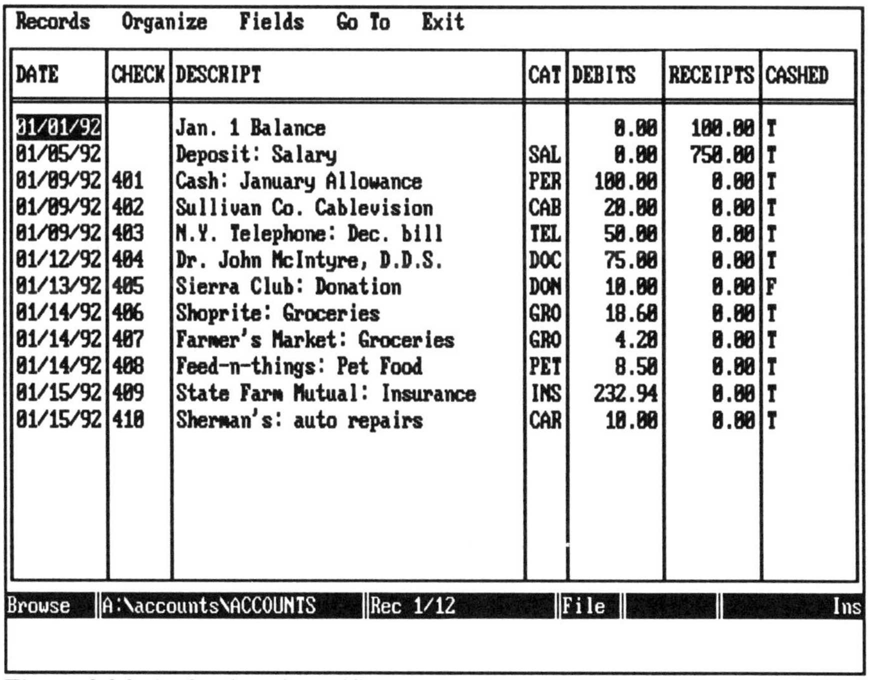
Records Organize Fields Go To Exit

DATE	CHECK	DESCRIPT	CAT	DEBITS	RECEIPTS	CASHED
01/01/92		Jan. 1 Balance		0.00	100.00	T
01/05/92		Deposit: Salary	SAL	0.00	750.00	T
01/09/92	401	Cash: January Allowance	PER	100.00	0.00	T
01/09/92	402	Sullivan Co. Cablevision	CAB	20.00	0.00	T
01/09/92	403	N.Y. Telephone: Dec. bill	TEL	50.00	0.00	T
01/12/92	404	Dr. John McIntyre, D.D.S.	DOC	75.00	0.00	T
01/13/92	405	Sierra Club: Donation	DON	10.00	0.00	F
01/14/92	406	Shoprite: Groceries	GRO	10.60	0.00	T
01/14/92	407	Farmer's Market: Groceries	GRO	4.20	0.00	T
01/14/92	408	Feed-n-things: Pet Food	PET	8.50	0.00	T
01/15/92	409	State Farm Mutual: Insurance	INS	232.94	0.00	T
01/15/92	410	Sherman's: auto repairs	CAR	10.00	0.00	T

Browse A:\accounts\ACCOUNTS Rec 1/12 File Ins

Figure 2.26 BROWSE of modified database ACCOUNTS with original records having new values in the cashed field

EDITING YOUR DATABASE

```
Records   Organize   Fields   Go To   Exit
| DATE     | CHECK | DESCRIPT                        | CAT | DEBITS | RECEIPTS | CASHED |
| 01/16/92 | 411   | NYSEG: Utilities                | UTI | 110.12 |   0.00   | F      |
| 01/16/92 | 412   | West Side Vets                  | PET |  30.00 |   0.00   | F      |
| 01/18/92 |       | Deposit: Travel Expense Reimb.  | REI |   0.00 |  38.25   | T      |
| 01/19/92 | 413   | Dr. Isaacs, M.D. (eye doct)     | DOC |  40.00 |   0.00   | T      |
| 01/19/92 |       | Deposit: Salary                 | SAL |   0.00 | 750.00   | T      |
| 01/20/92 | 414   | Cash: Gas & Tolls               | CAR |  34.65 |   0.00   | T      |
| 01/20/92 | 415   | Sullivan's: Dept. Store         | GIF |  25.66 |   0.00   | F      |
| 01/22/92 | 416   | Action Video                    | ENT |  18.59 |   0.00   | F      |
| 01/22/92 | 417   | MBNA Payment Services:Cred. Card| HOU | 100.00 |   0.00   | F      |
| 01/25/92 | 418   | Many Happy Returns: Tax Prep.   | TAX | 105.00 |   0.00   | F      |
| 01/25/92 | 419   | NYC Parking Violations Bur.     | PER |  35.00 |   0.00   | F      |
| 01/27/92 | 420   | Great American: Groceries       | GRO |  39.92 |   0.00   | F      |
| 01/28/92 | 421   | Trading Post: Maintenance items | MAI |  20.47 |   0.00   | F      |

Browse   A:\accounts\ACCOUNTS   Rec 13/25   File                               Ins
```

Figure 2.27 Additional records added to database ACCOUNTS.dbf

The BROWSE mode gives us a quick way of moving through the database. Select the "Go To" menu option in the BROWSE menu using **Alt-G**. Now we see a number of menu selections for moving about the database. For example, if we select the "Last record" item as shown in Figure 2.28, and strike the Enter key, we immediately go to the bottom-most record at the end of the database (see Figure 2.29).

Likewise, if we select the "Top record" menu item as shown in Figure 2.30, we'll go to the very first record of the database as we see in Figure 2.31.

We can also move to specific records in the database by choosing the "Record number" menu item shown in Figure 2.32. However this requires you to know the record number of the record to which you want to go.

The way I often use to move about in a large database quickly is to do what is called a "Forward search" or a "Backward search". If we're at the beginning of the database, as shown in

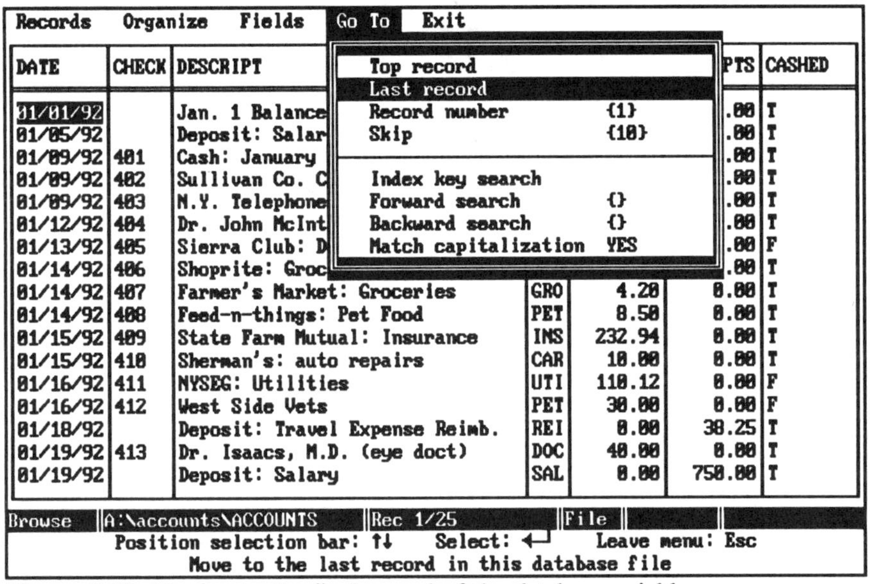

EDITING YOUR DATABASE

Records	Organize	Fields	Go To	Exit			
DATE	CHECK	DESCRIPT	Top record			PTS	CASHED
			Last record				
01/01/92		Jan. 1 Balance	Record number	{1}		.00	T
01/05/92		Deposit: Salar	Skip	{10}		.00	T
01/09/92	401	Cash: January				.00	T
01/09/92	402	Sullivan Co. C	Index key search			.00	T
01/09/92	403	N.Y. Telephone	Forward search	{}		.00	T
01/12/92	404	Dr. John McInt	Backward search	{}		.00	T
01/13/92	405	Sierra Club: D	Match capitalization	YES		.00	F
01/14/92	406	Shoprite: Groc				.00	T
01/14/92	407	Farmer's Market: Groceries		GRO	4.20	0.00	T
01/14/92	408	Feed-n-things: Pet Food		PET	8.50	0.00	T
01/15/92	409	State Farm Mutual: Insurance		INS	232.94	0.00	T
01/15/92	410	Sherman's: auto repairs		CAR	18.00	0.00	T
01/16/92	411	NYSEG: Utilities		UTI	110.12	0.00	F
01/16/92	412	West Side Vets		PET	30.00	0.00	F
01/18/92		Deposit: Travel Expense Reimb.		REI	0.00	38.25	T
01/19/92	413	Dr. Isaacs, M.D. (eye doct)		DOC	40.00	0.00	T
01/19/92		Deposit: Salary		SAL	0.00	750.00	T

Browse A:\accounts\ACCOUNTS   Rec 1/25   File
Position selection bar: ↑↓   Select: ↵   Leave menu: Esc
Move to the last record in this database file

Figure 2.28 Moving to the final record of the database quickly

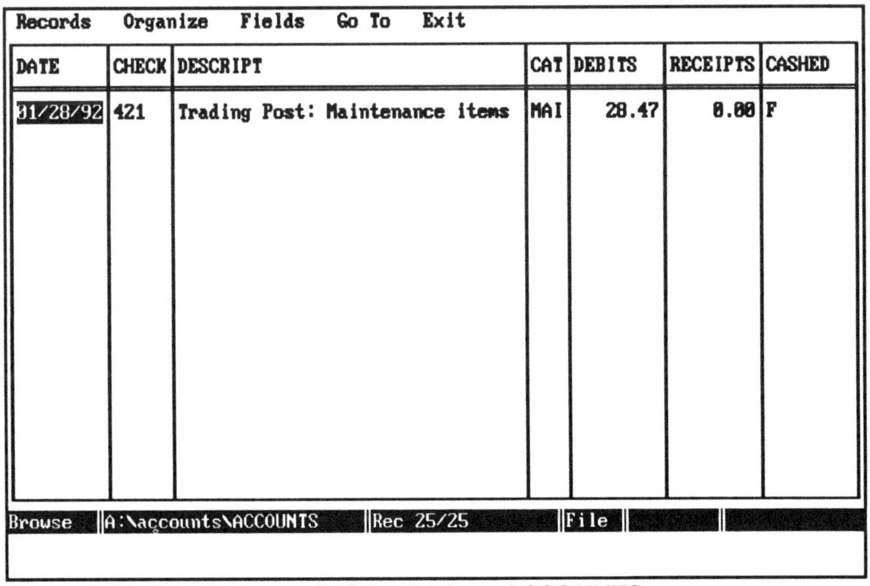

Records	Organize	Fields	Go To	Exit			
DATE	CHECK	DESCRIPT		CAT	DEBITS	RECEIPTS	CASHED
01/28/92	421	Trading Post: Maintenance items		MAI	28.47	0.00	F

Browse A:\accounts\ACCOUNTS   Rec 25/25   File

Figure 2.29 The final record of the database ACCOUNTS

64   EDITING YOUR DATABASE

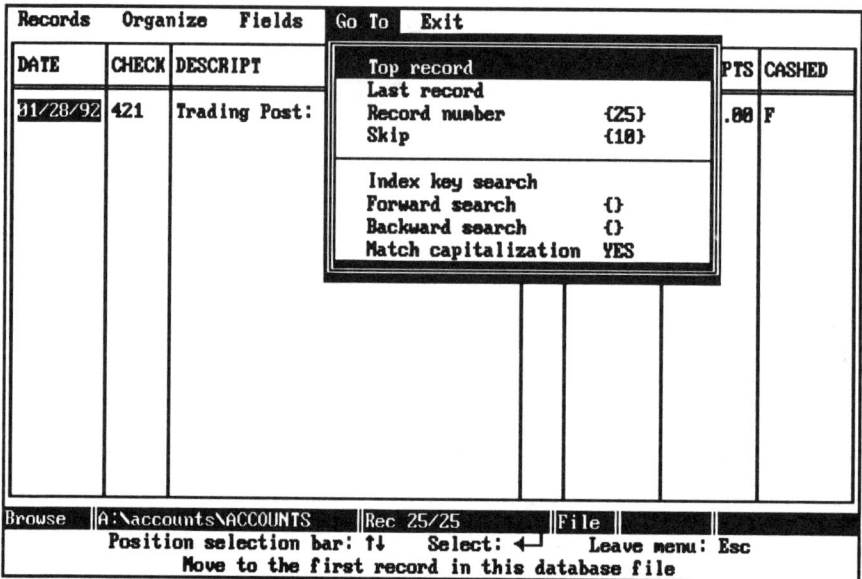

Records	Organize	Fields	Go To	Exit				
DATE	CHECK	DESCRIPT					PTS	CASHED
01/28/92	421	Trading Post:	Top record				.00	F
			Last record					
			Record number	{25}				
			Skip	{10}				
			Index key search					
			Forward search	{}				
			Backward search	{}				
			Match capitalization	YES				

```
Browse   A:\accounts\ACCOUNTS   Rec 25/25   File
         Position selection bar: ↑↓   Select: ↵   Leave menu: Esc
         Move to the first record in this database file
```

Figure 2.30 Moving to the beginning of the database quickly

Records	Organize	Fields	Go To	Exit			
DATE	CHECK	DESCRIPT		CAT	DEBITS	RECEIPTS	CASHED
01/01/92		Jan. 1 Balance			0.00	100.00	T
01/05/92		Deposit: Salary		SAL	0.00	750.00	T
01/09/92	401	Cash: January Allowance		PER	100.00	0.00	T
01/09/92	402	Sullivan Co. Cablevision		CAB	20.00	0.00	T
01/09/92	403	N.Y. Telephone: Dec. bill		TEL	50.00	0.00	T
01/12/92	404	Dr. John McIntyre, D.D.S.		DOC	75.00	0.00	T
01/13/92	405	Sierra Club: Donation		DON	10.00	0.00	F
01/14/92	406	Shoprite: Groceries		GRO	18.60	0.00	T
01/14/92	407	Farmer's Market: Groceries		GRO	4.20	0.00	T
01/14/92	408	Feed-n-things: Pet Food		PET	8.50	0.00	T
01/15/92	409	State Farm Mutual: Insurance		INS	232.94	0.00	T
01/15/92	410	Sherman's: auto repairs		CAR	10.00	0.00	T
01/16/92	411	NYSEG: Utilities		UTI	110.12	0.00	F
01/16/92	412	West Side Vets		PET	30.00	0.00	F
01/18/92		Deposit: Travel Expense Reimb.		REI	0.00	38.25	T
01/19/92	413	Dr. Isaacs, M.D. (eye doct)		DOC	40.00	0.00	T
01/19/92		Deposit: Salary		SAL	0.00	750.00	T

```
Browse   A:\accounts\ACCOUNTS   Rec 1/25   File
```

Figure 2.31 The beginning of the database ACCOUNTS in BROWSE

EDITING YOUR DATABASE

Figure 2.32, then we need to move the cursor to the column on which we wish to search. For the ACCOUNTS database, the CHECK number column is an obvious field on which to search. First, move the cursor to the CHECK field and select the menu item "Forward Search", as shown in Figure 2.33. Striking the Enter key, a window opens with the question, "Enter search string: ". If what we want is check number 415, we type this in here as indicated in Figure 2.34. Striking the Enter key once more, we find ourselves at check number 415 as shown in Figure 2.35.

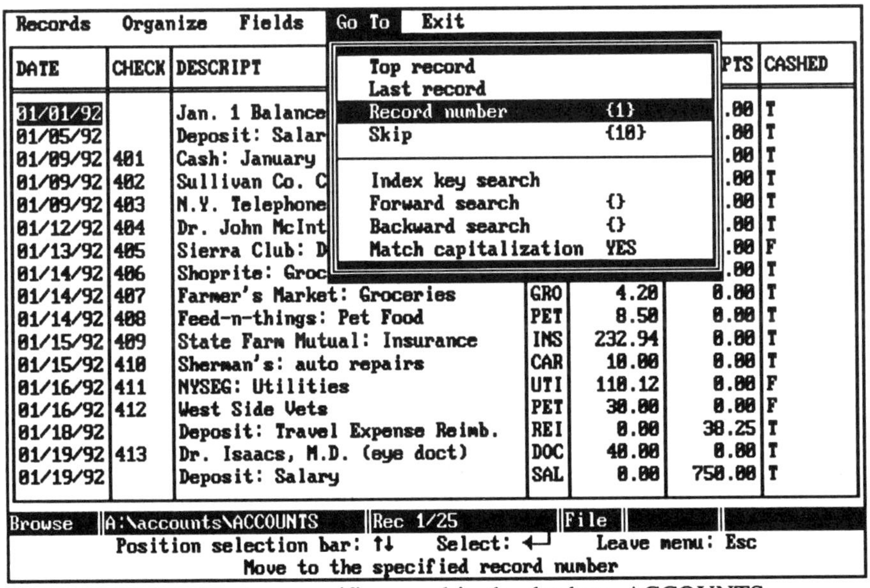

Figure 2.32 Moving to a specific record in the database ACCOUNTS

Obviously, if we were at the end of the database, we would use a "Backward search" to find the record we wanted. As you can see, the BROWSE mode gives us some powerful tools for navigating around a database quickly.

66 EDITING YOUR DATABASE

Records	Organize	Fields	Go To	Exit			
DATE	CHECK	DESCRIPT	Top record			PTS	CASHED
			Last record				
01/01/92		Jan. 1 Balance	Record number	{1}		.00	T
01/05/92		Deposit: Salar	Skip	{10}		.00	T
01/09/92	401	Cash: January				.00	T
01/09/92	402	Sullivan Co. C	Index key search			.00	T
01/09/92	403	N.Y. Telephone	Forward search	{}		.00	T
01/12/92	404	Dr. John McInt	Backward search	{}		.00	T
01/13/92	405	Sierra Club: D	Match capitalization	YES		.00	F
01/14/92	406	Shoprite: Groc				.00	T
01/14/92	407	Farmer's Market: Groceries		GRO	4.20	0.00	T
01/14/92	408	Feed-n-things: Pet Food		PET	8.50	0.00	T
01/15/92	409	State Farm Mutual: Insurance		INS	232.94	0.00	T
01/15/92	410	Sherman's: auto repairs		CAR	10.00	0.00	T
01/16/92	411	NYSEG: Utilities		UTI	110.12	0.00	F
01/16/92	412	West Side Vets		PET	30.00	0.00	F
01/18/92		Deposit: Travel Expense Reimb.		REI	0.00	38.25	T
01/19/92	413	Dr. Isaacs, M.D. (eye doct)		DOC	40.00	0.00	T
01/19/92		Deposit: Salary		SAL	0.00	750.00	T

Browse A:\accounts\ACCOUNTS Rec 1/25 File
Position selection bar: ↑↓   Select: ↵   Leave menu: Esc
Search this field for the specified string from the current record forward

Figure 2.33 Doing a Forward Search in the BROWSE Mode

Records	Organize	Fields	Go To	Exit			
DATE	CHECK	DESCRIPT	Top record			PTS	CASHED
			Last record				
01/01/92		Jan. 1 Balance	Record number	{1}		.00	T
01/05/92		Deposit: Salar	Skip	{10}		.00	T
01/09/92	401	Cash: January				.00	T
01/09/92	402	Sullivan Co. C	Index key search			.00	T
01/09/92	403	N.Y. Telephone	Forward search	{}		.00	T
01/12/92	404	Dr. John McInt					
01/13/92	405	Sierra Club: D	Enter search string: 415				
01/14/92	406	Shoprite: Groc					
01/14/92	407	Farmer's Market: Groceries		GRO	4.20	0.00	T
01/14/92	408	Feed-n-things: Pet Food		PET	8.50	0.00	T
01/15/92	409	State Farm Mutual: Insurance		INS	232.94	0.00	T
01/15/92	410	Sherman's: auto repairs		CAR	10.00	0.00	T
01/16/92	411	NYSEG: Utilities		UTI	110.12	0.00	F
01/16/92	412	West Side Vets		PET	30.00	0.00	F
01/18/92		Deposit: Travel Expense Reimb.		REI	0.00	38.25	T
01/19/92	413	Dr. Isaacs, M.D. (eye doct)		DOC	40.00	0.00	T
01/19/92		Deposit: Salary		SAL	0.00	750.00	T

Browse A:\accounts\ACCOUNTS Rec 1/25 File
Zoom: F9   Accept: ↵   Cancel: Esc
Search this field for the specified string from the current record forward

Figure 2.34 A Forward Search for check number 415 in ACCOUNTS

EDITING YOUR DATABASE

```
Records   Organize   Fields   Go To   Exit
```

DATE	CHECK	DESCRIPT	CAT	DEBITS	RECEIPTS	CASHED
01/20/92	415	Sullivan's: Dept. Store	GIF	25.66	0.00	F
01/22/92	416	Action Video	ENT	10.59	0.00	F
01/22/92	417	MBNA Payment Services:Cred. Card	HOU	100.00	0.00	F
01/25/92	418	Many Happy Returns: Tax Prep.	TAX	105.00	0.00	F
01/25/92	419	NYC Parking Violations Bur.	PER	35.00	0.00	F
01/27/92	420	Great American: Groceries	GRO	39.92	0.00	F
01/28/92	421	Trading Post: Maintenance items	MAI	20.47	0.00	F

```
Browse   A:\accounts\ACCOUNTS   Rec 19/25   File
```

Figure 2.35 Record containing check number 415 found

2.8 Summary

In this chapter we presented the **MODIFY STRUCTURE** command which allowed us to add fields, delete fields, and edit existing fields. The **DISPLAY ALL** command was introduced to allow us to display the database one screen page at a time. Finally, we looked at the **BROWSE** command in more depth.

Two means of deleting records were presented. The preferred method is to view the record while in the Edit or Browse mode. In this way you can see exactly who or what it is you are deleting.

The **BROWSE** mode was shown to provide not only such editing aids as "Lock" and "Freeze", but also the ability to move about the database quickly and to do searches.

The reader should now have the ability to Create and Modify database structures, append new data, delete obsolete data, edit existing data, and navigate around the database.

2.9 Review

In Chapter 2 we have covered the following commands:

BROWSE FIELD	INSERT
DELETE RECORD ...	LIST FIELD ...
DISPLAY	MODIFY STRUCTURE
DISPLAY ALL FIELD ...	PACK
DISPLAY ALL	RECALL ALL
GOTO	RECALL RECORD ...
INSERT BEFORE	

These are some more commonly used dBASE commands. Add them to your glossary of commands. You will want to use them frequently.

2.10 Laboratory Work

Follow all the steps outlined in this chapter making the modifications indicated to the structure of the database **COMPCLAS**. In addition, type in the field data for the new fields, ADDRESS and CITY_ST_ZP.

Modify the structure of ACCOUNTS, make the editing changes indicated, and add in the additional records to the database. (See Figure 2.27) Using LIST ... TO PRINT, print out hard copies of the structure of the new database, as well as the contents of it.

2.11 Exercises

Now that we've created this mailing list we begin to see possibilities that we hadn't noticed before. Shown below is the Mailist format with some additional fields we would like to incorporate into our new "improved" mailing list.

EDITING YOUR DATABASE

Field #	Field Name	Type	Width
1	First	Character	12
2	Last	Character	12
3	Mail_Addr	Character	22
4	City	Character	11
5	State	Character	2
6	Zip	Character	6
7	Country	Character	15
8	Ship_Addr	Character	30
9	Home_Phone	Character	12
10	Work_Phone	Character	18
11	Birthday	Date	8
12	Comments	Memo	10
13	Card	Logical	1

1. Using the procedure outlined in class, modify the structure of MAILIST.DBF to create a new file that has the structure shown above.

2. Add 15 more names of your own choice to Mailist to bring the total up to 26 names. Include your own name and address as one of the twenty-six.

3. LIST your expanded database on the printer and hand it in.

4. Print out a copy of the structure of MAILIST.DBF and hand that in.

5. Now delete Woody Woodpecker *permanently* from your database.

6. LIST only the following fields on the printer, and hand in the hard copy: First, Last, Mail_addr, City, State, Zip, and Card.

CHAPTER 3

ORDERING A DATABASE

3.0 Topics Covered in Chapter 3

Sorting a database.

Sorting on more than one field.

Sorting in Descending order.

Erasing files.

Indexing a database.

Indexing on Multiple fields.

Creation of a Production or Multiple Index.

Combining Date fields with Character fields in an Index.

Combining Numeric fields with Character fields in an Index.

Converting Logical fields to Character fields in an Index.

Indexing in Descending order.

Selecting the Master Index.

Deleting an Index Tag.

Indexing using the Unique Option.

Indexing using the FOR clause Option.

3.1 Sorting a Database

One of the most important features of a Database Management System (DBMS) is its ability to yield access to the database in any order that may be desired. It may very well be that you might wish to access the database in several different orders. For example, with the ACCOUNTS database, you will probably enter the transactions in chronological order. However, you might want to look at them in order of date, or in order of check number, or in order of category.

dBASE provides two ways of ordering a database: 1) **SORT**ing, and 2) **INDEX**ing. We will describe what it is to **SORT** a database and give a few examples, but the bulk of our study will be in the use of **INDEX**ing. The reasons for that will become apparent as we proceed.

In the dBASE language, to **SORT** a database is to create a second database which is in the desired order. The first database that you are trying to sort remains in its original order. We'll begin by opening COMPCLAS (shown in Figure 3.1).

. USE COMPCLAS

Now we'll **SORT** the database so that it is in order of LASTNAME. We'll call the new COMPCLAS database LASTNAME also to identify the fact that it is in that order. The syntax for this operation is:

. SORT ON LASTNAME TO LASTNAME

Do not confuse the field, LASTNAME (contained in "..ON LASTNAME.."), with the new database LASTNAME (contained in "..TO LASTNAME"). Having created this new database, we must now open it if we wish to access the data in the new sorted order.

. USE LASTNAME

ORDERING A DATABASE 73

Now browsing the database (see Figure 3.2), we see that it is indeed in the order of LASTNAME.

.BROWSE

Now suppose that we would like to access the data in the order of EVALUATION date. In the same manner we could **SORT** the database, LASTNAME, since it contains the same data as COMPCLAS. We'll call the new database, in the order of EVALUATION date, EVALDATE.

. SORT ON EVALUATION TO EVALDATE
. USE EVALDATE
. BROWSE

The result is shown in Figure 3.3

FIRSTNAME	LASTNAME	TERM_PROJ	EVALUATION	PROJ_GRADE	ADDRESS
Gladys	Naboa	T	12/15/92	93	324 Catskill T
Consuelo	Naboa	T	12/16/92	89	324 Catskill T
Derek	Caruthers	F	/ /	0	21 Spring Glen
Wendel	Little	T	12/17/92	87	1821 Cochecton
Jeremy	Witherspoon	T	12/19/92	82	821 Kiamesha C
Nancy	Hardwick	F	/ /	0	512 Delaware 0
Jonathan	Samuels	T	12/14/92	76	96 Rainbow's E
Matts	Engleberg	T	12/13/92	62	2821 Mountain
Mary Beth	Swazey	T	12/14/92	52	85 Cider Mill
Mary	Wong	F	/ /	0	321 Lakeside A

Figure 3.1 Browse of COMPCLAS in original order

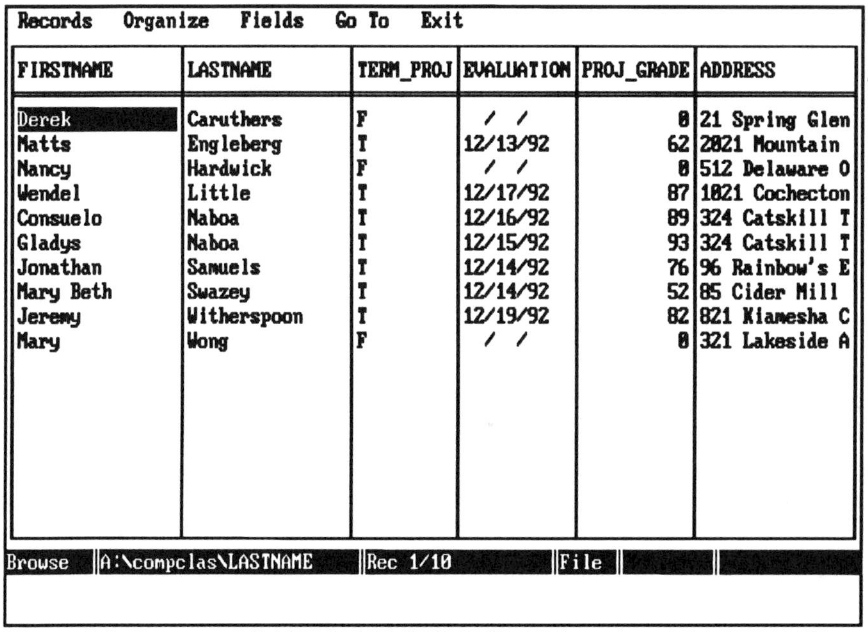

74 ORDERING A DATABASE

```
Records   Organize   Fields   Go To   Exit
```

FIRSTNAME	LASTNAME	TERM_PROJ	EVALUATION	PROJ_GRADE	ADDRESS
Derek	Caruthers	F	/ /	0	21 Spring Glen
Matts	Engleberg	T	12/13/92	62	2821 Mountain
Nancy	Hardwick	F	/ /	0	512 Delaware O
Wendel	Little	T	12/17/92	87	1821 Cochecton
Consuelo	Naboa	T	12/16/92	89	324 Catskill T
Gladys	Naboa	T	12/15/92	93	324 Catskill T
Jonathan	Samuels	T	12/14/92	76	96 Rainbow's E
Mary Beth	Swazey	T	12/14/92	52	85 Cider Mill
Jeremy	Witherspoon	T	12/19/92	82	821 Kiamesha C
Mary	Wong	F	/ /	0	321 Lakeside A

Browse A:\compclas\LASTNAME   Rec 1/10   File

Figure 3.2 Browse of LASTNAME (COMPCLAS in order of LASTNAME)

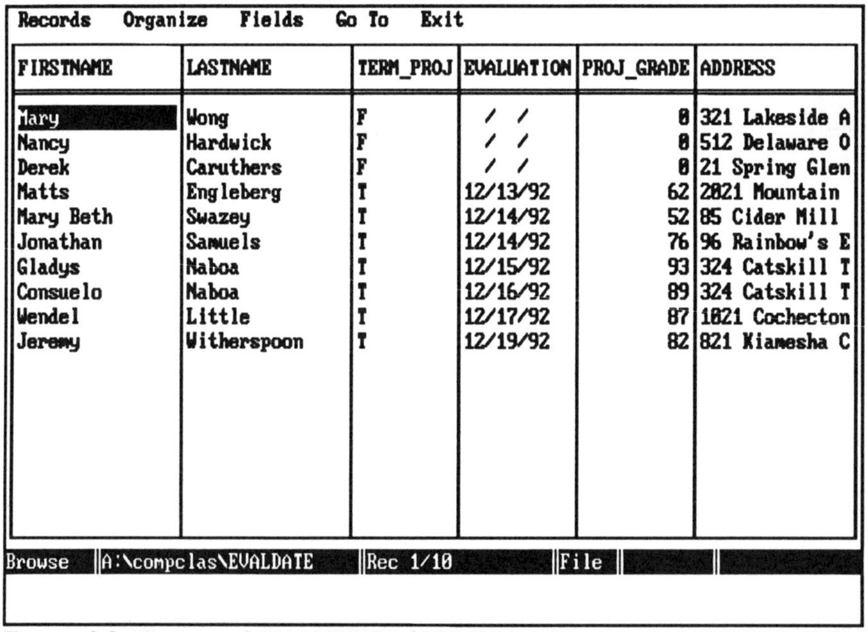

```
Records   Organize   Fields   Go To   Exit
```

FIRSTNAME	LASTNAME	TERM_PROJ	EVALUATION	PROJ_GRADE	ADDRESS
Mary	Wong	F	/ /	0	321 Lakeside A
Nancy	Hardwick	F	/ /	0	512 Delaware O
Derek	Caruthers	F	/ /	0	21 Spring Glen
Matts	Engleberg	T	12/13/92	62	2821 Mountain
Mary Beth	Swazey	T	12/14/92	52	85 Cider Mill
Jonathan	Samuels	T	12/14/92	76	96 Rainbow's E
Gladys	Naboa	T	12/15/92	93	324 Catskill T
Consuelo	Naboa	T	12/16/92	89	324 Catskill T
Wendel	Little	T	12/17/92	87	1821 Cochecton
Jeremy	Witherspoon	T	12/19/92	82	821 Kiamesha C

Browse A:\compclas\EVALDATE   Rec 1/10   File

Figure 3.3 Browse of EVALDATE (COMPCLAS in order of EVALUATION date)

Now suppose that we want the database ordered such that everyone is in order of EVALUATION date, but that those people who are coming on the same date should be in alphabetical order by LASTNAME. This is referred to as SORTing on multiple fields. The syntax is:

. SORT ON EVALUATION, LASTNAME TO EVALLAST
. USE EVALLAST
. BROWSE

Notice that the principal field, EVALUATION, comes first. The secondary field comes next. The name that we gave to this database has the name of the primary field for the first four letters, and the name of the secondary field for the next four letters. This gives the user an indication, at a glance, what the order of the database is. The result is shown in Figure 3.4. Notice that on December 14, both Jonathan Samuels, as well as Mary Beth Swazey, are scheduled to come for their evaluation. Note also that Samuels now precedes Swazey in order, whereas in Figure 3.3, Samuels did not.

We can also access data in reverse order if we desire. For example, teachers often like to look at grade data, but from highest to lowest. We can order the PROJ_GRADE data in reverse order by including the switch /D, which stands for descending (the default switch is always ascending or /A[15]). The syntax is:

. SORT ON PROJ_GRADE /D TO GRADE
. USE GRADE
. BROWSE

The result is shown in Figure 3.5.

---

[15] Because it is the default order, the /A (ascending order) switch never has to be specified. If no switch is given, it is always assumed to be in ascending order.

76 ORDERING A DATABASE

Records	Organize	Fields	Go To	Exit	
FIRSTNAME	LASTNAME	TERM_PROJ	EVALUATION	PROJ_GRADE	ADDRESS
Derek	Caruthers	F	/ /	0	21 Spring Glen
Nancy	Hardwick	F	/ /	0	512 Delaware O
Mary	Wong	F	/ /	0	321 Lakeside A
Matts	Engleberg	T	12/13/92	62	2821 Mountain
Jonathan	Samuels	T	12/14/92	76	96 Rainbow's E
Mary Beth	Swazey	T	12/14/92	52	85 Cider Mill
Gladys	Naboa	T	12/15/92	93	324 Catskill T
Consuelo	Naboa	T	12/16/92	89	324 Catskill T
Wendel	Little	T	12/17/92	87	1821 Cochecton
Jeremy	Witherspoon	T	12/19/92	82	821 Kiamesha C

Browse ‖A:\compclas\EVALLAST ‖Rec 1/10 ‖File‖

Figure 3.4 Browse of EVALLAST (COMPCLAS in order of EVALUATION date and LASTNAME)

Records	Organize	Fields	Go To	Exit	
FIRSTNAME	LASTNAME	TERM_PROJ	EVALUATION	PROJ_GRADE	ADDRESS
Gladys	Naboa	T	12/15/92	93	324 Catskill T
Consuelo	Naboa	T	12/16/92	89	324 Catskill T
Wendel	Little	T	12/17/92	87	1821 Cochecton
Jeremy	Witherspoon	T	12/19/92	82	821 Kiamesha C
Jonathan	Samuels	T	12/14/92	76	96 Rainbow's E
Matts	Engleberg	T	12/13/92	62	2821 Mountain
Mary Beth	Swazey	T	12/14/92	52	85 Cider Mill
Derek	Caruthers	F	/ /	0	21 Spring Glen
Mary	Wong	F	/ /	0	321 Lakeside A
Nancy	Hardwick	F	/ /	0	512 Delaware O

Browse ‖A:\compclas\GRADE ‖Rec 1/10 ‖File‖   Ins

Figure 3.5 Browse of GRADE (COMPCLAS in order of PROJ_GRADE)

ORDERING A DATABASE 77

Beware of the fact that normally higher case letters, A-Z, come before lower case letters, a-z. This means that the name dePardieu would come after the name Zabaar in a normal alphabetical sort. To make your **SORT** case insensitive, you will want to use the switch, /C.

If we were to type **DIR** at the dot prompt to see a listing of all the databases present in our directory, we would see five databases listed now: COMPCLAS, LASTNAME, EVALDATE, EVALLAST, and GRADE. (See Listing 3.1)

. **DIR**

Database Files	# Records	Last Update	Size
COMPCLAS.DBF	10	01/12/92	1320
LASTNAME.DBF	10	01/12/92	1320
EVALDATE.DBF	10	01/12/92	1320
EVALLAST.DBF	10	01/12/92	1320
GRADE.DBF	10	01/12/92	1320

Listing 3.1 Listing of all the databases in \COMPCLAS directory

What has happened is that our simple COMPCLAS database has proliferated and spawned four more clones. Worse than that, for every **.DBF** file there is also a **.DBT** file by the same name, so we now have 10 files instead of two. Since we have not nearly exhausted the possible number of ways that you could order COMPCLAS, you can see that we could indeed end up with an unwieldy number of files.

This is not so serious if the databases are small, but if they are quite large, then space becomes a real consideration.

A more serious problem arises however. The very concept of a database has been violated here. One of the characteristics of a database is that it is supposed to eliminate data redundancy. Instead of eliminating it, we have increased it five-fold.

The problem with data redundancy is this. Suppose that we update the database in order of LASTNAME, because that is the database order in which we wish to edit, then COMPCLAS no longer remains our Master database. Now we had better erase COMPCLAS and the other databases. If we don't, there is a chance that we might accidently refer to one of the other databases thinking that they were the most current. In such a situation the chances for data loss are enormous.

The safest rule to follow is: **THERE SHOULD NEVER BE MORE THAN ONE MASTER DATABASE!** This is one good reason to not use **SORT** to order a database.

Another problem associated with sorting is that unless you specify otherwise, you end up with a second database the same size as the first. This may not be a difficulty for small databases like **COMPCLAS, ACCOUNTS,** and **MAILIST**, but for large databases it can pose quite a problem. Right now I have two databases on my hard disk, each of which takes up about 2 megabytes of space. However, right now I have just under 1 megabyte of space left on my hard disk. Therefore it would be physically impossible, not to mention impractical, for me to sort either of these databases.

A final problem with sorting is that it is a time consuming process. It turns out that indexing a database is far quicker than sorting it mainly because you're dealing with fewer fields. Almost exclusively, if you want a database ordered, you **INDEX** it!

3.2 Erasing a Database

To underscore this point, we will now clean up our directory and remove all of those new sorted databases that we have created. We will **ERASE** each of these files, one by one, from the dot prompt. In this way we won't be confused as to which COMPCLAS database we should be using. First, make sure that COMPCLAS is closed, as you can't **ERASE** an open database.

. USE

ORDERING A DATABASE 79

Now we're ready to start eradicating all our spurious databases. The commands are:

. ERASE LASTNAME.DBF
. ERASE EVALDATE.DBF
. ERASE EVALLAST.DBF
. ERASE GRADE.DBF

Note that we have to include the extension **.DBF** in each case, as that is part of the name which identifies the particular file that you want to **ERASE**. We're not done yet because there also exists all the **.DBT** files associated with the **.DBF** files we just erased. So we have to repeat the procedure for the **.DBT** files.

. ERASE LASTNAME.DBT
. ERASE EVALDATE.DBT
. ERASE EVALLAST.DBT
. ERASE GRADE.DBT

When we type **DIR** at the dot prompt in order to see the databases in our current directory listed, we should see that only one now exists: COMPCLAS.DBF.[16] (Of course, COMPCLAS.DBT also exists although it will not be listed with the **DIR** command.)

. **DIR**

```
Database Files    # Records    Last Update    Size
COMPCLAS.DBF            10      01/12/92       1320
```

Listing 3.2 The only database left in the \COMPCLAS directory

---

[16]If for any reason you find other databases present, it would be good, at this point, to **ERASE** them. They have no business in the COMPCLAS directory.

3.3 Indexing a Database

An **INDEX** is an ordered list based on a particular field or key. Suppose, for example, we wanted to **INDEX** our database **COMPCLAS** on the field **LASTNAME**. (The unordered **COMPCLAS** is shown in Figure 3.1.) An **INDEX** is created which generates a list of the record numbers of all the records in the database in order of **LASTNAME**. The list generated from Figure 3.1 would look like that shown in Table 3.1. Note that the list is in alphabetical order. The order of the record numbers in the list defines the order in which the records themselves will appear as we **BROWSE, EDIT, LIST, DISPLAY ALL,** or print out the contents of our database.

Table 3.1 COMPCLAS Indexed on LASTNAME

Record #	Key Contents
3	Caruthers
8	Engleberg
6	Hardwick
4	Little
1	Naboa
2	Naboa
7	Samuels
9	Swazey
5	Witherspoon
10	Wong

3.3.1 Creating Individual (.NDX) Indexes

Table 3.1 is effectively the index of **COMPCLAS** on the key **LASTNAME**. The INDEX we created is a another file, but because it contains only two fields (the Record Number and the key), it is considerably smaller than our database which could have up to 255 fields. So we can think of an INDEX as a thin database, two fields wide. An individual INDEX has the extension **.NDX**. Because of this new extension, we will not be prone to confuse it with our databases which have the extensions **.DBF** and **.DBT** . We need to give our INDEX a name, so since we indexed on **LASTNAME**, we shall give it the name **LASTNAME.NDX** . The command for making an individual index is:

. INDEX ON LASTNAME TO LASTNAME

The BROWSE of the result is shown in Figure 3.6. Note that the first record is indeed Record 3, Caruthers.

3.3.2 Indexing on Two Character Fields

Suppose we want to **INDEX** on more than one field just as we did when we were sorting. Since there are only two fields in an INDEX, we must combine the multiple fields on which we are indexing.

Records Organize Fields Go To Exit

FIRSTNAME	LASTNAME	TERM_PROJ	EVALUATION	PROJ_GRADE	ADDRESS
Derek	Caruthers	F	/ /	0	21 Spring Glen
Matts	Engleberg	T	12/13/92	62	2021 Mountain
Nancy	Hardwick	F	/ /	0	512 Delaware O
Wendel	Little	T	12/17/92	87	1021 Cochecton
Gladys	Naboa	T	12/15/92	93	324 Catskill T
Consuelo	Naboa	T	12/16/92	89	324 Catskill T
Jonathan	Samuels	T	12/14/92	76	96 Rainbow's E
Mary Beth	Swazey	T	12/14/92	52	85 Cider Mill
Jeremy	Witherspoon	T	12/19/92	82	821 Kiamesha C
Mary	Wong	F	/ /	0	321 Lakeside A

Browse | A:\compclas\COMPCLAS | Rec 3/10 | File

Figure 3.6 Browse of COMPCLAS Indexed on LASTNAME

ORDERING A DATABASE

For example, suppose we want to **INDEX** on **FIRSTNAME** as the primary field, and **LASTNAME** as the secondary field. Let's make the INDEX name **FIRSTLAS** to acknowledge its primary and secondary fields. The command for doing this is:

. INDEX ON FIRSTNAME + LASTNAME TO FIRSTLAS

The + sign means that we have combined the two fifteen character wide fields, **FIRSTNAME** and **LASTNAME**, to form one field which is 30 characters long. This combining of character strings, one following the other, is referred to as concatenation. Table 3.2 shows what **FIRSTLAS.NDX** essentially looks like. The key field actually looks like what is shown, space for space, and character for character.

The BROWSE of the result is shown in Figure 3.7.

```
Records   Organize   Fields   Go To   Exit
FIRSTNAME      LASTNAME      TERM_PROJ  EVALUATION  PROJ_GRADE  ADDRESS
Consuelo       Naboa         T          12/16/92    89          324 Catskill T
Derek          Caruthers     F            /  /       0          21 Spring Glen
Gladys         Naboa         T          12/15/92    93          324 Catskill T
Jeremy         Witherspoon   T          12/19/92    82          821 Kianesha C
Jonathan       Samuels       T          12/14/92    76          96 Rainbow's E
Mary           Wong          F            /  /       0          321 Lakeside A
Mary Beth      Swazey        T          12/14/92    52          85 Cider Mill
Matts          Engleberg     T          12/13/92    62          2821 Mountain
Nancy          Hardwick      F            /  /       0          512 Delaware O
Wendel         Little        T          12/17/92    87          1821 Cochecton

Browse  A:\compclas\COMPCLAS   Rec 2/10   File
```

Figure 3.7 Browse of COMPCLAS Indexed on FIRSTNAME + LASTNAME

Table 3.2 COMPCLAS indexed on fields FIRSTNAME + LASTNAME

Record #	Key Contents	
2	Consuelo	Naboa
3	Derek	Caruthers
1	Gladys	Naboa
5	Jeremy	Witherspoon
7	Jonathan	Samuels
10	Mary	Wong
9	Mary Beth	Swazey
8	Matts	Engleberg
6	Nancy	Hardwick
4	Wendel	Little

3.4 Use of a Multiple or Production (.MDX) Index

One of the things that is happening as we create individual indexes is that they begin to proliferate just as COMPCLAS spawned so many databases when we were sorting. I am often confronted with multiple database systems which have ten or more indices among two or more databases. I find it inefficient to work with so many individual indexes as so much time is spent keeping track of which index goes with which database.

A solution to this problem has been created in dBASE4. This is the use of the Multiple or Production Index file. This one file, with an **.MDX** extension, can contain up to 47 individual index files. Since dBASE IV gives the Multiple Index file the same name as the database (i.e. COMPCLAS.MDX), we will never become confused as to which index goes with which database, nor will we get buried in a myriad of individual index files.

Each of the individual indexes contained in the Multiple Index is referred to with a **TAG**. The key word **TAG** is substituted for the word **TO** when we create the index. A tag can be up to ten (10) characters long. An example will demonstrate how this is done.

3.4.1 Making a Multiple Index on LASTNAME + FIRSTNAME

Looking at Figure 3.6, we notice that although the students are in alphabetical order by LASTNAME, those having the same last name are not in alphabetical order by FIRSTNAME. Note that Gladys Naboa precedes Consuelo Naboa in the list. So to make sure that everyone is in alphabetical order first by LASTNAME and then by FIRSTNAME, we must **INDEX** on the two fields. Table 3.3 shows what the effective index looks like.

To generate this index as a Multiple Index the syntax is:

. INDEX ON LASTNAME + FIRSTNAME TAG LASTFIRST

where we have given LASTFIRST as the tag name of our index. Figure 3.8 shows us the browse of COMPCLAS with the LASTFIRST **TAG** active. Note that Consuelo and Gladys are now in alphabetical order.

FIRSTNAME	LASTNAME	TERM_PROJ	EVALUATION	PROJ_GRADE	ADDRESS
Derek	Caruthers	F	/ /	0	21 Spring Glen
Matts	Engleberg	T	12/13/92	62	2821 Mountain
Nancy	Hardwick	F	/ /	0	512 Delaware O
Wendel	Little	T	12/17/92	87	1821 Cochecton
Consuelo	Naboa	T	12/16/92	89	324 Catskill T
Gladys	Naboa	T	12/15/92	93	324 Catskill T
Jonathan	Samuels	T	12/14/92	76	96 Rainbow's E
Mary Beth	Swazey	T	12/14/92	52	85 Cider Mill
Jeremy	Witherspoon	T	12/19/92	82	821 Kiamesha C
Mary	Wong	F	/ /	0	321 Lakeside A

Figure 3.8 Browse of COMPCLAS Indexed on LASTNAME + FIRSTNAME

Table 3.3 COMPCLAS Indexed on LASTNAME + FIRSTNAME

Record #	Key Contents	
3	Caruthers	Malcolm
8	Engleberg	Matts
6	Hardwick	Nancy
4	Little	Wendel
2	Naboa	Consuelo
1	Naboa	Gladys
7	Samuels	Jonathan
9	Swazey	Mary Beth
5	Witherspoon	Jeremy
10	Wong	Mary

3.4.2 Indexing on a Date Field and Character Field

Suppose we wanted to look at the students in the order of date of evaluation, and we would like those appearing on the same date to be in alphabetical order, last name first. Were we just to **INDEX** on the date field, **EVALUATION**, and call the INDEX EVALUATION, then the command would be simply:

. INDEX ON EVALUATION TAG EVALUATION

However, if we want to combine the date field with character fields like we did with **LASTNAME** and **FIRSTNAME**, then life is not so easy. The rule is, you can only combine fields of similar types. That is to say, character fields can only be combined with character fields. Hence, we must transform our date field into a character field. This can be done by means of a Function.

A Function is an operation which transforms one piece of data into another piece of data. A Function always has parentheses surrounding the field or expression which you want to transform.

This field or expression is referred to as the "argument" of the function. The function that we would like to use is the **Date TO** character String function: **DTOS()**.

DTOS(EVALUATION) makes a character string out of the **EVALUATION** date. Furthermore, it orders the date as follows: "YYYY/MM/DD". This means that when we **INDEX** on it, the chronological order will be correct. So now we are free to concatenate that string to the **LASTNAME** and **FIRSTNAME** strings. We will call the resulting TAG **EVALASTFIR** . The command to generate this INDEX is:

. INDEX ON DTOS(EVALUATION) + LASTNAME + FIRSTNAME TAG EVALASTFIR

Table 3.4 shows the key field that would be generated for **EVALASTFIR**. The length of the key is 38 characters long (two 15 character fields plus one 8 character date field) and is shown letter for letter, space for space, just how it would appear in the INDEX. The BROWSE of the result is shown in Figure 3.9.

Table 3.4 COMPCLAS indexed on DTOS(EVALUATION) + LASTNAME + FIRSTNAME

Record #	Key Field	
3	Caruthers	Derek
6	Hardwick	Nancy
10	Wong	Mary
8	19921213Engleberg	Matts
7	19921214Samuels	Jonathan
9	19921214Swazey	Mary Beth
1	19921215Naboa	Gladys
2	19921216Naboa	Consuelo
4	19921217Little	Wendel
5	19921219Jeremy	Witherspoon

It should be noted that there is a 100 character limit to the size of the field expression that generates an INDEX. The field expression used in this example, DTOS(EVALUATION) + LASTNAME + FIRSTNAME, is only 40 characters long so 100 characters provides ample space to generate most any INDEX we choose.

3.4.3 Indexing on Numeric and Character Fields

Now suppose we want to **INDEX** people in order of **PROJ_GRADE**, but for those receiving the same grade (or no grade at all), we would like them to be in alphabetical order, last name first. Once again, were we to **INDEX** on just the Project Grade and call the resulting INDEX, **GRADE,** then the command would be simply:

. INDEX ON PROJ_GRADE TAG GRADE

However, **PROJ_GRADE** is a numeric field, and hence cannot be combined directly with a character field. A transformation must be made using the String Function: **STR()**. The syntax of this function is: **STR**(*numeric expression,width*). This function takes a numeric expression and converts it into a character string whose width is determined by the number following the comma. Note that this function has two arguments[17]. Performing this function on our Project Grade, we would obtain: **STR(PROJ_GRADE,3)**.

Now we are free to combine this result with the other two character fields. If we call our resulting index tag **GRADLASTFI** (note that we can tell by the tag name that the index is made up of the fields: GRADE + LASTNAME + FIRSTNAME), then the command to generate it is:

.INDEX ON STR(PROJ_GRADE,3) + LASTNAME + FIRSTNAME TAG GRADLASTFI

---

[17] If our numeric field had digits after the decimal point, then the STR() function would have a third argument indicating the number of decimal places.

```
| Records   Organize   Fields   Go To   Exit              |
| FIRSTNAME  | LASTNAME   | TERM_PROJ | EVALUATION | PROJ_GRADE | ADDRESS        |
| Derek      | Caruthers  | F         | / /        | 0          | 21 Spring Glen |
| Nancy      | Hardwick   | F         | / /        | 0          | 512 Delaware O |
| Mary       | Wong       | F         | / /        | 0          | 321 Lakeside A |
| Matts      | Engleberg  | T         | 12/13/92   | 62         | 2821 Mountain  |
| Jonathan   | Samuels    | T         | 12/14/92   | 76         | 96 Rainbow's E |
| Mary Beth  | Swazey     | T         | 12/14/92   | 52         | 85 Cider Mill  |
| Gladys     | Naboa      | T         | 12/15/92   | 93         | 324 Catskill T |
| Consuelo   | Naboa      | T         | 12/16/92   | 89         | 324 Catskill T |
| Wendel     | Little     | T         | 12/17/92   | 87         | 1821 Cochecton |
| Jeremy     | Witherspoon| T         | 12/19/92   | 82         | 821 Kiamesha C |

Browse   A:\compclas\COMPCLAS   Rec 3/10   File
```

Figure 3.9 Browse of COMPCLAS Indexed on DTOS(EVALUATION) + LASTNAME + FIRSTNAME

Table 3.5 shows the key field that would be generated for **GRADLASTFI**. The length of the key is 33 characters long (two 15 character fields plus one 3 character numeric field) and is shown letter for letter, space for space, just how it would appear in the INDEX itself. Figure 3.10 shows the Browse of COMPCLAS ordered in this way. Note that Caruthers, Hardwick, and Wong, who all have the same zero grade, are in alphabetical order.

3.4.4 Indexing on a Logical Field

The logical field is one on which you cannot INDEX directly. It must first be converted to a character string, just as we did with the date and numeric fields when we combined them with character fields. To do this we need to use a three argument function called the Immediate **IF** function: **IIF(„)**. It's syntax is as follows: **IIF**(*logical expression, output if true, output if false*).

ORDERING A DATABASE

Table 3.5 COMPCLAS Indexed on
STR(PROJ_GRADE,3)+LASTNAME+FIRSTNAME

Record #	Key Field	
3	0Caruthers	Derek
6	0Hardwick	Nancy
10	0Wong	Mary
9	52Swazey	Mary Beth
8	62Engleberg	Matts
7	76Samuels	Jonathan
5	82Witherspoon	Jeremy
4	87Little	Wendel
2	89Naboa	Consuelo
1	93Naboa	Gladys

In this particular case the function with its arguments would be: **IIF(TERM_PROJ, "Y", "N")**. If TERM_PROJ is True, then the function will output the character **Y**, and if it is False, then it will output the character **N**. The INDEX instruction would take the form:

. INDEX ON IIF(TERM_PROJ, "Y", "N") TAG TERM_PROJ

Table 3.6 shows what the index would look like. Figure 3.11 shows the Browse of the result. Obviously, if you wanted to, you could also concatenate on the name fields so that the group that did do a Term Project would be in order alphabetically, as well as the group that didn't.

3.4.5 Indexing in Descending Order

dBASE IV allows one the option to INDEX in descending order as well as ascending. This is done by simply putting the word **DESCENDING** at the end of the INDEX instruction. For example, let's INDEX COMPCLAS by PROJ_GRADE in descending order.

90 ORDERING A DATABASE

```
| Records   Organize   Fields   Go To   Exit                                              |
| FIRSTNAME  | LASTNAME    | TERM_PROJ | EVALUATION | PROJ_GRADE | ADDRESS          |
| Derek      | Caruthers   | F         |    /  /    |          0 | 21 Spring Glen   |
| Nancy      | Hardwick    | F         |    /  /    |          0 | 512 Delaware O   |
| Mary       | Wong        | F         |    /  /    |          0 | 321 Lakeside A   |
| Mary Beth  | Swazey      | T         | 12/14/92   |         52 | 85 Cider Mill    |
| Matts      | Engleberg   | T         | 12/13/92   |         62 | 2021 Mountain    |
| Jonathan   | Samuels     | T         | 12/14/92   |         76 | 96 Rainbow's E   |
| Jeremy     | Witherspoon | T         | 12/19/92   |         82 | 821 Kiamesha C   |
| Wendel     | Little      | T         | 12/17/92   |         87 | 1021 Cochecton   |
| Consuelo   | Naboa       | T         | 12/16/92   |         89 | 324 Catskill T   |
| Gladys     | Naboa       | T         | 12/15/92   |         93 | 324 Catskill T   |
| Browse   A:\compclas\COMPCLAS   Rec 3/10   File                                Ins     |
```

Figure 3.10 Browse of COMPCLAS Indexed on STR(PROJ_GRADE,3) + LASTNAME + FIRSTNAME

Table 3.6 COMPCLAS Indexed on IIF(TERM_PROJ, "Y", "N")

Record #	Key Contents
3	N
6	N
10	N
1	Y
2	Y
4	Y
5	Y
7	Y
8	Y
9	Y

ORDERING A DATABASE

The command would be:

. INDEX ON PROJ_GRADE TAG GRADE DESCENDING

When you execute this command, dBASE will tell you that the tag **GRADE** already exists. It will ask you if you wish to overwrite this tag. Strike the Enter key indicating that you do wish to do this. Figure 3.12 shows the Browse of the grades in descending order.

3.5 Selecting the Master Index in a Production (.MDX) Index

The very first time that we INDEX a database creating a TAG, an **.MDX** Production Index file is created. In addition, the index TAG that was just created becomes the MASTER Index. This means that everything will be ordered by that particular index TAG. This condition will remain true until we close the database, create a new index, or **SET** the **ORDER** to another index TAG. For example, suppose the current Master Index Tag for COMPCLAS is

FIRSTNAME	LASTNAME	TERM_PROJ	EVALUATION	PROJ_GRADE	ADDRESS
Derek	Caruthers	F	/ /	0	21 Spring Glen
Nancy	Hardwick	F	/ /	0	512 Delaware O
Mary	Wong	F	/ /	0	321 Lakeside A
Gladys	Naboa	T	12/15/92	93	324 Catskill T
Consuelo	Naboa	T	12/16/92	89	324 Catskill T
Wendel	Little	T	12/17/92	87	1821 Cochecton
Jeremy	Witherspoon	T	12/19/92	82	821 Kiamesha C
Jonathan	Samuels	T	12/14/92	76	96 Rainbow's E
Matts	Engleberg	T	12/13/92	62	2021 Mountain
Mary Beth	Swazey	T	12/14/92	52	85 Cider Mill

Figure 3.11 Browse of COMPCLAS Indexed on IIF(TERM_PROJ,"Y","N")

```
 Records   Organize   Fields   Go To   Exit
| FIRSTNAME | LASTNAME   | TERM_PROJ | EVALUATION | PROJ_GRADE | ADDRESS         |
|-----------|------------|-----------|------------|------------|-----------------|
| Gladys    | Naboa      | T         | 12/15/92   | 93         | 324 Catskill T  |
| Consuelo  | Naboa      | T         | 12/16/92   | 89         | 324 Catskill T  |
| Wendel    | Little     | T         | 12/17/92   | 87         | 1821 Cochecton  |
| Jeremy    | Witherspoon| T         | 12/19/92   | 82         | 821 Kiamesha C  |
| Jonathan  | Samuels    | T         | 12/14/92   | 76         | 96 Rainbow's E  |
| Matts     | Engleberg  | T         | 12/13/92   | 62         | 2821 Mountain   |
| Mary Beth | Swazey     | T         | 12/14/92   | 52         | 85 Cider Mill   |
| Mary      | Wong       | F         | / /        | 0          | 321 Lakeside A  |
| Nancy     | Hardwick   | F         | / /        | 0          | 512 Delaware O  |
| Derek     | Caruthers  | F         | / /        | 0          | 21 Spring Glen  |

 Browse   A:\compclas\COMPCLAS     Rec 1/10        File                    Ins
```

Figure 3.12 Browse of COMPCLAS Indexed DESCENDING on PROJ_GRADE

GRADE. If we want to change the Master Index to LASTFIRST, then we need to execute the command:

. **SET ORDER TO LASTFIRST**

The result of doing this **SET ORDER** command is to create the ordering shown in Figure 3.8. If we desire to switch back to the GRADE Tag, then we need only execute:

. **SET ORDER TO GRADE**

Now the ordering is back to what it was in Figure 3.12.

The beauty of a Production Index is that regardless of which index, if any, is the current Master Index, all indexes in the Production Index will be updated each time a record is edited, appended to, or deleted from the database. In this way we don't have to worry about whether an index TAG is current or not. Effectively, it will always be current (as long as you don't exceed 47 index Tags). This feature is not true of the individual (**.NDX**) indexes.[18]

If you wish to return the database to its "natural order", then you need only type:

. **SET ORDER TO**

This releases the control of all the index tags, but because the Production Index is still open, all of the index tags will continue to be updated as the database is updated.

If you want to know exactly what indexes exist in the Multiple Index, and on what they were indexed, you need only type:

. **DISPLAY STATUS**

The result of doing this is shown in Figure 3.13. Note that we have five index TAGs in our Multiple Index COMPCLAS.MDX. You can see that the keys for each of them are displayed to the right of the index TAG. The DISPLAY STATUS command goes on to display more information than we're interested in right now. To avoid these additional screens you need only hit the **Esc** key.

Short of deleting the Production Index, there is no way you can turn off the Production Index as long as the database, to which the Production Index belongs, is open. When the database is closed with the **USE** command, then the Production Index is also closed.

After having created a Production Index, each time we open the database, the Production Index is automatically opened too. The database will remain in its "natural order" (the order in which the data was entered) until a particular order is selected.

---

[18]This inconvenience is another reason why we will not be using the individual (.NDX) indexes in our work.

```
Currently Selected Database:
Select area: 1, Database in Use: A:\COMPCLAS\COMPCLAS.DBF   Alias: COMPCLAS
Production   MDX file:  A:\COMPCLAS\COMPCLAS.MDX
             Index TAG:     LASTFIRST  Key: lastname+firstname
             Index TAG:     EVALASTFIR Key: dtos(evaluation) + lastname + firstna
me
             Index TAG:     TERM_PROJ  Key: iif(term_proj,"Y","N")
             Index TAG:     GRADLASTFI Key: str(proj_grade,3) + lastname + firstn
ame
             Index TAG:     GRADE Key: proj_grade (Descending)
             Memo file:     A:\COMPCLAS\COMPCLAS.DBT

File search path:
OS Working drive/directory : A:\COMPCLAS
Default disk drive: A:
Print destination: PRN:
Margin =      0
Refresh count =    0
Reprocess count =   0
Number of files open =    5
Press any key to continue...
Command  A:\compclas\COMPCLAS    Rec 1/10       File
         Type a dBASE IV command and press the ENTER key (←⏎)
```

Figure 3.13 Result of Executing: DISPLAY STATUS with COMPCLAS Open

3.5.1 Selecting Individual (.NDX) Indexes

On the other hand, if you wish to open another index file, (e.g. the individual index LASTNAME.NDX) then you must use the command:

. SET INDEX TO LASTNAME

Now the index, LASTNAME.NDX is the Master Index, even though the Production Index, COMPCLAS.MDX, is still open. (The order of the database is now as shown in Figure 3.6) Furthermore, any changes to the database will be incorporated into both LASTNAME.NDX as well as all the indexes within COMPCLAS.MDX. If you wish to close the individual index LASTNAME.NDX, you need only type:

. SET INDEX TO

ORDERING A DATABASE

The individual indexes are all off now and won't be updated if any additions, deletions, or changes are made to our database. However, the Production Index still continues to remain open.

The only advantage of the individual index is that you can turn it off. This is also its disadvantage too. The reason that you might want to turn an index off is because the updating of an entire Production Index file every time the database is updated can cause some time delay. Were you to wait until all the changes were made, and then re-index, you might conceivably save time.

However, the errors that can be made because one of the individual indexes didn't get updated "as it should have" far offset, in my opinion, the time delays that one usually encounters utilizing the Production Index.

3.6   Deleting Indexes

There is an overhead to having a large number of indexes. Besides the fact that each additional index takes up disk space, each additional index added to a Production Index is automatically updated each time a change is made to the database. This updating takes time, so obviously we don't want to carry more indexes than we need.

We now have two indexes that index COMPCLAS on PROJ_GRADE: GRADLASTFI and GRADE. Since we really only need one, let's eliminate GRADLASTFI which is in ascending order. The syntax of the DELETE TAG instruction is: **DELETE TAG** *Tagname*. In the case of the tag GRADLASTFI we would type:

. DELETE TAG GRADLASTFI

Displaying the status now shows that the index GRADLASTFI is now gone (see Figure 3.14).

. DISPLAY STATUS

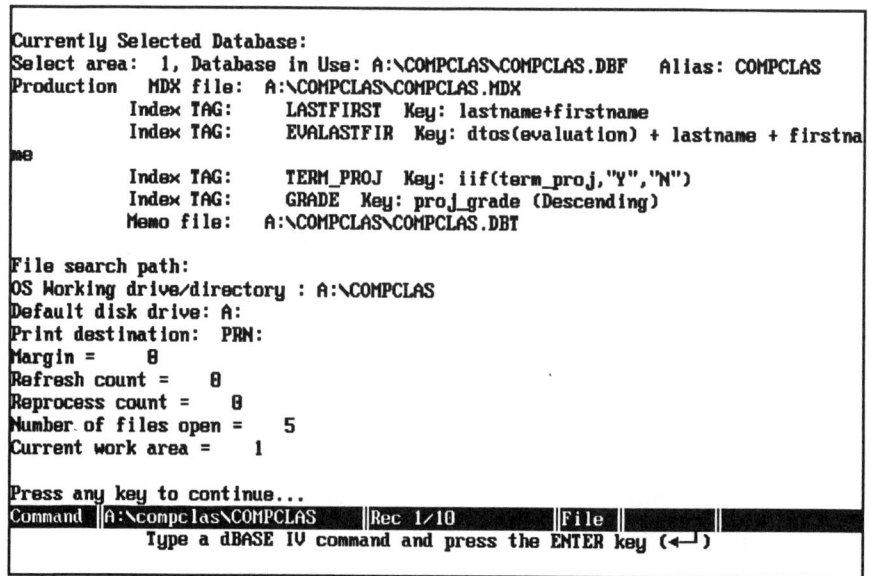

Figure 3.14   DISPLAY STATUS of COMPCLAS after deleting TAG GRADLASTFI

To get rid of an individual index, we simply ERASE it, just as we erased the extra databases we made as a result of using the SORT command. Since we have no further use for the two individual indexes, LASTNAME.NDX and FIRSTLAS.NDX, we'll ERASE them both.

. ERASE LASTNAME.NDX
. ERASE FIRSTLAS.NDX

The only indexes that we'll be dealing with from this point on are contained in the Production Index, COMPCLAS.MDX.

3.7   Example II: Use of INDEXing Options in ACCOUNTS Database

There are three options available to an index in dBASE IV. The first of these, the **DESCENDING** option, we have already seen. The second of these is the **UNIQUE** option.

ORDERING A DATABASE 97

3.7.1 Use of the UNIQUE Option

The **UNIQUE** option allows us to look at only the first occurrence of each record having a particular field value. For example, in the ACCOUNTS database (see Figure 3.15), there are 17 different categories a check or a deposit can have. Since it would be easy to forget one of these categories, it would be nice to have a quick easy way to refer to a list of the UNIQUE occurrences of each CATegory.

DATE	CHECK	DESCRIPT	CAT	DEBITS	RECEIPTS	CASHED
01/01/92		Jan. 1 Balance		0.00	100.00	T
01/05/92		Deposit: Salary	SAL	0.00	750.00	T
01/09/92	401	Cash: January Allowance	PER	100.00	0.00	T
01/09/92	402	Sullivan Co. Cablevision	CAB	20.00	0.00	T
01/09/92	403	N.Y. Telephone: Dec. bill	TEL	50.00	0.00	T
01/12/92	404	Dr. John McIntyre, D.D.S.	DOC	75.00	0.00	T
01/13/92	405	Sierra Club: Donation	DON	10.00	0.00	F
01/14/92	406	Shoprite: Groceries	GRO	18.60	0.00	T
01/14/92	407	Farmer's Market: Groceries	GRO	4.20	0.00	T
01/14/92	408	Feed-n-things: Pet Food	PET	8.50	0.00	T
01/15/92	409	State Farm Mutual: Insurance	INS	232.94	0.00	T
01/15/92	410	Sherman's: auto repairs	CAR	10.00	0.00	T
01/16/92	411	NYSEG: Utilities	UTI	110.12	0.00	F
01/16/92	412	West Side Vets	PET	30.00	0.00	F
01/18/92		Deposit: Travel Expense Reimb.	REI	0.00	38.25	T
01/19/92	413	Dr. Isaacs, M.D. (eye doct)	DOC	40.00	0.00	T
01/19/92		Deposit: Salary	SAL	0.00	750.00	T

Figure 3.15 Browse of ACCOUNTS in "Natural order"

Let's open ACCOUNTS and create such a UNIQUE list. First we want to index on CAT since we would like the list in alphabetical order. But since we only want UNIQUE occurrences of each CATegory, we place the key word UNIQUE at the end.

. USE ACCOUNTS
. INDEX ON CAT TAG CAT UNIQUE
. LIST OFF FIELD CAT

Listing the field CAT after having created the Index shows just the list that we desired (see Figure 3.16).

98   ORDERING A DATABASE

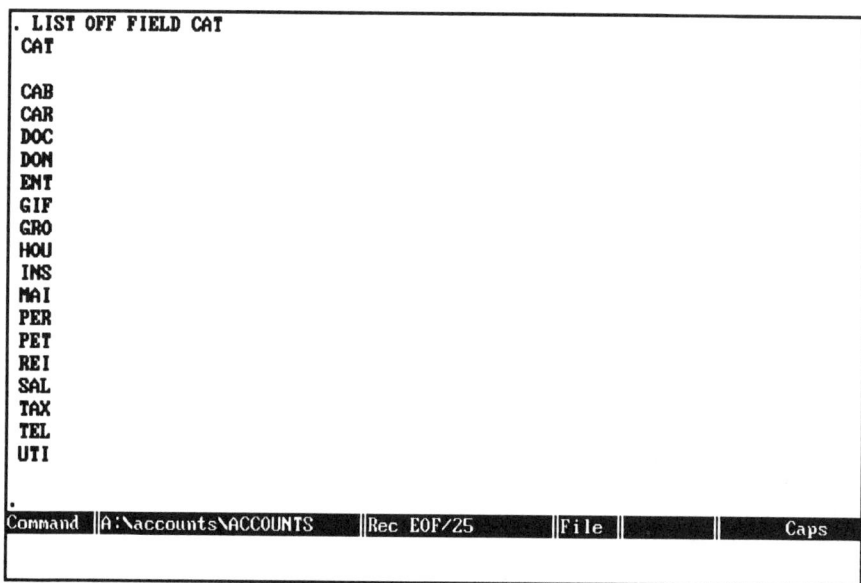

Figure 3.16 LIST of ACCOUNTS INDEXed on CATegory UNIQUE

3.7.2 Use of the FOR Option

There is one more extremely powerful option that is available to us in dBASE IV. This is the **FOR** option. It allows us to select just which records we want to access out of the entire database. This is done by creating a shortened index which has in it references to only those database records that we want, and omitting references to those database records that we do not want.

For example, suppose we wanted to look at DEBITS and RECEIPTS separately. This is done by adding a **FOR** clause to the end of our INDEX instruction. In the case of DEBITS, we are interested in only those records in which the DEBITS field is not 0. This can be said using the following clause: **FOR DEBITS <> 0**. The **<>** symbols means "not equal to". Indexing the DEBITS on CHECK number, our instruction becomes:

. INDEX ON CHECK TAG DEBITS FOR DEBITS <> 0

ORDERING A DATABASE

```
Records   Organize   Fields   Go To   Exit
```

DATE	CHECK	DESCRIPT	CAT	DEBITS	RECEIPTS	CASHED
01/09/92	401	Cash: January Allowance	PER	100.00	0.00	T
01/09/92	402	Sullivan Co. Cablevision	CAB	20.00	0.00	T
01/09/92	403	N.Y. Telephone: Dec. bill	TEL	50.00	0.00	T
01/12/92	404	Dr. John McIntyre, D.D.S.	DOC	75.00	0.00	T
01/13/92	405	Sierra Club: Donation	DON	10.00	0.00	F
01/14/92	406	Shoprite: Groceries	GRO	18.68	0.00	T
01/14/92	407	Farmer's Market: Groceries	GRO	4.20	0.00	T
01/14/92	408	Feed-n-things: Pet Food	PET	8.58	0.00	T
01/15/92	409	State Farm Mutual: Insurance	INS	232.94	0.00	T
01/15/92	410	Sherman's: auto repairs	CAR	10.00	0.00	T
01/16/92	411	NYSEG: Utilities	UTI	110.12	0.00	F
01/16/92	412	West Side Vets	PET	30.00	0.00	F
01/19/92	413	Dr. Isaacs, M.D. (eye doct)	DOC	40.00	0.00	T
01/20/92	414	Cash: Gas & Tolls	CAR	34.65	0.00	T
01/20/92	415	Sullivan's: Dept. Store	GIF	25.66	0.00	F
01/22/92	416	Action Video	ENT	10.59	0.00	F
01/22/92	417	MBNA Payment Services:Cred. Card	HOU	100.00	0.00	F

```
Browse   A:\accounts\ACCOUNTS   Rec 3/25   File
```

Figure 3.17 Browse of ACCOUNTS Indexed using option FOR DEBITS<>0

```
Records   Organize   Fields   Go To   Exit
```

DATE	CHECK	DESCRIPT	CAT	DEBITS	RECEIPTS	CASHED
01/01/92		Jan. 1 Balance		0.00	100.00	T
01/05/92		Deposit: Salary	SAL	0.00	750.00	T
01/18/92		Deposit: Travel Expense Reimb.	REI	0.00	38.25	T
01/19/92		Deposit: Salary	SAL	0.00	750.00	T

```
Browse   A:\accounts\ACCOUNTS   Rec 1/25   File
```

Figure 3.18 ACCOUNTS indexed using option FOR RECEIPTS<>0

A Browse of the first 17 checks is shown in Figure 3.17. As you can see, only checks are listed, the deposits are not displayed. As long as the index tag DEBITS is the Master Index, there is no way to access or display any of the deposits whatsoever. It is as though they do not exist. However, as soon as the order is changed to another index tag, the deposits will reappear.

To create the corresponding index for deposits alone, since we don't have a check number to order them by, we will use the DATE. Again, we are looking for entries **FOR** which the RECEIPTS field is not zero. Our instruction becomes:

. **INDEX ON DATE TAG RECEIPTS FOR RECEIPTS <> 0**
. **BROWSE**

Figure 3.18 shows a browse of just the resulting RECEIPTS.

As you can see, the INDEX is a most powerful tool used in accessing as well as ordering a database.

3.8 Summary

In this chapter we have covered sorting and indexing. We have seen that we can order items on any field, or any combination of fields except the MEMO field. When we combine fields in an index, we must convert them all to character strings in the process of combining them.

We have seen that we can sequence items in either ascending or descending order. We can also create indexes in which only unique occurrences of particular field values are accessed.

Finally we have seen that we can control exactly which records we want to access in an index through the use of the FOR clause.

3.9 Review

In Chapter 3 we have introduced two new powerful ordering instructions and several commands that support these ordering instructions:

> **DELETE TAG** *tagname*
> **DIR**
> **DISPLAY STATUS**
> **ERASE** *filename*
> **INDEX ON ...**
> **SET INDEX TO**
> **SET INDEX TO** *indexname*
> **SET ORDER TO**
> **SET ORDER TO** *tagname*
> **SORT ON ...**

Be sure to add these commands to your glossary of commonly used dBASE commands. In addition, the following functions were introduced in this chapter:

> **DTOS()**   **IIF(,,)**   **STR(,)**

You will want to add these to your glossary of functions as they are ones we will be using frequently.

3.10 Laboratory Work

Follow all the steps outlined in this chapter. Generate all the index tags: LASTFIRST, EVALASTFIR, TERM_PROJ, and GRADE for the COMPCLAS database. In addition, generate all the index tags associated with the database ACCOUNTS: CHECK, CAT, DEBITS, and RECEIPTS.

3.11 Exercises

1. Sort MAILIST on the primary field FIRST and on the secondary field LAST. Print out a hard copy using the command:

   . LIST OFF FIELD FIRST,LAST, MAIL_ADDR,CITY,STATE,ZIP,CARD TO PRINT

2. Index MAILIST on the fields LAST + FIRST. Call your index tag LASTFIRST. Print out a hard copy of the result.

3. Index your list on the fields ZIP + LAST + FIRST in descending order. Call your index tag ZIPLASTFIR. Hand in a hard copy of the result.

4. Index your list on the fields ZIP + FIRST + LAST in ascending order **FOR** only those individuals who will be receiving a card. (Hint: use the FOR clause, **FOR CARD** at the end of the INDEX instruction.) Make a hard copy and hand it in.

CHAPTER 4

COLUMNAR REPORTS

4.0　Topics Covered in Chapter 4

Using the Report Generator to make simple Columnar reports.

Making Quick Layouts.

Previewing Reports within the Report Generator.

Moving Fields in the Report Form.

Creating Groups and Subtotals in the Report Form.

Creating Calculated Fields in a Report Form.

Using the Hidden Display Attribute in a Report Form.

Using Summary Functions to make Running Sums.

4.1 The Report Form Generator

The reports we have generated to this point have been done with the limited capacity of the **LIST TO PRINT** instruction. This results in a not very elegant hard copy report which might be useful for in-house purposes, but is not something you would want to send out professionally. The Report Form generator can generate three different types of reports: a columnar report where information is printed in columns, a "mailmerge" report where information is dropped into a form letter type template, and a free form report where record information can be laid out in any form the user would like.

In this chapter, we are going to concentrate on the most common of report forms, the simple columnar report. This will give the user an idea of what the possibilities are from this most powerful report form generator. We will be returning to the report form generator later to look at some of the more sophisticated uses to which it can be put.

So far, we have come across six different extensions to our dBASE files (See Table 4.1).

Table 4.1 dBASE file extensions encountered in Chapters 1-3

Extension	Description	Example
.DBF	Database File	COMPCLAS.DBF
.DBT	Database Memo File	COMPCLAS.DBT
.BAK	Backup Database File	COMPCLAS.BAK
.TBK	Backup Memo File	COMPCLAS.TBK
.NDX	Individual Index File	LASTNAME.NDX
.MDX	Multiple Index File	COMPCLAS.MDX

The **.DBF** file is the main, fixed field length database that we originally created. The **DBF** stands for "Data Base File." The **.DBT** file is the file created by the presence of the Memo file, COMMENTS. All of the variable length memos get placed in this file. The **DBT** stands for "Data Base Text".

In addition, when we did a MODIFY STRUCTURE command, we generated two backups of these two original files. The backup of COMPCLAS.DBF is called COMPCLAS.BAK . The backup of COMPCLAS.DBT is called COMPCLAS.TBK . These last two files may be erased from your disk if you want the extra space or would like to remove the extra clutter.

We are now going to be introduced to three more extensions, all associated with the Report Form. The way that dBASE IV goes about producing a report form is to first allow you to visually produce a report form in the report form generator. This report form has the extension **.FRM** .

From this report form, an actual program is created using dBASE IV instructions, which will generate the desired report. This file has the extension, **.FRG** . If we had the time and patience, we could produce such a program ourselves. However, that would be quite a time consuming process. I have spent days writing report generating programs that would take minutes to produce using the Report Form Generator.

Finally, dBASE IV then translates this program into the machine code that it actually uses to execute our report. This **.FRO** file is the compiled or executable code. We will talk more about this when we actually get into programming. Since dBASE handles this all automatically, it is not something that we have to worry about. However; as we get further into dBASE IV, we will see the file types begin to proliferate, so it is good to know what they are all for.

106 COLUMNAR REPORTS

4.1.1 Creating a Columnar Report

Listing 4.1 shows us exactly the report that we wish to generate. We shall now go through the steps necessary in order to generate this report using the Report Form Generator.

```
01/19/93                COMPUTER CLASS REPORT


FIRST NAME     LAST NAME        TERM      EVALUATION    PROJECT
                                PROJECT      DATE        GRADE

Gladys         Naboa              Y        12/15/92        93
Consuelo       Naboa              Y        12/16/92        89
Derek          Caruthers          N          /  /           0
Wendel         Little             Y        12/17/92        87
Jeremy         Witherspoon        Y        12/19/92        82
Nancy          Hardwick           N          /  /           0
Jonathan       Samuels            Y        12/14/92        76
Matts          Engleberg          Y        12/13/92        62
Mary Beth      Swazey             Y        12/14/92        52
Mary           Wong               N          /  /           0

                                             AVERAGE:      54
```

Listing 4.1 Columnar Report that we desire to make of COMPCLAS

To get into the Report Form Generator, you must first open a database. So let us open **COMPCLAS** once more.

. **USE COMPCLAS**

Having done that, the report form is created by the command: **CREATE REPORT** followed by the name of the report. So we must choose a name for our report form. Since we plan to make more than one report form, we'll call this report form **COLUMNAR**, so it will describe exactly what it is.

COLUMNAR REPORTS

Our report form file will have the name: **COLUMNAR.FRM**. To create this report form, we type at the dot prompt:

. CREATE REPORT COLUMNAR

This causes the screen shown in Figure 4.1 to appear.

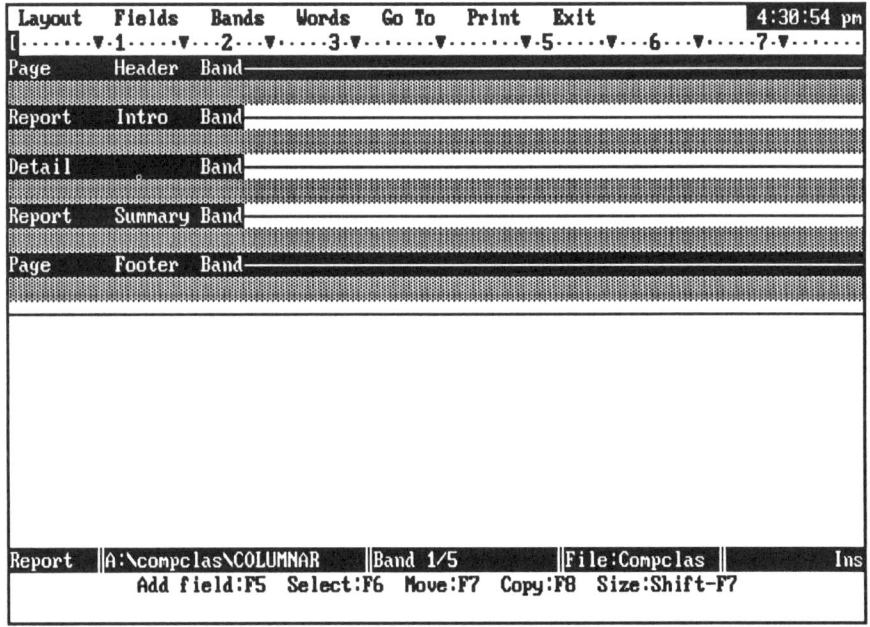

Figure 4.1 Opening Screen of Report Form Generator

Note that five bands are shown in the working area of the screen. These are:

Page Header Band
Report Intro Band
Detail Band
Report Summary Band
Page Footer Band

The Page Header Band is where we place the title that we want to appear on every page of our report. We will start by entering into this band the title of our report, "COMPUTER CLASS REPORT". Since we want to see it appear in the center of the page, we'll place it right in the center of the screen (see Figure 4.2). What you type on this screen is what will appear in the report.

Next we want to put a label at the top of all the columns in the report identifying what each column represents. This also is done in the Page Header Band. First we need to create more space in that band so that we can type in these column headings. With our cursor positioned just after the report title, we use the **Ctrl-N** keystroke pair to insert a new row. Do this four times to give us plenty of working space in this band. The result is shown in Figure 4.3.

We shall label the column containing the field FIRSTNAME, "FIRST NAME". Although we were restricted in making field names not use spaces, no such restriction applies to how we label columns. As FIRSTNAME does not appear in the dictionary, and

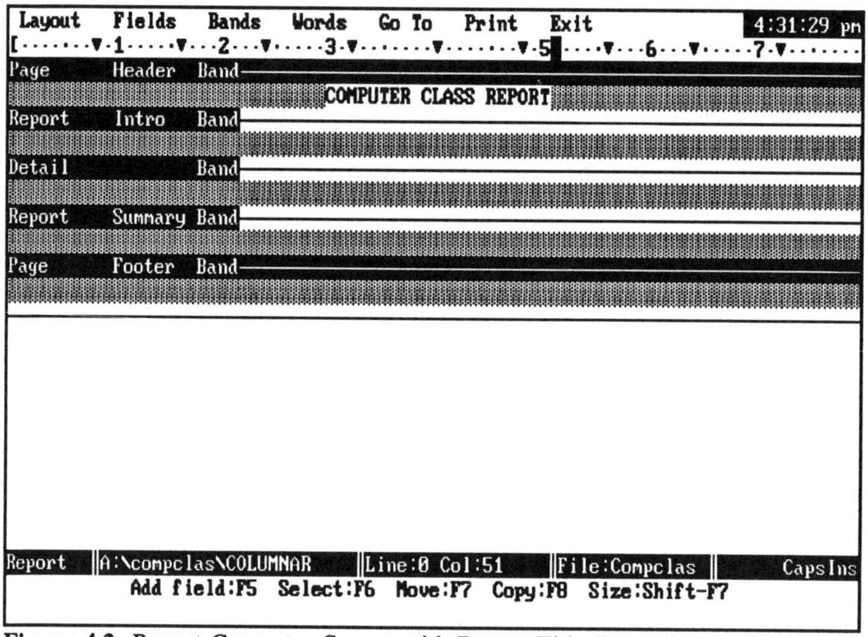

Figure 4.2 Report Generator Screen with Report Title Entered

as we would like to use good grammar, we will spell the heading putting a space between FIRST and NAME. Note that we position this heading two rows below the report title (see Figure 4.4).

The Report Intro Band is used only for information that one would like to put at the beginning of the report, but not on any subsequent pages. Since we have no information of that nature in this report, we will delete this band. This is done by moving the cursor down to the blank line immediately below the Report Intro Band and striking the keystroke pair: **Ctrl-Y** . The resulting screen is shown in Figure 4.5.

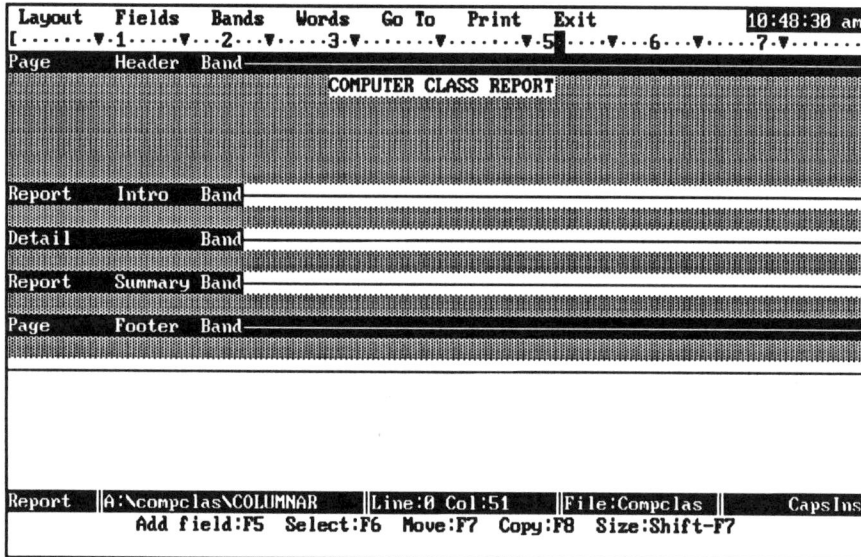

Figure 4.3 Inserting four blank lines in the Page Header Band

The Detail Band contains precisely the field data (or calculated data) that we wish to see for each record. Since what we want is the Field, FIRSTNAME, we must use the "Field" menu option shown in the menu at the top of the screen in order to do this. First we move the cursor so that it is in the blank row below the Detail Band in precisely the same column as the "F" in "FIRST NAME". Striking the **Alt-F** keystroke pair, we bring down the window shown in Figure 4.6.

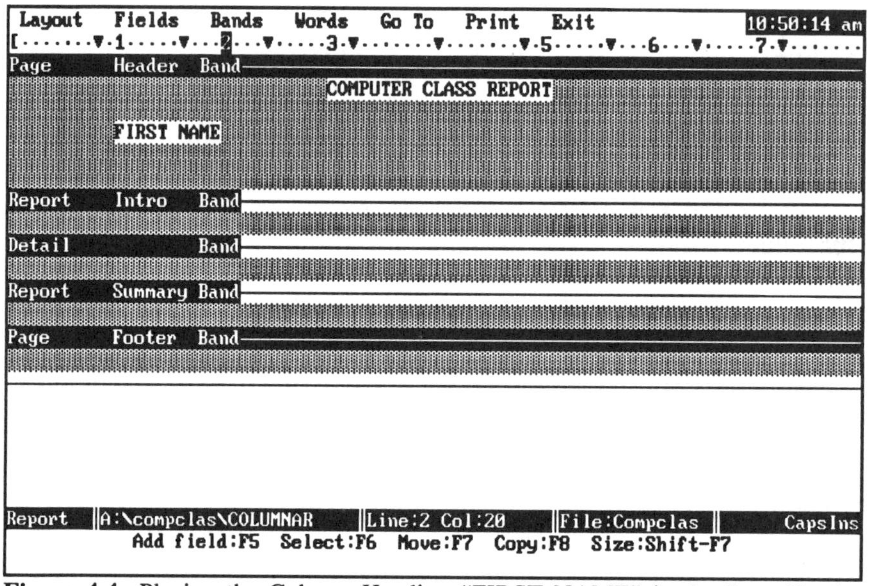

Figure 4.4 Placing the Column Heading "FIRST NAME" in the Page Header band

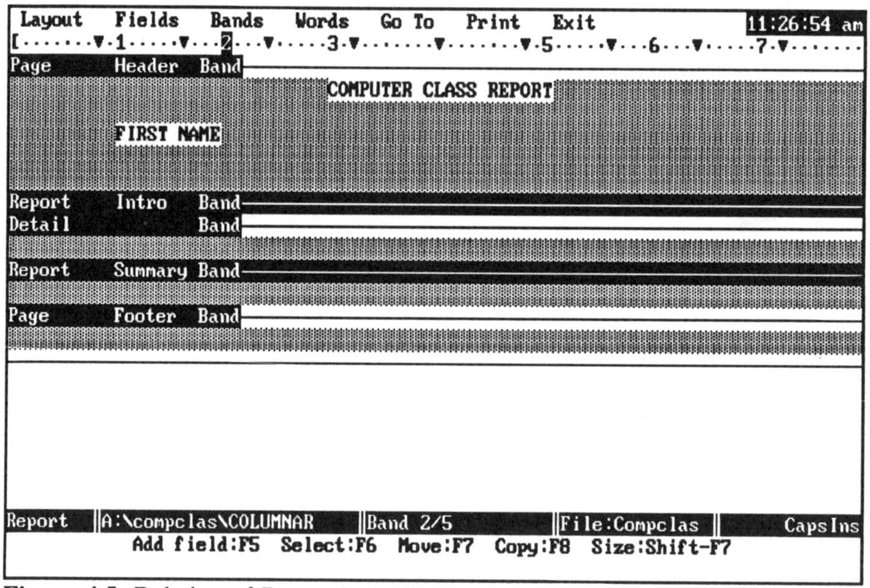

Figure 4.5 Deletion of Report Intro Band using Ctrl-Y

COLUMNAR REPORTS

Note that the highlighted item is the one we want, "Add field". Striking the Enter key, we get the field selection screen. Moving the cursor down to the FIRSTNAME selection, we get the screen shown in Figure 4.7. Striking the Enter key, we get the field attributes menu window shown in Figure 4.8. Since there is nothing that we need to do to alter the field attributes, we will accept the attributes as they are by striking the **Ctrl-End** keystroke pair (indicated in the box below the menu). The final result is that the field gets inserted into the Detail Band as shown in Figure 4.9. Note that it takes the form of XXXXXXXXXXXXXXX which indicates a field of 15 characters.

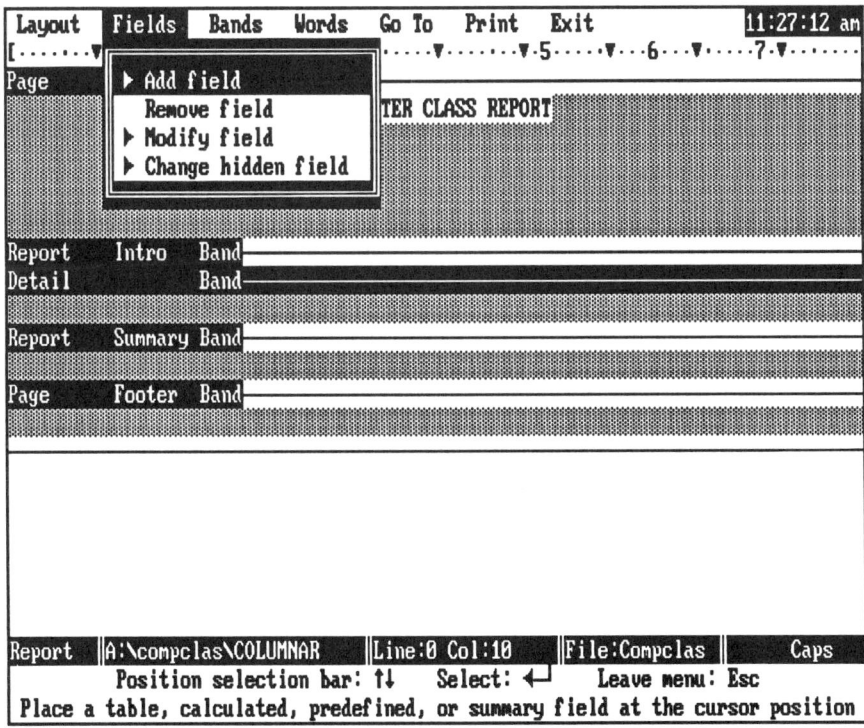

Figure 4.6 Selecting "Add field" menu item from the "Fields" menu

112   COLUMNAR REPORTS

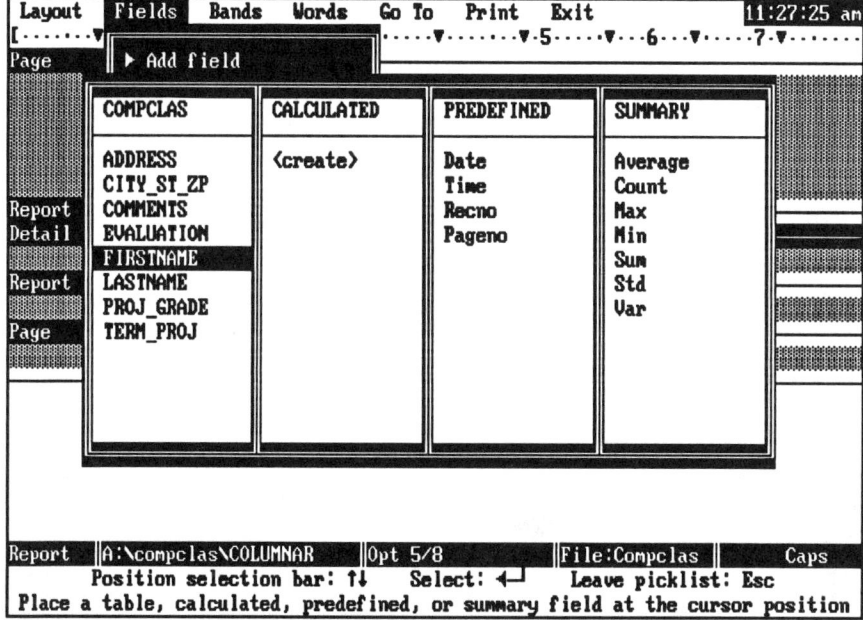
Figure 4.7 Selecting the FIRSTNAME field for the Detail Band

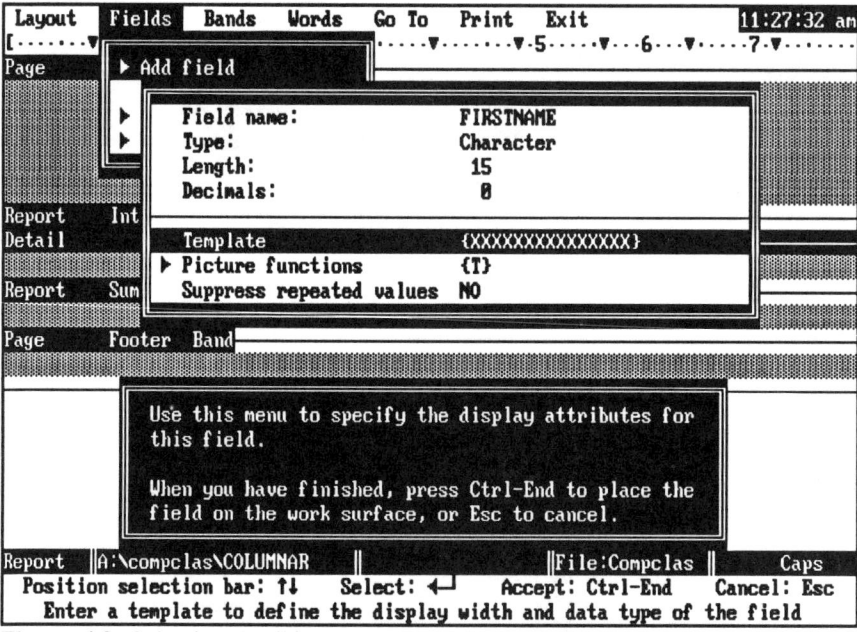
Figure 4.8 Selecting the Display attributes of the FIRSTNAME field

COLUMNAR REPORTS

```
Layout   Fields  Bands   Words   Go To   Print   Exit           11:27:40 am
[......▼.1.....▼...2...▼█....3.▼......▼......▼.5.....▼...6...▼.....7.▼......
Page     Header  Band
                         COMPUTER CLASS REPORT

         FIRST NAME


Report   Intro   Band
Detail           Band
         XXXXXXXXXXXXXXX
Report   Summary Band


Page     Footer  Band





Report   A:\compclas\COLUMNAR    Line:0 Col:25    File:Compclas      CapsIns
         Add field:F5  Select:F6  Move:F7  Copy:F8  Size:Shift-F7
```

Figure 4.9 Report Form after adding field LASTNAME to Detail Band

We repeat the same process that we went through in order to put in the "FIRST NAME" heading and FIRSTNAME field for the "LAST NAME" heading and LASTNAME field. In the third column, we want to enter the data for the logical field, TERM_PROJ. Since the heading, "TERM PROJECT", is 12 characters wide, while the actual data is only 1 character, we will put the heading on two lines so that it take up less space. See Figure 4.10.

Now, just below the heading "PROJECT" we can add the logical field, TERM_PROJ, to the detail band. The result of doing this is shown on the Detail Band in Figure 4.10. Note that a "Y" appears here. This "Y" is a symbol for a logical value that will either take on the value of "Y" or "N" in the report itself.

In the same way, we can add two more columns, one for EVALUATION date, and the other for the data of the field PROJ_GRADE. The final result is shown in Figure 4.11. Note that the date data for the field EVALUATION is represented by the

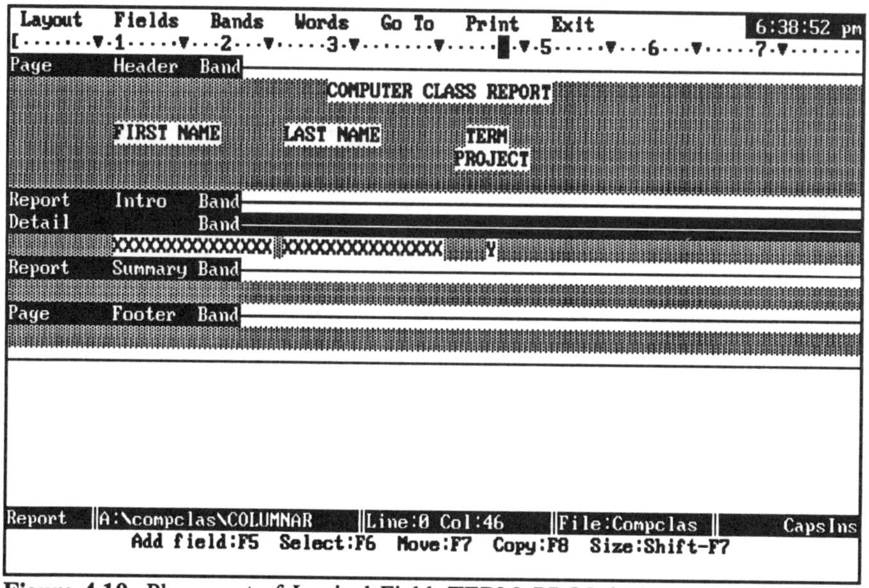

COLUMNAR REPORTS

Figure 4.10 Placement of Logical Field, TERM_PROJ, in Report Form

symbol, "MM/DD/YY", while the numeric data of the field, PROJ_GRADE, is represented by the symbols: "999". This is all the data from the database COMPCLAS that we actually want to put into this particular report.

Now that we're done with the design of the main body of the report, it would be nice for us to be able to display the average of all the grades at the very end of the report. This is done by adding a field to the Summary Band immediately below the PROJ_GRADE field in the Detail Band. Placing our cursor there, and then selecting the "Add field" menu item from the "Fields" menu option as usual, we obtain the screen shown in Figure 4.12.

Now, using the right arrow key, we carefully move our cursor to the column labeled "SUMMARY". There we select the first menu item, "Average", as shown in Figure 4.12. Striking the Enter key, we get the screen shown in Figure 4.13. Here we move the cursor down to the option, "Field to summarize on". Striking the Enter key, we then get the screen shown in Figure 4.14.

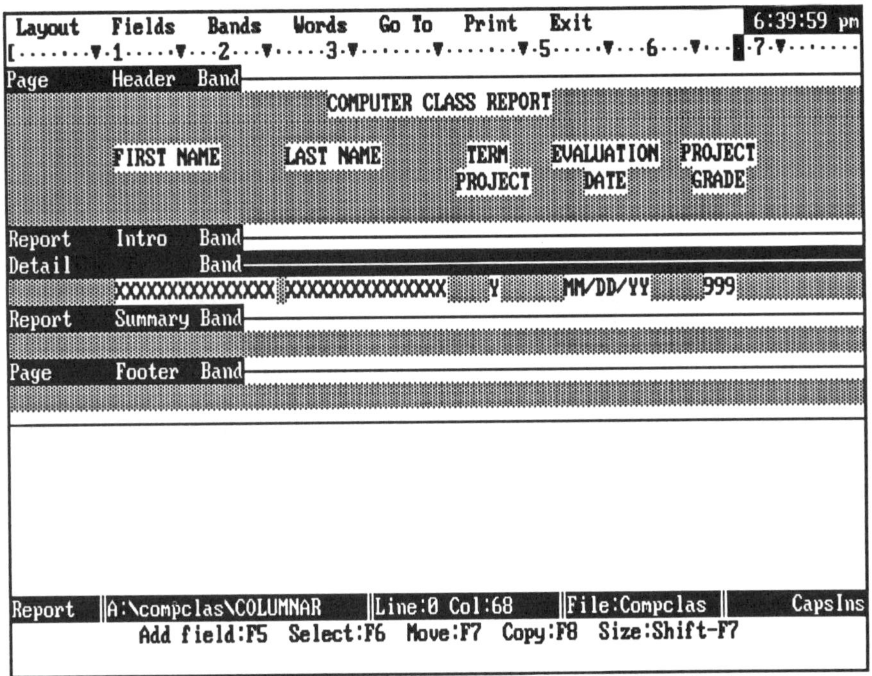

COLUMNAR REPORTS

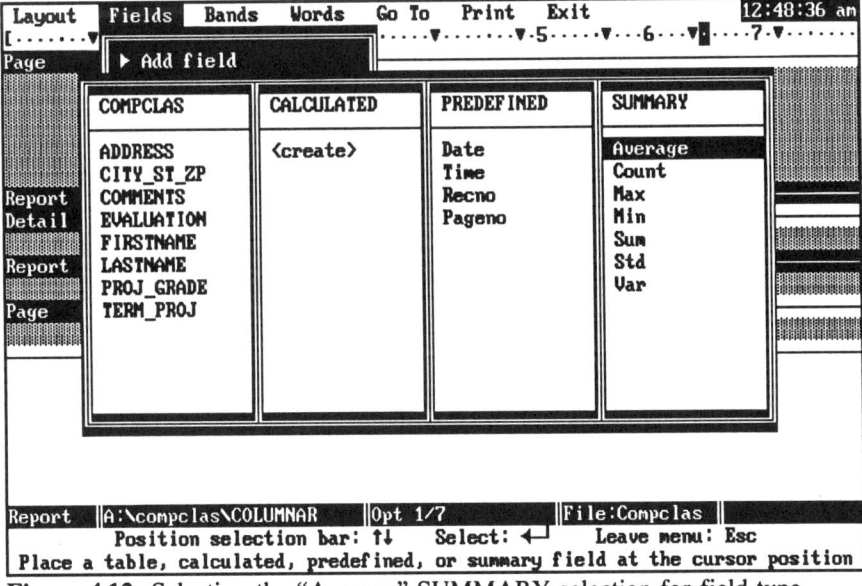

Figure 4.11 Report Form COLUMNAR after adding in all desired columns

Figure 4.12 Selecting the "Average" SUMMARY selection for field type

Now we move the cursor down to the field, PROJ_GRADE, as shown in Figure 4.14, and we hit the Enter key once more. This returns us to the Display Attributes screen. Now we must make one more change, and that is in the way the average of the Project Grade gets displayed. To do this we move down to the option on the menu labeled "Template" as shown in Figure 4.15.

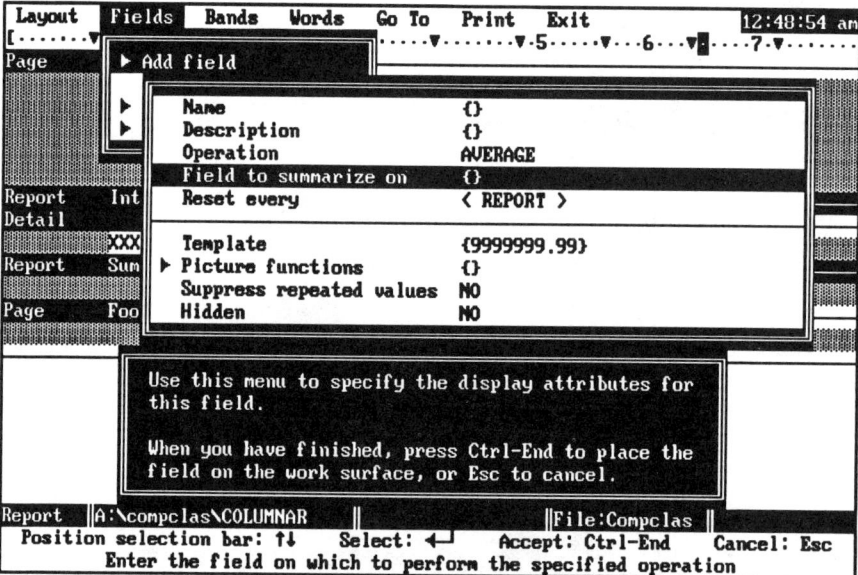

Figure 4.13 Selecting the "Field to summarize on" option

Here, the default way the average is going to be displayed, "9999999.99", is shown to be using a width of 10 digits with two decimal places. Since our average will never be in excess of 100, the report will look far better if we reduce this template to "999". This is done by using the Backspace or Delete key to remove the unwanted nines (see Figure 4.16).

Now we simply strike the Enter key to confirm our change, and then strike the **Ctrl-End** key combination to end our menu selection. The resulting report form is shown in Figure 4.17.

Now if we exit from the Report Form Generator the way we usually do (strike **Alt-E** and then hit the Enter key), we return to the

COLUMNAR REPORTS

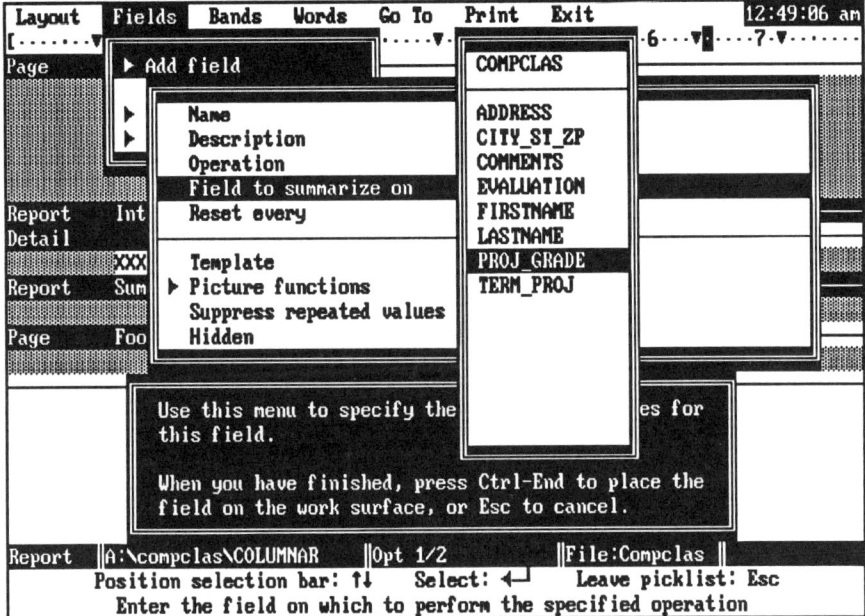

Figure 4.14 Choosing the Field "PROJ_GRADE" as the Field on which to Summarize

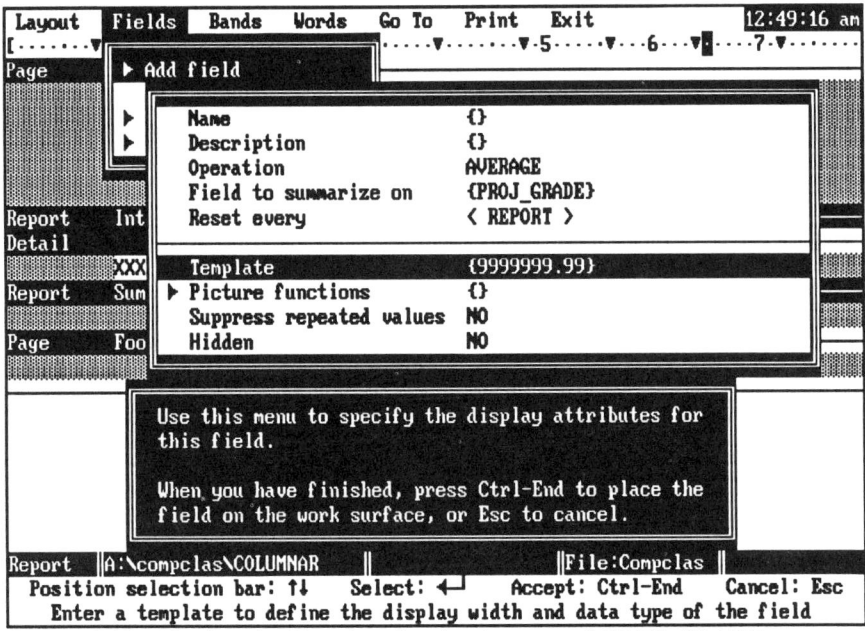

Figure 4.15 Altering the Template for the Average of PROJ_GRADE

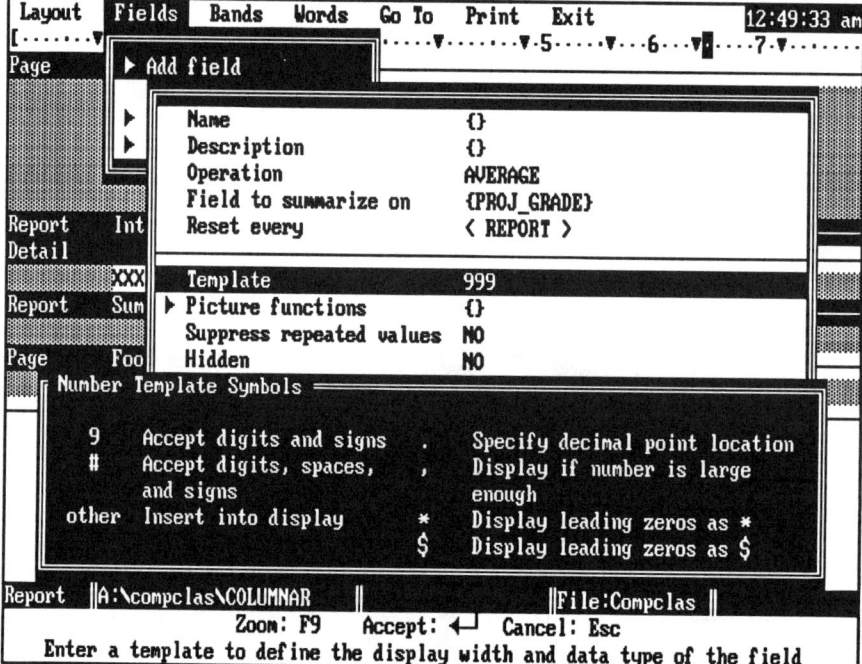

Figure 4.16 Changing the Average of PROJ_GRADE Template to "999"

dot prompt. There we can print out this report. The syntax for the command to actually print out the report is: **REPORT FORM** *filename* **TO PRINT** . In this particular case we would type:

. REPORT FORM COLUMNAR TO PRINT

Listing 4.2 shows what will actually be printed out.

4.1.2 Modifying Report Forms

This first pass looks reasonably good, but we'd like to improve on the spacing and put the date in the upper left hand corner so that we get precisely what was shown in Listing 4.1. To do this we must modify our report form. The syntax of the command to modify a report form is: **MODIFY REPORT** *filename*. In our case it would be:

. MODIFY REPORT COLUMNAR

COLUMNAR REPORTS 119

```
Layout    Fields   Bands    Words    Go To    Print    Exit              6:40:49 pm
[.......▼.1.....▼...2...▼......3.▼......▼......▼.5.....▼...6...▼....▼.7.▼......
Page      Header   Band
                                    COMPUTER CLASS REPORT

             FIRST NAME     LAST NAME        TERM      EVALUATION   PROJECT
                                             PROJECT      DATE       GRADE

Report    Intro    Band
Detail             Band
             XXXXXXXXXXXXXXX XXXXXXXXXXXXXXX    Y         MM/DD/YY     999
Report    Summary  Band
                                                                      999
Page      Footer   Band




Report   A:\compclas\COLUMNAR     Line:0 Col:68     File:Compclas         CapsIns
         Add field:F5  Select:F6  Move:F7  Copy:F8  Size:Shift-F7
```

Figure 4.17 Report Form Columnar after having added an Average of PROJ_GRADE to the Report Summary Band

```
                       COMPUTER CLASS REPORT
    FIRST NAME    LAST NAME         TERM      EVALUATION   PROJECT
                                    PROJECT      DATE       GRADE
    Gladys        Naboa              Y         12/15/92      93
    Consuelo      Naboa              Y         12/16/92      89
    Derek         Caruthers          N           /  /         0
    Wendel        Little             Y         12/17/92      87
    Jeremy        Witherspoon        Y         12/19/92      82
    Nancy         Hardwick           N           /  /         0
    Jonathan      Samuels            Y         12/14/92      76
    Matts         Engleberg          Y         12/13/92      62
    Mary Beth     Swazey             Y         12/14/92      52
    Mary          Wong               N           /  /         0
                                                              54
```

Listing 4.2 Print out of COMPCLAS using the Report Form shown in Figure 4.16

This takes us back to the screen of Figure 4.17. First let's add the date to the upper left hand corner of the report form. Move the cursor so that it sits two spaces directly above the "F" in "FIRST NAME", in the Page Header Band. Then select the "Field" option of the menu with **Alt-F** and the "Add field" item of the drop down window menu as we normally do whenever we add a new field to the report form. This gives us our field selection screen shown in Figure 4.18.

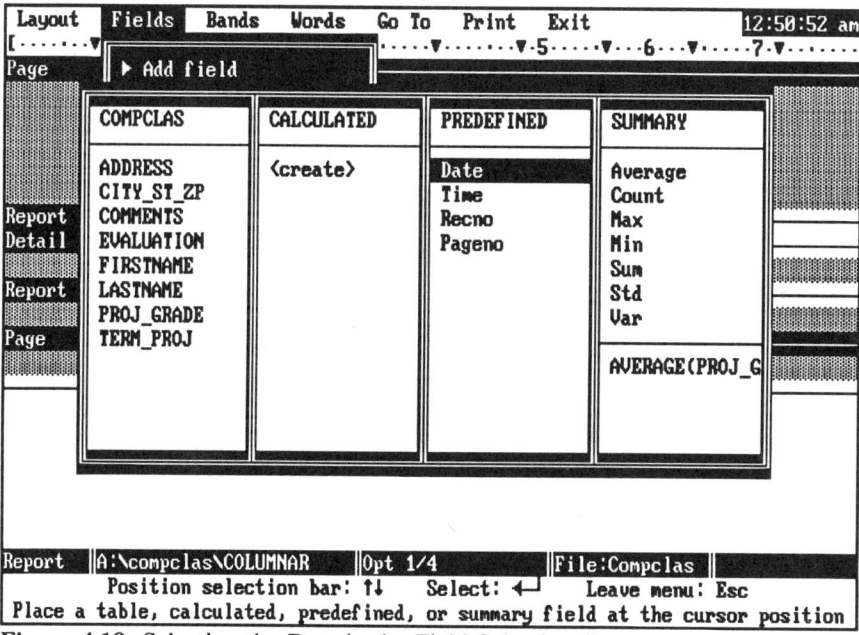

Figure 4.18 Selecting the Date in the Field Selection Screen

This time we move the cursor over to the column labeled "Predefined", and select the item labeled: "Date" as see in Figure 4.18. Striking the Enter key, we get the "Display Attributes" screen of Figure 4.19. Accepting the attributes as they are by striking **Ctrl-End,** we get the date added to the upper left hand corner of the report form as seen in Figure 4.20.

Now all we need to do is to create a space just before the final average as seen in Listing 4.1. This is done by moving the cursor down to the beginning of the Report Summary line containing

COLUMNAR REPORTS

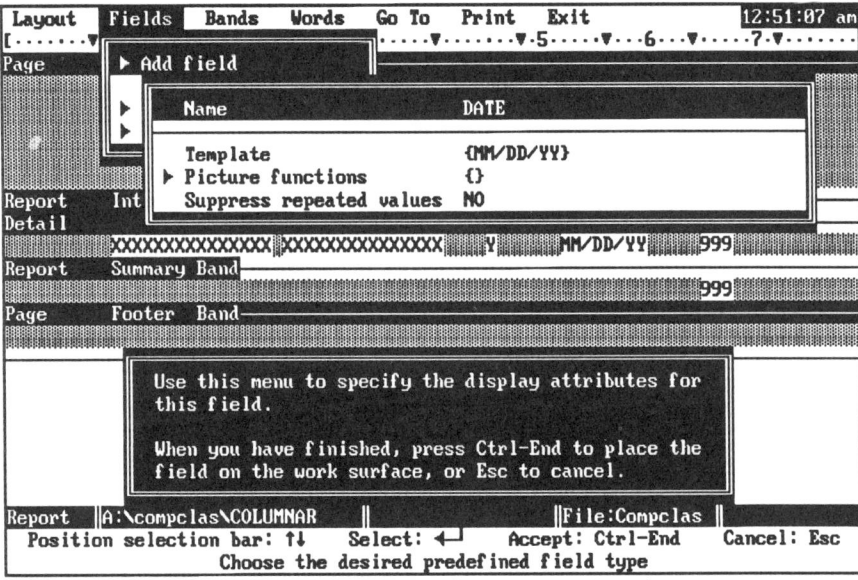

Figure 4.19 "Display Attributes" screen for the Date Function

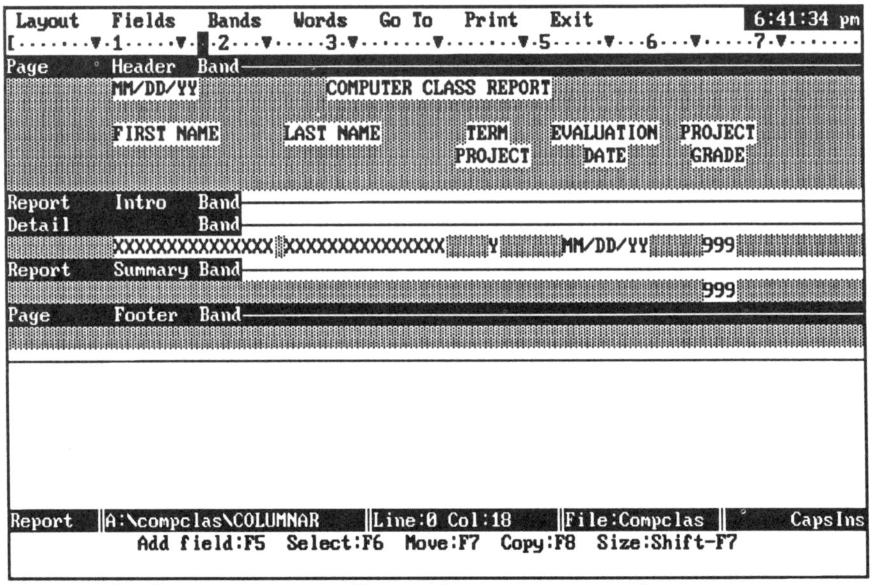

Figure 4.20 Report Form with Date added to the upper left corner

the average and striking the keystroke pair **Ctrl-N**. Finally, type in the word "Average: " just preceding where the "999" template for average is placed. The final result is shown in Figure 4.21.

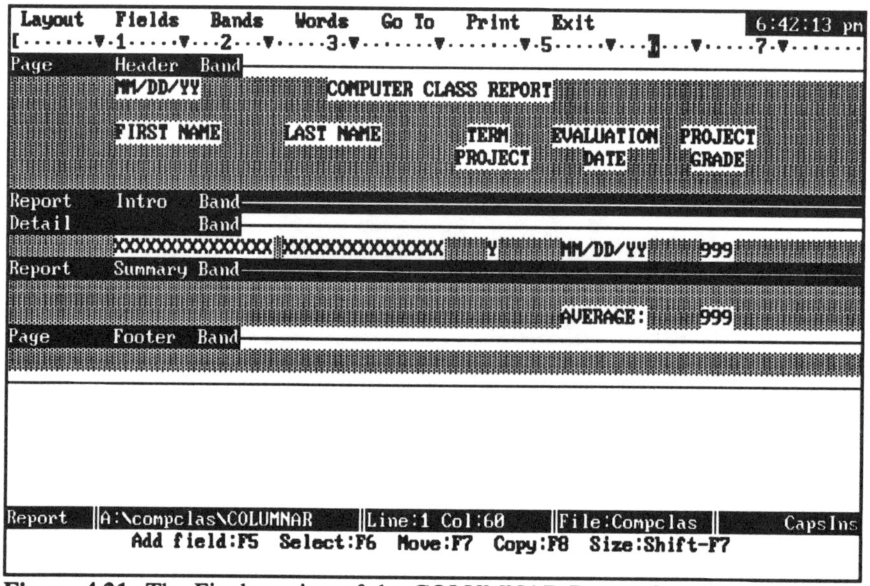

Figure 4.21 The Final version of the COLUMNAR Report for COMPCLAS

Saving and Exiting from the Report Form Generator, we print out the final version of the report typing:

. **REPORT FORM COLUMNAR TO PRINT**

The result is shown in Listing 4.1.

4.2 Example II: Quick Layout for ACCOUNTS Database

If you have a database with a small number of fields, then it may be faster for you to make what is called a "Quick Layout". In a Quick Layout for a columnar report, dBASE IV simply lays out all the fields in the database in a simple report format using the field names as the column headings. Obviously, if your fields are too wide, or if you have too many of them, then the report that is generated will exceed the width of your paper. Usually some sort of modification needs to be made to a Quick Layout so that it looks acceptable.

COLUMNAR REPORTS 123

Given these caveats, the Quick Layout is a fast way of generating a report. Let us generate a Quick Layout for the ACCOUNTS database. First, let's move to the \ACCOUNTS subdirectory and open up the ACCOUNTS database:

. **SET DIRECTORY TO \ACCOUNTS**
. **USE ACCOUNTS**

Now let's create another report form called ACCOUNTS.

. **CREATE REPORT ACCOUNTS**

The opening screen that we get is similar to what we got in Figure 4.1. The only difference is that on the status line we see that we are dealing with an ACCOUNTS report form in the \ACCOUNTS directory.

Now we will choose the menu option "Layout" which is in the upper left hand corner of the screen. We do this in the usual way by striking the keystroke pair: **Alt-L** . This gives us the screen we see in Figure 4.22. Selecting the "Quick layout" menu item as shown, we strike the Enter key. The next screen that appears is shown in Figure 4.23. This allows us to choose between a columnar layout, a form layout, or a mailmerge layout. Selecting the "Column layout" as shown, strike the Enter key. The result is the report form shown in Figure 4.24.

Let's look at the report generated by this report form. We do not have to leave the Report Form Generator in order to do this, nor do we have to actually print the report on paper. We can pull down the "Print" menu option window by striking the **Alt-P** keystroke pair as shown in Figure 4.25. Selecting the "View report on screen" menu item (as shown), and striking the Enter key causes the report to be displayed screen by screen. The first screen of the resulting report is shown in Figure 4.26.

In examining the first page of the report, note that the field name "CASHED" wraps around onto the next line. This is because there just wasn't enough room on this 80 column screen for the all

COLUMNAR REPORTS

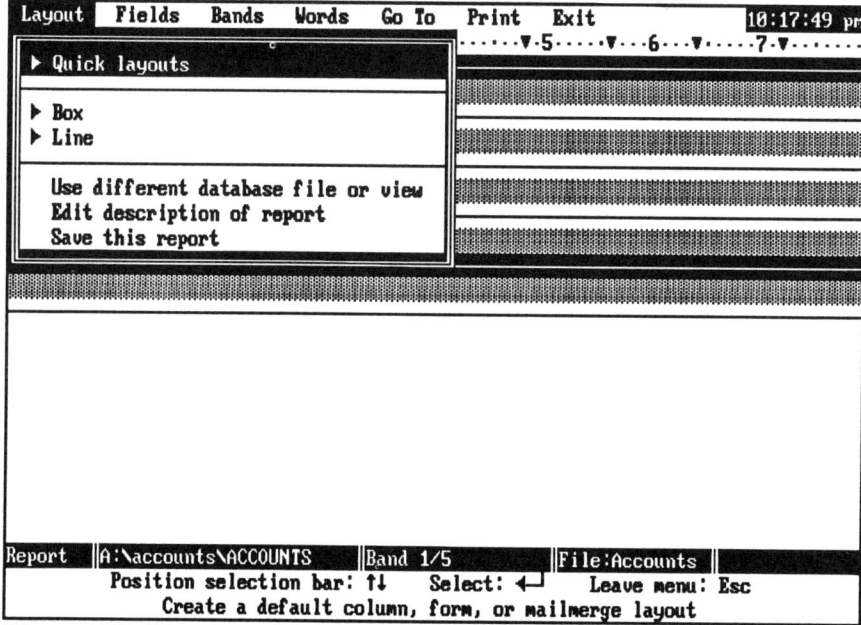

Figure 4.22 Choosing a "Quick Layout" in the "Layout" Menu Option.

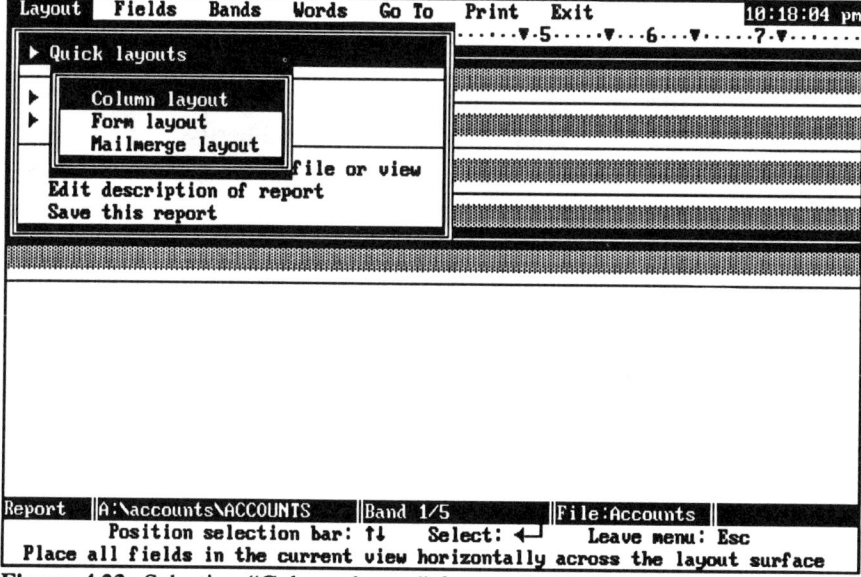

Figure 4.23 Selecting "Column layout" for our Quick Layout format

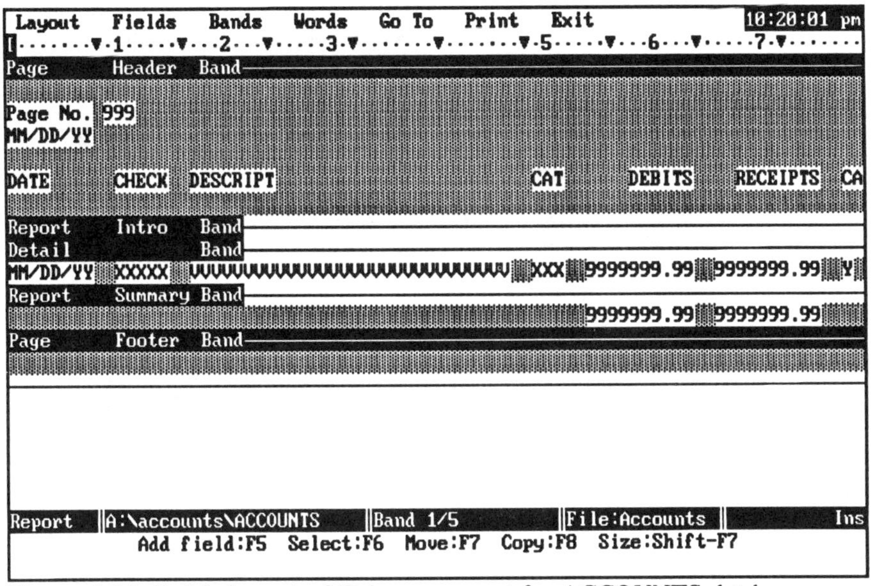

COLUMNAR REPORTS 125

Figure 4.24 Quick Layout of Columnar report for ACCOUNTS database

the fields with their field names to appear in a columnar fashion. However, as you can see, we're close to a final product. Looking further you see that the columns for DEBITS and RECEIPTS are wider than they need be (we assume that no check nor receipt will be in excess of $99,999.99).

We will solve this problem simply by changing the field width of both the DEBITS and RECEIPTS columns from 10 digits to 8 so that everything fits in. This is done by first putting the cursor on the DEBITS field in the Detail Band line. When this happens the entire field switches into reverse video as shown in Figure 4.27. Now the "Fields" option on the menu is selected (**Alt-F**), and the "Modify field" menu item is selected as shown in Figure 4.28.

Striking the Enter key, we get the screen attributes menu shown in Figure 4.29. Move the cursor key down to the template for DEBITS, as shown. Note that it is currently 10 digits long (including the decimal point). Strike the Enter key to select the template. Now move the cursor so that it is in the area to the left of the decimal point. Strike the Backspace or Delete key twice to

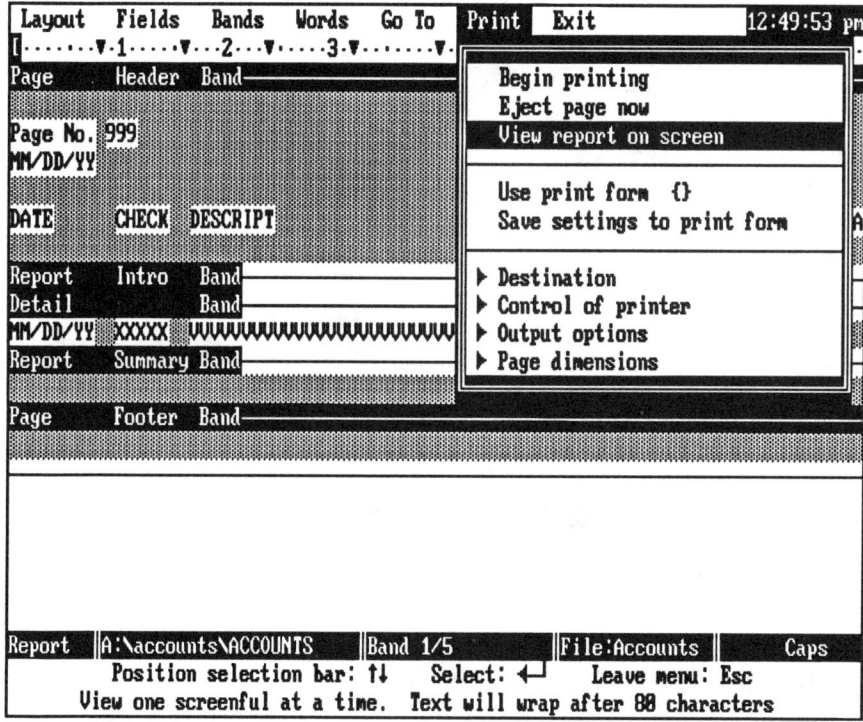

Figure 4.25 Selecting "View report on screen" as a Print option

reduce the number of nines by 2 as is shown in Figure 4.30. Strike the Enter key to deselect the template, and the **Ctrl-End** key to take us back to the report form.

Note that in the report form, the number of digits in the DEBITS field in the Detail Band has indeed been reduced by two. (See Figure 4.31) Repeating this same process for the DEBITS field in the Report Summary Band as well as for the RECEIPTS field in both the Detail as well as Report Summary Bands we get the result shown in Figure 4.32.

Now that we've made the fields smaller, we can move them to the left in order to create more space on the right for the CASHED field. This is done by placing the cursor in the DEBITS field in the Detail Band once more as shown in Figure 4.32.

```
Page No.  1
01/23/93

DATE       CHECK  DESCRIPT                    CAT    DEBITS    RECEIPTS   CA
SHED

01/01/92          Jan. 1 Balance                       0.00     100.00    Y
01/05/92          Deposit: Salary             SAL      0.00     750.00    Y
01/09/92   401    Cash: January Allowance     PER    100.00       0.00    Y
01/09/92   402    Sullivan Co. Cablevision    CAB     20.00       0.00    Y
01/09/92   403    N.Y. Telephone: Dec. bill   TEL     50.00       0.00    Y
01/12/92   404    Dr. John McIntyre, D.D.S.   DOC     75.00       0.00    Y
01/13/92   405    Sierra Club: Donation       DON     10.00       0.00    N
01/14/92   406    Shoprite: Groceries         GRO     18.60       0.00    Y
01/14/92   407    Farmer's Market: Groceries  GRO      4.20       0.00    Y
01/14/92   408    Feed-n-things: Pet Food     PET      8.50       0.00    Y
01/15/92   409    State Farm Mutual: Insurance INS   232.94       0.00    Y
01/15/92   410    Sherman's: auto repairs     CAR     10.00       0.00    Y
01/16/92   411    NYSEG: Utilities            UTI    110.12       0.00    N
01/16/92   412    West Side Vets              PET     30.00       0.00    N
01/18/92          Deposit: Travel Expense Reimb. REI   0.00      38.25    Y
01/19/92   413    Dr. Isaacs, M.D. (eye doct) DOC     40.00       0.00    Y
01/19/92          Deposit: Salary             SAL      0.00     750.00    Y
                  Cancel viewing: ESC,  Continue viewing: SPACEBAR
```

Figure 4.26 The first screen of the report, ACCOUNTS, using the "View report on screen" menu item of the "Print" menu option

Looking at the bottom of the screen, notice that striking the **F6** key selects the field that we wish to operate on. So we strike the **F6** key followed by the Enter key. Looking at the bottom of the screen once more, notice that to move the field one strikes the **F7** key. Striking the **F7** key we can now move the entire field to the left one space by striking the left arrow key once. When we hit the Enter key to confirm our new position, the question appears at the bottom of the screen, "Delete covered text and fields? (Y/N)", as shown in Figure 4.33. Answer by striking **Y**. The result is shown in Figure 4.34.

Doing the same for the DEBITS field in the Report Summary Band, as well as the RECEIPTS fields (move 2 spaces to the left) and the CASHED field (move 5 spaces to the left), we get the result shown in Figure 4.35.

Now all that needs to be done is to move the column headings for DEBITS, RECEIPTS and CASHED to the left so that

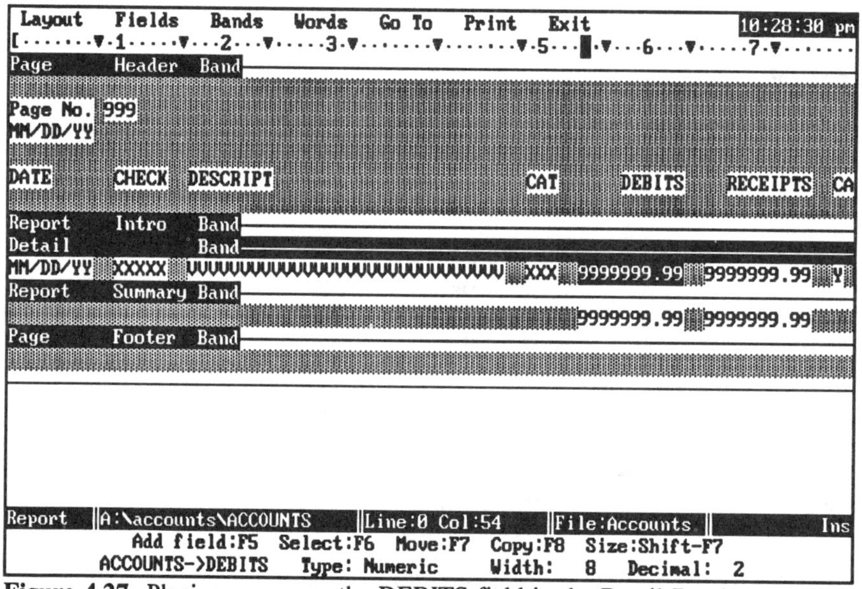

128   COLUMNAR REPORTS

Figure 4.27 Placing cursor on the DEBITS field in the Detail Band

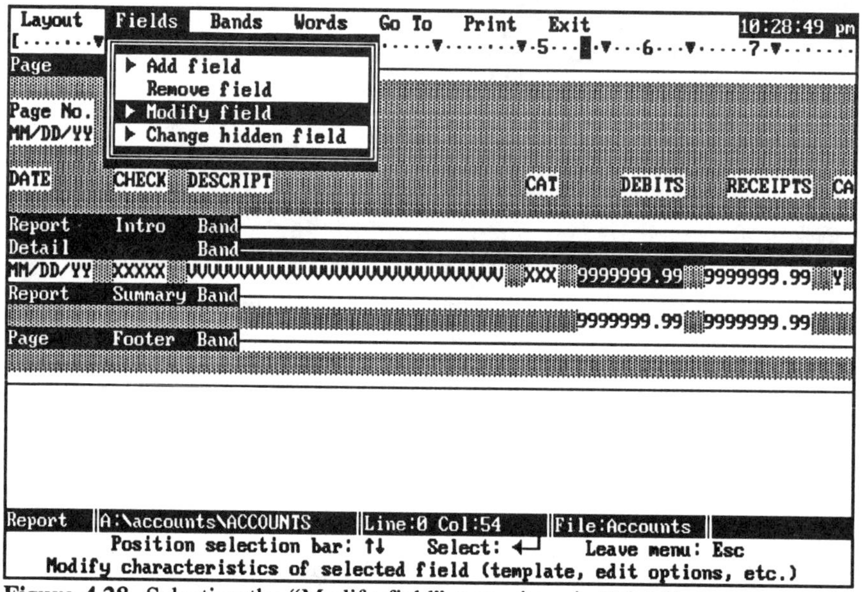

Figure 4.28 Selecting the "Modify field" menu item in "Field" menu

COLUMNAR REPORTS 129

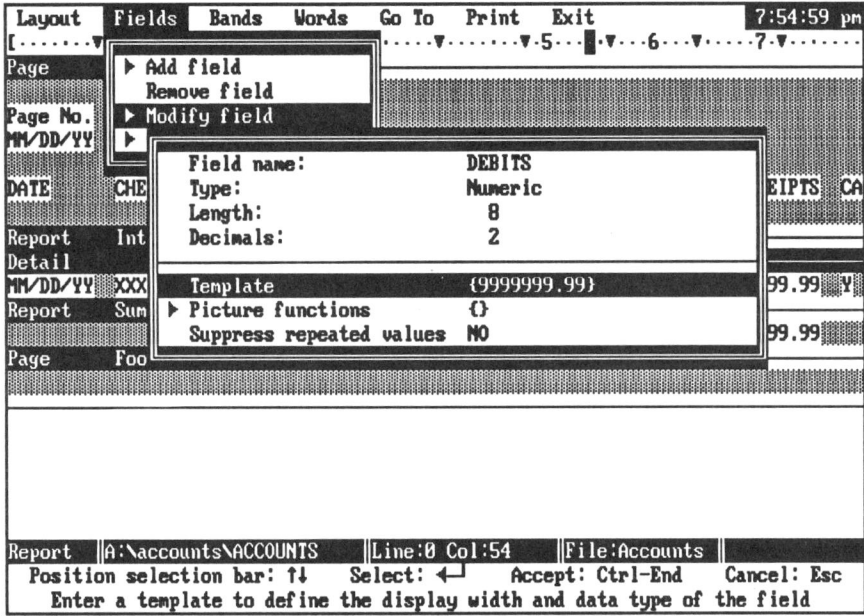

Figure 4.29 Selecting the Template of the DEBITS field

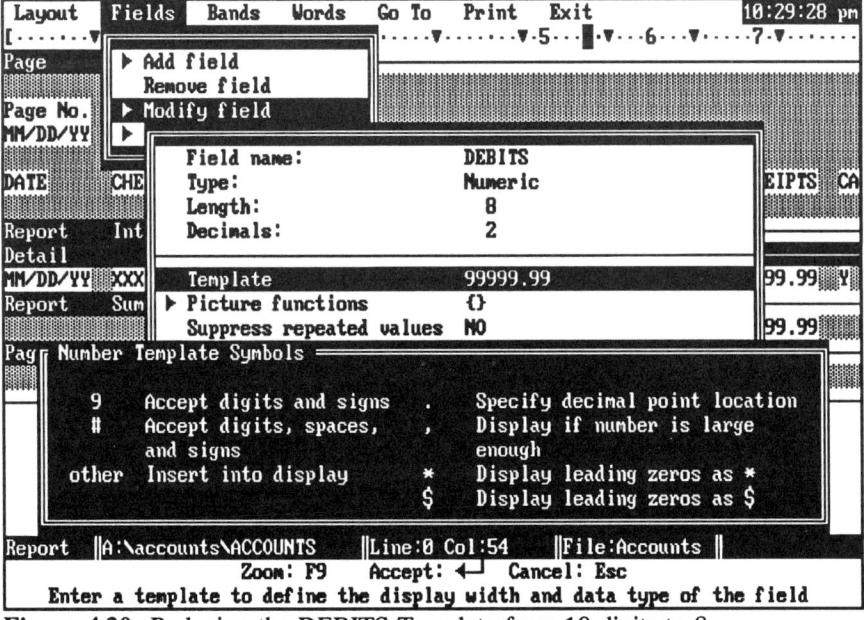

Figure 4.30 Reducing the DEBITS Template from 10 digits to 8

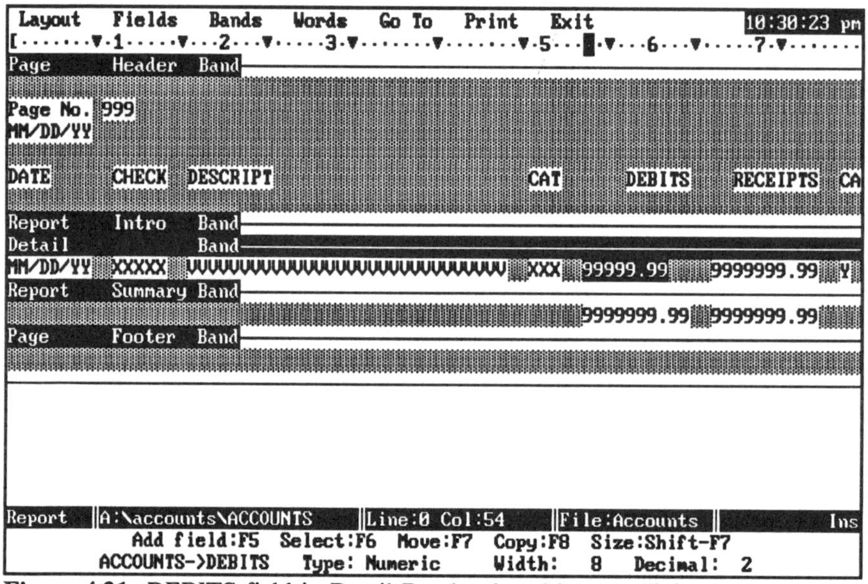

130   COLUMNAR REPORTS

Figure 4.31 DEBITS field in Detail Band reduced by two digits

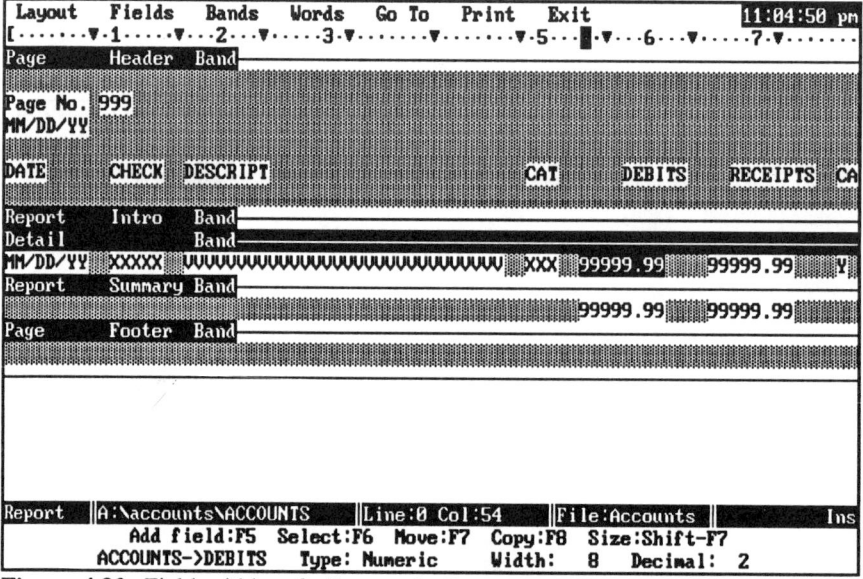

Figure 4.32 Field widths of all numeric fields reduced by 2 digits

COLUMNAR REPORTS

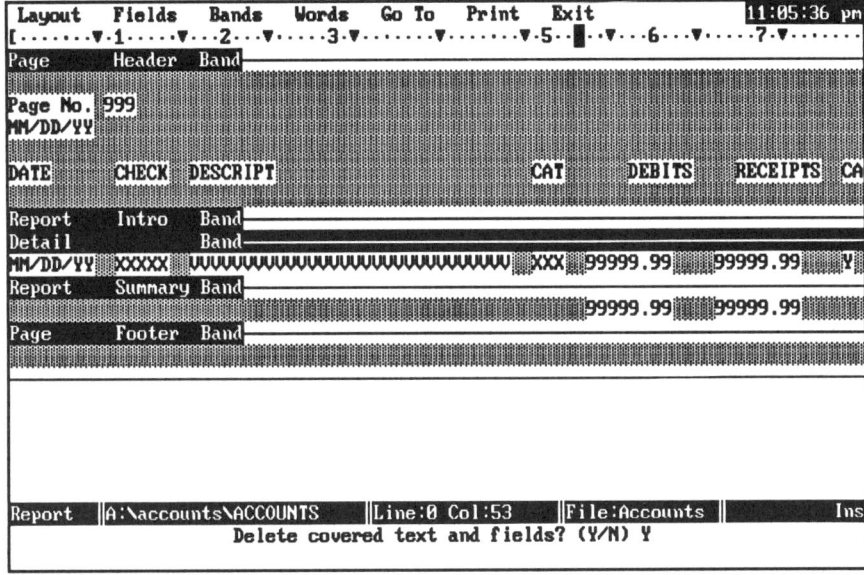

Figure 4.33 Answering question, "Delete covered test and fields?"

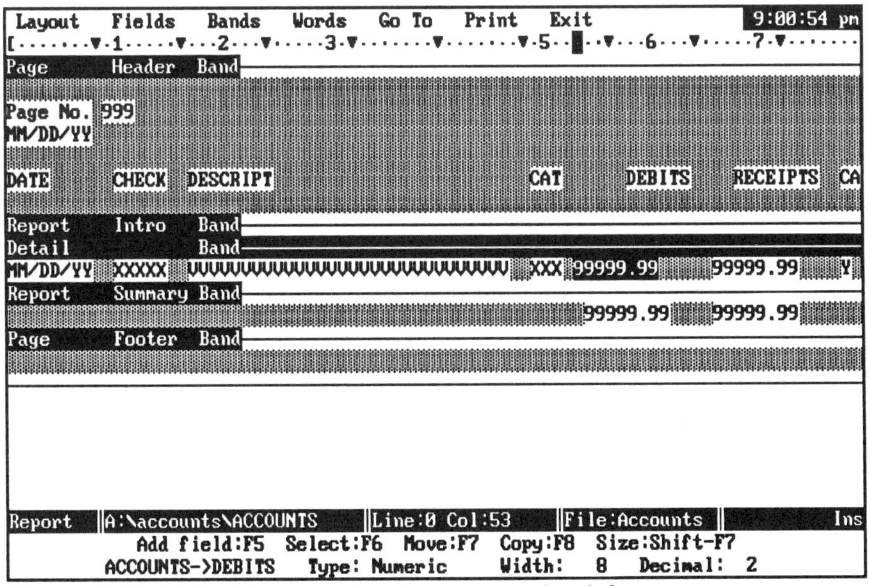

Figure 4.34 Field DEBITS in Detail Band moved to left one space

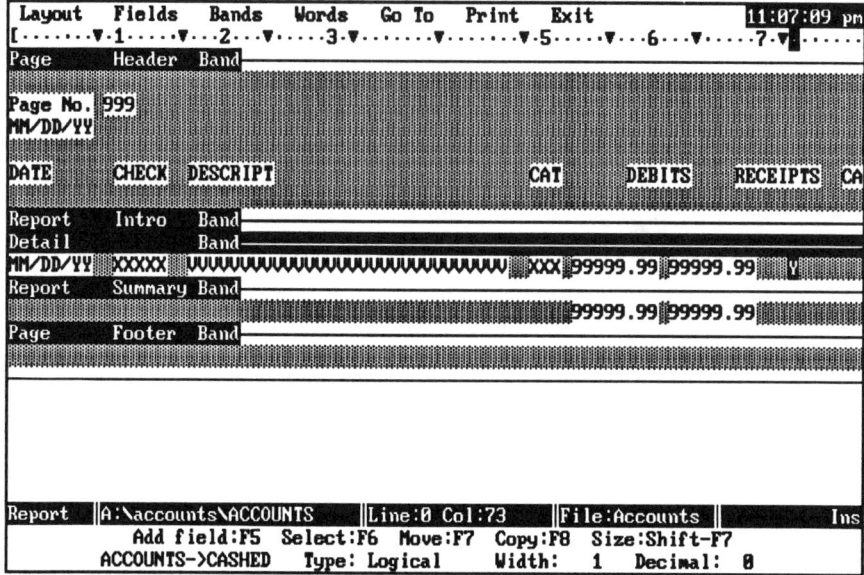

Figure 4.35 Report form ACCOUNTS after having moved DEBITS, RECEIPTS, CASHED fields to the left

they are directly over their respective fields. This is easily done by using the **F6** key once more. For the case of the word "DEBITS", we first place the cursor under the "D", then we strike the **F6** key. It is now necessary to use the right arrow key to extend the block of characters that we wish to move to include all six letters of the word "DEBITS". Once blocked, we precede as we did before, striking the Enter key, then striking the **F7** key, and hitting the left arrow key until the word is exactly where we want it to be. The same may be done for the column headings "RECEIPTS" and "CASHED". The final report form, ACCOUNTS, is shown in Figure 4.36. Note that we have typed in the report title, ACCOUNTS, in the middle of the top line.

Exiting and saving the report form ACCOUNTS (**Alt-E**, Enter), we can now print out our result. Executing the command:

. REPORT FORM ACCOUNTS TO PRINT

we get the result shown in Listing 4.3. Note that at the bottom of the report we get the sum of all the DEBITS as well as the sum of

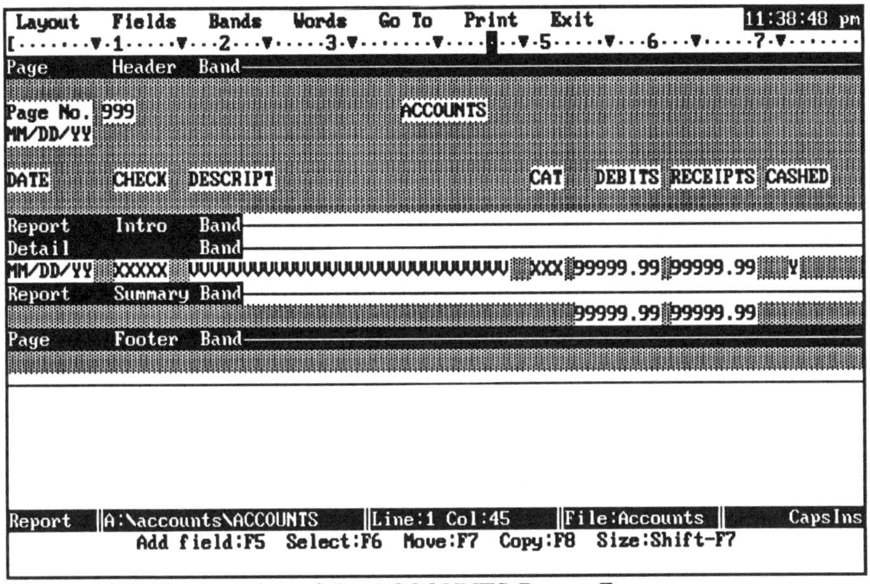

Figure 4.36 Final version of the ACCOUNTS Report Form

all the RECEIPTS. This sum was generated by the DEBITS and RECEIPTS fields in the Report Summary Band. The default when creating a Quick Layout is always to generate the sum of all numeric fields in the Report Summary Band.

4.2.1 Using Group Bands with Subtotals

It is often desirable to group like categories of records together and generate subtotals within these groups. In the case of ACCOUNTS, it would be nice to see how much we've spent or received in each of our CAT field categories. We reenter our report with:

. MODIFY REPORT ACCOUNTS

This time we select the "Bands" menu option using the keystroke pair: **Alt-B** . The resulting window menu is shown in Figure 4.37. Since we want to add a group band to the report form, all we need to do is to hit the Enter key. The screen that results, shown in Figure 4.38, asks us how we want to group the records in

COLUMNAR REPORTS

```
Page No.   1                         ACCOUNTS
01/19/93

DATE       CHECK   DESCRIPT                        CAT   DEBITS  RECEIPTS  CASHED

01/01/92           Jan. 1 Balance                          0.00    100.00   Y
01/05/92           Deposit: Salary                 SAL     0.00    750.00   Y
01/09/92   401     Cash: January Allowance         PER   100.00      0.00   Y
01/09/92   402     Sullivan Co. Cablevision        CAB    20.00      0.00   Y
01/09/92   403     N.Y. Telephone: Dec. bill       TEL    50.00      0.00   Y
01/12/92   404     Dr. John McIntyre, D.D.S.       DOC    75.00      0.00   Y
01/13/92   405     Sierra Club: Donation           DON    10.00      0.00   N
01/14/92   406     Shoprite: Groceries             GRO    18.60      0.00   Y
01/14/92   407     Farmer's Market: Groceries      GRO     4.20      0.00   Y
01/14/92   408     Feed-n-things: Pet Food         PET     8.50      0.00   Y
01/15/92   409     State Farm Mutual: Insurance    INS   232.94      0.00   Y
01/15/92   410     Sherman's: auto repairs         CAR    10.00      0.00   Y
01/16/92   411     NYSEG: Utilities                UTI   110.12      0.00   N
01/16/92   412     West Side Vets                  PET    30.00      0.00   N
01/18/92           Deposit: Travel Expense Reimb.  REI     0.00     38.25   Y
01/19/92   413     Dr. Isaacs, M.D. (eye doct)     DOC    40.00      0.00   Y
01/19/92           Deposit: Salary                 SAL     0.00    750.00   Y
01/20/92   414     Cash: Gas & Tolls               CAR    34.65      0.00   Y
01/20/92   415     Sullivan's: Dept. Store         GIF    25.66      0.00   N
01/22/92   416     Action Video                    ENT    10.59      0.00   N
01/22/92   417     MBNA Payment Services:Cred.     HOU   100.00      0.00   N
                   Card
01/25/92   418     Many Happy Returns: Tax Prep.   TAX   105.00      0.00   N
01/25/92   419     NYC Parking Violations Bur.     PER    35.00      0.00   N
01/27/92   420     Great American: Groceries       GRO    39.92      0.00   N
01/28/92   421     Trading Post: Maintenance       MAI    28.47      0.00   N
                   items
                                                        1088.65   1638.25
```

Listing 4.3 Report generated by command: REPORT FORM ACCOUNTS TO PRINT

the report. As highlighted, we choose the option, "Field value" on which to group.

After striking the Enter key, we get the screen shown in Figure 4.39. Using the down arrow key to select **CAT**, we strike the Enter key once more. The resulting modified report form is shown in Figure 4.40.

Note that two bands have been added: the "Group 1 Intro Band", and the "Group 1 Summary Band". The Group Intro Band precedes every group, while the Group Summary Band follows at the end of every group. Figure 4.41 shows what we would like to do with the two bands. Notice that we precede the group indicating with which category, CAT, we're dealing. At the end of each group, to summarize, we include a subtotal of both the DEBITS and RECEIPTS fields.

COLUMNAR REPORTS

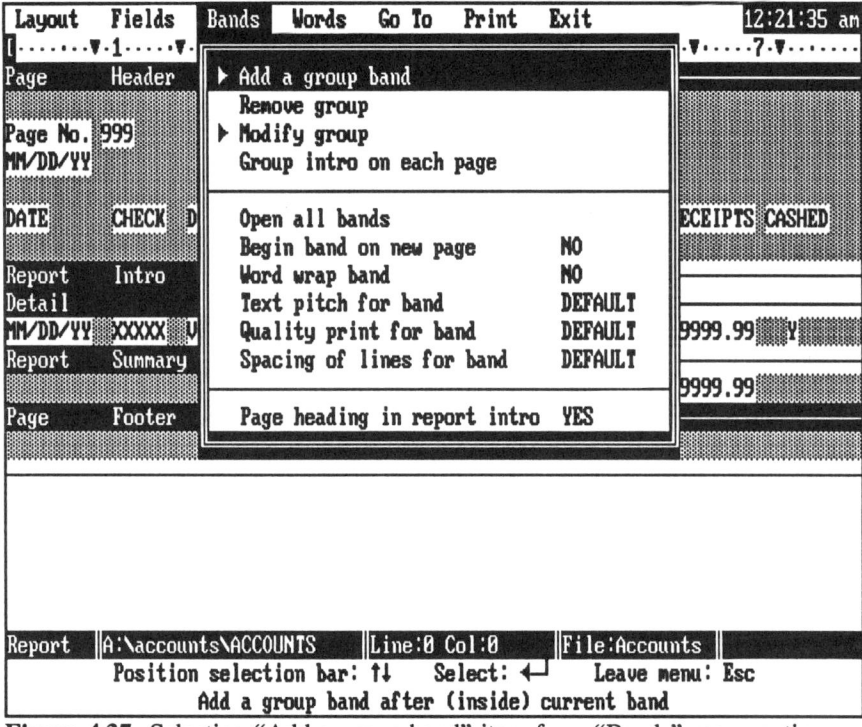

Figure 4.37 Selecting "Add a group band" item from "Bands" menu option

The CAT field is added to the Group Intro Band in the usual way one would add a database field to a Detail Band. The DEBITS and RECEIPTS fields are added to the Group Summary Band in the same way that we added the average of PROJ_GRADE to the Report Summary Band. Specifically, in the case of the DEBITS field in the Group Summary Band, we select from the summary column of the "Add field" window, the "Sum" menu item as shown in Figure 4.42.

Striking the Enter key, we get the Display Attributes screen shown in Figure 4.43. Here we select DEBITS as the field to summarize on as shown in Figure 4.44. In addition, we reduce the size of the template to 8 digits as indicated in Figure 4.45. These steps are repeated for the RECEIPTS field in the Group Summary Band. As a result of adding these fields to the Group Intro and Group Summary Bands, we get the desired report form shown in Figure 4.41.

COLUMNAR REPORTS

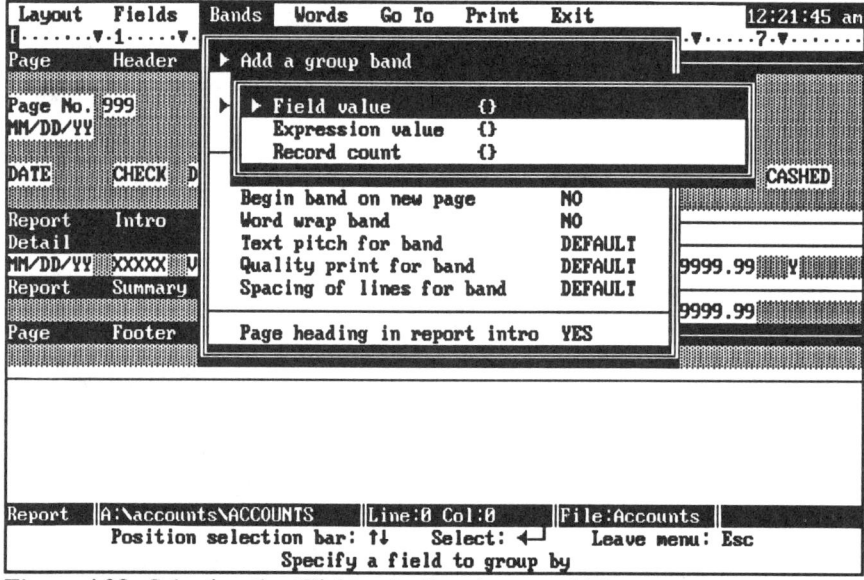

Figure 4.38 Selecting the "Field value" option on which to group

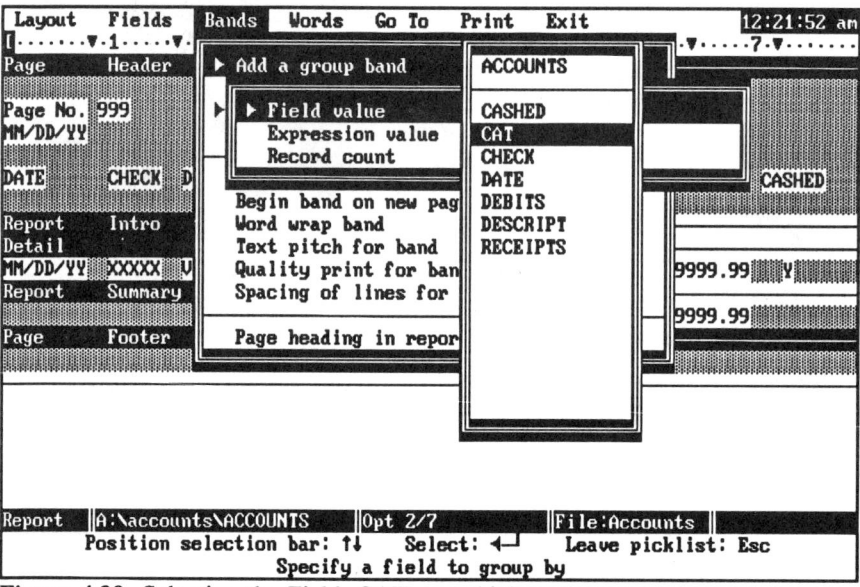

Figure 4.39 Selecting the Field, CAT, on which to group

COLUMNAR REPORTS

```
Layout   Fields  Bands  Words  Go To  Print  Exit           11:53:19 pm
[······▼·1·····▼·····2···▼·····3·▼······▼······▼·5·····▼···6···▼·····7·▼······
Page     Header  Band─────────────────────────────────────────────────────

Page No. 999                            ACCOUNTS
MM/DD/YY
DATE     CHECK   DESCRIPT                     CAT  DEBITS RECEIPTS CASHED
Report   Intro   Band─────────────────────────────────────────────────────
Group 1  Intro   Band─────────────────────────────────────────────────────

Detail           Band─────────────────────────────────────────────────────
MM/DD/YY XXXXX   UUUUUUUUUUUUUUUUUUUUUUUUUUU   XXX  99999.99 99999.99    V
Group 1  Summary Band─────────────────────────────────────────────────────

Report   Summary Band─────────────────────────────────────────────────────
                                                   99999.99 99999.99
Page     Footer  Band─────────────────────────────────────────────────────



Report   A:\accounts\ACCOUNTS   Line:3 Col:0    File:Accounts      CapsIns
          Add field:F5  Select:F6  Move:F7  Copy:F8  Size:Shift-F7
```

Figure 4.40 Report Form ACCOUNTS with Group bands added

```
Layout   Fields  Bands  Words  Go To  Print  Exit           12:26:01 am
[······▼·1·····▼·····2···▼·····3·▼······▼······▼·5·····▼···6···▼·····7·▼······
Page     Header  Band─────────────────────────────────────────────────────

Page No. 999                            ACCOUNTS
MM/DD/YY
DATE     CHECK   DESCRIPT                     CAT  DEBITS RECEIPTS CASHED
Report   Intro   Band─────────────────────────────────────────────────────
Group 1  Intro   Band─────────────────────────────────────────────────────
Category: XXX
Detail           Band─────────────────────────────────────────────────────
MM/DD/YY XXXXX   UUUUUUUUUUUUUUUUUUUUUUUUUUU   XXX  99999.99 99999.99    V
Group 1  Summary Band─────────────────────────────────────────────────────
                                                   99999.99 99999.99
Report   Summary Band─────────────────────────────────────────────────────
                                                   99999.99 99999.99
Page     Footer  Band─────────────────────────────────────────────────────



Report   A:\accounts\ACCOUNTS   Line:0 Col:70   File:Accounts         Ins
          Add field:F5  Select:F6  Move:F7  Copy:F8  Size:Shift-F7
```

Figure 4.41 Adding fields to the Group Intro and the Group Summary bands

138 COLUMNAR REPORTS

Since we have the category, CAT, in the Group Intro Band, there is no reason to repeat it on every line of the Detail Band. So we may eliminate the CAT field from the Detail Band. This is done by simply moving the cursor to the CAT field and striking the Delete key. We also want to remove the heading, "CAT", in the Page Header Band. Next, we place the word, "Subtotal: ", just before the subtotals of DEBITS and RECEIPTS. Finally, we want to have a space between groups, so another line is added to the Group Summary Band. This is done by moving the cursor all the way to the right side of the screen, in the Group Summary band, and then striking the keystroke pair: **Ctrl-N** . The resulting report form is shown in Figure 4.46. We may now Exit and save the ACCOUNTS report form (**Alt-E**, Enter).

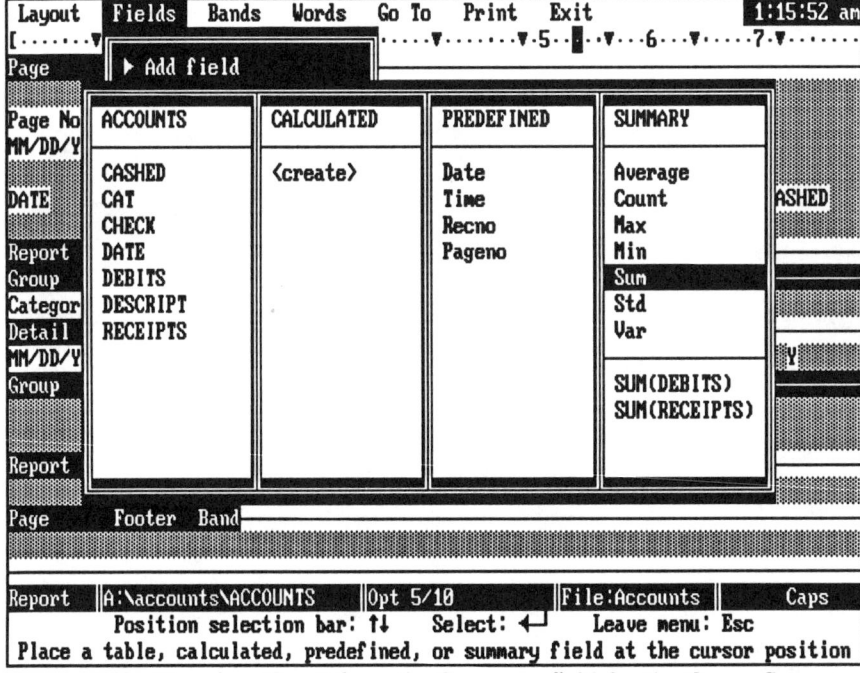

Figure 4.42 Choosing "Sum" from the Summary field for the Group Summary of DEBITS

4.2.2 Printing a Group Report

A prerequisite for printing a group report is that the database be ordered in the same order on which it is grouped. In the case of our ACCOUNTS report form and database, we must insure the fact that the database is indexed in the order of CAT. Since we do not possess an index on CAT in our Multiple Index (we do have one indexed on CAT unique, but we don't want a unique index here), we must create one. So we execute the command:

. INDEX ON CAT TAG CATEGORY

Now that the database is indexed properly, we are ready to generate a copy of our report. Once again the command is:

. REPORT FORM ACCOUNTS TO PRINT

The resulting report is shown in Listings 4.4A and 4.4B.

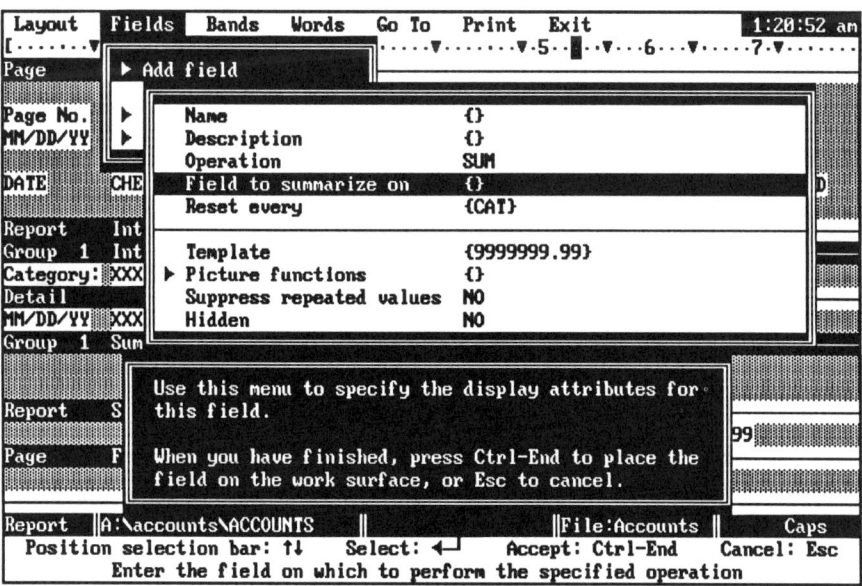

Figure 4.43 Choosing the "Field to summarize on" in the Display Attributes Screen

140 COLUMNAR REPORTS

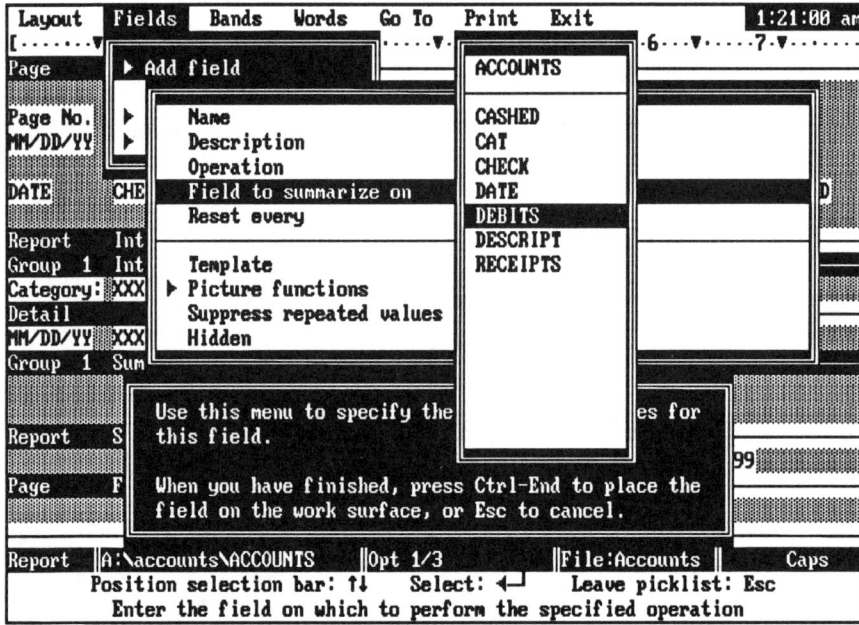

Figure 4.44 Choosing DEBITS to be the "Field to summarize on" in the Group Summary band

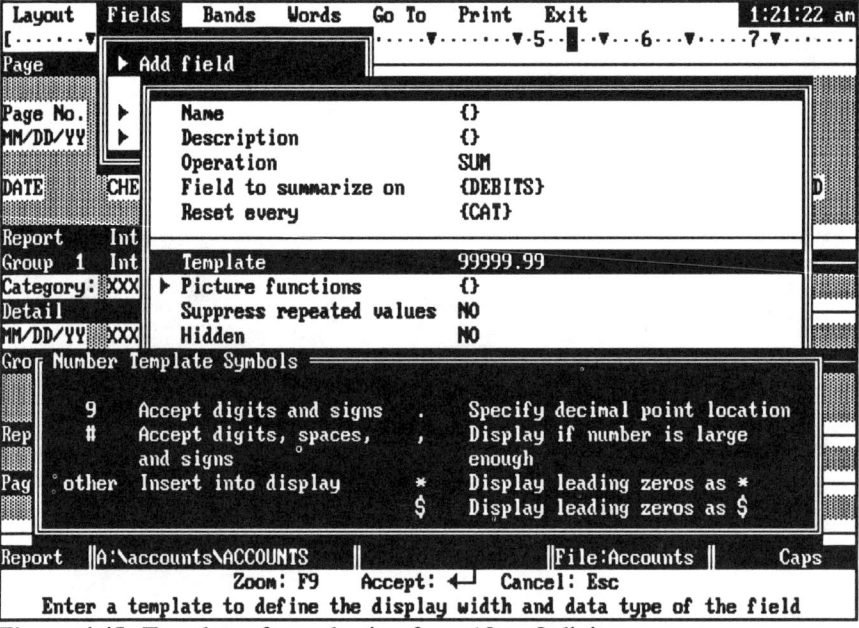

Figure 4.45 Template after reduction from 10 to 8 digits

COLUMNAR REPORTS

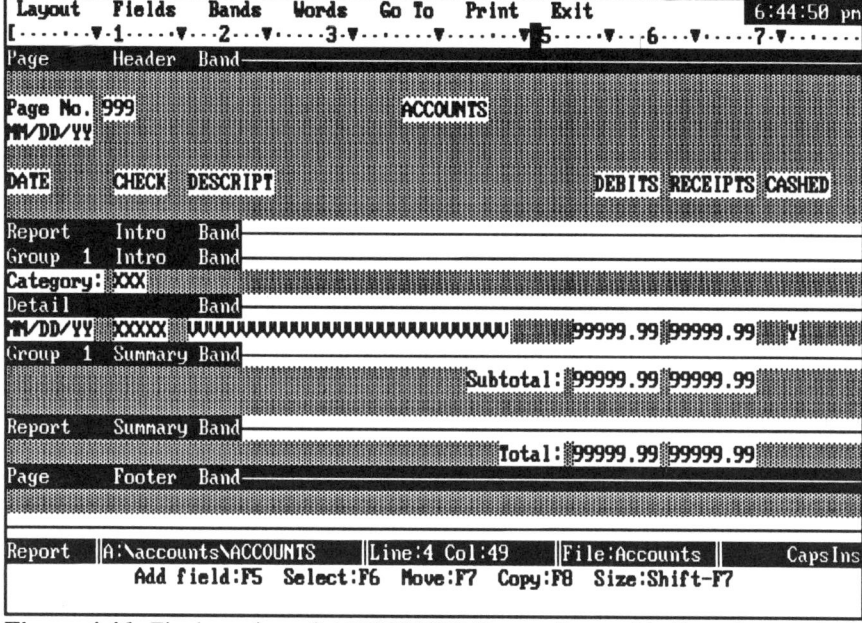

Figure 4.46 Final version of ACCOUNTS Report form with Grouping on CAT

4.3 Example II: Use of the Calculated Field in a Report Form

What would be really useful to us would be to create a report which not only has most of the data present in the ACCOUNTS report form but would also give us the running balance in our account. Let's start by using the report form that we've already created and adding some modifications to it. Since we want to keep the report form ACCOUNTS.FRM for future use, we will start by making a copy of it. We will call the new report form, LEDGER.FRM. We'll use the **COPY FILE** instruction to do this.

. COPY FILE ACCOUNTS.FRM TO LEDGER.FRM

Now we can open up the report form LEDGER with the command:

. MODIFY REPORT LEDGER

```
Page No.  1                        ACCOUNTS
01/24/93

DATE      CHECK  DESCRIPT                        DEBITS  RECEIPTS  CASHED
Category:
01/01/92         Jan. 1 Balance                    0.00    100.00    Y
                                      Subtotal:    0.00    100.00

Category: CAB
01/09/92  402    Sullivan Co. Cablevision         20.00      0.00    Y
                                      Subtotal:   20.00      0.00

Category: CAR
01/15/92  410    Sherman's: auto repairs          10.00      0.00    Y
01/20/92  414    Cash: Gas & Tolls                34.65      0.00    Y
                                      Subtotal:   44.65      0.00

Category: DOC
01/12/92  404    Dr. John McIntyre, D.D.S.        75.00      0.00    Y
01/19/92  413    Dr. Isaacs, M.D. (eye doct)      40.00      0.00    Y
                                      Subtotal:  115.00      0.00

Category: DON
01/13/92  405    Sierra Club: Donation            10.00      0.00    N
                                      Subtotal:   10.00      0.00

Category: ENT
01/22/92  416    Action Video                     10.59      0.00    N
                                      Subtotal:   10.59      0.00

Category: GIF
01/20/92  415    Sullivan's: Dept. Store          25.66      0.00    N
                                      Subtotal:   25.66      0.00

Category: GRO
01/14/92  406    Shoprite: Groceries              18.60      0.00    Y
01/14/92  407    Farmer's Market: Groceries        4.20      0.00    Y
01/27/92  420    Great American: Groceries        39.92      0.00    N
                                      Subtotal:   62.72      0.00

Category: HOU
01/22/92  417    MBNA Payment Services:Cred.     100.00      0.00    N
                 Card
                                      Subtotal:  100.00      0.00
```

Listing 4.4A Page 1 of REPORT FORM ACCOUNTS grouped on CAT

The screen we see is, of course, a duplicate of Figure 4.46, except that the report form now has the name LEDGER.FRM. We want to delete the group we added previously, but before we can do this we must blank out the Group Intro Band and the Group Summary Band. This can be done by using the keystroke pair **Ctrl-Y** within the Group Intro and Group Summary Bands. Once they are blank, our screen should essentially look like that of Figure 4.40.

Now we are ready to delete the Group 1 Bands. This is done by selecting the "Band" menu option once more using the **Alt-B**

```
Page No.   2                    ACCOUNTS
01/24/93
DATE       CHECK  DESCRIPT                         DEBITS  RECEIPTS  CASHED
Category:  INS
01/15/92   409    State Farm Mutual: Insurance     232.94    0.00      Y
                                       Subtotal:   232.94    0.00

Category:  MAI
01/28/92   421    Trading Post: Maintenance         28.47    0.00      N
                  items
                                       Subtotal:    28.47    0.00

Category:  PER
01/09/92   401    Cash: January Allowance          100.00    0.00      Y
01/25/92   419    NYC Parking Violations Bur.       35.00    0.00      N
                                       Subtotal:   135.00    0.00

Category:  PET
01/14/92   408    Feed-n-things: Pet Food            8.50    0.00      Y
01/16/92   412    West Side Vets                    30.00    0.00      N
                                       Subtotal:    38.50    0.00

Category:  REI
01/18/92          Deposit: Travel Expense Reimb.     0.00   38.25      Y
                                       Subtotal:     0.00   38.25

Category:  SAL
01/05/92          Deposit: Salary                    0.00  750.00      Y
01/19/92          Deposit: Salary                    0.00  750.00      Y
                                       Subtotal:     0.00 1500.00

Category:  TAX
01/25/92   418    Many Happy Returns: Tax Prep.    105.00    0.00      N
                                       Subtotal:   105.00    0.00

Category:  TEL
01/09/92   403    N.Y. Telephone: Dec. bill         50.00    0.00      Y
                                       Subtotal:    50.00    0.00

Category:  UTI
01/16/92   411    NYSEG: Utilities                 110.12    0.00      N
                                       Subtotal:   110.12    0.00

                                          Total:  1088.65 1638.25
```

Listing 4.4B Page 2 of REPORT FORM ACCOUNTS grouped on CAT

keystroke pair. The resulting screen is shown in Figure 4.47. Selecting the "Delete Band" option, as indicated, we strike the Enter key. One last thing we must do is put back the CAT field in the Detail Band and its heading in the Page Header Band. When this is accomplished, the screen that appears is again Figure 4.36.

As a first pass, the report that we are seeking to make is shown in Listing 4.5. Notice that the CASHED field column is gone, and in its place is a new column labeled BALANCE. BALANCE is the field heading for a calculated field. Note that this is only a column heading in the Report Summary, but not in the

144   COLUMNAR REPORTS

detail lines. The field is said to be "Hidden" as far as the detail lines are concerned. Using the backspace key or Delete key we can alter the report form so that it appears as in Figure 4.48. Here we have typed in the new column heading, "BALANCE".

We are now ready to create the new calculated field called DIFFERENCE. DIFFERENCE is equal to: RECEIPTS - DEBITS. Even though the DIFFERENCE does not appear in the report in the detail lines, nonetheless it must be defined. As usual, we use the keystroke pair **Alt-F** to bring up the "Fields" menu. Likewise we select the "Add field" menu item. This gives us the screen shown in Figure 4.49. Now we have selected the <create> option in the CALCULATED column.

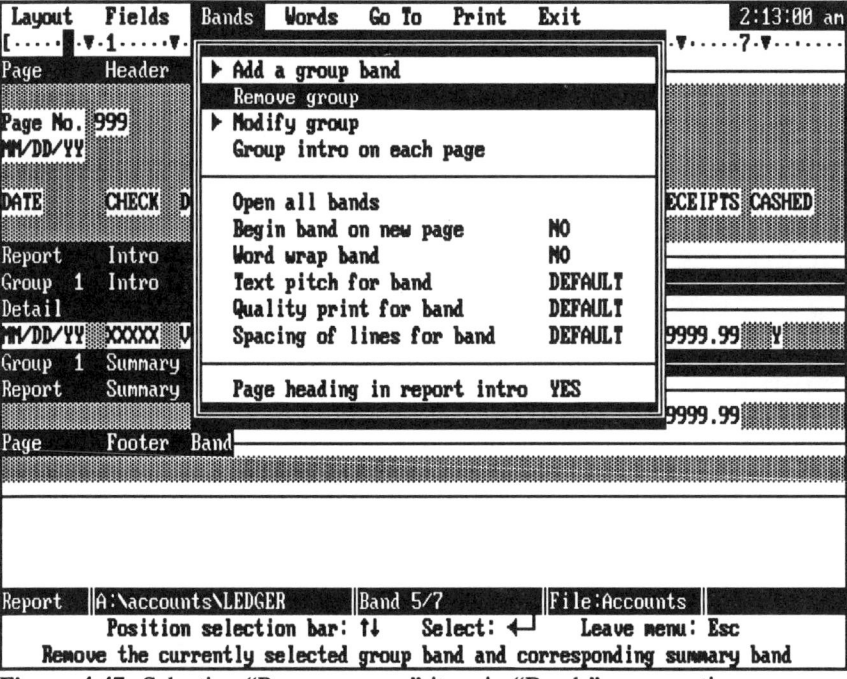

Figure 4.47 Selecting "Remove group" item in "Bands" menu option

COLUMNAR REPORTS 145

```
Layout  Fields  Bands  Words  Go To  Print  Exit              11:23:30 pm
[......▼.1.....▼...2...▼.....3.▼......▼.......▼.5.....▼...6...▼.....7.▼......
Page    Header  Band

Page No. 999
MM/DD/YY

DATE       CHECK  DESCRIPT                            CAT  DEBITS  RECEIPTS  BALANCE

Report   Intro   Band
Detail           Band
MM/DD/YY XXXXX  UUUUUUUUUUUUUUUUUUUUUUUUUUUUUUU  XXX  99999.99 99999.99
Report   Summary Band
                                                      99999.99 99999.99
Page     Footer  Band




Report   A:\accounts\LEDGER       Band 1/5       File:Accounts         CapsIns
         Add field:F5  Select:F6  Move:F7  Copy:F8  Size:Shift-F7
```

Figure 4.48 Report Form LEDGER before adding Calculated field

```
Page No.  1                     LEDGER
01/19/91

DATE      CHECK DESCRIPT                    CAT  DEBITS RECEIPTS BALANCE

01/01/92        Jan. 1 Balance                     0.00   100.00
01/05/92        Deposit: Salary             SAL    0.00   750.00
01/09/92  401   Cash: January Allowance     PER  100.00     0.00
01/09/92  402   Sullivan Co. Cablevision    CAB   20.00     0.00
01/09/92  403   N.Y. Telephone: Dec. bill   TEL   50.00     0.00
01/12/92  404   Dr. John McIntyre, D.D.S.   DOC   75.00     0.00
01/13/92  405   Sierra Club: Donation       DON   10.00     0.00
01/14/92  406   Shoprite: Groceries         GRO   18.60     0.00
01/14/92  407   Farmer's Market: Groceries  GRO    4.20     0.00
01/14/92  408   Feed-n-things: Pet Food     PET    8.50     0.00
01/15/92  409   State Farm Mutual: Insurance INS 232.94     0.00
01/15/92  410   Sherman's: auto repairs     CAR   10.00     0.00
01/16/92  411   NYSEG: Utilities            UTI  110.12     0.00
01/16/92  412   West Side Vets              PET   30.00     0.00
01/18/92        Deposit: Travel Expense Reimb. REI 0.00    38.25
01/19/92  413   Dr. Isaacs, M.D. (eye doct) DOC   40.00     0.00
01/19/92        Deposit: Salary             SAL    0.00   750.00
01/20/92  414   Cash: Gas & Tolls           CAR   34.65     0.00
01/20/92  415   Sullivan's: Dept. Store     GIF   25.66     0.00
01/22/92  416   Action Video                ENT   10.59     0.00
01/22/92  417   MBNA Payment Services:Cred. HOU  100.00     0.00
01/25/92  418   Many Happy Returns: Tax Prep. TAX 105.00    0.00
01/25/92  419   NYC Parking Violations Bur. PER   35.00     0.00
01/27/92  420   Great American: Groceries   GRO   39.92     0.00
01/28/92  421   Trading Post: Maintenance   MAI   28.47     0.00
                                                 1088.65 1638.25 549.60
```

Listing 4.5 Hard Copy from REPORT FORM LEDGER

Striking the Enter key we get the "Display Attributes" menu options. We select "YES" for the "Hidden" attribute by moving the cursor down to the "Hidden" menu item and striking the Enter key (See Figure 4.50). The reason that we are hiding the DIFFERENCE is because we are not interested in seeing: RECEIPTS - DEBITS in every detail line as it is not a true balance. Only the sum of all of the receipts minus the sum of all the debits is the true balance, and this will occur in the Report Summary line. Nonetheless, in order to have a summary, we must have DIFFERENCE as a calculated field.

We will accept the rest of the Display Attributes menu options by striking the **Ctrl-End** keystroke pair. The resulting screen looks exactly like Figure 4.48 because the field that was added is "Hidden".

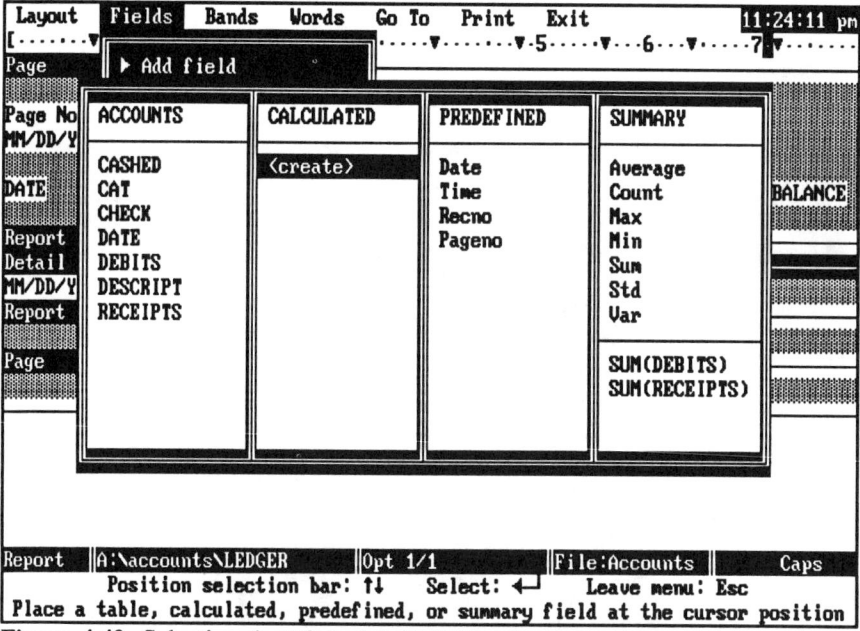

Figure 4.49 Selecting the "Calculated" field column

COLUMNAR REPORTS

Now we move the cursor down to the Report Summary Band, immediately below the "BALANCE" heading. Once more we select the "Fields" menu option (**Alt-F**), and the "Add field" menu item. This brings up the screen shown in Figure 4.51. Note that this time we choose the "Sum" as a summary function.

Strike the Enter key and the screen of Figure 4.52 appears. Selecting the "Field to summarize on" item, we hit the Enter key, select DIFFERENCE, and strike Enter once more. Likewise, we move down to the template menu item and make it 8 digits long as opposed to its default of 10 digits (see Figure 4.53).

Striking **Ctrl-End** to accept our adjustments, we get the report form shown in Figure 4.54. Note that the calculated balance now appears in the Report Summary Band. In addition, we have added the appropriate title, "LEDGER" to our report form. We can exit and save our report form LEDGER (**Alt-E**). When we generate the report from this report form, we get the listing shown in Listing 4.5.

. REPORT FORM LEDGER TO PRINT

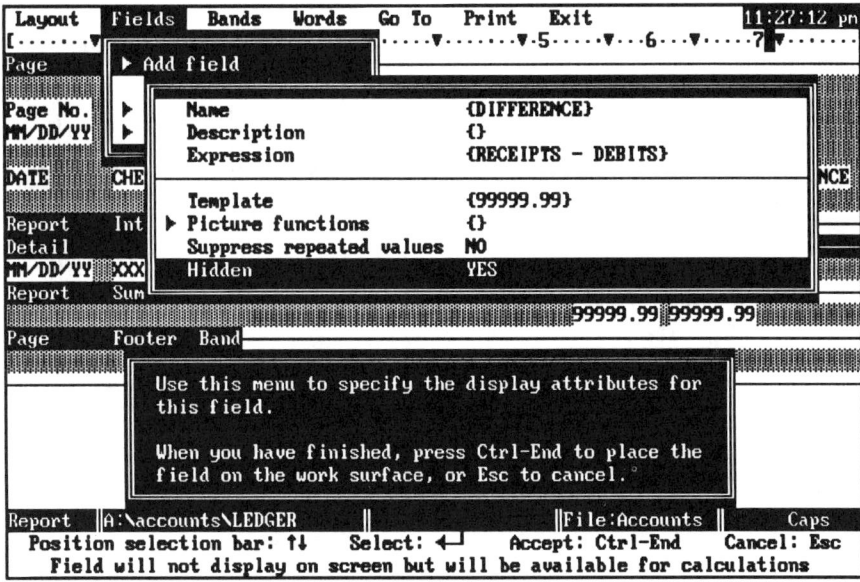

Figure 4.50 Selecting "Hidden" for a display attribute of DIFFERENCE for the Detail lines

148 COLUMNAR REPORTS

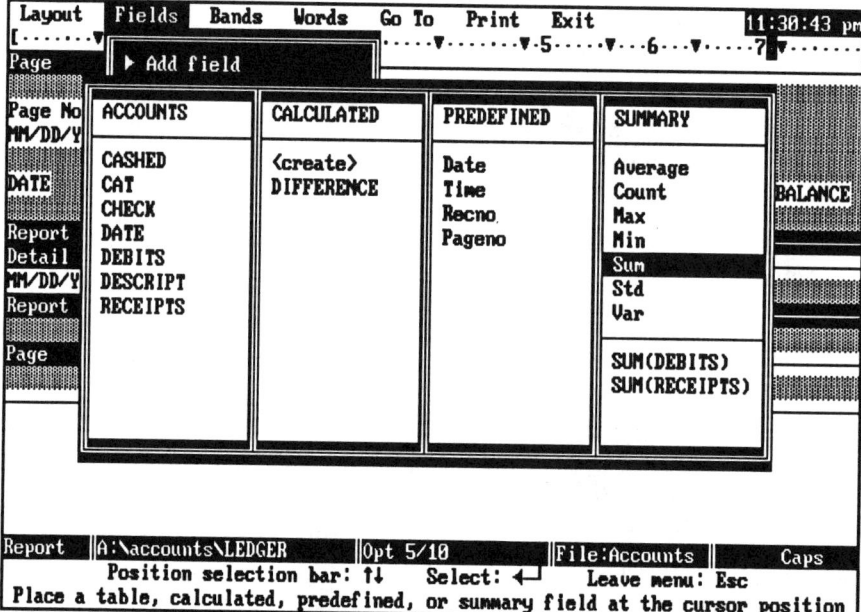

Figure 4.51 Selecting the "Sum" option for the Report Summary line

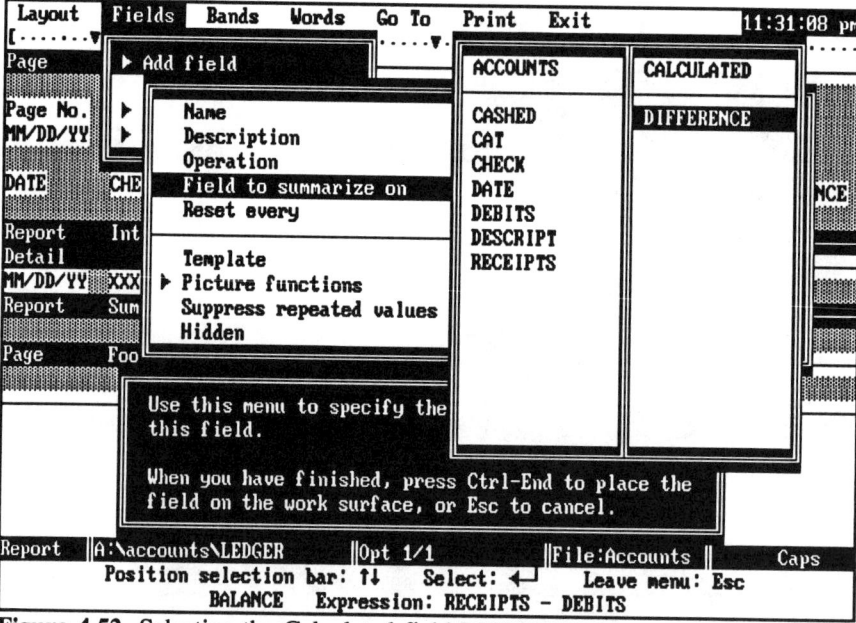

Figure 4.52 Selecting the Calculated field DIFFERENCE

COLUMNAR REPORTS

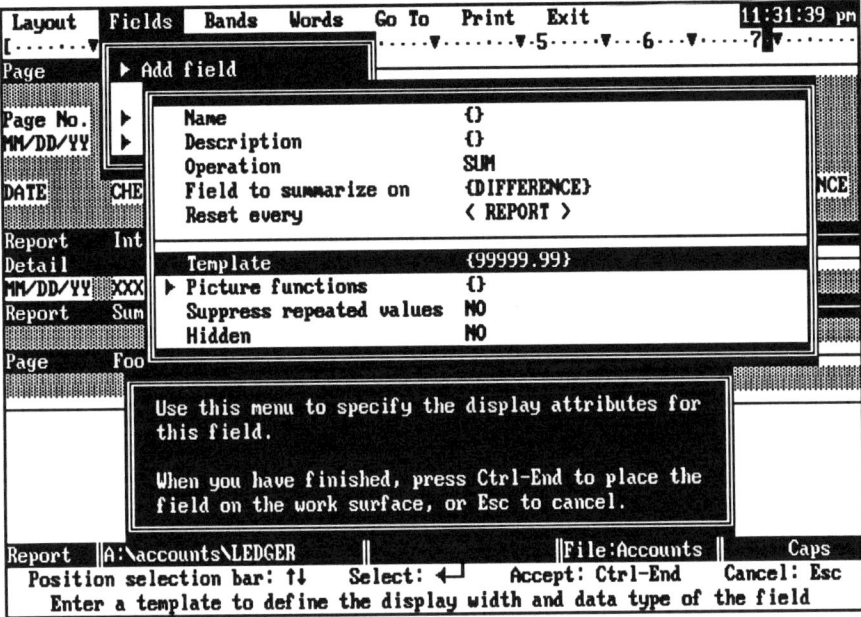

Figure 4.53 Changing the Template from 10 digits to 8

4.3.1 Use of a Running Sum of a Field in the Detail Line

The one thing that is missing from the report of Listing 4.5 is that a ledger normally has the running balance on every line, not just at the bottom. dBASE IV provides us with the means of placing the running sum of a field in the Detail Band provided that we have generated the Summary Sum function of that field. By generating the sum of DIFFERENCE in the Report Summary Band, we have created the Summary Sum function of DIFFERENCE which we can now use.

Let's put the cursor in the Detail Band just above where the sum of the balance resides in the Report Summary Band. (This is where the "Hidden" difference would have gone were it not hidden.) Striking the **Alt-F** keystroke pair to bring up the "Add field" menu item and pressing the Enter key, we get the screen shown in Figure 4.55. Note that this time we have highlighted the **SUM(DIFFERENCE)** function in the summary column.

150   COLUMNAR REPORTS

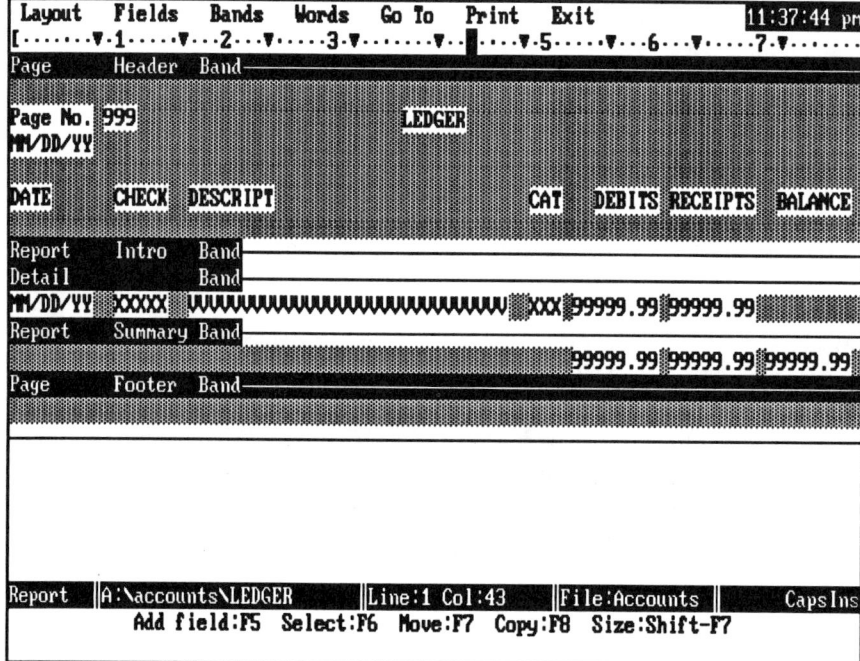

Figure 4.54 Report Form LEDGER Without the Running Balance

Striking the Enter key we get the Display Attributes screen shown in Figure 4.56. The attributes shown will give us the running sum that we desire, so we accept those attributes by striking the **Ctrl-End** keystroke pair. The final version of the report form is shown in Figure 4.57.

Executing the REPORT FORM command gives us our final ledger report shown in Listing 4.6.

. REPORT FORM LEDGER TO PRINT

COLUMNAR REPORTS 151

```
Page No.   1                    LEDGER
02/01/93

DATE      CHECK  DESCRIPT                      CAT   DEBITS  RECEIPTS  BALANCE

01/01/92         Jan. 1 Balance                        0.00    100.00   100.00
01/05/92         Deposit: Salary               SAL     0.00    750.00   850.00
01/09/92  401    Cash: January Allowance       PER   100.00      0.00   750.00
01/09/92  402    Sullivan Co. Cablevision      CAB    20.00      0.00   730.00
01/09/92  403    N.Y. Telephone: Dec. bill     TEL    50.00      0.00   680.00
01/12/92  404    Dr. John McIntyre, D.D.S.     DOC    75.00      0.00   605.00
01/13/92  405    Sierra Club: Donation         DON    10.00      0.00   595.00
01/14/92  406    Shoprite: Groceries           GRO    18.60      0.00   576.40
01/14/92  407    Farmer's Market: Groceries    GRO     4.20      0.00   572.20
01/14/92  408    Feed-n-things: Pet Food       PET     8.50      0.00   563.70
01/15/92  409    State Farm Mutual: Insurance  INS   232.94      0.00   330.76
01/15/92  410    Sherman's: auto repairs       CAR    10.00      0.00   320.76
01/16/92  411    NYSEG: Utilities              UTI   110.12      0.00   210.64
01/16/92  412    West Side Vets                PET    30.00      0.00   180.64
01/18/92         Deposit: Travel Expense Reimb REI     0.00     38.25   218.89
01/19/92  413    Dr. Isaacs, M.D. (eye doct)   DOC    40.00      0.00   178.89
01/19/92         Deposit: Salary               SAL     0.00    750.00   928.89
01/20/92  414    Cash: Gas & Tolls             CAR    34.65      0.00   894.24
01/20/92  415    Sullivan's: Dept. Store       GIF    25.66      0.00   868.58
01/22/92  416    Action Video                  ENT    10.59      0.00   857.99
01/22/92  417    MBNA Payment Services:Cred.   HOU   100.00      0.00   757.99
                 Card
01/25/92  418    Many Happy Returns: Tax Prep. TAX   105.00      0.00   652.99
01/25/92  419    NYC Parking Violations Bur.   PER    35.00      0.00   617.99
01/27/92  420    Great American: Groceries     GRO    39.92      0.00   578.07
01/28/92  421    Trading Post: Maintenance     MAI    28.47      0.00   549.60
                 items
                                                    1088.65   1638.25   549.60
```

Listing 4.6 Final version of hard copy from REPORT FORM LEDGER

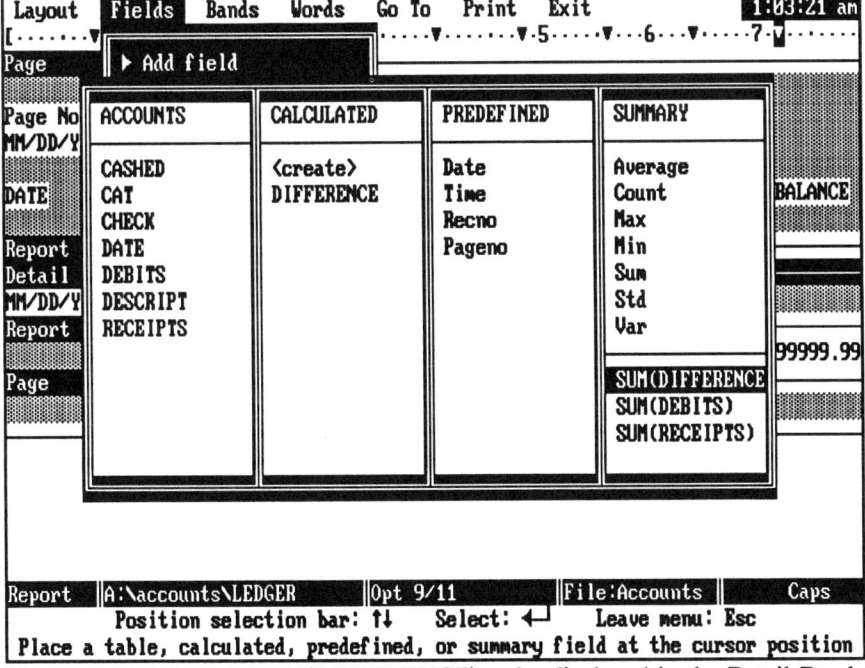

Figure 4.55 Selecting SUM(DIFFERENCE) to be displayed in the Detail Band

152   COLUMNAR REPORTS

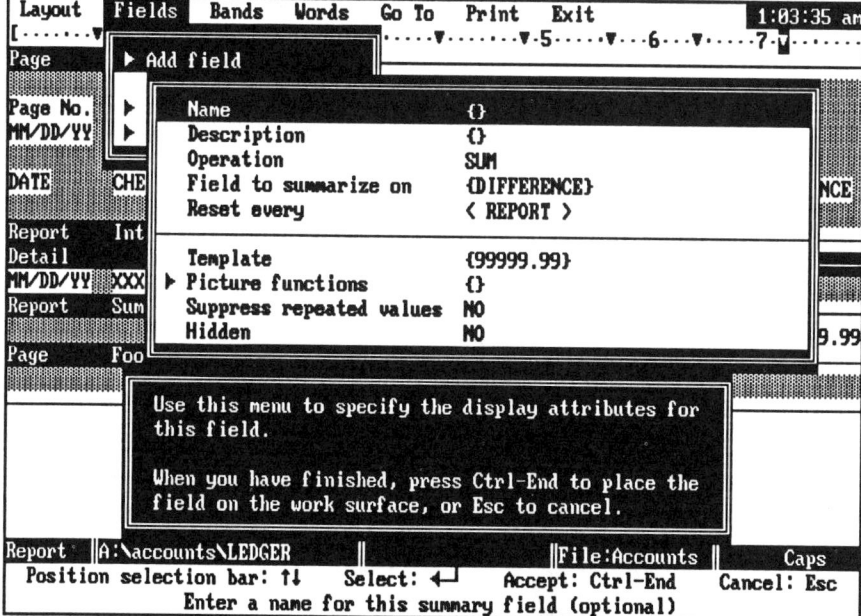

Figure 4.56 Display of Attributes for the SUM(DIFFERENCE) to be displayed in the Detail Band

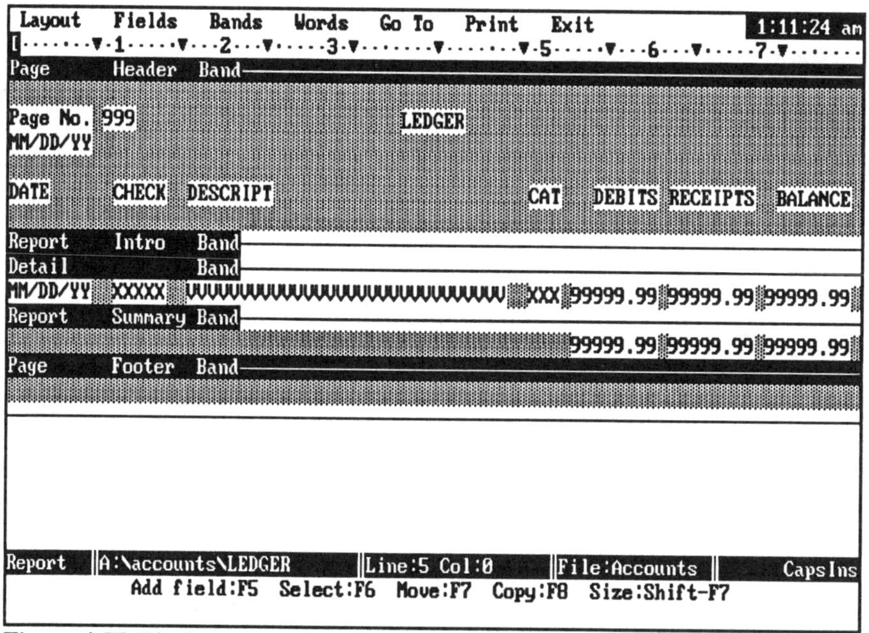

Figure 4.57 Final version of the Report Form Ledger with a Running Sum of the Difference

COLUMNAR REPORTS

4.4 Summary

In this chapter we have learned to make simple columnar reports with summary lines at the end. Next, we learned how to make quick layouts. Then we acquired the skill of moving fields about in the report form. We found, with little difficulty, we could make group reports with subtotals.

We learned how to make calculated fields. We then saw how we could hide a field so that it didn't appear on the report. Finally, we learned how to use the summary functions that we had generated to create a running total on the detail line. This enabled us to create a true ledger as a report.

4.5 Review

In Chapter 4 we have covered the following commands:

> **COPY FILE** *filename1* **TO** *filename2*
> **CREATE REPORT** *filename*
> **MODIFY REPORT** *filename*
> **REPORT FORM** *filename*
> **REPORT FORM** *filename* **TO PRINT**
> **SET DIRECTORY TO**

We will be using these commands frequently. Be sure to add them to your glossary of commands.

4.6 Laboratory Work

Follow all the steps outlined in this chapter generating the report form COLUMNAR.FRM, as well as the printed output associated with it.

Generate both the simple report form ACCOUNTS.FRM, as well as the grouped report form ACCOUNTS.FRM. Print out the hard copy for both versions of ACCOUNTS.FRM.

Generate the report form LEDGER.FRM and its associated printout of the ACCOUNTS database.

4.7 Exercises

We shall now generate some reports on your **MAILIST** data.

1. Create a columnar report form called MAILIST.FRM and generate a printed report. It should have the date in the upper left hand corner. Make the title include your own name (e.g. "MAC'S MAILING LIST"). Be sure that it is indexed in order of ZIP + LAST + FIRST names. Hand it in. You need only include the fields:

    LAST
    FIRST
    MAIL_ADDR
    CITY
    STATE
    ZIP

2. Modify the structure of MAILIST.FRM so that you can print out the value of the **CARD** field. (In order to get all this on one line, you will have to reduce the size of one or more of the other fields in your report form. For example, if your mailing addresses are all less than 22 characters then reducing the Address field width, in the report, would facilitate this. This will give you the space you need to add the additional field. Note: In some cases you will lose space because the column heading is longer than the length of the field (e.g. **STATE**). This problem can be overcome by using the abbreviation: "ST" for the column heading in the report.)

3. Using your modified report form structure print out the new report. It should be indexed on zip code as the primary field and by first name and last name as the secondary and tertiary fields, but in *descending alphabetical order*. Hand this in.

4. Modify your report once more adding group bands. Group your database on zip code. Be sure to order your database by ascending zip, then print out your grouped report. Hand this in.

CHAPTER 5

CONDITIONAL REPORTS & SEARCHES

5.0   Topics Covered in Chapter 5

Using the FOR clause in selecting records.

Using the SET FILTER instruction in selecting records.

Using relational operators.

Using logical operators.

Presenting Arithmetic operators.

Doing Calculations on a database.

Using the CALCULATE command and its associated functions.

Doing LOCATE searches.

Doing Indexed searches.

5.1 Selecting Records in a Database

We touched on selecting records when we introduced the **FOR** clause in our discussion of indexes. We saw that using this clause at the end of the indexing command allowed us to choose which records we wanted to include in the index and which we wanted to exclude. Once the index was created it was as though those records, that had not been included, did not exist anymore.

The power of the **FOR** clause, in selecting records, far exceeds its use in indexing. This clause is used in a vast number of commands including some we've already had, such as EDIT and REPORT FORM. It would be difficult to overstate the importance of the **FOR** clause. For this reason we will spend some time getting to know the Relational Operators and Logical Operators which are used in record selection. This is the language of logic and should be clearly understood if the user is going to be able to extract precisely the data he or she wants from the database.

We will begin our discussion by introducing Conditional Reports which are reports that include only selected records in a database.

5.2 Conditional Reports

The problem with the report we generated in Listing 4.1 is that it averages in the Project Grades of those three students who didn't hand in a Term Project. What we'd like to do is to avoid those particular students in the report. In this way the average would indeed reflect an average of only those who handed in the Term Project.

Just as we did in indexing, we can add a "FOR" clause to the REPORT FORM *filename* command. This will enable us to filter out the Project Grades of those students who received none. Our REPORT FORM command becomes:

. REPORT FORM COLUMNAR FOR TERM_PROJ TO PRINT

For those records where TERM_PROJ is True, the records will be printed out. Those where TERM_PROJ is False will be skipped. The result of executing this command is shown in Listing 5.1.

```
01/19/93            COMPUTER CLASS REPORT

  FIRST NAME      LAST NAME         TERM      EVALUATION   PROJECT
                                   PROJECT       DATE       GRADE

  Gladys          Naboa              Y        12/15/92       93
  Consuelo        Naboa              Y        12/16/92       89
  Wendel          Little             Y        12/17/92       87
  Jeremy          Witherspoon        Y        12/19/92       82
  Jonathan        Samuels            Y        12/14/92       76
  Matts           Engleberg          Y        12/13/92       62
  Mary Beth       Swazey             Y        12/14/92       52

                                                AVERAGE:     77
```

Listing 5.1 Report of only those students handing in Term Projects using the final COLUMNAR report form

5.2.1 The HEADING Clause

The only thing missing in Listing 5.1 is a title which clearly indicates the conditional nature of this report. For that reason we will add another clause called the **HEADING**. The HEADING clause allows us to place a title, temporarily, into the Report Intro Band of the report form. The syntax for the HEADING clause is: **HEADING** *textline* . In this case the command might become:

. **REPORT FORM COLUMNAR FOR TERM_PROJ HEADING "STUDENTS HANDING IN TERM PROJECTS" TO PRINT**

The hard copy resulting from adding this HEADING is shown in Listing 5.2. Note: When using the HEADING clause, it is important that the very top line of the report form be blank, or dBASEIV version 1.5 will display an error message.

```
01/26/93              COMPUTER CLASS REPORT

              STUDENTS HANDING IN TERM PROJECTS

    FIRST NAME        LAST NAME         TERM       EVALUATION
    PROJECT
                                        PROJECT    DATE       GRADE

    Matts             Engleberg         Y          12/13/92     62
    Wendel            Little            Y          12/17/92     87
    Consuelo          Naboa             Y          12/16/92     89
    Gladys            Naboa             Y          12/15/92     93
    Jonathan          Samuels           Y          12/14/92     76
    Mary Beth         Swazey            Y          12/14/92     52
    Jeremy            Witherspoon       Y          12/19/92     82

                                                   AVERAGE:     77
```

Listing 5.2 REPORT FORM COLUMNAR FOR TERM_PROJ with Heading

5.2.2 Relational Operators

As another example of a conditional report, let's print out a report meeting the following three conditions:

1. The report should contain all those students who received a passing grade on their Term Project. We will take a passing grade to be a 60 or better.

2. Furthermore, let's put an additional **HEADING** at the top of the report saying: "STUDENTS RECEIVING PASSING GRADE ON TERM PROJECT".

3. Finally, let's print the report in alphabetical order with **LASTNAME** as the primary field and **FIRSTNAME** as the secondary.

The condition of 60 or better will require a **FOR** statement of the form: **FOR PROJ_GRADE >= 60** . The **>=** means Greater Than or Equal To and is called a relational operator. The expression **PROJ_GRADE >= 60** takes on the value of True when the **PROJ_GRADE** is greater than or equal to **60**. Otherwise it takes on the value of False. A complete list of all the relational operators is given in Table 5.1.

The second condition is satisfied using the **HEADING** option in the **REPORT FORM** command. Finally the third option will be satisfied if we use our Set Index Tag to LASTFIRST. We must always Set our Index Order before we execute the REPORT FORM command:

. **SET ORDER TO LASTFIRST**

Now we are ready to execute our REPORT FORM instruction.

. **REPORT FORM COLUMNAR FOR PROJ_GRADE >= 60 HEADING "STUDENTS RECEIVING PASSING GRADE ON TERM PROJECT" TO PRINT**

The result is shown in Listing 5.3.

Table 5.1 List of Relational Operators

Operator	Operator's Function
<	Less than
>	Greater than
=	Equal to
<> or #	Not Equal to
<=	Less than or equal to
>=	Greater than or equal to
$	Contains

5.2.3 Use of the SET FILTER Command

What the **FOR** clause does is create a temporary filter which allows certain records to be accessed and others to be skipped. As soon as the command in which the **FOR** clause appears is over, the filter disappears. However, it is possible to SET a FILTER which does not disappear until another command explicitly tells it to stop filtering. This is the **SET FILTER TO** ... command.

What follows the words **SET FILTER TO** is exactly the same kind of expression that follows the word **FOR** in a **FOR** clause. You would use the **SET FILTER TO** command in a situation where you wanted this filtration to last for more than one command.

A good example of this is using the report form generator, itself, for the purpose of previewing reports. The benefit of doing this is to give a screen output of a report and of course to save paper. For example the following procedure would display on the screen what was printed out on hard copy in the previous section:

. **SET FILTER TO PROJ_GRADE >= 60**
. **MODIFY REPORT COLUMNAR**

```
01/26/91              COMPUTER CLASS REPORT
       STUDENTS RECEIVING PASSING GRADE ON TERM PROJECT
     FIRST NAME      LAST NAME        TERM     EVALUATION   PROJECT
                                     PROJECT      DATE       GRADE

       Matts         Engleberg          Y       12/13/92       62
       Wendel        Little             Y       12/17/92       87
       Consuelo      Naboa              Y       12/16/92       89
       Gladys        Naboa              Y       12/15/92       93
       Jonathan      Samuels            Y       12/14/92       76
       Jeremy        Witherspoon        Y       12/19/92       82

                                                 AVERAGE:      82
```

Listing 5.3 REPORT FORM COLUMNAR FOR PROJ_GRADE >= 60

CONDITIONAL REPORTS & SEARCHES 163

Once in the report form, the **Alt-P** keystroke pair is used to select the "Print" option. Then the "View report on screen" menu item is selected (see Figure 5.1). When the Enter key is struck, Figure 5.2 shows what appears on the screen.

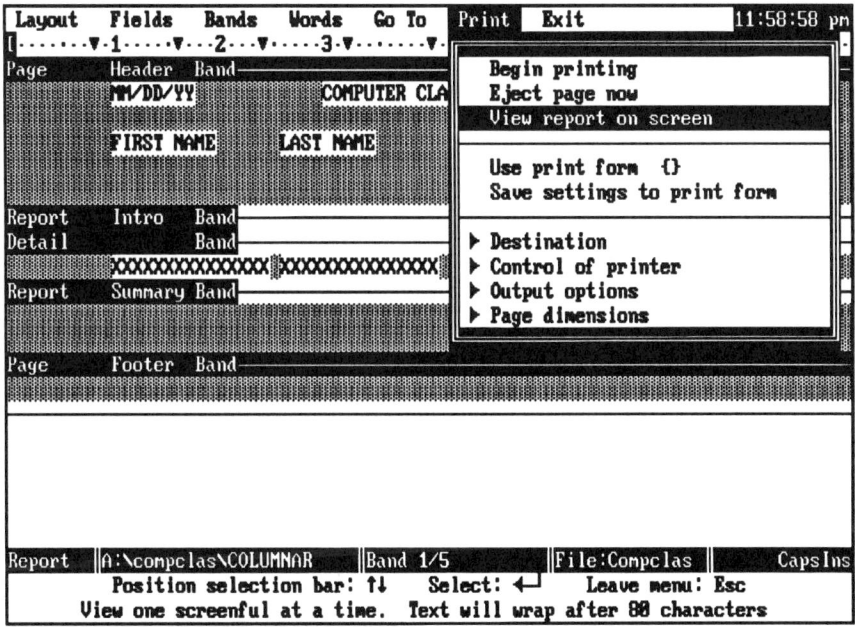

Figure 5.1 Selecting the "View report on screen" menu item

As you can see, except for the fact that the **HEADING** does not appear as it did using the REPORT FORM COLUMNAR FOR... command, the output is the same. Of course, if you really wanted the HEADING in the screen view, you would only need to type it directly into the Report Intro Band.

5.2.4 Conditional Report Using a Date Function

Suppose we are interested in knowing which students are being evaluated on December 14. This requires a relational operation involving a date function. In order to change a date we entered as characters into a date type field, we will need to use a date function. The function we must use is: **CTOD()** which stands

164   CONDITIONAL REPORTS & SEARCHES

```
 01/29/91            COMPUTER CLASS REPORT

 FIRST NAME    LAST NAME      TERM     EVALUATION   PROJECT
                             PROJECT      DATE       GRADE

 Gladys        Naboa            Y       12/15/92      93
 Consuelo      Naboa            Y       12/16/92      89
 Wendel        Little           Y       12/17/92      87
 Jeremy        Witherspoon      Y       12/19/92      82
 Jonathan      Samuels          Y       12/14/92      76
 Matts         Engleberg        Y       12/13/92      62

                                        AVERAGE:      82




               Cancel viewing: ESC,  Continue viewing: SPACEBAR
```

Figure 5.2 Viewing report COLUMNAR of COMPCLAS on screen with the filter: **PROJ_GRADE >= 60**

for Character TO Date. The expression becomes: **EVALUATION = CTOD("12/14/92")** . This expression takes on the value of True for every record in which the **EVALUATION** date is **12/14/92**, and False for all other records.

The **CTOD("12/14/92")** converts the character string "12/14/92" into a date having the date value of December 14, 1992. Making use of this function, our filter command becomes:

. SET FILTER TO EVALUATION = CTOD("12/14/92")
. MODIFY REPORT COLUMNAR

Selecting the "View report on screen" menu item as before we get the result shown in Figure 5.3.

```
01/29/91              COMPUTER CLASS REPORT

       FIRST NAME     LAST NAME      TERM      EVALUATION   PROJECT
                                     PROJECT   DATE         GRADE

       Jonathan       Samuels        Y         12/14/92     76
       Mary Beth      Swazey         Y         12/14/92     52

                                               AVERAGE:     64




       Cancel viewing: ESC,   Continue viewing: SPACEBAR
```

Figure 5.3 Viewing report COLUMNAR of COMPCLAS on screen with the filter: **EVALUATION = CTOD("12/14/92")**

5.2.5 Conditional Report Using the Substring Relational Operator

Now suppose we are interested in making a report of only those students living in a particular zip code area. The difficulty with this task is that the zip code is not a distinct field, but rather it is imbedded in the **CITY_ST_ZP** field. Since we're interested only in the zip code and nothing that precedes it, we must use the substring comparison relational operator, **$** .

Suppose, for example, we are interested in the records of those people living at the zip code: "12782". To access records with this particular substring we would use the filter expression: **"12782"$CITY_ST_ZP** . This would locate only those records in which the substring "12782" appeared in the field **CITY_ST_ZP**. The exact SET FILTER command that we would use here is:

. **SET FILTER TO "12782"$CITY_ST_ZP**
. **MODIFY REPORT COLUMNAR**

166   CONDITIONAL REPORTS & SEARCHES

The result of doing the "View report on screen" is shown in Figure 5.4.

5.2.6 Use of the Logical Function LIKE(,) in a Filter

A logical function is a function which returns a logical value of .T. or .F.. dBASE IV has many logical functions, any of which may be used in a filter. As an example of this, the **LIKE(,)** function is a means by which two character strings may be compared to each other.

LIKE(,) permits the use of wildcards. "?" is a wildcard that you can substitute for any character that you wish to leave unspecified. For example, suppose that we wish to make a conditional report of all those students who have an EVALUATION date in December, 1992.

```
01/29/91            COMPUTER CLASS REPORT

FIRST NAME     LAST NAME      TERM      EVALUATION   PROJECT
                              PROJECT      DATE       GRADE

Gladys         Naboa            Y        12/15/92       93
Consuelo       Naboa            Y        12/16/92       89

                                         AVERAGE:       91




              Cancel viewing: ESC,  Continue viewing: SPACEBAR
```
Figure 5.4 Viewing report COLUMNAR of COMPCLAS on screen with the filter: **"12782"$CITY_ST_ZP**

The wildcard string that we are going to compare to the EVALUATION field is: "12/??/92". Note that we don't care which day in December, 1992, the evaluation takes place. Since we don't care, we put in "??" to substitute for the values that may be present. When the comparison is made, everything in the string "12/??/92", except the "??", will be compared to the string of the field EVALUATION. Those dates which compare exactly will be included in our report, those that don't, won't.

Now we must use another function to convert the date field, EVALUATION, into a character field. Since the form the character field must take is: "MM/DD/YY", we need to use the function: **DTOC()**. This function transforms a **D**ate field in**TO** the desired Character string. The filter then is described by:

. **SET FILTER TO LIKE("12/??/92", DTOC(EVALUATION))**

Going into our report generator with:

. **MODIFY REPORT COLUMNAR**

and doing a "View report on screen", we get the result shown in Figure 5.5. Note that no records having blank dates now appear.

As we have seen, using logical fields, relational operators, and logical functions, we have the ability to create a filter that will select just those records we want to appear in a report. Our filter can be applied temporarily with the FOR clause, or indefinitely using the SET FILTER TO ... command.

The most important thing to remember about the SET FILTER TO ... command is to turn it off when you no longer need it on. This is done by simply typing: **SET FILTER TO** , with no expression following. At the same time we'll also return the database to its "Natural Order".

. **SET FILTER TO**
. **SET ORDER TO**

```
01/29/91            COMPUTER CLASS REPORT

        FIRST NAME    LAST NAME      TERM      EVALUATION   PROJECT
                                    PROJECT       DATE       GRADE

        Gladys        Naboa           Y        12/15/92       93
        Consuelo      Naboa           Y        12/16/92       89
        Wendel        Little          Y        12/17/92       87
        Jeremy        Witherspoon     Y        12/19/92       82
        Jonathan      Samuels         Y        12/14/92       76
        Matts         Engleberg       Y        12/13/92       62
        Mary Beth     Swazey          Y        12/14/92       52

                                                AVERAGE:      77




              Cancel viewing: ESC,  Continue viewing: SPACEBAR
```

Figure 5.5 Viewing report COLUMNAR of COMPCLAS on screen with the filter: **LIKE("12/??/92", DTOC(EVALUATION))**

5.3 Calculations

Conditional reports are not the only commands that make use of the selecting of records in a database. There is a family of commands that perform arithmetic operations on an entire database.

5.3.1 The COUNT Command

The **COUNT** command allows us to get a count of all the records that meet certain criteria. For example, suppose we want to know the number of students who turned in Term Projects. All we need do is type: **COUNT FOR TERM_PROJ** and the **COUNT** command will report the number of students for which this is true. What we would see on the screen in response to this command is shown below:

. **COUNT FOR TERM_PROJ**
   7 records

(Note, if nothing appears when you execute this command, then the **TALK** must be off, and you need to type: **SET TALK ON** at the dot prompt.)

Likewise, if you want to get a **COUNT** of the number of people who did not turn in Term Projects, then you need to negate the Logical Field **TERM_PROJ**. This is done by placing the **Logical Operator .NOT.** in front of the field name. The resulting command and its response would be:

. **COUNT FOR .NOT. TERM_PROJ**
   3 records

Finally, suppose we wanted to know the number of students that are going to be evaluated on 12/14/92 and 12/15/92. Again we will have to make use of the **CTOD()** function. Notice that we have two criteria here. When we have more than one criterion, we have to combine them with one of two **Logical Operator**s: either the **.AND.** operator or the **.OR.** operator.

One way we could get the result we want is by asking dBASE to **COUNT FOR** the students being evaluated on 12/14/92 *or* the students being evaluated on 12/15/92. The command and its response would look like:

. **COUNT FOR EVALUATION = CTOD("12/14/92") .OR.**
     EVALUATION = CTOD("12/15/92")
   3 records

Another way we could get the result we would like is by doing a **COUNT FOR** the students being evaluated on or after

12/14/92 *and* on or before 12/15/92. The command and its response would look like:

. COUNT FOR EVALUATION >= CTOD("12/14/92") .AND. EVALUATION <= CTOD("12/15/92")
   3 records

5.3.2 Logical Operators

As you can see, logical operators are often necessary in order to connect together the expressions containing the relational operators with which we have been working. To clearly indicate the logical nature of these operators, the dot has been placed on either side of the words, **.AND., .OR.,** and **.NOT..** Table 5.2 lists these operators and their results.

5.3.3 The SUM Command

Now suppose you wanted to find the average grade given to all those people who turned in a Term Project. One way to go about that would be to add up all the grades in the field **PROJ_GRADE**, and then divide that sum by the count that we obtained earlier for all of those handing in a Term Project.

Table 5.2 Logical Operators and their Results

Logical Operator	Function
X .AND. Y	Gives a .T. if and only if X=.T. and Y=.T.
X .OR. Y	Gives a .T. if either X=.T. or Y=.T. or both
.NOT. X	Gives .F. if X=.T. or gives .T. if X=.F.

To obtain the **SUM** of a numeric field, one need only type: **SUM** *NumericFieldName* at the dot prompt. In the case of **COMPCLAS** the command would be:

. SUM PROJ_GRADE

PROJ_GRADE
    541

Now all we need do is to divide our sum, 541, by the count of the number of people who turned in Term Projects, 7, and we will have the result we seek. To display this result, we make use of the **?** (or Print) command. To do division, we use the forward slash, / . The command becomes:

. ? 541/7
    77.29

5.3.4 Arithmetic Operators

We have just encountered our first arithmetic operator, the / or division sign. Table 5.3, shown below, gives a list of all the arithmetic operators in dBASE.

Table 5.3 Arithmetic Operators in dBASE

Arithmetic Operator	Function
+	Addition
-	Subtraction
*	Multiplication
/	Division
** or ^	Exponentiation

Suppose we wanted to find the volume of a sphere. As you may recall from Geometry, the equation is:

$$V = {}^4/_3 \, \Pi * R^3$$

If the radius were 10 inches, then the way we would evaluate it in dBASE would be:

. ? (4/3)*3.14159*10^3
   4188.79

Notice the use of the parentheses. They are used for grouping in both arithmetic and logical operations.

5.3.5 The AVERAGE Command

We could have done the operation in section 5.3.3 a lot more easily by simply using the **AVERAGE** command. This command will do all the work for us. However, we do need to specify the **FOR TERM_PROJ** clause in order to **AVERAGE** only those students who turned in a Term Project. The command and response would be:

. AVERAGE PROJ_GRADE FOR TERM_PROJ

   PROJ_GRADE
   77.29

Note that the syntax is: **AVERAGE** followed by the numeric field over which the average will take place followed by the conditions, if any.

5.3.6 Use of the CALCULATE Command

One of the problems with the COUNT, SUM, and AVERAGE commands is that each command must pass through the entire database in order to get a result. Suppose you wanted to

CONDITIONAL REPORTS & SEARCHES

execute two or more of these commands, then you would have to make two or more passes through the database. For a large database, this could mean having these calculations take two or three times as long as they need to take.

dBASE IV solves this problem with the **CALCULATE** command. This command allows all of the arithmetic functions that can be applied to the entire database, to be done in a single pass through the database. In addition, it expands the number of arithmetic functions available to the user. Table 5.4 gives a complete list of the arithmetic functions available to the user.

The syntax for this instruction is: **CALCULATE** *function1, function2, ...* **FOR** *LogicalExpression* . For example, suppose we wanted to know, in addition to the count and the average, the minimum, maximum, and standard deviation of the Project Grade scores (PROJ_GRADE) for those people who handed in Term Projects. The command and its response would look like:

. **CALCULATE CNT(), AVG(PROJ_GRADE),**
　　MAX(PROJ_GRADE), MIN(PROJ_GRADE),
　　STD(PROJ_GRADE) FOR TERM_PROJ

Table 5.4 Arithmetic Functions available through CALCULATE command

Function	Description	Argument Field Type
AVG( )	Average	Numeric
CNT( )	Count	None
MAX( )	Maximum value	Numeric
MIN( )	Minimum value	Numeric
NPV( )	Net Present Value	Numeric
STD( )	Standard Deviation	Numeric
SUM( )	Sum	Numeric
VAR( )	Variance	Numeric

CNT()   AVG(PROJ_GRADE)   MAX(PROJ_GRADE)
MIN(PROJ_GRADE) STD(PROJ_GRADE)
   7   77.29   93   52   14.02

Note that among the functions, all have a numeric field for an argument except the **CNT()** function which has no argument. This is because the Count function only counts the number of records selected by the FOR clause, but does not operate on any particular field. However as all functions *must have left and right parentheses*, the Count function must still have () following the CNT.

5.4   Searches

In small databases, like the ones we've been using, one can BROWSE through the database to find what one is looking for. I have even used this technique to find information in databases of several hundred records. However, there comes a point at which it is easier to let the machine do the searching for you. I would never dream of paging through a database I have of over 13,000 records. For this the dBASE search commands are indispensable.

5.4.1   Searching Using the **LOCATE** Instruction

There are two types of search commands in dBASE. The first is the **LOCATE FOR** instruction. The word **FOR** is included because **LOCATE** doesn't have much meaning without a condition. The syntax of the instruction is **LOCATE FOR** *logicalexpression* .

Suppose we wanted to **LOCATE** the student record on Jonathan Samuels. We would simply say:

. **LOCATE FOR LASTNAME = "Samuels"**
Record =   7

CONDITIONAL REPORTS & SEARCHES

Checking with Figure 5.6, we find that Samuels is the seventh record in the list. Hence Record = 7 is accurate.

FIRSTNAME	LASTNAME	TERM_PROJ	EVALUATION	PROJ_GRADE	ADDRESS
Gladys	Naboa	T	12/15/92	93	324 Catskill T
Consuelo	Naboa	T	12/16/92	89	324 Catskill T
Derek	Caruthers	F	/ /	0	21 Spring Glen
Wendel	Little	T	12/17/92	87	1821 Cochecton
Jeremy	Witherspoon	T	12/19/92	82	821 Kiamesha C
Nancy	Hardwick	F	/ /	0	512 Delaware O
Jonathan	Samuels	T	12/14/92	76	96 Rainbow's E
Matts	Engleberg	T	12/13/92	62	2821 Mountain
Mary Beth	Swazey	T	12/14/92	52	85 Cider Mill
Mary	Wong	F	/ /	0	321 Lakeside A

Browse A:\compclas\COMPCLAS Rec 1/10 File

Figure 5.6 Browse of COMPCLAS in its Natural Order

If we wanted to **LOCATE** the record on Consuelo Naboa, we would have to search on two fields, as there are two Naboas. The command would be:

. **LOCATE FOR LASTNAME = "Naboa" .AND.**
   FIRSTNAME = "Consuelo"
Record =   2

If we want to **LOCATE** the person who is being evaluated on 12/19/92, then we would type:

. **LOCATE FOR EVALUATION = CTOD("12/19/92")**
Record =   5

176 CONDITIONAL REPORTS & SEARCHES

If we wanted to **LOCATE** a student who did "A" work on the Term Project, then we might type:

. **LOCATE FOR PROJ_GRADE >= 89**
Record =   1

Now since there may be more than one person for whom this is so, and since the **LOCATE** command only finds the first person, we need to use the **CONTINUE** command to find all subsequent records that satisfy the **FOR** criterion.

. **CONTINUE**
Record =   2

Executing **CONTINUE** once more we get the following message:

. **CONTINUE**

End of LOCATE scope

Clearly, the **CONTINUE** command was unable to find any more records satisfying that criterion.

5.4.2 Searching Using the **FIND** and **SEEK** Commands

The principal difficulty with the LOCATE instruction is that for large databases it can be slow as it goes through every record of the database, one by one, until it finds the first record meeting its criteria. On my database of more than 13,000 records this can take as long as 2 minutes on a PC-AT.

A far faster way of searching is using the **FIND** or **SEEK** command. In order to use this command, the database must be indexed on the field on which you are searching. This requirement satisfied, the search should never take longer than a matter of seconds regardless of how many records there are in the database. For large databases, that is quite an improvement in speed.

CONDITIONAL REPORTS & SEARCHES 177

The syntax for the **FIND** command is: **FIND** *CharacterString*. However, you must be sure that the index tag is set to the proper index before you execute your **FIND** instruction. For example, we can find the record of Jonathan Samuels by executing:

. **SET ORDER TO LASTFIRST**
. **FIND Samuels**
. **DISPLAY FIELD LASTNAME, FIRSTNAME, EVALUATION, PROJ_GRADE**

Record# LASTNAME   FIRSTNAME   EVALUATION   PROJ_GRADE
   7   Samuels   Jonathan   12/14/92   76

(Since the **FIND** command does not announce the record it has found, I've followed the **FIND** command with a **DISPLAY FIELD** command so that we could see which record was found.)

Suppose we want to find Consuelo Naboa. Again we would first have to have the index tag, **LASTFIRST** as the Master Index. For this search we will use the **SEEK** command. The difference between the **SEEK** and **FIND** commands is that the **SEEK** command requires quotes around any text string that is being sought. The syntax of the **SEEK** command is: **SEEK** *expression*. If the *expression* is a character string, then it needs to begin and end with either single or double quotes or with brackets. In the case of finding Consuelo Naboa we would execute:

. **SEEK "Naboa   Consuelo"**
. **DISPLAY FIELD LASTNAME, FIRSTNAME, EVALUATION, PROJ_GRADE**

Record# LASTNAME   FIRSTNAME   EVALUATION   PROJ_GRADE
   2   Naboa   Consuelo   12/16/92   89

Note that the first field, **LASTNAME**, required that we use all 15 places before we could begin the **FIRSTNAME** field. This is because the index was created by concatenating (adding one string to the end of the other) the **LASTNAME** and the **FIRSTNAME** strings.

We can use the **SEEK** command to find records that have been indexed on a date field. Since we have not as yet indexed our database on a pure date field, we had better do that first.

. INDEX ON EVALUATION TAG EVALUATION

Now suppose we wanted to find the individual whose work was to be evaluated on 12/19/92. We would type:

. SEEK CTOD("12/19/92")
. DISPLAY FIELD LASTNAME, FIRSTNAME, EVALUATION, PROJ_GRADE

Record#	LASTNAME	FIRSTNAME	EVALUATION	PROJ_GRADE
9	Witherspoon	Jeremy	12/19/92	82

The case where we have difficulty with **FIND** or **SEEK** is when we have a range that we wish to search over, and we're not sure of the particular value that began that range. For example, if we wanted to find those students who did "A" work on the Term Project, we cannot **SEEK** those students who did 89 or better. We can only **SEEK** those students who got a **PROJ_GRADE** of 89, 90, 91, etc.

On the other hand, if we know for certain that someone has achieved a grade of 93, then we can **SEEK** that grade and know that each grade after that grade will be equal to or lower in value because we indexed it in descending order of grade. In this case we must set the index tag GRADE as our Master Index.

. **SET ORDER TO GRADE**
. **SEEK 93**
. **DISPLAY FIELD LASTNAME, FIRSTNAME, EVALUATION, PROJ_GRADE**

Record#	LASTNAME	FIRSTNAME	EVALUATION	PROJ_GRADE
1	Naboa	Gladys	12/15/92	93

If we now want to look at any further records in this category (89 or higher), all we need to do is to execute the command **SKIP**. This command moves us to the next record in indexed sequence. Executing it we obtain:

. **SKIP**
Record No.   2
. **DISPLAY FIELD LASTNAME, FIRSTNAME, EVALUATION, PROJ_GRADE**

Record#	LASTNAME	FIRSTNAME	EVALUATION	PROJ_GRADE
2	Naboa	Consuelo	12/16/92	89

Were we to execute the **SKIP** instruction once more we would get the following result:

. **SKIP**
Record No.   4
. **DISPLAY FIELD LASTNAME, FIRSTNAME, EVALUATION, PROJ_GRADE**

Record#	LASTNAME	FIRSTNAME	EVALUATION	PROJ_GRADE
4	Little	Wendel	12/17/92	87

Since this record is clearly out of the range we were searching, we know that we have passed through all the records that had Project Grades of 89 or above.

5.4.3 LOCATE Search versus INDEX Search

You might ask, since the **FIND** and **SEEK** instructions are so much quicker than the **LOCATE** instruction, why would we ever want to use the **LOCATE** instruction? The reason is that no index need exist for a **LOCATE** instruction and indexing takes time, much more time than it takes to **LOCATE** a record.

Also, if you have 40 different types of searches that you do, that may mean carrying around and updating 40 different indexes, which can take a lot of time.

So the moral is: if you are going to do a particular search often, and you don't experience too much delay from dBASE doing the updating of the Multiple Index, then go ahead and create an index for the search. On the other hand, if you do a particular search seldom, and/or you have a great number of indexes and the overhead from dBASE in updating your indexes is noticeable, then use a **LOCATE** search.

5.5 Summary

In this chapter we have covered conditional reports, calculation commands, and both LOCATE as well as indexed searches. In addition, we have covered relational operators, logical operators, and arithmetic operators.

Among the calculation commands we covered were COUNT, SUM, AVERAGE, and the CALCULATE command which allowed us to use several new calculation functions. Among these new calculation functions were MAX(), MIN(), VAR(), and STD().

All of these commands made use of record selection which is done by creating a temporary filter using the FOR clause, or a persistent filter created by the SET FILTER TO ... instruction.

CONDITIONAL REPORTS & SEARCHES

5.6 Review

In Chapter 5 we have covered the following commands:

> **AVERAGE**
> **CALCULATE**
> **CONTINUE**
> **COUNT**
> **FIND**
> **LOCATE FOR**
> **SEEK**
> **SET FILTER TO** *LogicalExpression*
> **SET FILTER TO**
> **SKIP**
> **SUM**

In addition, we have encountered some new functions which should be entered into your glossary of dBASE functions:

> **AVG()**
> **CNT()**
> **CTOD()**
> **DTOC()**
> **LIKE(,)**
> **MAX()**
> **MIN()**
> **STD()**
> **SUM()**

5.7 Laboratory Work

Follow all the steps outlined in this chapter creating all the conditional reports, performing all the calculations, and doing both the LOCATE as well as indexed searches.

5.8 Exercises

1. Using your modified report form structure for MAILIST, print out a report meeting the following criteria. Hand this in.

    a) It should be ordered in ascending zip code order as the primary field and in ascending alphabetical order on LASTNAME and FIRSTNAME as the secondary and tertiary fields.

    b) Add the **HEADING** to the Report Intro Band of your report which says: "PEOPLE RECEIVING CARDS THIS YEAR"

    c) Print out only those people who will be receiving cards.

2. Print out a second report from your MAILIST database, in the same order, of those people *not* receiving cards this year. This report should have the heading, "PEOPLE NOT RECEIVING CARDS THIS YEAR". Hand this in also.

3. Using the ACCOUNTS database, make a report showing all the checks written for groceries. This report should have the HEADING, "GROCERY EXPENSES". Hand this in.

4. Print a report from the ACCOUNTS database showing all the RECEIPTS only. Label this report, "ACCOUNT CREDITS". Hand this in.

CHAPTER 6

LABELS, MAILMERGE REPORTS & FORMS

6.0 Topics Covered in Chapter 6

Creating Labels using the Label Form Generator.

Creating Mailmerge Reports using the Mailmerge Report Form Generator.

Using Date Functions to create the Date form desired.

Creating customized Screens using the Screen Generator.

Control of the screen using the Format file.

6.1 Label Form Generator

There is another type of report generator which is available to us in dBASE. This type of report will print out information on one record after another record without creating any page breaks or page ejects. This is the type of report that is designed for mailing labels in particular.

Suppose we want to drop a card to all those who did a Term Project just to let them know when their evaluation date is. Since we have all the address information in our database, it would be very simple to let the computer print out the mailing labels. This is accomplished by means of the **LABEL FORM** generator.

6.1.1 Creating a Label Form

Let us start by opening the database COMPCLAS. (If you don't remember how to do this, please refer to Chapter 1.) The syntax for creating a mailing label is the command **CREATE LABEL** *LabelName*. We'll choose the name COMPCLAS as the name of our labels. This should create no confusion as the extension, **.LBL**, will be added to the filename for identification[19]. Executing the command:

. CREATE LABEL COMPCLAS

we get the label generation screen shown in Figure 6.1.

The first step in creating a label is to select the proper label dimensions. You can buy labels in many common styles, most of which are included in the Dimensions Menu. We select the Dimensions Menu option by striking the keystroke pair: **Alt-D**. Figure 6.2 shows the resulting screen.

---

[19]Just as with the report form generator, two more files will be created. The label form generator will create a source program with the extension **.LBG**. That program will, in turn, be compiled into machine language, and the file will be given the extension **.LBO**.

LABELS, MAILMERGE REPORTS & FORMS

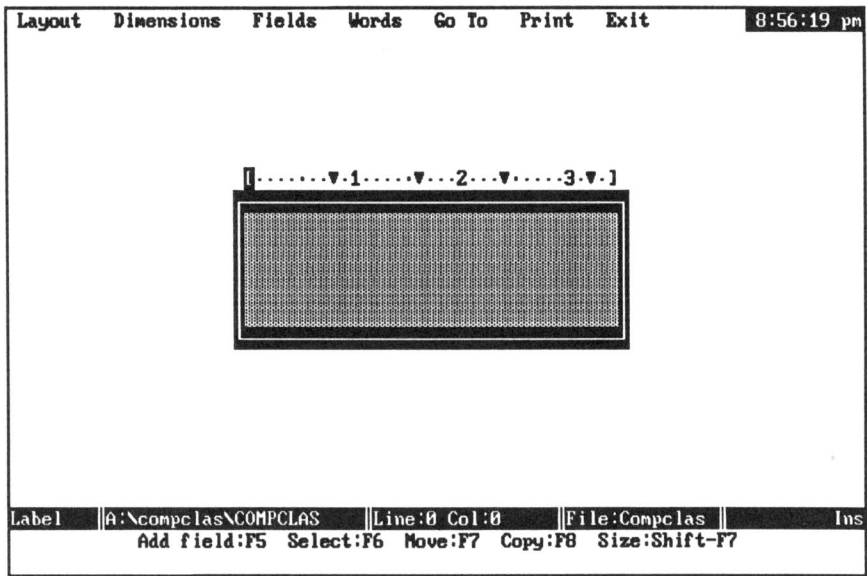

Figure 6.1 Label Form Generator opening screen

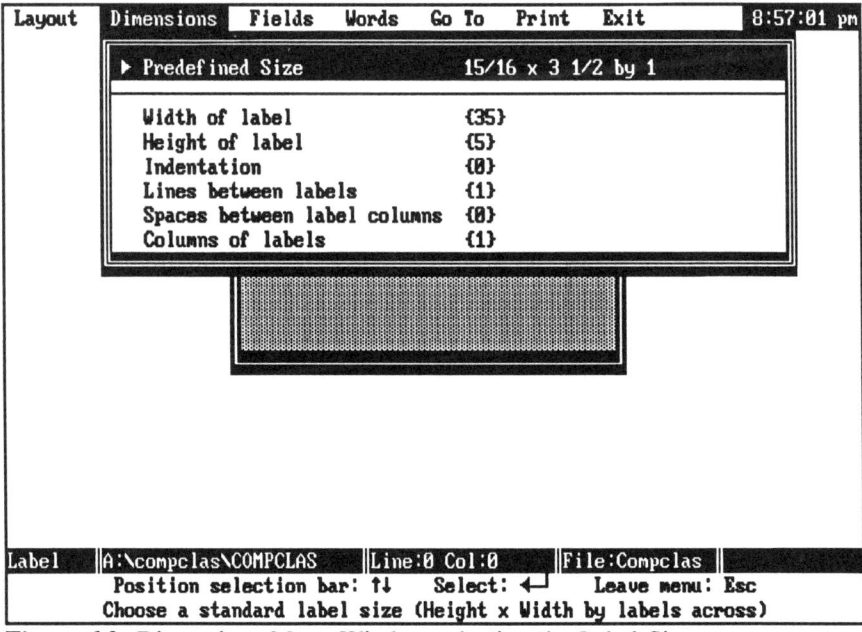

Figure 6.2 Dimensions Menu Window selecting the Label Size

186 LABELS, MAILMERGE REPORTS & FORMS

Note that we can either choose the "Predefined Size" which is currently highlighted, or we can arrow down to the menu below and precisely specify what dimensions we want for our labels (or report). We will choose the "Predefined Size" menu item.

With the default label dimension highlighted, we strike the Enter key to give us the list of common label styles and dimensions. Figure 6.3 shows us the screen that results. Note that there are 7 different sizes of labels. Labels can be bought 1, 2, or 3 across a sheet. We have chosen the standard 15/16" x 3.5" label with two across the sheet.

Striking the Enter key with our selection highlighted returns us to the screen of Figure 6.1. We are now ready to lay out our label. Naturally, we want our label to be laid out with our fields in the standard mailing address order:

>   FIRSTNAME LASTNAME
>   ADDRESS
>   CITY_ST_ZP

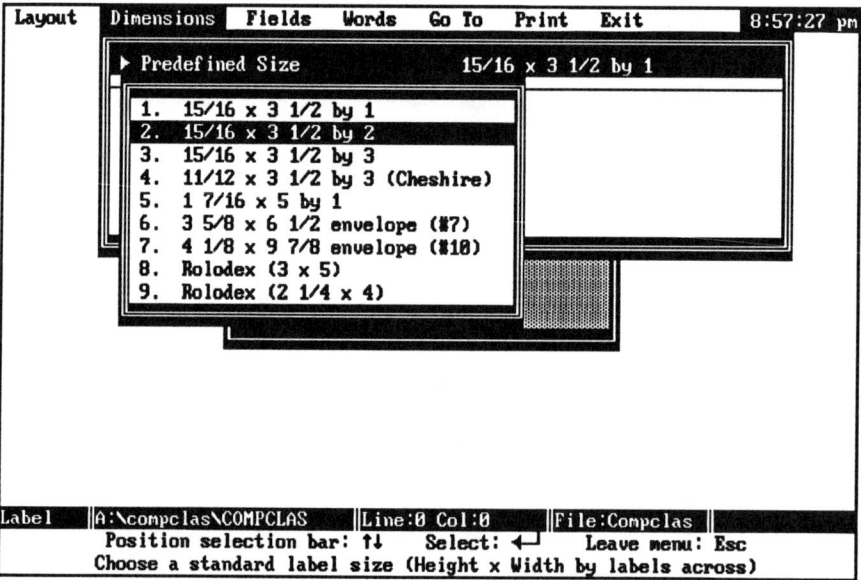

Figure 6.3 Choosing the label 15/16" x 3.5" with two across the page

LABELS, MAILMERGE REPORTS & FORMS 187

To do this we select the "Field" menu option, as we did with our report form, using the **Alt-F** keystroke pair. This gives us the screen shown in Figure 6.4. Striking the Enter key once more, we get the field selection screen shown in Figure 6.5. The first field that we are selecting is clearly the FIRSTNAME field.

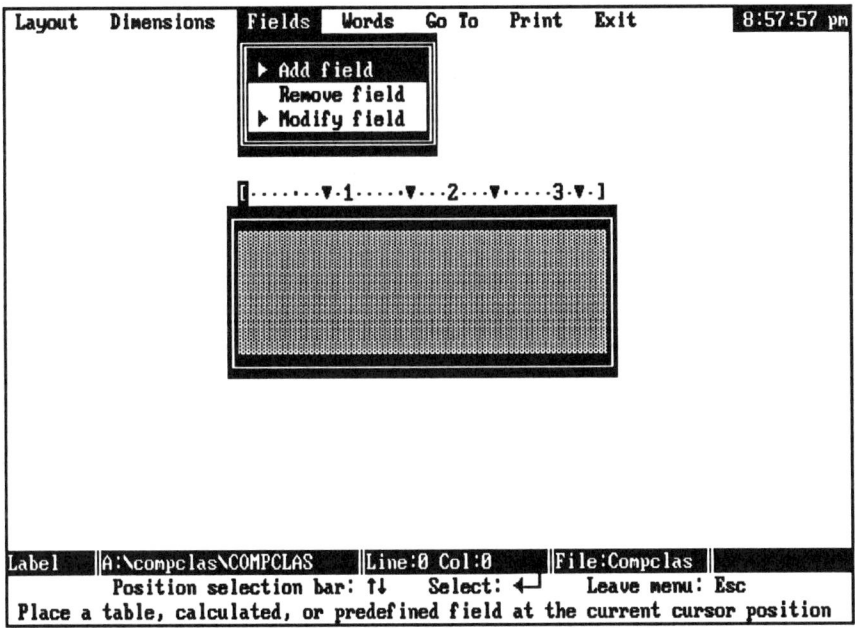

Figure 6.4 Selecting the "Add field" Menu item in the Field menu

Striking the Enter key we get the Display Attributes screen shown in Figure 6.6. Accepting these default attributes, we strike the keystroke pair **Ctrl-End** and return to the label form screen with the field, FIRSTNAME, added to it (see Figure 6.7).

Using the right arrow key we can move over one space and then add the field, LASTNAME, in the same way that we entered the FIRSTNAME field. The result is shown in Figure 6.8. In a similar manner we add the ADDRESS field to the second line and the CITY_ST_ZP field to the third line of the label form. The final version of our first pass at a label form is shown in Figure 6.9.

188 LABELS, MAILMERGE REPORTS & FORMS

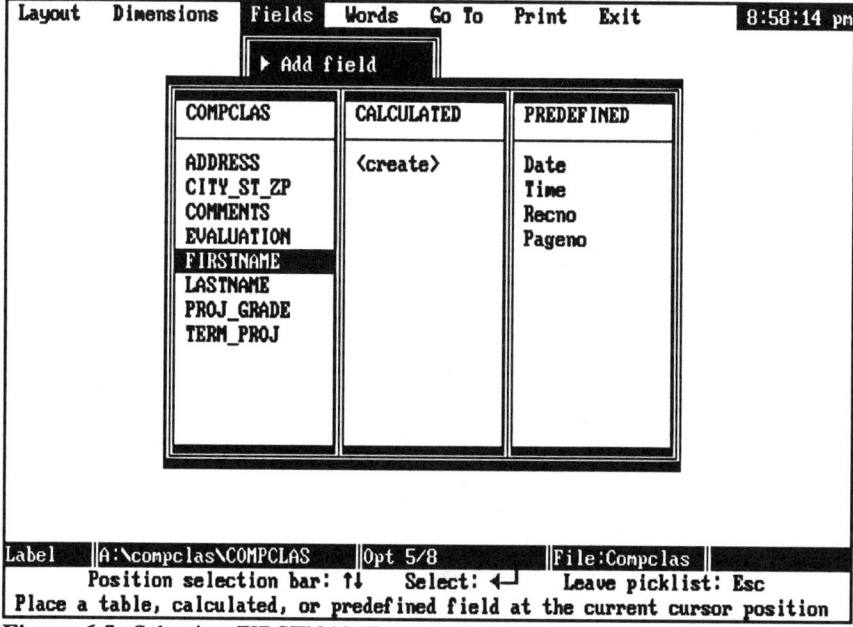
Figure 6.5 Selecting FIRSTNAME as the field to be entered in the Label

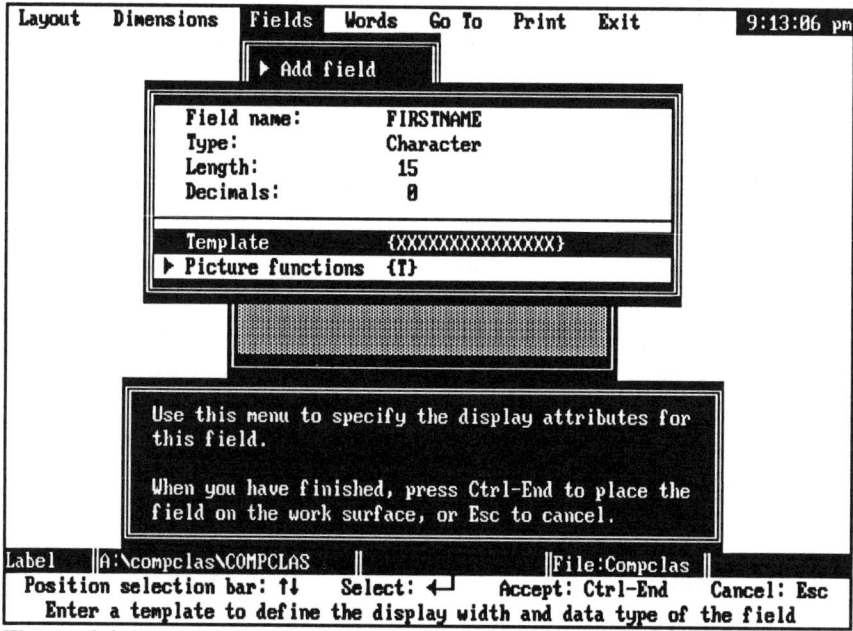
Figure 6.6 The Display Attributes screen for the field FIRSTNAME

LABELS, MAILMERGE REPORTS & FORMS 189

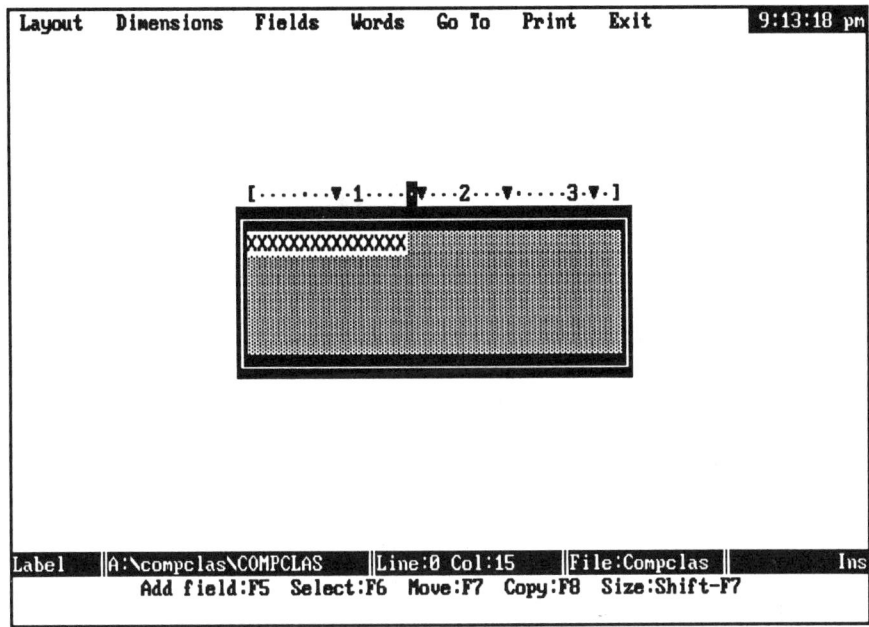

Figure 6.7 Label Form with LASTNAME field added

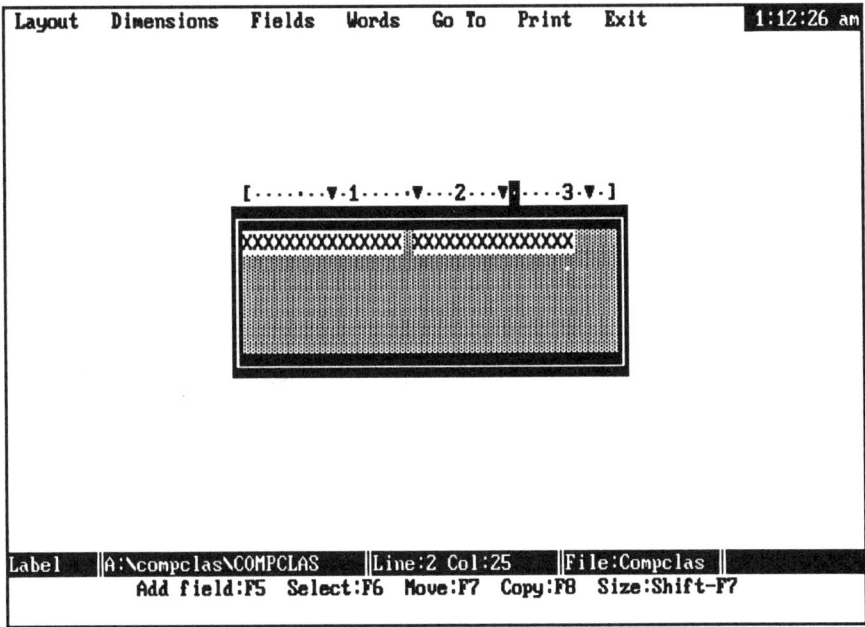

Figure 6.8 LASTNAME positioned one space to right of FIRSTNAME by the cursor movement key

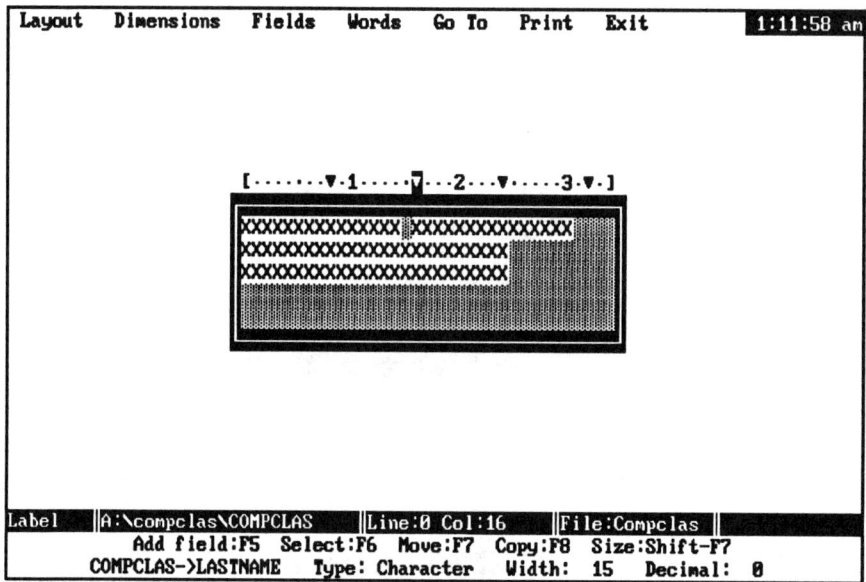
Figure 6.9 First attempt at a complete Label Form for COMPCLAS

We are now ready to print out our first set of labels to see what we get. Exiting from the Label Form Generator in the usual way (**Alt-E** followed by Enter), we return to the dot prompt. Now we can execute the command that actually generates the labels. The syntax is: **LABEL FORM** *LabelName*. If we direct it towards the printer, then we get the result shown in Listing 6.1.

. LABEL FORM COMPCLAS TO PRINT

Examining Listing 6.1, we notice that there is too much space between the FIRSTNAME and LASTNAME fields. We should have expected that not only the first name would be printed out, but so would all the spaces in the FIRSTNAME field. We clearly do not want those spaces, so we will have to **MODIFY** our **LABEL** form. This is done with the **MODIFY LABEL** *LabelName* command[20].

. MODIFY LABEL COMPCLAS

---

[20]The command MODIFY LABEL can be used to actually create the label form in the first place, just as the MODIFY REPORT command can be used to actually create a report. In this way only one command needs to be remembered for both purposes.

```
Gladys          Naboa           Consuelo        Naboa
324 Catskill Terrace            324 Catskill Terrace
Sundown, NY  12782              Sundown, NY  12782


Derek           Caruthers       Wendel          Little
21 Spring Glen Road             1021 Cochecton Street
Cooks Falls, NY  12728          Jeffersonville,  NY 12748


Jeremy          Witherspoon     Nancy           Hardwick
821 Kiamesha Circle             512 Delaware Overlook
Glen Spey, NY  12737            Callicoon, NY  12723


Jonathan        Samuels         Matts           Engleberg
96 Rainbow's End                2021 Mountain View
Roscoe, NY  12776               Mountaindale, NY  12758


Mary Beth       Swazey          Mary            Wong
85 Cider Mill Lane              321 Lakeside Avenue
North Branch, NY  12766         Swan Lake, NY  12783
```

Listing 6.1 Printed output of first pass at LABEL FORM COMPCLAS

Returning to the screen of Figure 6.9, we find that the problem is that we used the right arrow cursor key to separate the two fields, FIRSTNAME and LASTNAME, by one space. The key here is to actually use the spacebar to create this separation. Striking the spacebar key at the blank space in between FIRSTNAME and LASTNAME fields gives us the result shown in Figure 6.10.

Now we exit once again (**Alt-E**, Enter), and we enter the **LABEL FORM** command at the dot prompt to print out our labels. Remembering the fact that we want to only print out labels for those

192   LABELS, MAILMERGE REPORTS & FORMS

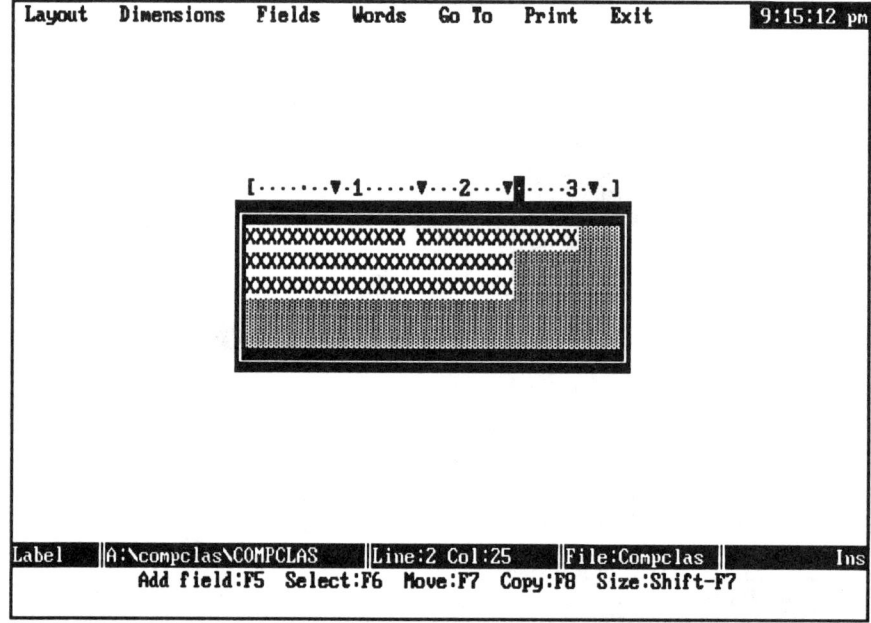

Figure 6.10 The final version of the LABEL FORM for COMPCLAS

students who actually have Evaluation Dates scheduled with the professor, we add in the appropriate FOR clause. Our command becomes:

. LABEL FORM COMPCLAS FOR TERM_PROJ TO PRINT

The output that results from this command is shown in Listing 6.2. Notice that the first and last names have no extra spaces between them and appear just as we would like them to. The key thing to learn, in this process, is that if we want to avoid extra spaces between fields, we must connect adjacent fields by the characters of our choosing (e.g. spaces and commas), not by using the cursor movement keys and leaving blanks.

6.1.2 Printing Sample Labels

Before printing out the labels, it is useful to make sure the printer is lined up, so that we don't waste a lot of labels unnecessarily. To check out how our labels are lined up, we may

```
Gladys Naboa                    Consuelo Naboa
324 Catskill Terrace            324 Catskill Terrace
Sundown, NY  12782              Sundown, NY  12782



Wendel Little                   Jeremy Witherspoon
1021 Cochecton Street           821 Kiamesha Circle
Jeffersonville,  NY 12748       Glen Spey, NY  12737



Jonathan Samuels                Matts Engleberg
96 Rainbow's End                2021 Mountain View
Roscoe, NY  12776               Mountaindale, NY  12758



Mary Beth Swazey
85 Cider Mill Lane
North Branch, NY  12766
```

Listing 6.2 Output of final version of LABEL FORM COMPCLAS

use the **SAMPLE** clause to print out how the top row of labels will line up. The **LABEL FORM** command becomes:

. LABEL FORM COMPCLAS SAMPLE FOR TERM_PROJ TO PRINT

Figure 6.11 shows what appears on the screen. What appears on the printer are only the asterisks. If they appear well centered on your labels, then type **N** in answer to the question: "Do you want more samples? (Y/N)". If you need to move the labels or readjust the carriage, then answer **Y** to that question and another set of labels will be printed out. After typing **N**, the output of Listing 6.2 will once more be printed.

194 LABELS, MAILMERGE REPORTS & FORMS

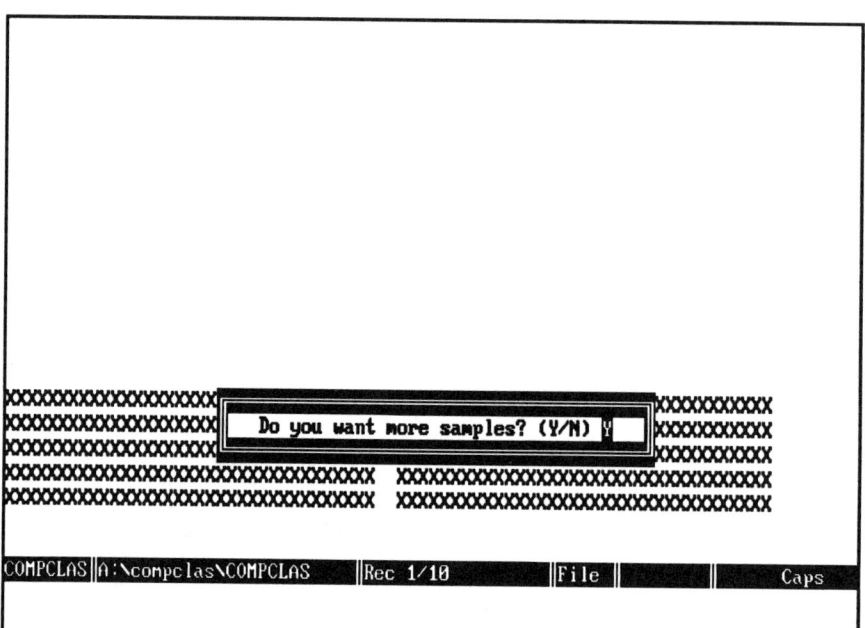

Figure 6.11 Screen resulting from Printing out of Sample Label Template Patterns to see if Labels are properly aligned on the printer

As you can see, in this way mailing labels can be easily and quickly produced. However, this is not the only use to which the **LABEL FORM** generator can be put. It can be used in cases where information is to be printed continuously with no attention made to page beginnings or endings. I often print out memorandums, which have a wide circulation, using the Label Form generator. By getting five or six memos to a sheet, I can save quite a bit of paper.

6.2 Mailmerge Report Form

Now that we have mailing labels to put on letters to write to the students in the class, this brings up the question of how do we go about writing the personalized letters to the individual students. Among the Quick Layouts available to us is one called "Mailmerge". This will enable us to write a general "boilerplate" letter into which we insert personalized information from each of the records of the COMPCLAS database.

LABELS, MAILMERGE REPORTS & FORMS   195

Let's go right into the report form generator, calling our new report form LETTER.

. CREATE REPORT LETTER

After encountering the initial screen, we select the "Layout" menu option using **Alt-L** as usual. Striking the Enter key with the "Quick Layouts" menu item selected we get the screen of Figure 6.12.

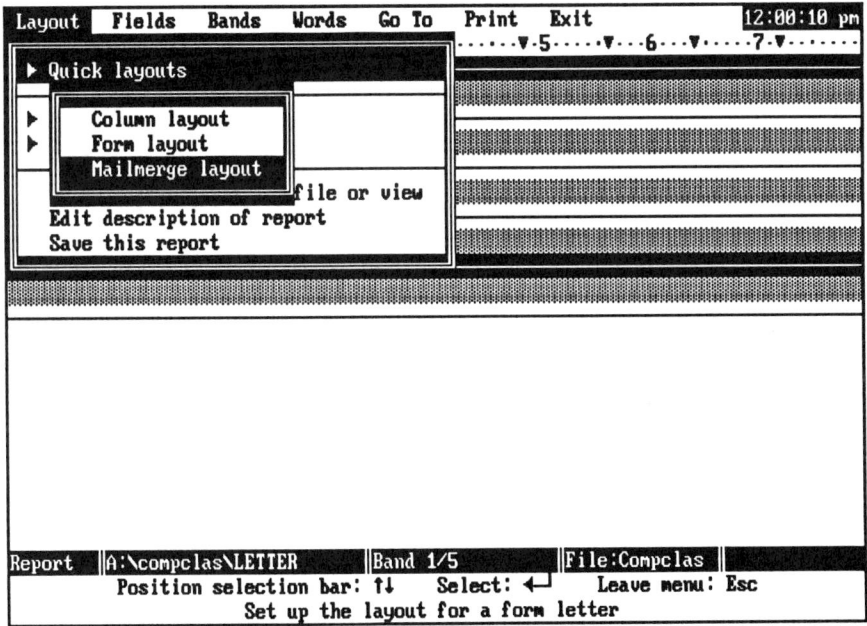

Figure 6.12 Selecting "Mailmerge layout" as the Quick layout form

Here we have selected the "Mailmerge layout" from the menu. Striking the Enter key we get the mailmerge screen of the report generator (see Figure 6.13). Note that all the bands, except for the detail band, are closed with no space to type in. In a mailmerge we are only interested in the Detail Band. Notice also that the area given to us in the Detail Band is not shaded as it was when we did the columnar report. The effect of removing the shaded area is to make the entire band an active area in which we will do some rudimentary "word processing".

196 LABELS, MAILMERGE REPORTS & FORMS

We will start by putting the system date, as a predefined field, in the upper right hand corner. (If you have forgotten how to do this, please refer to section 4.1.) Next we'll put in the FIRSTNAME and LASTNAME fields at the beginning of the next line. Note that we have assumed a margin for ourselves of 0.8" from the left. Next we add the ADDRESS and the CITY_ST_ZP fields on the following two lines. (We use the exact same procedure here that we used in the previous section in creating mailing labels.) After the word "Dear", we add the field FIRSTNAME, once more, followed by a ",". The result of this is shown in Figure 6.14.

Now we are ready to type the body of our letter. So we just proceed to type as we would in any word processor. Figure 6.15 shows the script that we have typed up to the point where we want to insert our EVALUATION date field from COMPCLAS. As usual, we select the "Fields" menu option with **Alt-F**, and strike the Enter key with the "Add field" menu item highlighted.

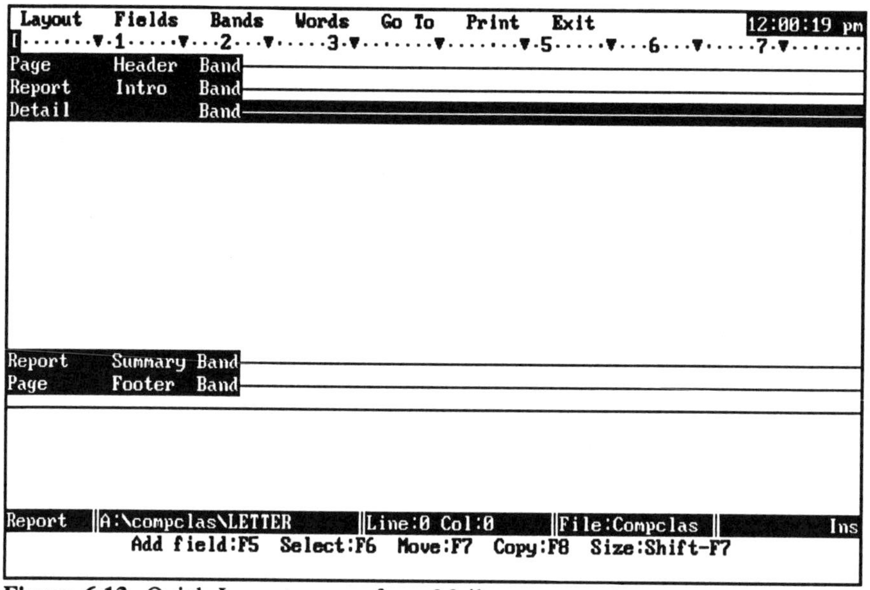

Figure 6.13 Quick Layout screen for a Mailmerge report

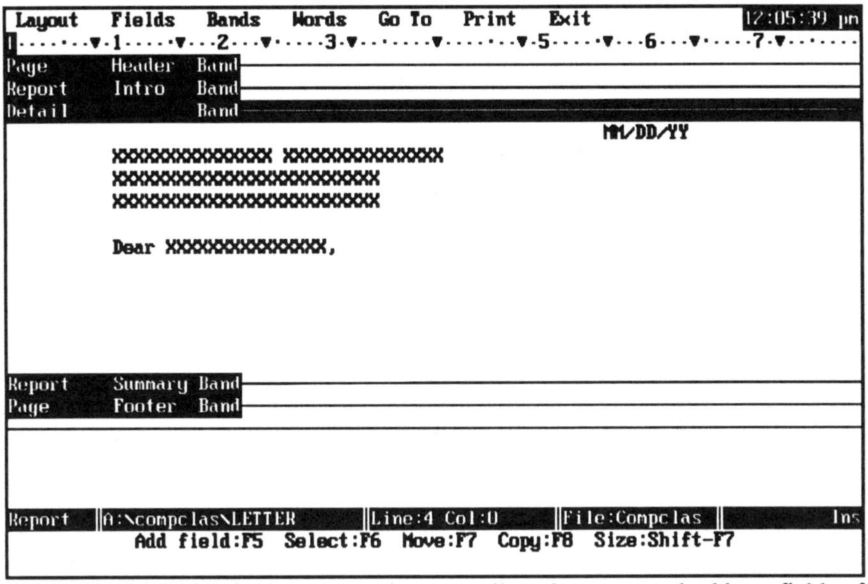

LABELS, MAILMERGE REPORTS & FORMS   197

Figure 6.14 Placing in the current date as well as the name and address fields of the student in COMPCLAS, along with the Salutation

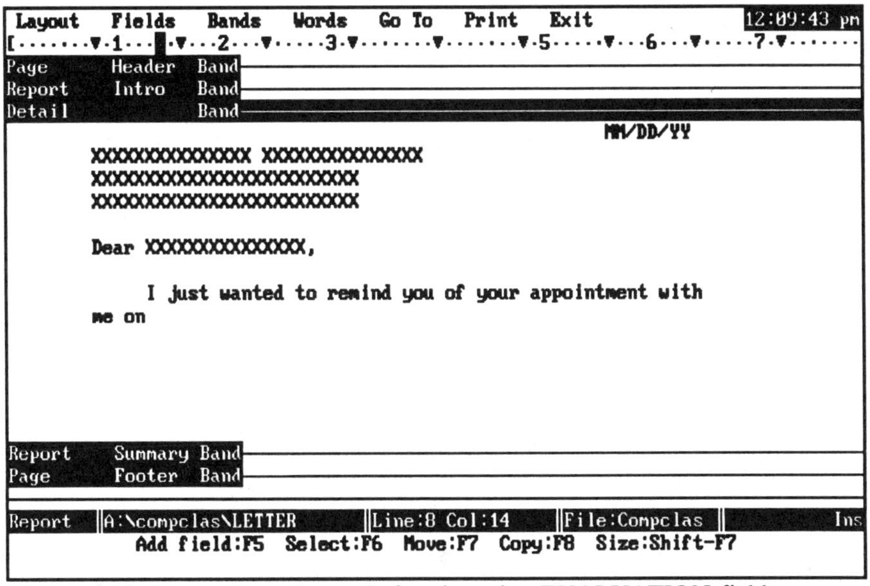

Figure 6.15 Report Form Letter before inserting EVALUATION field

198 LABELS, MAILMERGE REPORTS & FORMS

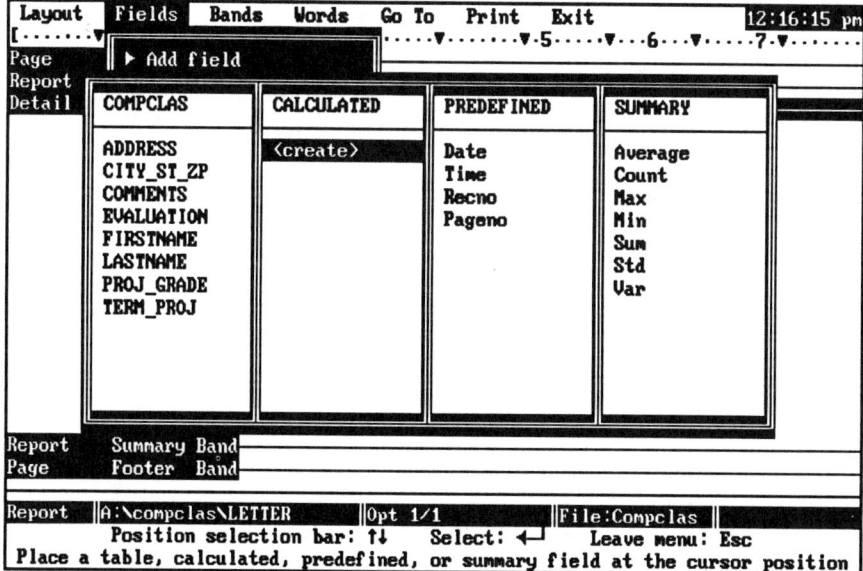

Figure 6.16 Selecting the CALCULATED field option for the EVALUATION date field

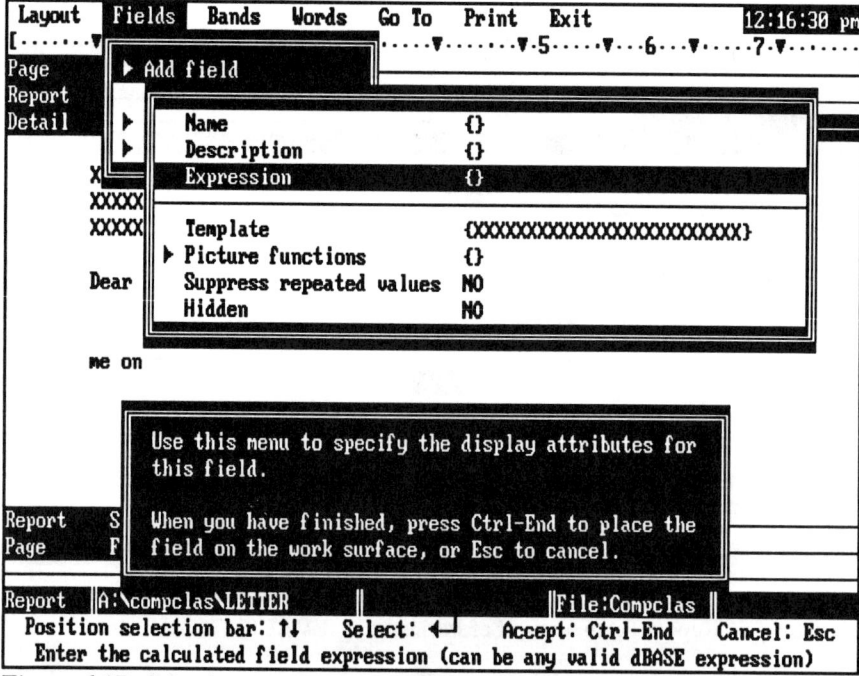

Figure 6.17 Selecting the Expression option for EVALUATION

We now obtain the field selection screen shown in Figure 6.16. Note that we have opted to create a CALCULATED field. The reason that we are making a calculated field, rather than simply taking the field EVALUATION in its regular format, is because using the template: "MM/DD/YY" in the body of a letter is a rather awkward way to refer to a date. We prefer to write a date out, in the form: *"DayOfWeek, MonthName NumericDay"*. For example, the date "12/14/92" would be written as: "Monday, December 14". This format has a much more natural sound to it, but it does require our calculating some date functions. Striking the Enter key with the **<create>** option highlighted, we get the display attributes screen shown in Figure 6.17.

Our ploy will be to create three calculated fields: the first for the *DayOfWeek*, the second for the *MonthName*, and the third for the *NumericDay*. First we'll calculate the *DayOfWeek*. There is no need to give a name to this calculated field because we won't be referring to it again. For this reason, Figure 6.17 shows that we have gone right to the Fields Expression option. Striking Enter we open up the option so we can type in the desired function. This is shown in Figure 6.18.

The function that we will be using is the date function, **CDOW()**. This stands for Character Day Of Week. Figure 6.18 shows our having entered: **CDOW(EVALUATION)**. With that date function entered, we want to reduce the size of the template from twenty-five X's to nine. We choose nine, because no day of the week contains more than nine letters in English. The final Display Attributes screen is shown in Figure 6.19. Striking the **Ctrl-End** keystroke pair to accept the Display Attributes as amended, we get the *DayOfWeek* calculated field added to our boilerplate letter, as shown in Figure 6.20.

Since we want to separate the day of week from the month by a comma, we have typed a comma following the *DayOfWeek* field. Now we are ready to add in the calculated field, *MonthName*. We go through the same procedure as we did for the *DayOfWeek* calculated field to get to the Display Attributes screen. This time we choose the date function, **CMONTH()**. This stands for Character

200 LABELS, MAILMERGE REPORTS & FORMS

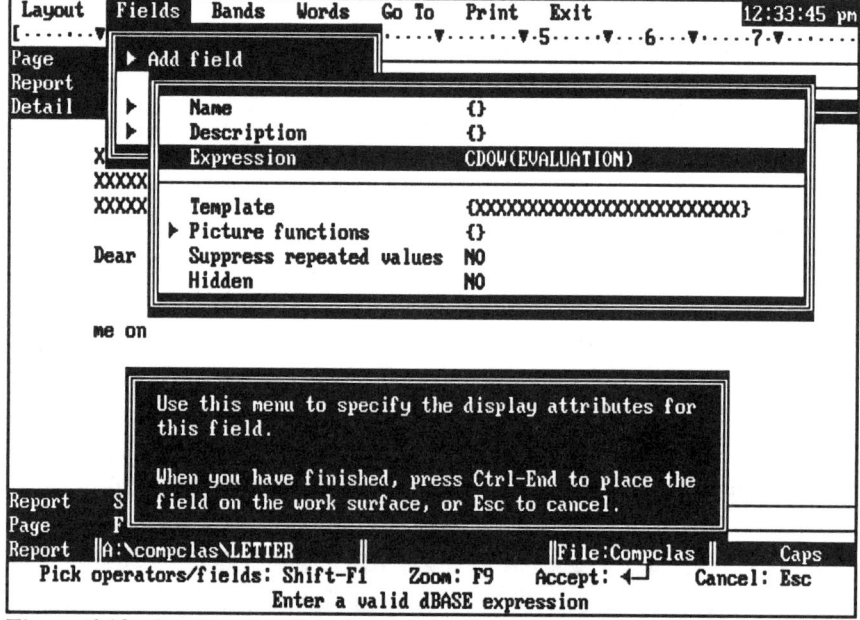

Figure 6.18 Creating the Calculated field CDOW(EVALUATION)

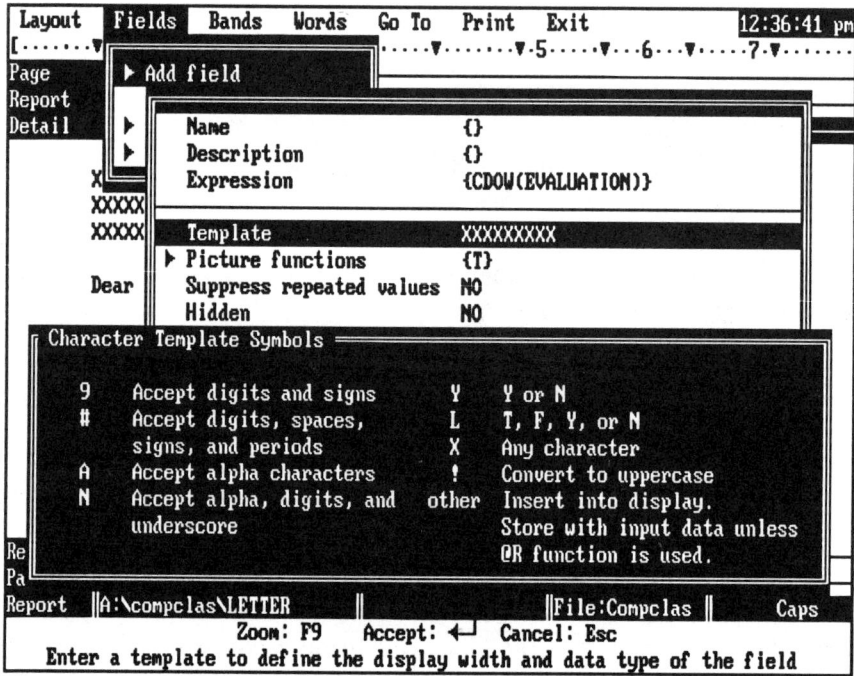

Figure 6.19 Reducing the template width from 25 to 9 characters

LABELS, MAILMERGE REPORTS & FORMS 201

```
Layout  Fields  Bands  Words  Go To  Print  Exit           12:37:00 pm
[.......▼.1.....▼...2...▼.....3.▼......▼.....▼.5....▼...6...▼....7.▼.......
Page        Header  Band
Report      Intro   Band
Detail              Band
                                                    MM/DD/YY
        XXXXXXXXXXXXXX XXXXXXXXXXXXXX
        XXXXXXXXXXXXXXXXXXXXXXXX
        XXXXXXXXXXXXXXXXXXXXXXXX

        Dear XXXXXXXXXXXXXX,

            I just wanted to remind you of your appointment with
        me on XXXXXXXX,




Report      Summary Band
Page        Footer  Band
Report      ||A:\compclas\LETTER    ||Line:8 Col:24  ||File:Compclas||    CapsIns
             Add field:F5  Select:F6  Move:F7  Copy:F8  Size:Shift-F7
```

Figure 6.20 Letter with Calculated field CDOW(EVALUATION) added

MONTH. Figure 6.21 shows our having entered: **CMONTH(EVALUATION).** Since no month name has more than nine letters, we have reduced the size of the template from 25 X's down to nine. Again we accept that Display Attributes screen with **Ctrl-End.**

Once more we repeat the process to arrive at the Display Attributes screen for the calculated field, *NumericDay*. Figure 6.22 shows what we have entered. Here, we have used the function: **DAY()** to generate the numeric day of the week. We reduced the template to two digits as no numeric day is in excess of 31 (which is two digits long). We once more accept the Display Attributes screen of Figure 6.22 with **Ctrl-End.** The current stage of our letter is shown in Figure 6.23.

202 LABELS, MAILMERGE REPORTS & FORMS

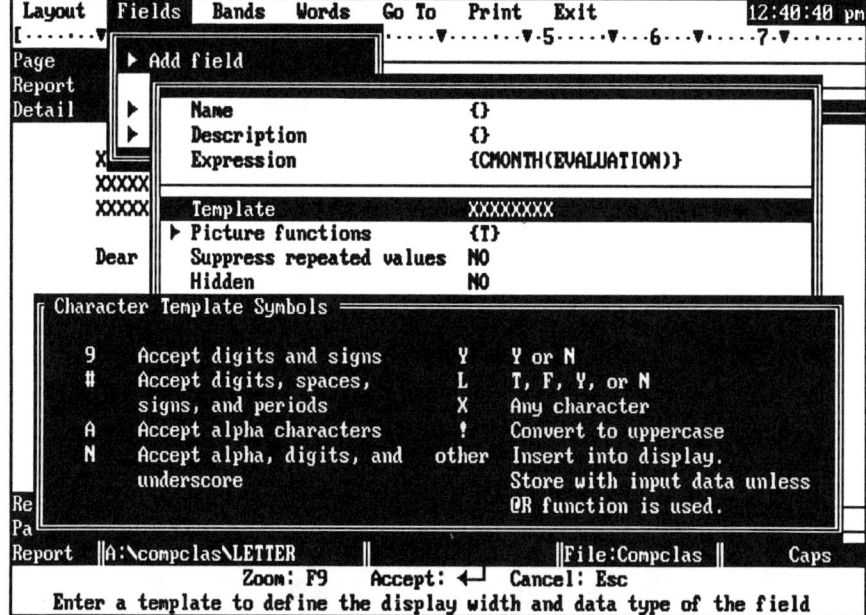

Figure 6.21 Creating the Calculated field CMONTH(EVALUATION) with 9 spaces in the template

Adding the remaining text to the letter we get the final "Mailmerge" report form shown in Figure 6.24.[21] Saving the report form in the usual way (**Alt-E**, Enter), we return to the dot prompt.

Now we're ready to print out all our letters. This is done using the standard REPORT FORM command. Since we only want to create letters for those who did term projects, the command becomes:

. REPORT FORM LETTER FOR TERM_PROJ TO PRINT

The first of the seven letters in the report is shown in Listing 6.3.

---

[21]There is an annoying bug in the mailmerge layout in dBASE 4.1. If any lines have a blank character printed on them because you hit the spacebar, but no other characters on them, the report form will not compile, and will give an error message. Hence, be sure all blank lines in the report have no spaces typed in them whatsoever.

LABELS, MAILMERGE REPORTS & FORMS 203

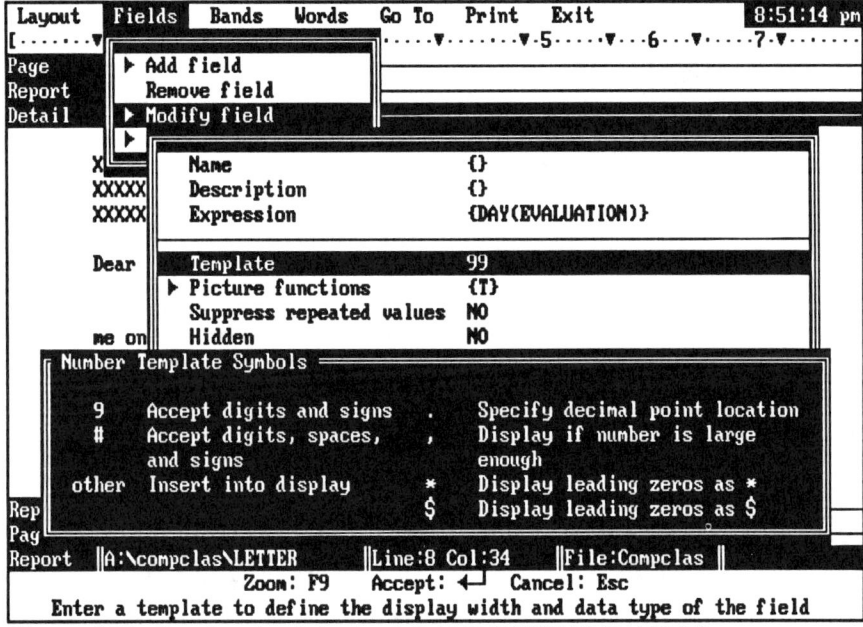

Figure 6.22 Creating the Calculated field DAY(EVALUATION)

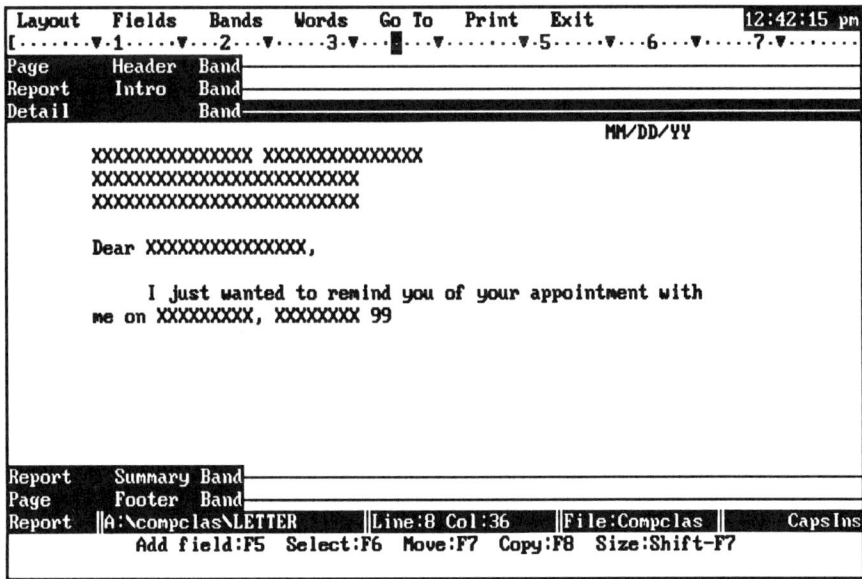

Figure 6.23 Letter with three Calculated date fields included

```
┌─────────────────────────────────────────────────────────────────┐
│ Layout   Fields   Bands   Words   Go To   Print   Exit  12:44:23 pm│
│┌·····▼·1·····▼···2···▼·······3·▼········▼······▼·5····▼··6···▼····7·▼·······│
││Page     Header  Band                                            │
││Report   Intro   Band                                            │
││Detail           Band                                            │
│                                               MM/DD/YY           │
│        XXXXXXXXXXXXXXX XXXXXXXXXXXXXX                            │
│        XXXXXXXXXXXXXXXXXXXXXXXX                                  │
│        XXXXXXXXXXXXXXXXXXXXXXXX                                  │
│                                                                  │
│        Dear XXXXXXXXXXXXXX,                                      │
│                                                                  │
│            I just wanted to remind you of your appointment with  │
│        me on XXXXXXXX, XXXXXXX 99, for the purpose of evaluating │
│        your Term Project. We can meet in my office at 1 PM. If   │
│        you have any problem with this date or time, please let me│
│        know. I look forward to seeing you then.                  │
│                                                                  │
│                                    Yours Sincerely,              │
│                                                                  │
│┌Report   Summary  Band                                           │
││Page     Footer   Band                                           │
││Report  ║A:\compclas\LETTER  ║Line:14 Col:0 ║File:Compclas║   Ins│
│         Add field:F5  Select:F6  Move:F7  Copy:F8  Size:Shift-F7 │
└─────────────────────────────────────────────────────────────────┘
```

Figure 6.24 Final version of "Mailmerge" report form

6.2.1 Importing a Text File Letter into the Mailmerge Layout

Often people prefer to write their letters using their own particular word processor. The question becomes, how does one import the document into the mailmerge layout of the dBASE IV report form generator? This is a simple process. The only thing that the user need do is to generate a DOS text file[22] from their word processor. This is a standard option in all word processors, so it should prove no problem.

After having created the "Mailmerge layout", then one need only select the "Words" menu option, and then select the "Write/read text file" menu item as shown in Figure 6.25. After the text file has been read into the mailmerge layout, the database fields may be inserted as desired.

---

[22]This is often known as an ASCII (American Standard Code for Information Interchange) file.

> 12/01/92
> Gladys Naboa
> 324 Catskill Terrace
> Sundown, NY 12782
>
> Dear Gladys,
>
> I just wanted to remind you of your appointment with me on Tuesday, December 15, for the purpose of evaluating your Term Project. We can meet in my office at 1 PM. If you have any problem with this date or time, please let me know. I look forward to seeing you then.
>
> Yours Sincerely,

Listing 6.3 The first of the seven letters printed in the Mailmerge

6.3   The Screen Generator

Just as we were able to use a report form generator to generate customized reports, in the same way we can use the Screen Format generator to generate customized EDIT and APPEND screens.

Why, you may ask, would one want to create customized screens? What's wrong with the EDIT and APPEND screens that we've been using? There are three reasons why we might want to make a customized screen: (1) to be able to view and Edit Memo fields on the same screen as the rest of the data; (2) to be able to place more data on one screen; 3) esthetics.

206   LABELS, MAILMERGE REPORTS & FORMS

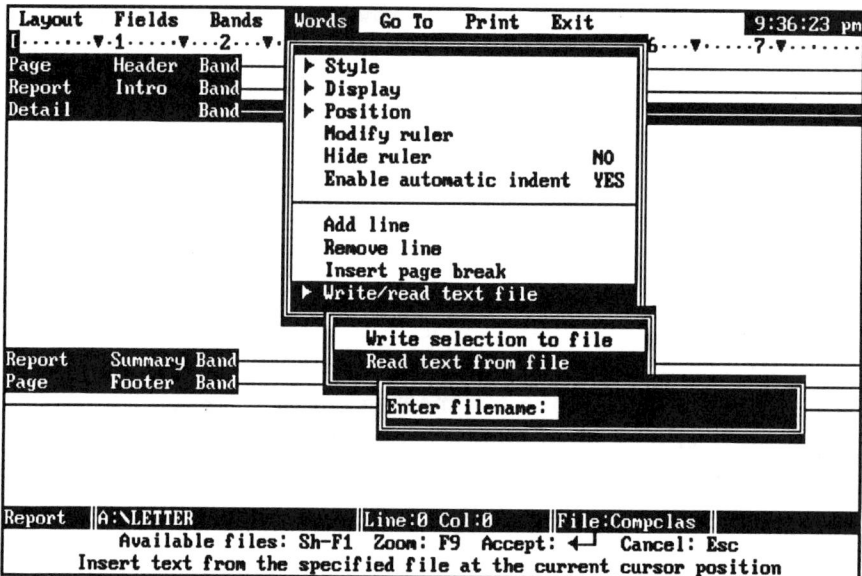

Figure 6.25 Selecting the "Write/read text file" menu item in the a Mailmerge layout

If our database had more than 21 fields, then our dBASE default data screen would need more than one screen page to display the data. We would find ourselves paging back and forth between screens looking at our data, as well as entering it. However, if we make a customized screen, then we could easily put the equivalent of three default screen pages on one screen. This would save us a lot of paging back and forth.

With respect to esthetics, note how, in Figure 2.7, all the data is bunched together in the upper left hand corner. This is the sequential data screen that dBASE gives you by default. We have an entire screen of 25 rows by 80 columns with which to work. Why bunch everything up in one corner, when it is easier on the eyes to spread it out?

To enter the Screen Format Generator, we type: **CREATE SCREEN** *ScreenName* at the dot prompt. Choosing, **COMPCLAS** as the name of our screen format file, we type:

. CREATE SCREEN COMPCLAS

LABELS, MAILMERGE REPORTS & FORMS

The opening screen of the screen generator is shown in Figure 6.26. The techniques that we will use here are similar to those that we employed in designing the mailmerge report. Our approach will be to place the name of a field directly before the field itself and to arrange the fields in an orderly, logical sequence. We will start by typing the name of the first field, "First Name: ", two lines down from the top on the left as see in Figure 6.27. We never use the top line because dBASE uses much of that line for other purposes.

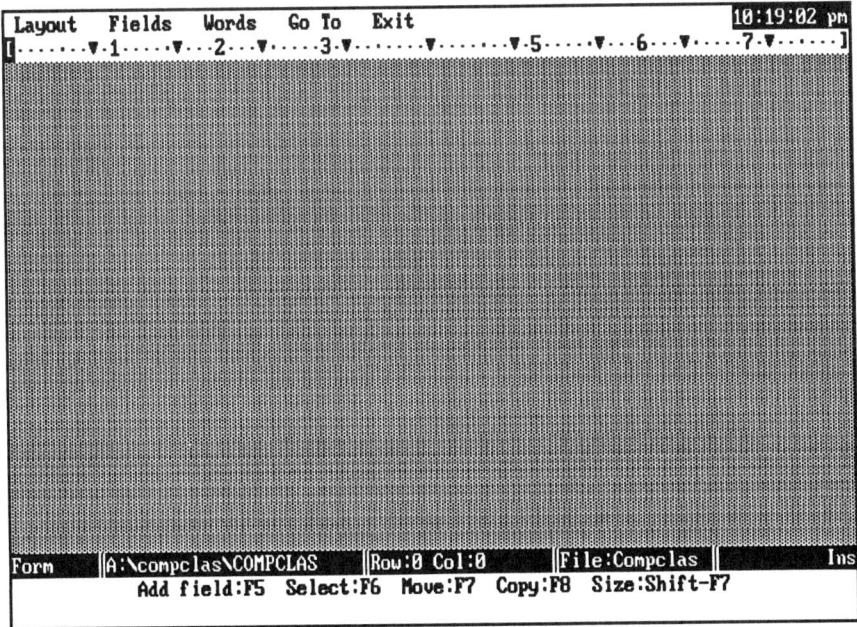

Figure 6.26 Opening screen of the Screen Generator

We add the field: FIRSTNAME, to the screen just two spaces beyond the field name, in the usual manner. Using the keystroke pair, **Alt-F**, followed by Enter, we get the menu of field choices shown in Figure 6.28. Selecting FIRSTNAME, and striking the Enter key, we get the Display Attributes screen shown in Figure 6.29. Accepting the default attributes as is, we strike the keystroke pair, **Ctrl-End**. Figure 6.30 shows the screen with the FIRSTNAME field added.

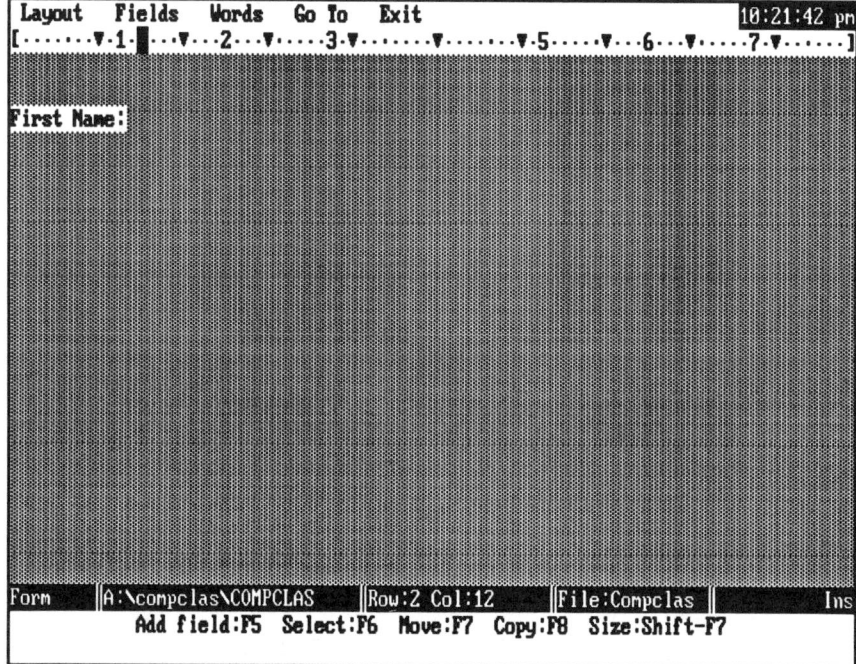

Figure 6.27 Entering the first Field Name in the Screen Design

Next, we space over to the right and type in the field name: "Last Name". Using the same procedure as we did for the FIRSTNAME, we add in the field LASTNAME. The result of doing this is shown in Figure 6.31.

In the same manner, we proceed adding all the fields in our database to the screen, spreading them out in a way that makes good use of the screen space and is pleasing to the eye. It is usually best to try and line things up, column wise, as much as possible. In Figure 6.32, note that I placed the ADDRESS field immediately below the FIRSTNAME field, and the CITY_ST_ZP field below the LASTNAME field.

The one field that we have left to add is the MEMO field, COMMENTS. We could simply add it in the same way it appears in the EDIT screen (see Figure 2.7). However, we want to be able to see the contents of the MEMO field on the EDIT screen itself, so there is a variation in the way in which we add this field.

LABELS, MAILMERGE REPORTS & FORMS

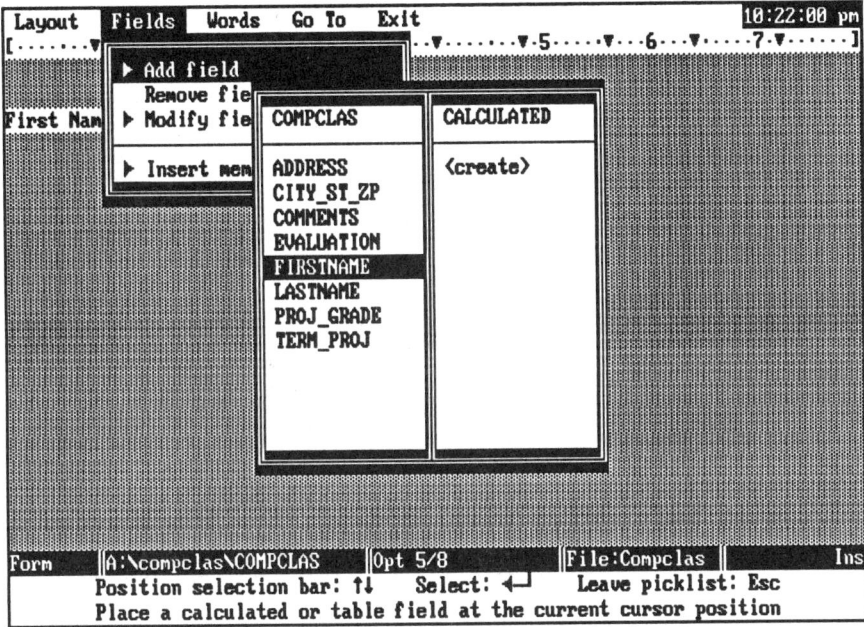

Figure 6.28 Selecting the field FIRSTNAME to be added to the screen

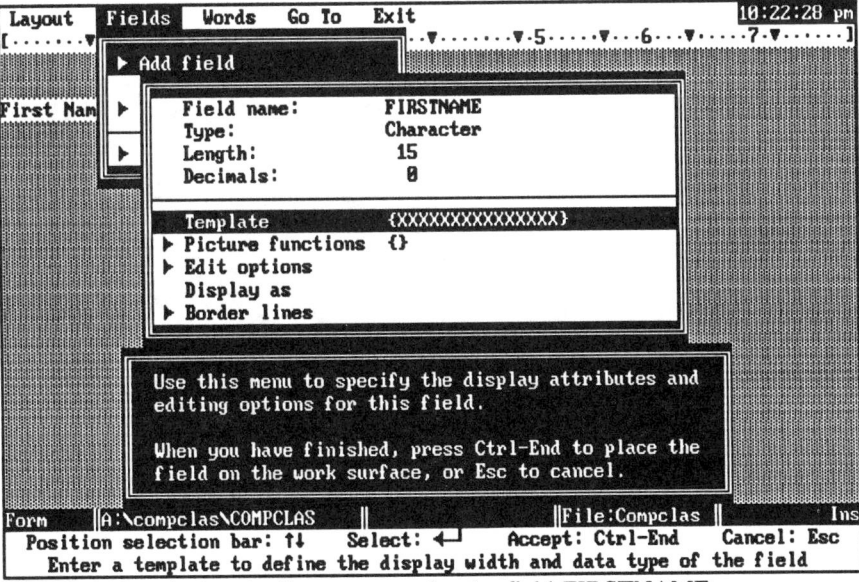

Figure 6.29 Display Attributes screen for the field FIRSTNAME

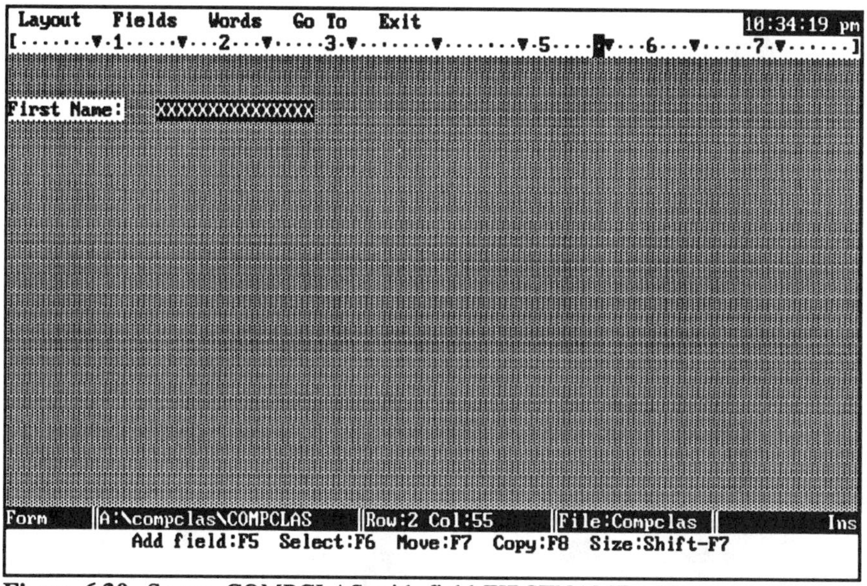

210 LABELS, MAILMERGE REPORTS & FORMS

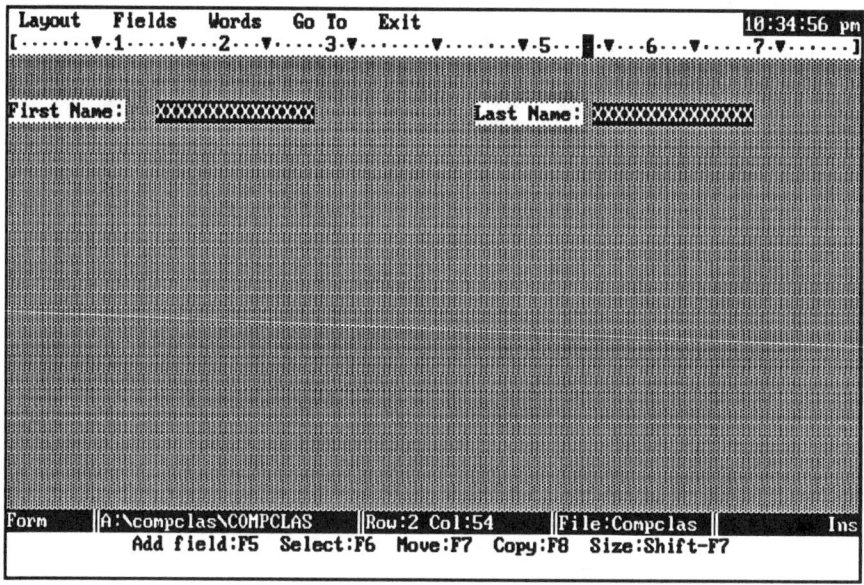

Figure 6.30 Screen COMPCLAS with field FIRSTNAME added

Figure 6.31 Screen COMPCLAS with first two fields added

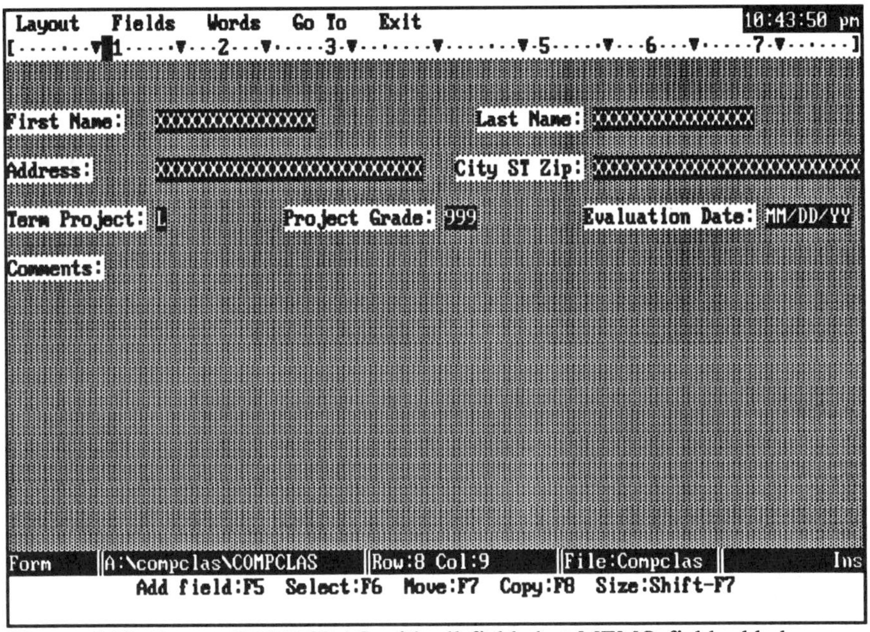

LABELS, MAILMERGE REPORTS & FORMS 211

Figure 6.32 Screen COMPCLAS with all fields but MEMO field added

We proceed to add the COMMENTS field in the usual way until we get to the Display Attributes screen shown in Figure 6.33. In the menu item labeled "Display", which is shown highlighted, note that the default setting is: "Marker". We want to change that to "Window". This is done by striking the Enter key with that menu item selected. Immediately, "Window" appears as the setting as seen in Figure 6.34.

Accepting the display attributes as modified, we strike **Ctrl-End**. Figure 6.35 shows what appears on our screen as a result. Note the directions down on the navigation line at the bottom of the screen: "Position upper left of menu window with cursor keys, complete with ENTER". Since the upper left hand corner of our window is exactly where we want it to be, we strike the Enter key.

Next we get the message on the navigation line: "Stretch memo window with cursor keys, complete with ENTER". In response to these directions, we hold down the right arrow stretching the window across to the right hand side of the screen. Then we

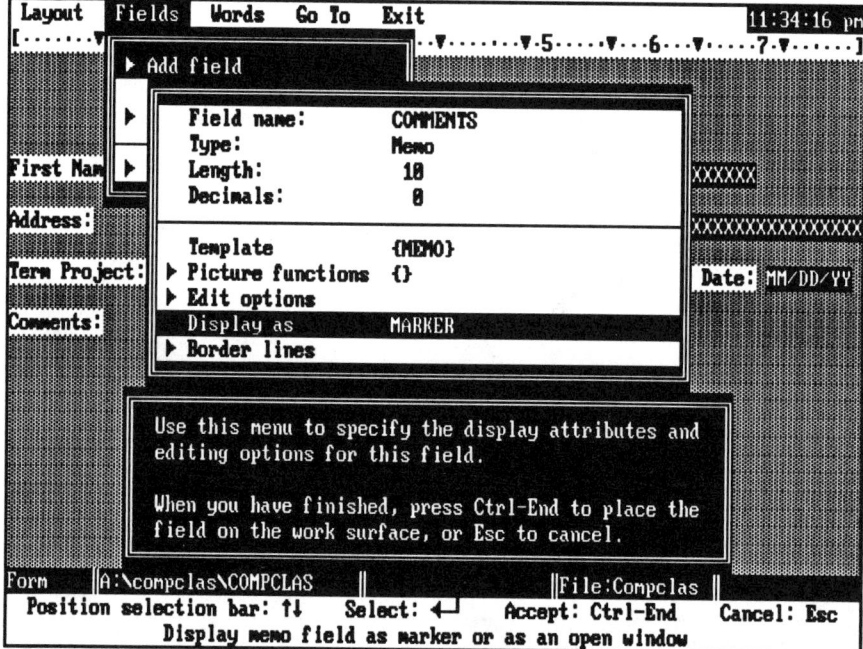

Figure 6.33 "Display as" menu item selected in Display Attributes

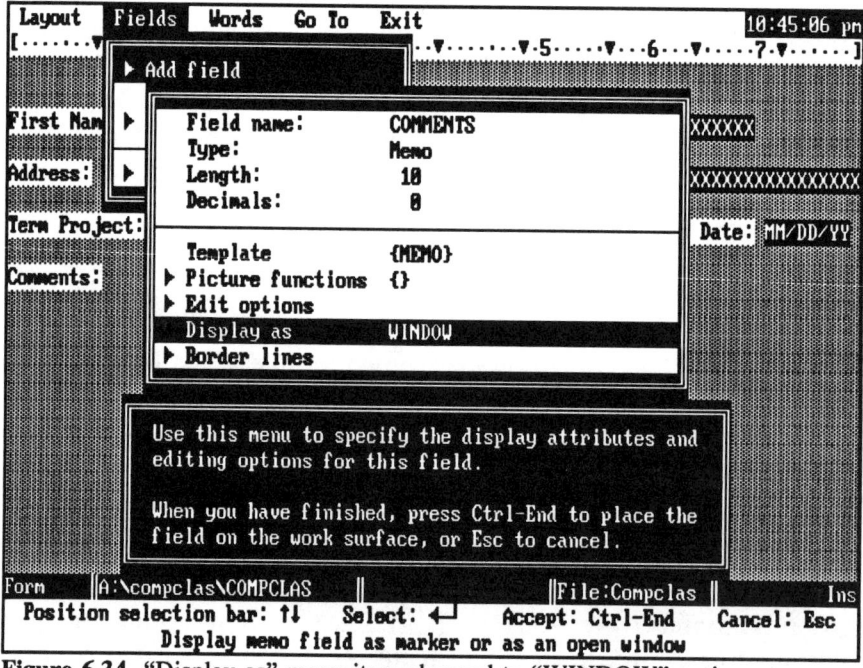

Figure 6.34 "Display as" menu item changed to "WINDOW" option

depress the down arrow stretching the window downwards until it is the width we want. Figure 6.36 shows the result of stretching this window. Since it is now the size we want, we strike the Enter key once more. Figure 6.37 shows the completed window.

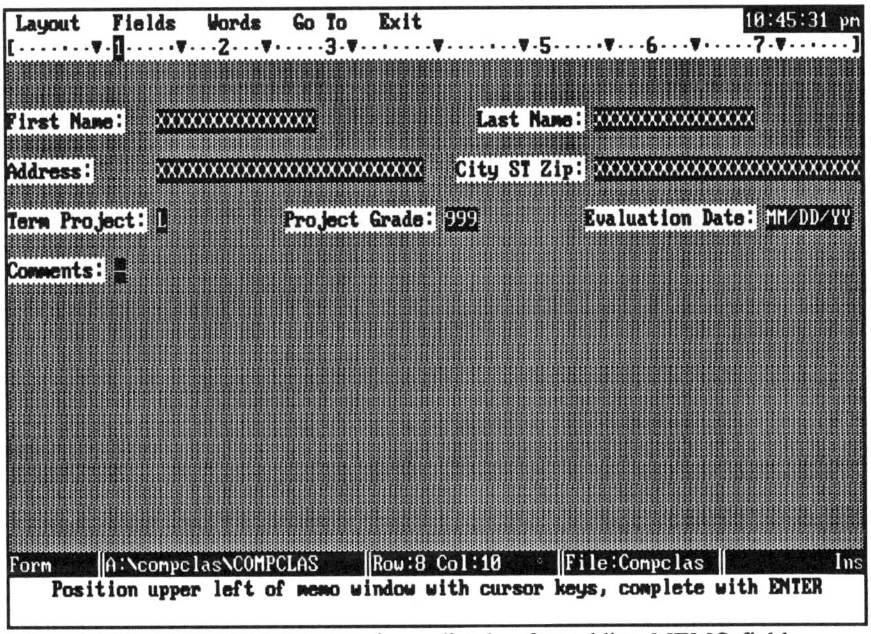

Figure 6.35 COMPCLAS screen immediately after adding MEMO field

We now exit from the screen generator in the usual way (**Alt-E**, Enter). Next we type: EDIT at the dot prompt to see what the screen that we have designed actually looks like.

. **EDIT**

Figure 6.38 shows Record 1 displayed using our new screen. On first inspection, we may be pleased with the results, but it sits just a little high on the screen. Let's lower the entire screen by two lines, just to center it a bit better. To do this we must return to the screen generator. As you might guess, the syntax for the command to modify our screen is: **MODIFY SCREEN** *ScreenName*. In our case the command is:

. **MODIFY SCREEN COMPCLAS**

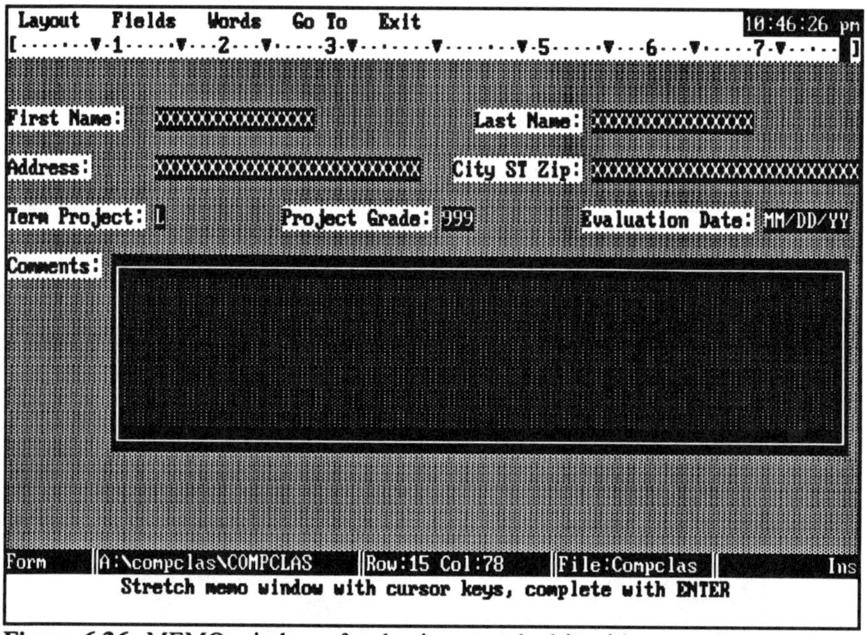

214 LABELS, MAILMERGE REPORTS & FORMS

Figure 6.36 MEMO window after having stretched it with cursor keys

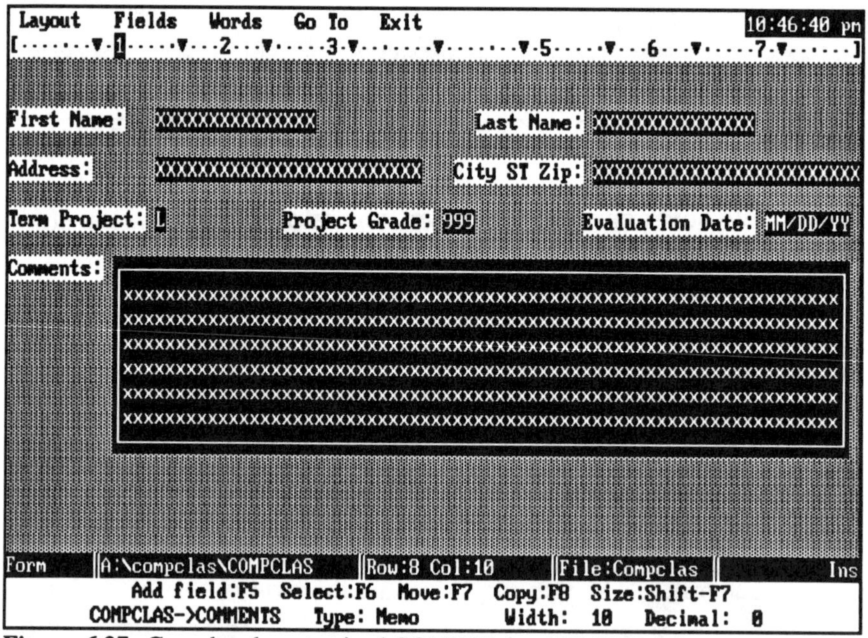

Figure 6.37 Completed customized SCREEN for COMPCLAS

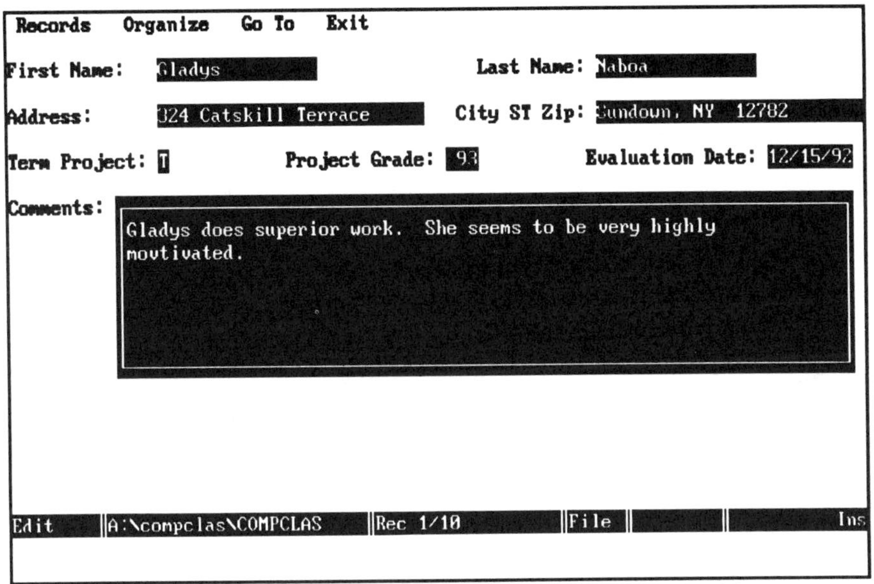

LABELS, MAILMERGE REPORTS & FORMS   215

```
Records   Organize   Go To   Exit
First Name:  Gladys              Last Name: Naboa
Address:     324 Catskill Terrace City ST Zip: Sundown, NY  12782
Term Project: 1    Project Grade: 93   Evaluation Date: 12/15/92
Comments:
             Gladys does superior work.  She seems to be very highly
             moutivated.




Edit     A:\compclas\COMPCLAS   Rec 1/10      File                      Ins
```

Figure 6.38 EDIT mode with new customized Screen COMPCLAS

We make this modification in two parts. First we must move the MEMO window down two lines, then we can move the rest of the screen all at once. Moving the cursor down to the window, we strike the **F6** key to select the window as indicated by the message down on the navigation line. Then we hit the Enter key. Next we strike the **F7** key to move the window. Now we strike the down arrow key twice which moves the window downward. Striking the Enter key to confirm our move results in the screen shown in Figure 6.39.

Now move the cursor up to the top of the screen. In this position we will insert two lines using the **Ctrl-N** keystroke pair. The final result is shown in Figure 6.40. Exit from the screen generator in the normal way (**Alt-E**, Enter). Now we will examine our final product looking at Record 2 which has a blank MEMO field. To bring up Record 2 in the EDIT mode we type:

. **EDIT 2**

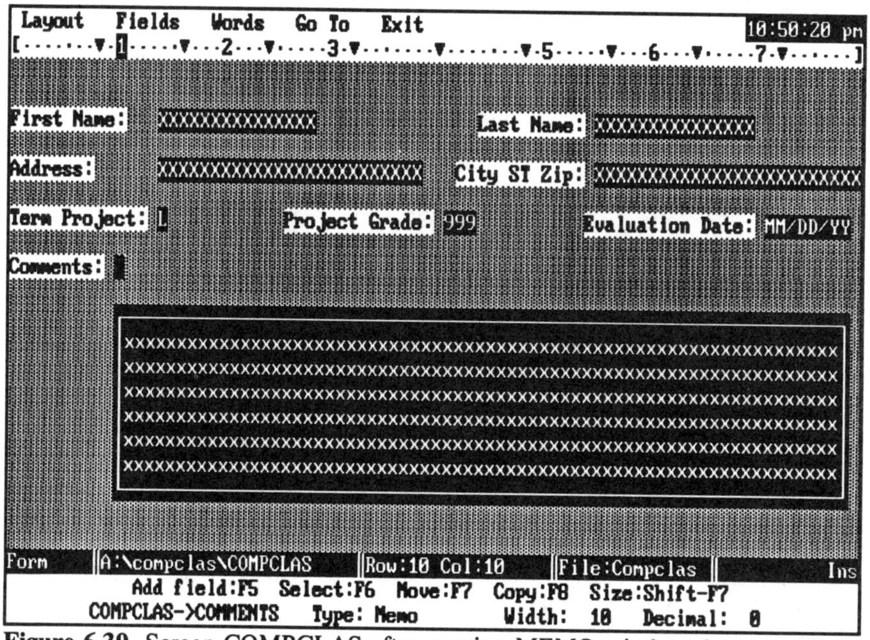

Figure 6.39 Screen COMPCLAS after moving MEMO window down two lines

The EDIT of Record 2 is shown in Figure 6.41. Notice that the screen is more evenly centered, vertically, than it was after our first pass at a screen design. Striking the Enter key 7 times takes us down to the MEMO field for COMMENTS. If we want to enter a comment, however, merely starting to type will not work. In order to open the window so that we can type into it, we strike the **F9** key. The result of doing this is shown in Figure 6.42. As we can see, the MEMO editor has simply moved into the window and is now open for business.

Now we type in a comment on Consuelo's work which is shown in Figure 6.43. To exit from the MEMO field we need only type the keystroke pair: **Ctrl-End**. This closes the window but displays the contents of the COMMENTS MEMO field.

This customized screen will stay in control as long as the database, COMPCLAS, is open. However, the next time we enter dBASE, it will not automatically be activated. In order to activate our customized screen, we must turn on the FORMAT File.

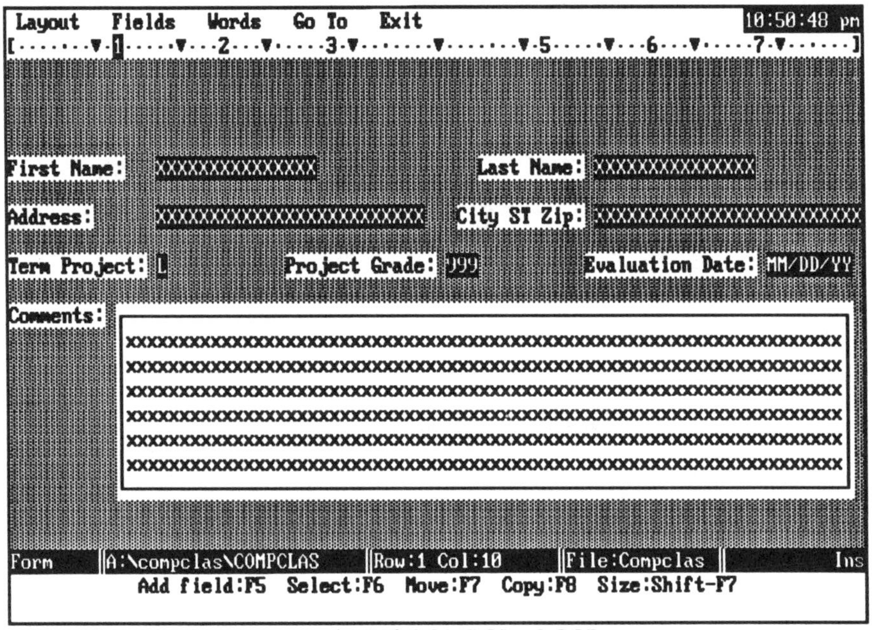

LABELS, MAILMERGE REPORTS & FORMS 217

Figure 6.40 Final Screen Design of COMPCLAS.SCR

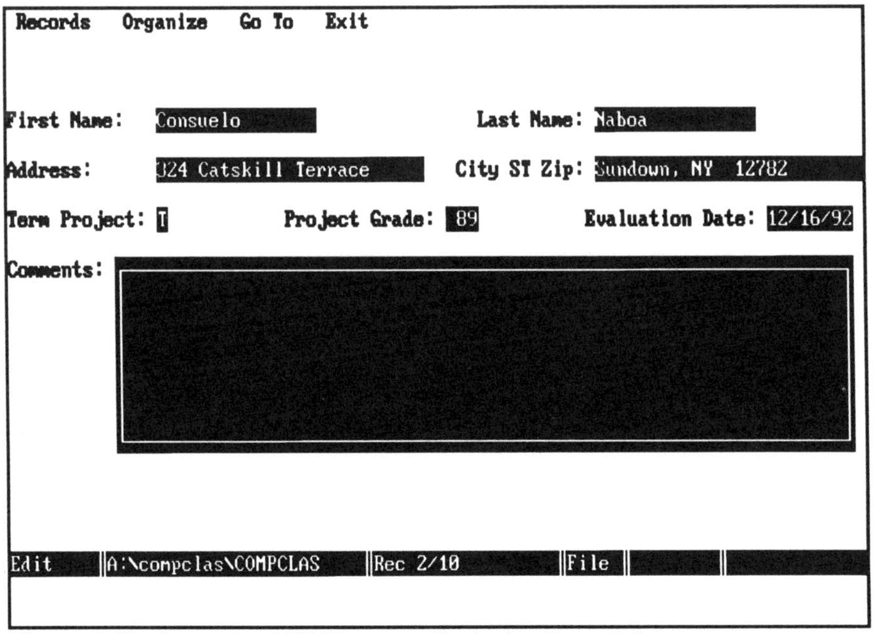

Figure 6.41 Customized EDIT screen displaying Record 2

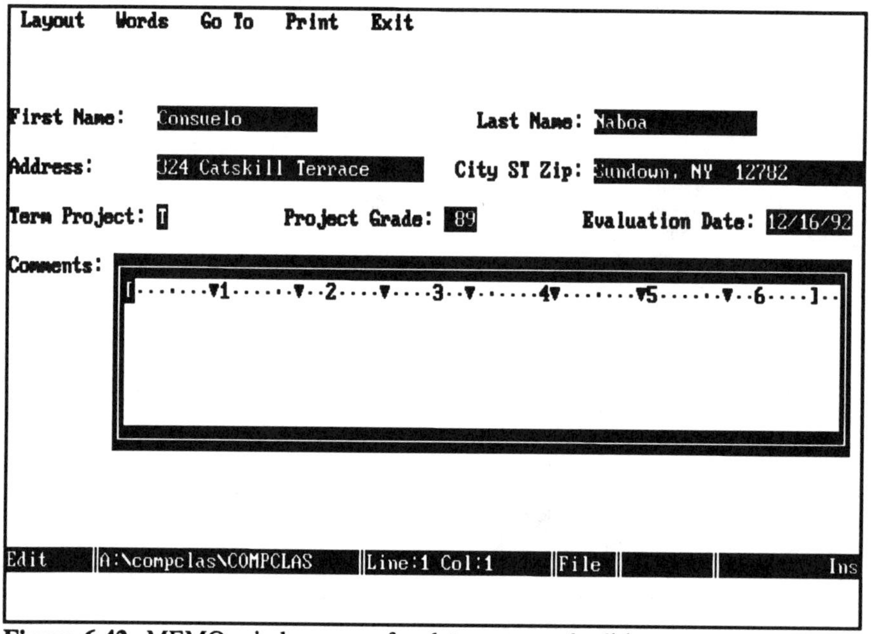

218 LABELS, MAILMERGE REPORTS & FORMS

Figure 6.42 MEMO window open for data entry and editing

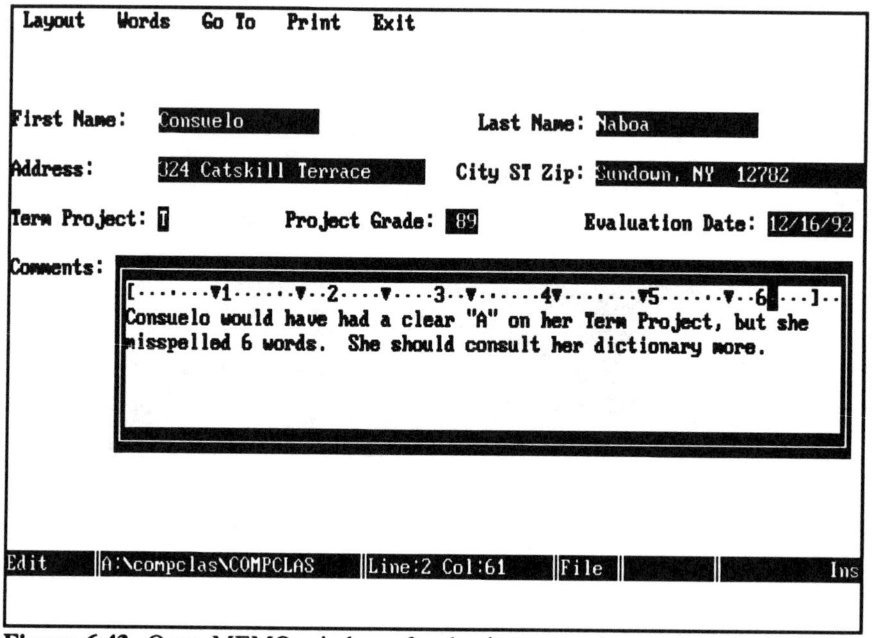

Figure 6.43 Open MEMO window after having entered a comment

One further point should be noted. You'll notice that our customized edit screen exhibits a status bar. The thing that determines whether a status bar is on or not, in the customized screen, is whether the status was set to "ON" when we entered the Screen Generator. In other words, if we do not wish a status bar to appear in our customized screen, we should execute the instruction: **SET STATUS OFF** before initially executing: **CREATE SCREEN COMPCLAS** .

6.3.1 The Format File

The file created by the Screen Generator has an extension of **.SCR** (in our case the file was called COMPCLAS.SCR). When we exited from the screen generator with Alt-E, a program was created which actually controls the screen. This program is called the FORMAT file, and it has the extension of **.FMT** (in this case the file is called COMPCLAS.FMT). This program is then compiled into machine language, just as the report form and label form programs were compiled, resulting in a file with the extension **.FMO** (producing COMPCLAS.FMO).

After leaving the screen generator, the format file is set on, and so it controls the display of the APPEND, EDIT, and INSERT screens. However, if you quit from dBASE and then enter it again, the format file will not be activated. So after you open your database, you must then SET your FORMAT file on. This is done with the command: **SET FORMAT TO** *ScreenName*. In our case the command would take the form:

. **SET FORMAT TO COMPCLAS**

Likewise, when we wish to turn the customized screen control off, we use the command: **SET FORMAT TO.**

. **SET FORMAT TO**

220 LABELS, MAILMERGE REPORTS & FORMS

In this way we see how we can customize our screen in the same way that we designed our reports. This gives us a lot of control over our display just as we had with our printed output.

Figure 6.44 shows our customized edit screen for Record 2 with the window closed.

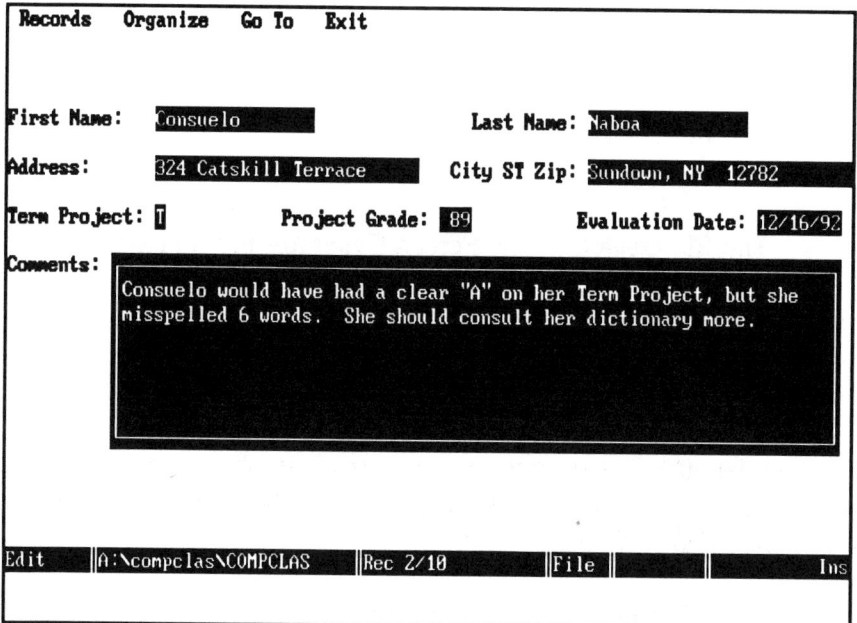

Figure 6.44 Customized Edit Screen for Record 2 with Window closed

6.4 Summary

In this chapter we have learned how to use the LABEL Form Generator to generate labels or other reports that ignore paging. In addition, we learned how to create mailmerge documents so that we could do mass mailings with a personalized touch. Finally, we learned how to customize our screen and generate a format file that would control how our EDIT, APPEND, and INSERT screens would appear to the user.

LABELS, MAILMERGE REPORTS & FORMS   221

6.5 Review

In Chapter 6 the commands we covered were:

>   **CREATE LABEL** *FileName*
>   **CREATE SCREEN** *ScreenName*
>   **LABEL FORM** *FileName*
>   **MODIFY LABEL** *FileName*
>   **MODIFY SCREEN** *ScreenName*
>   **SET FORMAT TO**
>   **SET FORMAT TO** *FormatFileName*

Add these commands to your glossary of commonly used dBASE commands. In addition, the following date functions were introduced in this chapter.

>   **CDOW()**
>   **CMONTH()**
>   **DAY()**

You will want to add these to your glossary of functions also.

6.6 Laboratory Work

Step through the procedures outlined in this chapter to create the mailing labels in section 6.1 and the mailmerge letter designed in section 6.2. Finally, create a customized screen for the COMPCLAS database as outlined in section 6.3.

6.7 Exercises

1. Create a mailing label format, called MAILIST.LBL, that will print out a mailing list for all those in your database. Assume that the label size you will be using is: 3 1/2" X 15/16" X 2 across. Be sure your database is indexed on the

fields ZIP + LAST + FIRST, FOR those people receiving cards. Print out a copy of these mailing labels on regular paper (there is no need to use real mailing labels), and hand them in.

2. For your database, MAILIST, create a mailmerge report form having the type of output shown in Listing 6.4. Note that the date [use the date function: DATE()] and the name "Donald" are **FIELDS** that are imbedded in the mailmerge text. Print out the first two letters of the report, and hand them in. (Hint: This can be done by using the **FOR** clause: **FOR RECNO()<=2** in our REPORT FORM command as long as the database is in its natural order.)

February 6, 1993

Dear **Donald**,

It's been ages since I got around to writing. I want you to know that I think about you often, even though my correspondence may not show it. Who would believe time could fly so quickly.

And how are you? How is everything going? What do you hear from our old friends?

I just wanted to touch base and let you know everything was OK with me. Hope to see you in the not too distant future.

Yours With Love,

Listing 6.4 An Example of the First Letter to be printed by the Mailmerge Report Form For MAILIST

LABELS, MAILMERGE REPORTS & FORMS   223

3. Design a customized screen for your MAILIST database, like the one shown in Figure 6.45. Be sure to print out a copy of the screen by striking the keystroke pair: **Shift PrtSc** when your formatted screen is showing in the EDIT mode. Hand in this printed screen.

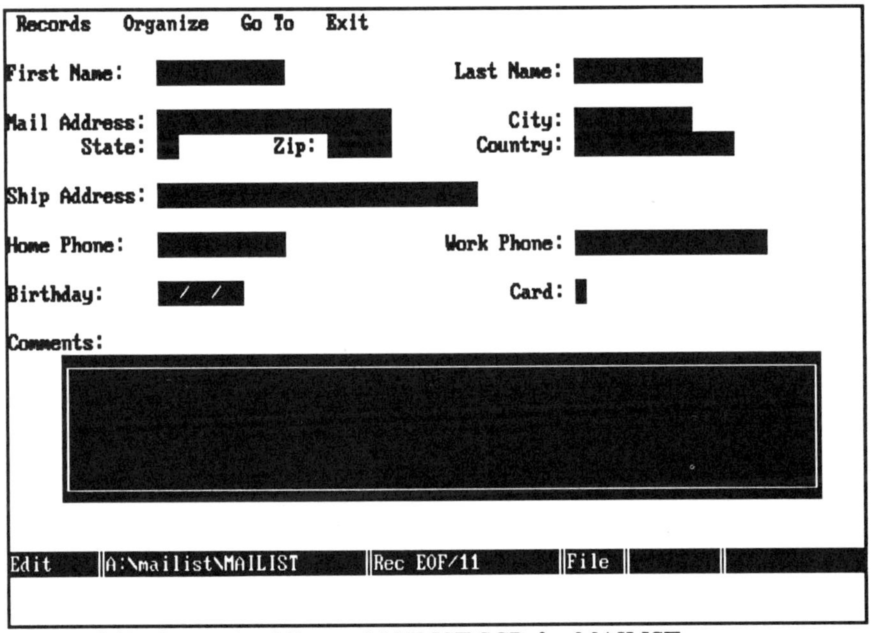

Figure 6.45 Customized Screen MAILIST.SCR for MAILIST

CHAPTER 7

COMMAND FILES & MEMORY VARIABLES

7.0 **Contents of Chapter 7**

Introducing the Command File.

Use of the WAIT instruction.

Introduction of user defined Memory Variables.

Modification of System Memory Variables.

Introduction of the @, SAY, GET and READ commands.

Design of a Command File which does a Search and Edit.

Design of a Menu Driver Command File.

7.1 Introduction to Command Files

By now you may have noticed that some things that we try to accomplish may require the execution of a number of commands from the dot prompt. If we have to go through these steps often, then typing these same steps over and over can get quite tedious. Sometimes these steps require some thought. To have to repeat this thinking process is analogous to re-inventing the wheel. A command file is a way of capturing all the steps that we use in accomplishing a task and saving them so that we can use them over and over again.

7.1.1 Creating an "Add Records" Command File

As an example of this, here are the steps that we would have to go through in order to do a simple APPEND instruction using our new format file. (Remember that we must start from scratch here, we can't assume anything has been done for us already.)

USE COMPCLAS   && Open the database
SET FORMAT TO COMPCLAS   && Turn on Format File
APPEND   && Go into the Append mode
SET FORMAT TO   && Turn off the Format File
USE   && Close the database

The **&&** marks the beginning of a comment[23]. Note that everything that we did at the beginning, we undid at the end. This is the usual rule in a command file.

As you can see, just to do something simple like add a record to a database requires 5 steps, and a lot of typing. However, if we put these five steps into a command file, then we only have to type them once. To open a command file we use the command: **MODIFY COMMAND** *Filename* . Giving our command file the name: **COMPADD**, we have:

---

[23]In a command file, everything beyond the "&&" is ignored by dBASE. The comments were just placed here to make it clear why each step was taken.

COMMAND FILES & MEMORY VARIABLES   227

. MODIFY COMMAND COMPADD

In Figure 7.1, we see that we have entered into the dBASE command file editor. As this file does not yet exist, we have a blank screen. Typing in these commands, we have the screen shown in Figure 7.2. Note the three lines at the top, beginning with an asterisk: *. These are comments and are skipped when the command file is executed. We end a command file with the command, RETURN.

Although a single command file will operate perfectly well without the RETURN command, it does serve the purpose of marking where the command file ends. When we concatenate a group of command files together to form a procedure file, as we will in Chapter 10, its presence becomes indispensable. For now we will consider it simply good form to always include the RETURN command at the end of each command file. As Figure 7.3 indicates, we exit in the usual way: **Alt-E**, Enter. This returns us to the dot prompt.

Figure 7.1 Opening a new file in the Command File Editor

228 COMMAND FILES & MEMORY VARIABLES

```
 Layout   Words   Go To   Print   Exit
[..█....v1.....v..2....v....3..v.....4v.......v5.....v..6....v....7..v......
* COMPADD.PRG
* This program Opens the Database COMPCLAS and Appends Records to it.
*
USE COMPCLAS
SET FORMAT TO COMPCLAS
APPEND
SET FORMAT TO
USE
RETURN




                                                                                


 Program  A:\compclas\COMPADD      Line:10 Col:4                    CapsIns
```

Figure 7.2 The Command File COMPADD.PRG in the Command File Editor

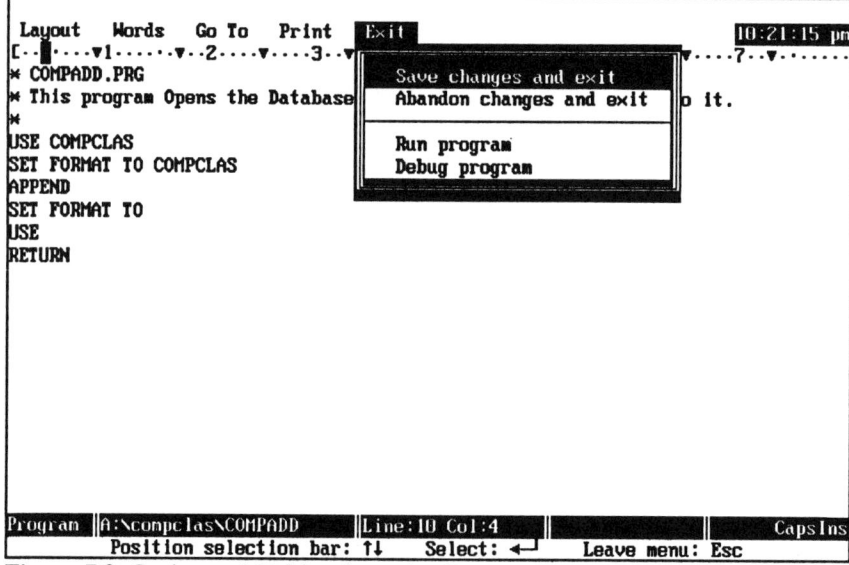

Figure 7.3 Saving and Exiting from the Command File Editor

COMMAND FILES & MEMORY VARIABLES   229

The file that has been created in this way has the extension **.PRG**, which stands for "Program". This file is often referred to as the "Source Code". When this program is executed, dBASE translates it into a version written in machine language. This is referred to as the "compiled" version. This is the program that is then executed, and it has the same name with an extension of **.DBO**. To execute this command file, we simply use the key word, **DO**, followed by the name of the command file. In this case the command would be:

. **DO COMPADD**

The result of doing this instruction is, of course, to take us into the APPEND mode as seen in Figure 7.4. When we're done appending, we return to the dot prompt as usual, our work done, and the file closed.[24]

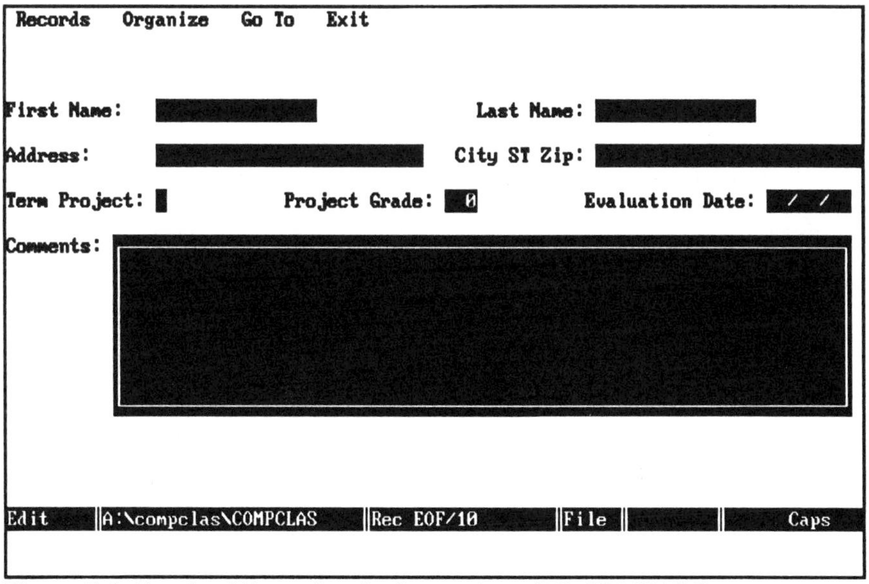

Figure 7.4 Result of Executing the Instruction: DO COMPADD

---

[24]The presence of the status bar in the customized screen results from the fact that the status bar was present when the screen was initially made. Had the status bar been off when it was made, there would be no status bar present in the screen.

7.1.2 Use of the WAIT Command in the COMPPACK Command File

Some actions, though simple to execute, are of such a drastic nature, that we want to place some protection around them to insure the fact that they are not executed by mistake. A good example of this is the PACK instruction.

PACK is a very drastic instruction because the effect of executing it is irrevocable. Anywhere from 0 to all the records in your database may be removed simply by typing these four letters. Because of this fact, we want to ask a question of the user to the effect, "Do You Really Want To Do This?" This makes the user think twice before executing this command to which there is no appeal.

A useful instruction that allows such a question to be asked is the **WAIT** instruction. This instruction is only used in command files, and has the effect of pausing the instruction execution, and prompting the user with a question or a comment. The syntax of the instruction is: **WAIT** *prompt*, where *prompt* is a character string beginning and ending with quotes.

In addition, we precede the **WAIT** instruction with another new instruction, **CLEAR**, which clears the screen. In this way we're assured of the fact that the prompt will appear at the top of the screen with no other garbage littering our view. Finally, we stick another CLEAR command at the end of the command file to leave a clean screen when we are done with our work. Figure 7.5 shows the kind of command file we might want to write to insure the fact that the user has a chance to think twice about his or her action.

Again, notice that we always begin a command file with comments reminding the user of the purpose of the command file as well as its name. Executing the command file, COMPPACK.prg, we get the screen shown in Figure 7.6.

. **DO COMPPACK**

COMMAND FILES & MEMORY VARIABLES 231

```
Layout  Words  Go To  Print  Exit
* COMPPACK.PRG
* This program PACKS the database COMPCLAS after making an inquiry
*
USE COMPCLAS
CLEAR
WAIT "Press Enter If You Want To Remove All Your Deletions (Hit Esc if Not)!"
PACK
USE
CLEAR
RETURN
```

Figure 7.5 The Command File: COMPPACK.PRG

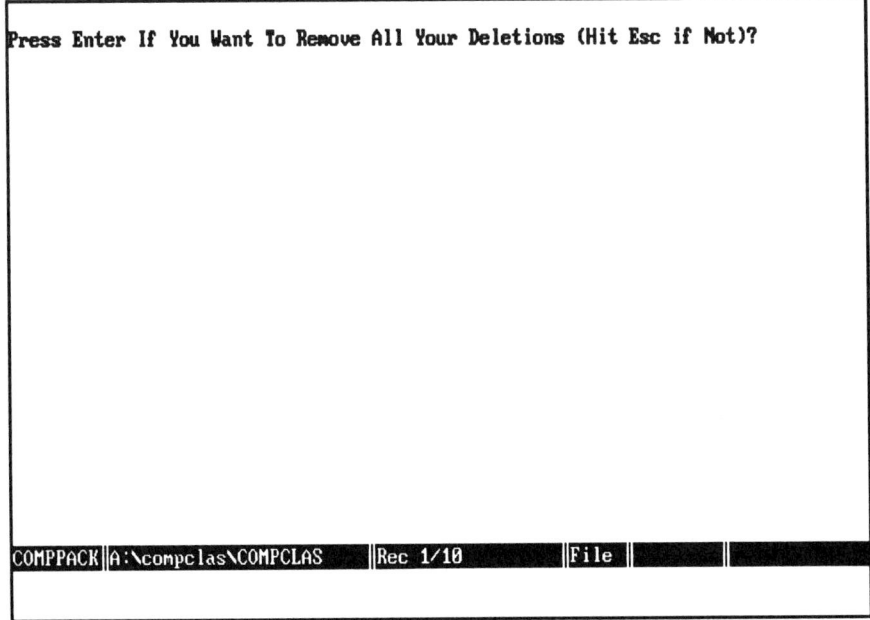

Figure 7.6 Screen Resulting from the execution of: DO COMPPACK.PRG

Although we prompt the user to press the Enter key, striking any key but the Esc key will cause the desired action to take place. If the Esc key is struck, then we get the screen shown in Figure 7.7. This is not a very elegant way to go about changing our minds on executing a PACK, but striking the Enter key will get us out of it. We'll discuss more elegant techniques in succeeding chapters.

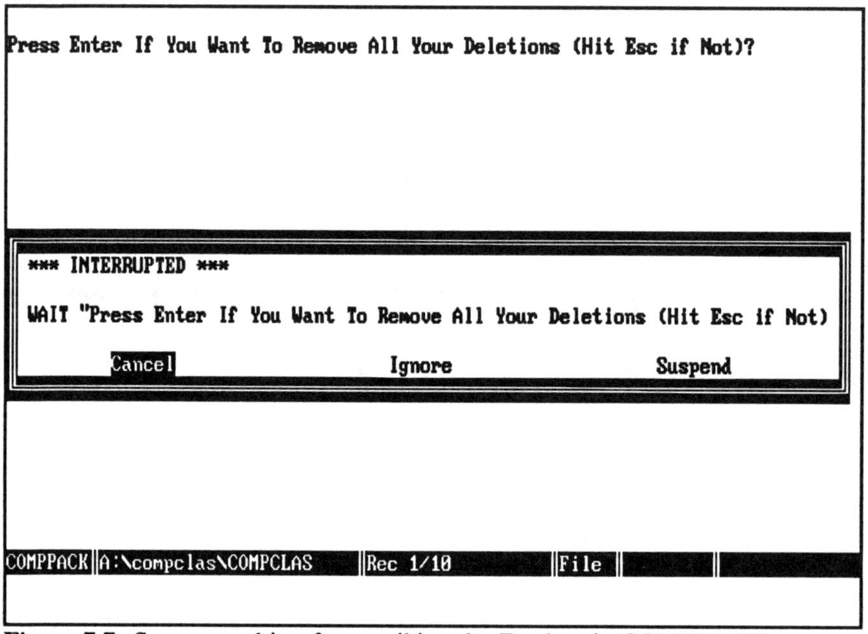

```
Press Enter If You Want To Remove All Your Deletions (Hit Esc if Not)?




┌──────────────────────────────────────────────────────────────────┐
│ *** INTERRUPTED ***                                              │
│ WAIT "Press Enter If You Want To Remove All Your Deletions (Hit Esc if Not) │
│      Cancel              Ignore                    Suspend       │
└──────────────────────────────────────────────────────────────────┘



COMPPACK  A:\compclas\COMPCLAS    Rec 1/10      File
```

Figure 7.7 Screen resulting from striking the Esc key in COMPPACK

7.2 Memory Variables

In the writing of command files we soon find the need to remember and save some of the values that we manipulate. Up to now, the only way we've been saving values is by storing them as fields in a database. However, not all values that we generate do we want to save in a database. For this reason dBASE has available memory variables which store the intermediate results that occur.

A memory variable may be stored using the **STORE** command. The syntax for **STORE** is: **STORE** *value* **TO** *MemoryVariable* . For example, suppose that we want to use the

COMMAND FILES & MEMORY VARIABLES   233

value of Pi over and over again in doing calculations. We can save Pi as a memory variable as follows:

. **STORE 3.14159 TO PI**

Likewise, we can store a value to the radius of a sphere:

. **STORE 10 TO RADIUS**

Then we can generate the volume of a sphere using a general formula as follows:

. **STORE 4/3*PI*RADIUS^3 TO VOLUME**

When we are ready to display the result, we need only type:

. **? VOLUME**
   4188.79

7.2.1 Use of System Memory Variables

If we want to look at all the memory variables that we have stored in memory, we may do that with the **DISPLAY MEMORY** command. Executing this command, we get the screen shown in Figure 7.8.

. **DISPLAY MEMORY**

At the top of the screen we see the three memory variables that we defined. However, at the bottom of the screen we see the beginning of a list of System Memory Variables. If we strike the Enter key once more, we see the rest of this list (See Figure 7.9).

The system memory variables begin with an underscore: _. These variables presently contain the default settings of all the printer controls. One, in particular, has been costing us a lot of paper. Looking toward the bottom of Figure 7.9, the system

```
        User Memory Variables
VOLUME     pub   F       4188.79  (4188.786666666670000)
RADIUS     pub   N          10    (10.000000000000000)
PI         pub   N           3.14 (3.141590000000000)

  3 out of 500 memvars defined (and 0 array elements)


        User MEMVAR/RTSYM Memory Usage

  2800 bytes used for 1 memvar blocks (max=10)
   850 bytes used for 1 rtsym blocks (max=10)
     0 bytes used for 0 array element memvars
     0 bytes used for 0 memvar character strings

  3650 bytes total

        Print System Memory Variables
_BOX       pub   L   .T.
_TABS      pub   C   ""
_PCOLNO    pub   N          21    (21.000000000000000)
Press any key to continue...
```

Figure 7.8 Executing DISPLAY MEMORY after defining Memory Variables

```
_PLINENO    pub   N           17    (17.000000000000000)
_PAGENO     pub   N            6    (6.000000000000000)
_ALIGNMENT  pub   C   "LEFT"
_INDENT     pub   N            0    (0.000000000000000)
_RMARGIN    pub   N           79    (79.000000000000000)
_LMARGIN    pub   N            0    (0.000000000000000)
_WRAP       pub   L   .F.
_PLOFFSET   pub   N            0    (0.000000000000000)
_PLENGTH    pub   N           66    (66.000000000000000)
_PCOPIES    pub   N            1    (1.000000000000000)
_PSPACING   pub   N            1    (1.000000000000000)
_PEPAGE     pub   N        32767    (32767.000000000000)
_PBPAGE     pub   N            1    (1.000000000000000)
_PECODE     pub   C   ""
_PSCODE     pub   C   ""
_PADVANCE   pub   C   "FORMFEED"
_PWAIT      pub   L   .F.
_PEJECT     pub   C   "BEFORE"
_PQUALITY   pub   L   .F.
_PPITCH     pub   C   "DEFAULT"
_PDRIVER    pub   C   "Generic.PR2"
_PFORM      pub   C   ""

Press any key to continue...
```

Figure 7.9 DISPLAY MEMORY (page 2) showing System Memory Variables

memory variable, **_peject**, is set to "BEFORE". This means that before any printing takes place, a sheet of paper is ejected from the printer. On most printers this is unnecessary as the previous user (or the system if connected into a Local Area Network) has aligned the paper so that it is ready to go. To save us this sheet of paper, we will change the default setting of **_peject** to "NONE".

. _PEJECT = "NONE"

Now a page eject will not take place before the printing begins. Notice that we used a different syntax for the memory assignment. The = assignment operator has the same effect as the **STORE** command. The two commands are interchangeable.

7.2.2 Design of the Print Report Command File: COMPREPO.prg

Now that we have control of the System Memory Variables, we are in a better position to print reports as we'd like them to be. Figure 7.10 shows a command file that will first set a system memory variable, order the database by LASTNAME + FIRSTNAME, then prompt the user to check the printer and finally print the report.

Executing the command: **DO COMPREPO**, we get the screen shown in Figure 7.11.

. **DO COMPREPO**

The output from this program is shown in Listing 4.1.

7.2.3 Design of the Label and Mailmerge Command Files

With a slight change we can easily make the command files, COMPLABL, and COMPMAIL. The only alteration we need to make is in the "FORM" command which actually does the printing.

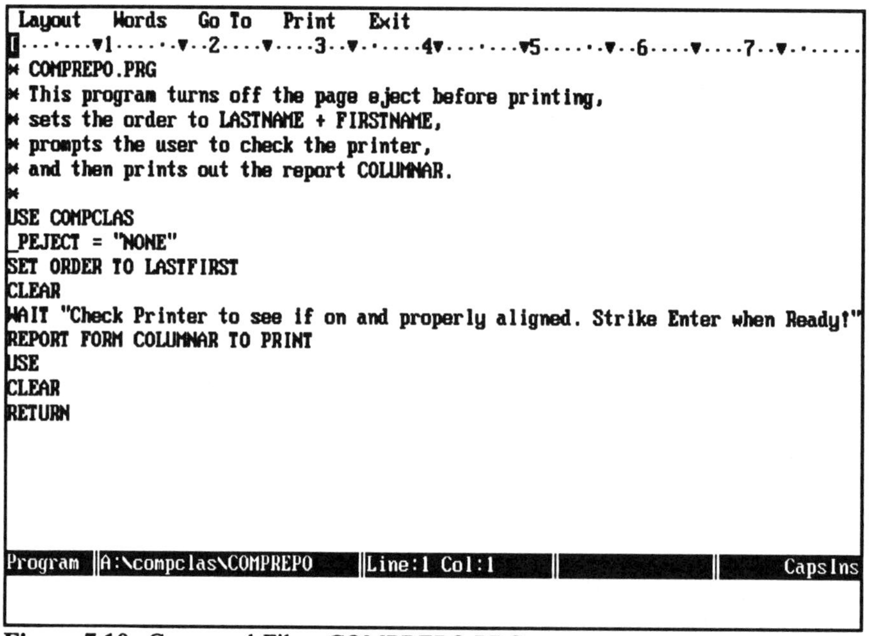

236 COMMAND FILES & MEMORY VARIABLES

```
Layout   Words   Go To   Print   Exit
[]......▼1......▼..2....▼....3..▼.......4▼........▼5......▼..6....▼....7..▼......
* COMPREPO.PRG
* This program turns off the page eject before printing,
* sets the order to LASTNAME + FIRSTNAME,
* prompts the user to check the printer,
* and then prints out the report COLUMNAR.
*
USE COMPCLAS
_PEJECT = "NONE"
SET ORDER TO LASTFIRST
CLEAR
WAIT "Check Printer to see if on and properly aligned. Strike Enter when Ready!"
REPORT FORM COLUMNAR TO PRINT
USE
CLEAR
RETURN


Program  A:\compclas\COMPREPO      Line:1 Col:1                    CapsIns
```

Figure 7.10 Command File: COMPREPO.PRG

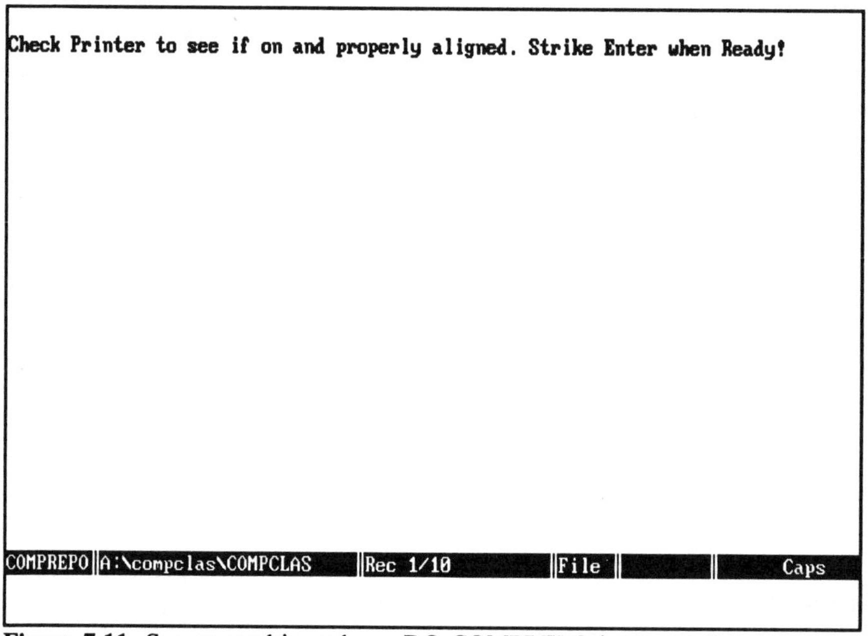

```
Check Printer to see if on and properly aligned. Strike Enter when Ready!




















COMPREPO  A:\compclas\COMPCLAS    Rec 1/10          File               Caps
```

Figure 7.11 Screen resulting when: DO COMPREPO is executed

COMMAND FILES & MEMORY VARIABLES 237

In both cases we want a FOR clause that limits the letters to go only to those people who are doing Term Projects. In the case of COMPLABL.prg, the command becomes:

. **LABEL FORM COMPCLAS FOR TERM_PROJ TO PRINT**

Similarly, for COMPMAIL.prg, the command becomes:

. **REPORT FORM LETTER FOR TERM_PROJ TO PRINT**

The two command files are shown in Figures 7.12 and 7.13 respectively.

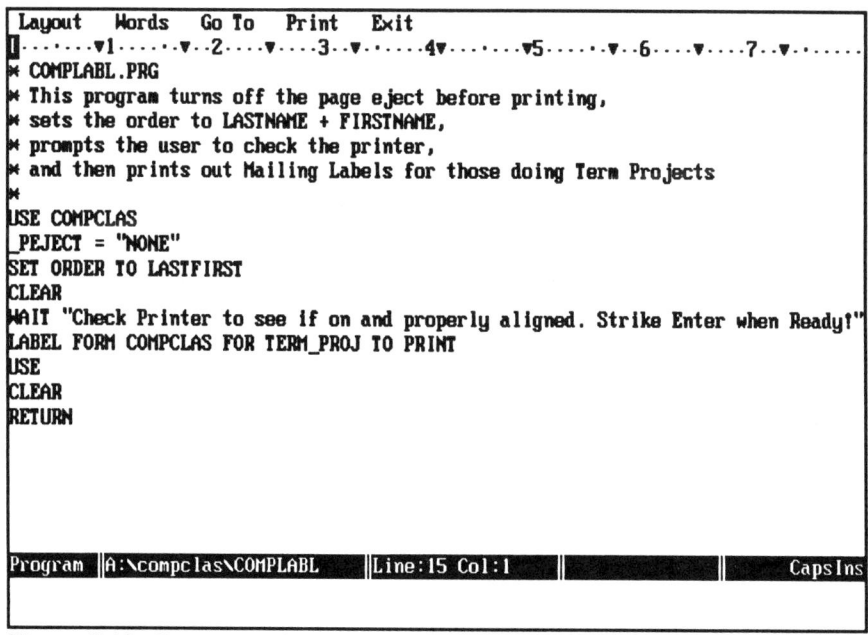

Figure 7.12 Command File: COMPLABL.PRG

238 COMMAND FILES & MEMORY VARIABLES

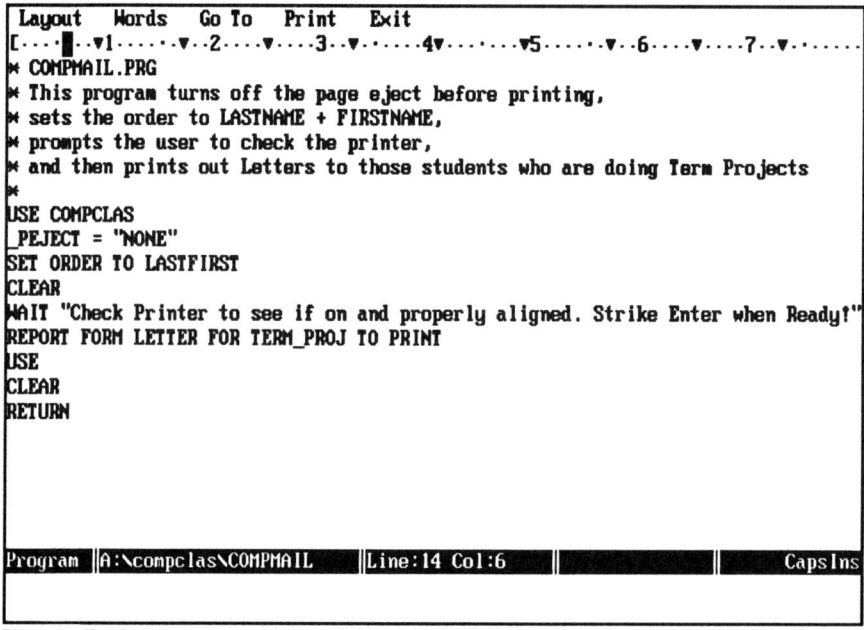

Figure 7.13 Command File: COMPMAIL.PRG

7.3 Design of a Search/Edit Command File

One of the things that we would like to be able to do is to find a particular record quickly and then be able to Edit it. In a database of only ten students, stepping through the database until you find the person you're looking for is no problem. But as the database increases in size, the need for such a procedure becomes quickly apparent.

In order to do a search, we have to be able to input data into the command file. For this reason, we have need of some keyboard input and screen output instructions.

7.3.1 The @ and SAY Display Instructions

The WAIT instruction did indeed display a message on the screen. However, we had little control over where the message was placed on the screen. This problem is rectified by the powerful pair

COMMAND FILES & MEMORY VARIABLES

of instructions, @ and **SAY**. The @ instruction tells dBASE where to move the cursor on the screen. The syntax for the @ instruction is: *@ RowNumber,ColumnNumber* .

The **SAY** command immediately follows the @ command and displays whatever character string follows it just as the WAIT command does. Unlike the WAIT command, it does not pause for a response.

Listing 7.1 shows a short command file which demonstrates how these two instructions work together. The topmost row on the screen is row 0, while the bottommost row is row 24 (in a 25 row screen). The leftmost column on the screen is column 0 while the rightmost column is column 79 (in an 80 column screen). With this in mind, Figure 7.14 shows what this command file displays on the screen.

```
* ATSAYDEM.PRG
* This program demonstrates the use of the
* @ and SAY commands
*
SET STATUS OFF
CLEAR
@  0,0   SAY "Upper Left Hand Corner"
@  0,57  SAY "Upper Right Hand Corner"
@ 12,37  SAY "Middle"
@ 24,0   SAY "Lower Left Hand Corner"
@ 24,57  SAY "Lower Right Hand Corner"
@  1,0
WAIT [ ]
SET STATUS ON
RETURN
```

Listing 7.1 ATSAYDEM.PRG demonstrates @ and SAY commands

As you can see, the @ **0,0** placed the cursor in the upper left hand corner of the screen so that the words, "Upper Left Hand Corner" would appear starting at that location. Likewise, the @ **0,57** placed the cursor 23 characters short of the upper right hand corner of the screen so that the 23 character string, "Upper Right Hand Corner" would fit on row 0 without running off the screen. In the same way, the @ **24,57** placed the cursor 23 characters shy of the bottom right so that the words, "Lower Right Hand Corner" would appear as shown. Finally, the @ **12,37** placed the cursor right smack dab in the middle of the screen so that the word "Middle" would be there.

The purpose of the @ **1,0** command, by itself, is to move the cursor back up to line 1 and clear that particular line. In this way the **WAIT ""** instruction, which holds everything on the screen until a key is struck, doesn't cause the screen to scroll upwards. We turn the Status off at the beginning so we can start with a pure blank screen.

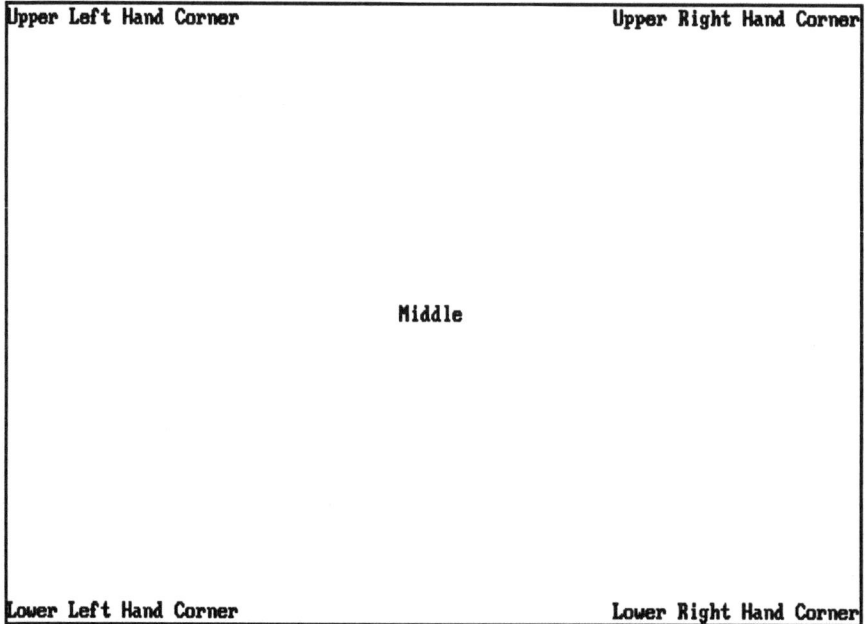

Figure 7.14 Screen resulting from executing: DO ATSAYDEM

7.3.2 The GET and READ Instructions

Just as the **SAY** command causes a message or a variable to be output to the screen, the **GET** command causes whatever is entered from the keyboard to be displayed on the screen. We have already, unknowingly, used the **GET** command when we created the format file: COMPCLAS.FMT. After we generated the screen that we liked with the screen generator, dBASE4 translated that screen into COMPCLAS.FMT. Every place that we had placed a field on the screen, that place was translated into a **GET** instruction.

If we do a MODIFY COMMAND on the format file, COMPCLAS.FMT, we'll see the @, **SAY** and **GET** statements that do the job of giving us our customized screens. In Figure 7.15, looking at lines 32-51 (shown on the screen), we see the commands that gave us the screen shown in Figure 7.4. Everything that is in reverse video, in Figure 7.4, is there because of a **GET** statement. All the field labels, shown in normal video, are there by virtue of the **SAY** statements. One may think of **SAY** statements as output commands and **GET** statements as input commands.

The **PICTURE** clause controls the formatting of the display of the variable in the **GET** command. In this case the **PICTURE** clause is unnecessary since the formatting specified by the **PICTURE** clause is the default width of the field variables to begin with. Hence, this format file would work just as well without the **PICTURE** clauses. The **WINDOW** clause, on the bottom line of Figure 7.15, is what created the window for the memo field in Figure 7.4. These clauses will be discussed in more detail in subsequent chapters.

The function of the **READ** command is to transfer all the data stored on the screen by the **GET** instructions into either field or memory variables. Although the **READ** command is not necessary in a format file, it is necessary in a command or .PRG file. Under default conditions, the contents of up to 128 **GET** instructions

242 COMMAND FILES & MEMORY VARIABLES

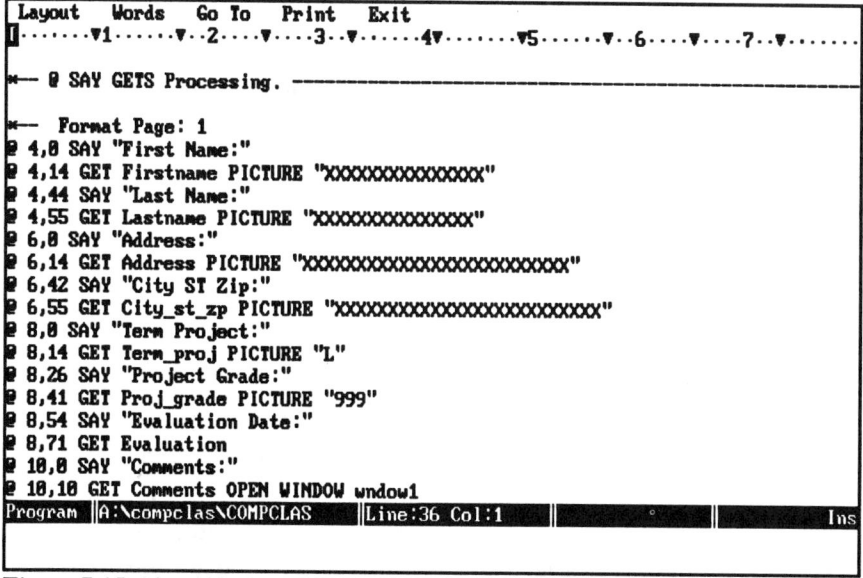

Figure 7.15 Lines 32-51 of COMPCLAS.FMT showing use of @, SAY and GET commands

can be entered by means of one **READ** instruction. As a result, the **READ** instruction always comes at the end of a list of **GET** instructions.

We now have the tools to do our edit command file, COMPEDIT.

7.3.3 The Design of COMPEDIT.PRG

Our edit command file will try to locate an individual in the **COMPCLAS** database. If the search is successful, the command file will announce its successful location and display it in EDIT mode. If it is not successful, then it will announce its failure to find the record and will display the last record in the database in EDIT mode.

Since our database is a short one, the **LOCATE** command will be used rather than the **FIND** (or **SEEK**) command. The command file is shown in Figure 7.16.

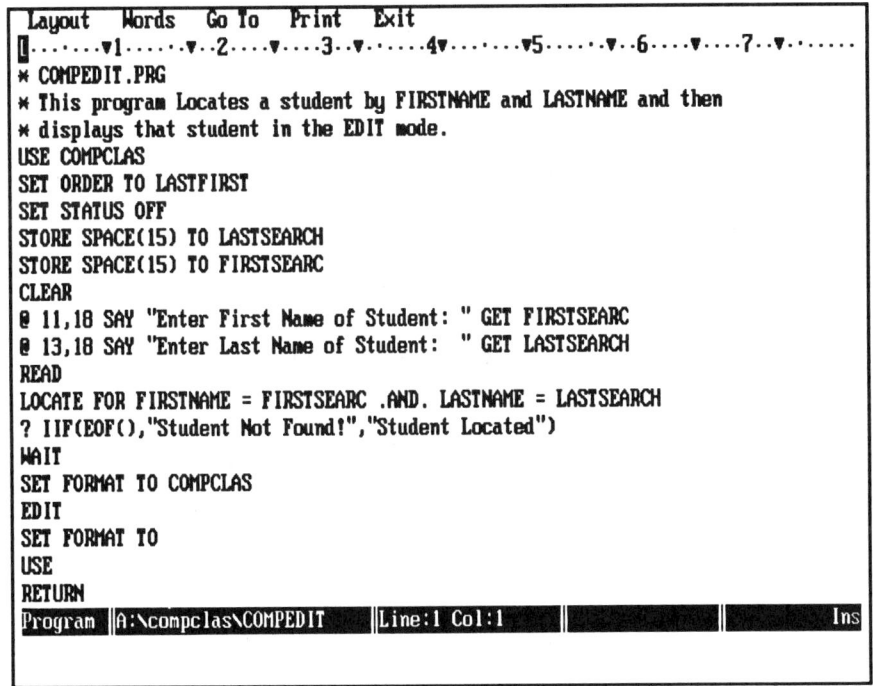

Figure 7.16 First pass at COMPEDIT.prg

We start by saving 15 blank spaces to two memory variables: **LASTSEARCH**, and **FIRSTSEARC** . This is done by means of the **SPACE()** function. This allows us to type names into the same number of spaces that exist in the width of the LASTNAME and FIRSTNAME fields. The next thing we do, after clearing the screen, is to make use of the @, **SAY** and the **GET** commands. By choosing rows 11 and 13, in which to put the prompts for first name and last name, we center the questions vertically in the middle of the screen. By starting in column 18, we center the questions horizontally. Notice that we put the **GET** commands immediately after the **SAY** command is executed, rather than using a separate @ command.

The sequence is terminated with the **READ** command. This causes whatever has been entered on the screen to be actually input into our two new variables: **FIRSTSEARC** and **LASTSEARCH**.

Now **FIRSTSEARC** and **LASTSEARCH** represent the first and last names of a student for whom we are searching. **FIRSTNAME** and **LASTNAME** represent the fields of **COMPCLAS** in which we are searching for those names. Hopefully, in one of the records in our database, a match will occur between **FIRSTNAME** and **FIRSTSEARC** and also between **LASTNAME** and **LASTSEARCH**. This is the function of our **LOCATE** command. It's job is to **LOCATE** that match.

Now there are two possibilities: 1) The record was not found; 2) The record was found. If the record was not found, then that means that the **LOCATE** instruction has searched through the database and is now at the end of the database File. If we're at the end of the file, this means that the logical function, **EOF()**, is true. On the other hand, if a match was found, then the **LOCATE** instruction has us sitting at that particular record and we are *not* at the end of the file. This means that the logical function, **EOF()**, would now be false.

Using the **IIF()** function that we utilized in Chapter 3, we can print out whether or not the record was located based on whether or not the **EOF()** is true or false. If the **EOF()** is true, it means that the record was not found, which is what the **IIF()** function will print out. If the **EOF()** is false, then the record was indeed located and the last argument of the **IIF()** function is what will be printed out.

Finally, we tack on a **WAIT** command to hold the result on the screen so that we may examine it. Executing our command file:

. **DO COMPEDIT**

we get the screen shown in Figure 7.17. If we type in a name we know to be in the file, Jeremy Witherspoon, then we get the result shown at the bottom of the screen[25]. Striking any key as indicated, we get the edit of the desired record as seen in Figure 7.18.

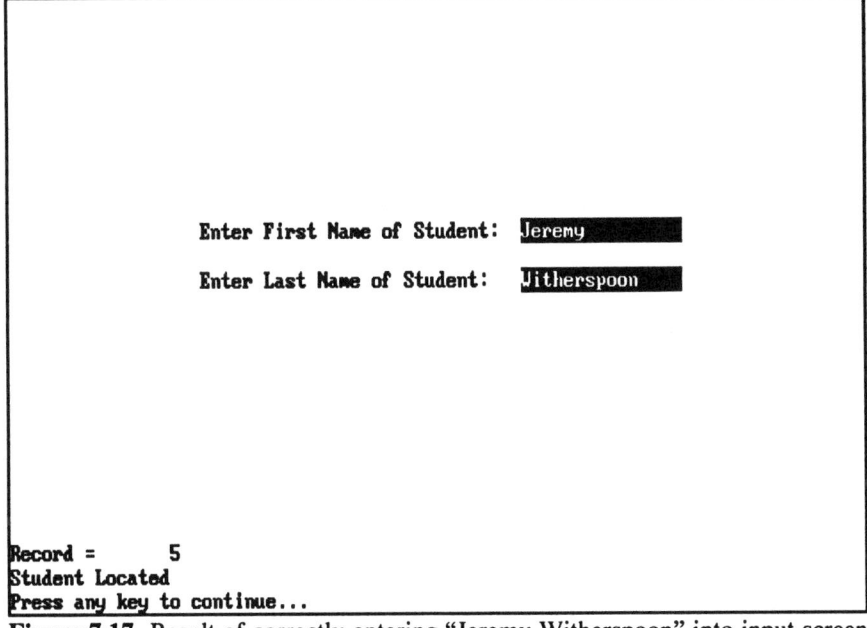

Figure 7.17 Result of correctly entering "Jeremy Witherspoon" into input screen of COMPEDIT.prg

There are two problems with **COMPEDIT** as it is now written. The first problem is that we have to write the name exactly as it appears in the database, letter for letter, case for case (the first letter must be upper case, all succeeding letters must be lower case). For example, in Figure 7.19 we type in JEREMY WITHERSPOON, all in upper case letters, and the result of the search is shown below.

The second problem is that we can't search on only **LASTNAME** or only **FIRSTNAME**. We have to remember both

---

[25]Note the prompt at the bottom of Figure 7.17, "Press any key to continue...". This is the default prompt of the WAIT command. This prompt can be eliminated by typing: WAIT "" .

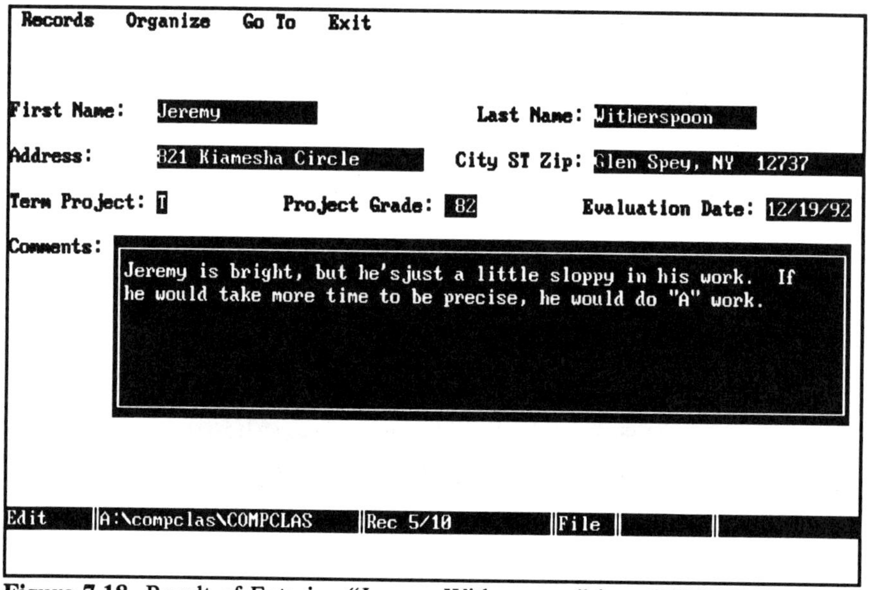

Figure 7.18 Result of Entering "Jeremy Witherspoon" into COMPEDIT

names and type them in. Figure 7.20 shows what happens when we type in just the first name.

These two problems can be easily remedied with the use of two functions. To make our command file case blind (i.e. so that it will ignore whether we type in upper or lower case), we can use the **UPPER()** function. We must use this on both the field names, **FIRSTNAME** and **LASTNAME**, as well as on our memory variables, **FIRSTSEARC** and **LASTSEARCH**. Since everything gets transposed into upper case, we are always comparing upper case names with upper case names.

The second problem is arrested by trimming off all trailing blanks in the name memory variables. This is done with the **TRIM()** function. Since the **LOCATE** command only compares for as many characters as exist in the variable on the right hand side of the relation, if we leave the **LASTSEARCH** memory variable entirely blank, then the **LOCATE** instruction will do no comparison at all for the **LASTNAME**. Since the **TRIM(LASTSEARCH)** will have zero width, there is nothing to compare. Listing 7.2 shows the

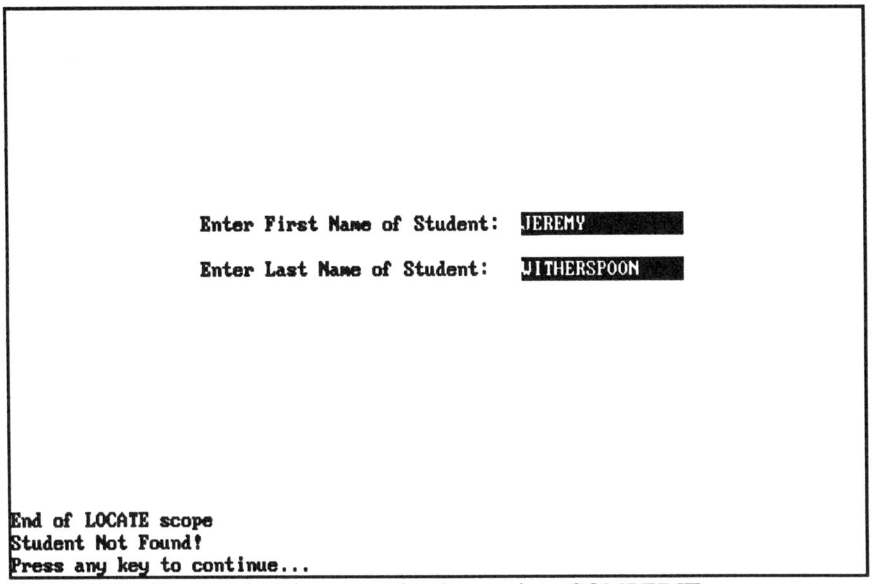

```
                    Enter First Name of Student:  JEREMY
                    Enter Last Name of Student:   WITHERSPOON




End of LOCATE scope
Student Not Found!
Press any key to continue...
```
Figure 7.19 Result of typing name in all caps into COMPEDIT.prg

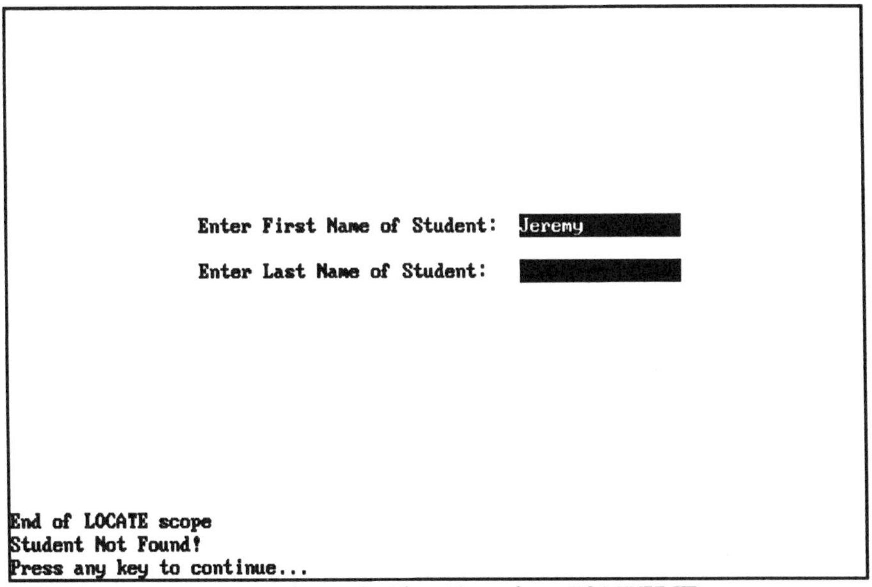

```
                    Enter First Name of Student:  Jeremy
                    Enter Last Name of Student:   




End of LOCATE scope
Student Not Found!
Press any key to continue...
```
Figure 7.20 Result of typing only First Name into COMPEDIT.prg

final result for **COMPEDIT.prg** with our two functions in place. (Note the use of the semicolon, **;** , to continue the LOCATE instruction onto the next line.) This listing is produced by means of redirecting the **TYPE** *Filename* **TO PRINT** command, as follows:

. **TYPE COMPEDIT.PRG TO PRINT**

```
* COMPEDIT.PRG
* This program Locates a student by
* FIRSTNAME and LASTNAME and
* then displays that student in the EDIT
* mode.
USE COMPCLAS
SET ORDER TO LASTFIRST
SET STATUS OFF
STORE SPACE(15) TO LASTSEARCH
STORE SPACE(15) TO FIRSTSEARC
CLEAR
@ 11,18 SAY "Enter First Name of Student: ";
  GET FIRSTSEARC
@ 13,18 SAY "Enter Last Name of Student:  ";
  GET LASTSEARCH
READ
LOCATE FOR UPPER(FIRSTNAME) = TRIM(UPPER(FIRSTSEARC));
  .AND. UPPER(LASTNAME) = TRIM(UPPER(LASTSEARCH))
? IIF(EOF(),"Student Not Found!","Student Located")
WAIT
SET FORMAT TO COMPCLAS
EDIT
SET FORMAT TO
USE
RETURN
```

Listing 7.2 Final Version of COMPEDIT.prg using UPPER() and TRIM()

COMMAND FILES & MEMORY VARIABLES 249

As an added benefit of the **TRIM()** function, we need not even type in an entire First Name into **FIRSTSEARC** in order for there to be a match. The **LOCATE** instruction will only match for as many letters as we do type in. Figure 7.21 shows what results when we type in the first three letters of Jeremy's first name in the wrong case.

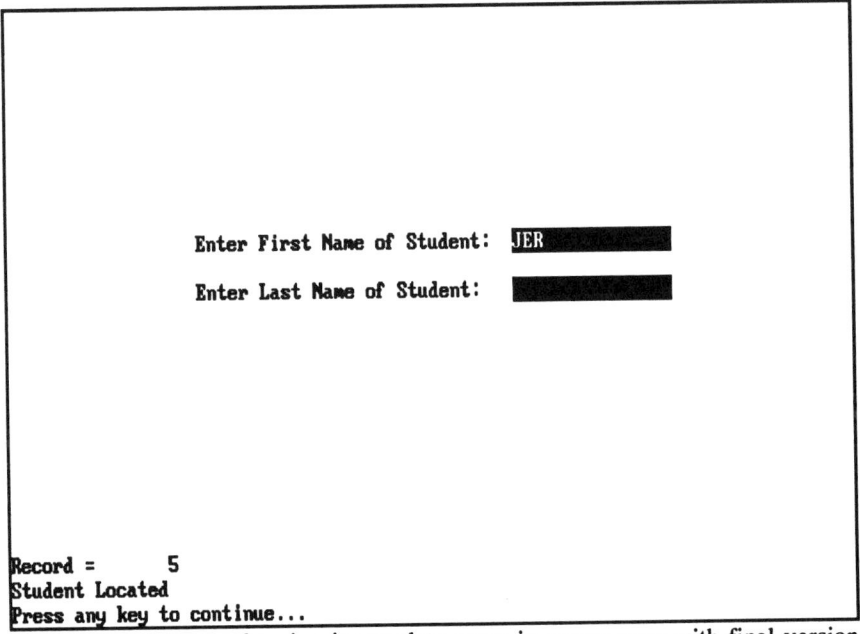

Figure 7.21 Result of typing incomplete name in wrong case with final version of COMPEDIT.prg

You may wonder why we went to all this trouble to write this command file when it is so easy to use the **LOCATE** instruction at the dot prompt. The answer will become apparent in the next section, when we put it all together into a menu driven system.

7.4 Design of a Menu Driving Command File

We have just created six command files which can do the work of the COMPCLAS system. The command files are given in Table 7.1.

Table 7.1 List of all the COMPCLAS Command Files

PROGRAM	USE
COMPADD.PRG	Appends new records
COMPEDIT.PRG	Searches and Edits records
COMPPACK.PRG	Eliminates deleted records
COMPREPO.PRG	Prints columnar report
COMPMAIL.PRG	Prints out Mailmerge letter
COMPLABL.PRG	Prints out mailing labels

The purpose of these command files is to make our life simpler so that we will not have to repeat all the commands that go into each of the command files, nor even have to remember what the commands are. However, now we have a new problem, we have to remember the names of the six command files listed in Table 7.1. What use are these programs to us if we can't remember what they are called? Though remembering names like EDIT, LOCATE, REPORT FORM, etc. is bad enough, remembering arcane names like COMPPACK and COMPLABL can be even worse.

So to make life easier on us, we are going to create a menu command file which will do all the remembering for us. In this way all we will have to do is to remember the name of *one* command file. We will call this command file: COMPMENU. A listing of COMPMENU.prg is shown in Listing 7.3. The screen produced when COMPMENU is executed is shown in Figure 7.22.

To create this menu, we first turn off the status bar and CLEAR the screen so that all that appears on the screen will be the menu. Next we define the menu using the **DEFINE MENU** command. We will call our menu "Main". We could have called it anything, but since this is the main menu for COMPCLAS, the name "Main" seemed fitting.

COMMAND FILES & MEMORY VARIABLES 251

The **MESSAGE** clause puts a message on the bottom of the screen which we will use for a title to our menu, "COMPUTER CLASS SYSTEM". The syntax of this instruction is: **DEFINE MENU** *MenuName* **MESSAGE** *MessageText* .

Our next step is to define each of the pads that appear on the screen of Figure 7.22. As there are seven pads arranged in vertical order, we will need seven **DEFINE PAD** instructions. Each of the pads must have a name, so we have given them the names of what we do in each of the pads: Add, Edit, Pack, Report, Letter, Labels, and Exit. In addition, we define the prompts that appear on the screen of Figure 7.22 in this instruction. Finally we define the row and column number where we want the pad to begin. In order to center the pads, we start the pads in column 33, and at row 6 skipping every other row.

The next thing that we must do is to define what action will be taken when the highlighted pad is selected by striking the Enter key. The **ON SELECTION PAD** command is where we tell dBASE which of our command files to run for us. The syntax of

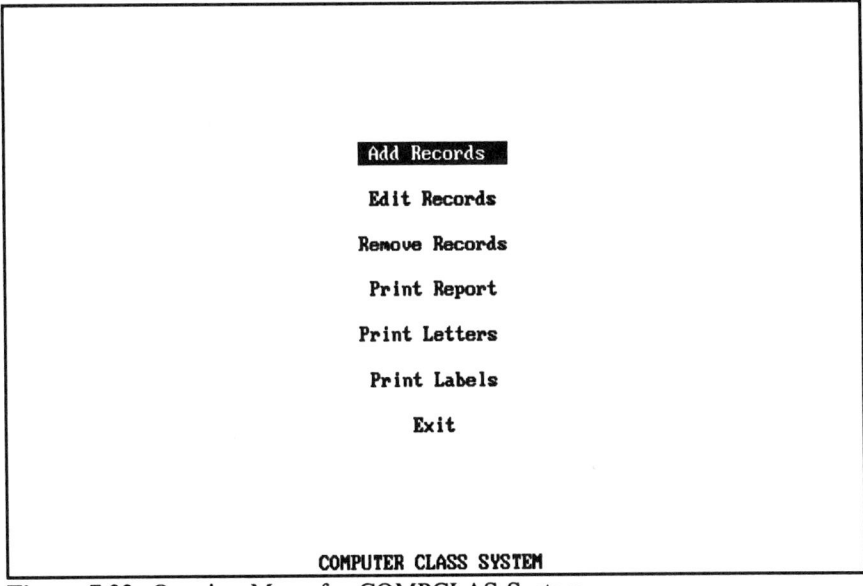

Figure 7.22 Opening Menu for COMPCLAS System

```
* COMPMENU.PRG
* This defines the Main menu for COMPCLAS SYSTEM
*
SET STATUS OFF
CLEAR

DEFINE MENU Main MESSAGE "COMPUTER CLASS SYSTEM"

DEFINE PAD Add    OF Main PROMPT  " Add Records  " AT  6,33
DEFINE PAD Edit   OF Main PROMPT  " Edit Records " AT  8,33
DEFINE PAD Pack   OF Main PROMPT  "Remove Records" AT 10,33
DEFINE PAD Report OF Main PROMPT  " Print Report " AT 12,33
DEFINE PAD Letter OF Main PROMPT  "Print Letters " AT 14,33
DEFINE PAD Labels OF Main PROMPT  " Print Labels " AT 16,33
DEFINE PAD Exit   OF Main PROMPT  "     Exit     " AT 18,33

* Definition of Action taken by each Pad when selected

ON SELECTION PAD Add    OF Main Do COMPADD
ON SELECTION PAD Edit   OF Main Do COMPEDIT
ON SELECTION PAD Pack   OF Main Do COMPPACK
ON SELECTION PAD Report OF Main Do COMPREPO
ON SELECTION PAD Letter OF Main Do COMPMAIL
ON SELECTION PAD Labels OF Main DO COMPLABL
ON SELECTION PAD Exit   OF Main DEACTIVATE MENU

ACTIVATE MENU MAIN

SET STATUS ON
RETURN
```

Listing 7.3 The Menu Driver for the COMPCLAS System: COMPMENU.prg

this instruction is: **ON SELECTION PAD** *PadName* **OF** *MenuName ActionToTake* . Each of our command files is assigned to a particular **ON SELECTION PAD** instruction. The last **ON SELECTION PAD EXIT** instruction defines the action to take if we use "Exit". As you can see, the action that we want taken is given in the command: **DEACTIVATE MENU.**

Following the DEFINE statements and the ON SELECTION PAD statements we activate the menu with the command: **ACTIVATE** *MenuName*, where in our case the menu name is "Main". That completes our menu definition.

When we Exit from the menu by using the down arrows to select the pad labeled "Exit" (see Figure 7.23), we execute the

DEACTIVATE MENU command. This causes program execution to jump to the instructions immediately following the **MAIN** instruction. Here we turn the Status Bar back on and then **RETURN** from our command file. The **RETURN** command causes us to return back to whatever called our command file. Since COMPMENU is the only command file that will actually be executed from the dot prompt, **RETURN** will simply return us to the dot prompt.

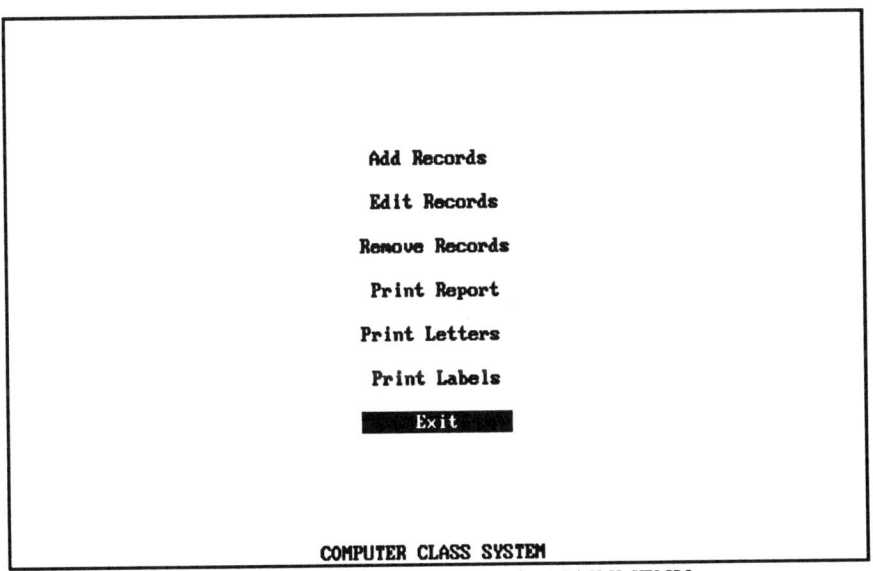

Figure 7.23 Selecting the "Exit" menu option in MAINMENU.prg

Our COMPCLAS system will now be executed by simply typing:

. DO COMPMENU

By using the up and down arrow keys[26], we may choose our menu option and execute it. Each time one of our command files is executed, the operation returns to the main menu of COMPMENU.

---

[26]In an earlier dBASE IV version, 1.0, the left and right arrow keys are the only ones that function to move the cursor around the pads. Use the right arrow key to move down a pad, the left arrow key to ascend a pad.

The beauty of our COMPCLAS system is that the user does not even have to know anything about dBASE IV in order to use it. Hence a user, who does not know dBASE (nor wants to know), can easily use a piece of software written in the dBASE IV language. In fact, they don't even have to deal with the dot prompt. All that needs to be typed at the DOS prompt is:

A:\COMPCLAS> **DBASE COMPMENU**

This takes us right into the COMPCLAS system avoiding even having to use the command: DO COMPMENU. If you were to replace the **RETURN** at the end of Listing 7.3 with a QUIT command, then the user would not have to deal with any dBASE commands whatsoever.

As you can see, without having much programming experience at all, one can put together a customized application fairly easily. In this way others, who do not know dBASE, can do these applications. As we shall see in succeeding chapters, we can make these systems as powerful and as user friendly as we would like.

7.5 Summary

In this chapter we have been introduced to the command file as a simple sequence of commands. We have seen the power of being able to contain a series of complicated steps all in one file which we execute with a **DO** *CommandFile* instruction. We learned to use the Command File Editor to make these files.

Then we introduced both the user defined, as well as the system memory variables, and saw their applicability to command files. We introduced the @, SAY, GET, READ family of input/output instructions.

Armed with these tools we wrote six command files to run the Computer Class System. We then put all these programs together by means of a menu driving command file. In this way we were able to generate a customized menu driven system that would do all the functions that we had developed for the COMPCLAS system. This system could, in turn, be operated by one who knew virtually nothing about dBASE.

We have now covered sufficient material on sequential command files that the reader should be able to create systems that do most of the simple file handling that occurs in most cases. The use of the menu program allows one to keep the system orderly and manageable.

In virtually every database that I use at all repeatedly, I create around it such a menu driven system. In this way I am continually reminded of what programs I have written and what my options are. In cases where I do not write such menu driven systems, my programs usually fall into disuse and are soon forgotten. Many times I have had to "reinvent the wheel" because I didn't keep track of the command files that I had already composed.

The reader is now in a good position to create simple sequential menu driven systems of his or her own with no further instruction. If, however, there is a desire to learn how to program in dBASE, to use selection and iteration, and create more powerful programs, then the reader is invited to read on.

7.6 Review

In Chapter 7 we have introduced the following commands:

>*@ RowNumber,ColumnNumber*
>**ACTIVATE MENU** *MenuName*
>**CLEAR**
>**DEACTIVATE MENU**
>**DEFINE MENU...**
>**DEFINE PAD...**
>**DISPLAY MEMORY**

> **GET**
> **MODIFY COMMAND** *FileName*
> **ON SELECTION PAD...**
> **READ**
> **RETURN**
> **SAY** *TextString*
> **STORE** *Value* **TO** *MemoryVariable*
> **TYPE** *Filename* **TO PRINT**
> **WAIT** *TextString*

Add these instructions to your glossary of dBASE commands. In addition we have introduced the following functions:

> **EOF()**
> **SPACE()**
> **TRIM()**
> **UPPER()**

These should be added to your glossary of dBASE functions.

7.7 Laboratory Work

Follow all the steps outlined in this chapter, creating the menu program, **COMPMENU.prg**, and all the command files that it drives: **COMPADD.prg, COMPEDIT.prg, COMPPACK.prg, COMPREPO.prg, COMPLABL.prg,** and **COMPMAIL.prg**. Try running the system, and make sure that all the modules work properly.

7.8 Exercises

1. Write a menu program for MAILIST, called MAILMENU.prg that should create the following menu screen:

    ```
                    Append Records

                    Edit Records

                    Pack Records

                   Print Mailing List

                 Print General Letter

                 Print Mailing Labels

                         Quit

                 MAILING LIST SYSTEM
    ```

    Make a hard copy of the printout of the program, and hand it in. (Note: a printout of MAILMENU.prg may be produced by executing the instruction: **TYPE MAILMENU.PRG TO PRINT**)

2. Create each of the sub-programs that execute append, edit, pack, print list, print letter and print labels. Call these sub-programs: MAILADD, MAILEDIT, MAILPACK, MAILREPO, MAILETTR and MAILABEL. These programs should look very similar to the ones we've done for COMPCLAS. (Be careful of the width of the memory variables in Mailedit.) Hand in hard copies of the programs.

7.9 Term Project

As a term project select some topic for which you would like to create a system. It can be something to do with your work, a hobby, or something for you personally. Here are just a few of the topics that past students have picked for their term projects.

Airline Reservations
Archives
Articulation Agreements
Attendance Monitoring in
 High School
Automobile Parts Inventory
Booking of Conference
 Rooms
Bottle Labeling
Business Travel Accounting
Certificate
Check Reconciliation
Compliance List for State
Course Listings
Course Grades
Door Key Inventory
Eligibility List for
 Probation
Employee Vital Statistics
Fire Department Course
 Currency
Football Teams' Statistics
Golf Handicap
 Computation
Health Department
 Violation Listings
Hookup, Disconnect &
 Repair List for Cable TV

Hotel Room Status
Hotel Arrival & Departures
Job Tracking
Library
Livery Driver Schedules
Manpower Allocation
Menus for Catering
 Organization
Milk Production
Payroll
Personnel
Physician Patient
 Accounting
Project Listings
Real Estate
Recipes
Snow Telephone Chain for
 a High School
Student Union List
Student Advisees
Teacher Workload
Transportation Bookings
Uniform Ordering
Vehicle Schedules
Video Rental
Volunteer Ambulance
 Corps.
Voter Registration

Most of these topics are ones for which a modest file handling system can be easily designed and implemented during the remainder of the semester. Obviously, some of these topics, such as Airlines Reservations, if done as a full blown system could take years of work to do. This list is by no means exhaustive of the possibilities which are literally endless. In fact, the student is encouraged to come up with a project not on the list. In any case the topic should be one that the student finds engaging, stimulating, and do-able in the remaining time allotted to the course.

CHAPTER 8

SELECTION

8.0 Contents of Chapter 8

The Flow Chart is Introduced as a Didactic tool.

The three basic programming structures are presented.

Binary Selection using IF—ELSE—ENDIF is presented. COM_EDIT.PRG demonstrates its use.

Multiple Selection using DO CASE structure is presented. COM_BROW.PRG demonstrates its use.

INPUT, ACCEPT, and WAIT data entry instructions are introduced.

SAVE, RESTORE, and RELEASE commands are introduced.

The REPLACE command is presented. COMUPDAT.PRG demonstrates use of INPUT, ACCEPT, WAIT and REPLACE.

262   SELECTION

8.1   Structured Programming

Up to this point all we have written are simple sequential command files. Simple sequences of commands are the most elementary of the programming structures. As we have seen, a complete system can be written using this structure alone. Figure 8.1 shows a graphical representation of the simple sequence.

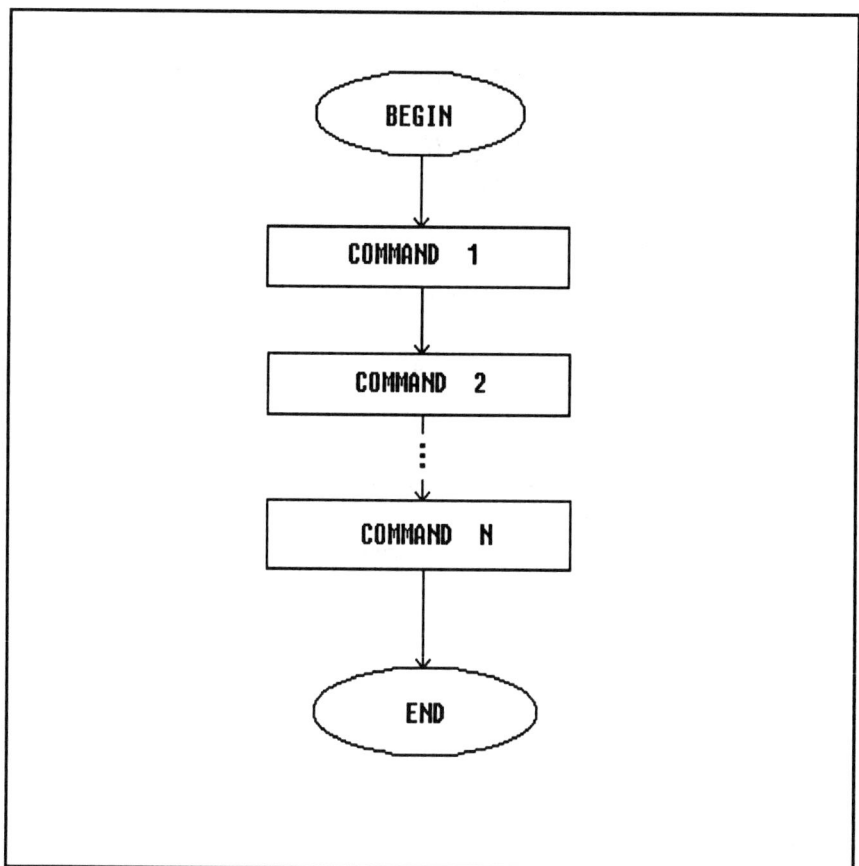

Figure 8.1 The Simple Sequence Programming Structure

SELECTION

In structured programming there are three and only three structures that are used. By now we are very familiar with the simple sequence. The second structure is the selection structure. This structure is shown in Figure 8.2 and is the topic of this chapter.

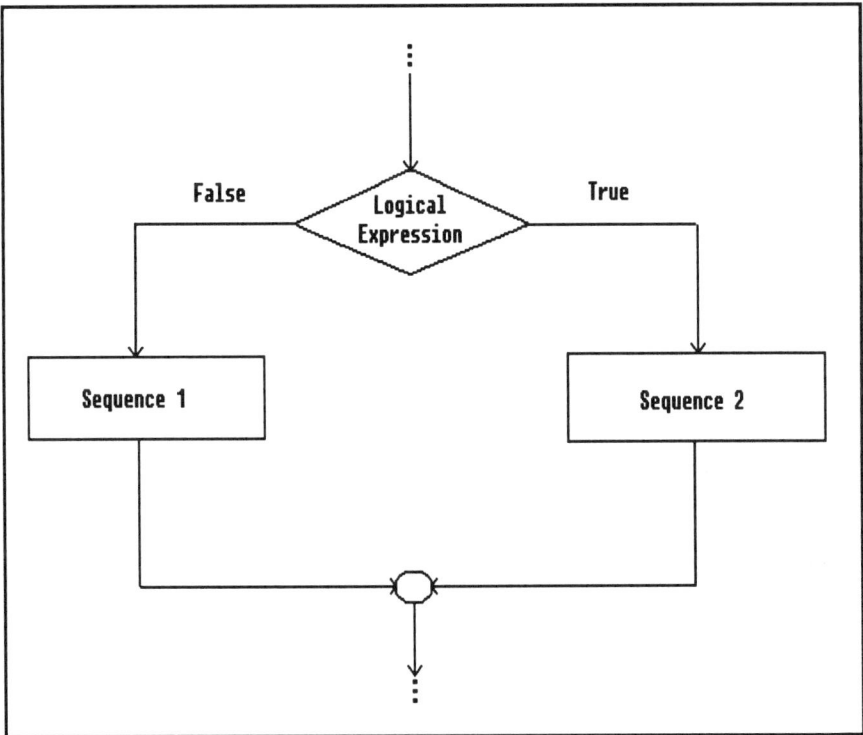

Figure 8.2 The Binary Selection Programming Structure

The third and final structure that is used in structured programming is Iteration or "The Loop". This structure is shown in Figure 8.3 and will be the topic of Chapter 9. It is what allows us to repeat sequences of commands over and over again in a program.

I cannot emphasize enough the fact that if you learn these three structures well, you will know essentially everything there is to know about structured programming. The rest is simply detail. However, we will spend the rest of this book elaborating on this detail. For now, let us concentrate on learning these structures, then everything else will fall into place.

264   SELECTION

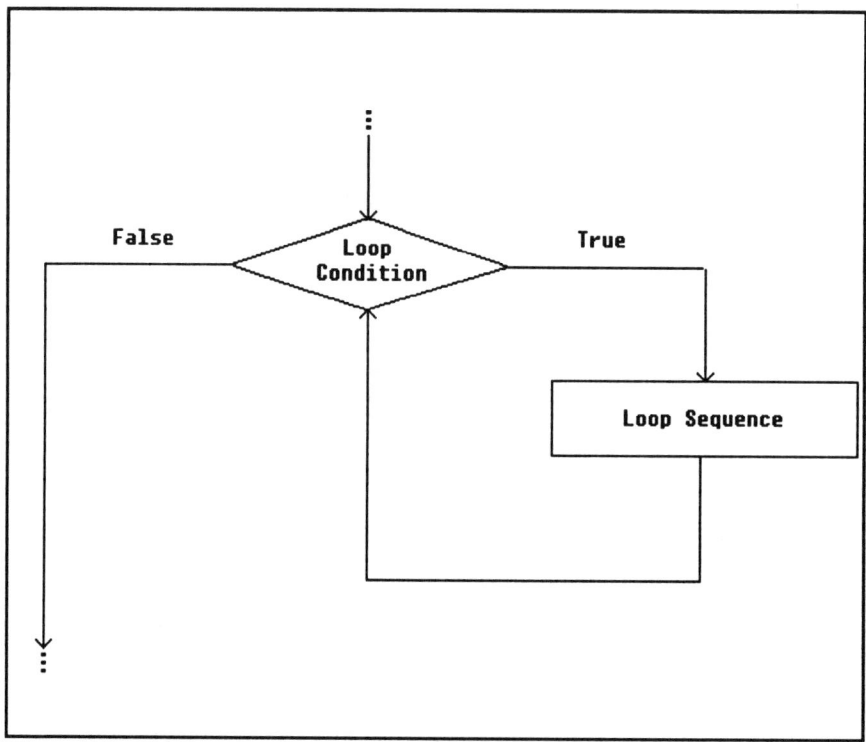

Figure 8.3 The Iteration Programming Structure—The Loop

8.2   Flow Charts

The diagrams shown in Figures 8.1—8.3 are referred to as Flow Diagrams or Flow Charts. They show the flow of the program as the command sequence starts at the beginning and goes on to the end of the program.

A flow diagram always begins and ends with an oval symbol as shown in Figure 8.1. These are referred to as terminators.

A single command or even a sequence of commands is shown as a rectangle and is referred to as a process. For example, all of the commands in Figure 8.1: 1, 2, ..., N could be bunched together into a single box and be referred to as Process 1.

SELECTION

In Figure 8.2 and 8.3 we introduce a decision making symbol, the diamond shaped element, which is used in selection as well as loops. If the logical expression contained in the decision symbol is true, then we execute the instructions in one path; if the logical expression is false, then we proceed on the other path.

The round circle is referred to as a connector to which the operation returns when the selection process is through. This is the essential part of selection and a requirement of structured programming. After the selection, all the operations must merge once again at one and only one point. If there is a branch, but no merger afterwards, then the primary rule of structured programming has been violated. Fortunately, dBASE is designed to operate in a structured way, so we won't have to worry about this, at least for a while.

The symbol for input and output is shown in Figure 8.4. We see that a typical program consists of entering some data, processing it, and then outputting the results.

The group of symbols contained in Figures 8.1—8.4 is referred to as the ANSI (American National Standards Institute) flow chart symbols.

8.3   Binary Selection

The simplest type of selection is binary selection where we are testing to see if a logical expression is true or not.

For example, suppose we have a logical memory variable called **SUNNYDAY** . If **SUNNYDAY** is true, then we may go and execute the command file known as **PICNIC** , if it is not true, then we won't, but rather we'll proceed immediately to what we would have done after the picnic. This is called the binary selection, single process structure. The flow chart of this decision making process is shown in Figure 8.5.

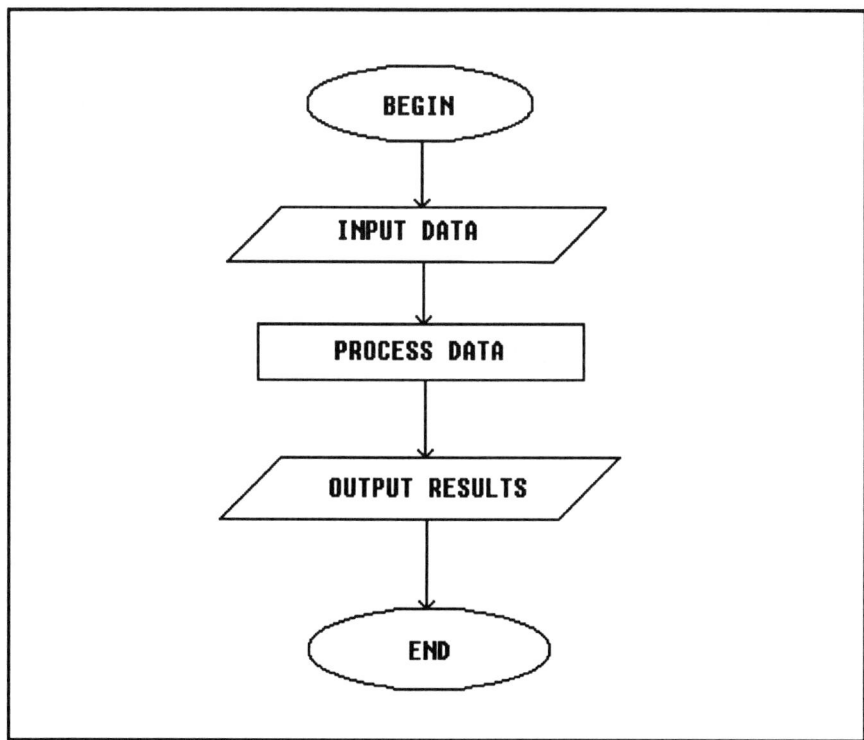

Figure 8.4 Standard Program Structure

The dBASE command that executes this decision making process is called: **IF—ENDIF**. The syntax of the instruction is:

IF *LogicalExpression*
  Process
ENDIF

where Process can be any sequence of commands. For our example, the **IF** statement would be:

IF SUNNYDAY
  DO PICNIC
ENDIF

We can also have a binary selection, dual process structure which allows an either/or decision making process. For example, if it is not a **SUNNYDAY**, we might have the alternative of going to

SELECTION

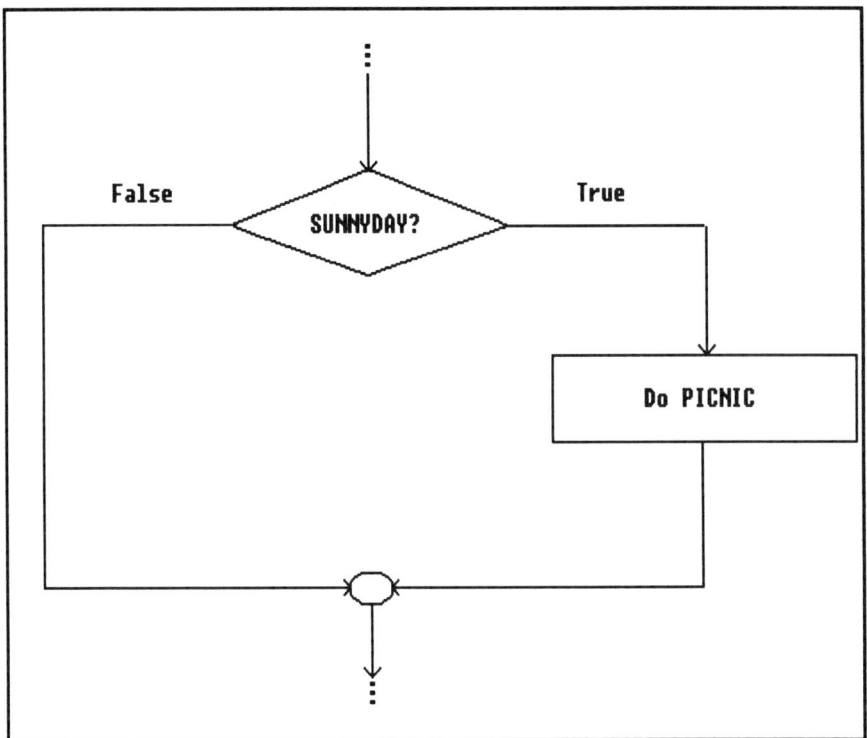

Figure 8.5 Binary Selection—Single Process

a movie instead. This example is shown in Figure 8.6. The syntax for the **IF—ELSE—ENDIF** instruction is:

IF *LogicalExpression*
  Process1
ELSE
  Process2
ENDIF

In our example the **IF** statement would be:

IF SUNNYDAY
  DO PICNIC
ELSE
  DO MOVIE
ENDIF

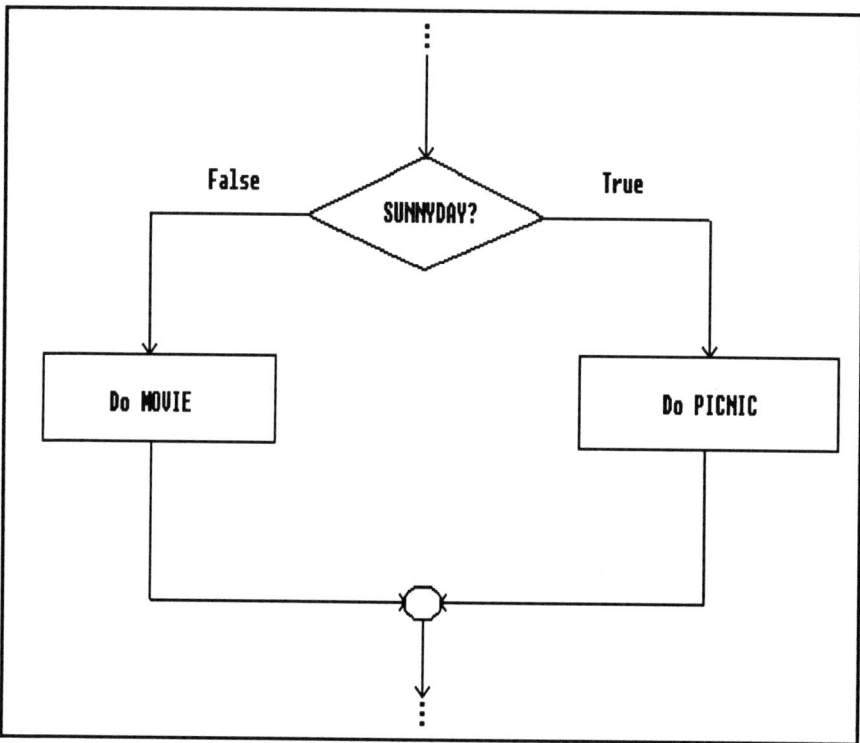

Figure 8.6 Binary Selection—Dual Process

The syntax does not require that we indent the processes from the **IF—ELSE—ENDIF**. However, the indentations do underscore the fact that these are the two distinct processes which are contained in our flow diagram. Indenting, in this way, reduces the likelihood of error and makes the program far more readable. For this reason, indenting in a selection statement is strongly encouraged.

8.4 Example of Binary Selection, COM_EDIT.prg

We are now going to start writing a group of more sophisticated programs for our **COMPCLAS** system in order to improve upon it. To distinguish this group from those we initially wrote in Chapter 7, we shall give them all names starting with **COM_** . The first of these will be **COM_EDIT.prg**.

SELECTION

The problem with the original version of **COMPEDIT.prg**, that we wrote in Chapter 7, is that regardless of whether we found the person for whom we were searching or not, we still went into the EDIT mode. We'd like to correct this problem by including the selection programming structure in the program design.

The overall design of **COM_EDIT.PRG** is indicated in the flow chart shown in Figure 8.7. The program gives us the option of searching for a record that we would like to edit by name, or simply starting at the top of the file. So the first step is to enter whether or not we would like to do a search.

At the decision element we examine the result of what we input, and if a search for a particular name was requested, then we go off to the right. Here we order the database so that the LASTFIRST tag is the Master Index. This is to be sure that we can search by name. The next step is to enter the person's name, and then create a search key (make everything upper case and trim off trailing blanks), and finally we search for a record in the database that has the same name as the one we entered at the keyboard.

If we enter that we do not want to do a search, then we would go off to the left after the decision element and remain at the top of the file. Regardless of whether we search or not, we end up together again at the merge element and we approach the next decision element.

The question to be answered is whether or not we found the record that we were looking for. If we ended up at the end of the file, then we did not find the record that we were looking for. If that is the case, we simply display an error message and return to the calling program or the dot prompt.

If on the other hand, we are not at the end of the file, then indeed we have found the record that we were searching for, or we are simply at the top of the file. In either case we leave the decision element and head towards the left. Here we turn on our format file to format our screen. Now we can go directly into the edit mode. Upon leaving the edit mode, we turn off the format file. We then return back to the calling program or the dot prompt.

SELECTION

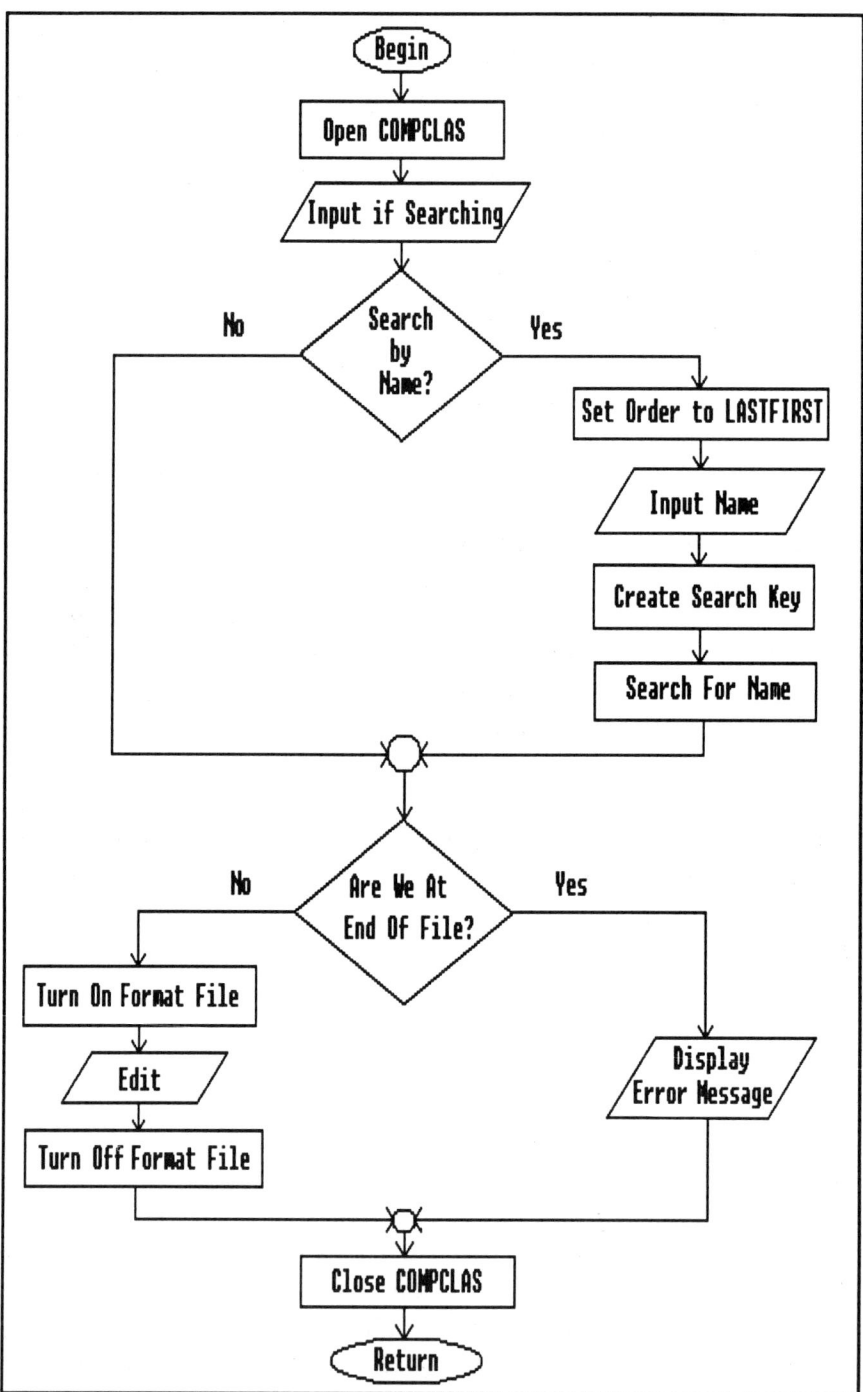

Figure 8.7 Flow chart for COM_EDIT.prg

Translating this into dBASE commands, we get the program shown in Listing 8.1. As you can see we used the **IF—ELSE—ENDIF** structure twice to handle our two binary selections. For the most part, the program should be self explanatory.

In order to SEEK on both LASTNAME and FIRSTNAME we need to combine these two names together to form a key which we call **NAMESEARCH**. We will do this by entering the name **LASTSEARCH** and then enter the name **FIRSTSEARC** if there is one. To do this, and make the search case blind, as we did in Chapter 7, we need to be certain that everything is in upper case. As a result, the search key, **NAMESEARCH**, is given by:

NAMESEARCH = UPPER(TRIM(LASTSEARCH + FIRSTSEARC))

The reason for trimming the concatenation of the two memory variables is to allow for the user to enter only a few letters of the total name, rather than the exact last name and first name. If one does not enter any first name for **FIRSTSEARC**, then just a fraction of the last name may be entered for **LASTSEARCH**. However, note that if any of the first name is entered into **FIRSTSEARC**, then the entire last name must be entered into **LASTSEARCH**. This is a limitation of the indexed search as compared to the locate search that we used in Chapter 6.

If we're going to upper case the search key, then we also have to be sure that the index, when it is made, is also totally upper cased. For this reason we re-index COMPCLAS so that the index tag LASTFIRST looks like this:

INDEX ON UPPER(LASTNAME + FIRSTNAME) TAG LASTFIRST

Now the **SEEK NAMESEARCH** command will find the name entered, if it does exist.

```
* COM_EDIT.prg
* This routine allows one to edit COMPCLAS.dbf
* Records can be searched by a particular Name or
* sequentially.
* If a Search is chosen then the Order is set to
* LASTFIRST.
*
USE COMPCLAS
STORE .T. TO BYNAME
CLEAR
@ 12,15 SAY [Do You Want To Search By Name (Y/N): ];
        GET BYNAME
READ
IF BYNAME
   SET ORDER TO LASTFIRST
   STORE SPACE(15) TO LASTSEARCH
   STORE SPACE(15) TO FIRSTSEARC
   CLEAR
   @ 11,24 SAY "Enter Last Name:  " GET LASTSEARCH
   @ 13,24 SAY "Enter First Name: " GET FIRSTSEARC
   READ
   STORE UPPER(TRIM(LASTSEARCH + FIRSTSEARC)) TO;
        NAMESEARCH
   SEEK NAMESEARCH
ENDIF          && byname
IF .NOT. EOF()
   SET FORMAT TO COMPCLAS
   EDIT
   SET FORMAT TO
ELSE
   CLEAR
   @ 12,17 SAY "Unable to Find: " + TRIM(LASTSEARCH);
       +", "+ FIRSTSEARC
   WAIT
ENDIF          && not eof
USE
RETURN
```

Listing 8.1 Program COM_EDIT.prg

SELECTION

If the search failed to find a record, then the error message is generated with the following SAY command:

@ 12,24 SAY "Unable to Find: " + TRIM(LASTSEARCH) + ;
", " + FIRSTSEARC

This prints out the words "Unable to Find: " and then the Name (typed in at the beginning). This is printed out on row 24 of the screen, and the message is held there by the WAIT command until a key is struck at the keyboard.

Take note of the fact that after each ENDIF statement there is a comment that indicates which **IF** statement the ENDIF is ending. This comment is not required by dBASE. However, it is a very good idea if you have multiple selection statements in your program. Typing these comments makes the program clearer to read and less prone to error.

8.5 Multiple Selection—The DO CASE Structure

Often we wish to choose one of many possible choices. One way to do this is to use multiple **IF** statements. For example, suppose we wish to choose one of three ways to index our database: 1) by name, 2) by grade, 3) by evaluation date. We could enter our choice into a memory variable called **WHICHINDEX**. Then the decision making part of our program might look like:

```
IF WHICHINDEX = "1"
   SET ORDER TO LASTFIRST
ENDIF    && 1
IF WHICHINDEX = "2"
   SET ORDER TO GRADE
ENDIF    && 2
IF WHICHINDEX = "3"
   SET ORDER TO EVALUATION
ENDIF    && 3
```

This method will work although it is a bit tedious. It is also slow to execute because the operation must pass through each of the **IF** statements even after the desired **IF** statement was located and executed. A faster way of doing the same thing would be to use a series of nested **IF** statements as follows:

```
IF WHICHINDEX = "1"
   SET ORDER TO LASTFIRST
ELSE
   IF WHICHINDEX = "2"
      SET ORDER TO GRADE
   ELSE
      IF WHICHINDEX = "3"
         SET ORDER TO EVALUATION
      ENDIF      && 3
   ENDIF      && 2
ENDIF      && 1
```

This executes more quickly because as soon as the desired **IF** statement is found, the operation skips the next **ELSE** clause and returns to the **ENDIF** series. However, when the nesting starts getting three or more layers deep, it becomes much more difficult to read and understand.

There is another structure which was made for multiple selection and is quite readable as well as fast executing. This is the **CASE** statement. It's syntax is as follows:

```
DO CASE
   CASE condition1
      <Commands1>
   CASE condition2
      <Commands2>
   CASE condition3
      <Commands3>
      .
      .
      .
   CASE conditionN
      <CommandsN>
   OTHERWISE
      <Commands0>
ENDCASE
```

The **OTHERWISE** clause is optional and is used when one wants to execute a command(s) if none of the above CASEs are satisfied.

Our program fragment example would then be written:

```
DO CASE
   CASE WHICHINDEX = '1'
      SET ORDER TO LASTFIRST
   CASE WHICHINDEX = '2'
      SET ORDER TO GRADE
   CASE WHICHINDEX = '3'
      SET ORDER TO EVALUATION
ENDCASE
```

Notice how compact and clear this statement is. It certainly is easier to follow than a bunch of nested **IF** statements. Figure 8.8 shows a flow diagram of this program fragment.

If we add to our program fragment the modules shown in the flow chart in Figure 8.9, we end up with: **COM_BROW.prg**. This is a browse module which can be ordered in any one of three ways. The program resulting from this Flow Chart is shown in Listing 8.2. Note that a menu was added to the front end of this program. This menu requires the user to type in his or her selection: "1", "2", or "3" to select the desired ordering.

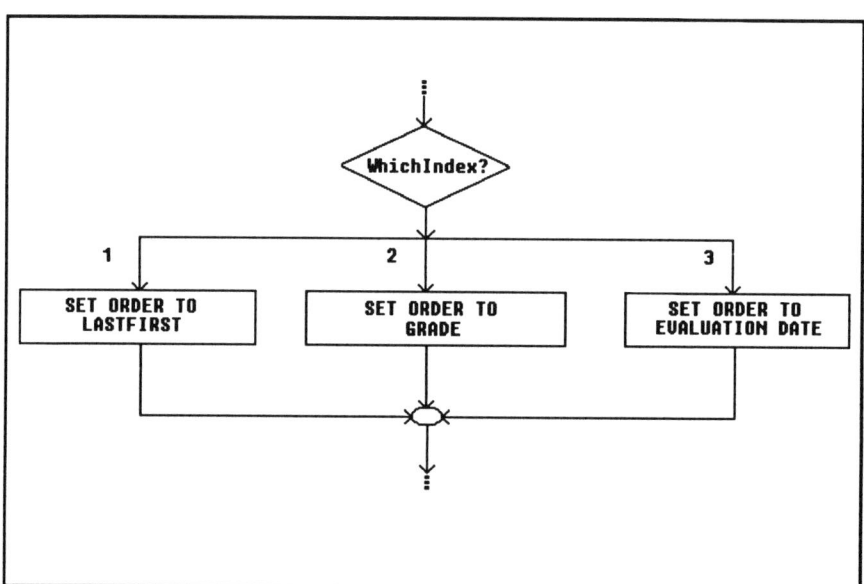

Figure 8.8 Multiple Selection Example Using CASE Statement

8.6 Alternative Data Entry Commands

The only data entry command that we have discussed so far is the **GET** command. Although perhaps the most useful of the data entry commands, **GET** has some disadvantages: 1) It requires that you define a memory variable first (if you are doing data entry to a memory variable), 2) It requires a **SAY** instruction to prompt the user as to what is to be entered, 3) It requires a **READ** instruction to read the data into the memory variables. For example, if we want to enter a date for the term project evaluation, then the following three program lines are required.

STORE CTOD(" / / ") TO EVALDATE
@ 12,16 SAY "Enter the Date For Project ;
    Evaluation: " GET EVALDATE
READ

For a date memory variable, this can't be avoided. However, this is a lot of overhead if you just want to enter a number or some characters. For this reason we have three specialized data entry instructions that will enter data with a minimum of commands.

SELECTION

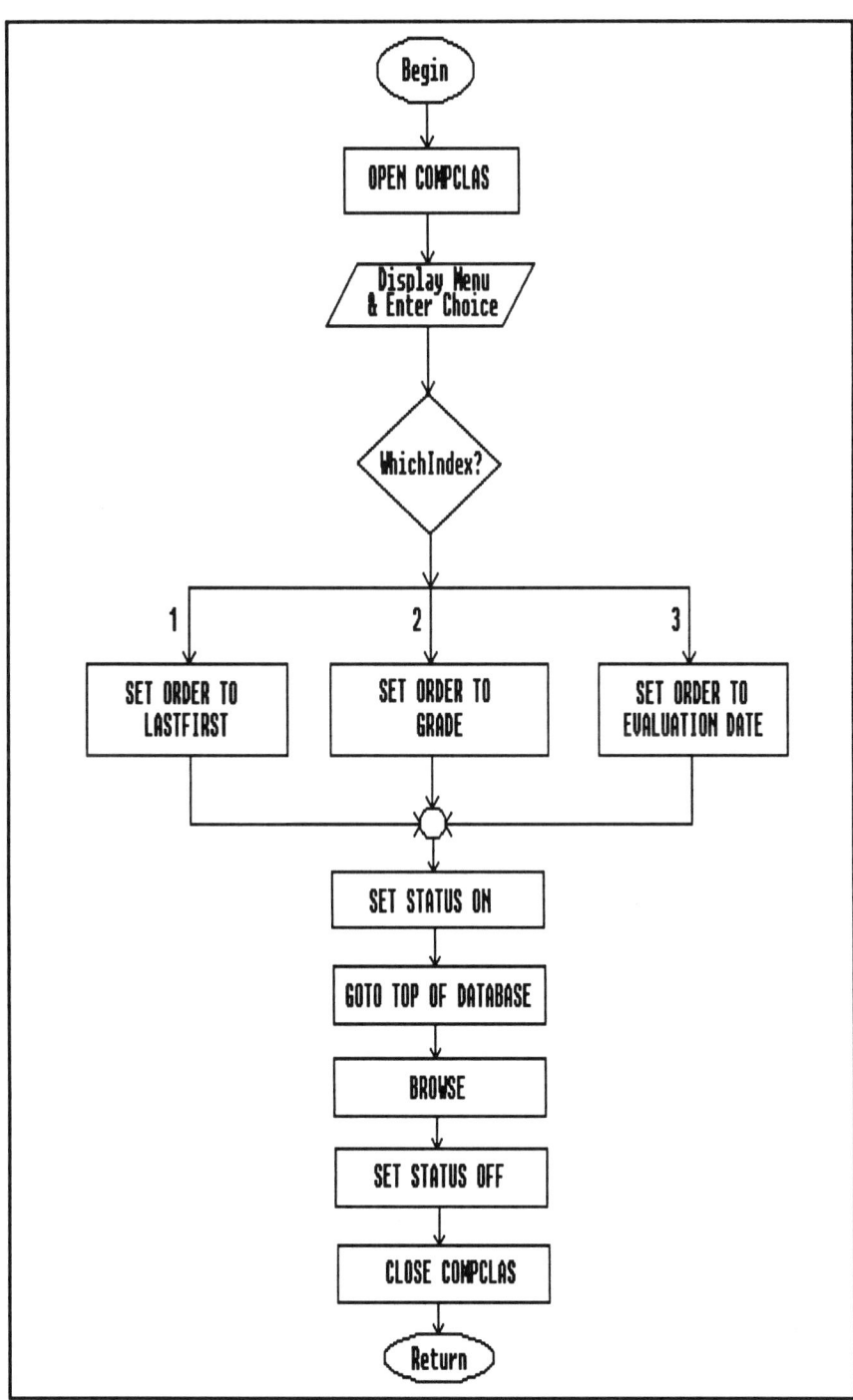

Figure 8.9 Flow Chart of COM_BROW.prg

```
* COM_BROW.prg
* This module allows the user to select one of three
* indices to be in control, demonstrating the use of
* the CASE statement.  It then goes into the
* Browse mode.
*
USE COMPCLAS
STORE [1] TO WHICHINDEX
CLEAR
@ 01,30 SAY "COMPCLAS ORDERING MENU"
@ 09,16 SAY "< 1 >  Order by Last Name, First Name"
@ 11,16 SAY "< 2 >  Order by Project Grade"
@ 13,16 SAY "< 3 >  Order by Evaluation Date"
@ 17,29 SAY "Which (1-3): " GET WHICHINDEX
READ
DO CASE
   CASE WHICHINDEX = '1'
      SET ORDER TO LASTFIRST
   CASE WHICHINDEX = '2'
      SET ORDER TO GRADE
   CASE WHICHINDEX = '3'
      SET ORDER TO EVALUATION
ENDCASE
SET STATUS ON
GOTO TOP
BROWSE
SET STATUS OFF
USE
RETURN
```

Listing 8.2 Program COM_BROW.prg which also Orders COMPCLAS.DBF

8.6.1 The INPUT Command

INPUT is a simple way of entering numeric data[27] into a program. It does not require that you define a memory variable first, nor does it need any other instructions to assist it in its work. Furthermore, like the STORE command, it can be executed from the dot prompt.

---

[27] The INPUT command will allow other data types to be entered, however, the manner in which you do this defines the data type. For example, to enter text data, you must precede and terminate your data entry with quotes. Because of its sensitivity to the manner of entering other data types, its only recommended use is for entering numeric data.

SELECTION

The syntax is: **INPUT** *"prompt"* **TO** *NumberVariable* where *prompt* is simply the prompt that we have been putting in the **SAY** command. For example, suppose we wanted to input into memory variables some new grades that have been turned in.

. **INPUT "Enter Grade: " TO NEWGRADE**
Enter Grade: **85**

The response to the command is shown on the next line. First there is the prompt: "Enter Grade: ", followed by the user, who in this case typed in **85**. (Notice that we could have accomplished the same task from the command line by using a **STORE** instruction. However, our intention will be to use the **INPUT** instruction to input data typed in from the keyboard into memory variables within programs. This task cannot be accomplished by the **STORE** instruction.) Using the **?** instruction, we can print out the value contained in our memory variable, **NEWGRADE**, just for verification.

. **? NEWGRADE**
   85

8.6.2 The ACCEPT Command

The **ACCEPT** command acts as an easy way to enter text data into a memory variable. Like the INPUT instruction, it needs no other supporting commands, and it can be executed from the dot prompt. The syntax is: **ACCEPT** *"prompt"* **TO** *TextVariable* . For example, we could enter a student's name as follows:

. **ACCEPT "Enter Student's Name: " TO STUDENAME**
Enter Student's Name: **MARY WONG**
. **? STUDENAME**
Mary Wong

Note that we do not need to type in quotes from the keyboard (as you had to in a STORE instruction). The memory variable created ends up being only as long as the number of letters you typed in.

This is different from the **GET** instruction which will load in trailing blanks if you do not type in all the characters into the space provided. For cases where you do not want those trailing blanks, **ACCEPT** is a good alternative to the **GET** instruction.

8.6.3 The WAIT Command Revisited

The humble **WAIT** command has a feature that we have ignored until now, and that is its ability to accept the single character key that is struck as input to a memory variable. The syntax is: **WAIT** *Prompt* **TO** *CharacterVariable* . This is a good means of entering a one character menu choice.

If we wanted to enter a True or False value using the **WAIT** instruction, we could do it as shown in the following program fragment:

WAIT "Did Student Do Term Project (Y/N): " TO TERMPROJ
IF UPPER(TERMPROJ) = "Y"
  STORE .T. TO TERMPROJ
ELSE
  STORE .F. TO TERMPROJ
ENDIF

Notice that when **TERMPROJ** was first typed in, it was done as a character variable, which is the only thing that a **WAIT** instruction can accept. It was then changed into a logical variable by the **IF—ELSE—ENDIF** selection statement that followed.

8.7   Saving, Restoring and Releasing Memory Variables

In these last two chapters we have been dealing with both field variables as well as memory variables. It is extremely important that the reader understand the difference between the two so as not to confuse them.

A field variable is the value that a particular field takes depending on which record of a database you are currently looking at. A field variable pertains to a database.

A memory variable is a value that is stored in memory for use at some future time. When you turn off the computer, all the memory variables will be lost (unless they have been **SAVED**), whereas the database field values will remain safely stored in their files.

The value of a field variable will change depending on which record you are looking at. The value of a memory variable will not change until you redefine it to have a different value.

Unless you adopt some naming convention, there is no way (unless you have memorized all of your database field names) to tell the difference between a field variable and a memory variable simply by looking at the name. Some people do use the convention of putting an "M" in front of all memory variables to make this distinction. An underscore, (_), preceding the variable name, is used to indicate a system memory variable.

The way to remind yourself what your current field variable names are is by typing: **DISPLAY STRUCTURE** at the dot prompt, as we have done in earlier chapters. Likewise, to see what your currently defined memory variables are, we simply type: **DISPLAY MEMORY** at the dot prompt (see Chapter 7).

Since these memory variables disappear as soon as you leave the dBASE environment, if you would like to save these for further use, they must be saved before you exit. The syntax of this instruction is: **SAVE TO** *MemoryFile* . For example we can save all our memory variables to the memory file **GRADDATA.MEM** as follows:

. SAVE TO GRADDATA

This automatically creates a new file **GRADDATA** with the extension **.MEM** . Now when you exit from dBASE, the variables will not be lost. When you return to dBASE, however, they must be RESTORED by means of the **RESTORE** command. The syntax is: **RESTORE FROM** *MemoryFile* . In our case we would type:

. **RESTORE FROM GRADDATA**

Our memory variables would then be restored to their previous glory.

On the other hand, we might want to **RELEASE** some or all of the variables from our current memory. As there are 2048 memory variables allowed in dBASE IV, it is unlikely that we might run out of memory variable space. But if we do need to make room for other memory variables, the **RELEASE** instruction is available to us. The syntax is: **RELEASE** *variable1, variable2, ... variableN*. If we wanted to release **STUDENAME** and **TERMPROJ** for example, we could type:

. **RELEASE STUDENAME, TERMPROJ**

On the other hand, if we wanted to release all the memory variables, then we would type: **RELEASE ALL** .
. **RELEASE ALL**

The main reason that one may not ever have to worry about releasing memory variables is that memory variables used in a program are released as soon as the program is done executing.

8.8 The REPLACE Command

Up till now, the only way we've been able to change field variables in a record is to do so in the EDIT mode. However, suppose that we wish to change one field in all the records in the data base. Doing this using either EDIT or BROWSE can be quite tedious. The **REPLACE** command gives us a means of doing it for all records at once. In addition, the **REPLACE** command can be executed from the dot prompt or from within a command file without having to deal with the full data entry screen.

The syntax for the **REPLACE** command is: **REPLACE** *FieldName* **WITH** *NewFieldValue* **FOR** *LogicalExpression* . For example, let's **REPLACE** Mary Wong's project grade (which was

SELECTION

0) with her new grade. Using the **REPLACE** command we would type:

. **REPLACE PROJ_GRADE WITH 85 FOR LASTNAME = "Wong" .AND. FIRSTNAME = "Mary"**

(Note that we used both the LASTNAME as well as the FIRSTNAME to completely specify the individual. If we did this for only the LASTNAME, and we were trying to **REPLACE** the grade for Consuelo Naboa, we would end up replacing it for Gladys also.)

We could also use the values stored in our memory variables that we so carefully saved. We'll **REPLACE** Mary Wong's EVALUATION date using the memory variable STUDENAME.

. **REPLACE EVALUATION WITH CTOD("12/20/92") FOR TRIM(FIRSTNAME) + " " + TRIM(LASTNAME) = STUDENAME**

Notice that here we had to trim our FIRSTNAME and LASTNAME so that it would be in a form identical to STUDENAME. In addition, we had to add a space in between the first and last names so that it would appear in exactly the same way that we typed in our value for STUDENAME, "Mary Wong".

8.8.1 Example Using the REPLACE Command for Block Replacements

Let's modify our database, COMPCLAS, to include one more field, **FINALGRADE**. We will choose it to be a character field of width one character. It is left as an exercise to the student to perform this modification. Insert **FINALGRADE** in between PROJ_GRADE and ADDRESS. Doing a BROWSE of the resulting database we get the result shown in Figure 8.10.

. **BROWSE**

284   SELECTION

```
Records   Organize   Fields   Go To   Exit
FIRSTNAME    LASTNAME      TERM_PROJ  EVALUATION  PROJ_GRADE  FINALGRADE  ADD
Gladys       Naboa         T          12/15/92    93          ▮           324
Consuelo     Naboa         T          12/16/92    89                      324
Derek        Caruthers     F            /  /       0                       21
Wendel       Little        T          12/17/92    87                      182
Jeremy       Witherspoon   T          12/19/92    82                      821
Nancy        Hardwick      F            /  /       0                      512
Jonathan     Samuels       T          12/14/92    76                       96
Matts        Engleberg     T          12/13/92    62                      282
Mary Beth    Swazey        T          12/14/92    52                       85
Mary         Wong          F          12/20/92    85                      321

Browse   A:\compclas\COMPCLAS   Rec 1/10   File
```

Figure 8.10 Browse of COMPCLAS with new field FINALGRADE added

If we display the structure of our modified COMPCLAS.dbf, we see the result displayed in Listing 8.3.

. DISPLAY STRUCTURE

```
Structure for database: A:\COMPCLAS\COMPCLAS.DBF
Number of data records:      10
Date of last update   : 02/18/91
Field   Field Name   Type         Width    Dec    Index
    1   FIRSTNAME    Character      15                N
    2   LASTNAME     Character      15                N
    3   TERM_PROJ    Logical         1                N
    4   EVALUATION   Date            8                Y
    5   PROJ_GRADE   Numeric         3                Y
    6   FINALGRADE   Character       1                N
    7   ADDRESS      Character      25                N
    8   CITY_ST_ZP   Character      25                N
    9   COMMENTS     Memo           10                N
** Total **                        104
```

Listing 8.3 Newly Modified Structure of COMPCLAS with FINALGRADE

```
* GIVEGRAD.PRG
* This assigns a letter grade to the FINALGRADE
depending on grade
* received for PROJ_GRADE.
*
USE COMPCLAS
REPLACE FINALGRADE WITH "a" FOR PROJ_GRADE >=89
REPLACE FINALGRADE WITH "b" FOR PROJ_GRADE >=79;
  .AND. PROJ_GRADE <89
REPLACE FINALGRADE WITH "c" FOR PROJ_GRADE >=69;
  .AND. PROJ_GRADE <79
REPLACE FINALGRADE WITH "d" FOR PROJ_GRADE >=59;
  .AND. PROJ_GRADE <69
REPLACE FINALGRADE WITH "f" FOR PROJ_GRADE < 59
RETURN
```

Listing 8.4 Program GIVEGRAD.prg Demonstrating REPLACE command

Now we are free to write a command file that REPLACEs the blank **FINALGRADE** with a letter grade depending on the numeric grade they received on their Term Project. We'll call this program GIVEGRAD.PRG (see Listing 8.4).

A BROWSE of the result is shown in Figure 8.11. Notice that we mistakenly gave FINALGRADEs to those people who elected to take a Final instead of the Term Project. We should change these back to blanks until the Final Exam grades are in. This can be done with the following **REPLACE** command.

. REPLACE FINALGRADE WITH " " FOR .NOT.
    TERM_PROJ

A BROWSE of the result is shown in Figure 8.12. In this way we can quickly execute global replacements in a database.

8.8.2 The REPLACE ALL Command

If we want to do a replacement in every record, we can use the **REPLACE ALL** command. The FOR clause no longer applies since we're operating on all records. The syntax is: **REPLACE**

286   SELECTION

```
Records   Organize   Fields   Go To   Exit
FIRSTNAME   LASTNAME     TERM_PROJ  EVALUATION  PROJ_GRADE  FINALGRADE  ADD
Gladys      Naboa        T          12/15/92    93          a           324
Consuelo    Naboa        T          12/16/92    89          a           324
Derek       Caruthers    F          /  /        0           f           21
Wendel      Little       T          12/17/92    87          b           182
Jeremy      Witherspoon  T          12/19/92    82          b           821
Nancy       Hardwick     F          /  /        0           f           512
Jonathan    Samuels      T          12/14/92    76          c           96
Matts       Engleberg    T          12/13/92    62          d           282
Mary Beth   Swazey       T          12/14/92    52          f           85
Mary        Wong         F          12/28/92    85          b           321

Browse    A:\compclas\COMPCLAS    Rec 1/10    File
```

Figure 8.11   Browse of COMPCLAS with FINALGRADEs assigned using REPLACE

ALL *FieldName* **WITH** *NewFieldValue* . In our case, note that we have put in lower case grades for the **FINALGRADE** field. What we would like to do is to make them all upper case. This can be accomplished by typing at the dot prompt:

. **REPLACE ALL FINALGRADE WITH**
    UPPER(FINALGRADE)

A browse of the final result is shown in Figure 8.13.

8.9   Program Example Using ACCEPT, INPUT, WAIT and REPLACE

We can now demonstrate the use of all of our data entry commands in the program, **COMUPDAT.prg** , shown in Listing 8.5.

Note that we use **ACCEPT** to enter character string data, **WAIT** to enter a single character, and **INPUT** to enter numbers.

```
┌─────────────────────────────────────────────────────────────────────┐
│ Records   Organize   Fields   Go To   Exit                          │
├──────────┬───────────┬─────────┬──────────┬──────────┬──────────┬───┤
│FIRSTNAME │LASTNAME   │TERM_PROJ│EVALUATION│PROJ_GRADE│FINALGRADE│ADD│
├──────────┼───────────┼─────────┼──────────┼──────────┼──────────┼───┤
│Gladys    │Naboa      │    T    │ 12/15/92 │    93    │    a     │324│
│Consuelo  │Naboa      │    T    │ 12/16/92 │    89    │    a     │324│
│Derek     │Caruthers  │    F    │   / /    │     0    │          │ 21│
│Wendel    │Little     │    T    │ 12/17/92 │    87    │    b     │102│
│Jeremy    │Witherspoon│    T    │ 12/19/92 │    82    │    b     │821│
│Nancy     │Hardwick   │    F    │   / /    │     0    │          │512│
│Jonathan  │Samuels    │    T    │ 12/14/92 │    76    │    c     │ 96│
│Matts     │Engleberg  │    T    │ 12/13/92 │    62    │    d     │202│
│Mary Beth │Swazey     │    T    │ 12/14/92 │    52    │    f     │ 85│
│Mary      │Wong       │    F    │ 12/20/92 │    85    │    b     │321│
│          │           │         │          │          │          │   │
├──────────┴───────────┴─────────┴──────────┴──────────┴──────────┴───┤
│Browse  A:\compclas\COMPCLAS   Rec 1/10      File                    │
└─────────────────────────────────────────────────────────────────────┘
```

Figure 8.12 Browse of FINALGRADEs of those who did Term Projects

However, we are forced to use **STORE—@—SAY—GET—READ** to enter date variables in a "user friendly" way.

We test for the end of the file just to be sure that our locate didn't fail. If we are at the end of the file, clearly, no match was found and an error message is printed out at the end of the program using the **? IIF(,,)** instruction that we have seen before.

If we are not at the end of the file, then the locate was successful and we **REPLACE** the three field variables: **TERM_PROJ, PROJ_GRADE,** and **EVALUATION** with the three memory variables: TERMPROJ, NEWGRADE and EVALDATE respectively.

Observe the use of the **IIF()** function to assign a logical variable to **TERM_PROJ** based on whether the letter typed in for TERMPROJ was a "Y" or not. This use of the **IIF()** function saves

```
Records   Organize   Fields   Go To   Exit
FIRSTNAME      LASTNAME        TERM_PROJ   EVALUATION   PROJ_GRADE   FINALGRADE   ADD
Gladys         Naboa           T           12/15/92     93           A            324
Consuelo       Naboa           T           12/16/92     89           A            324
Derek          Caruthers       F             /  /        0                        21
Wendel         Little          T           12/17/92     87           B            102
Jeremy         Witherspoon     T           12/19/92     82           B            821
Nancy          Hardwick        F             /  /        0                        512
Jonathan       Samuels         T           12/14/92     76           C            96
Matts          Engleberg       T           12/13/92     62           D            202
Mary Beth      Swazey          T           12/14/92     52           F            85
Mary           Wong            F           12/20/92     85           B            321

Browse   A:\compclas\COMPCLAS         Rec 1/10          File
```

Figure 8.13 Browse of FINALGRADEs using REPLACE to make Upper Case

us the use of a **IF—ELSE—ENDIF** binary selection instruction set and executes faster in the machine. Figure 8.14 shows the flow diagram for this program.

This program offers a comparison of the various data entry commands and the context of their use. Because of: 1) the screen control inherent in the **@—SAY—GET** commands, 2) the visual clarity of the number of characters permitted, 3) and the consistency of using only one type of command, the author's preference for the **@—SAY—GET** is apparent in this text. Nonetheless, the reader is encouraged to use whichever data entry command best suits his or her needs.

8.10 Summary

This chapter has concerned itself with both binary and multiple selection. The use of selection shows the power of a computer to make decisions based on the data presented. The **IF—ELSE—ENDIF** was introduced as an example of a command that executes binary selection.

```
* COMUPDAT.prg
* This updates the PROJ_GRADE, TERM_PROJ and
* EVALUATION fields.  The record is located
* by means of the Student's First and Last
* Names. This Program demonstrates the use
* of each of the data entry commands:
* ACCEPT, INPUT, WAIT, and SAY, as well as
* the use of the REPLACE command.  Also note
* use of semicolons to continue a command to
* the next line.
*
USE COMPCLAS
STORE CTOD("  /  /  ") TO EVALDATE
CLEAR
ACCEPT "Enter Student's Name [First Last]:";
   TO STUDENAME
WAIT "Has the Student Completed the Term ;
   Project (Y/N): " TO TERMPROJ
INPUT "Enter Student's New Grade: " ;
   TO PROJGRADE
@ 4,0 SAY "Enter Date of Student ;
   Evaluation: " GET EVALDATE
READ
LOCATE FOR UPPER(TRIM(FIRSTNAME) + " " +;
   TRIM(LASTNAME)) = UPPER(STUDENAME)
IF .NOT. EOF()
   REPLACE PROJ_GRADE WITH PROJGRADE
   REPLACE EVALUATION WITH EVALDATE
   REPLACE TERM_PROJ WITH ;
      IIF(UPPER(TERMPROJ)="Y",.T.,.F.)
ENDIF
CLEAR
? IIF(EOF(),"Unable to Locate " +;
   STUDENAME, "Replacement Successful")
WAIT
RETURN
```

Listing 8.5 Program COMUPDAT.prg using 4 different data entry Commands

290   SELECTION

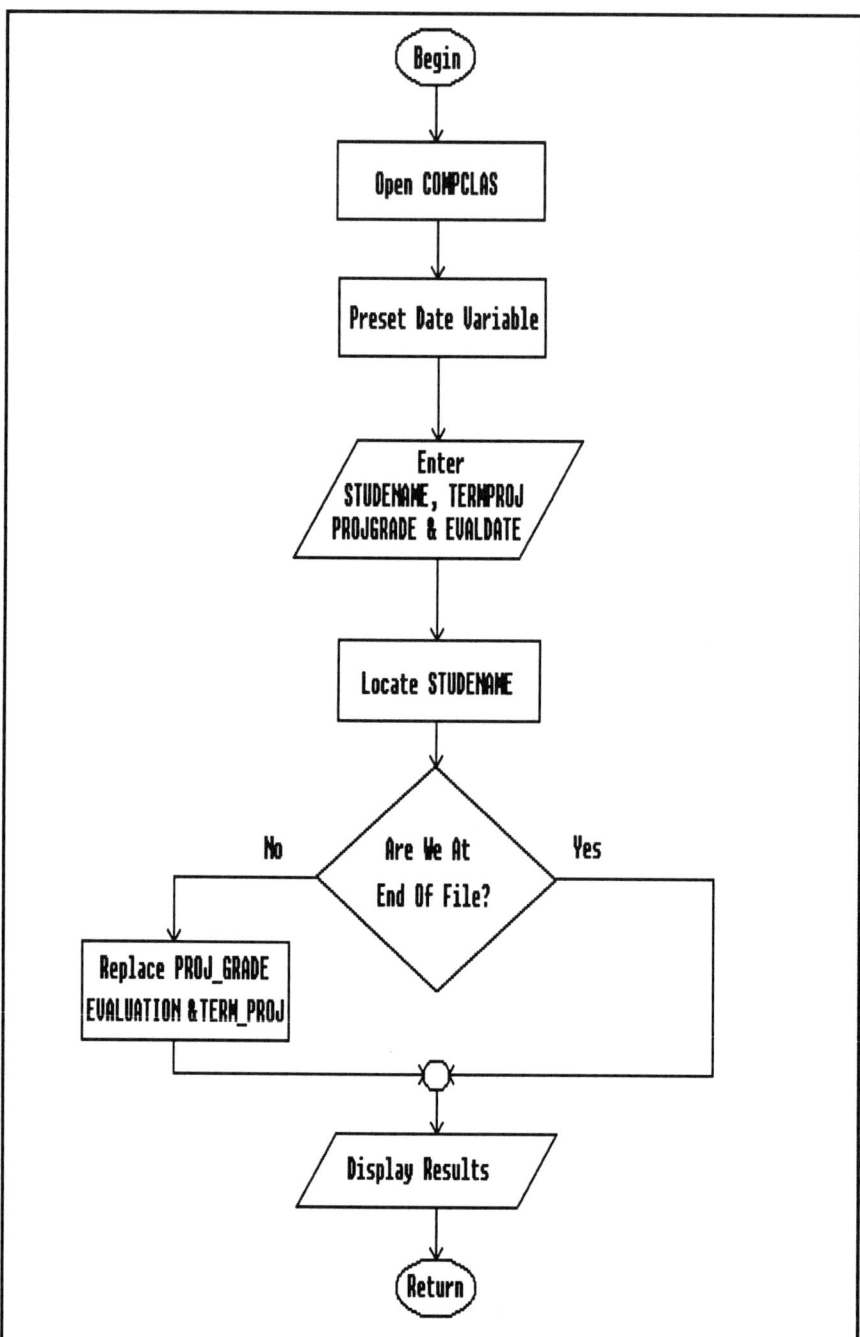

Figure 8.14 Flow Chart of COMUPDAT.prg

SELECTION 291

The concept of the flow chart was introduced as a didactic aid to the understanding of the execution flow in a program which uses selection as a structure. Although flow charts can be used to design programs in general, the difficulty in making any changes in them renders them of limited utility for use in large complicated designs.

The use of the **CASE** structure was presented as a means of executing multiple selections. The choice of **CASE** for menu programs is one of the more obvious uses of this powerful structure.

The concept of saving and restoring memory variables was presented. It was shown how unneeded memory variables could also be released.

Alternative data entry commands: **INPUT, ACCEPT**, and **WAIT** were presented along with their limitations.

The **REPLACE** command was presented as a means of doing global replacements in a database. All of the concepts of the chapter were put together in the final example of a database update program, **COMUPDAT.prg** . The **IIF()** instruction was shown to be useful as a means of avoiding the binary selection structure for either assignment or display commands.

8.11 Review

In Chapter 8 we have presented the following commands:
ACCEPT
CASE—ENDCASE
IF—ELSE—ENDIF
INPUT
RELEASE
REPLACE ALL
REPLACE
RESTORE FROM
SAVE
WAIT

Add these instructions to your glossary of dBASE programming commands.

8.12 Laboratory Work

Follow all the steps outlined in this chapter. Write and execute the programs: COM_EDIT.prg, COM_BROW.prg, and COMUPDAT.prg. Create the memory variables: NEWGRADE, STUDENAME, and TERMPROJ. SAVE them in the memory file GRADDATA, exit dBASE, return to dBASE and then RESTORE them once more.

8.13 Exercises

1. Write a program called MAIL_ED.prg which works along lines similar to COM_EDIT.prg. Hand in a hard copy of this program.

2. Write a program called MAILBROW.prg which works along lines similar to COM_BROW.prg. You may assume that you will be indexing your database, MAILLIST.dbf, as follows:

    a) INDEX ON UPPER(LAST) + UPPER(FIRST) ; TAG MAILAFI

    b) INDEX ON UPPER(FIRST) + UPPER(LAST) ; TAG MAILFILA

    c) INDEX ON ZIP + UPPER(LAST) + ; UPPER(FIRST) TAG MAILZILF

    Write your program using the CASE statement. Hand in a hard copy of this program.

3. Rewrite MAILBROW.prg so that it makes use of nested IF—ELSE—ENDIF statements rather than the CASE statement. Hand in a hard copy of this program.

8.14 Term Project

Decide on a topic for your term project. Meet with your instructor to get his or her reaction to your topic. You should have a clear idea of what it is that you would like to do. Don't choose a topic that is so open-ended that there is little hope for its completion by the end of the semester.

CHAPTER 9

ITERATION

9.0 **Topics Covered in Chapter 9**

The Loop is presented as a Programming Structure.

The DO WHILE Loop is presented.

The three conditions that a Structured Programming loop must satisfy are presented.

Six examples of programs using loops are presented, each demonstrating a different type of loop condition.

Use of the WHILE clause is demonstrated in order to speed up processing.

Examples of both Indexed as well as Range searches are presented.

Use of the SCAN—ENDSCAN loop is demonstrated.

296 ITERATION

9.1 Introduction to The Loop

In Chapter 8 it was mentioned that there are only three structures in structured programming. We have studied the first two: 1) simple sequence; 2) selection. Now we approach the third and final structure, iteration ("The Loop"). (See Figure 9.1)

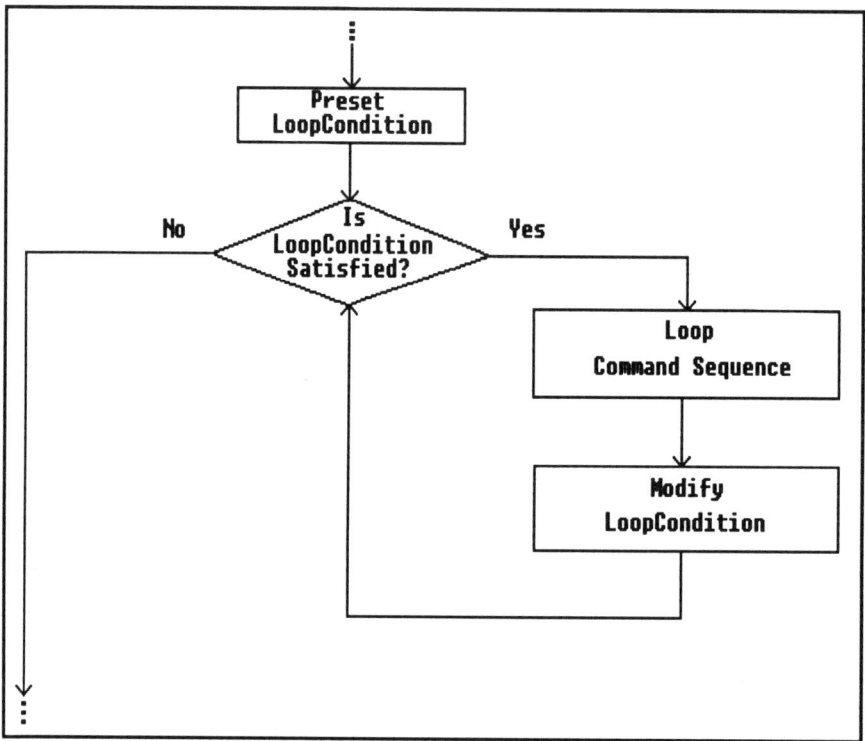

Figure 9.1 Programming Structure: The Loop

Iteration is what gives computers their real power, the ability to repeat a program segment over and over until a certain criterion is met. For example, suppose we had an employee data base of 1000 records, and we wanted to compute the salary for each employee. We could do this in one of two ways: 1) we could design the code to do the calculation for one employee, and then just copy this code over and over again 999 times (resulting in a very large unwieldy program), 2) or we could design the code to do the calculation for one employee, and imbed this in a loop with the instructions to execute this loop until each record in the file has been processed. The code that would be executed to compute the salary for a single employee would be imbedded in the box labeled Loop Command Sequence. Obviously the second method is a more compact as well as more elegant solution to this problem.

9.1.1 The **DO WHILE** Command

The command that dBASE uses for executing loops is the **DO WHILE** *LoopCondition* command. This command will allow an exit from a **DO WHILE** loop only when the *LoopCondition* no longer holds.

A **DO WHILE** loop begins with the command: **DO WHILE** *LoopCondition* and ends with the command: **ENDDO**.

There are three requirements for a **DO WHILE** loop:

1. The *LoopCondition* must be preset before entering the loop.

2. Within the loop the *LoopCondition* must be able to be modified.

3. The *LoopCondition* must, at some point, be able to take on a value that allows the loop to be exited.

The reason that the *LoopCondition* must be preset before entering the **DO WHILE** loop is because if it is not preset, then we may never be able to enter the loop to begin with. The box labeled Preset *LoopCondition* in Figure 9.1 is meant to satisfy this condition.

The reason that the *LoopCondition* must be able to be modified is because if it is not able to be modified, then program execution will never be able to leave the loop, and we will be stuck in an endless loop. The box labeled "Modify LoopCondition" is the element that changes the loop condition. The DO WHILE statement rechecks the loop condition each iteration to see if it should continue executing the loop.

ITERATION

Simply being able to modify the *LoopCondition* is not sufficient. One must be able to modify it in such a way that the loop can be ultimately exited.

9.1.2 Example of Use of **DO WHILE** Loop

Below is a listing for a program that checks to see if the user knows the correct password. If the user types in the correct password, then the operation continues, otherwise, the user is stuck in the loop and can only get out of it by striking the **Esc** key.

```
* PASSWORD.prg
* This program checks the word typed in with
* the PASSWORD.
* The PASSWORD is preset to be "NAUTILUS"
* Operation will return to the Calling
* Program Only if the correct
* Password is entered.  Otherwise operation
* will remain stuck in
* The program loop.
*
STORE .F. TO MATCH
DO WHILE .NOT. MATCH
  CLEAR
  ACCEPT "Enter the Password: " TO TRYPASSWRD
  STORE UPPER(TRYPASSWRD) TO TRYPASSWRD
  STORE IIF(TRYPASSWRD="NAUTILUS",.T.,.F.);
    TO MATCH
ENDDO
RETURN
```

Listing 9.1 Program PASSWORD.prg Demonstrating effect of a Loop

The flow chart for PASSWORD.prg is shown in Figure 9.2. Note that the "STORE .F. TO MATCH" statement corresponds to the preset *LoopCondition* box of Figure 9.1. The clause: ".NOT. MATCH" is our *LoopCondition*. The CLEAR and ACCEPT statements:

```
CLEAR
ACCEPT "Enter the Password:  " TO TRYPASSWRD
STORE UPPER(TRYPASSWRD) TO TRYPASSWRD
```

correspond to the box in Figure 9.1 labeled "Loop Command Sequence". Finally, the statement:

```
STORE IIF(TRYPASSWRD="NAUTILUS",.T.,.F.) TO MATCH
```

corresponds to the box labeled "Modify *LoopCondition*" in Figure 9.1. In Figure 9.2 this box is represented by an assignment process. Since it is possible to type in the correct password, the third requirement of a loop is satisfied.

Note that within a **DO WHILE** loop we indent everything between the **DO WHILE** and the **ENDDO** statements. This clearly delineates the beginning and end of the loop.

9.2 Design of a Delay Loop

Sometimes a loop will serve no other purpose than to cause an intended delay in the execution of a program. The program, **MESSAGE.prg**, demonstrates such a use. What we would like is for a message to appear and to be held on the screen for a few seconds while it is digested by the user and then for it to disappear once more.

The flow diagram for this module is shown in Figure 9.3, and the program itself is shown in Listing 9.2. After the maximum delay time is set, we display the message on line 12, "OUR OPERATOR WILL BE WITH YOU IN JUST ONE MOMENT!"

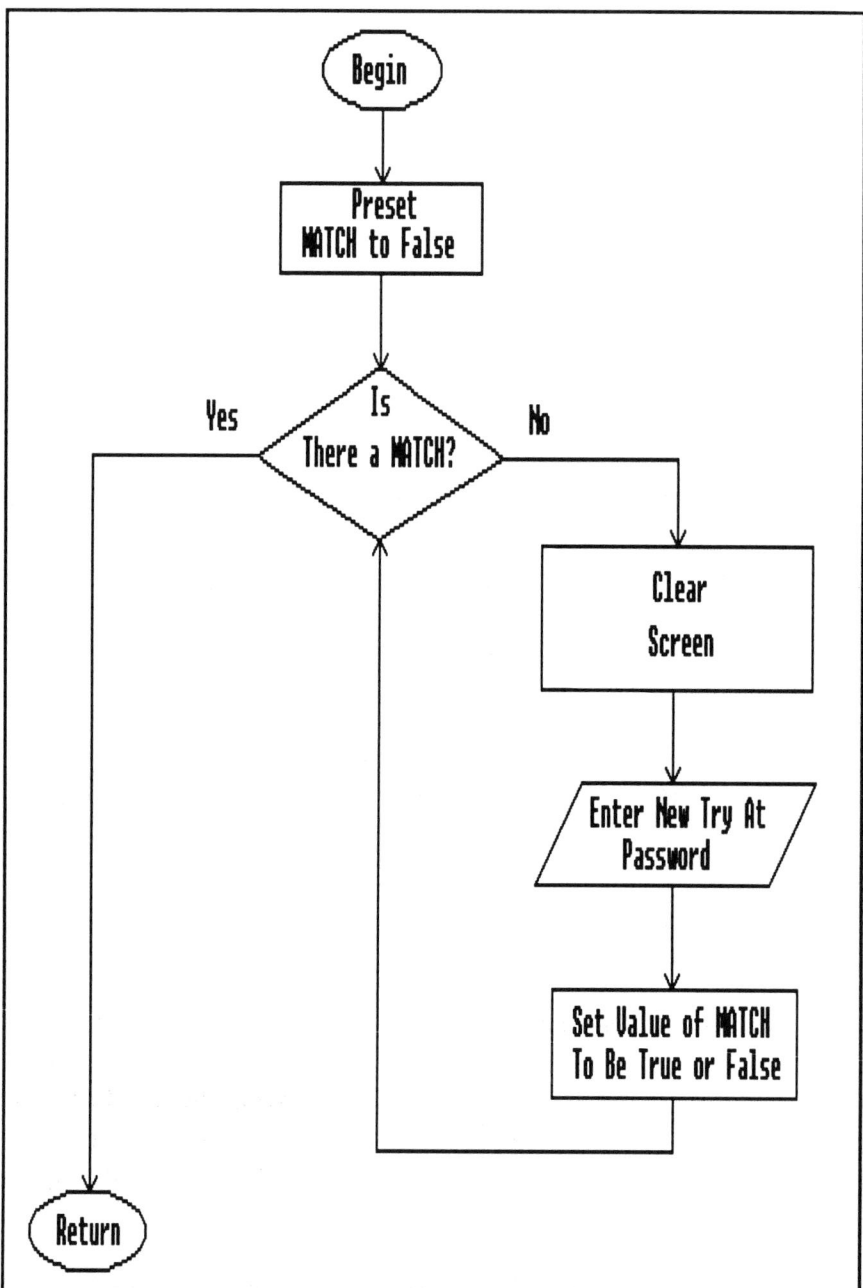

Figure 9.2 Flow Chart of PASSWORD.prg

```
* MESSAGE.prg
* This causes a message to be displayed for approx.
* 3 seconds
* MAXDELAY = 200 is suggested on a computer with a
* 8088 processor
* MAXDELAY = 400 is suggested on a computer with a
* 8086 processor
* MAXDELAY = 1200 is suggested on a computer with a
* 80286 processor.
* MAXDELAY = 2400 is suggested on a computer with a
* 80386 processor.
* MAXDELAY = 4000 is suggested on a computer with
* an 80486 processor.
SET TALK OFF
SET STATUS OFF
STORE 1200 TO MAXDELAY
CLEAR
@ 12,15 SAY "OUR OPERATOR WILL BE WITH YOU IN JUST;
            ONE MOMENT!"
STORE MAXDELAY TO DELAYCOUNT
DO WHILE DELAYCOUNT > 0
   STORE DELAYCOUNT - 1 TO DELAYCOUNT
ENDDO
CLEAR
SET STATUS ON
SET TALK ON
RETURN
```

Listing 9.2 MESSAGE.prg which demonstrates use of Delay Loop

Now we preset the *LoopCondition* for our loop, **DELAYCOUNT** to **MAXDELAY**. What we will do in the loop to modify our *LoopCondition* is to decrement the value of **DELAYCOUNT** by one each time we traverse the loop. This is done by use of the command: **STORE DELAYCOUNT - 1 TO DELAYCOUNT** . As you can see this will subtract 1 from DELAYCOUNT each time it is executed.

The third requirement of a loop is satisfied since the operation will continue looping until **DELAYCOUNT** has finally reached 0. After the loop has been exited, the screen is cleared once more and the operation terminates. The effect is to display the

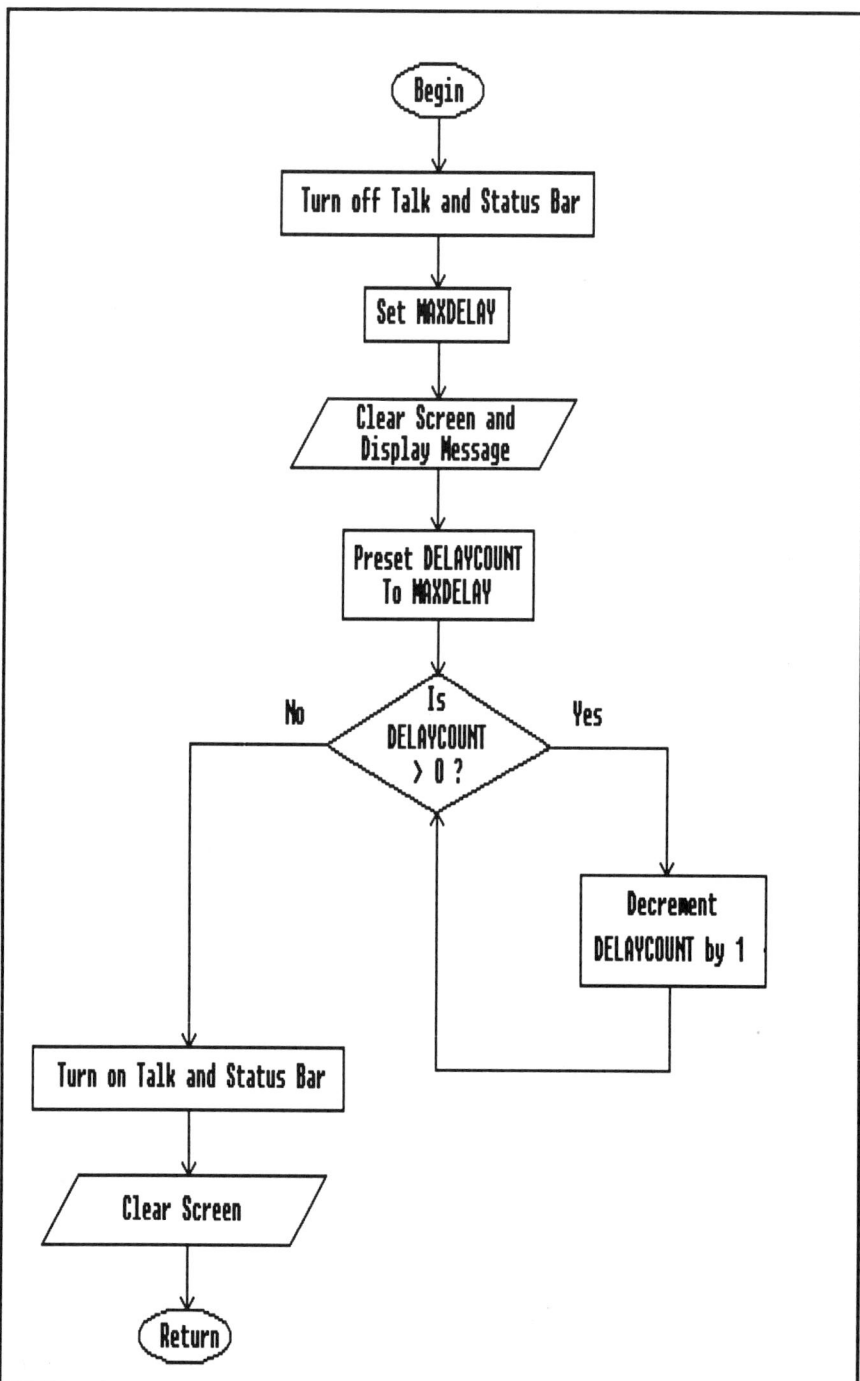

Figure 9.3 Flow Chart of MESSAGE.prg showing Delay Loop

ITERATION

Figure 9.4 Screen Displayed by MESSAGE.prg

screen shown in Figure 9.4 for a few seconds and then disappear returning the operation to the dot prompt.

9.3 Use of DO WHILE Loop with EOF() Function

A common use of the **DO WHILE** loop is with the EOF() function. As long as we are not at the end of the file we will perform a process on each record in the data base. When we reach the end, we will stop.

The following program, BALANCE.prg, takes our ACCOUNTS database which has been modified to contain a field called BALANCE and computes the BALANCE of the account record by record. The modified structure of the ACCOUNTS database is shown in Listing 9.3. The browse of the modified ACCOUNTS database is shown in Figure 9.5. Note that the $100 which had been in the RECEIPTS field in Record 1 as the opening balance, has been moved to the BALANCE field where it properly belongs.

```
Structure for database: A:\ACCOUNTS\ACCOUNTS.DBF
Number of data records:      25
Date of last update   : 02/24/91
Field  Field Name  Type         Width    Dec    Index
    1  DATE        Date             8                N
    2  CHECK       Character        3                N
    3  DESCRIPT    Character       32                N
    4  CAT         Character        3                N
    5  DEBITS      Numeric          8      2         N
    6  RECEIPTS    Numeric          8      2         N
    7  BALANCE     Numeric          8      2         N
    8  CASHED      Logical          1                N
** Total **                        72
```

Listing 9.3 Modified Structure of ACCOUNTS.DBF with field BALANCE

Records	Organize	Fields	Go To	Exit				
DATE	CHECK	DESCRIPT			CAT	DEBITS	RECEIPTS	BALANCE
01/01/92		Jan. 1 Balance				0.00	0.00	100.00
01/05/92		Deposit: Salary			SAL	0.00	750.00	.
01/09/92	401	Cash: January Allowance			PER	100.00	0.00	.
01/09/92	402	Sullivan Co. Cablevision			CAB	20.00	0.00	.
01/09/92	403	N.Y. Telephone: Dec. bill			TEL	50.00	0.00	.
01/12/92	404	Dr. John McIntyre, D.D.S.			DOC	75.00	0.00	.
01/13/92	405	Sierra Club: Donation			DON	10.00	0.00	.
01/14/92	406	Shoprite: Groceries			GRO	18.68	0.00	.
01/14/92	407	Farmer's Market: Groceries			GRO	4.20	0.00	.
01/14/92	408	Feed-n-things: Pet Food			PET	8.50	0.00	.
01/15/92	409	State Farm Mutual: Insurance			INS	232.94	0.00	.
01/15/92	410	Sherman's: auto repairs			CAR	10.00	0.00	.
01/16/92	411	NYSEG: Utilities			UTI	110.12	0.00	.
01/16/92	412	West Side Vets			PET	30.00	0.00	.
01/18/92		Deposit: Travel Expense Reimb.			REI	0.00	38.25	.
01/19/92	413	Dr. Isaacs, M.D. (eye doct)			DOC	40.00	0.00	.
01/19/92		Deposit: Salary			SAL	0.00	750.00	.

| Browse | A:\accounts\ACCOUNTS | Rec 1/25 | File | | Caps |

Figure 9.5 Browse of new ACCOUNTS.DBF

ITERATION

After the program, BALANCE.prg, has been run, the result will be that the field value for BALANCE, in every record of the database, will be the BALANCE as of the current transaction. The effect of this is that when a browse is done of ACCOUNTS, the line by line BALANCE can be viewed as it is in any ledger. The strategy for making this computation is shown in the flow chart pictured in Figure 9.6.

Comparing BALANCE.prg (see Listing 9.4) with the flowchart in Figure 9.1, we see that the "Preset LoopCondition" box is represented by the process labeled "Open ACCOUNTS" followed by "Skip to Next Record." This automatically moves the file pointer to Record Number 2 and gives the value of false to the function EOF(). In this way our EOF() function is preset to false so that program execution can enter the loop. (Unless there is only one record in the database.)

The "Loop Command Sequence" is represented by the two commands:

REPLACE BALANCE WITH OLDBALANCE +;
  RECEIPTS - DEBITS
OLDBALANCE = BALANCE

This takes the balance from the previous record (referred to as OLDBALANCE) and adds to it any RECEIPTS and subtracts from it any DEBITS in order to compute the new BALANCE. Now, since we're about to move onto the next record, it saves the current BALANCE as the OLDBALANCE. This will be used to compute the BALANCE of the next record in sequence.

The "Modify LoopCondition" process box of Figure 9.1 is represented here by the process labeled "SKIP to Next Record". **SKIP** is a command that moves the file pointer to the next record in sequence thus automatically modifying the **EOF()** function once we have moved through all the records in the data base. Since every file must have an end, the third condition of a loop is satisfied. After leaving the loop, the data base is closed.

306 ITERATION

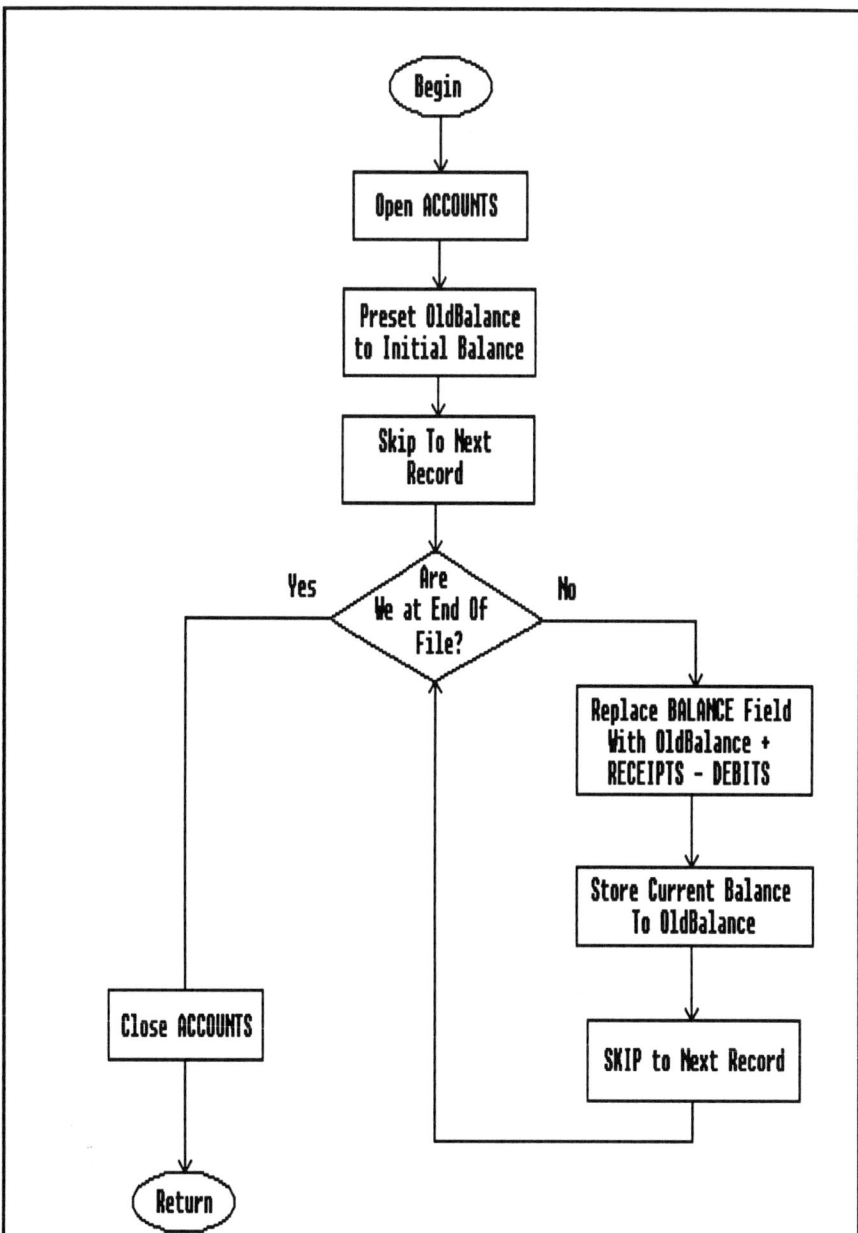

Figure 9.6 Flow Chart of BALANCE.prg

ITERATION

```
* BALANCE.PRG
* This computes and records the record by record
* Balance in the
* ACCOUNTS database, in its natural order.
* It is required that record 1 contain the correct
* opening Balance in the BALANCE field.
*
USE ACCOUNTS
STORE BALANCE TO OLDBALANCE
SKIP
DO WHILE .NOT. EOF()
    REPLACE BALANCE WITH OLDBALANCE +;
        RECEIPTS - DEBITS
    OLDBALANCE = BALANCE
    SKIP
ENDDO
USE
RETURN
```

Listing 9.4 Program BALANCE.prg

The result of executing BALANCE.prg is shown in Figures 9.7 and 9.8 where we see the running BALANCE throughout our ledger from the beginning (shown in reverse video in Figure 9.7) to the current BALANCE after the last check has been entered (shown in reverse video in Figure 9.8).

We should note that it is *not* a standard practice for a database to contain a field which is calculated from other fields in a database. Usually, one simply calculates the value that is needed as we did with the calculated field "BALANCE" in the report form in Chapter 4. However, if you want to see a ledger with a balance in it when you browse your ACCOUNTS database, then this is a way of doing it.

It should also be clear that this BALANCE field only has meaning when the database is in its natural order. If we browse an indexed version of ACCOUNTS, the BALANCE field will have no meaning in that case, and should not be displayed.

Records	Organize	Fields	Go To	Exit				
DATE	CHECK	DESCRIPT			CAT	DEBITS	RECEIPTS	BALANCE
01/01/92		Jan. 1 Balance				0.00	0.00	100.00
01/05/92		Deposit: Salary			SAL	0.00	750.00	850.00
01/09/92	401	Cash: January Allowance			PER	100.00	0.00	750.00
01/09/92	402	Sullivan Co. Cablevision			CAB	20.00	0.00	730.00
01/09/92	403	N.Y. Telephone: Dec. bill			TEL	50.00	0.00	680.00
01/12/92	404	Dr. John McIntyre, D.D.S.			DOC	75.00	0.00	605.00
01/13/92	405	Sierra Club: Donation			DON	10.00	0.00	595.00
01/14/92	406	Shoprite: Groceries			GRO	18.60	0.00	576.40
01/14/92	407	Farmer's Market: Groceries			GRO	4.20	0.00	572.20
01/14/92	408	Feed-n-things: Pet Food			PET	8.50	0.00	563.70
01/15/92	409	State Farm Mutual: Insurance			INS	232.94	0.00	330.76
01/15/92	410	Sherman's: auto repairs			CAR	10.00	0.00	320.76
01/16/92	411	NYSEG: Utilities			UTI	110.12	0.00	210.64
01/16/92	412	West Side Vets			PET	30.00	0.00	180.64
01/18/92		Deposit: Travel Expense Reimb.			REI	0.00	30.25	210.89
01/19/92	413	Dr. Isaacs, M.D. (eye doct)			DOC	40.00	0.00	170.89
01/19/92		Deposit: Salary			SAL	0.00	750.00	920.89

Browse A:\accounts\ACCOUNTS Rec 1/25 File Caps

Figure 9.7 First Browse Screen of ACCOUNTS after running BALANCE

Records	Organize	Fields	Go To	Exit				
DATE	CHECK	DESCRIPT			CAT	DEBITS	RECEIPTS	BALANCE
01/19/92		Deposit: Salary			SAL	0.00	750.00	920.89
01/20/92	414	Cash: Gas & Tolls			CAR	34.65	0.00	894.24
01/20/92	415	Sullivan's: Dept. Store			GIF	25.66	0.00	868.58
01/22/92	416	Action Video			ENT	10.59	0.00	857.99
01/22/92	417	MBNA Payment Services:Cred. Card			HOU	100.00	0.00	757.99
01/25/92	418	Many Happy Returns: Tax Prep.			TAX	105.00	0.00	652.99
01/25/92	419	NYC Parking Violations Bur.			PER	35.00	0.00	617.99
01/27/92	420	Great American: Groceries			GRO	39.92	0.00	578.07
01/28/92	421	Trading Post: Maintenance items			MAI	28.47	0.00	549.60

Browse A:\accounts\ACCOUNTS Rec 25/25 File Caps

Figure 9.8 Second Screen of ACCOUNTS.DBF after running BALANCE

9.4 The Deletion Program—COM_DELE.prg

We will now write a program that is designed to delete and pack records in the COMPCLAS system. Such a program will make it more obvious, as well as easier for the uninitiated dBASE user, to delete records. This program will allow one to: 1) search for a record by name; 2) examine the record before choosing to mark it for deletion; 3) repeat these two steps as many times as desired; 4) execute these deletions by packing the database if desired.

Figure 9.9 shows the flow chart for the Delete Record program. Listing 9.5 shows the program steps. Note that it combines nested **IF—ELSE—ENDIF** statements within a **DO WHILE** loop. The first step is to open the data base and set the order to the name index whose tag is LASTFIRST. Note that we can do this in the single instruction: **USE COMPCLAS ORDER LASTFIRST**.

We then preset the *LoopCondition* to "N" so that the **DO WHILE** *LoopCondition* will be satisfied as we enter the loop. In this case the *LoopCondition* is: **UPPER(FINISHED) <> 'Y'**. We use the UPPER() function so that regardless of whether the user inputs an upper or a lower case **Y** it will be recognized. Notice that saying: **FINISHED <> 'Y'** is the same as saying: **.NOT. FINISHED = 'Y'**. In either case, if **FINISHED = 'N'** then, the loop condition is satisfied.

Next we enter the last and first name of the student as shown in Figure 9.10. We then trim and upper case the name entered to form the **LASTSEARCH** and **FIRSTSEARC** keys which we will use to **SEEK** the student record we desire. If we are not at the end of the file after we do the **SEEK**, then we must have located the record. In this case we display enough fields of the record so that a positive I.D. can be made that this is indeed the record we wish to eliminate. If it is the record we want to delete, then we can answer either "Y" or "N" to the question "Delete It?". On the other hand, if we did end up at the end of the file, then we did not find the record.

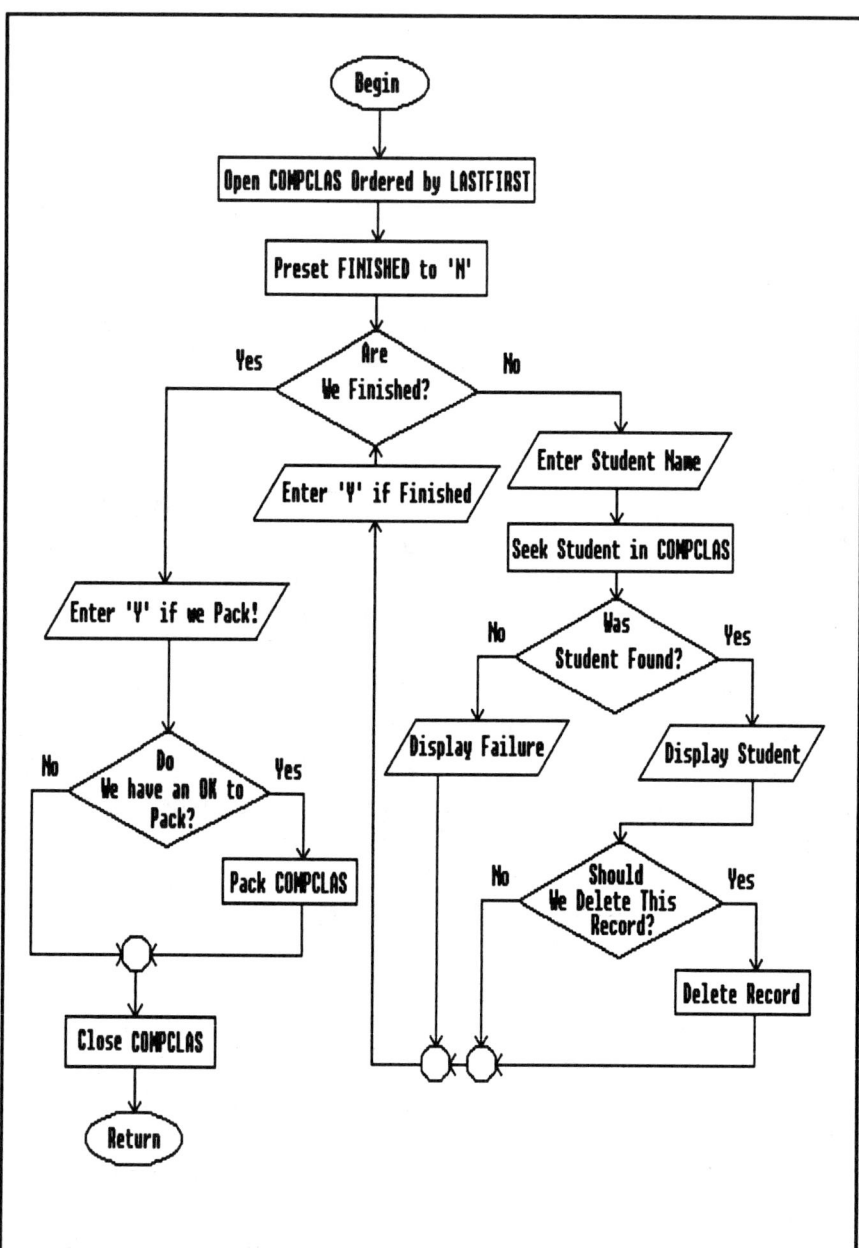

Figure 9.9 Flow Chart of COM_DELE.prg

```
*
*  COM_DELE.PRG
*  This Program Finds, Deletes and Packs Records
*
SET STATUS OFF
USE COMPCLAS ORDER LASTFIRST
STORE 'N' TO FINISHED
DO WHILE UPPER(FINISHED) <> 'Y'
   STORE SPACE(15) TO LASTSEARCH
   STORE SPACE(15) TO FIRSTSEARC
   CLEAR
   @ 11,24 SAY "Enter Last Name:  " GET LASTSEARCH
   @ 13,24 SAY "Enter First Name: " GET FIRSTSEARC
   READ
   STORE UPPER(TRIM(LASTSEARCH + FIRSTSEARC)) TO;
         NAMESEARCH
   SEEK NAMESEARCH
   IF .NOT. EOF()
      CLEAR
      @ 02,24 SAY 'COMPCLAS RECORD DELETION SCREEN'
      @ 04,00 SAY 'Student First Name: '+ FIRSTNAME
      @ 04,40 SAY 'Student Last Name: ' + LASTNAME
      @ 06,00 SAY 'Term paper? ' +;
                  IIF(TERM_PROJ,'Y','N')
      @ 06,40 SAY 'Evaluation Date: ' +;
                  DTOC(EVALUATION)
      @ 08,00 SAY 'Project Grade: ' +;
                  STR(PROJ_GRADE,3)
      @ 20,00
      WAIT [Delete it? (Y/N): ] TO DELETEIT
      CLEAR
      IF UPPER(DELETEIT) = 'Y'
         DELETE
      ENDIF          && deleteit='Y'
   ELSE
      CLEAR
      @ 12,20 SAY NAMESEARCH + ' COULD NOT BE ;
                  FOUND...'
   ENDIF             && .not. eof()
   @ 21,00
   WAIT [Finished? (Y/N): ] TO FINISHED
ENDDO                && finished<>'Y'
CLEAR
@ 11,0
WAIT [Do you wish to Execute Your Deletions (Y/N): ];
     TO PACKTHEMIN
IF UPPER(PACKTHEMIN) = 'Y'
   PACK
ENDIF             && packthemin='Y'
USE
RETURN
```

Listing 9.5 Program COM_DELE.prg

312   ITERATION

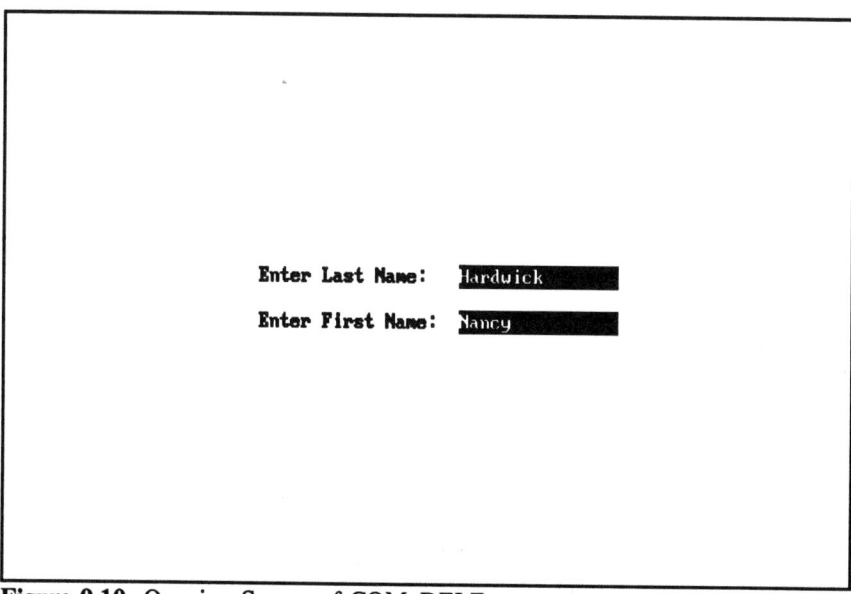

Figure 9.10 Opening Screen of COM_DELE.prg

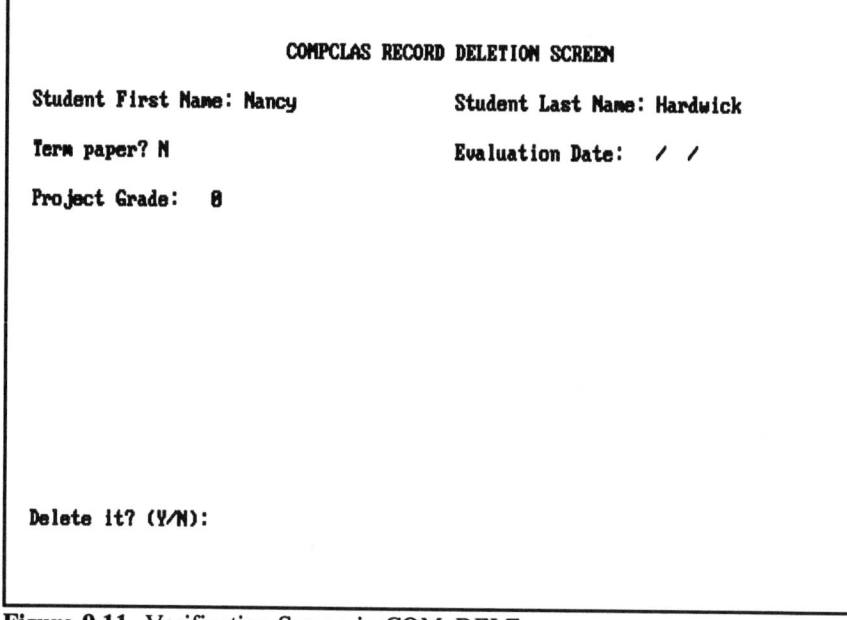

Figure 9.11 Verification Screen in COM_DELE.prg

In either case we then get to decide if we wish to delete some more records or not. In this way, a whole series of records can be deleted before any packing is done. The parallelogram in Figure 9.9 labeled "Enter 'Y' if Finished?" allows us to modify the *LoopCondition* so that we can leave the loop if we desire.

Once we have left the loop, the last decision is whether we wish to execute these deletions by packing the data base or not. If we answer 'Y' to the question of "Do you wish to Execute Your Deletions", then the PACK takes place; otherwise it is skipped, leaving the records we indicated, still marked for deletion.

As an example, suppose we choose to delete Nancy Hardwick's record from our data base. Figure 9.10 shows us entering in her name for the initial search. In Figure 9.11 we have Nancy Hardwick's record up for deletion. Having answered "Y" to the question, "Delete It?" we then see the screen shown in Figure 9.12. To the question, "Finished?" we type "Y" once more. Finally we see the screen shown in Figure 9.13, which asks us if we wish to execute our deletions. To this question we will answer "N", leaving Nancy marked for deletion but not as yet removed from the data base.

9.5 Design of a Fast Indexed Search Program

The indexed search is a fast search since the SEEK operation can go directly to the desired record without searching through the entire database. However, the SEEK operation only finds the first occurrence of the desired item. To obtain subsequent records having the same search criterion, we must use other means.

Fortunately an indexed database is in the order of the key by which it is indexed. Since the key happens to be the item we are searching for, all of the records satisfying our search criterion are in consecutive indexed order.

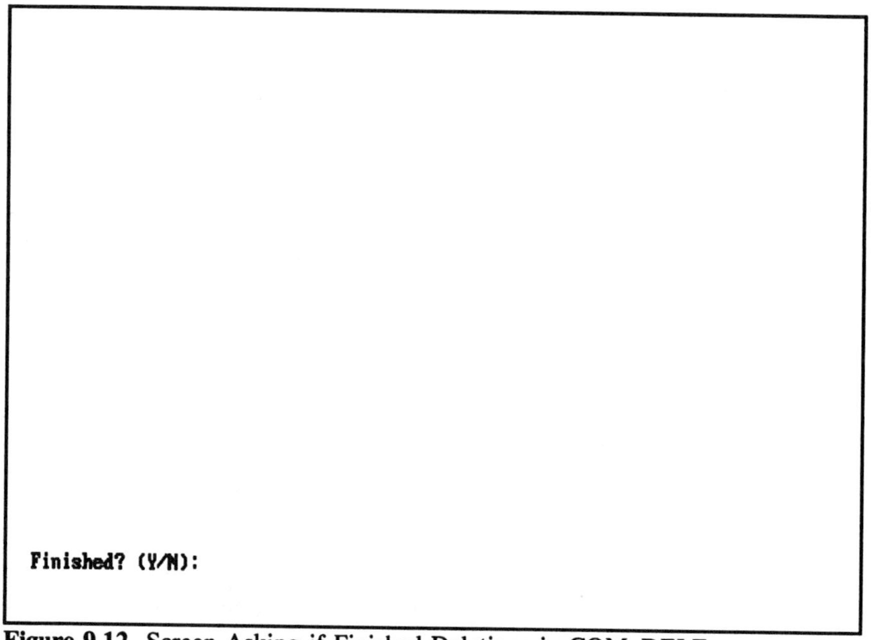

```
Finished? (Y/N):
```

Figure 9.12 Screen Asking if Finished Deletions in COM_DELE.prg

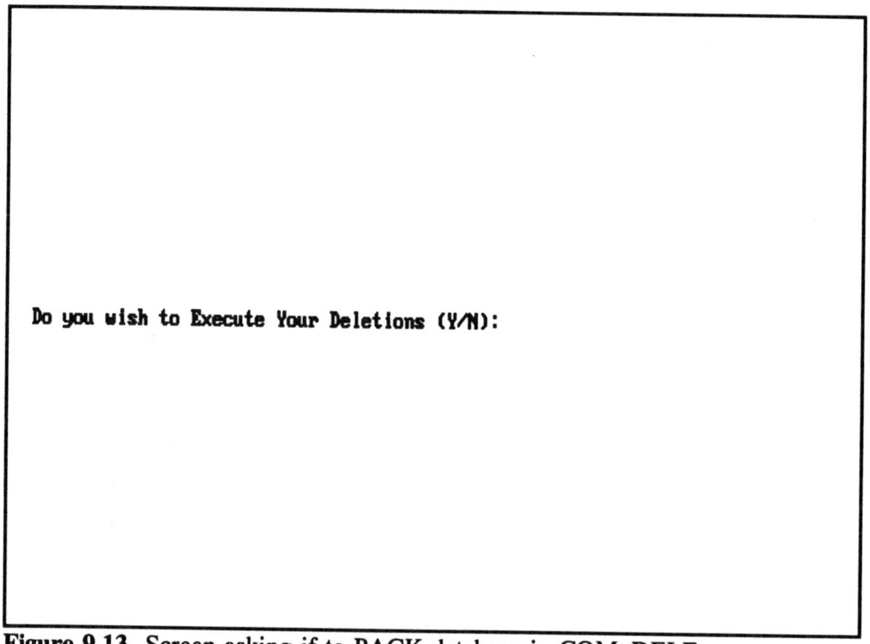

```
Do you wish to Execute Your Deletions (Y/N):
```

Figure 9.13 Screen asking if to PACK database in COM_DELE.prg

Because of this fact, one way of displaying all of these records is to begin by SEEKing the first record, and then using the SKIP instruction to display all subsequent records until we find one which no longer matches our search criterion. However, there is even an easier way of limiting our search to just those records satisfying our search criterion, and that is by means of the **LOCATE WHILE** instruction.

9.5.1 The **LOCATE WHILE** Instruction

The **LOCATE WHILE** *Criterion* instruction limits the scope of the search to include only the consecutive records satisfying the search criterion. As soon as the search criterion is no longer satisfied, the search activity ceases. This is in stark contrast to the **LOCATE FOR** instruction which searches starting at the beginning of the database and continues on until the end of the database looking for the desired item and wasting a lot of processing time as it is doing so.

In the indexed search, the first record satisfying the criterion is immediately found using the **SEEK** or **FIND** instruction. Then the **LOCATE WHILE** instruction is invoked. Finally, all subsequent records satisfying the criterion are found with successive applications of the **CONTINUE** instruction.

For example, suppose that we wish to access all records having the EVALUATION date of {12/14/92}[28]. The sequence we would follow is:
SET ORDER TO EVALUATION
SEEK {12/14/92}
LOCATE WHILE EVALUATION = {12/14/92}
.
CONTINUE
.
CONTINUE
etc.

---

[28] {12/14/92} is an expression equivalent to the function: CTOD("12/14/92").

The **SEEK** finds the first record, then the **LOCATE WHILE** instruction is invoked which allows us to locate all subsequent consecutive records for which the evaluation date is 12/14/92. As soon as a record is located for which the evaluation date is no longer 12/14/92, the end of the locate scope is encountered. The means of determining when the end of the locate scope has been encountered is by use of the **FOUND()** function.

9.5.2 Use of the **FOUND()** Function

As long as a **SEEK, FIND, LOCATE,** or a **CONTINUE** instruction successfully encounters a record satisfying its criterion, the **FOUND()** function will have a value of **True**. As soon as no record satisfying the criterion is encountered, the value of the **FOUND()** function becomes **False**. The program fragment containing our loop which locates all records satisfying our criterion looks like:

```
SET INDEX TO EVALUATION
SEEK {12/14/92}
LOCATE WHILE EVALUATION = {12/14/92}
DO WHILE FOUND()
    .
    . {This part displays each record satisfying the criterion}
    .
    CONTINUE
ENDDO
```

What makes the **FOUND()** function so powerful is that, unlike the **EOF()** function, the search does not have to continue until the end of the file in order to break out of the loop. As soon as the **LOCATE WHILE** *criterion* is no longer satisfied, the loop is terminated.

9.5.3 An Example of Indexed Search—COM_EVAL.prg

The flow diagram for COM_EVAL.prg is shown in Figure 9.14, while the program itself is given in Listing 9.6. We begin by entering the date for which we'd like to search. In this case we

ITERATION

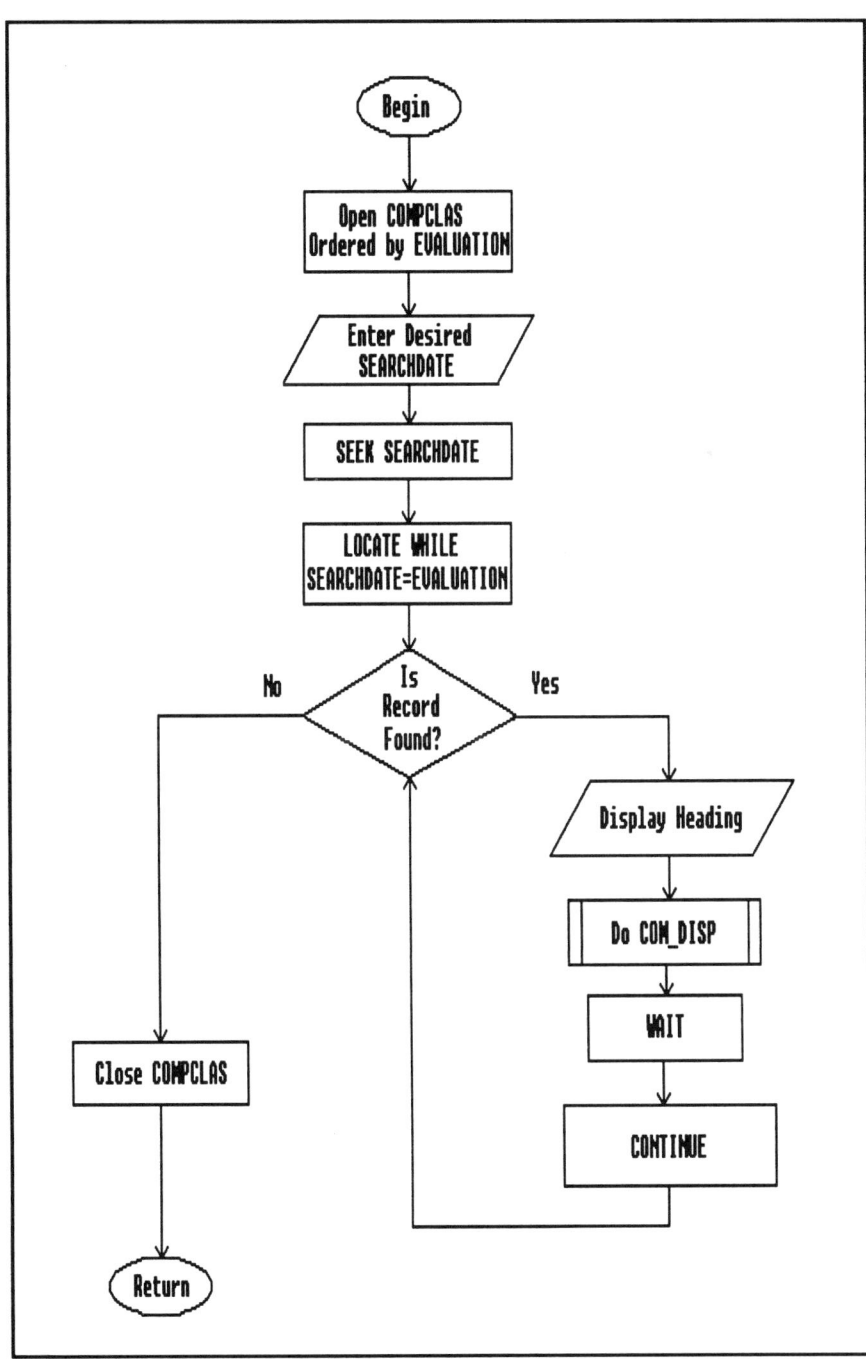

Figure 9.14 Flow Chart of COM_EVAL.prg

preset our input date variable, SEARCHDATE, to a blank. The opening screen, showing this display, is shown in Figure 9.15. Here we have entered the date, "12/14/92".

```
* COM_EVAL.prg
* This Program searches for all records where
* evaluation dates are those specified by the
* user.  The records are then displayed on the
* screen.  This demonstrates the use of an
* Indexed Search using SEEK followed by a LOCATE
* WHILE instruction.  In addition it calls another
* sub-module, COM_DISP.prg which displays the
* contents of a particular record.
*
SET STATUS OFF
USE COMPCLAS ORDER EVALUATION
STORE CTOD("  /  /  ") TO SEARCHDATE
CLEAR
@12,15 SAY "Enter Evaluation Date You Wish To Find:";
       GET SEARCHDATE
READ
SEEK SEARCHDATE
LOCATE WHILE EVALUATION = SEARCHDATE
DO WHILE FOUND()
   CLEAR
   @ 1,22 SAY "Students To Be Evaluated on " +;
      DTOC(SEARCHDATE)
   DO COM_DISP
   WAIT
   CONTINUE
ENDDO
USE
RETURN
```

Listing 9.6 Program COM_EVAL.prg

ITERATION 319

```
            Enter Evaluation Date You Wish To Find:  12/14/92
```

Figure 9.15 Opening Screen For COM_EVAL.prg

```
                    Students To Be Evaluated on 12/14/92

First Name:   Mary Beth              Last Name: Swazey

Address:      85 Cider Mill Lane     City ST Zip: North Branch, NY  12766

Term Project: T        Project Grade: 52      Evaluation Date: 12/14/92

Comments:
Mary Beth clearly did not put any effort into her
project. Her attendance has been very spotty
also.




Press any key to continue...
```
Figure 9.16 Record Found by COM_EVAL.prg for date: "12/14/92"

Next, we open the database ordered by the date index, EVALUATION. We then **SEEK** the **SEARCHDATE** that we entered at the opening screen. Since **SEEK** starts at the top of the database, we can be sure if there are any records in the database that satisfy our search criterion, they will be found. We then invoke the **LOCATE WHILE EVALUATION = SEARCHDATE** command. Since the pointer is currently pointing to a record that is satisfying this criterion (or it is at the end of the file), our current record is the one that has been located.

Now we are ready to display the record that satisfies our date criterion. This is done by executing the program COM_DISP.prg, which is shown in Listing 9.7. This listing was copied directly from our format file, COMPCLAS.FMT, that we first examined in Figure 7.15. COM_DISP.prg was obtained from Figure 7.15 by replacing every **GET** with a **SAY**.

There is one display statement in COM_DISP.prg which is an exception. This is the one which displays the contents of the memo field, COMMENTS. This is because the contents of a memo field cannot be displayed with the SAY command. The cursor is then placed at the bottom of the screen so that the comment made by the WAIT instruction will appear as far from the record data as possible.

After we have executed COM_DISP.prg, we hold the display on the screen with the **WAIT** command until a key is struck. After a key is struck, we **CONTINUE** doing our **LOCATE WHILE** command. If the next record in sequence is found to satisfy our evaluation date criterion, then **FOUND()** will be **true**. If the next record does not satisfy this criterion, then **FOUND()** will be **false**, and the loop will be exited.

If we strike the Enter key after entering "12/14/92", we find that the record of Jonathan Samuels is displayed. If we strike the Enter key once more, we find that Mary Beth Swazey also meets this criterion. The display for her case is shown in Figure 9.16.

```
* COM_DISP.PRG
* This displays the contents of a COMPCLAS record on
* the screen.  It was obtained by copying a portion
* of COMPCLAS.FMT, and changing all the GETs to SAYs.
* The only exception is the Memo field, COMMENTS,
* which can only be displayed with the ? command.
* Cursor is positioned at the bottom of the screen
* upon exiting.
*
@ 4,0  SAY "First Name:"
@ 4,14 SAY Firstname PICTURE "XXXXXXXXXXXXXXX"
@ 4,44 SAY "Last Name:"
@ 4,55 SAY Lastname PICTURE "XXXXXXXXXXXXXXX"
@ 6,0  SAY "Address:"
@ 6,14 SAY Address PICTURE   ;
          "XXXXXXXXXXXXXXXXXXXXXXXXX"
@ 6,42 SAY "City ST Zip:"
@ 6,55 SAY City_st_zp PICTURE   ;
          "XXXXXXXXXXXXXXXXXXXXXXXXX"
@ 8,0  SAY "Term Project:"
@ 8,14 SAY Term_proj PICTURE "L"
@ 8,26 SAY "Project Grade:"
@ 8,41 SAY Proj_grade PICTURE "999"
@ 8,54 SAY "Evaluation Date:"
@ 8,71 SAY Evaluation
@ 10,0 SAY "Comments:"
? Comments
@ 23,0
RETURN
```

Listing 9.7 Display Sub-Module: COM_DISP.prg

9.6 Use of the SCAN—ENDSCAN Instruction

The search loop in COM_EVAL.prg can be simplified by the means of another type of loop, the **SCAN** loop. We can replace these instructions in Listing 9.6:

```
LOCATE WHILE EVALUATION = SEARCHDATE
DO WHILE FOUND()
   CLEAR
   @ 1,22 SAY "Students To Be Evaluated on " +;
          DTOC(SEARCHDATE)
   DO COM_DISP
   WAIT
   CONTINUE
ENDDO
```

with the following instructions:

```
SCAN WHILE EVALUATION = SEARCHDATE
   CLEAR
   @ 1,22 SAY "Students To Be Evaluated on " +;
          DTOC(SEARCHDATE)
   DO COM_DISP
   WAIT
ENDSCAN
```

Note that the two instructions, **SCAN** and **ENDSCAN**, have replaced the four instructions: LOCATE, DO WHILE ..., CONTINUE, and ENDDO. This loop thus makes our instruction sequence a bit more compact. We shall employ its use in the design of a range search program.

9.6.1 The Design of a Range Search Program

When a variable range of values are being sought, rather than just a fixed range, an indexed search is no longer practical. This is because it takes longer to index the database on the new range desired than it does simply to SCAN the database. For this reason, we have to fall back on our slower LOCATE type of search[29].

However, what we can do is to put the records into indexed order, and then once the first record is located, we know that all records satisfying the criterion are immediately adjacent to that record or are non-existent. We have a couple of options open to us in this case. The first is to use, as we did in the previous section, the **LOCATE WHILE** instruction to encounter all of the subsequent records satisfying our criterion. The other is to use the **SCAN** loop.

---

[29]That is unless the user has some "trick" by which he or she can locate the first record satisfying the range criterion without doing an exhaustive record by record search. Methods for speeding up such searches fill volumes of books.

9.6.2 Example: The Design of COM_GRAD.prg

The technique for designing a range search program to find all records where the PROJ_GRADE is greater than or equal to a LOWERGRADE and less than or equal to a HIGHERGRAD is almost identical to that used in designing the fast indexed search routine. As a matter of fact, all one needs do is to replace the following lines found in COM_EVAL.prg:

```
USE COMPCLAS ORDER EVALUATION
STORE CTOD("  /  /  ") TO SEARCHDATE
CLEAR
@ 12,15 SAY "Enter Evaluation Date You Wish To
          Find: " GET SEARCHDATE
READ
SEEK SEARCHDATE
LOCATE WHILE EVALUATION = SEARCHDATE
```

with these lines:

```
USE COMPCLAS ORDER GRADE
STORE 0 TO LOWERGRADE
STORE 100 TO HIGHERGRAD
CLEAR
@ 10,18 SAY "From What Grade do you want to;
     Search:  " GET LOWERGRADE PICTURE '999'
@ 14,18 SAY "Up to What Grade do you want to;
     Search:  " GET HIGHERGRAD PICTURE '999'
READ
LOCATE FOR PROJ_GRADE>=LOWERGRADE .AND.;
     PROJ_GRADE<=HIGHERGRAD
LOCATE WHILE PROJ_GRADE>=LOWERGRADE .AND.;
     PROJ_GRADE<=HIGHERGRAD
```

and the desired program, COM_GRAD.prg, will be complete. Note that the SEEK statement in COM_EVAL.prg has been replaced by a LOCATE statement in COM_GRAD.prg. Otherwise the two approaches are pretty much the same.

However, we want to show how we would use the **SCAN—ENDSCAN** loop in the LOCATE case.

9.6.3 Use of the **SCAN—ENDSCAN** Loop for a LOCATE Search

Figure 9.17 shows the flow diagram for COM_GRAD, and the program itself is shown in Listing 9.8. We begin by opening COMPCLAS ordered by GRADE. Next we select the lower and upper limits of the grade ranges in which we would like to search. We set the defaults from a grade of "0" up to a grade of "100", just to cover the complete range. We then narrow the range of the search by typing in the values selected. Figure 9.18 shows the opening screen for COM_GRAD with the default values indicated. Figure 9.19 shows us having entered 80 for our low range of search and 90 for the high range.

Note that we have narrowed the numeric memory variables, LOWERGRADE and HIGHERGRAD, down to a width of three in the screen display. Normally, an integer variable will have a default width of 10. The use of the **PICTURE** clause after the **GET** command changes the default width accordingly. By saying **PICTURE '999'**, it indicates that the numeric variable should be three digits wide with no decimal point. In general the **PICTURE** clause is used to alter the display of the **SAY** or **GET** command from the default format of the variable displayed, be it numeric or character, memory variable or field variable.

Note that because we are using a LOCATE statement to find the first occurrence of the record satisfying the range criteria, for a large database (more than a few thousand records), the delay may be significant. The LOCATE statement is:

LOCATE FOR PROJ_GRADE >= LOWERGRADE .AND. ;
  PROJ_GRADE <= HIGHERGRAD

```
* COM_GRAD.prg
* This sub-module searches for all records
* where grades are in the range specified by
* the user.  The records are then displayed
* on the screen.  This demonstrates the use
* of the SCAN - ENDSCAN loop structure
*
SET STATUS OFF
USE COMPCLAS ORDER GRADE
STORE 0 TO LOWERGRADE
STORE 100 TO HIGHERGRAD
CLEAR
@ 10,18 SAY "From What Grade do you want to;
   Search:   " GET LOWERGRADE PICTURE '999'
@ 14,18 SAY "Up to What Grade do you want;
   to Search: " GET HIGHERGRAD PICTURE '999'
READ
LOCATE FOR PROJ_GRADE>=LOWERGRADE .AND.;
          PROJ_GRADE<=HIGHERGRAD
SCAN WHILE PROJ_GRADE>=LOWERGRADE .AND.;
          PROJ_GRADE<=HIGHERGRAD
   CLEAR
   @ 1,22 SAY "Students With Grades From ";
     + STR(LOWERGRADE,3) + " To " +;
     STR(HIGHERGRAD,3)
   DO COM_DISP
   WAIT
ENDSCAN
USE
RETURN
```

Listing 9.8 Program COM_GRAD.prg using SCAN—ENDSCAN structure

326 ITERATION

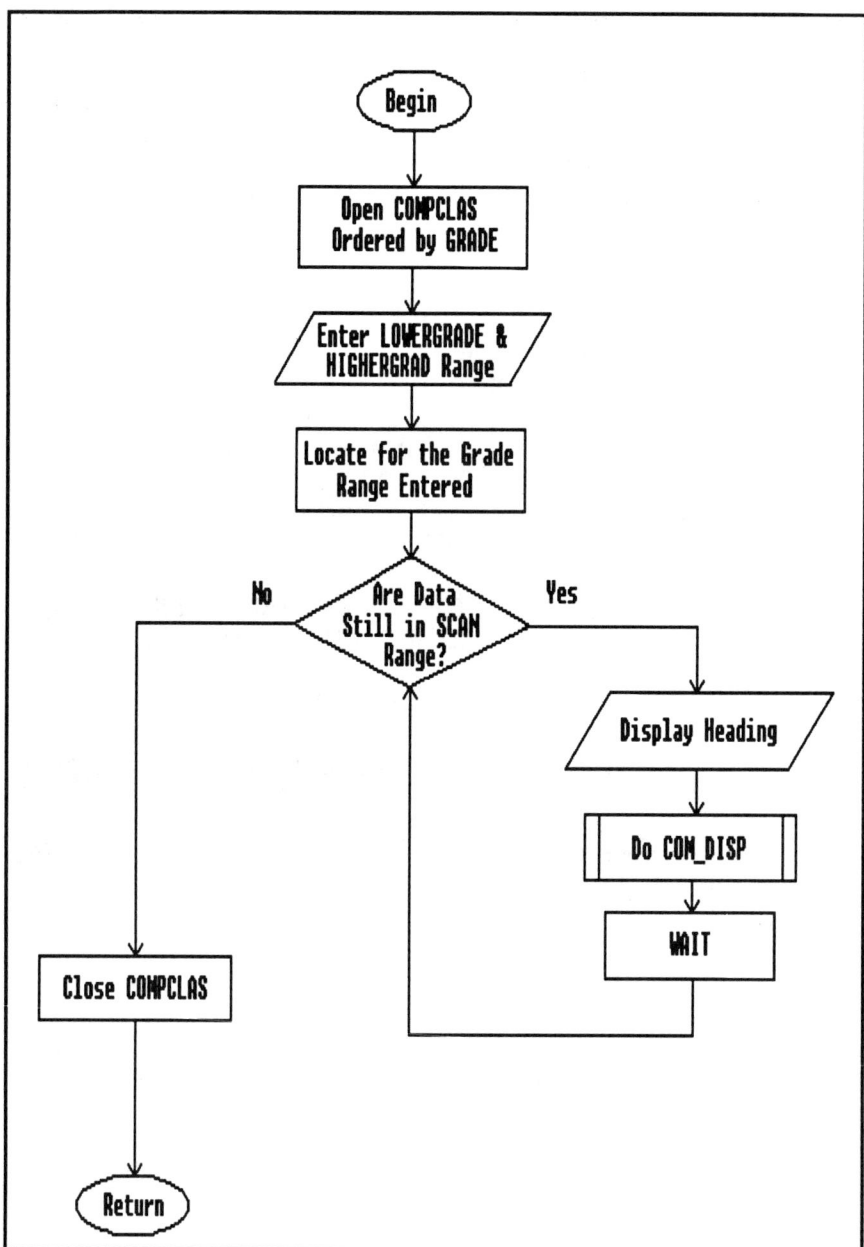

Figure 9.17 Flow Chart of COM_GRAD.prg

ITERATION 327

```
        From What Grade do you want to Search:   [ 0 ]


        Up to What Grade do you want to Search:  [100]
```

Figure 9.18 Opening Screen For COM_GRAD.prg

```
        From What Grade do you want to Search:   [80]


        Up to What Grade do you want to Search:  [90]
```

Figure 9.19 COM_GRAD after entering Desired Lower & Upper Range

This statement will locate the first record that contains a value of PROJ_GRADE greater than or equal to whatever we typed in for the LOWERGRADE and less than or equal to whatever we typed in for the HIGHERGRAD. We follow this statement immediately with:

SCAN WHILE PROJ_GRADE >= LOWERGRADE .AND. ;
    PROJ_GRADE <= HIGHERGRAD

This begins our loop but will terminate the loop as soon as the criteria are no longer satisfied. In this way we will not have to continue searching onward until the end of the file.

Except for the title displayed at the top of the screen, the rest of this program operates in exactly the same manner as COM_EVAL.prg. If, for example, we typed in 80 for the lower range and 90 for the upper range, then the screen title will be: "Students With Grades From 80 To 90".

Figure 9.20 shows the first screen that appears in our search for project grades between 80 and 90. Notice that the students are listed in descending order of grade.

9.6.4 Use of the **SCAN FOR** ... Loop

If we do not care about terminating the search as soon as the last record satisfying the criteria has been located, then we can make our code even more abbreviated. Listing 9.9 shows how we can replace the LOCATE FOR statement in the **SCAN FOR** loop.

The program, COMPGRAD.prg, will execute a bit slower than COM_GRAD.prg since it will continue searching even after all the records satisfying the criterion have been found. However, note that it is no longer necessary to have COMPCLAS ordered by the GRADE index tag. Since order is not important using **SCAN FOR**, this would enable you, if you so chose, to order all the students passing the criteria alphabetically.

```
                    Students With Grades From   80 To   90

First Name:   Consuelo                    Last Name: Naboa

Address:      324 Catskill Terrace        City ST Zip: Sundown, NY  12782

Term Project: T         Project Grade:  89        Evaluation Date: 12/16/92

Comments:
Consuelo would have had a clear "A" on her Term
Project, but she misspelled 6 words.  She should
consult her dictionary more.




Press any key to continue...
```

Figure 9.20 Display of 1st Record Meeting Range Criterion in COM_GRAD.prg

```
* COMPGRAD.prg
* This sub-module searches for all records where
* grades are in the range specified by the user.
* The records are then displayed on the screen.  This
* demonstrates the use of the SCAN FOR ...--ENDSCAN
* loop structure
*
SET STATUS OFF
USE COMPCLAS
STORE 0 TO LOWERGRADE
STORE 100 TO HIGHERGRAD
CLEAR
@ 10,18 SAY "From What Grade do you want to Search:  ";
            GET LOWERGRADE PICTURE '999'
@ 14,18 SAY "Up to What Grade do you want to Search: ";
            GET HIGHERGRAD PICTURE '999'
READ
SCAN FOR PROJ_GRADE >= LOWERGRADE .AND. PROJ_GRADE;
    <= HIGHERGRAD
   CLEAR
   @ 1,22 SAY "Students With Grades From " +;
     STR(LOWERGRADE,3) + " To " + STR(HIGHERGRAD,3)
   DO COM_DISP
   WAIT
ENDSCAN
USE
RETURN
```

Listing 9.9 COMPGRAD.prg demonstrates use of SCAN FOR Loop

Although anything that can be done using the **SCAN** loop can be done using the **DO WHILE** loop, the **SCAN** loop does make for tighter code, hence less chance of making errors.

9.7 Remarks on the use of the WHILE Clause

The use of the **WHILE** clause extends well beyond its use in the LOCATE and SCAN instructions. The following global instructions that we have already introduced support the use of the **WHILE** clause:

> **AVERAGE**
> **CALCULATE**
> **COUNT**
> **DELETE**
> **DISPLAY**
> **LIST**
> **LOCATE**
> **REPLACE**
> **SCAN**
> **SORT**
> **SUM**

The means of using the **WHILE** clause is the same in each case. Unless the database is in sorted order on the key with which you are operating, the index needs to be on. One begins by searching for the first record satisfying the criteria, then the instruction is invoked with the **WHILE** clause. As soon as all the records in sequence which satisfy the criteria are processed, the operation ceases.

In indexed systems, the use of the **WHILE** clause over the simple **FOR** clause is encouraged to speed up whatever global operation is being done.

9.8 Summary

In this chapter we have introduced the concept of iteration. The command that allows us to iterate is the DO WHILE loop. We learned the three conditions that a Do While loop must fulfill in order to be considered consistent with the principles of "Structured Programming".

Using the DO WHILE loop, we found we could use such diverse loop conditions as: a password, counting down to zero, End Of File, a "Y" or "N" answer to whether or not you want to quit, or whether or not a record satisfying a particular criteria is still being Found.

We learned that we could speed up a search by using the WHILE clause. We also found that we could use fewer steps in a search loop by using the SCAN—ENDSCAN commands.

We have now wrapped up our discussion of structured programming with the presentation of the loop. With the addition of the loop and selection structures, we have the full power we need to write any kind of program that we wish to create.

9.9 Review

In Chapter 9 we have presented the following commands:

> **DO WHILE** *LoopCondition*
> **ENDDO**
> **ENDSCAN**
> **LOCATE WHILE** *SearchCondition*
> **SCAN FOR** *SearchCondition*
> **SCAN WHILE** *LoopCondition*
> **USE** *FileName* **ORDER** *TagName*

Add these instructions to your glossary of dBASE programming commands. In addition, the following function was introduced in this chapter.

FOUND()

Add this to your glossary of dBASE functions.

9.10 Laboratory Work

Follow all the steps outlined in this chapter. Write and run the programs: PASSWORD.prg, MESSAGE.prg, BALANCE.prg, COM_DELE.prg, COM_EVAL.prg, and COM_GRAD.prg.

9.11 Exercises

1. Write the program, MAIL_DEL.prg, for the MAILIST system along lines similar to those used for COM_DELE.prg. Hand in a hard copy of this program.

2. Write the program, MAILZIP.prg, for the MAILIST system along lines similar to those used for COM_GRAD.prg. The program should search and display those records greater than or equal to a lower zip code value and less than or equal to an upper zip code value. The user should be able to input the upper and lower ranges for the zip code from the keyboard.

    a) Hand in a copy of MAILZIP.prg.

    b) Hand in a copy of MAILDISP.prg (the program module which actually displays the record on the screen after it has been located).

3. Write the program, MAILCARD.prg, for the MAILIST system along lines similar to those used for COM_EVAL.prg. The program should search and display either those records for which CARD is true, or those records for which CARD is false. The user should be able to input from the keyboard

which of those two conditions he or she wants to display. Hand in a copy of this program.

9.12 Term Project

Hand in a list of all the actions that you want your system to be able to accomplish. Each of these actions will refer to a program, or group of programs, that you will be writing. Each should be labeled with an eight character, or less, name. Each should contain a brief description of what it will do. For example:

PROJEDIT	Will search for records by account # and edit them
PROJADD	Will append new records to the project database
etc.	etc.

CHAPTER 10

SYSTEM ORGANIZATION

10.0   Topics Covered in Chapter 10

The System Structure Chart is introduced.

A Menu Driver with Pop-up Windows is Designed.

A Sub-Menu Driver within a Window is Presented.

The Program Structure Chart shows the organization of all the programs used by the system.

The Use of Procedures is demonstrated.

An entire system of Programs is replaced by one Procedure File.

A Procedure Driver is developed to run the Procedure File.

A working system is created out of only the Object Files compiled by the dBASE IV pseudo compiler.

10.1 Bottom Up Systems Design

Most systems designers like to talk about "Top Down" systems's design. This is where the systems designer has analyzed the needs of the user and has designed a new system that will do the desired job meeting the specifications of the client. This requires that the designer obtain, before he or she starts designing, a clear idea of exactly what the final goals of the system are to be. However, that requires that the client know precisely what the system should do.

It is a wonderful thing when a systems designer encounters a client who is so clear on his or her objectives. Among those people who may be new to computer use, I more often find people who have a vague or somewhat limited idea of what they want their system to do. As we work on the various tasks that they want their system to perform, they will begin to see what the possibilities are and become more creative in what they want their system to do. To build a system in this way is often called "prototyping" or "Bottom Up" systems design. This is particularly true of people who build their own systems and continually find a need to enhance these systems.

In working in this manner, the need soon arises to bring some order out of the chaos of the design process. We did this in Chapter 7 by organizing six of the programs that we wrote with a menu program that tied them all together. However, Chapters 8 and 9 have added three additional and two replacement programs to our COMPCLAS system. To simply add them to our already existing menu would create a menu of ten choices[30] with the threat of more modules to come.

At some point it becomes desirable to break a large menu into a group of small submenus. In this way the user starts by making some choices about the broad categories in which he or she

---

[30] It is a generally accepted convention that a single menu should not contain more than seven different actions to be performed.

wishes to work and then gets down to the detail in subsequent submenus. This way of organizing one's system has the benefit of being less daunting to the new user than one large menu of ten or more choices. It also has the benefit of allowing for indefinite system expansion in a "user friendly" way.

10.2 The Systems Structure Chart

Figure 10.1 shows the original system structure that was produced by the system of programs created in Chapter 7. Figure 10.2 shows a way in which we can organize all the relevant programs in the COMPCLAS system, including those developed in Chapters 8 and 9, so that they fall into a logical order. Such a design also allows for further expansion which is certain to occur.

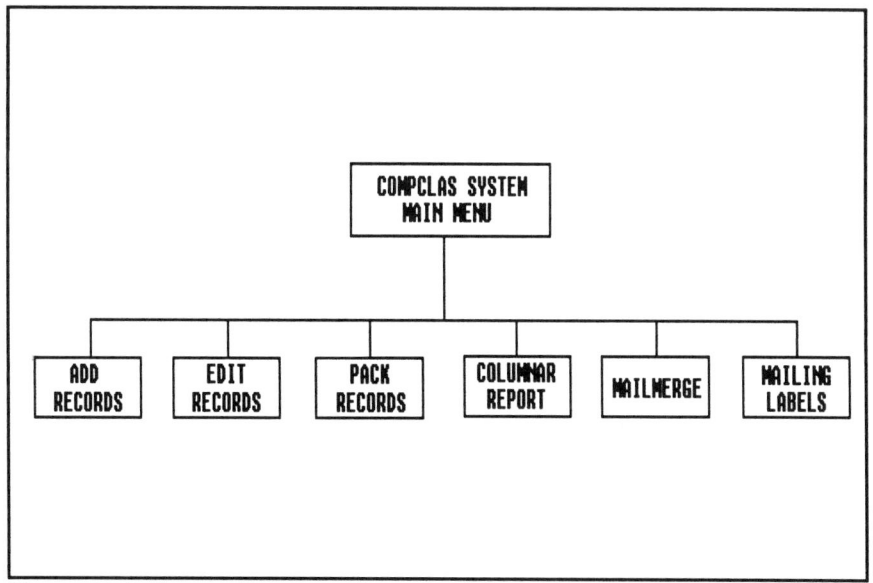

Figure 10.1 System Structure Chart of Original COMPCLAS System

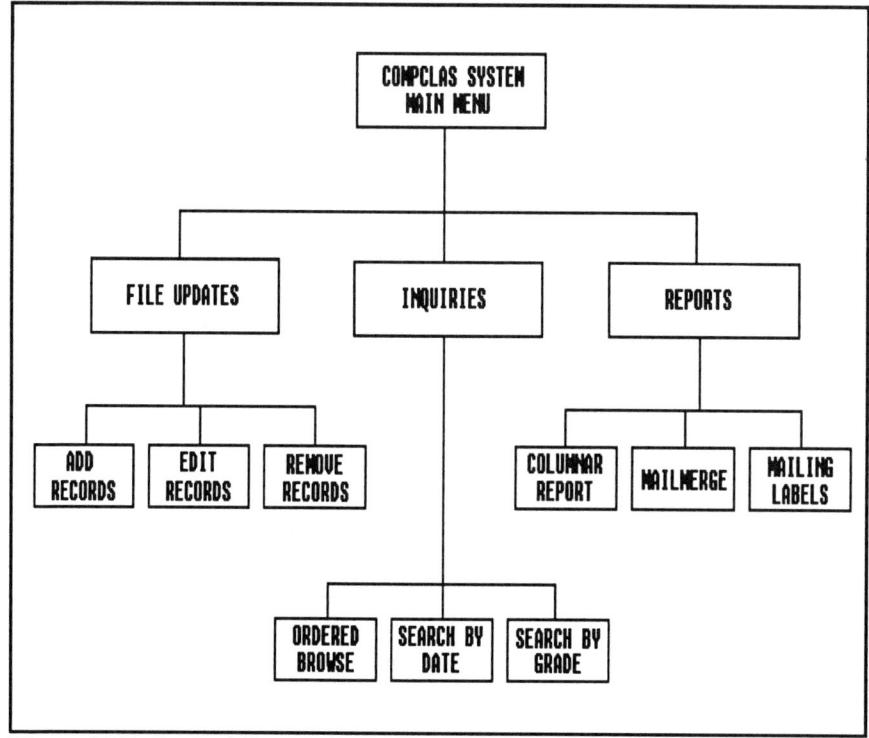

Figure 10.2 Revised System Chart For COMPCLAS System

Notice that we have taken all of the programs having to do with updating the system: the appending of new records, the editing of existing records, and the deletion of records, and have put them together under a menu heading of "File Updates". These are file maintenance operations and are usually used together.

All the reports also form a homogeneous grouping, and are logically placed together under a menu heading of "Reports".

The data queries are not quite so homogeneous. The Evaluation Date search and the Project Grade search are clearly queries that are logically similar. The "Ordered Browse" might be considered a query, but it does allow for editing and appending, so it might better be put with the "File Updates" grouping (see Figure 10.3). This is the type of design decision that the system designer frequently must make.

SYSTEM ORGANIZATION

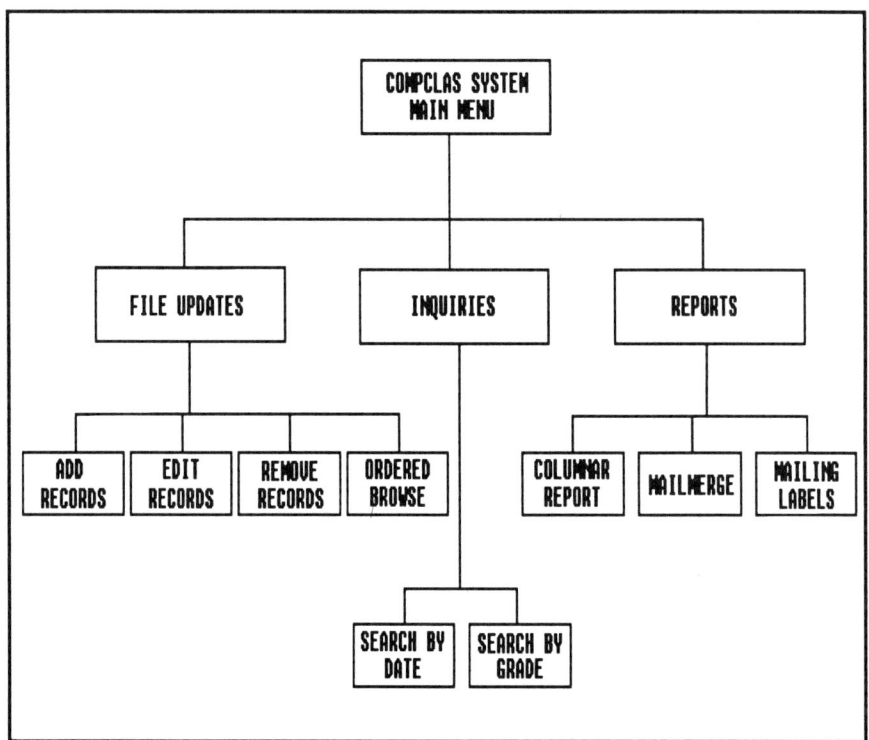

Figure 10.3 Alternate Grouping of COMPCLAS Submodules in New System

The user is now confronted with a clear menu of only three choices for starters. In subsequent menus, at worst, the user only has to decide between one of four items.

Now we need to develop a menu driver program that can handle not only the main menu, but also submenus too. This is the subject of the next section.

10.3 Menu Driver Program with Pop-Up Windows

We shall now develop a menu driver program that implements the alternate system structure chart shown in Figure 10.3. The program, called COM_MENU.prg, is shown in Listing 10.1. This program represents an enhancement of the menu that we developed in Chapter 7, COMPMENU.prg.

We begin as we did with COMPMENU.prg, by defining the menu and its pads. However, this time we elect to make this a horizontal menu. In this way the pop-up windows can descend vertically, just below the pads that allow access to them. (See Figure 10.4)

Below each pad a pop-up is activated as seen in the statement:

ON PAD Update OF Main Activate Pop-up Updatpop

Next the pop-up is defined as in the statement:

DEFINE Pop-up Updatpop FROM 13,05 MESSAGE "File Maintenance"

Then the individual bars of the pop-up are defined with the statements:

DEFINE BAR 1 OF Updatpop PROMPT "Add Records"
DEFINE BAR 2 OF Updatpop PROMPT "Edit Records"
DEFINE BAR 3 OF Updatpop PROMPT "Delete Records"
DEFINE BAR 4 OF Updatpop PROMPT "Browse Records"

Next, the action taken by the pop-up is given by the instruction:

ON SELECTION POP-UP Updatpop Do UPDACASE

Finally, the menu is **ACTIVATE**d.

When the menu driving program, COM_MENU.prg is executed, the first pad with its respective pop-up menu is shown. Executing:

. DO COM_MENU

we get the result shown in Figure 10.4. Moving the cursor to the right one keystroke at a time results in the screens shown in Figures 10.5, 10.6, and 10.7.

SYSTEM ORGANIZATION

```
* COM_MENU.prg
* This defines the menu for COMPCLAS
* It includes a Horizontal Menu with Popup Windows
*
SET STATUS OFF
CLEAR

@ 2,28 SAY "COMPUTER CLASS MAIN MENU"

* Define the Menu with its pads

DEFINE MENU Main
DEFINE PAD Update OF Main PROMPT " Update Records ";
   AT 12,05
DEFINE PAD Search OF Main PROMPT "Search Records" AT 12,25
DEFINE PAD Print  OF Main PROMPT "Print Reports"  AT 12,45
DEFINE PAD Exit   OF Main PROMPT "Exit"           AT 12,70

* Assign popups to the pads

ON PAD Update OF Main Activate Popup Updatpop
ON PAD Search OF Main Activate Popup Searcpop
ON PAD Print  OF Main Activate Popup Printpop

* Define Exit pad's popup and first bar

DEFINE POPUP Updatpop FROM 13,05 MESSAGE "File Maintenance"
DEFINE POPUP Searcpop FROM 13,25 MESSAGE "Search Options"
DEFINE POPUP Printpop FROM 13,45 MESSAGE "Report Options"

DEFINE BAR 1 OF Updatpop PROMPT "Add Records"
DEFINE BAR 2 OF Updatpop PROMPT "Edit Records"
DEFINE BAR 3 OF Updatpop PROMPT "Delete Records"
DEFINE BAR 4 OF Updatpop PROMPT "Browse Records"

DEFINE BAR 1 OF Searcpop PROMPT "Grade Search"
DEFINE BAR 2 OF Searcpop PROMPT "Date Search"

DEFINE BAR 1 OF Printpop PROMPT " Columnar  "
DEFINE BAR 2 OF Printpop PROMPT " Mailmerge "
DEFINE BAR 3 OF Printpop PROMPT "  Labels   "

ON SELECTION POPUP Updatpop Do UPDACASE
ON SELECTION POPUP Searcpop DO SEARCASE
ON SELECTION POPUP Printpop DO PRINCASE
ON SELECTION PAD Exit OF Main DEACTIVATE MENU

ACTIVATE MENU MAIN

SET STATUS ON
RETURN
```

Listing 10.1 Expanded Main Menu Program: COM_MENU.prg

342   SYSTEM ORGANIZATION

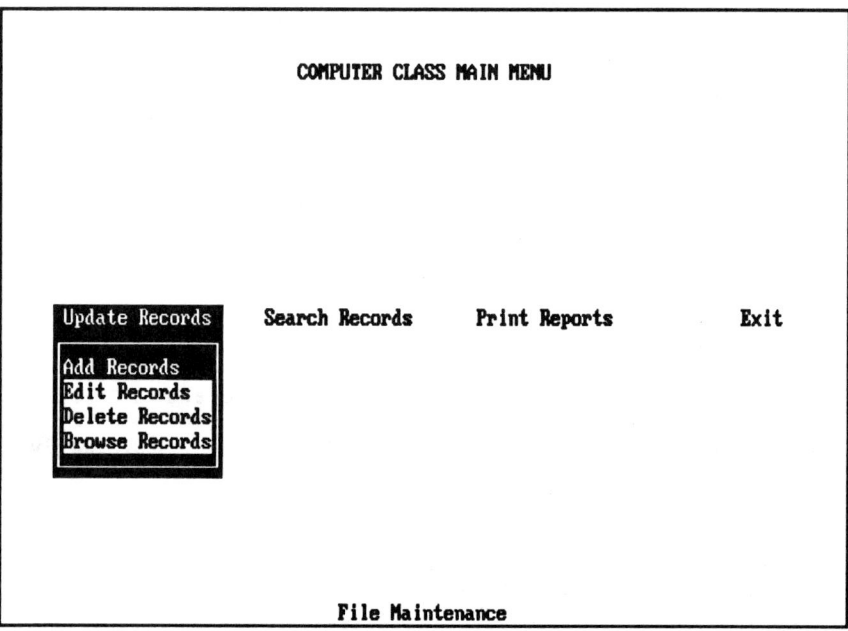

Figure 10.4 Opening Screen for COM_MENU.PRG

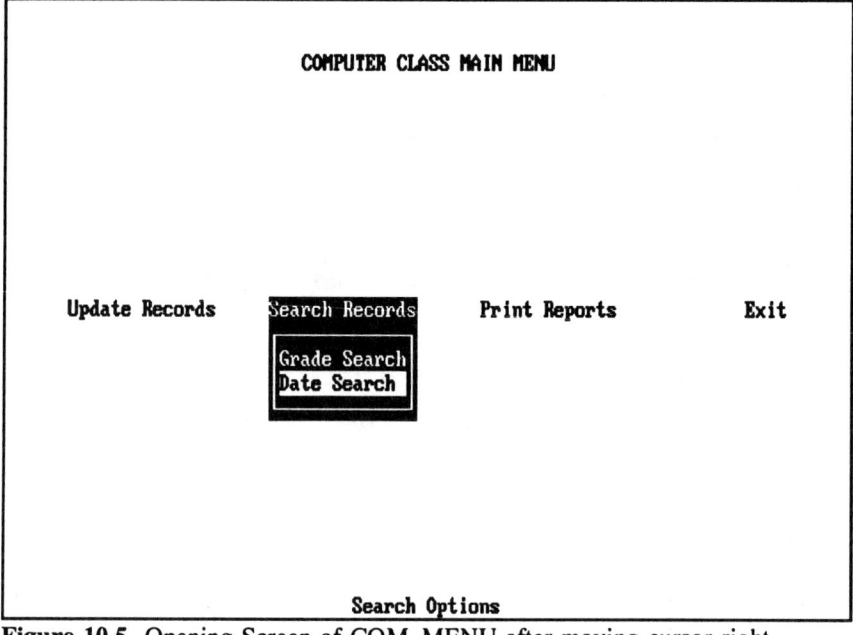

Figure 10.5 Opening Screen of COM_MENU after moving cursor right

SYSTEM ORGANIZATION

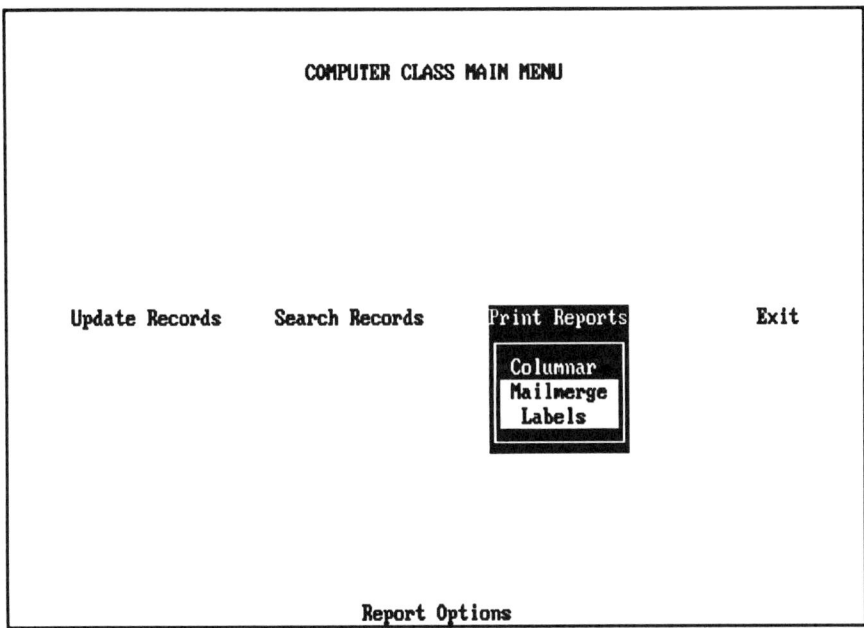

Figure 10.6 Menu of COM_MENU after striking right cursor key twice

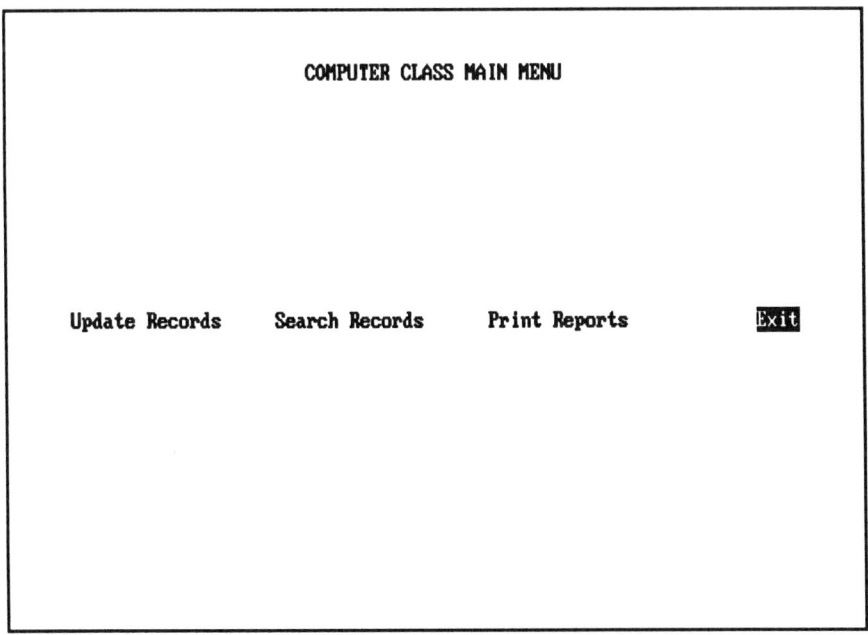

Figure 10.7 Selecting Rightmost Menu option in COM_MENU.prg

344 SYSTEM ORGANIZATION

By striking the down and up cursor movement keys, we may select any of the menu options appearing in the pop-up window that is open. For example, striking the down arrow key three times in Figure 10.4 then would cause the "Browse Records" option to be selected (see Figure 10.8). Striking the Enter key would cause the program, COM_BROW.prg, to be executed.

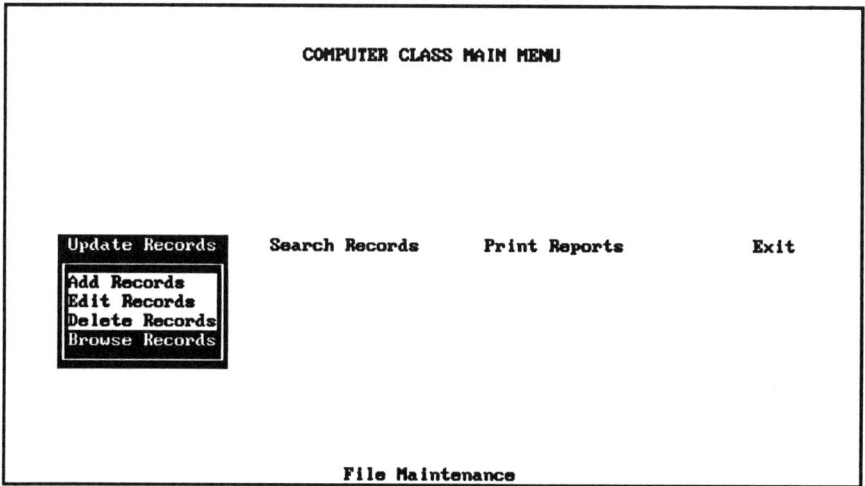

Figure 10.8 Selecting the "Browse Records" Popup menu item

10.3.1 Design of Menu Sub-Modules

The program, COM_MENU.prg, contains the three lines:

ON SELECTION POP-UP Updatpop Do UPDACASE
ON SELECTION POP-UP Searcpop DO SEARCASE
ON SELECTION POP-UP Printpop DO PRINCASE

These imply the existence of three sub-programs: UPDACASE.prg, SEARCASE.prg, and PRINCASE.prg. These are the sub-modules that actually determine which of the programs of the COMPCLAS system actually get executed.

Listing 10.2 shows the program UPDACASE.prg, Listing 10.3 shows SEARCASE.prg, and Listing 10.4 shows PRINCASE.prg.

```
* UPDACASE.prg
* This is the selection CASE statement for
* File Maintenance
*
SAVE SCREEN TO COMPSCREEN
DO CASE
   CASE BAR()=1
      DO COMPADD
   CASE BAR()=2
      DO COM_EDIT
   CASE BAR()=3
      DO COM_DELE
   CASE BAR()=4
      DO BROWMENU
ENDCASE
RESTORE SCREEN FROM COMPSCREEN
RETURN
```

Listing 10.2 Program UPDACASE.prg which determines which file Maintenance Function to Perform

```
* SEARCASE.PRG
* This is the selection CASE statement for
* the searches
*
SAVE SCREEN TO COMPSCREEN
DO CASE
   CASE BAR()=1
      DO COM_GRAD
   CASE BAR()=2
      DO COM_EVAL
ENDCASE
RESTORE SCREEN FROM COMPSCREEN
RETURN
```

Listing 10.3 Program SEARCASE.prg which determines which Search program to run

```
* PRINCASE.prg
* This is the selection CASE statement for
* the Printed Reports
*
SAVE SCREEN TO COMPSCREEN
DO CASE
    CASE BAR()=1
        DO COMPREPO
    CASE BAR()=2
        DO COMPMAIL
    CASE BAR()=3
        DO COMPLABL
ENDCASE
RESTORE SCREEN FROM COMPSCREEN
RETURN
```

Listing 10.4 Program: PRINCASE.prg which determines which Report to Print

Note that each of these programs basically amounts to a CASE statement. We begin by saving the main screen we created in COM_MENU.prg with the statement: **SAVE SCREEN TO COMPSCRN**. When we're done with the CASE statement, we **RESTORE** this screen with the command **RESTORE SCREEN FROM COMPSCRN**. In this way, the screen of the main menu is preserved intact after each menu item is selected and executed.

The new function: **BAR()**, is introduced. **BAR()** takes on an integer value determined by which bar in the pop-up menu was selected when the Enter key was struck.

In the case of UPDACASE.prg, we call a new program called BROWMENU.prg, rather than the COM_BROW.prg that was designed in Chapter 8. COM_BROW.prg asks you to type in a number to determine which option you want to take in the menu. This approach is inconsistent with how menus have been handled in Chapters 7 and 10. Instead we will develop another menu in which the menu option is chosen by the position of the cursor key. In order to do this, we will create a separate small window in which to put this menu.

10.4 Use of Windows in Sub-Menus

One of the ways to continue to use "cursor selected menus" is to create a window in which the new menu appears. This menu can be defined in much the same way as the original COMPMENU.prg was defined in Chapter 7.

Listing 10.5 shows the program BROWMENU.prg.

We begin by creating a window. This is done in the statements:

DEFINE WINDOW BrowWind From 18,06 to 23,19
ACTIVATE WINDOW BrowWind

The position of the upper left hand corner of the window—row 18, column 6—and the lower right hand corner of the window—row 23, column 19—is specified in the **FROM 18,06 to 23,19** clause. The window is then activated by the: **ACTIVATE WINDOW** *WindowName* command.

From this point onwards, any specification of row and column refers to a position within this window. The interior of the upper left hand corner of the window is now referred to as **0,0** regardless of where the window itself might be positioned on the screen. This is seen in the subsequent statements:

DEFINE PAD Name of SubMain PROMPT " Name "
  AT 0,1
DEFINE PAD Eval of SubMain PROMPT "Evaluation"
  AT 1,1
DEFINE PAD Grade of SubMain PROMPT " Grade "
  AT 2,1
DEFINE PAD Exit of SubMain PROMPT " Exit "
  AT 3,1

```
* BROWMENU.PRG
* This is a Sub-Menu for the Ordered
* Browse.  The Sub_Menu is contained
* within a defined Window.
*
* Create the Window
DEFINE WINDOW BrowWind From 18,06 to 23,19
ACTIVATE WINDOW BrowWind

* Create the Sub-Menu
DEFINE MENU SubMain MESSAGE   ;
   "Choose Index Order"
DEFINE PAD Name of SubMain PROMPT   ;
   "    Name    " AT 0,1
DEFINE PAD Eval of SubMain PROMPT   ;
   "Evaluation" AT 1,1
DEFINE PAD Grade of SubMain PROMPT ;
   "    Grade    " AT 2,1
DEFINE PAD Exit of SubMain PROMPT   ;
   "    Exit    " AT 3,1
ON SELECTION PAD Name of SubMain    ;
   DO NAMEBROW
ON SELECTION PAD Eval of SubMain    ;
   DO EVALBROW
ON SELECTION PAD Grade of SubMain   ;
   DO GRADBROW
ON SELECTION PAD Exit of SubMain    ;
   DEACTIVATE MENU
ACTIVATE MENU SUBMAIN

* After Deactivation of Sub-Menu, Turn off
* the Window
DEACTIVATE WINDOW BROWWIND
RETURN
```

Listing 10.5 Program: BROWMENU.prg creates a Sub-Menu in a Window

Note that we began our first Pad, "Name", at position **0,1** within the window.

The program fragment:

```
DEFINE MENU SubMain MESSAGE "Choose Index Order"
DEFINE PAD Name of SubMain PROMPT "  Name  ";
   AT 0,1
DEFINE PAD Eval of SubMain PROMPT "Evaluation";
   AT 1,1
DEFINE PAD Grade of SubMain PROMPT "  Grade  ";
   AT 2,1
DEFINE PAD Exit of SubMain PROMPT "  Exit  ";
   AT 3,1
ON SELECTION PAD Name of SubMain DO NAMEBROW
ON SELECTION PAD Eval of SubMain DO EVALBROW
ON SELECTION PAD Grade of SubMain DO GRADBROW
ON SELECTION PAD Exit of SubMain DEACTIVATE;
   MENU
ACTIVATE MENU SUBMAIN
```

is identical in substance to COMPMENU.prg which we developed in Chapter 7.

If we strike the Enter key with the "Browse" menu item selected in Figure 10.8, we get the window with its sub-menu displayed in Figure 10.9.

Note that Listing 10.5 implies the existence of the three subprograms: NAMEBROW.prg, EVALBROW.prg, and GRADBROW.prg. Listings 10.6, 10.7 and 10.8 show these sub-modules.

Just as we did with the sub-modules to the main menu program, we begin and end with STORE and RESTORE-ing our sub-menu screen. Notice that in each of these programs, we must next execute the command: **DEACTIVATE WINDOW** *WindowName*. If we did not do this, then the entire browse of the database would appear in the small window we created in Figure

350 SYSTEM ORGANIZATION

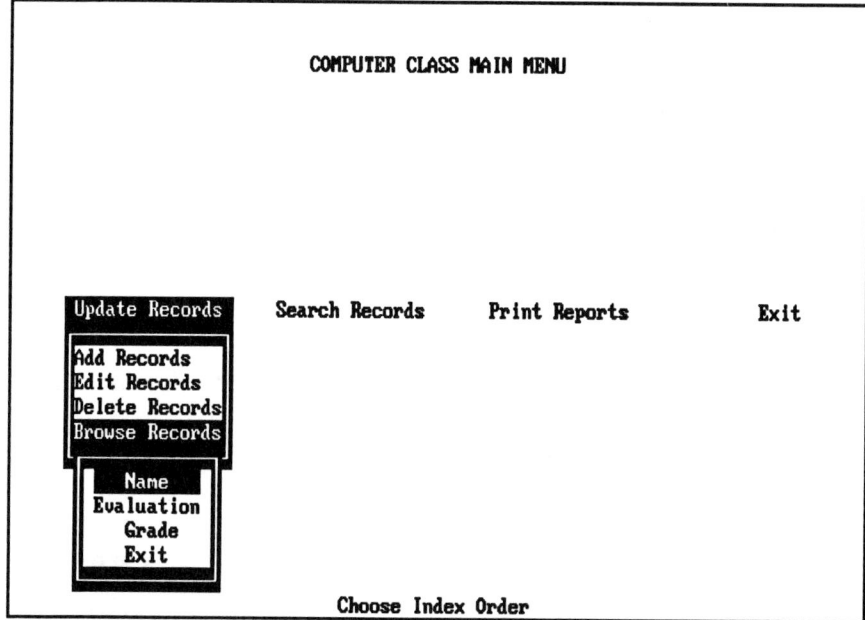

Figure 10.9 Program UPDACASE.prg creating SubMenu in Window

10.9 After we have done our browse in each case, we execute the command ACTIVATE WINDOW *WindowName* once more. Thus when we return to the calling program, BROWMENU.prg, we return within the framework of our sub-menu contained in our window.

As you can see, this type of menu building can be repeated indefinitely to any level that you might want to go. Note that windows do not have to be placed immediately below the menu popup that called them but can be placed anywhere on the screen.

10.5 Program Structure Chart

In the previous section we replaced the program GRADBROW.prg with a new window menu driver, BROWMENU.prg, which in turn called three sub-modules: NAMEBROW, GRADBROW, and EVALBROW. Revising our system structure chart, we find that the system now has the structure shown in Figure 10.10

```
* NAMEBROW.PRG
* This does a Browse of COMPCLAS.DBF in
* order of LASTFIRST
* It begins by deactivating the Window, and
* ends by activating it once more.
*
SAVE SCREEN TO BROWSCREEN
DEACTIVATE WINDOW BROWWIND
SET STATUS ON
USE COMPCLAS ORDER LASTFIRST
BROWSE
USE
SET STATUS OFF
ACTIVATE WINDOW BROWWIND
RESTORE SCREEN FROM BROWSCREEN
RETURN
```

Listing 10.6 Program: NAMEBROW.prg which Browses Ordered by LASTFIRST

The program structure chart shows the hierarchy of programs that actually implement the system structure chart (see Figure 10.11). Note that although the program structure chart and the system structure chart look very similar to each other, there is not always a one to one correspondence between the two. The display submodule, COM_DISP, although not really different from the COM_EVAL and COM_GRAD routines from a systems point of view, is indeed a separate program, functionally. As such it would appear in the program structure chart even though it does not appear in the system structure chart.

The program structure chart allows us to see, at a glance, the relationship between all the program modules we have written for the system. In this way we can not only keep an overview of the system, but we can see where individual programs fit into the overall system quickly.

Were it not for such tools as the program structure chart, as our system grows more and more complex, we would soon lose

```
* EVALBROW.PRG
* This does a Browse of COMPCLAS.DBF in
* order of EVALUATION
* Date.  It begins by deactivating the
* Window, and ends by
* activating it once more.
*
SAVE SCREEN TO BROWSCREEN
DEACTIVATE WINDOW BROWWIND
SET STATUS ON
USE COMPCLAS ORDER EVALUATION
BROWSE
USE
SET STATUS OFF
ACTIVATE WINDOW BROWWIND
RESTORE SCREEN FROM BROWSCREEN
RETURN
```

Listing 10.7 Program: EVALBROW.prg which Browses ordered by Evaluation Date

track of the programs that make it up and how they relate to each other. The importance of keeping such an overview cannot be stressed enough.

10.6   Use of Procedures in dBASE

One of the characteristics of dBASE is that it is "disk access intense", which is to say that it goes to the disk very frequently. Each time that you call a new program module, or open or close a database that's been altered, dBASE accesses the disk. Since accessing the disk takes orders of magnitude longer than accessing the RAM[31] (Random Access Memory, or Primary memory), if speed is a consideration, then you will want to minimize the frequency with which dBASE will have to access the disk.

---

[31]Typical disk access times are in the order of tens of milliseconds for a hard disk and hundreds of milliseconds for a floppy. Typical RAM access times are in the order of tens of nanoseconds (i.e. a million times as fast).

SYSTEM ORGANIZATION

```
* GRADBROW.PRG
* This does a Browse of COMPCLAS.DBF in
* order of PROJ_GRADE
* It begins by deactivating the Window, and
* ends by activating it once more.
*
SAVE SCREEN TO BROWSCREEN
DEACTIVATE WINDOW BROWWIND
SET STATUS ON
USE COMPCLAS ORDER GRADE
BROWSE
USE
SET STATUS OFF
ACTIVATE WINDOW BROWWIND
RESTORE SCREEN FROM BROWSCREEN
RETURN
```

Listing 10.8 Program: GRADBROW.prg which Browses ordered by PROJ_GRADE

There are two ways of doing this. One is to write large programs, which by their very nature will be complex. This way is not recommended. You will notice that none of the programs written in this book has exceeded one sheet of 8 $\frac{1}{2}$" X 11" paper in length. As programs become longer, the probability of error goes up not proportionately, but much faster than that. It usually takes more than twice as long to debug a two page program as it would for a one page program. This is because errors often interact with each other. So we want to keep our programs tight and use sub-modules wherever needed to simplify our understanding.

The second way to minimize access to the disk is by putting as much of the program up in memory as possible. This can be done by means of procedures.

Another of the most prominent features of dBASE is the number of files that it generates. Our COMPCLAS system now has seventeen .PRG files which make up the source code for the programs alone. Just as the production index has at least kept the number of index files from proliferating, in the same way we can

354   SYSTEM ORGANIZATION

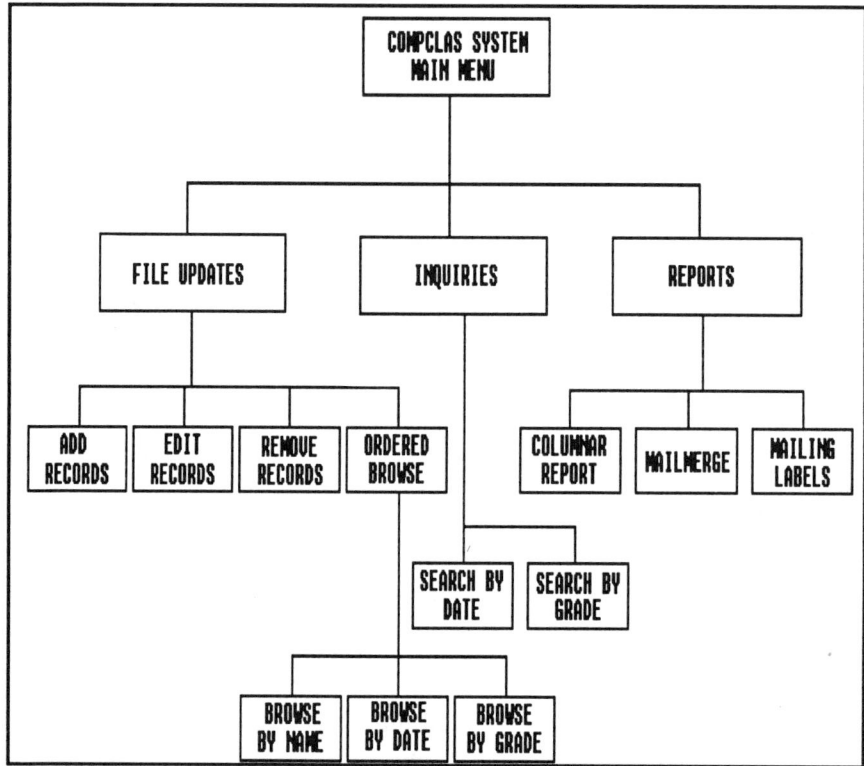

Figure 10.10 Further Revised System Structure Chart for COMPCLAS

merge all of the program files together into one single file. This too is accomplished by the use of procedures in dBASE.

For a small system like the COM_MENU system, one could easily put each of the programs into one procedure file. Since a procedure file can contain up to 1170 procedures, basically available memory is the limiting factor as to how many programs you can string together to form a procedure file. In a very large program, one could make more than one procedure file and just open and close each one of them as needed.

A procedure is designated by placing at the beginning of the module the instruction, **PROCEDURE** *ProcedureName* . Each of the procedure modules are listed together in one file called the *ProcedureFile* . Next, the *ProcedureFile* is placed into memory by the command: **SET PROCEDURE TO** *ProcedureFile* .

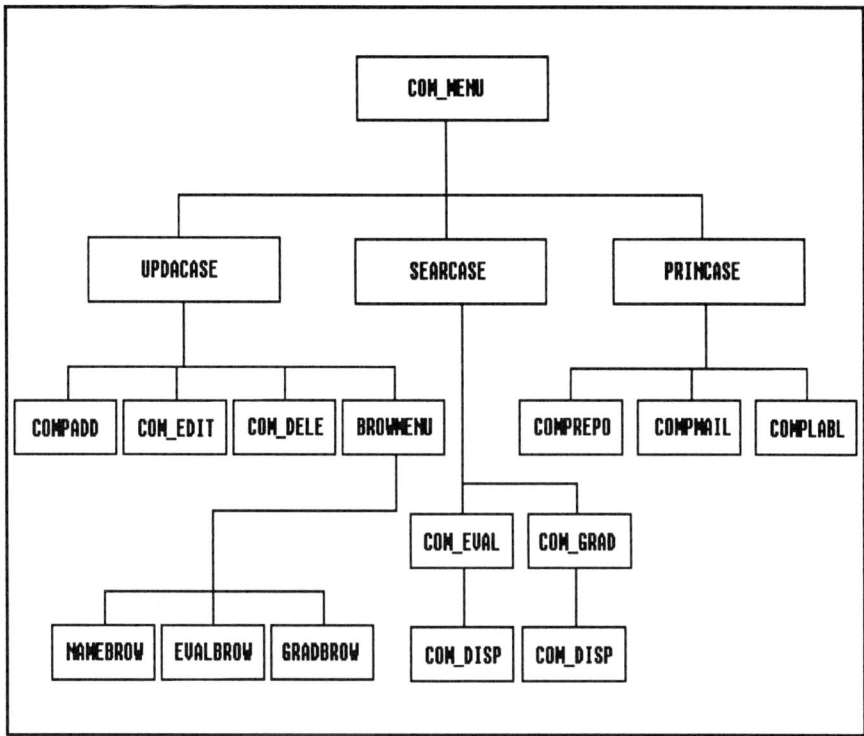

Figure 10.11 Program Structure Chart for the COMPCLAS System

Let's go ahead and make procedures out of each of our seventeen .PRG files. This is done by putting all our programs together to form one conglomerate file.

10.6.1 Appending Programs Together to Form COM_PROC.PRG

We can create our procedure file, COM_PROC.prg by simply taking all the programs contained in the program structure tree shown in Figure 10.11 and appending each one to our **COM_PROC.prg** file. We begin by going into the dBASE text editor with:

.MODIFY COMMAND COM_PROC

Choosing the "Words" menu selection, we depress the **Alt-W** keystroke pair (see Figure 10.12). We then choose the menu item

"Write/read text file", and strike the Enter key once more. Next we choose the "Read text from file" option, and finally we type in the filename. As the order of entering these files is arbitrary, we'll simply start at the top and work our way down. Hence we type in: **COM_MENU.PRG** where it says "Enter filename:".

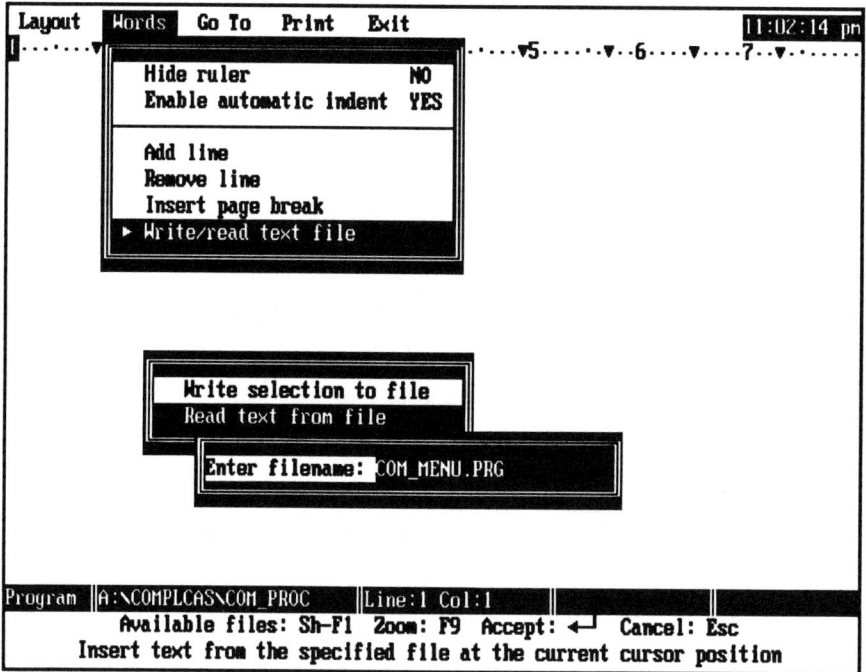

Figure 10.12 Loading in the file COM_MENU.prg into COM_PROC.prg

Striking the Enter key we load in the file, **COM_MENU.PRG**. Using the Page Up key to get to the top of the file, we must add one new line to the file to identify it as a procedure rather than a program. Overtyping the first line which says, "*COM_MENU.prg", we type the words: **PROCEDURE COM_MENU**. The result is shown in Figure 10.13.

Now paging down to the bottom of the file, and striking the Enter key a couple of more times to create some space between procedures, we are now ready to append the next program in the new COMPCLAS system. Looking down on the next row of programs in Figure 10.11, we choose to append **UPDACASE.prg** as

SYSTEM ORGANIZATION

```
 Layout   Words   Go To   Print   Exit
[......v1......v.2....v....3..v.....4v.......v5......v..6....v....7..v.....
PROCEDURE COM_MENU
* This defines the menu for COMPCLAS
* It includes a Horizontal Menu with Popup Windows
*
SET STATUS OFF
CLEAR

@ 2,28 SAY "COMPUTER CLASS MAIN MENU"

* Define the Menu with its pads

DEFINE MENU Main
DEFINE PAD Update OF Main PROMPT " Update Records " AT 12,05
DEFINE PAD Search OF Main PROMPT "Search Records" AT 12,25
DEFINE PAD Print  OF Main PROMPT "Print Records"  AT 12,45
DEFINE PAD Exit   OF Main PROMPT "Exit"           AT 12,70

* Assign popups to the pads

ON PAD Update OF MAIN Activate Popup Updatpop
Program  A:\COMPCLAS\COM PROC     Line:1 Col:19
```

Figure 10.13 COM_MENU.prg with the line inserted at the top: **PROCEDURE COM_MENU**

the next program. Going through the same set of steps as we did entering COM_MENU.prg, we obtain the screen shown in Figure 10.14.

Once again, moving the cursor up to the beginning of UPDACASE.prg, we insert the words: **PROCEDURE UPDACASE**. The result is shown in Figure 10.15. In a similar manner, we continue doing this for all seventeen programs shown in Figure 10.11. The result is one large procedure file called COM_PROC.prg, consisting of seventeen procedures, rather than seventeen separate program files.

10.6.2 Design of a Procedure Driver Program

Now all that remains to be done is to write a program that opens our procedure file and runs it. This program is shown in Listing 10.9.

358 SYSTEM ORGANIZATION

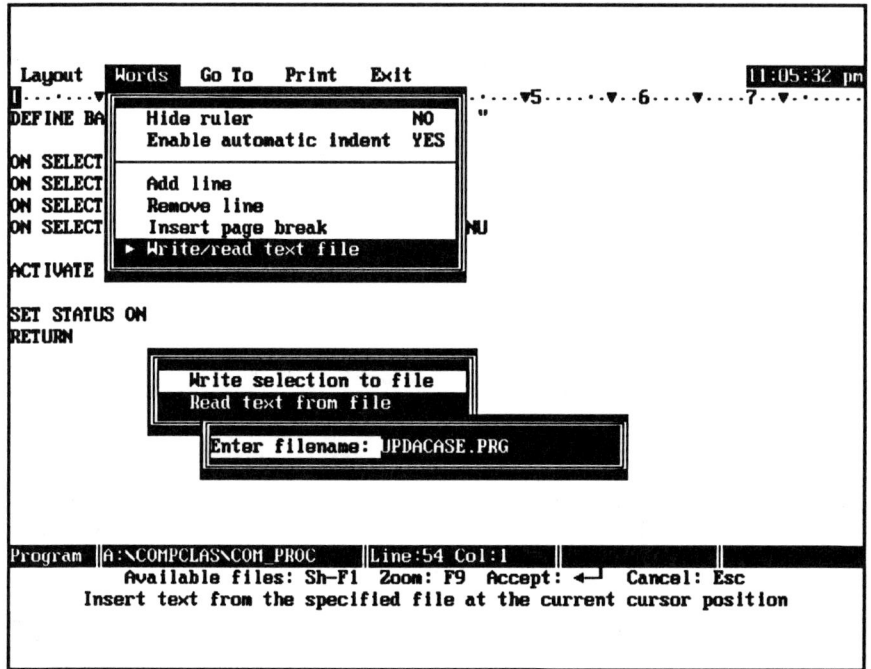

Figure 10.14 Appending UPDACASE.prg into COM_PROC.prg

```
* COMPMAIN.PRG
* This turns on the PROCEDURE FILE,
* COM_PROC, and runs the system.
*
SET PROCEDURE TO COM_PROC
DO COM_MENU
SET PROCEDURE TO
RETURN
```

Listing 10.9 COMPCLAS Initiating Program: COMPMAIN.prg

```
 Layout   Words   Go To   Print   Exit
[······v1······v·▌2····v····3··v·····4v·······v5·····v··6····v····7··v······
RETURN

PROCEDURE UPDACASE
* This is the selection CASE statement for File Maintenance
*
SAVE SCREEN TO COMPSCREEN
DO CASE
   CASE BAR()=1
      DO COMPADD
   CASE BAR()=2
      DO COM_EDIT
   CASE BAR()=3
      DO COM_DELE
   CASE BAR()=4
      DO BROWMENU
ENDCASE
RESTORE SCREEN FROM COMPSCREEN
RETURN

 Program  ||A:\COMPCLAS\COM_PROC  ||Line:53 Col:19 ||
```

Figure 10.15 Procedure File COM_PROC.prg after having appended UPDACASE.prg

Note that all COMPMAIN.prg does is to SET the PROCEDURE to the COM_PROC procedure file. Then it proceeds to execute COM_MENU, which in turn executes the rest of the system. When the user exits from the system, execution returns to COMPMAIN.prg, and the procedure file is turned off, thus ending the program.

Two improvements in the system should be noted. The first is that instead of having seventeen individual .PRG files (and seventeen additional .DBO files), we now have only two .PRG files (and two .DBO files). The second improvement should be an improvement in execution speed, particularly if you are operating on a floppy disk system. Instead of having to go to the disk each time a new module is executed, it goes to the disk just twice: once for COMPMAIN.prg and once for COM_PROC.prg. After that program execution occurs strictly from memory. (However, it will still have to go to the disk for the database file as well as for the report forms and the format file.)

360 SYSTEM ORGANIZATION

A word of warning here. Don't place all your programs into a procedure file until the system has been fully debugged. It is much easier to debug single programs than a conglomerate file.

10.7 Comments About Compiled Code in dBASE IV

The payoff from all our effort is a group of "Object Code" files which are the result of the dBASE IV pseudo compiler's work. The word "pseudo" is used because the "Object Code" produced is not executable by itself[32]. It still needs the presence of the dBASE IV system program, or a RUNTIME module called RUNTIME.EXE[33], in order to execute these programs.

The "Object Code" files are the files that will actually "run" the system. As such, it is not necessary to give to any user the "Source Code" which we so painstakingly created (the .PRG files). In this way you can keep the way you programmed your system a proprietary secret. The only files that we will need for our system will be the files with the extensions: .DBF, .DBT, .DBO, .MDX, .FRO, .LBO, and .FMO .

Just to make this point, let's create a new directory with only these files in the directory. In this way we can see that system operation depends on these files alone. We will call our new directory, **COMPILED**. To create a new directory, and transfer the files, let's QUIT from dBASE and execute the following DOS commands:

```
A:\COMPCLAS> MD \COMPCLAS\COMPILED
A:\COMPCLAS> CD \COMPCLAS\COMPILED
A:\COMPCLAS\COMPILED>COPY\COMPCLAS\COMPCLAS.DBF
A:\COMPCLAS\COMPILED> COPY \COMPCLAS\COMPCLAS.DBT
A:\COMPCLAS\COMPILED> COPY \COMPCLAS\COMPCLAS.MDX
```

---

[32] A "true" compiler will yield executable code which can run without the aid of any further programs.

[33] RUNTIME.EXE is available only with the "Developer's Version" of dBASE IV.

SYSTEM ORGANIZATION

A:\COMPCLAS\COMPILED> COPY \COMPCLAS\COM_PROC.DBO
A:\COMPCLAS\COMPILES> COPY \COMPCLAS\COMPMAIN.DBO
A:\COMPCLAS\COMPILED> COPY \COMPCLAS*.FRO
A:\COMPCLAS\COMPILED> COPY \COMPCLAS\COMPCLAS.LBO
A:\COMPCLAS\COMPILED> COPY \COMPCLAS\COMPCLAS.FMO

We used the DOS **COPY** command because we could use a wildcard, *, with it. The wildcard, *, used with an extension like *.DBO, means "any" filename with the extension .DBO. Now if we were to RUN the DOS Directory command, **DIR**:

A:\COMPCLAS\COMPILED> **DIR**

we would get the screen shown in Listing 10.10.

```
Directory of  A:\COMPCLAS\COMPILED

.              <DIR>         03-10-92    9:46p
..             <DIR>         03-10-92    9:46p
COMPCLAS DBF             1362 02-25-92   12:07a
COM_PROC DBO             9696 03-10-92    9:43p
COMPMAIN DBO              244 03-10-92    9:43p
COMPCLAS DBT             4096 02-25-92   12:07a
COMPCLAS FMO             1744 03-10-92    9:44p
LETTER   FRO             5112 02-03-92    8:55p
COLUMNAR FRO             4652 01-29-92    6:43p
COMPCLAS LBO             5864 02-03-92    1:18a
COMPCLAS MDX            12288 02-18-92   11:36a
       11 File(s)        96256 bytes free
```

Listing 10.10 List of "Object" files needed to run COMPCLAS System

Notice that the size of COM_PROC.prg, which contains all the modules that make up our system, is less than 10,000 bytes in size. This amounts to quite a consolidation in disk space.

Now go back into dBASE and try running the skeleton system. This can be done directly from the A> prompt by typing DBASE followed by the name of the topmost program. In our case the command would be:

A:\COMPCLAS\COMPILED> **DBASE COMPMAIN**

The beauty of this method of entering dBASE is that the user does not have to know anything about dBASE itself in order to use the program. If you were to put the command: **QUIT**, instead of **RETURN**, at the end of **COMPMAIN.prg**, then the user would never even see the dot prompt.

The system should now perform just as it did before with no time spent in further compilation. It is in this form that dBASE IV should demonstrate the speed of which it is capable. Another word of warning is in order here. *Don't place all your compiled programs into a COMPILED directory until the system is fully debugged and working perfectly.* This is the very last step in any system implementation.

10.8 Summary

In Chapter 10 we have discussed system organization. We began by introducing the system structure chart. We showed how we could organize the conglomeration of all the programs written for the COMPCLAS system by using a simple main menu with additional sub-menus for each of the actions to be performed.

We saw that one way we could go to a third level of menus, or beyond, was to use a windowing technique in which to contain these sub-menus.

Next we looked at the program structure chart which actually implements the system structure chart we devised previously. This chart contained additional subprograms to be performed that were not directly implied by the system structure chart.

Next, we saw how we could tidy things up a bit by putting all our seventeen disparate programs into one procedure file. This not only made our system more compact, but also sped up the execution of the system.

Finally, we saw that we only needed the "Object Files" in order to run our system. This not only conserved space but maintained the confidentiality of how we did our programming.

10.9 Review

In Chapter 10 we encountered the following new commands:

>**ACTIVATE WINDOW** *WindowName*
>**DEFINE BAR** *BarNumber*
>**DEFINE POP-UP** *Pop-upName*...
>**DEFINE WINDOW** *WindowName*
>**ON PAD** *PadName*...
>**PROCEDURE** *ProcedureName*
>**RESTORE SCREEN FROM** *ScreenName*
>**SAVE SCREEN TO** *ScreenName*
>**SET PROCEDURE TO** *ProcedureName*

Add these new commands to your glossary of dBASE IV instructions. In addition, the following function was introduced:

>**BAR()**

Add this function to your glossary of dBASE IV functions.

10.10 Laboratory Work

Create the two menu driving programs: COMPMENU.prg and BROWMENU.prg. In addition, write the CASE programs that determine which of our program functions get performed: UPDACASE.prg, SEARCASE.prg, and PRINCASE.prg. Also write the individual Browse routines: NAMEBROW.prg, EVALBROW.prg, and GRADBROW.prg.

Finally, create the procedure file, COM_PROC.prg, as well as the procedure driver, COMPMAIN.prg. After the system has been tested, move all object files (those whose extensions end in the letter "O") to a new subdirectory: \COMPCLAS\COMPILED. Add to these the COMPCLAS.DBF, COMPCLAS.DBT, and COMPCLAS.MDX files, and run the system.

10.11 Exercises

1. Along lines similar to those used in the design of the system structure chart for COMPCLAS, design a system structure chart for MAILIST. Make sure that it is organized in such a way that there are no more than seven options in any menu. The actions to be performed by this system should include:

    Appending Records
    Editing Records
    Deleting Records
    Browsing Records
    Searching for People By CARD
    Searching for People By Zip code
    Generate General Report
    Generate Mailing Labels
    Generate Mailmerge Letters

2. Create a program structure chart for the MAILIST system. The program structure chart should include the following programs:

SYSTEM ORGANIZATION

> MAILADD.prg
> MAIL_ED.prg
> MAIL_DEL.prg
> MAILBROW.prg
> MAILCARD.prg
> MAILZIP.prg
> MAILREPO.prg
> MAILETTR.prg
> MAILABEL.prg

3. Along lines similar to those used in the design of COM_MENU.prg, write a menu driver program, MAIL_MEN.prg, which will drive your MAILIST system. Hand in a hard copy of this program.

4. Along lines similar to those used to design BROWMENU.prg, redesign MAILBROW.prg so that it becomes a menu driver in a window driving the modules CARDBROW.prg, NAMEBROW.prg and ZIPBROW.prg. Hand in hard copies of all four of these programs.

5. Merge all your MAILIST programs together into a procedure file called MAILPROC.prg. Print out a copy of the first two procedures in that file, and hand them in.

6. Write the procedure driver: MAILMAIN.prg. Hand in a hard copy of this program.

10.12 Term Project

Hand in a copy of the system structure chart for your term project.

CHAPTER 11

CONTROLLING YOUR ENVIRONMENT

11.0   Topics Covered in Chapter 11

The SET Mode is Introduced.

DISPLAY STATUS shows the state of the SET switches.

SET FUNCTION TO demonstrates how one can assign commands to the various function keys.

Control of the Color Display is presented.

The CONFIG.DB file is introduced along with its own command language.

DBSETUP.EXE Routine is introduced as a menu driven way of creating the CONFIG.DB file.

Password Protection is integrated into the program system.

A System Backup Program shows the utility of executing DOS commands within the dBASE environment.

The ability to modify program commands on the fly is demonstrated with the introduction of Macros.

11.1 The SET Command

In writing programs, we often modify the environment in which we work by means of the **SET** command. We frequently start our programs with lists of options ("switches") to SET. For example, it is not unusual to start the main menu module with a list of SETs like:

SET TALK OFF
SET BELL OFF
SET STATUS OFF
SET CONFIRM ON
SET SAFETY OFF

The first three SETs we've used before. **SET CONFIRM ON** makes us strike the Enter key for each entry we input without automatically going on to the next command. This gives us an extra measure of safety where we can review our entry to be sure that we've got it right before executing it. The last SET allows us to copy a file or remake an index without dBASE confirming with us if we really want to do this.

There are many more environmental (SET) commands than these. If we would like to see the status of our environment at any time, we need only type **DISPLAY STATUS**, which will display the status on three separate screens. We can also type **LIST STATUS TO PRINT** to get a printout of the STATUS. Figures 11.1, 11.2 and 11.3 show the result of having executed **DISPLAY STATUS** after having opened the database COMPCLAS.

. **USE COMPCLAS**
. **DISPLAY STATUS**

Note that among other things, the following information is supplied:

1. The database that is open and its memo file, if any;

CONTROLLING YOUR ENVIRONMENT 369

2. The various index Tags of the Production Index as well as any individual indexes that might be open;

3. The current drive as well as directory;

4. The present status of all the Status switches;

5. A list of how the function keys are presently programmed.

As you can see, there are many status switches that we can set with the **SET** command. To define them all is beyond the scope of this text, and the user is referred to the dBASE IV manual or to such texts as: DBASE IV PROGRAMMER'S INSTANT REFERENCE 2ND EDITION, Alan Simpson, Sybex Inc., San Francisco, 1991.

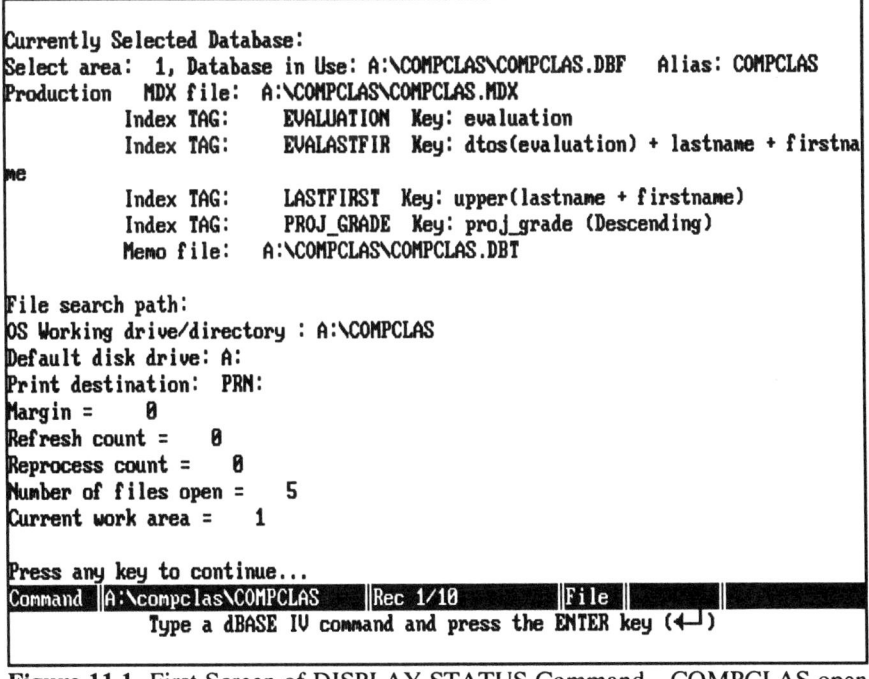

Figure 11.1 First Screen of DISPLAY STATUS Command—COMPCLAS open

370 CONTROLLING YOUR ENVIRONMENT

11.1.1 The SET Mode

dBASE IV provides us with an easy means of re-assigning the default settings. The process is initiated with the **SET** command and puts us immediately into the **SET** mode. If we type at the dot prompt:

. **SET**

we immediately obtain the screen shown in Figure 11.4. As you can see, this mode allows us to change all the default settings whose current state appeared to us when we executed: **DISPLAY STATUS**.

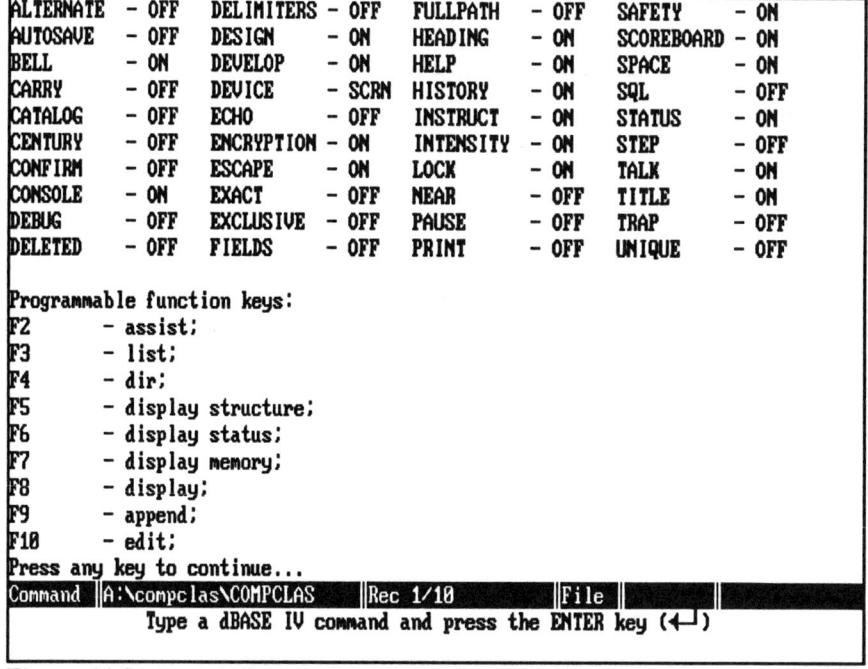

Figure 11.2 Second Screen of DISPLAY STATUS showing status of all SET Switches

CONTROLLING YOUR ENVIRONMENT 371

```
Press any key to continue...
CTRL-F1  -
CTRL-F2  -
CTRL-F3  -
CTRL-F4  -
CTRL-F5  -
CTRL-F6  -
CTRL-F7  -
CTRL-F8  -
CTRL-F9  -
CTRL-F10 -
SHIFT-F1 -
SHIFT-F2 -
SHIFT-F3 -
SHIFT-F4 -
SHIFT-F5 -
SHIFT-F6 -
SHIFT-F7 -
SHIFT-F8 -
SHIFT-F9 -
.
Command  A:\compclas\COMPCLAS    Rec 1/10    File
         Type a dBASE IV command and press the ENTER key (⏎)
```

Figure 11.3 Third Screen of DISPLAY STATUS showing empty Function key Assignments

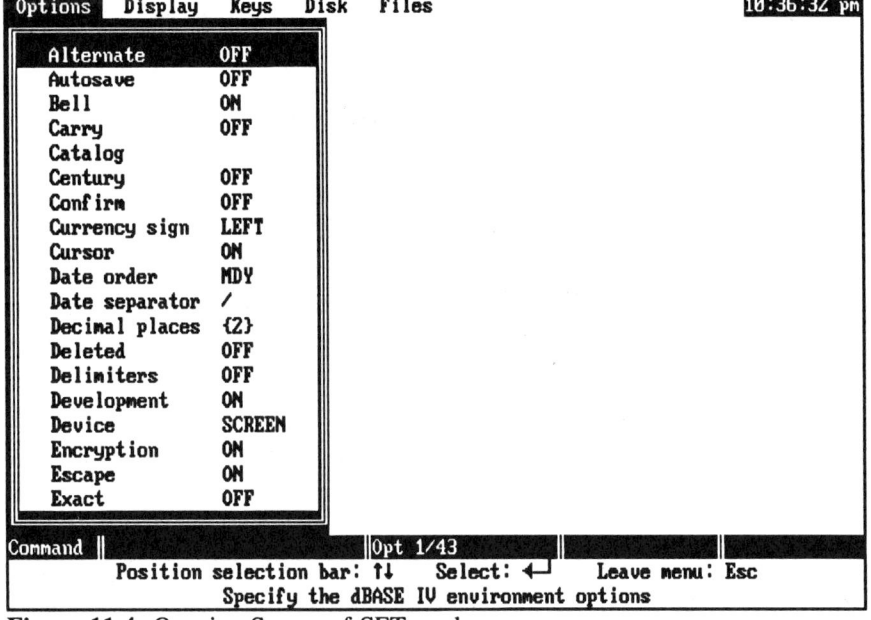

Figure 11.4 Opening Screen of SET mode

However, it is not recommended that one use the **SET** mode in the context of a program, as it gives the user the opportunity to set the defaults in a way that might be disastrous to the data. One of the functions of a program is to limit the choices that a user has, not to expand them. For this reason we will use individual commands to change the status of the system rather than use the shotgun approach offered to us by the **SET** mode.

11.1.2 The **SET FUNCTION TO** Command

Figures 11.2 and 11.3 indicate that we may define the function keys 2-10 as we like. This can be done for the function key alone, or as a keystroke pair with **Shift** or **Ctrl** as shown in Figure 11.3. dBASE IV reserves the key **F1** for the Help screen, but allows use of CTRL-F1 and SHIFT-F1.

We see what the default settings for the function keys are from Figure 11.2. As I only find the default settings for keys **F5** and **F6** useful, I am prone to redefine the rest of them by means of the **SET FUNCTION TO** command. The syntax for this command is: **SET FUNCTION** *KeyNumber* **TO** *"StringDefinition"*.

For example, suppose we wanted to program the command: **DIR *.*** to function key **F2** . This is done by typing:

. **SET FUNCTION 2 TO "DIR *.*;"**

The reason for the ";" is because the semicolon represents the striking of the Enter key. Since we don't want to have to follow the striking of the F2 key with the pressing of the Enter key every time, we incorporate the Enter key into the command definition itself. Having defined F2 in this way, the result of pressing it is shown in Figure 11.5.

The string definition of a function key may be up to 238 characters long. We may also execute more than one command with one function key. For example, as I am often using the MODIFY COMMAND instruction, this is a good one to program. However,

CONTROLLING YOUR ENVIRONMENT 373

```
ATSAYDEM.DBO      ATSAYDEM.PRG      BROWMENU.PRG      BROWMENU.DBO
COLUMNAR.FRO      COLUMNAR.FRM      COLUMNAR.FRG      COMPADD.PRG
COMPADD.DBO       COMPCLAS.SCR      COMPCLAS.DBO      COMPCLAS.FRO
COMPCLAS.FRM      COMPCLAS.FMO      COMPCLAS.LBG      COMPCLAS.LBO
COMPCLAS.PRG      COMPCLAS.DBT      COMPCLAS.FMT      COMPCLAS.LBL
COMPCLAS.FRG      COMPCLAS.MDX      COMPCLAS.DBF      COMPEDIT.PRG
COMPEDIT.DBO      COMPGRAD.DBO      COMPGRAD.PRG      COMPLABL.PRG
COMPLABL.DBO      COMPMAIL.DBO      COMPMAIL.PRG      COMPMENU.DBO
COMPMENU.PRG      COMPPACK.DBO      COMPPACK.PRG      COMPREPO.DBO
COMPREPO.PRG      COM_BROW.DBO      COM_BROW.PRG      COM_DELE.DBO
COM_DELE.PRG      COM_DISP.DBO      COM_DISP.PRG      COM_EDIT.PRG
COM_EDIT.DBO      COM_EVAL.DBO      COM_EVAL.PRG      COM_GRAD.PRG
COM_GRAD.DBO      COM_MENU.PRG      COM_MENU.DBO      COM_PROC.DBO
COM_PROC.PRG      EVALBROW.DBO      EVALBROW.PRG      FREEFORM.FRM
FREEFORM.DBO      FREEFORM.FRG      FREEFORM.PRG      FREEFORM.FRO
GRADBROW.PRG      GRADBROW.DBO      LETTER.FRG        LETTER.FRO
LETTER.FRM        MESSAGE.DBO       MESSAGE.PRG       NAMEBROW.DBO
NAMEBROW.PRG      PRINCASE.DBO      PRINCASE.PRG      SEARCASE.PRG
SEARCASE.DBO      UPDACASE.PRG      UPDACASE.DBO

    133269 bytes in     75 files
    161792 bytes remaining on drive
```

Figure 11.5 Result of Executing DIR *.* from dot prompt

I often try to modify procedure files which are currently on, so I must turn them off first. Hence the following command pair I find useful as a definition for SHIFT-F9:
. **SET FUNCTION SHIFT-F9 TO "SET PROCEDURE TO; MODIFY COMMAND "**

11.1.3 Setting a Color Display[34]

In dBASE, we can set the foreground color as well as the background color. In addition, the part of the screen that is enhanced (e.g. the status bar and the GET boxes are in enhanced mode) can also have its foreground and background colors set.

The syntax for the SET COLOR TO command is: **SET COLOR TO** *Foreground/Background, EnhancedForeground/ EnhancedBackground {, Border}*[35]. A list of available colors is shown in Table 11.1.

---

[34]This only applies to computers having color monitors.

[35]In a CGA screen the border surrounding the screen can be independently set also.

374 CONTROLLING YOUR ENVIRONMENT

For example, suppose we wanted to set the foreground color to yellow, and the background color to magenta. In addition, suppose we want our enhanced foreground color to be blue, and the enhanced background color to be white.

. SET COLOR TO GR+/RB, B/W

Table 11.1 Colors Available in SET COLOR TO Instruction

COLOR	CODE
Black	N
Blue	B
Green	G
Cyan	BG
Blank	X
Red	R
Magenta	RB
Brown	GR
White	W
Blinking	*
High Intensity	+
Yellow	GR+

Try this for yourself, and experiment with different colors that might be more to your liking than white on black or blue.

11.2 The CONFIG.DB File

Now that we know that we can control the dBASE environment to a large extent, we also realize that there are so many parameters to deal with that it is not something that we want to do manually every time we start a session in dBASE. Usually speaking, there's a particular default setup that feels right for the user, and that's the one that he or she would like to be greeted by each time he or she enters dBASE. Fortunately, there is a file that can be made that contains all the desired parameters which will be set up automatically upon entering dBASE. This file is called the **CONFIG.DB** file.

CONTROLLING YOUR ENVIRONMENT

This file can be generated in the same way as our command files have been written, in the text editor, MODIFY COMMAND. To enter the CONFIG.DB file, type:

. MODIFY COMMAND CONFIG.DB

The actual command syntax that we execute in a CONFIG.DB file is different from the normal syntax that we use in our command files. For example, the defaults that I like to put in a typical CONFIG.DB file are summarized by the equivalent sequence of commands from the dot line shown in Listing 11.1.

```
. SET BELL OFF
. SET CONFIRM ON
. SET STATUS ON
. SET EXCLUSIVE ON
. SET FUNCTION 2 TO "DIR *.*;"
. SET FUNCTION 4 TO "DIR *.PRG;"
. SET COLOR TO W/B, R/W
```

Listing 11.1 Sequence of Initial Sets

The equivalent commands in a CONFIG.DB file are shown in Listing 11.2.

```
BELL = OFF
CONFIRM = ON
STATUS = ON
EXCLUSIVE = ON
F2 = "DIR *.*;"
F4 = "DIR *.PRG;"
COLOR = W/B, R/W
```

Listing 11.2 CONFIG.DB equivalent of Listing 11.1

Notice the use of the equals sign rather than the use of the word SET.

With this CONFIG.DB file in existence, each time you enter dBASE, this file will be executed before any other file. The result is that the user obtains the desired defaults with no effort on the users part aside from creating the file to begin with.

In addition, there are some default settings that can be executed only in the CONFIG.DB file. The two that I particularly like to make use of, are the text editor default, and the memo file word processor default. These allow one to use some word processor other than the limited dBASE word processor, MODIFY COMMAND.

The CONFIG.DB command for specifying the default text editor is: **TEDIT** = *AlternateTextEditor* . The *AlternateTextEditor* that I usually use is the Norton Editor which is invoked by the command: **NE +1**. The CONFIG.DB command to execute for this particular text editor would be:

TEDIT = NE +1

The CONFIG.DB command for specifying the default word processor for memo fields is: **WP** = *AlternateWordProcessor*. Supposing you wanted to use WordStar 3.3[36] as your default word processor (the command used to invoke WordStar is: **WS**). The CONFIG.DB command to execute for this particular word processor would be:

WP = WS

Another thing the CONFIG.DB file can do that the SET command cannot do is to alter the default prompt from the familiar

---

[36] On a normally configured machine using 640K for DOS memory, dBASE IV does not leave enough memory to use a more modern word processor such as Word Perfect 5.1.

dot. This is done by specifying: **PROMPT** = *PromptString* . For example, if we wanted to make our prompt become: **RELAX:** , we would put into our CONFIG.DB file:

PROMPT = RELAX:

Since the number of spaces that you type in on the line after the word **RELAX** actually appears with the prompt on the screen, be careful of the spacing. I have put in *one* space after the colon so that the commands that I type will not run up against the prompt, **RELAX:** , itself.

One more thing that the CONFIG.DB file will do for you is to automatically execute any command you would like upon entry into dBASE. The syntax for this is: **COMMAND** = *InitialCommand* . For example, if you would like to execute the main menu module of COMPCLAS upon entering dBASE automatically, this can be done by choosing: **DO COM_MENU** as the *InitialCommand* :

COMMAND = DO COM_MENU

Listing 11.3 shows the combination of all these commands into one CONFIG.DB file.

```
BELL = OFF
CONFIRM = ON
STATUS = ON
EXCLUSIVE = ON
F2 = "DIR *.*;"
F4 = "DIR *.PRG;"
COLOR = W/B, R/W
TEDIT = NE +1
WP = WS
PROMPT = RELAX:
COMMAND = DO COM_MENU
```

Listing 11.3 CONFIG.DB initiates COMPCLAS System upon entry into dBASE

378   CONTROLLING YOUR ENVIRONMENT

Now, upon typing **dBASE** at the **A>** prompt, the first thing that we will see after the usual opening screen is displayed for ten seconds is the opening menu of COM_MENU.prg as shown in Figure 11.6. The appealing feature of the CONFIG.DB file, in this case, is that the user now does not have to know anything about dBASE in order to use the system that has been created. All the user must do is to follow the instructions of the menu driven system which, hopefully, will be user friendly enough to direct the novitiate through all the proper steps.

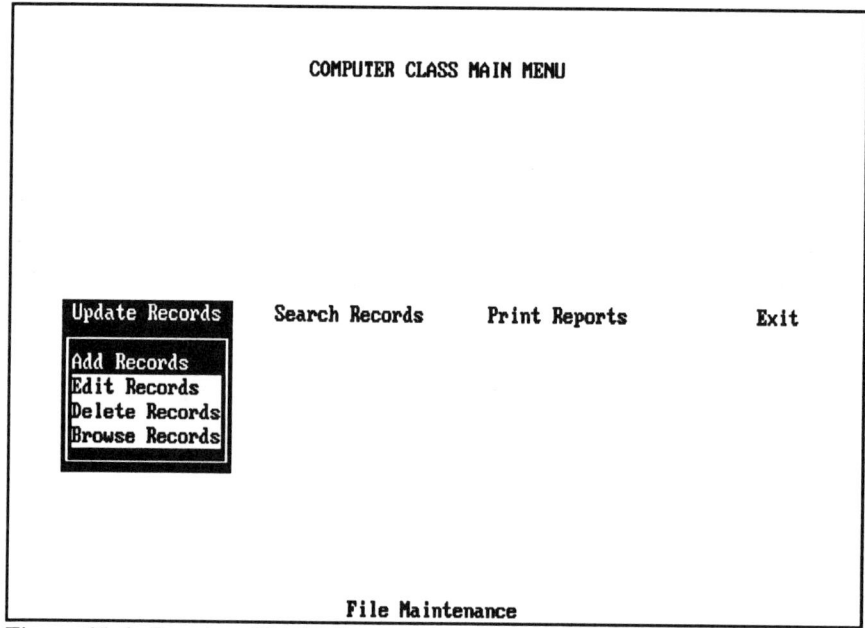

Figure 11.6 Opening dBASE Screen when using CONFIG.DB of Listing 11.3

When it comes time to look at a particular memo, and the memo field is selected in the Edit mode, then the screen that will appear is the one belonging to the default word processor, as specified in the CONFIG.DB file. For the CONFIG.DB file of Listing 11.3, the screen, that would appear when the COMMENTS field of Record 1 is selected, is shown in Figure 11.7.

CONTROLLING YOUR ENVIRONMENT 379

After the user exits from COM_MENU.prg, the following prompt is now seen on the screen for the first time.

RELAX:

Suppose it is desired to edit the file CONFIG.DB once more. Typing at the **RELAX:** prompt:

RELAX: MODIFY COMMAND CONFIG.DB

results in the screen shown in Figure 11.8. This is the editing screen of the Norton Editor.

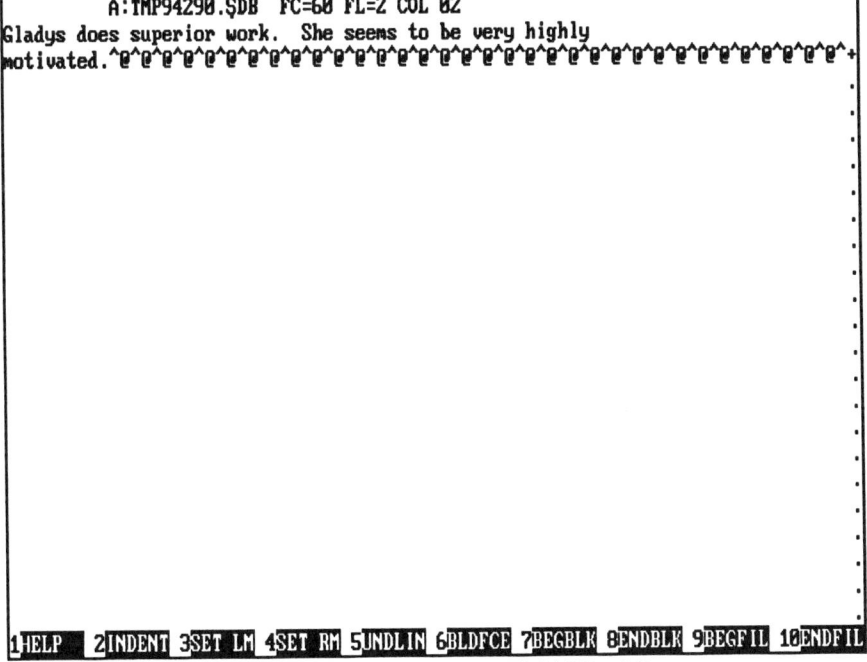

Figure 11.7 WordStar 3.3 used as the Memo Field Word Processor

```
BELL = OFF
CONFIRM = ON
STATUS = ON
EXCLUSIVE = ON
F2 = "DIR *.*;"
F4 = "DIR *.PRG:*
TEDIT = NE +1
WP = WS
PROMPT = RELAX:
COMMAND = DO COM_MENU









Line=1    Col=1         A:COMPCLAS\CONFIG.DB        Insert    WW=Off
```

Figure 11.8 Example of a CONFIG.DB file

The example shown in Listing 11.3 shows only a small sample of the possible commands available in a CONFIG.DB file. Table 11.2 shows a list of those configuration commands that can *only* be set from within a CONFIG.DB file. They have no SET counterpart within dBASE IV.

In the next section we describe a menu driven method for creating the CONFIG.DB file, DBSETUP.

11.2.1 DBSETUP Routine

From the DOS (**A>**) prompt, we can access the dBASE utility program: **DBSETUP.EXE**. We shall use this utility to modify our existing CONFIG.DB configuration file. Since the new dBASE IV word processor which is used for memo fields is sufficient for most needs, we'll modify the CONFIG.DB file to remove the choice of **WS** as our default word processor. Invoking DBSETUP:

CONTROLLING YOUR ENVIRONMENT

Table 11.2 Configuration Commands with no SET counterpart

BUCKET	*n*	{1K to 31K, default is 2K}
COMMAND	*command*	
DO	*n*	{1 to 256, default is 20}
EEMS	ON/OFF	Accesses Extended or Expanded Memory
EXPSIZE	*n*	{100 to 2000, default is 100}
FILES	*n*	{15 to 99, default is 99}
GETS	*n*	{35 to 1023, default is 128}
INDEXBYTES	*n*	{2K to 128K, default is 2K}
PDRIVER	*FileName*	
PRINTER	*PrinterFileName*	
PROMPT	*PromptString*	
RESETCRT	ON/OFF	
SQLDATABASE	*SqlDatabaseName*	
SQLHOME	*PathName*	
TEDIT	*AlternateModifyCommandEditor*	
WP	*AlternateMemoWordProcessor*	

A:\COMPCLAS> **DBSETUP**

we get the opening screen shown in Figure 11.9.

Selecting the "Modify Existing CONFIG.DB" file, as indicated, by striking the Enter key, we enter the DBSETUP main menu system. Using the right arrow to move over to the menu option entitled "General", we get the screen shown in Figure 11.10. Examining this screen note that the defaults shown reflect what is already in the CONFIG.DB file created in the previous section: 1) CONFIRM is ON and 2) COMMAND is DO COM_MENU. Striking the PgDn key until the last of the menu items is reached, we obtain the screen shown in Figure 11.11. Here we see that the **WP** default is indeed **WS**.

Striking the Enter key, we get the screen shown in Figure 11.12. Using the backspace key to erase the **WS** and striking the Enter key once more, we obtain the screen shown in Figure 11.13, where no external word processor has been selected.

382 CONTROLLING YOUR ENVIRONMENT

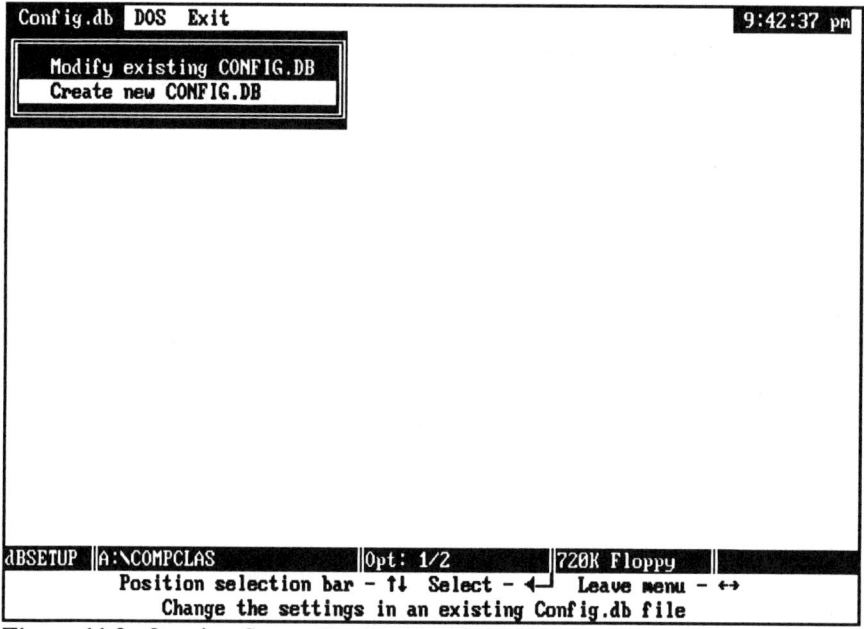

Figure 11.9 Opening Screen For DBSETUP.EXE

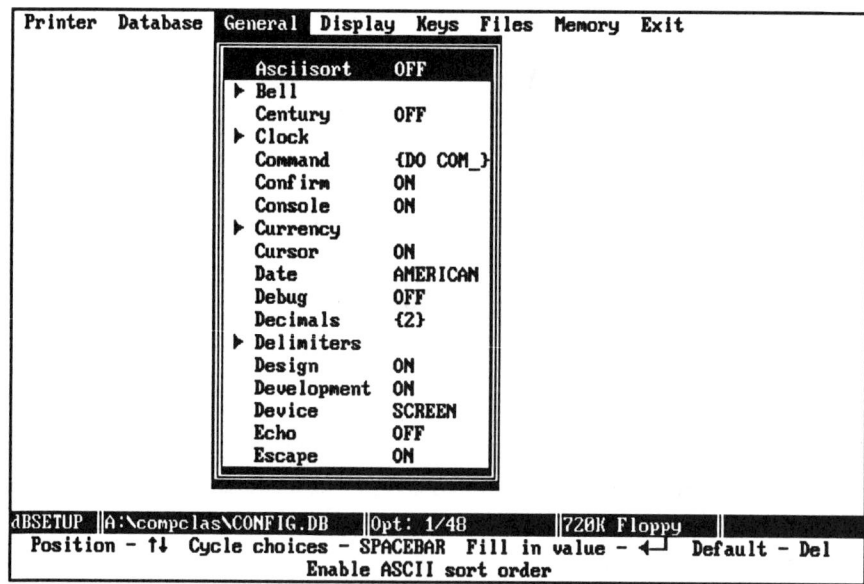

Figure 11.10 The "General" Sub-Menu of DBSETUP.EXE

CONTROLLING YOUR ENVIRONMENT

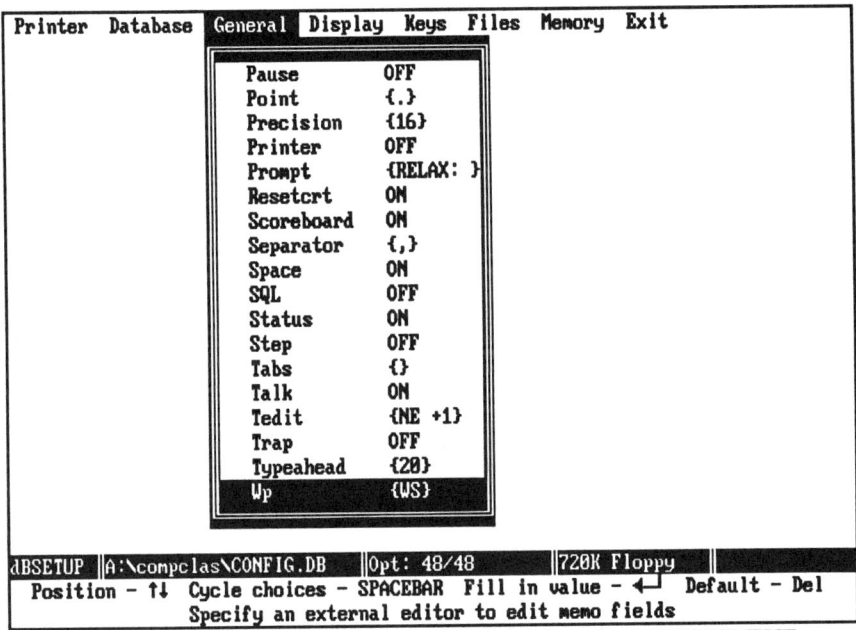

Figure 11.11 The Bottom of the "General" Sub-Menu in DBSETUP.EXE

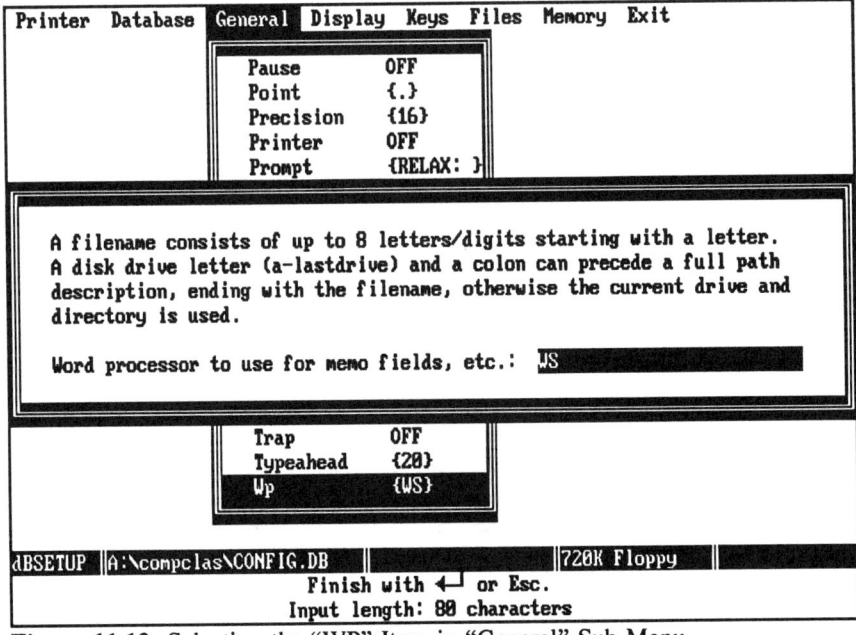

Figure 11.12 Selecting the "WP" Item in "General" Sub-Menu

384   CONTROLLING YOUR ENVIRONMENT

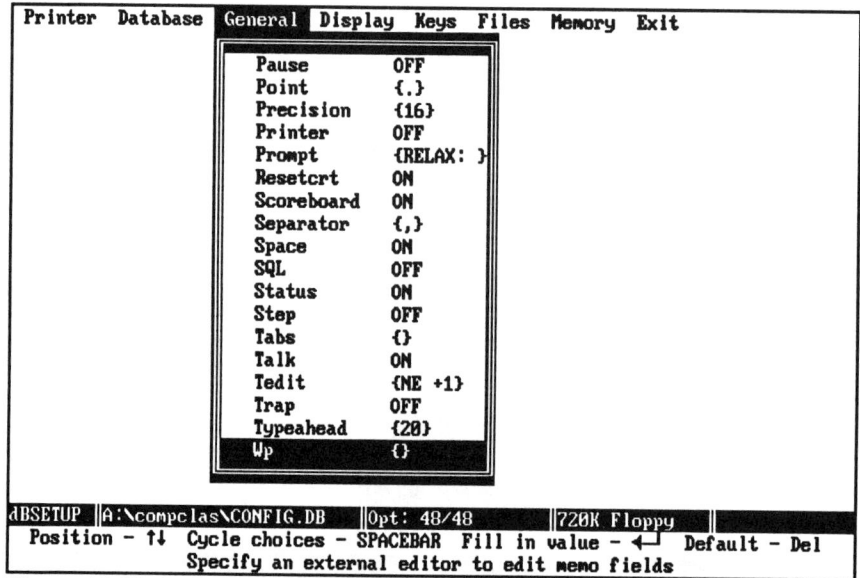

Figure 11.13 Default of "WP" changed back to the null condition

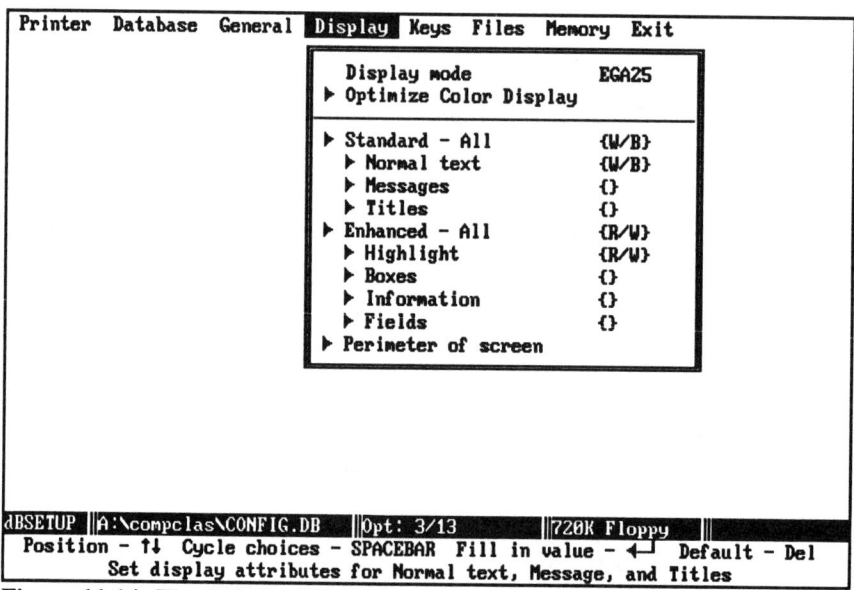

Figure 11.14 The "Display" Sub-Menu of DBSETUP.EXE

CONTROLLING YOUR ENVIRONMENT 385

Striking the right arrow once, we move over to the "Display" sub-menu, and notice that the color defaults we selected are displayed in Figure 11.14. Striking the right arrow once more, we see that the "Keys" sub-menu is displayed, and the two function key assignments we made for F2 and F4 are also shown (see Figure 11.15)

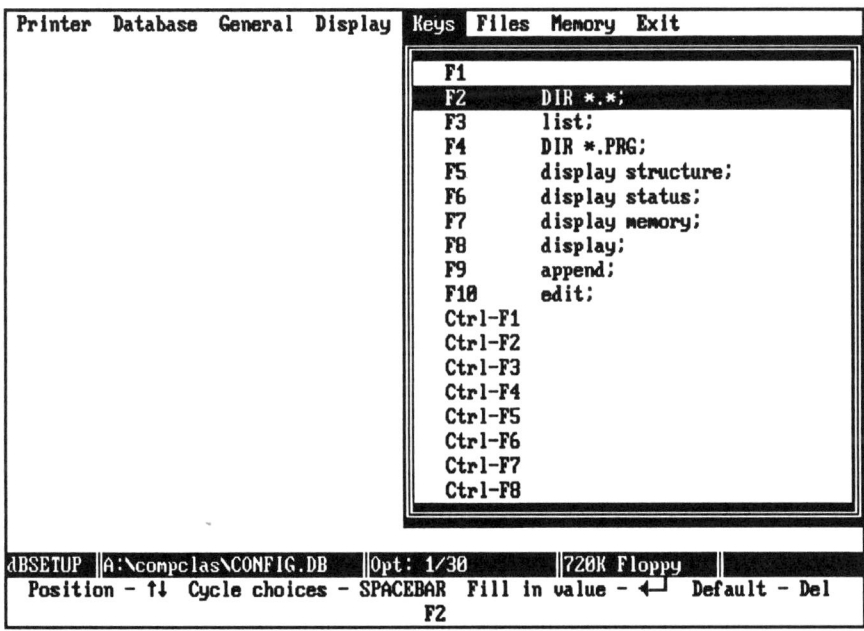

Figure 11.15 The "Keys" Sub-Menu of DBSETUP.EXE

The remaining menu options: "Printer", "Database", "Files", and "Memory", are left for the reader to investigate. A more detailed discussion of these options, as well as those of Table 11.2, may be obtained from the DBASE IV LANGUAGE REFERENCE (comes with dBASE IV software).

The resulting version of our CONFIG.DB file is shown in Figure 11.16. Note that DBSETUP.EXE has alphabetized our commands and added some comments. In addition it replaced the command: **COLOR = W/B, R/W** with the two commands:

COLOR OF NORMAL   = W/B
COLOR OF HIGHLIGHT = R/W

386　CONTROLLING YOUR ENVIRONMENT

```
*
*         dBASE IV Configuration File
*         Sunday March 17, 1991
*

COLOR OF NORMAL        = W/B
COLOR OF HIGHLIGHT     = R/W
COMMAND                = DO COM_MENU
CONFIRM                = ON
EXCLUSIVE              = ON
F2                     = "DIR *.*;"
F4                     = "DIR *.PRG;"
PROMPT                 = RELAX:
STATUS                 = ON
TEDIT                  = NE +1




Line=1    Col=1            A:COMPCLAS\CONFIG.DB         Insert   WW=Off
```
Figure 11.16 Final version of CONFIG.DB generated by DBSETUP.EXE

The DBSETUP.EXE gives us an easy way to generate our CONFIG.DB file as well as a means of displaying all our options. Nonetheless, the ability to modify the CONFIG.DB file using the MODIFY COMMAND editor directly does become necessary in special cases such as the **TEDIT = NE +1** command. The **+1** can be added manually in MODIFY COMMAND, but DBSETUP.EXE will not accept it if it is initially entered in that environment.

If the CONFIG.DB is created, or placed in the directory where dBASE IV is located, then it will be the CONFIG.DB file for dBASE IV regardless of the directory or drive you are using it in. However, if a CONFIG.DB file is created in a particular directory, such as COMPCLAS, then it becomes the CONFIG file for only that specific directory and takes precedence over any other CONFIG.DB.

11.3　Password Protection

Suppose you share a computer's hard disk with a number of other individuals. However, you would like to protect your files

CONTROLLING YOUR ENVIRONMENT 387

from unauthorized access. A first line of defense is the use of the password.

We have already seen one example of the use of a password in Chapter 8. However, in this example, the user was trapped in a loop until he or she came up with the correct password. It would be far more useful to return the user to the DOS prompt immediately if the correct password is not entered. Listing 11.4 shows an enhanced version of COMPMAIN.prg called COM_PASS.prg, that checks on a PASSWORD before allowing someone to execute our COM_MENU system.

After initializing by setting off Talk and Status, we preset the password. We do this right up front to facilitate our changing its value in the future. Next we prompt for the entry of the password. Then immediately, the screen is turned off with the **SET CONSOLE OFF** command so that no one will be able to see what the password is that we are typing. Having entered the password, the **SET CONSOLE ON** command is executed, turning the console back on, and the comparison is made.

If the password is correct, then the main menu procedure, COM_MENU, is executed. Otherwise an error message is placed on the screen. The **WAIT ()** command causes the operation to pause until a key is struck without giving any prompt whatsoever to the user.

Note that **COM_PASS.prg** ends with the QUIT command. This causes the operation to leave dBASE and return to DOS upon termination of the COMPCLAS indexed system. If we modify Listing 11.4 such that the Command that is executed is: **COMMAND = COM_PASS** (rather than: COMMAND = COM_MENU), then the user will never be confronted with dBASE or its dot prompt. After the opening credits, the actual application program, COMPCLAS, will be the only thing seen.

Figure 11.17 shows the screen that is obtained upon the execution of **DO COM_PASS** or by entering dBASE with the modified CONFIG.DB file.

```
* COM_PASS.prg
* This module checks to see if the password
* entered is correct.  If it is, operation
* is allowed to proceed to COM_MENU.
* If not, operation is returned to the
* command line.
*
SET TALK OFF
SET STATUS OFF
* Set the system Password. Use UPPER CASE!
STORE "ROSEBUD" TO PASSWORD
*
CLEAR
@ 12,29 SAY "Enter Your Password: "
SET CONSOLE OFF
ACCEPT [] TO TRYPASSWRD
SET CONSOLE ON
IF UPPER(TRYPASSWRD) = PASSWORD
   SET PROCEDURE TO COM_PROC
   DO COM_MENU
   SET PROCEDURE TO
ELSE
   CLEAR
   @ 12,31 SAY "Invalid Password!"
   WAIT []
   QUIT
ENDIF
SET STATUS ON
SET TALK ON
RETURN
```

Listing 11.4 COM_PASS—A Password protected Front End to COM_MENU

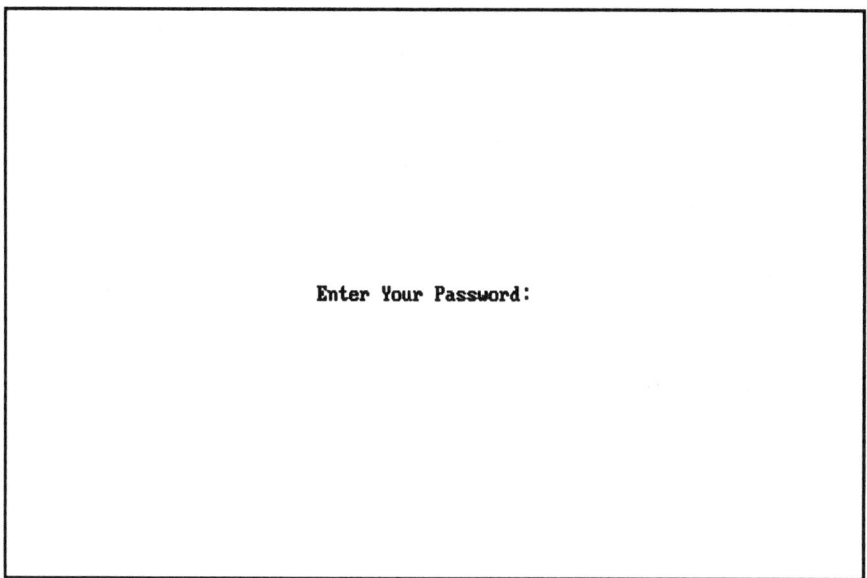

Figure 11.17 Opening Screen of COM_PASS.prg

11.4 Backing Up Your System

In as much as floppy diskettes are media which may be exposed to extremes of heat and cold, dust, magnetic fields, as well as general misuse, their reliability is usually the weakest link in the computer system. I've had a student wipe out an entire semester's work simply by placing her one and only data diskette inside a book which was accidentally degaussed by the librarian at the checkout counter of a library.

Backups should be made of all data, as well as programs, that have any value at all to the user. Even the best hard disk drive will eventually fail. There are myriad backup programs for backing up large database files which reside on the hard disk. Discussion of these is beyond the scope of this text.

11.4.1 Backing Up a Floppy Diskette

Backing up, or making a simple copy of a database system that resides on a single floppy disk is simplicity itself. The DOS command to execute the disk copy is: **DISKCOPY** *Drive1*: *Drive2*: where *Drive1*: can be either **A:** or **B:** and *Drive2*: can be either **A:** or **B:**. The new diskette will be formatted as the copy is being made. The command is executed at the A> prompt:

A:\COMPCLAS> **DISKCOPY A: B:**

Caution should be taken to not try to **DISKCOPY** from one format to another. For example, one would not try to **DISKCOPY** from a 3.5" diskette in Drive **A:** to a 5.25" diskette in drive **B:**. **DISKCOPY** will only work with like formats.

If the computer you are using does not have a drive **B:**, or if drive **B:** is a different type of drive than drive **A:**, then both *drive1*: and *drive2*: can be **A:**. The operation will prompt you to replace the **Source** disk in drive **A:** with the **Target** disk at the appropriate times. Following the prompts given by the DOS **DISKCOPY** a duplicate disk is easily obtained. The command executed from the A> prompt would be:

A:\COMPCLAS> **DISKCOPY A: A:**

11.4.2 Backing Up Between Different Types of Media

Suppose you wish to back up a hard disk to a floppy, or from a 5¼" floppy to a 3½" floppy. This is a change of media, hence the DISKCOPY command cannot be used here. For this we need to use the venerable DOS **COPY** command. Executing the command: **COPY *.*** *Drive:* will copy any file with any extension, in the current directory, to the diskette on drive *Drive:*. For example, if we wish to back up the current directory to drive B:, then the command would become:

A:\COMPCLAS> **COPY *.* B:**

11.5 Running DOS Commands While in dBASE

As we have seen, the DOS commands, with their use of wildcards, have greater power than the dBASE utility commands, which, with the exception of the **DIR** command, do not support wildcards. Then there are the DOS commands which have no counterpart in dBASE, such as **DISKCOPY**. As a result, it is often more expedient to leave dBASE and execute the DOS utility commands than to stay and use the dBASE utility commands.

Fortunately, there is a way of executing DOS commands, as well as other programs, from within the dBASE environment. In this way we do not have to leave dBASE in order to execute our favorite DOS commands. The dBASE command that performs this magic is the **RUN** command. By simply typing the word **RUN** before the DOS command, it causes the operation to return to the operating system for the execution of the command, and then to return to dBASE for the next succeeding command. Its syntax is: **RUN** *ExternalProgram*, where *ExternalProgram* is either a DOS command or any **.exe**, **.com**, or **.bat** file.

For example, if we wanted to execute **DISKCOPY A: A:** from within dBASE, we would type:

. **RUN DISKCOPY A: A:**

In as much as the **RUN** command does not limit itself to just DOS commands, we can **RUN** our favorite program right from within dBASE, with the proviso that the program not take up more memory than dBASE will allow. For example, one could not run Word Perfect from within dBASE IV (in normal DOS memory). Both Word Perfect and dBASE IV take up far to much space to permit the other to run simultaneously.

Also, when dBASE gives up memory in order to do a **RUN**, it intends to get it back when the **RUN** is completed. Because memory resident programs, such as SideKick, do not return the memory that they take when they are executed, they should not be executed from within dBASE by the **RUN** command.

The **"RUN"** command may also be written **"!"**, which saves a couple of keystrokes. Consider the program, BACKUP.prg, shown in Listing 11.5 [37].

BACKUP.prg first determines what your source and target drives will be. It then checks to see if either the source or the target drive is a hard disk (drive is C: or higher). If that is so, then we're dealing in cross media and cannot use the DISKCOPY command. The first IIF() statement makes the determination if we're dealing with a hard drive. If we are, then CROSSMEDIA is set to .T..

If we are not dealing with a hard drive, then there is still the possibility that we are dealing with cross media. Drive A: might be a 3½" drive, while drive B: might be a 5¼" drive (or vice versa). However, if both the source drive as well as the target drive are the same, then we're definitely not dealing with cross media, so CROSSMEDIA can be set to .F. But if the source and target drives are different, then we must ask the question of the user, "Are Both Diskette Drives The Same Type?" (i.e. are they homogeneous?). If the answer is "Y", then CROSSMEDIA is .F., but if the answer is "N", then CROSSMEDIA is .T. . The expression: **CROSSMEDIA = .NOT. HOMOGENOUS**, accomplishes this task. We now know whether we are dealing with cross media or not.

If we are dealing with cross media (CROSSMEDIA is True), then we simply prepare to execute a **COPY *.*** command. If it is false, then we prepare to do a **DISKCOPY**. The preparation of the COPY or DISKCOPY command involves the use of a macro. To fully understand the use of a macro, we have devoted the next section to its discussion.

---

[37]This program was written to demonstrate two new concepts (macros, and the RUN command). It is far more complicated than it has to be. Simplifying this program for a specific machine configuration is assigned as an exercise to the reader at the end of the chapter.

```
* BACKUP.PRG
* This module will back up the current dBASE directory
* It makes use of the DOS DISKCOPY, and COPY commands
* It is executed by means of the dBASE RUN command
* It makes use of Macros
*
STORE [A] TO SOURCEDRIV
STORE [B] TO TARGETDRIV
CLEAR
@ 11,20 SAY "Which drive is the Source Diskette on: " ;
   GET SOURCEDRIV
@ 13,20 SAY "Which drive is the Target Diskette on: " ;
   GET TARGETDRIV
READ
STORE UPPER(SOURCEDRIV) TO SOURCEDRIV
STORE UPPER(TARGETDRIV) TO TARGETDRIV
HARDDRIVE = IIF(TARGETDRIV>'B' .OR. SOURCEDRIV>'B',.T.,.F.)
IF HARDDRIVE
   CROSSMEDIA = .T.
ELSE
   SAMEDRIVE = IIF(TARGETDRIV = SOURCEDRIV,.T.,.F.)
   IF SAMEDRIVE
      CROSSMEDIA = .F.
   ELSE
      STORE .T. TO HOMOGENOUS
      CLEAR
      @ 12,20 SAY "Are Both Diskette Drives The Same Type:";
              GET HOMOGENOUS
      READ
      CROSSMEDIA = .NOT. HOMOGENOUS
   ENDIF
ENDIF
* Prompt User To Place Backup Diskette In Drive
IF CROSSMEDIA
   IF TARGETDRIV <= 'B'
      STORE "Place Backup Diskette In Drive " + TARGETDRIV;
            TO QUE
      CLEAR
      @ 12,0
      WAIT QUE
   ENDIF
   STORE " *.* " + TARGETDRIV + ":" TO ARGUMENT
   RUN COPY &ARGUMENT
ELSE
   STORE SOURCEDRIV + ": " + TARGETDRIV + ":" TO ARGUMENT
   RUN DISKCOPY &ARGUMENT
ENDIF
RETURN
```

Listing 11.5 Program: BACKUP.prg which backs up your system

11.5.1 Macros

Our difficulty is that the two arguments of the COPY or DISKCOPY command are not known before the command is to be executed. Up till now we have always known what command we were going to execute at the time that we wrote the program. In this case we will have to create the command, on the fly, while the program is being executed. It is the existence of the macro that allows us to create a "variable" argument to a command.

The way this is done is by making a single character string by concatenating the character variables that contribute to it. In the command: **STORE " *.* " + TARGETDRIV + ":" TO ARGUMENT**, we create an ARGUMENT which takes on the following values:

TARGETDRIV	ARGUMENT
A	*.* A:
B	*.* B:
C	*.* C:
etc.	etc.

The effect of placing the **&** (ampersand) sign in front of the string variable, **ARGUMENT**, in the statement: **RUN COPY &ARGUMENT**, is to cause the contents of the ARGUMENT variable to replace the words &ARGUMENT in the command. For example, if the TARGETDRIV was A, then the **RUN COPY &ARGUMENT** becomes: **RUN COPY *.* A:**, and that is the command that actually gets executed.

In the same manner, in the command: **STORE SOURCEDRIV + ":" + TARGETDRIV + ":" TO ARGUMENT**, we create an ARGUMENT that can take on any of the following values:

CONTROLLING YOUR ENVIRONMENT

SOURCEDRIV	TARGETDRIV	ARGUMENT
A	A	A: A:
A	B	A: B:
B	A	B: A:
B	B	B: B:

Once again, the effect of placing the & in front of the string variable, **ARGUMENT**, in the statement: **RUN DISKCOPY &ARGUMENT** , is to cause the contents of the ARGUMENT variable to replace the words &ARGUMENT in the command. For example, if the SOURCEDRIV were A, and the TARGETDRIV were B, then the **RUN DISKCOPY &ARGUMENT** becomes: **RUN DISKCOPY A: B:** , and that is the command that gets executed.

Basically what the macro does is to substitute the value given to the variable for the variable itself. It's syntax is: *&Variable* . In our case the *Variable* is **ARGUMENT** . The value of the variable is pre-defined in an earlier statement in the program.

By means of macros we can use variable arguments in our instructions. Another example of the use of macros is shown in the program fragment below:

```
STORE [    ] TO WHICHFILE
CLEAR
@ 12,20 SAY "Enter Name Of Database To Be Opened:  " GET ;
   WHICHFILE
READ
USE &WHICHFILE
```

As you can see, this program fragment will open any data base that is entered in response to the prompt: "Enter Name of Database To Be Opened:".

Macros can also be executed from the command line. A macro can be used to substitute a few short keystrokes for a long complicated instruction. For example, suppose the memory variable, **R**, is defined as follows:

. R = "REPORT FORM COMPCLAS FOR TERM_PROJ TO PRINT"

Then whenever one wants to generate a COMPCLAS report, all one has to do is to type:

. &R

which is a lot faster than typing out the instruction itself.

In the case of our BACKUP.prg program, by concatenating the colons and the space between the drive letters to conform to the DOS syntax, we have created the memory variable **ARGUMENT**, which contains the desired argument to the DOS **DISKCOPY** or **COPY** command.

The **RUN** command allowed us to execute, from within dBASE IV itself, a DOS command. In this way, dBASE allows you to do all the chores that are the specialty of some other application program or operating system, without ever leaving dBASE. There is no reason why **BACKUP.prg** for example, could not become part of the **COMPCLAS** system and be compiled with it. This is the final topic of this chapter.

11.6 Modification of COMPCLAS System to Include BACKUP.prg

The ability to back itself up should be a part of any computer system. All you have to do is to lose the contents of a database just once to fully understand the truth of this maxim. In this spirit we shall refine our COMPCLAS System one more time.

Listing 11.6 shows a modified version of COM_PASS.prg which we will call COM_MAIN.prg. This version includes the inquiry, "Do You Want To Backup COMPCLAS?" In this way the user is confronted with this question each time he or she enters the system. If the answer is "Y", then BACKUP.prg is executed, otherwise not.

Figure 11.18 shows our most recent revision of the COMPCLAS System Structure Chart.

```
* COM_MAIN.prg
* This module checks to see if the password entered
* is correct.  If it is, the user is queried about
* Backing Up the system, and operation is allowed
* to proceed to COM_MENU.
* If not, operation is returned to the command line.
*
SET TALK OFF
SET STATUS OFF
* Set the system Password. Use UPPER CASE only!
STORE "ROSEBUD" TO PASSWORD
*
CLEAR
@ 12,29 SAY "Enter Your Password: "
SET CONSOLE OFF
ACCEPT [ ] TO TRYPASSWRD
SET CONSOLE ON
IF UPPER(TRYPASSWRD) = PASSWORD
   STORE .F. TO BACKITUP
   CLEAR
   @ 12,20 SAY "Do You Want To Back Up the System: ";
           GET BACKITUP
   READ
   IF BACKITUP
      DO BACKUP
   ENDIF
   SET PROCEDURE TO COM_PROC
   DO COM_MENU
   SET PROCEDURE TO
ELSE
   CLEAR
   @ 12,31 SAY "Invalid Password!"
   WAIT [ ]
ENDIF
SET STATUS ON
SET TALK ON
QUIT
```

Listing 11.6 COM_MAIN.prg—The opening Module to COMPCLAS System

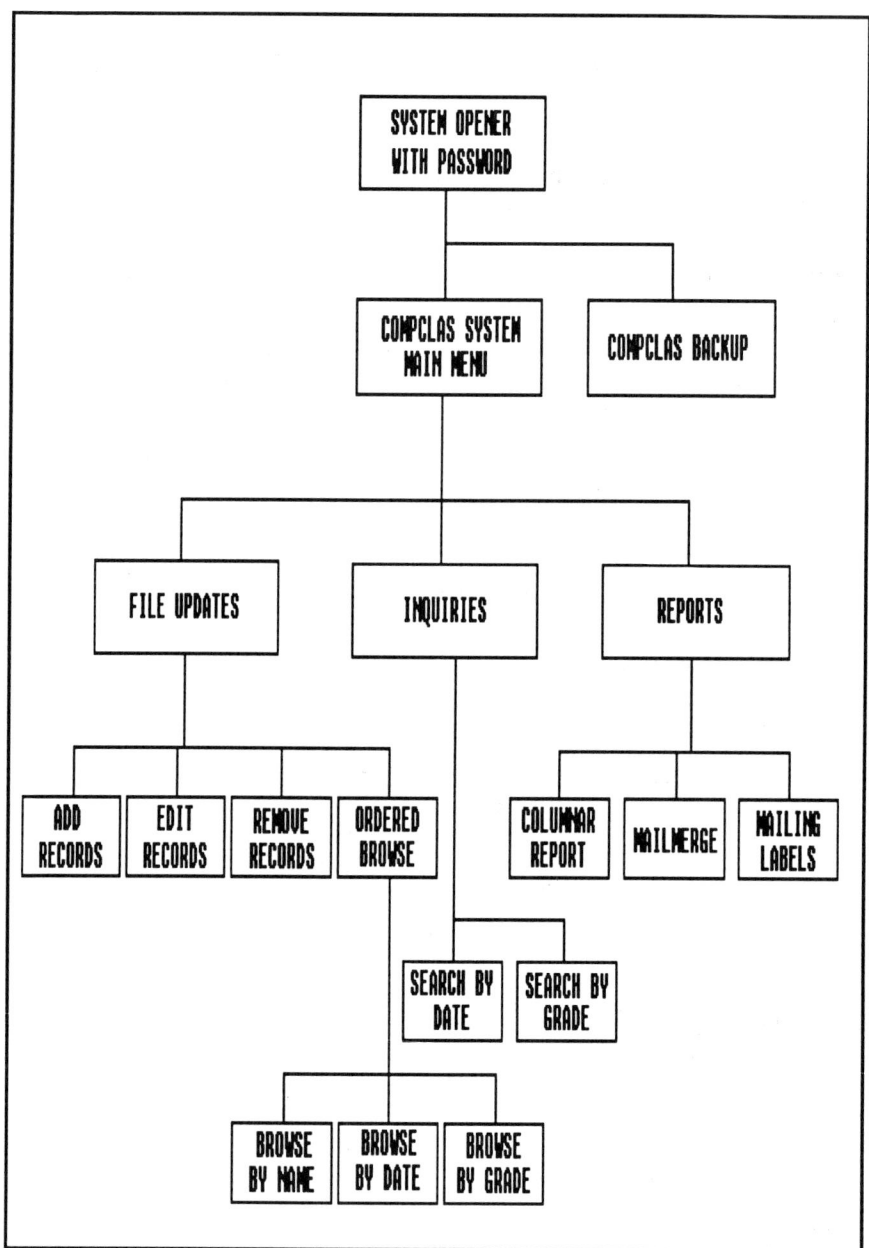

Figure 11.18 Enhanced System Structure Chart For COMPCLAS System

CONTROLLING YOUR ENVIRONMENT

11.7 Summary

In Chapter 11 we have discussed how to control the environment of dBASE itself. The many uses of the **SET** instruction were discussed, as well as the use of the **SET** mode.

The **CONFIG.DB** file was introduced as a means to customize the defaults of the dBASE environment automatically each time dBASE is entered. The **DBSETUP.EXE** program was presented as a means of generating the CONFIG.DB file from a menu of options.

The use of password protection was discussed, and an example of a password protected system was demonstrated.

The concept of backing up the system was emphasized, and it was demonstrated how to execute DOS commands, with their wildcards, from within the dBASE environment. In creating a BACKUP program, the utility of the macro was introduced. The macro was shown to be a means of allowing variable arguments in dBASE commands.

11.8 Review

In Chapter 11 we presented the following commands:
> **LIST STATUS**
> **RUN**
> **SET**
> **SET CONFIRM ON/OFF**
> **SET COLOR TO** *a/b,c/d*
> **SET CONSOLE ON/OFF**
> **SET FUNCTION** *n* **TO** *function*

Add these to your glossary of dBASE commands.

Additionally, a list of commands which can be used in the CONFIG.DB file was presented in Listing 11.3. This can be a separate list in your glossary of commands.

Add the DOS command **DISKCOPY** to your glossary of DOS commands.

Finally, the macro function, **&** , was introduced. Note of its function should also be made in your glossary.

11.9 Laboratory Work

Following the text, execute all the commands and programs given as examples. Create the CONFIG.DB file shown in Listing 11.2. Write and execute the programs, COM_PASS.prg, BACKUP.prg, and COM_MAIN.prg.

11.10 Exercises

1. Write a CONFIG.DB file for the directory which contains your MAILIST system. Hand it in. It should include at least seven commands including the following:

    a) A command to DO MAIL_MEN upon entry into dBASE;

    b) Define a prompt of your choosing;

    c) Set the decimals to 5 (the default value of 2). Try doing some math (do a division) and demonstrate the result of your new default value.

    d) Pick four more defaults (your choice) to put into your CONFIG.DB file.

2. Write a program called BACKMAIL.prg which will back up the MAILIST system. It should be specific to your use of MAILIST. (It doesn't need to have all the possibilities that BACKUP.prg includes. It can do either a DISKCOPY or a COPY. Hand this in.

CONTROLLING YOUR ENVIRONMENT   401

3. Write a front end to your indexed MAILIST system called MAILCALL.prg and hand it in. It should include the following:

   a) Password protection;

   b) Setting the procedure file, MAILPROC, on;

   c) Option of calling BACKMAIL.prg.

4. Redraw the system structure chart for the MAILIST System. It should take into account the new BACKMAIL module.

11.11 Term Project

Hand in an updated version of the system chart for your project. This should reflect any changes you've had in your thinking about what your system should contain in light of the points made in this chapter. Also hand in *one* of the completed modules for your system.

CHAPTER 12

DEBUGGING & DOCUMENTATION

12.0 Topics Covered in Chapter 12

DEBUG is introduced.

The SET ECHO ON and SET DEBUG ON pair of commands is shown to generate a trace of the program execution.

Helpful comments are added to Format Files to increase user "friendliness".

On-Line Help/Reference screens are employed using the ON KEY LABEL command to access them.

Documentation is discussed, and the minimal set of system documentation is outlined.

The documentation utility, SNAP is presented which generates most of the desired system documentation required.

12.1 Debugging

In compiling our programs we eliminated all of our syntax errors. However, what we did not eliminate was our runtime errors, the actual errors in logic that we detect in the debugging process.

With a runtime error, sometime after we strike the key telling the computer to execute the program, the error occurs, and the anticipated result is not obtained. Furthermore, the location of the actual error is not given to us.

Usually, one of two things occur: 1) either the program gets executed, but the desired result is in error; 2) or program execution gets into a long or endless loop and we have to strike the Escape key in order to get out. When that happens we get, what should now be the familiar error message asking the question, should we "Cancel", "Ignore", or "Suspend" operation.

Striking **C** for Cancel will get us out of the program but does not tell us where or why things went wrong. With the help of **DEBUG** we can narrow down the source of the difficulty very quickly.

12.1.1 Using the **Debugger**

dBASE IV has a full-fledged built in debugger called **DEBUG**. It is activated by executing the desired program replacing the word **DEBUG** for the word **DO**. It's syntax is: **DEBUG** *ProgramName* .

For example, suppose that we were having difficulty getting COM_MAIN.prg to accept our password. Since we're certain that we've been typing it in right, let's use **DEBUG** to find out what the problem is. We enter COM_MAIN.prg by typing:

. DEBUG COM_MAIN

DEBUGGING & DOCUMENTATION

Immediately, we get the screen shown in Figure 12.1. Note that the screen is broken down into four windows. The editing window at the top left shows the program being executed. The Help window at the top right shows the available commands that can be used in **DEBUG**. The display window in the middle left is where we can type in the variables whose values we want to know as we proceed through the program. Finally, the bottom window shows the status of where we're at. It is also the place where we type in what action we want to take place.

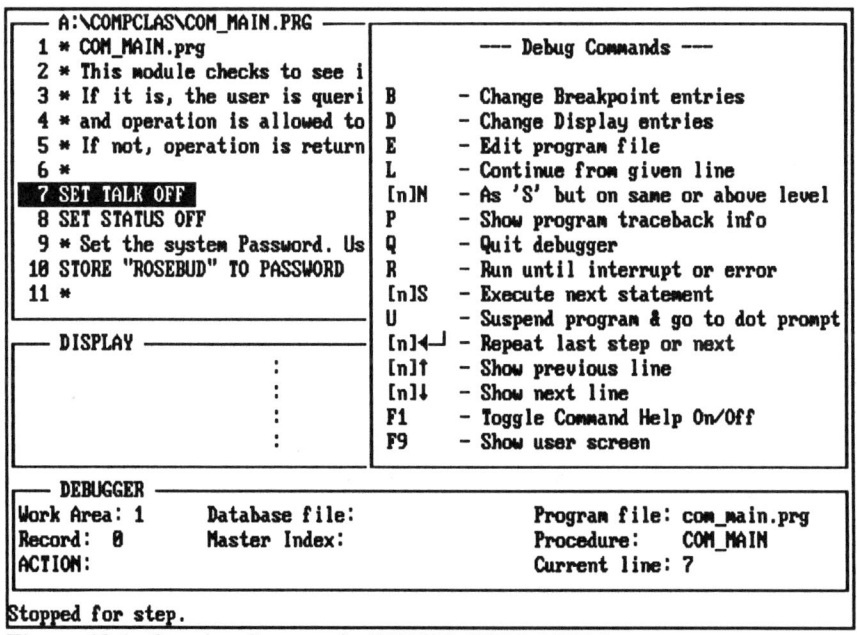

Figure 12.1 Opening Screen of: DEBUG COM_MAIN

Striking **D** to go to the display window, we type in the two variables that we are tracking in this program: PASSWORD and TRYPASSWRD. Having typed those in, we strike **Ctrl-End** to return to the action window at the bottom. Looking at Figure 12.2, note that we have uncovered one more window. The Breakpoint window in the middle right is where we type in the condition under which we want the operation to pause so that we can look at what's happening. We go to that window by typing **B** at the action line. As you can see from Figure 12.2, we have typed in: **LINENO() = 17**. The function: **LINENO()** returns the line number in the program. Since we're interested in what happens at line 17, where the decision is made as to whether or not the password we typed in is equivalent to the password that is imbedded in the program, we have typed in this expression as our condition for stopping the operation. Type **Ctrl-End** once more to return execution to the action line.

Note that **DEBUG** makes the comment, "Variable not found", after each of the two variables whose values we want displayed. This is because we have not reached the point in the program where these values have even been defined yet. As you can see, the operation is paused at line 7, the first executable line of the program.

We are now ready to begin the execution of the program. From Figure 12.1 we see that the command to do this is: **R**. Typing **R** and then entering in the password as requested by COM_MAIN.prg, we find the operation pauses with the screen shown in Figure 12.3.

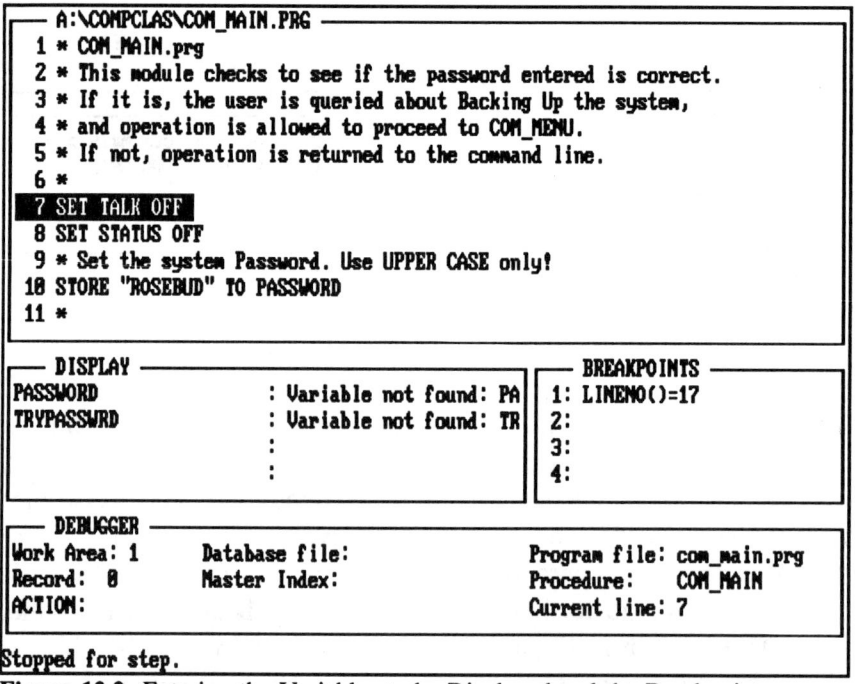

Figure 12.2 Entering the Variables to be Displayed and the Breakpoint

DEBUGGING & DOCUMENTATION

```
┌─ A:\COMPCLAS\COM_MAIN.PRG ──────────────────────────────────┐
│ 15 ACCEPT [] TO TRYPASSWRD                                  │
│ 16 SET CONSOLE ON                                           │
│ 17 IF TRYPASSWRD = PASSWORD                                 │
│ 18    STORE .F. TO BACKITUP                                 │
│ 19    CLEAR                                                 │
│ 20    @ 12,20 SAY "Do You Want To Back Up the System: " GET BACKITUP │
│ 21    READ                                                  │
│ 22    IF BACKITUP                                           │
│ 23       DO BACKUP                                          │
│ 24    ENDIF                                                 │
│ 25    SET PROCEDURE TO COM_PROC                             │
└─────────────────────────────────────────────────────────────┘
┌─ DISPLAY ─────────────────────────┐ ┌─ BREAKPOINTS ─────────┐
│ PASSWORD       : ROSEBUD          │ │ 1: LINENO()=17        │
│ TRYPASSWRD     : rosebud          │ │ 2:                    │
│                :                  │ │ 3:                    │
│                :                  │ │ 4:                    │
└───────────────────────────────────┘ └───────────────────────┘
┌─ DEBUGGER ────────────────────────────────────────────────────┐
│ Work Area: 1    Database file:        Program file: com_main.prg │
│ Record:    0    Master Index:         Procedure:    COM_MAIN     │
│ ACTION:                               Current line: 17           │
└──────────────────────────────────────────────────────────────────┘
Breakpoint: 1
```

Figure 12.3 Operation halting at the Breakpoint: LINENO()=17

In the display window we immediately see what our problem is. There is a case difference between the PASSWORD = "ROSEBUD" in the program and the TRYPASSWRD = "rosebud" we typed in. This is a problem that we can handle easily by editing our program. We do this by typing **E** at the action line. This takes us into editing mode with the program COM_MENU.prg. We replace the line: **IF TRYPASSWRD = PASSWORD** with: **IF UPPER(TRYPASSWRD) = PASSWORD,** as shown in Figure 12.4.

Having made the password what we type in from the keyboard case insensitive, we can now try executing our newly edited line 17 by striking the Enter key. The result is that we go to line 18, as shown in Figure 12.5, just as we should when we type in the proper password. Since we have now passed that hurdle, we can either quit from **DEBUG,** or continue on by striking **R** once more as the action to take.

```
┌─ A:\COMPCLAS\COM_MAIN.PRG ─────────────────────────────────────────────┐
│[......▼1.....▼..2█...▼...3..▼......4▼.......▼5......▼..6...▼...7..▼....│
│* Set the system Password. Use UPPER CASE only!                         │
│STORE "ROSEBUD" TO PASSWORD                                             │
│*                                                                       │
│CLEAR                                                                   │
│@ 12,29 SAY "Enter Your Password: "                                     │
│SET CONSOLE OFF                                                         │
│ACCEPT [] TO TRYPASSWRD                                                 │
│SET CONSOLE ON                                                          │
│IF UPPER(TRYPASSWRD) = PASSWORD                                         │
├─ DISPLAY ─────────────────────────┬─ BREAKPOINTS ──────────────────────┤
│PASSWORD              : ROSEBUD    │ 1: LINENO()=17                     │
│TRYPASSWRD            : rosebud    │ 2:                                 │
│                      :            │ 3:                                 │
│                      :            │ 4:                                 │
├─ DEBUGGER ─────────────────────────────────────────────────────────────┤
│Work Area: 1    Database file:          Program file: com_main.prg      │
│Record:    0    Master Index:           Procedure:    COM_MAIN          │
│ACTION:    E                            Current line: 17                │
└────────────────────────────────────────────────────────────────────────┘
Breakpoint:  1
```

Figure 12.4 Editing line 17 in DEBUG COM_MAIN

```
┌─ A:\COMPCLAS\COM_MAIN.PRG ─────────────────────────────────────────────┐
│ 15 ACCEPT [] TO TRYPASSWRD                                             │
│ 16 SET CONSOLE ON                                                      │
│ 17 IF UPPER(TRYPASSWRD) = PASSWORD                                     │
│ 18    STORE .F. TO BACKITUP                                            │
│ 19    CLEAR                                                            │
│ 20    @ 12,20 SAY "Do You Want To Back Up the System: " GET BACKITUP   │
│ 21    READ                                                             │
│ 22    IF BACKITUP                                                      │
│ 23       DO BACKUP                                                     │
│ 24    ENDIF                                                            │
│ 25    SET PROCEDURE TO COM_PROC                                        │
├─ DISPLAY ─────────────────────────┬─ BREAKPOINTS ──────────────────────┤
│PASSWORD              : ROSEBUD    │ 1: LINENO()=17                     │
│TRYPASSWRD            : rosebud    │ 2:                                 │
│                      :            │ 3:                                 │
│                      :            │ 4:                                 │
├─ DEBUGGER ─────────────────────────────────────────────────────────────┤
│Work Area: 1    Database file:          Program file: com_main.prg      │
│Record:    0    Master Index:           Procedure:    COM_MAIN          │
│ACTION:                                 Current line: 18                │
└────────────────────────────────────────────────────────────────────────┘
Stopped for step.
```

Figure 12.5 Stepping operation forward by striking Enter key

DEBUGGING & DOCUMENTATION 409

Suppose we wanted to stop the operation at a line in a program called by the opening program rather than the opening program itself. For example, suppose that we wanted to look at a possible bug in BACKUP.prg, even though we are starting with COM_MAIN.prg as before. This is done by simply changing our breakpoint condition to include the program name as well as the line number. This is done with the **PROGRAM()** function. This function takes on the value of the Program currently being executed. It's syntax is: **PROGRAM()** = *ProgramName* . In this case we would type for Breakpoint 1: **PROGRAM() = "BACKUP" .AND. LINENO()=32** if we want to stop at line 32 in BACKUP.prg (See Figure 12.6).

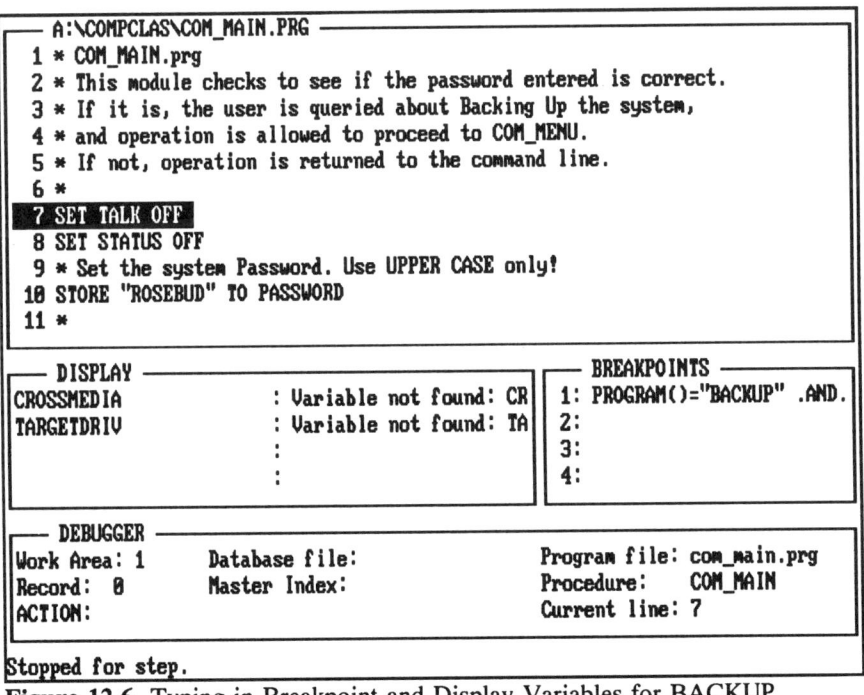

Figure 12.6 Typing in Breakpoint and Display Variables for BACKUP

In this case we are interested in the variables: CROSSMEDIA and TARGETDRIV which are used in the IF statement made in line 32 of BACKUP. These have been entered in the display window. Striking the **R** key, we run the program, and find that it indeed breaks at line 32 in BACKUP.prg (See Figure 12.7).

```
┌─ A:\COMPCLAS\BACKUP.PRG ─────────────────────────────────────────┐
│ 30 ENDIF                                                         │
│ 31 * Prompt User To Place Backup Diskette In Drive               │
│ 32 IF CROSSMEDIA .AND. TARGETDRIV <= 'B'                         │
│ 33    STORE "Place Backup Diskette In Drive " + TARGETDRIV TO QUE│
│ 34    CLEAR                                                      │
│ 35    @ 12,0                                                     │
│ 36    WAIT QUE                                                   │
│ 37 ENDIF                                                         │
│ 38 IF CROSSMEDIA                                                 │
│ 39    STORE " *.* " + TARGETDRIV + ":" TO ARGUMENT               │
│ 40    RUN COPY &ARGUMENT                                         │
└──────────────────────────────────────────────────────────────────┘
┌─ DISPLAY ────────────────────┐ ┌─ BREAKPOINTS ──────────────────┐
│ CROSSMEDIA        : T        │ │ 1: PROGRAM()="BACKUP" .AND.    │
│ TARGETDRIV        : B        │ │ 2:                             │
│                   :          │ │ 3:                             │
│                   :          │ │ 4:                             │
└──────────────────────────────┘ └────────────────────────────────┘
┌─ DEBUGGER ───────────────────────────────────────────────────────┐
│ Work Area: 1    Database file:       Program file: backup.prg    │
│ Record:    0    Master Index:        Procedure:    BACKUP        │
│ ACTION:                              Current line: 32            │
└──────────────────────────────────────────────────────────────────┘
Breakpoint: 1
```

Figure 12.7 DEBUG Execution Paused on line 32 in BACKUP.prg

It is not always necessary or desirable to make a breakpoint dependent on a line number in a program. Often, we want to have a breakpoint when a certain condition is met like a variable taking on a particular value. For example, we might have chosen the condition: .NOT. CROSSMEDIA for our breakpoint.

As you can see there is a lot of flexibility in **DEBUG**, and it is indeed a powerful tool with which to find runtime errors in your system.

DEBUGGING & DOCUMENTATION 411

12.1.2 Use of SET TRAP Command to Locate Errors

The standard runtime error message, "Cancel, Ignore, Suspend", gives us very little information as to what and where the problem is. On the other hand, if we were to execute: **SET TRAP ON** at the beginning of the program, then when a runtime error did occur, the operation would go directly into DEBUG. This, in turn, would tell us what program and with which instruction we are having problems and would further allow us to use the full power of the DEBUG to find the problem.

In addition if **SET TRAP** is **ON**, then were you to simply hit the Escape key, it would carry you into DEBUG. In this way you can activate DEBUG during any suspicious part of your program that you would like to more closely scrutinize.

12.1.3 Obtaining a Printed Trace of Your Program Execution

Suppose what you wanted to do is to trace the execution of your program as it proceeded through the code. If you wanted to do it step by step, then **DEBUG** would be the easiest tool to use. However, if you want a "paper trail" of how the execution proceeded, then another tool that is useful in debugging is the **SET ECHO ON** command combined with the **SET DEBUG ON** command.

What the **SET ECHO ON** does is to echo to the screen each command as it is executed. The program commands will be painted right on the screen on top of your normal program screen display. To set the **ECHO** on we simply type at the command line:

. SET ECHO ON

Now we follow that by executing the program that we wish to execute. For example, if we type at the command line:

. DO COM_MENU

the result is shown in Figure 12.8.

```
12 DEFINE PAD Update OF Main PROMPT " Update Records " AT 12,05
13 DEFINE PAD Search OF Main PROMPT "Search Records" AT 12,25
14 DEFINE PAD Print  OF Main PROMPT "Print Reports"  AT 12,45
15 DEFINE PAD Exit   OF Main PROMPT "Exit"           AT 12,70
19 ON PAD Update OF Main Activate Popup Updatpop
20 ON PAD Search OF Main Activate Popup Searcpop
21 ON PAD Print  OF Main Activate Popup Printpop
25 DEFINE POPUP Updatpop FROM 13,05 MESSAGE "File Maintenance"
26 DEFINE POPUP Searcpop FROM 13,25 MESSAGE "Search Options"
27 DEFINE POPUP Printpop FROM 13,45 MESSAGE "Report Options"
29 DEFINE BAR 1 OF Updatpop PROMPT "Add Records"
30  Update Records UpdaSearch Recordsdit RePrint Reports         Exit
31 DEFINE BAR 3 OF Updatpop PROMPT "Delete Records"
32 DEFINE BAR 4 OF Updatpop PROMPT "Browse Records"
34 DEFINE BAR 1 OF Searcpop PROMPT "Grade Search"
35 DEFINE BAR 2 OF Searcpop PROMPT "Date Search"
37 DEFINE BAR 1 OF Printpop PROMPT " Columnar  "
38 DEFINE BAR 2 OF Printpop PROMPT " Mailmerge "
39 DEFINE BAR 3 OF Printpop PROMPT " Labels    "
41 ON SELECTION POPUP Updatpop Do UPDACASE
42 ON SELECTION POPUP Searcpop DO SEARCASE
43 ON SELECTION POPUP Printpop DO PRINCASE
44 ON SELECTION PAD Exit OF Main DEACTIVATE MENU
46 ACTIVATE MENU MAIN
```

Figure 12.8 Execution of: DO COM_MENU with SET ECHO ON

However, as you can see, the interleaving of the echoed commands and the screen text makes the actual program execution a bit confusing to look at, as well as quite busy. A way of nicely solving this problem is to print out all the echoed commands to the printer rather than to the screen. This is done using the **SET DEBUG ON** command.

With the **SET DEBUG ON** command in operation, the operation continues normally on the screen while the printer follows the program execution, printing out each command as we go along. **SET DEBUG ON** is always used in conjunction with **SET ECHO ON**. Hence the two should be executed together before beginning program execution. Note: Be sure your printer is on! If it is not, program execution will get hung up. In this example, we will be tracing the operation in the program COM_MAIN.prg. We begin by typing:

. **SET ECHO ON**
. **SET DEBUG ON**
. **DO COM_MAIN**

If we were to type in the wrong password, then the resulting printout of the execution trace would be that shown in Listing 12.1.

```
 7 SET TALK OFF
 8 SET STATUS OFF
10 STORE "ROSEBUD" TO PASSWORD
12 CLEAR
13 @ 12,29 SAY "Enter Your Password: "
14 SET CONSOLE OFF
15 ACCEPT [] TO TRYPASSWRD
16 SET CONSOLE ON
17 IF UPPER(TRYPASSWRD) = PASSWORD
30 ELSE
31    CLEAR
32    @ 12,31 SAY "Invalid Password!"
33    WAIT []
34 ENDIF
35 SET STATUS ON
36 SET TALK ON
37 RETURN
```

Listing 12.1 Trace of COM_MAIN.prg when wrong password is typed in

Now we can easily follow the commands being executed on the printer while we watch the normal program execution on the screen.

12.1.4 Use Modular Programming to Minimize Errors

The length of time that it takes to find an error in a program is not directly proportional to the length of the program. Assuming that you average one programming bug per page of code (you are a good programmer indeed if that is your average), then in a two page program there will likely be two errors. It will probably take more than twice the time to find the two errors as it would to find one error on one page. For one thing, the errors might interact with each other making finding them more complicated.

For this reason, it is better to write many small program modules than a few large programs. You will, on the average, spend less time and make fewer errors debugging many small modules than you will debugging a few large ones. You will notice that no program presented in this book exceeds one page in length. Although there is no fixed rule here, I am of the opinion that if a program takes more than one page to write, it is probably too long and should be broken down into smaller pieces. This is particularly true for a person who is just starting to learn a programming language.

As soon as you start nesting loops within each other, and your selection statements start nesting more than two deep, things become very complicated very quickly. Resorting to writing additional modules rather than nesting three or more loops within each other will make your system less confusing and less error prone.

In response to the argument that making additional modules increases execution time, it is pointed out that if these modules are made into procedures and placed in a single module, then the increase in execution time is nil.

12.2 Creating Help and Reference Screens

A good applications program should be as self-documenting as possible. This means that the user should be able to follow the menu, the various data update screens, as well as any reference screens, and be able to operate the system without having to refer to some external manual or instruction sheet. The system should be as complete and as user friendly as possible.

Along these lines, we will be taking our COMPCLAS system and making it conform to this standard. COMPCLAS may seem like too small and trivial a database on which to justify our expending so much effort and time. The intention here is that if the student is presented with one system that is well designed, she or he will carry these design techniques over to all the rest of the work that the student does which may include systems well deserving of such attention.

12.2.1 Creating Help Screens

One of the easiest ways to create a Help screen, is to simply add helpful comments to the bottom of the format file(s). This is easily accomplished by typing in the desired "Help" using the screen generator that was used to generate the format file initially.

The one complication is the fact that the "Help" that may be included for the format file used to APPEND new records may be different than the "Help" that would be appropriate for the format file used to EDIT already existing records. In a case like this, it would become necessary to create two separate format files, one for APPENDing and one for EDITing. This task is easily accomplished by executing the following commands:

. COPY FILE COMPCLAS.SCR TO COM_ADD.SCR
. COPY FILE COMPCLAS.SCR TO COM_EDIT.SCR

This gives us two screen files, **COM_ADD.SCR** and **COM_EDIT.SCR**. From these we can generate our new format files, **COM_ADD.FMT** and **COM_EDIT.FMT**, with our "Help Menu" written on them. Using the same techniques that we learned in Chapter 6, we can simply add to the bottom of the screen the few keystrokes that one needs to know to APPEND and EDIT data. The resulting screens that appear in the screen generator for the APPEND and EDIT cases are shown in Figures 12.9 and 12.10 respectively.

The next thing that we have to do is to modify our two programs, **COMPADD.prg** and **COM_EDIT.prg**, such that they invoke our new format files, **COM_ADD.FMT** and **COM_EDIT.FMT** respectively. Listings 12.2 and 12.3 show the modified programs.

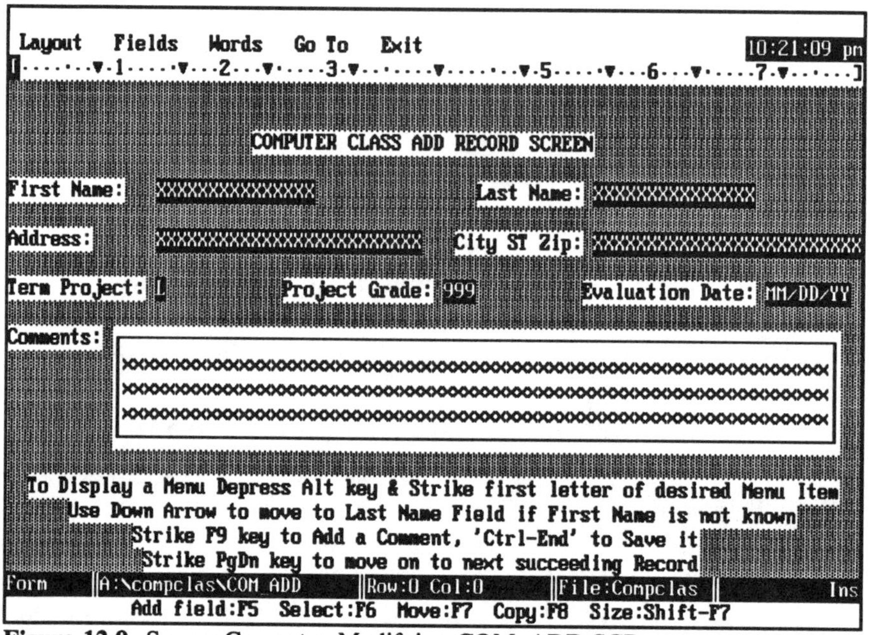

416   DEBUGGING & DOCUMENTATION

Figure 12.9 Screen Generator Modifying COM_ADD.SCR

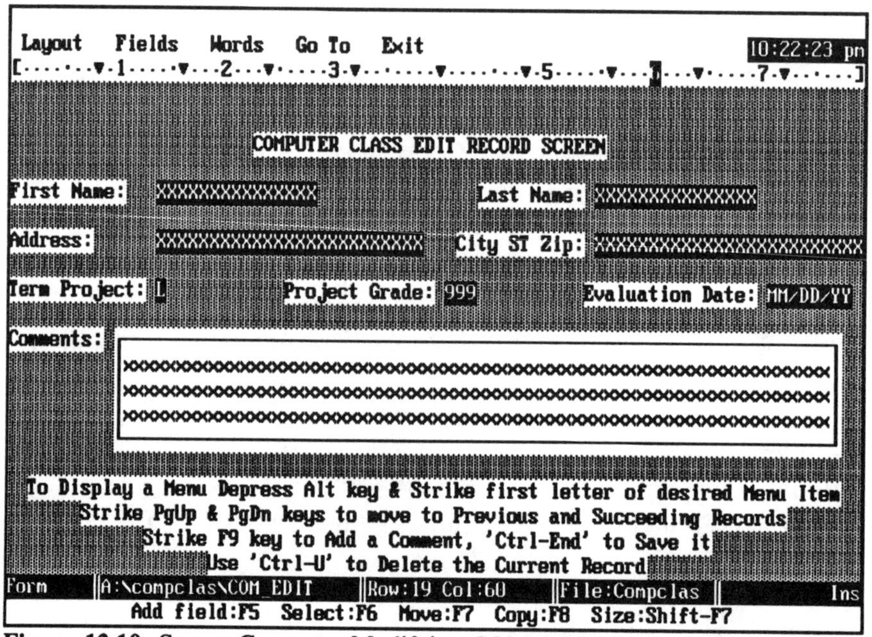

Figure 12.10 Screen Generator Modifying COM_EDIT.SCR

DEBUGGING & DOCUMENTATION 417

```
* COMPADD.PRG
* This program Opens the Database COMPCLAS
* and Appends to it.
* It makes use of the format file:
* COM_ADD.FMT.
*
USE COMPCLAS
SET FORMAT TO COM_ADD
APPEND
SET FORMAT TO
USE
RETURN
```

Listing 12.2 Modified version of COMPADD.prg using COM_ADD.FMT

Executing the "Add Record" and "Edit Record" options off of the menu of COM_MENU.prg, we get the screens shown in Figures 12.11 and 12.12 respectively.

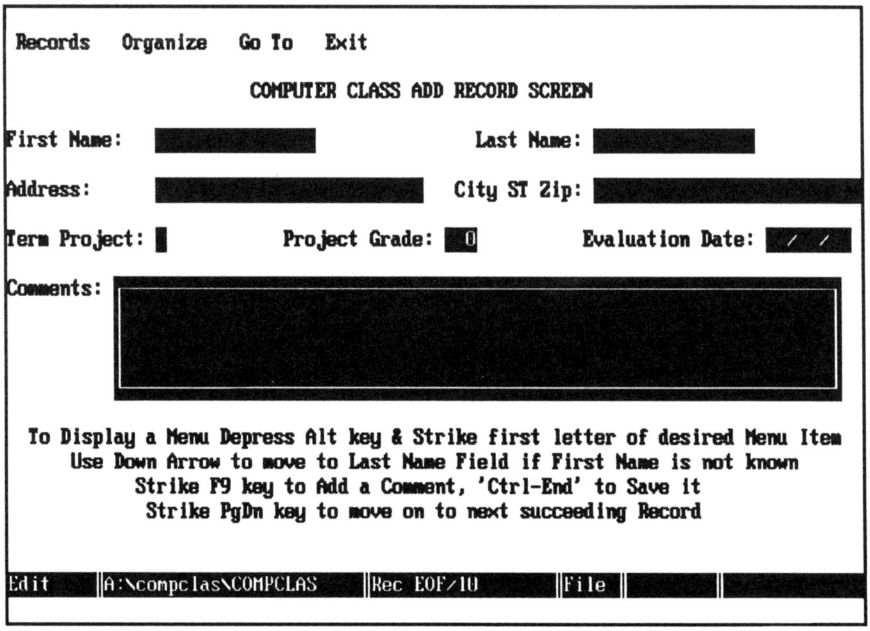

```
Records   Organize   Go To   Exit
                COMPUTER CLASS ADD RECORD SCREEN
First Name: [          ]         Last Name: [          ]
Address:    [          ]         City ST Zip: [          ]
Term Project: [ ]    Project Grade: [ 0 ]   Evaluation Date: [ / / ]
Comments:   [                                              ]

     To Display a Menu Depress Alt key & Strike first letter of desired Menu Item
     Use Down Arrow to move to Last Name Field if First Name is not known
           Strike F9 key to Add a Comment, 'Ctrl-End' to Save it
           Strike PgDn key to move on to next succeeding Record

 Edit    A:\compclas\COMPCLAS     Rec EOF/10      File
```

Figure 12.11 APPEND mode with SET FORMAT TO COM_ADD

```
* COM_EDIT.PRG
* This routine allows one to edit COMPCLAS.dbf
* Records can be searched by a particular Name or
* sequentially. If a Search is chosen then the
* Order is set to LASTFIRST.
* It uses the Format File COM_EDIT.FMT
*
USE COMPCLAS
STORE .T. TO BYNAME
CLEAR
@ 12,15 SAY [Do You Want To Search By Name (Y/N):] ;
   GET BYNAME
READ
IF BYNAME
   SET ORDER TO LASTFIRST
   STORE SPACE(15) TO LASTSEARCH
   STORE SPACE(15) TO FIRSTSEARC
   CLEAR
   @ 11,24 SAY "Enter Last Name:  " GET LASTSEARCH
   @ 13,24 SAY "Enter First Name: " GET FIRSTSEARC
   READ
   STORE UPPER(TRIM(LASTSEARCH + FIRSTSEARC)) TO ;
                 NAMESEARCH
   SEEK NAMESEARCH
ELSE
   GOTO TOP
ENDIF          && byname
IF .NOT. EOF()
   SET FORMAT TO COM_EDIT
   EDIT
   SET FORMAT TO
ELSE
   CLEAR
   @ 12,17 SAY "Unable to Find: " + TRIM(LASTSEARCH);
                         +" "+ FIRSTSEARC
WAIT
ENDIF          && not eof
USE
RETURN
```

Listing 12.3 Modified version of COM_EDIT.prg using COM_EDIT.FMT

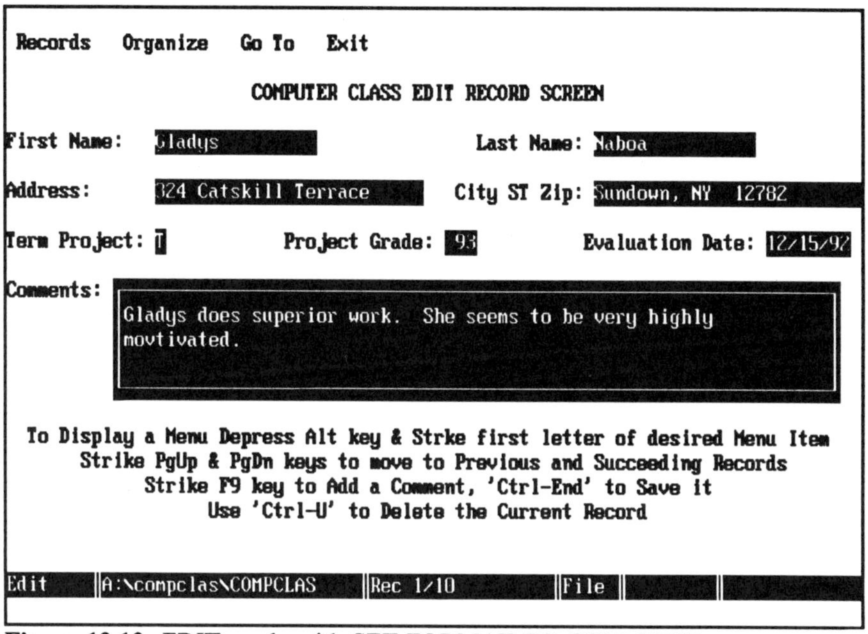

DEBUGGING & DOCUMENTATION 419

Figure 12.12 EDIT mode with SET FORMAT TO COM_EDIT

With the information shown on these screens, a person with no knowledge of dBASE could append new records, as well as edit old ones, with no further instruction.

12.2.2 Creating Reference/Help Screens

Quite often, in a system, there is a need to consult reference material so that naming conventions are uniform, whether it be department codes or department names in an inventory system, or commodity abbreviations in a brokerage system, etc. It is desirable that the Help screen be accessed from any point within the system simply by applying one keystroke.

dBASE makes available to us both the Escape key, as well as all the Function keys for just such purposes. Because the Escape key is used so much in the debugging process, I find it preferable to use the Function keys to invoke any Help/Reference screens that I might want to use. The command: **ON KEY LABEL** *FunctionKey*

DO *ProgramName*, allows us to make use of a Function key as the "Hot key". For example, were we to invoke the command: **ON KEY LABEL F10 DO** *ProgramName*, then at any point within the program, the special module, *ProgramName*, can be executed simply by striking the F10 Function key.

In the COMPCLAS system we will put in only one Reference/Help screen. However, in principle, as many can be entered as desired. Our Reference/Help screen will give the correct way to type in names, dates and grades, when doing searches.

Figure 12.13 shows the Reference/Help screen that we'll be using for the COMPCLAS system.

```
                    COMPUTER CLASS HELP SCREEN
                    When Searching For Records:

1. On Name:     The Entire Last Name MUST be typed in Before a
                First Name can be entered. Entering only a
                portion of the Last Name is allowed if and only
                if NO First Name is entered. For Example, the
                following are allowed:

   Example:     Enter Last Name: WITHERSPOON
                Enter First Name: JER

   Example:     Enter Last Name: WITH
                Enter First Name:

2. On Date:     Type in the entire Date in the format: MM/DD/YY
   Example:     Enter Evaluation Date You Wish To Find: 12/15/92

3. On Grade:    Type in an Integer Grade from: 0 to 100
   Example:     From What Grade do you want to Search:  88
```

Figure 12.13 Help Screen From COM_HELP.PRG when F10 key is struck

DEBUGGING & DOCUMENTATION

To generate the text that we see on the screen we will employ the **TEXT** and **ENDTEXT** instructions. These two instructions allow us to display or print out any text that appears between them. Listing 12.4 shows us the program fragment that will generate the screen shown in Figure 12.13.

```
TEXT
                    COMPUTER CLASS HELP SCREEN
                      When Searching For Records:


   1.  On Name:   The Entire Last Name MUST be typed in Before a
                  First Name can be entered.  Entering only a
                  portion of the Last Name is allowed if and only
                  if NO First Name is entered.  For Example, the
                  following are allowed:

       Example:   Enter Last Name:  WITHERSPOON
                  Enter First Name: JER


       Example:   Enter Last Name:  WITH
                  Enter First Name:


   2.  On Date:   Type in the entire Date in the format: MM/DD/YY
       Example:   Enter Evaluation Date You Wish To Find: 12/15/92


   3.  On Grade:  Type in an Integer Grade from: 0 to 100
       Example:   From What Grade do you want to Search:  80
ENDTEXT
```

Listing 12.4 Program Fragment Generating Screen Shown In Figure 12.13

In addition to this program fragment we add some comments at the top, plus the following lines of code:

```
SAVE SCREEN TO ESCREEN
OPENWIND = WINDOW()
IF LEN(OPENWIND) > 0
   DEACTIVATE WINDOW &OPENWIND
ENDIF
CLEAR
```

What this does is first SAVE the screen that we had been viewing before we went to the Help screen. Next we test to see if a Window is open. This is important, because if we do have a Window open, then the entire Help screen may try to be squeezed inside that Window. Since this is not only undesirable, but usually impossible, we want to be sure that if a Window is open that it gets closed. Since we need to remember if the Window was open when we leave the program, we save the original condition of the Window to the memory variable, OPENWIND. This is done in the statement: **OPENWIND = WINDOW()**, where the function, **WINDOW()** yields a character string containing the name of the open Window. If there is no Window open, then a character string of zero characters is returned.

Next, we test to see if OPENWIND is a string variable of more than 0 characters. If it is, then a window has been opened. In this case we deactivate this window. The **LEN**(*CharacterString*) is a function that will tell us the length of the *CharacterString* argument.

If the length was greater than zero, then a window was opened, in which case we deactivate whatever window this was. Since OPENWIND holds the name of the open window, using the macro **&OPENWIND**, will indeed cause whatever the window was to be deactivated (in our case the window was BROWWIND).

Likewise, at the end of COM_HELP.PRG, we insert the following commands to return the screen to its original state before returning to the program from whence the operation came.

```
WAIT ""
IF LEN(OPENWIND) > 0
  ACTIVATE WINDOW &OPENWIND
ENDIF
RESTORE SCREEN FROM ESCREEN
RETURN
```

The WAIT "" command, of course, holds the Help message on the screen until we're ready to exit from Help. Next, our memory variable, **OPENWIND**, is examined to see if it contained the name of our system Window. If it did, then the Window is turned back on. If it didn't, then it isn't turned on. In any case the SCREEN is restored, and we RETURN to the program from where we exited to get the Help/Reference screen. The resulting program, COM_HELP.PRG, is shown in Listing 12.5.

Now the only thing left to do is to modify COM_MENU.prg such that it invokes the **ON KEY LABEL F10 DO COM_HELP** command.

The modified version of **COM_MENU.prg** is shown in Listing 12.6. Note the additional command:

@ 23,29 SAY 'Strike F10 For Help'

which prompts the user to the existence of a Help Screen.

Finally, note that we must turn off the **F10** key before leaving the program. If we don't then every time we strike the **F10** key in the future, we will run **COM_HELP**. This is done with the command:

ON KEY LABEL F10

```
* COM_HELP.PRG
* This displays the Search Help Screen used when editing,
* deleting or searching by Evaluation date or by Project Grade.
* This includes a test to see if a window is open. If it is,
* then the window is shut, and reopened at the close.
*
SAVE SCREEN TO ESCREEN
OPENWIND = WINDOW()
IF LEN(OPENWIND) > 0
   DEACTIVATE WINDOW &OPENWIND
ENDIF
CLEAR
TEXT
                        COMPUTER CLASS HELP SCREEN
                          When Searching For Records:

   1. On Name:   The Entire Last Name MUST be typed in Before a
                 First Name can be entered. Entering only a
                 portion of the Last Name is allowed if and only
                 if NO First Name is entered. For Example, the
                 following are allowed:

      Example:   Enter Last Name:  WITHERSPOON
                 Enter First Name: JER

      Example:   Enter Last Name:  WITH
                 Enter First Name:

   2. On Date:   Type in the entire Date in the format: MM/DD/YY
      Example:   Enter Evaluation Date You Wish To Find: 12/15/92

   3. On Grade:  Type in an Integer Grade from: 0 to 100
      Example:   From What Grade do you want to Search:  80
ENDTEXT
WAIT []
IF LEN(OPENWIND) > 0
   ACTIVATE WINDOW &OPENWIND
ENDIF
RESTORE SCREEN FROM ESCREEN
RETURN
```

Listing 12.5 COM_HELP.PRG Displays Help Screen

```
* COM_MENU.prg
* This defines the menu for COMPCLAS
ON KEY LABEL F10 DO COM_HELP
SET STATUS OFF
CLEAR
@ 2,28  SAY "COMPUTER CLASS MAIN MENU"
@ 23,30 SAY "Strike F10 for Help"


* Define the Menu with its pads
DEFINE MENU Main
DEFINE PAD Update OF Main PROMPT " Update Records " AT 12,05
DEFINE PAD Search OF Main PROMPT "Search Records" AT 12,25
DEFINE PAD Print  OF Main PROMPT "Print Reports"  AT 12,45
DEFINE PAD Exit   OF Main PROMPT "Exit"           AT 12,70


* Assign popups to the pads
ON PAD Update OF Main Activate Popup Updatpop
ON PAD Search OF Main Activate Popup Searcpop
ON PAD Print  OF Main Activate Popup Printpop


* Define popups and bar prompts
DEFINE POPUP Updatpop FROM 13,05 MESSAGE "File Maintenance"
DEFINE POPUP Searcpop FROM 13,25 MESSAGE "Search Options"
DEFINE POPUP Printpop FROM 13,45 MESSAGE "Report Options"


DEFINE BAR 1 OF Updatpop PROMPT "Add Records"
DEFINE BAR 2 OF Updatpop PROMPT "Edit Records"
DEFINE BAR 3 OF Updatpop PROMPT "Delete Records"
DEFINE BAR 4 OF Updatpop PROMPT "Browse Records"


DEFINE BAR 1 OF Searcpop PROMPT "Grade Search"
DEFINE BAR 2 OF Searcpop PROMPT "Date Search"


DEFINE BAR 1 OF Printpop PROMPT " Columnar  "
DEFINE BAR 2 OF Printpop PROMPT " Mailmerge "
DEFINE BAR 3 OF Printpop PROMPT "  Labels   "


ON SELECTION POPUP Updatpop Do UPDACASE
ON SELECTION POPUP Searcpop DO SEARCASE
ON SELECTION POPUP Printpop DO PRINCASE
ON SELECTION PAD Exit OF Main DEACTIVATE MENU

ACTIVATE MENU MAIN
SET STATUS ON
ON KEY LABEL F10
RETURN
```

Listing 12.6 Revised Version of COM_MENU.PRG

426 DEBUGGING & DOCUMENTATION

Executing **COM_MENU**:

. DO COM_MENU

and selecting the "Browse Records" menu item in the "Update Records" Pad, we get the screen shown in Figure 12.14. Now, all we need to do is to strike the **F10** key and we get the screen shown in Figure 12.13. Striking any key will then return us to the Main Menu.

There do exist memory resident Help Screen programs[38], in the public domain, that are easy to use and to access. They're chief disadvantage is that they do take up additional memory space.

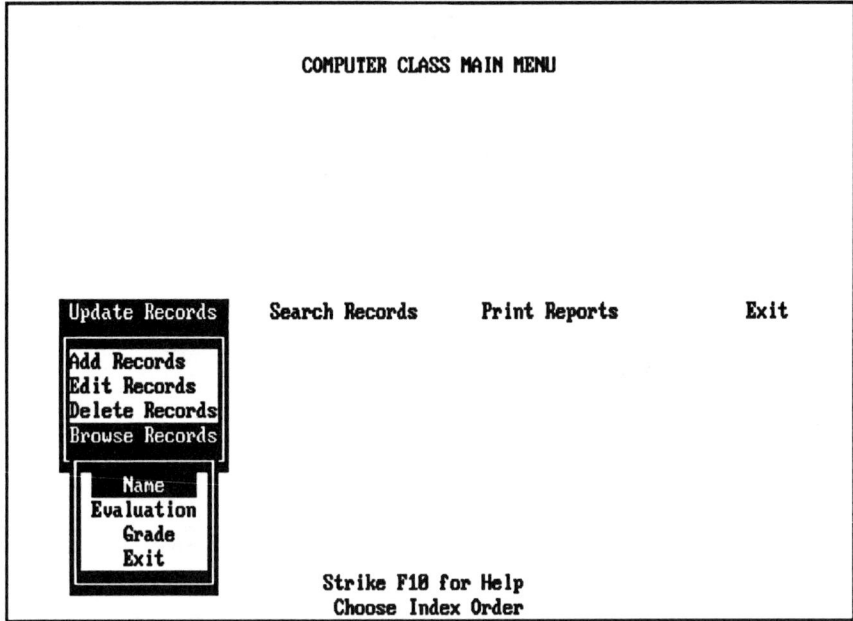

Figure 12.14 COM_MENU screen when "Browse" Option is selected

---

[38]The programs **PAINT.COM** and **HELP.COM**, available through Ziff Communications Co. (PC Magazine), will paint the screen much like the dBASE screen generator and then display the Help screen using the keystroke pair **Alt H**. **HELP.COM** will hold up to 16 help screens which may be accessed with the PgDn and PgUp keys.

12.3 Documentation

Once you have your system together and functioning, it should be documented. If other people will be using your system, then the price of not documenting your system is that you will always remain a slave to that system. Every time there is a bug, *you* will be called upon to fix it. Every time someone wants to modify the system in order to enhance it, *you* will be called upon to do the work. Unless you have the time, or your ego enjoys that type of gratification, it is best to document the system as thoroughly as necessary so that you can free yourself from it.

Of course, the other reason for documenting the system is so when you come back and look at what you did six months from now, you'll be able to figure it out[39].

Minimal documentation for a small system (of the order of magnitude that we have been dealing with in this text) should include the following:

1. A short narrative indicating exactly what your system does.

2. A users guide.

3. Sample reports generated by the system.

4. A program structure diagram listing all your program modules in a hierarchical fashion showing how they interrelate.

---

[39] When I was in graduate school, my faculty advisor gave me a program written in assembly language that did an Interpolation for a Fast Fourier Transform of the data that I was compiling. It was a complicated program that was completely undocumented. I tried to figure out how it worked but couldn't. I finally asked my advisor to document it for me. He said he would and took it home for the weekend. When he returned on Monday, he said that he simply couldn't figure out how he had done it. Not knowing what else to do, I labeled his program "Magic" and continued to use it.

5. A system structure chart or system structure diagram indicating how your system is logically organized.

6. A contents list of all the databases used in your system.

7. A list of all the indexes used and what their keys are.

8. Program listings with sufficient comments to be clearly readable written in structured programming style. They should contain the following comments:

    a) Program Name
    b) Author
    c) Date of last revision
    d) What program calls the particular module
    e) What sub-modules are called by the program
    f) What files are used by the program:
        i) Databases
        ii) Indexes
        iii) Format Files
        iv) Procedures
        v) Report Forms
        vi) Label Forms
    g) A clear explanation of what the program does

Now before you become overwhelmed by the above list, it should be pointed out that except for the first two items on the list, all the rest of the items either already exist, or can be made to exist in just a few minutes. That may seem like an incredible statement, but it's true. Read on!

12.3.1 Brief Narrative of System Function

A brief description of the function of COMPCLAS is provided in Text 12.1.

COMPCLAS - THE COMPUTER CLASS GRADING SYSTEM

COMPCLAS is a grading system that allows the user to enter the following student data:

    Name
    Address
    City, State & Zip
    Term Project Option
    Evaluation Date for Term Project
    Grade on Term Project
    Final Grade Given in Course
    Comments About the Student

The system maintains these files allowing the following file maintenance functions to occur:

    Adding New Student Records
    Editing Student Records
    Deleting Student Records
    Browsing Student Records

In addition, COMPCLAS allows the user to access and view student records by any of the following means:

    Name
    Grade Range
    Evaluation Date
    Order of Data Entry

COMPCLAS will print a class report, mailing labels, and a mailmerge letter.

COMPCLAS is in the public domain. The user needs to have either dBASE IV or the dBASE runtime module, RUNTIME.exe, in order to execute it. The system is password protected. For further information on COMPCLAS contact:

    Dr. Warren M. Littlefield
    Sullivan County Community College
    Loch Sheldrake, NY 12759

Text 12.1 Narrative Explaining the Function of COMPCLAS

12.3.2 User Instruction Guide

A system with a good menu system should be essentially self-explanatory and hence needs very little in the way of a user's guide. Text 12.2 is an example of a user's guide for COMPCLAS. A more complicated system might contain copies of each of the menu screens, the append and edit screens, with a few words of explanation for each of them.

12.3.3 Sample Reports

We've already generated a sample report (see Listing 4.1). Since our program is designed to do just that, we can print one out in minutes.

12.3.4 Program Structure Diagram

The program structure diagram is a hierarchical tree that shows each of the modules, the programs that call them, and the subprograms that they call. Such an outline is shown in Listing 12.7.

Granted, it would have taken me a while to type out this piece of documentation and draw in the lines. However, this was done for me by an ingenious piece of software called **SNAP**[40]. **SNAP** is a program which will document any system of programs written in the dBASE II, III, IV, Clipper, Foxplus or FoxPro. The rest of the documentation will be created using **SNAP**.

---

[40]**SNAP** was written by Walter J. Kennamer and is in the public domain. Version **5.02**, may be downloaded from **COMPUSERVE** by specifying **GO FOXFORUM** and requesting the file **SNP502.EXE**. This is a compressed file of 293 Kbytes, which explodes into 36 files upon execution. In order to obtain this file, you must become a member of the Fox Forum. There is no charge for joining.

COMPCLAS USER'S INSTRUCTION GUIDE

In order to run COMPCLAS, you must have either a copy of dBASE IV, or a copy of the dBASE runtime module, RUNTIME.exe. Whichever one you use, it must be contained in the PATHWAY or in the current directory along with COMPCLAS. The diskette containing COMPCLAS contains the following files:

```
BACKUP.DBO         COMPCLAS.LBO
COLUMNAR.FRO       COMPCLAS.DBT
COM_ADD.FMO        COMPCLAS.DBF
COM_EDIT.FMO       COMPCLAS.MDX
COM_MAIN.DBO       CONFIG.DB
COM_PROC.DBO       LETTER.FRO
```

To run the system, put the COMPCLAS diskette in Drive A: and do

either 1 or 2:

1. Make sure that the directory containing either dBASE IV, or the runtime module RUNTIME.exe, is in the pathway contained in your AUTOEXEC.BAT file. Now type at the A> prompt:

   A> **DBASE COM_MAIN**   (if you have dBASE IV)
   A> **RUNTIME COM_MAIN** (if you have RUNTIME.exe)

-or-

2. Create the following batch file on your **COMPCLAS** diskette in Drive A. (Assuming that there is a copy of dBASE IV and it is in a directory called **\DBASE** on drive C:.) This is done by typing the following at the DOS A> prompt on drive A:

   A> **COPY CON: COMPCLAS.BAT**   \<Enter\>
   PATH = C:\DBASE   \<Enter\>
   DBASE COM_MAIN   \<Enter\>
   C:\AUTOEXEC   \<F6\>,\<Enter\>

   The drive and directory name should be changed to whatever is appropriate for your system. If you have RUNTIME instead of dBASE IV, then the third line should read: **RUNTIME COM_MAIN**   \<Enter\> . After the final line is entered, the **F6** function key should be struck and then the **Enter** key should be struck once more. (Note that the above will be done only this one time. After that the system is installed.) Now when you want to execute **COMPCLAS** simply type at the DOS A> prompt:
   A> **COMPCLAS**

Now type in the password that your version of COMPCLAS came with (see sealed envelope), and strike the enter key.

Text 12.2 COMPCLAS User's Installation & Instruction Guide

```
System: COMPUTER CLASS SYSTEM
Author: Dr. Warren M. Littlefield
04/01/91    00:25:46
Tree Diagram

------------------------------------------------------------
COM_MAIN.PRG
   ├──BACKUP.PRG
   └──COM_MENU      (procedure in COM_PROC.PRG)
         ├──COM_HELP.PRG
         ├──UPDACASE      (procedure in COM_PROC.PRG)
         │     ├──COMPADD       (procedure in COM_PROC.PRG)
         │     │    └──COM_ADD.FMT
         │     ├──COM_EDIT      (procedure in COM_PROC.PRG)
         │     │    └──COM_EDIT.FMT
         │     ├──COM_DELE      (procedure in COM_PROC.PRG)
         │     └──BROWMENU      (procedure in COM_PROC.PRG)
         │           ├──NAMEBROW       (procedure in
         │           ├──EVALBROW       (procedure in
         │           └──GRADBROW       (procedure in
         ├──SEARCASE      (procedure in COM_PROC.PRG)
         │     ├──COM_GRAD      (procedure in COM_PROC.PRG)
         │     │    └──COM_DISP       (procedure in
         │     └──COM_EVAL      (procedure in COM_PROC.PRG)
         │          └──COM_DISP       (procedure in
         └──PRINCASE      (procedure in COM_PROC.PRG)
               ├──COMPREPO       (procedure in COM_PROC.PRG)
               ├──COMPMAIL       (procedure in COM_PROC.PRG)
               └──COMPLABL       (procedure in COM_PROC.PRG)
```

Listing 12.7 Program Structure Diagram for COMPCLAS—TREE.DOC using Graphics characters option for Tree

DEBUGGING & DOCUMENTATION

The first step is to make another sub-directory of the **\COMPCLAS** directory called: **\COMPCLAS\DOCUMENT**. We want to keep our document files separate from our source files for two reasons. First, SNAP actually modifies the source programs adding header banners to them and optionally changing the case of the code. Second, the **\COMPCLAS** directory is cluttered enough as it is even without the documentation files that SNAP produces[41]. To produce the desired sub-directory, we type:

A> MD \COMPCLAS\DOCUMENT

Now we are ready to execute **SNAP**. This is done by typing **SNAP** at the DOS prompt:

A> **SNAP**

You are then presented with the opening screen shown in Figure 12.15. Striking the space bar, we obtain the identification entry screen shown in Figure 12.16.

Besides the first three lines of identification, we are required to type in the name of the topmost program module. This is, of course, COM_MAIN.prg. Next we need to type in the various pathnames. The default pathnames for the source code and the data are fine, so we'll let them be. However, the output files should go to our output directory, **A:\COMPCLAS\DOCUMENT**.

Finally, we need to identify the path where the **SNAP** files are located. If, for example, you have them on **B:** drive, then **B:** should be typed in[42]. If you have loaded them into the **\COMPCLAS** directory, then the default values shown in Figure

---

[41] If you have limited space on your diskette, you may put the system files, having the following extensions, on a separate diskette as these are the only ones needed for documentation purposes: **.DBF**; **.DBT**; **.MDX**; **.PRG**; **.FRG**; **.FMT**; and **.LBG**.

[42] This will not work on a standard 360 Kbyte 5¼" disk drive as SNAP needs more than the 360 Kbytes of disk space. It will work if B: is a 3½" disk drive or a high density 5¼" drive.

434   DEBUGGING & DOCUMENTATION

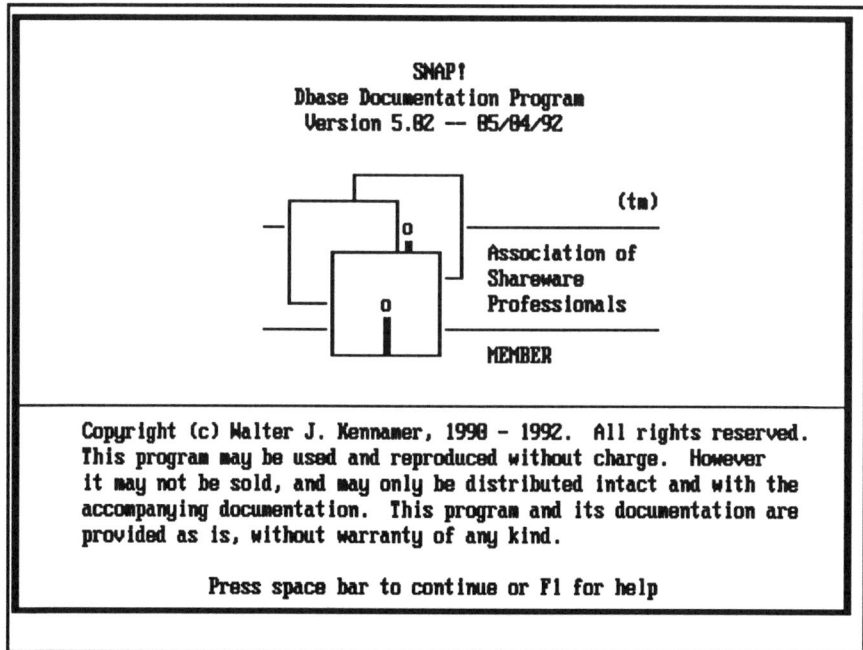

Figure 12.15 Opening Screen of SNAP

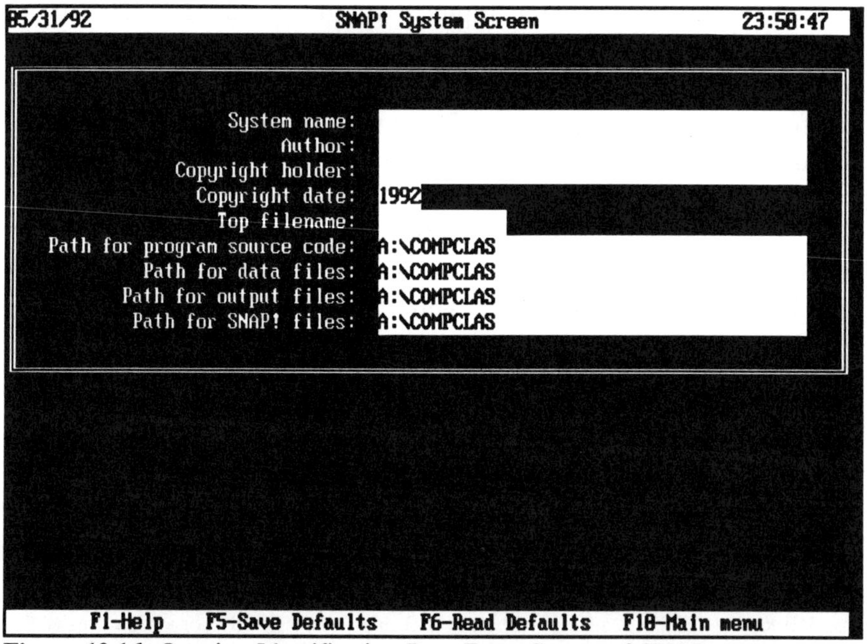

Figure 12.16 Opening Identification Data Entry Screen of SNAP

DEBUGGING & DOCUMENTATION

12.16 are fine. In our case, we will assume that they are contained in the **\DBASE** directory located on drive **C:**. Making this adjustment we end up with the screen shown in Figure 12.17.

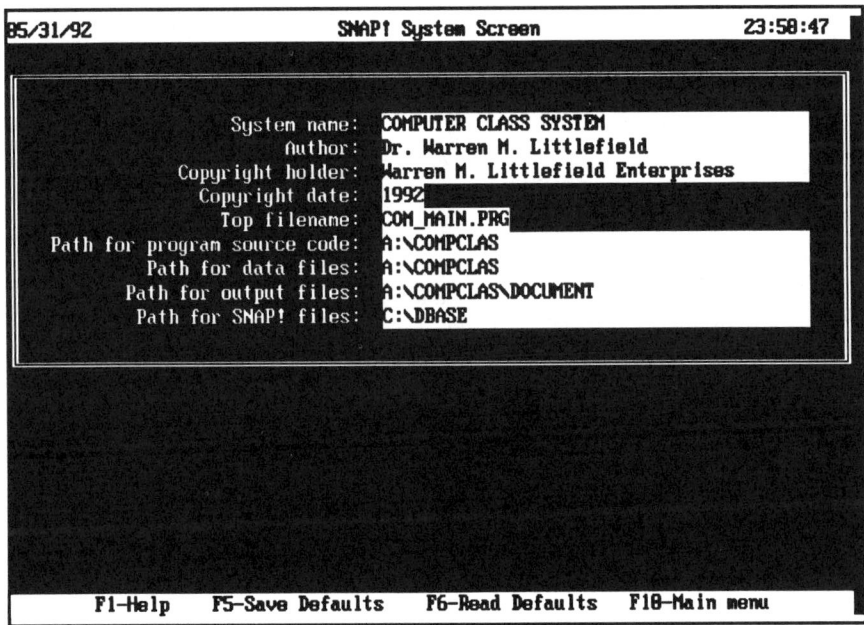

Figure 12.17 Completed Identification Screen of SNAP

Striking the **F10** key brings up the menu at the top of the screen. There are many options, but the one we wish to modify is found in the **Tree** menu. If we select the **Tree** menu as shown in Figure 12.18, then we get the menu with the default settings as shown in Figure 12.19.

The item whose setting we wish to change is the "Include Databases" option which we will set to **"N"**. Making this modification, we end up with the screen shown in Figure 12.20. Since we want to save these defaults for possible future use, let's strike the **F5** key as indicated. This causes a CONFIG.SNP file to be saved on the diskette. From now on when you enter SNAP in this directory, we will get the defaults and the system information screen that we have entered.

436   DEBUGGING & DOCUMENTATION

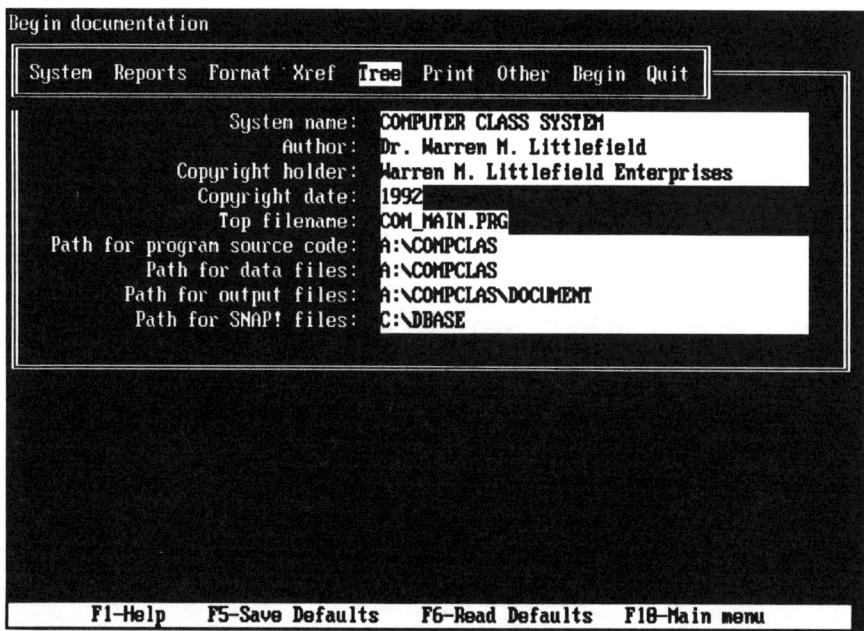

Figure 12.18 Selecting the "Tree" Menu option of SNAP

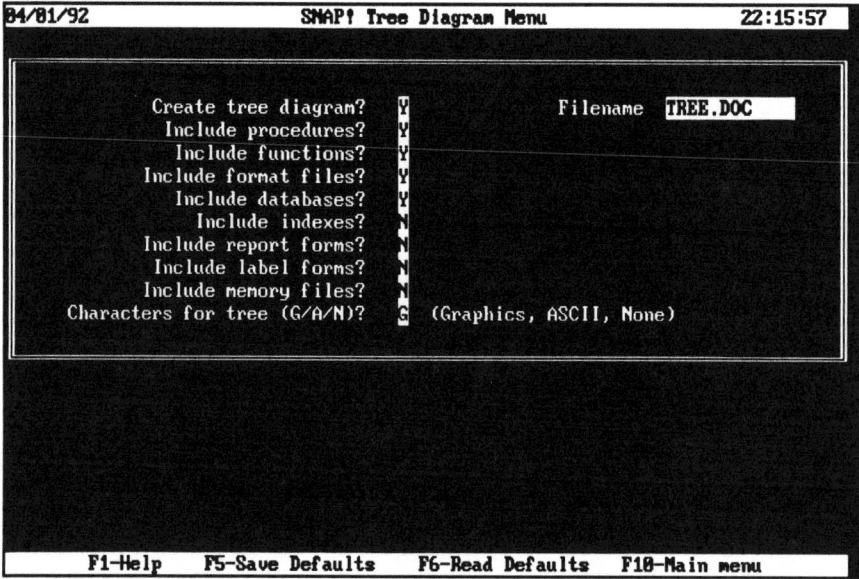

Figure 12.19 Default Menu for "Tree" menu option of SNAP

DEBUGGING & DOCUMENTATION

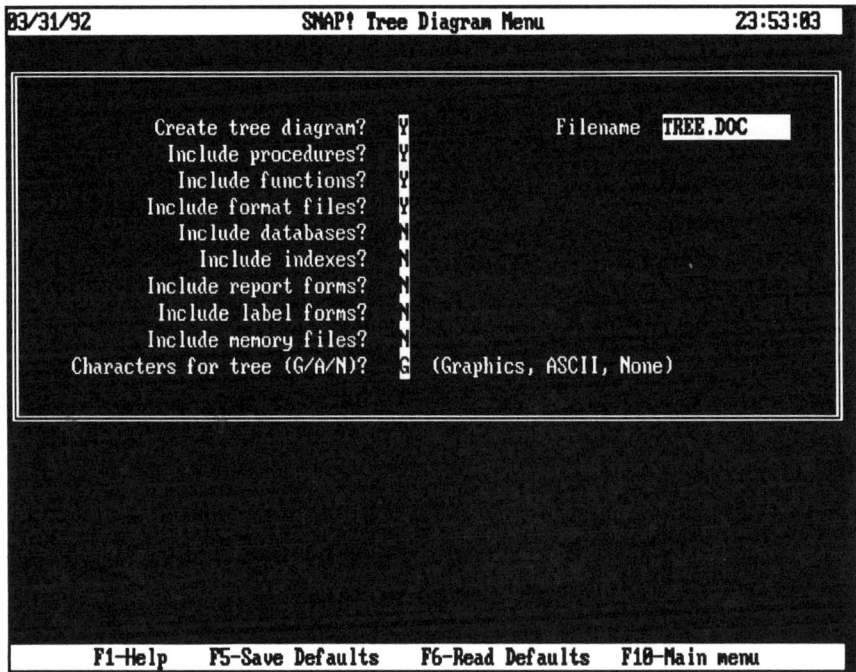

Figure 12.20 Tree Menu Option With Desired Default Settings

Now we are ready to begin our documentation run. Striking the **F10** key once more takes us back to the main menu. Now we move the cursor over to **Begin** and strike the Enter key as shown in Figure 12.21. **SNAP** then goes to work and generates more documentation than we have asked for.

Midway in the documentation process, SNAP prompts you, "Press space bar to continue" (See Figure 12.22). Do so!

After all the documentation is done, SNAP then tells you, "Press escape to exit, or any other key to begin printing source code" (See Figure 12.23). In response to this, ALWAYS STRIKE THE **ESC** KEY! The reason for this is that SNAP will immediately print out all the source listings in two different formats. For COMPCLAS alone, this amounts to over 70 pages of listings which is far more than we want or need. In the interests of paper and printer time we will always strike the **Esc** key. This takes us out of SNAP back to the DOS prompt.

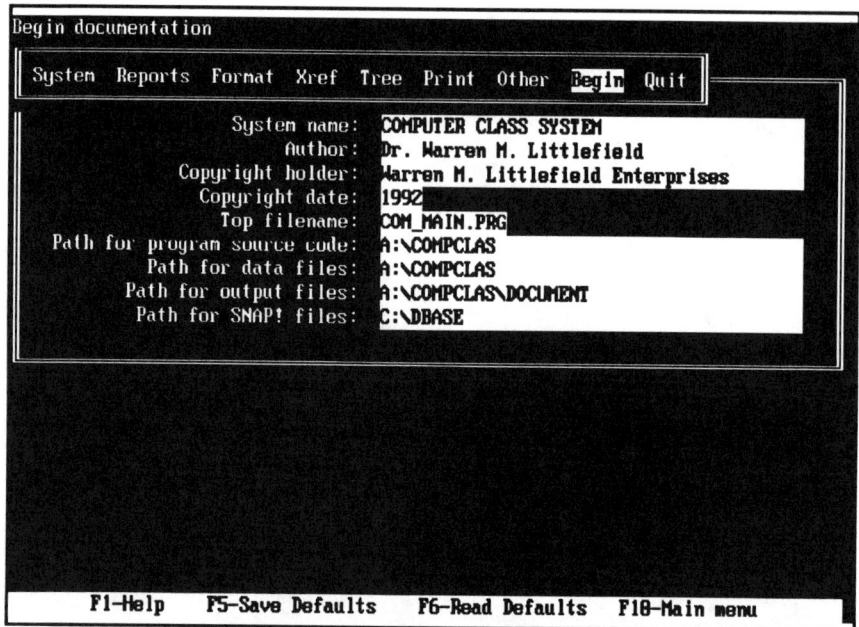

Figure 12.21 Selecting "Begin" menu option in SNAP

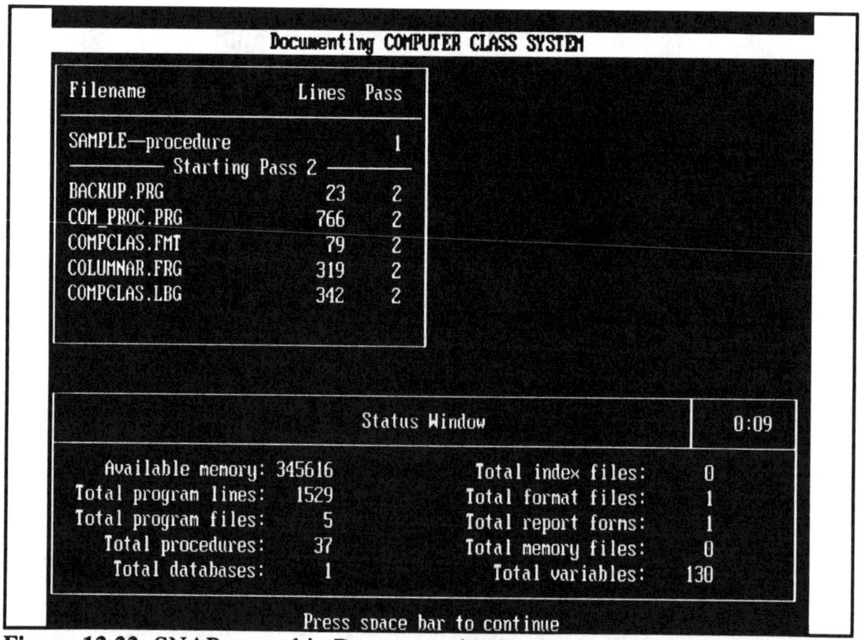

Figure 12.22 SNAP paused in Documentation Processing, waiting for Space Bar to be struck

DEBUGGING & DOCUMENTATION 439

```
                Documenting COMPUTER CLASS SYSTEM
 Filename              Lines  Pass
   Press escape to exit, or any other key to begin printing source code
 COM_PROC.PRG           766    2
 COMPCLAS.FMT            79    2
 COLUMNAR.FRG           319    2
 COMPCLAS.LBG           342    2


                        Status Window                 0:19
     Available memory: 347800       Total index files:   0
     Total program lines:  1529     Total format files:  1
     Total program files:     5     Total report forms:  1
     Total procedures:       37     Total memory files:  0
     Total databases:         1     Total variables:   130
```

Figure 12.23 SNAP paused, waiting for OK to Print Out all the Documentation—User should strike Esc key at this point

One of the pieces of documentation is called **TREE.DOC** . This is what has been shown in Listing 12.6. If you do not have a printer that handles graphics characters, you could change the bottom menu item in Figure 12.20 to an "A" for ASCII text characters. Then you would end up with the TREE in Listing 12.8.

12.3.5 System Structure Chart Diagram

Basically, the system structure diagram is a hierarchical tree structure showing the calling module and the modules called by the menu driven system. We drew the system structure chart back in Chapters 10 and 11 (see Figure 11.18). However, this document requires a small amount of drafting ability as well as some time to do neatly. The system structure diagram, on the other hand, is generated very quickly by simply removing from the program tree all of the items not included on your system menus.

```
System: COMPUTER CLASS SYSTEM
Author: Dr. Warren M. Littlefield
04/01/92   00:41:25
Tree Diagram
--------------------------------------------------------

COM_MAIN.PRG
+----BACKUP.PRG
+----COM_MENU      (procedure in COM_PROC.PRG)
     +----COM_HELP.PRG
     +----UPDACASE       (procedure in COM_PROC.PRG)
          +----COMPADD       (procedure in COM_PROC.PRG)
          |    +----COM_ADD.FMT
          +----COM_EDIT      (procedure in COM_PROC.PRG)
          |    +----COM_EDIT.FMT
          +----COM_DELE      (procedure in COM_PROC.PRG)
          +----BROWMENU      (procedure in COM_PROC.PRG)
               +----NAMEBROW      (procedure in
               +----EVALBROW      (procedure in
               +----GRADBROW      (procedure in
     +----SEARCASE       (procedure in COM_PROC.PRG)
          +----COM_GRAD      (procedure in COM_PROC.PRG)
          |    +----COM_DISP      (procedure in
          +----COM_EVAL      (procedure in COM_PROC.PRG)
          |    +----COM_DISP      (procedure in
     +----PRINCASE       (procedure in COM_PROC.PRG)
          +----COMPREPO      (procedure in COM_PROC.PRG)
          +----COMPMAIL      (procedure in COM_PROC.PRG)
          +----COMPLABL      (procedure in COM_PROC.PRG)
```

Listing 12.8 TREE.DOC with ASCII characters instead of Graphics

This can be done by copying **TREE.DOC** to **SYSTEM.DOC** and then removing the lines that don't pertain to the menu structure.

A> COPY TREE.DOC SYSTEM.DOC

Using "Modify Command" as the editor, the lines containing: 1) COM_HELP; 2) COM_DISP; and 3) COMPCLAS.FMT were removed by typing the keystroke pair **Ctrl Y** . In addition, any .PRG extensions and any procedure comments were removed. Finally, the chart was re-labeled: SYSTEM STRUCTURE DIAGRAM. The result is shown in Listing 12.9.

DEBUGGING & DOCUMENTATION

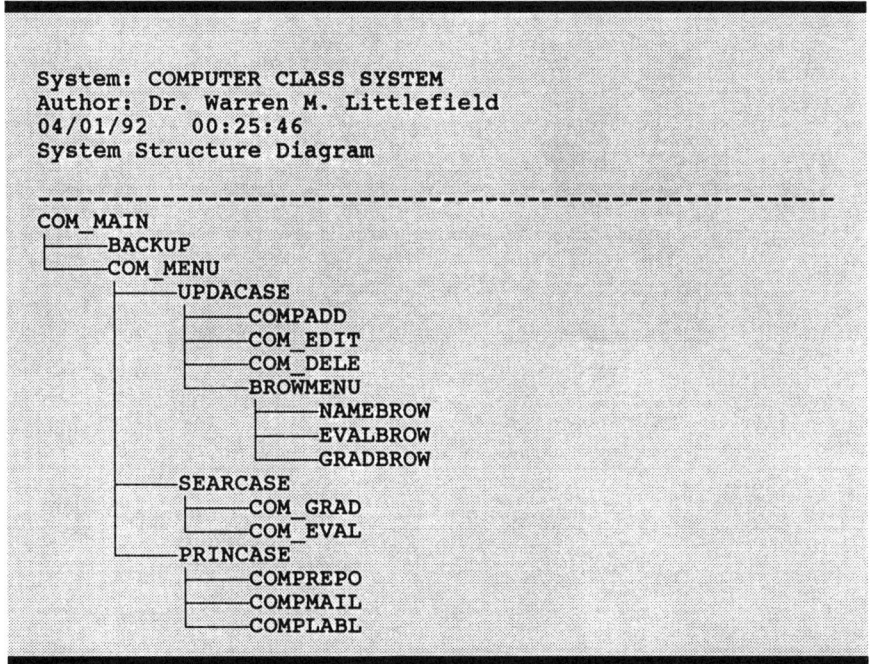

Listing 12.9 Preliminary System Structure Diagram for COMPCLAS System

An improved version of the system structure diagram may be obtained by replacing the somewhat arcane names we've used for the program modules with a full description of each level in our structure diagram. This final version is shown in Listing 12.10.

12.3.6 Database Contents List

This can be done by simply opening each of the databases in your system, and typing: **LIST STRUCTURE TO PRINT :**

. OPEN COMPCLAS
. LIST STRUCTURE TO PRINT
. EJECT

It also appears in a document created by **SNAP** called **DATADICT.DOC** . The top of the first page of **DATADICT.DOC** is shown in Listing 12.11.

```
System: COMPUTER CLASS SYSTEM
Author: Dr. Warren M. Littlefield
04/01/92   00:25:46
System Structure Diagram

-----------------------------------------------------------------
PERFORM COMPUTER CLASS SYSTEM APPLICATIONS
├──BACKUP
└──PERFORM COMPUTER CLASS FUNCTIONS
      ├──PERFORM FILE MAINTENANCE FUNCTIONS
      │      ├──ADD NEW RECORDS
      │      ├──EDIT RECORDS
      │      ├──REMOVE RECORDS
      │      └──BROWSE DATABASE
      │             ├──IN ORDER OF NAME
      │             ├──IN ORDER OF EVALUATION DATE
      │             └──IN ORDER OF GRADE
      ├──PERFORM INQUIRY FUNCTIONS
      │      ├──SEARCH BY GRADE
      │      └──SEARCH BY EVALUATION DATE
      └──PRINT OUT REPORTS
             ├──TYPE COLUMNAR REPORT
             ├──TYPE MAILMERGE LETTER
             └──TYPE OUT MAILING LABELS
```

Listing 12.10 Final Version of System Structure Chart for COMPCLAS

```
System: COMPUTER CLASS SYSTEM
Author: Dr. Warren M. Littlefield
04/01/92   00:40:22
Database Structure Summary

-----------------------------------------------------------------
1 database in the system
   COMPCLAS.DBF
-----------------------------------------------------------------
Structure for database : COMPCLAS.DBF
Number of data records :       10
      Last updated : 03/16/91 at 23:15
Field  Field name  Type        Width    Dec    Start     End
    1  FIRSTNAME   Character     15              1        15
    2  LASTNAME    Character     15             16        30
    3  TERM_PROJ   Logical        1             31        31
    4  EVALUATION  Date           8             32        39
    5  PROJ_GRADE  Numeric        3             40        42
    6  FINALGRADE  Character      1             43        43
    7  ADDRESS     Character     25             44        68
    8  CITY_ST_ZP  Character     25             69        93
    9  COMMENTS    Memo          10             94       103
** Total **                     104
```

Listing 12.11 Structure of COMPCLAS.DBF contained in DATADICT.DOC

DEBUGGING & DOCUMENTATION 443

12.3.7 List of all Indexes & their Keys

SNAP produces the index keys for all the indexes used by the system in a file called NDXSUMRY.DOC. Listing 12.12 shows the first part of that document[43].

```
System: COMPUTER CLASS SYSTEM
Author: Dr. Warren M. Littlefield
05/28/92    20:31:16
Multiple Index File Parameter Summary
------------------------------------------------------------
1 multiple index file in the system
   C:\SCCC\BOOK\COMPCLAS\COMPCLAS.MDX
------------------------------------------------------------

COMPCLAS.MDX          Last updated:  03/24/92 at 20:06
   Tag: Evaluation      (EVALUATION)
   Tag: Grade           (PROJ_GRADE)
   Tag: Lastfirst       (UPPER(LASTNAME+FIRSTNAME))

This multiple index file appears to be associated with
database(s):
        : COMPCLAS.DBF
```

Listing 12.12 Indexes used by COMPCLAS System Contained in NDXSUMRY.DOC

12.3.8 Fully Documented Program Listings

Typing all the required comments into each of the modules of our system would be a time consuming process were it not for SNAP. This ingenious piece of software does this for us automatically, at the same time that it generates the .DOC files.

Listing 12.13 shows how the module **COM_MAIN.prg** was rewritten. Notice that all the requirements of point 8 are

---

[43] A word of warning. GRADE was a descending key, but SNAP makes no mention of it. It would be good to add the words "(descending)" to the line containing the GRADE key.

automatically fulfilled. Also note that all variables were made lower case by **SNAP**. This is an option over which the user does have control.

As the first line of the old program:

* COM_MAIN.PRG

is contained in the banner inserted by **SNAP**, we have removed it from our text.

In the same manner we can print out the documented version of all the programs in the COMPCLAS system. Listing 12.14 shows the first page of the listing of SNAP's documentation of COM_PROC.prg. Note SNAP has inserted a header banner for not only the program file but also for each procedure. Printing out all our **SNAP** modified programs finishes off the minimal documentation requirements of our system.

12.3.9 Optional Documentation

Additional documentation provided by SNAP is listed in the **Reports** Menu option as shown in Figure 12.24.

12.4 Summary

In this chapter **DEBUG** has been introduced which allowed us to debug a program on-line. We saw that we could proceed up to a breakpoint, and then have it display the values of the various variables that we wish to monitor. We could then step through the program as desired, or have it proceed to another breakpoint. If we wished to trace the execution path of a program to where the bug occurred, we found that we could use the **SET ECHO ON** and **SET DEBUG ON** combination so that we could see each of the commands as the program was being executed.

```
*:*************************************************
*:           Program: COM_MAIN.PRG
*:
*:           System: COMPUTER CLASS SYSTEM
*:           Author: Dr. Warren M. Littlefield
*: Copyright (c) 1992, Warren M. Littlefield Enterprises
*: Last modified: 04/01/92        0:09
*:
*:           Calls: BACKUP.PRG
*:                : COM_HELP.PRG
*:                : COM_MENU  (procedure in COM_PROC.PRG)
*:
*: Documented 04/01/92 at 00:37        SNAP! version 5.02
*:*************************************************
* This module checks to see if the password entered
* is correct.  If it is, the user is queried about
* Backing Up the system.
SET TALK OFF
SET STATUS OFF
STORE "ROSEBUD" TO Password
CLEAR
@ 12,29 SAY "Enter Your Password: "
SET CONSOLE OFF
ACCEPT [] TO trypasswrd
SET CONSOLE ON
IF UPPER(trypasswrd) = Password
   STORE .F. TO backitup
   CLEAR
   @ 12,20 SAY "Do You Want To Back Up the System: ";
      GET backitup
   READ
   IF backitup
      DO backup
   ENDIF
   SET PROCEDURE TO com_proc
   ON KEY LABEL f10 DO com_help
   DO com_menu
   ON KEY LABEL f10
   SET PROCEDURE TO
ELSE
   CLEAR
   @ 12,31 SAY "Invalid Password!"
   WAIT []
ENDIF
SET STATUS ON
SET TALK ON
RETURN
*: EOF: COM_MAIN.PRG
```

Listing 12.13 COM_MAIN.prg as documented by SNAP

```
*:**************************************************************:
*: Procedure file: COM_PROC.PRG
*:
*:         System: COMPUTER CLASS SYSTEM
*:         Author: Dr. Warren M. Littlefield
*: Copyright (c) 1992, Warren M. Littlefield Enterprises
*:  Last modified: 04/01/92        0:31
*:
*:  Procs & Fncts: BROWMENU
*:               : COM_ADD
*:               : COM_DELE
*:               : COM_DISP
*:               : COM_EDIT
*:               : COM_EVAL
*:               : COM_GRAD
*:               : COM_MENU
*:               : COMPLABL
*:               : COMPMAIL
*:               : COMPGRAD
*:               : COMPREPO
*:               : EVALBROW
*:               : GRADBROW
*:               : NAMEBROW
*:               : PRINCASE
*:               : SEARCASE
*:               : UPDACASE
*:
*: Documented 04/01/92 at 00:38           SNAP! version 5.02
*:**************************************************************
*|**************************************************************
*|
*|      Procedure: COMPADD
*|
*|          Calls: COM_ADD.FMT
*|
*|           Uses: COMPCLAS.DBF
*|
*|      MDX files: COMPCLAS.MDX
*|
*|        Formats: COM_ADD.FMT
*|
*|**************************************************************
PROCEDURE compadd
* This program Opens the Database COMPCLAS and
* Appends Records.
*
```

Listing 12.14 First page of SNAP's documentation of COM_PROC.prg

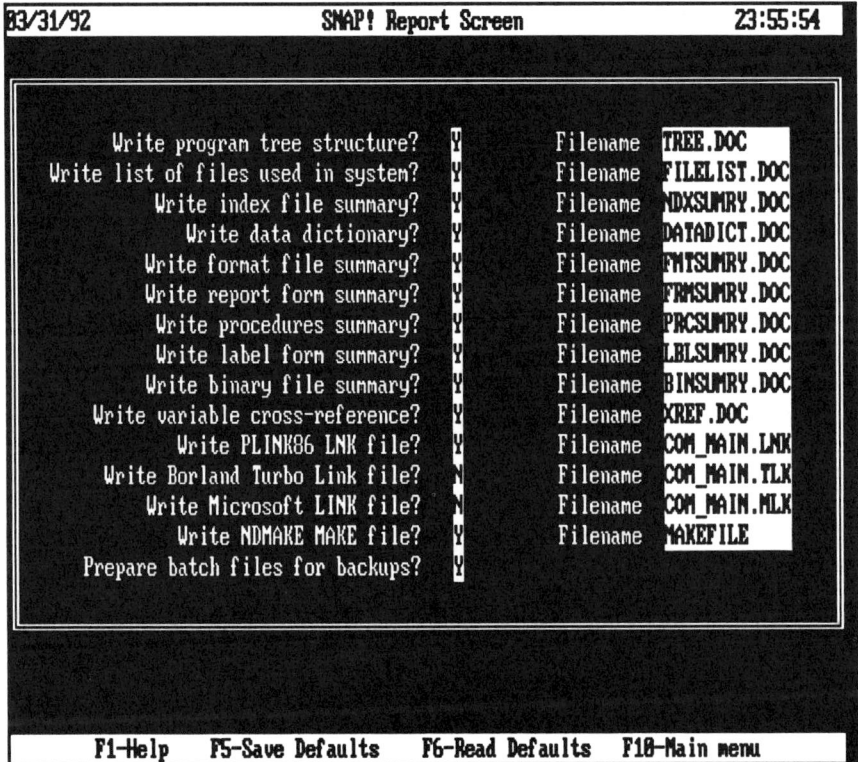

Figure 12.24 Documentation available from SNAP

Using **ON KEY LABEL** *LabelName* **DO** *ProgramName*, we were able to implement a Reference/Help screen, so that we could get Help at any point in the execution of the system. We also added some Help comments to our format screens.

Finally, we discussed the minimal documentation that a small system should contain. We found that by using the public domain software, **SNAP,** that we could generate the most tedious part of this documentation in a matter of minutes.

12.5 Review

In Chapter 12 we have presented the following new commands:

> **DEBUG** *ProgramName*
> **ENDTEXT**
> **ON KEY LABEL** *LabelName* **DO** *ProgramName*
> **SET ECHO ON/OFF**
> **SET DEBUG ON/OFF**
> **SET TRAP ON/OFF**
> **TEXT**

Add these instructions to your glossary of dBASE programming commands. In addition, add these new functions to your glossary of functions:

> **LEN()**
> **LINENO()**
> **PROGRAM()**
> **WINDOW()**

12.6 Laboratory Work

Go through the steps outlined in this chapter. Create the Reference/Help screen for COMPCLAS using your own name and address in the Help screen. Run SNAP on the COMPCLAS system. Print out all of the resulting documentation, and examine it.

12.7 Exercises

1. Debug your MAILIST system as necessary. Use the debugging commands presented in section 12.1.

2. Create a Reference/Help screen for your MAILIST system. Call your Help module, **MAILHELP.prg**. Use **ON KEY F10 DO MAILHELP** to invoke it. Hand in a hard copy of MAILHELP.prg.

DEBUGGING & DOCUMENTATION   449

3. Using SNAP (if you haven't as yet gotten a copy, you should get one), generate documentation for your MAILIST system. Hand it in.

12.8 Term Project

Completely debug your system project using the tools discussed in this chapter. Generate any Help or reference screens as needed. Fully document your system including all eight types of documentation.

CHAPTER 13

ACCOUNTS SYSTEM— MULTIPLE FILES

13.0 Topics Covered in Chapter 13

The concept of a "Top-Down" Systems Design is introduced.

A System Structure Chart for the ACCOUNTS System is developed.

Saved Memory variables are used to create Macros which select the desired Ledger Year.

Stubs are introduced as a means of debugging high level modules.

The TOTAL Command is introduced as a means of calculating Totals on each category in a Field.

The powerful SET RELATION TO command is presented as a means of tying two databases together in lockstep given that they have a common field.

The concept of a "Do Until" loop is presented, and its implementation is shown using DO WHILE .T. and the EXIT command.

The use of the Picture FUNCTION, used with the SAY Command, is introduced.

The use of the PICTURE template is examined in more detail, and it is used to get just the formatted output that we desire.

13.1 Top Down Systems Design

When we first introduced the system structure chart, we arrived at it from a "Bottom Up" systems design approach. This was necessitated from the fact that we were learning about the dBASE language as we went along. To start from a "Top Down" design approach presupposes a lot more knowledge about what the implementation possibilities are than we possessed. So the "Bottom Up" approach was used as a didactic technique. However, now we possess a much higher degree of sophistication of the dBASE IV programming language as well as of how to go about designing a system. As a result, we are now prepared to create an ACCOUNTS system around our ACCOUNTS database, using a "Top Down" approach.

We would like our system to accomplish the following tasks:

1. Display and update a "Checkbook" ledger
2. Re-balance the ledger after an update
3. Reconcile the ledger against the bank statement
4. Spread accounts into budgeted categories
5. Browse the budget and display the totals
6. Create a new set of databases from the old in order to start a new year
7. Switch databases from one calendar year to the next
8. Make Reports
   a) ledger report
   b) budget report
9. Make Inquiries
   a) search on category
   b) search on description
   c) search on outstanding checks

Notice that we have implied the existence of a second database, a budget database whose structure is shown in Listing 13.1.

Field	Field Name	Type	Width	Dec
1	CATEGORY	Character	18	
2	CAT	Character	3	
3	BUDGETED	Numeric	8	2
4	SPENT	Numeric	8	2
5	EXPECT_INC	Numeric	8	2
6	INCOME	Numeric	8	2

Listing 13.1 Structure of the Budget database

13.1.1 The Budget Database

The budget database contains all the budget categories that appear in our ACCOUNTS database, plus the field, CATEGORY, that fully describes the three character CAT field. In addition, it contains the field, BUDGETED, that accepts what our budgeted amounts are for each of the budget categories. It also contains the field, SPENT, in which all our calculated totals from the ACCOUNTS database, for each budget category, are placed. In this way we can compare how much we have spent in each category, to date, with the amount we allotted at the beginning of the calendar year. In a similar manner, it contains a field for expected income, EXPECT_INC, which contains the amount of income that we expect to receive during the calendar year. Finally, it contains the field, INCOME, which is a total of all the RECEIPTS to date from the database ACCOUNTS.

This lets us know, at any given minute, how we're doing on our budget, for both expenditures as well as income. In this way we can make informed decisions as to whether or not a particular purchase can be afforded. Listing 13.2 shows all the category items as well as their full description. You'll note that we have added a few more categories to the list.

CATEGORY	CAT
BLANK	
CABLE TV	CAB
CAR	CAR
DOCTORS	DOC
DONATIONS	DON
ENTERTAINMENT	ENT
GIFTS	GIF
GROCERIES	GRO
HOUSEHOLD	HOU
INSURANCE	INS
INTEREST	INT
LOAN	LOA
MAINTENANCE	MAI
OTHER	OTH
PERSONAL	PER
PET	PET
REIMBURSEMENTS	REI
SALARY	SAL
TAX	TAX
TELEPHONE	TEL
TRAVEL	TRA
UTILITIES	UTI

Listing 13.2 LIST OFF TO PRINT of BUDGET.DBF

13.1.2 System Structure Chart for ACCOUNTS System

In designing the system structure chart for the accounts system, we note that if we try to include all nine items listed into a main menu, then it becomes a very "busy" menu. Taking note of the fact that items 1—3 pertain only to the ACCOUNTS database, while items 4—5 pertain principally to the BUDGET database, this suggests the system structure chart shown in Figure 13.1.

Next, adding the entry module into the system with the usual backup option, we end up with a refined system structure chart shown in Figure 13.2.

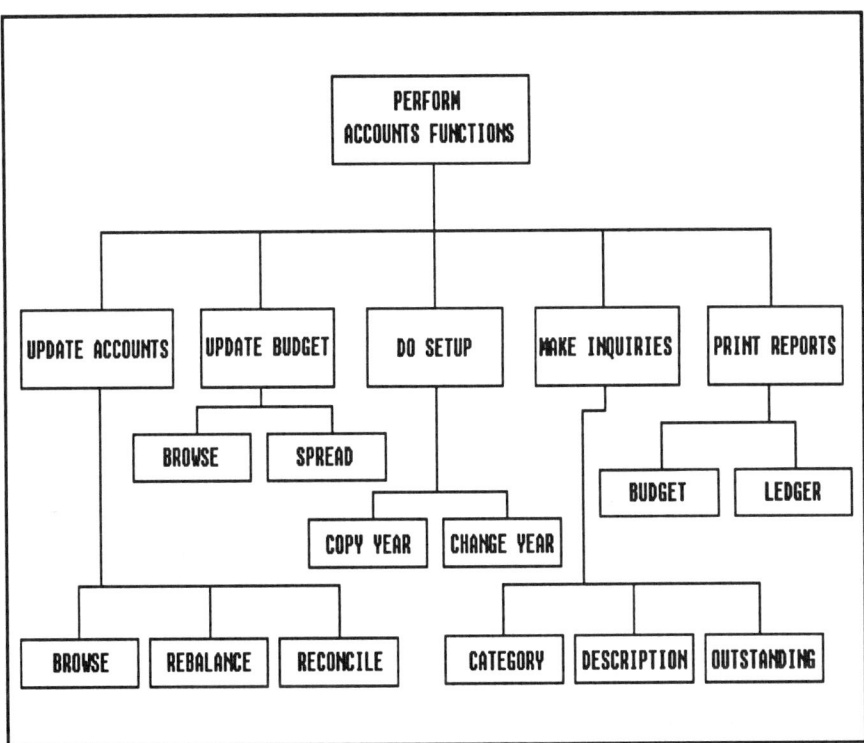

Figure 13.1 System Structure Chart for ACCOUNTS System

This, then, is the system that we will be implementing in this chapter. The program structure chart will turn out to be nearly identical to the system structure chart in appearance and is shown in Figure 13.3.

13.1.3 The Database ACCOUNTS.DBF

There are some extra features we would like to add to the ACCOUNTS system that would entail some modification of the ACCOUNTS database as we know it.

First, we wish to do check reconciliation at the end of each month. In order to do this, we must carry not only our checkbook balance but also the reconciled balance (i.e. the bank's balance of

456 ACCOUNTS SYSTEM—MULTIPLE FILES

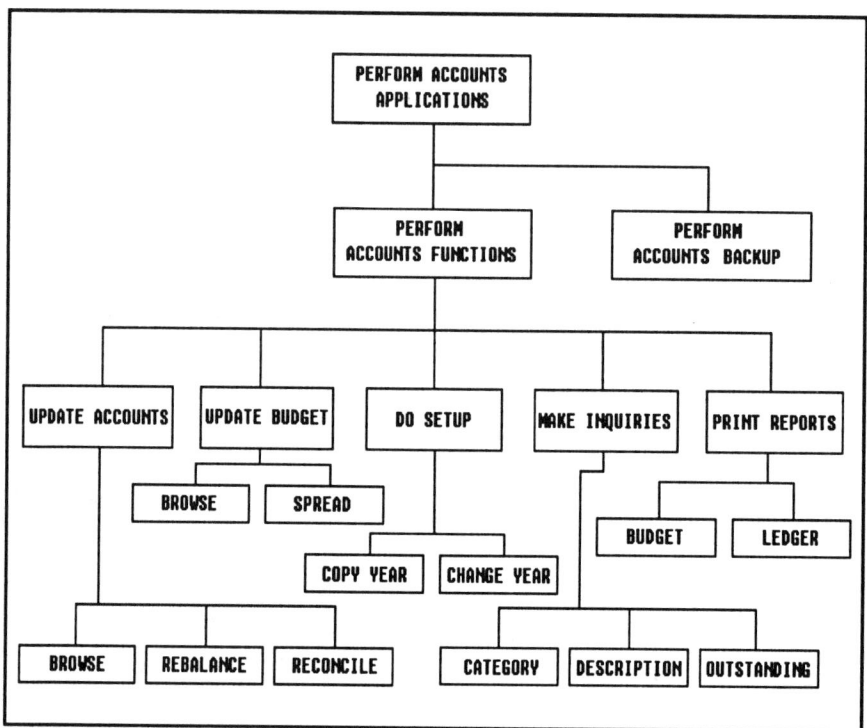

Figure 13.2 Refined System Structure Chart for ACCOUNTS System

our account which includes only checks that have been cashed at our bank). Hence we have to add a new field called RECONCILED. In the very first record of the ACCOUNTS database, in the RECONCILED field, we need to place the initial reconciled balance for the year. This is analogous to our having placed the initial balance for the year in the BALANCE field.

Second, quite often we will write a check which pays for items in several categories, not just one. A check to a credit card company is an example of this. One charge may be for a household item, while another might be for travel, while another might be for entertainment, etc. The question becomes, how does one go about making a spread of a single check. In order to do this, it becomes necessary to create a new field called BREAKDOWN. How we plan to use this new field will become apparent shortly.

ACCOUNTS SYSTEM—MULTIPLE FILES 457

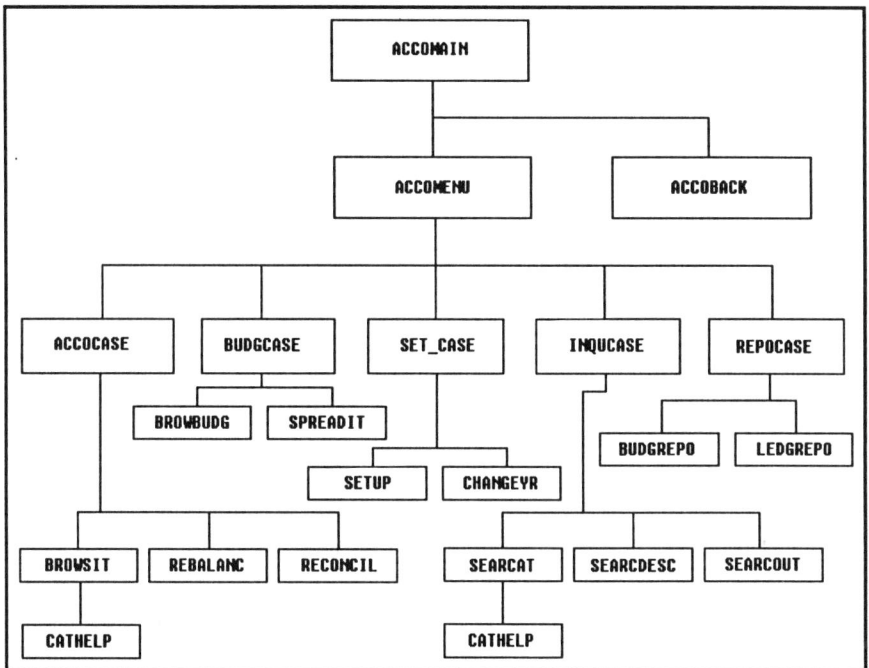

Figure 13.3 Program Structure Chart for ACCOUNTS System

The structure of our modified ACCOUNTS database is shown in Listing 13.3.

Field	Field Name	Type	Width	Dec
1	DATE	Date	8	
2	CHECK	Character	3	
3	DESCRIPT	Character	32	
4	CAT	Character	3	
5	DEBITS	Numeric	8	2
6	RECEIPTS	Numeric	8	2
7	BALANCE	Numeric	8	2
8	CASHED	Logical	1	
9	BREAKDOWN	Numeric	8	2
10	RECONCILED	Numeric	8	2

Listing 13.3 Modified Structure of ACCOUNTS.DBF

The main menu, ACCOMENU.prg, and its associated case statement programs: ACCOCASE.prg, BUDGCASE.prg, SETCASE.prg, INQUCASE.prg and REPOCASE.prg, contain no new concepts and so will be left as an exercise to the reader to write, as will the ACCOBACK.prg program. It is thus our job to write the programs that do the ACCOUNTS system work, as well as the main calling module: ACCOMAIN.prg. As we are demonstrating top-down design, we will begin with ACCOMAIN.

13.2 Use of Saved Memory Variables to Select Multiple Databases

One of the features of the ACCOUNTS system is that a separate LEDGER and a separate budget will be kept for each fiscal year. This means that there will be more than one account and one budget database. For example, for the year 1992, the accounts database would be called: ACCOUN92.DBF. Let's copy our old ACCOUNTS.DBF database to this new name:

.COPY FILE ACCOUNTS.DBF TO ACCOUN92.DBF

Since we do not wish to have to rewrite our programs each year to accommodate a new database, we must develop a way of handling this variable. There are two options open to us. The first is to have the program ask us which database we wish to open each time we enter the system. The second is to save a memory variable which contains the name of the database that we currently wish to access. Since we do not want to be troubled by the same question every time we enter the system, the latter method will be adopted.

Listing 13.4 shows the program, ACCOMAIN.prg.

We start by restoring some memory variables from a memory file called YEAR.MEM. This file contains the memory variable, THEYEAR, which contains the name of the default year of interest. For the year 1992, THEYEAR would take on the text value "92". From this we set the memory variable, WHICHYEAR, which we use

```
* ACCOMAIN.PRG
* This is the main entrance into the Accounts Budget System
* Restore Memory variable from YEAR
RESTORE FROM YEAR
WHICHYEAR = THEYEAR
* Create ACCOUNT and BUDGET memory variables from
* WHICHYEAR which is created from THEYEAR contained
* in the Memory file YEAR.
ACCOUNT = "ACCOUN" + WHICHYEAR
BUDGET = "BUDGET" + WHICHYEAR
SET TALK OFF
SET STATUS OFF
SET BELL OFF
SET CONFIRM ON
SET PROCEDURE TO ACCOPROC
DO ACCOMENU
SET PROCEDURE TO
CLEAR
@ 12,20 SAY "Do You Wish To Backup Accounts (Y/N): "
SET CONSOLE OFF
WAIT [] TO BACKITUP
SET CONSOLE ON
IF UPPER(BACKITUP) = "Y"
   DO ACCOBACK
ENDIF
SET CONFIRM OFF
SET BELL ON
SET STATUS ON
SET TALK ON
RETURN
```

Listing 13.4 Main Module for ACCOUNTS System ACCOMAIN.prg

within the program. The reason that we use a separate memory variable within the program is that we may change the particular year that we wish to look at, but we do not necessarily wish to change the default year (i.e. the year we automatically get each time we enter the program).

The next thing we do is to create the name of our current ACCOUNT database and BUDGET database. We do this simply by concatenating WHICHYEAR to the end of the words "ACCOUN" and "BUDGET".

After we do our usual sets, we open the procedure file which will eventually contain all the rest of the programs in this system. However, at this moment it does not exist. Nonetheless, if we wish to test this topmost module, we do have to create something for ACCOPROC.prg or the program will "bomb out" at this point. Likewise, we also need something named ACCOMENU.prg as well as ACCOBACK.prg in order to fully debug ACCOMAIN.prg.

If we have not as yet written these sub-programs, then we need to create stubs. The purpose of stubs is to enable us to fully test a program which calls other programs without having to write the other programs first.

13.3 Use of Stubs in Top Down Implementation

A stub is a "dummy" program which may pretend to do the desired function, but never does more than announce what the "Coming Attractions" are. For example, Listing 13.5 shows a stub that might be used for ACCOPROC.prg. Notice that it contains nothing more than a few comments and a RETURN statement. This is all that is necessary in order for ACCOMAIN.prg to function.

Listings 13.6 and 13.7 show what the stubs for ACCOMENU.prg and ACCOBACK.prg might look like. Note that their only function is to announce to the user what will eventually be done.

In this manner, the high level modules may be designed and tested without having to concern ourselves with the devilish details that await us at the lower levels.

```
* ACCOPROC.PRG
* This file will contain all the Procedures necessary to run
* the ACCOUNTS system.
*
RETURN
```

Listing 13.5 Stub for ACCOPROC.prg

```
* ACCOMENU.PRG
* This will contain the Main Menu for the
* ACCOUNTS system.
*
CLEAR
@ 12,21 SAY "COMING SOON!  THE GREAT ACCOUNTS MENU!"
WAIT []
CLEAR
RETURN
```

Listing 13.6 Stub for ACCOMENU.prg

```
* ACCOBACK.PRG
* This will contain the Backup Routine For the
* ACCOUNTS System
*
CLEAR
@ 12,21 SAY "SOON COMING!  THE GREAT BACKUP MODULE!"
WAIT []
CLEAR
RETURN
```

Listing 13.7 Stub for ACCOBACK.prg

462 ACCOUNTS SYSTEM—MULTIPLE FILES

In top-down design, the rule of thumb is always to put details off to later. In this way, one never loses sight of the "forest" of the system, for the "trees" of the details.

The next step is to design the main menu program, ACCOMENU.prg. As there is nothing new here, this design will be left to the reader. However, when ACCOMENU is executed, we should get an initial screen something like that shown in Figure 13.4.

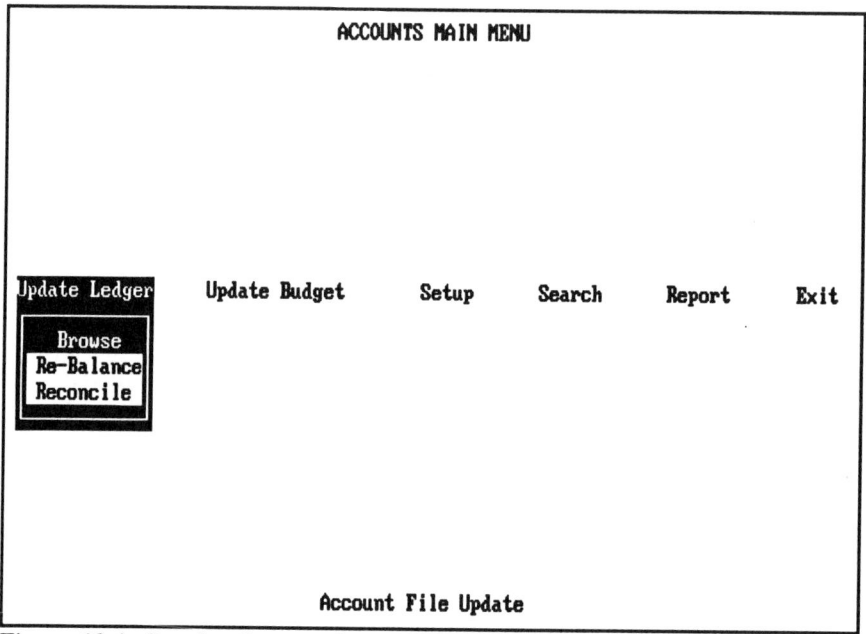

Figure 13.4 Opening Screen of ACCOMENU.prg

It should be emphasized, at this point, that it is important that ACCOMENU.prg, as well as: ACCOCASE.prg, BUDGCASE.prg, SETCASE.prg, INQUCASE.prg, and REPOCASE.prg be written at this time so that we can properly test the lowest level modules that will actually do the work. After this, stubs should be written for all of the lowest level programs being called by ACCOMENU. In this way the menu program can also be fully debugged before proceeding. The reader is encouraged to perform these steps.

Now we are ready for the design of the lowest level individual modules that actually do all the work.

13.4 Design of the Update Accounts Sub-Modules

We will begin with the design of the main data entry and data updating module, BROWSIT.prg, which browses the ACCOUNTS database. There will be no special ADD records or EDIT records module used here. Neither will there be a DELETE record module, as financial transactions should be voided, but not deleted. Everything will be done in BROWSIT.prg. This is a very natural way to approach the ACCOUNTS database; since when viewed in BROWSE it looks like a LEDGER, and in a ledger each time there is a new transaction, it is simply added to the bottom.

13.4.1 Design of BROWSIT.prg

Listing 13.8 shows the module BROWSIT.prg. Note that we start off with making the **F1** key the "hot" key for the Help module, CATHELP.prg. The **F1** key was chosen as it is the most common key used for Help in computer systems. Since there is no provision in a BROWSE screen to indicate which key is the Help key, it is best to use the most obvious one.

Next we use a macro, **&ACCOUNT**, to represent the particular ACCOUNTS database that we wish to open. Hence, **USE &ACCOUNT** effectively opens the desired ACCOUNTS database.

The usual reason for executing BROWSIT.prg will be to append a new transaction to the end of the ACCOUNTS database. For this reason we want to place ourselves near the end of the database. However, we don't want to end up at the bottom of the database, or all that we will be looking at is the last record of the database. This is a waste of the BROWSE screen. For this reason, we will back off sixteen records from the end of the database and enter BROWSE at this point. In this way we fill the screen with the most recent activity of the ledger. This is accomplished by the two commands:

```
GOTO BOTTOM
SKIP -16
```

```
* BROWSIT.PRG
* This program displays the check database in order of entry.
*
ON KEY LABEL F1 DO CATHELP
SET STATUS ON
SELECT 1
USE &ACCOUNT
GOTO BOTT
SKIP -16
BROWSE
SET STATUS OFF
ON KEY LABEL F1
RETURN
```

Listing 13.8 BROWSIT.prg for Data Update of ACCOUNTS Database

where **SKIP -16** is an example of the more general **SKIP** *n* command.

Finally, we go into BROWSE. Figure 13.5 shows what that might look like. Now suppose that we wish to enter a new transaction, but we forget what the various three letter category codes are. By striking the **F1** key, we immediately go into CATHELP.prg.

13.4.2 Design of CATHELP.prg—Use of Multiple Databases

The difference between CATHELP.prg and the previous Help screen we discussed in Chapter 12 is that while the previous Help screen was a static display, CATHELP.prg is a dynamic display of the BUDGET database. Since the ACCOUNT database is already open and in BROWSE mode, we need to **SELECT** a separate work area to open this second database. Listing 13.9 shows the program CATHELP.prg.

ACCOUNTS SYSTEM—MULTIPLE FILES 465

Records	Organize	Fields	Go To	Exit			
DATE	CHECK	DESCRIPT		CAT	DEBITS	RECEIPTS	BALANCE
01/14/92	407	Farmer's Market: Groceries		GRO	4.28	0.00	572.28
01/14/92	408	Feed-n-things: Pet Food		PET	8.50	0.00	563.78
01/15/92	409	State Farm Mutual: Insurance		INS	232.94	0.00	330.76
01/15/92	410	Sherman's: auto repairs		CAR	10.00	0.00	320.76
01/16/92	411	NYSEG: Utilities		UTI	110.12	0.00	210.64
01/16/92	412	West Side Vets		PET	30.00	0.00	180.64
01/18/92		Deposit: Travel Expense Reimb.		REI	0.00	30.25	210.89
01/19/92	413	Dr. Isaacs, M.D. (eye doct)		DOC	40.00	0.00	170.89
01/19/92		Deposit: Salary		SAL	0.00	750.00	920.89
01/20/92	414	Cash: Gas & Tolls		CAR	34.65	0.00	894.24
01/20/92	415	Sullivan's: Dept. Store		GIF	25.66	0.00	868.58
01/22/92	416	Action Video		ENT	10.59	0.00	857.99
01/22/92	417	MBNA Payment Services:Cred. Card		HOU	100.00	0.00	757.99
01/25/92	418	Many Happy Returns: Tax Prep.		TAX	105.00	0.00	652.99
01/25/92	419	NYC Parking Violations Bur.		PER	35.00	0.00	617.99
01/27/92	420	Great American: Groceries		GRO	39.92	0.00	578.07
01/28/92	421	Trading Post: Maintenance items		MAI	28.47	0.00	549.60
Browse	A:\accounts\ACCOUN92	Rec 9/25		File			

Figure 13.5 Ledger Browse Screen of BROWSIT.prg

We start CATHELP by saving the screen that we had in BROWSIT.prg. As we're interrupting a BROWSE, we have to be able to reproduce the screen from whence the operation exited when we are done with CATHELP. Next we turn off the Status Line since we don't want to see it on the HELP screen.

In order to be able to have two databases open simultaneously, it is necessary to create a second work area. This is done with the **SELECT** command. By saying **SELECT 2**, a second database workspace is created thus allowing both the BUDGET and the ACCOUNTS databases to be open simultaneously, albeit in separate workspaces.

Next we open the BUDGET database with it ordered by CAT. We need to be certain that at some point the following commands have been executed:

. **USE &BUDGET**
. **INDEX ON CAT TAG CAT**

```
* CATHELP.PRG
* This displays the categories for reference during data
* entry
*
SAVE SCREEN TO CSCREEN
SET STATUS OFF
CLEAR
SELECT 2
USE &BUDGET ORDER CAT
DISPLAY ALL OFF FIELD CATEGORY, CAT
WAIT
USE
SELECT 1
SET STATUS ON
RESTORE SCREEN FROM CSCREEN
RETURN
```

Listing 13.9 Help Module: CATHELP.prg for ACCOUNTS System

Now we simply **DISPLAY** the database allowing us to see all of the categories and their abbreviations. The WAIT command holds the screen until a key is struck. Then the second work space is cleared out and closed by the **USE** command. Next we turn the Status Line back on and RESTORE the screen. Finally we return to our BROWSE of the ACCOUNT database at exactly the point where we had exited.

13.4.3 Design of REBALANC.prg

One of the most frustrating and time consuming parts of keeping a checkbook is reconciling your personal balance with the balance shown on the bank statement. The difficulty lies in the fact that not everyone has cashed all the checks that you have written. So, although your balance reflects all the checks you have written plus all the deposits you have made, the bank's balance reflects only those checks that have been processed by the bank and those deposits that have cleared before your statement went out.

In order to reconcile the two, one normally adds to their balance all the checks that have not cleared the bank and subtracts all the deposits that have not cleared by the statement time. Finally one subtracts any service charges that might have been added by the bank for that month. The resulting adjusted balance should equal the bank's balance. In principle this is a pretty straightforward procedure. However, in practice, whenever I'm dealing with more than about a dozen checks a month, I make an arithmetic mistake that usually takes me an hour or so to find.

I've found that the length of time that it takes to reconcile a bank statement increases not simply with the number of checks but more like the square of the number of checks. One institution I've worked with handles nearly 1000 checks per month manually. It got so it took longer than a month for a single person to reconcile these checks by hand. Naturally they began to fall further and further behind. This is where a computer can really prove its worth. Using the following program, the length of time that they take has been reduced to about one day per month.

The technique is very simple. Every check and deposit that appears on the bank statement is marked on the computer by turning the CASHED field to .T. . Then only those records where the CASHED field is .T. are used to compute the reconciled balance. Any service charges are added in and their CASHED field is made .T. . The resulting reconciled balance should be identically equal to the bank's balance. We compute this reconciled balance at the same time as we compute our personal balance.

In Chapter 9 we designed the module, BALANCE.prg, which calculated the BALANCE column in our ledger. REBALANC.prg is an updated version of that program. This version not only computes both the personal as well as the reconciled balance, but also takes care of one other wrinkle that commonly occurs in writing checks.

Quite often, checks are written that encompass more than one budget category. This is particularly true with checks written to credit card companies. One of the charges may have been for entertainment, another may have been for home improvements, another for personal, etc. Yet when you go to pay your credit card bill, you do it with one check, not with three or more. So the question arises as to how to handle this situation. The answer is that a "spread" must be made of the check[44].

A "spread" is handled in the following manner. When the check is written, no category is assigned to the check, but the amount of the check is recorded in the DEBITS field. Immediately below the check is written how the check was spread, one record per budget category. On each of these lines a budget category is indicated. However, no amount is entered in the DEBIT field. Rather, each of the spread checks is entered in the field called: BREAKDOWN. When balances are computed, the DEBIT field is used, but when the budget categories are totalled, the BREAKDOWN field is used. Figure 13.6 shows how a check has been spread. Note that we have not as yet recalculated the balance.

We are now ready to look at the program, REBALANC.prg, which does this calculation. (See Listing 13.10.) Notice that this program is very similar to BALANCE.prg which we wrote in Chapter 9.

Note that REBALANC.prg differs from BALANCE.prg only in that it calculates not only the BALANCE field but also the RECONCILED field. In addition, it includes in the BREAKDOWN field the debited amount of every check that has a category in the CAT field.

---

[44]Using a similar technique with deposits can be avoided in as much as deposits do not need to be attributed to a single number like a check. Hence a deposit that contains more than one category may be entered in several pieces all adding up to the total deposit.

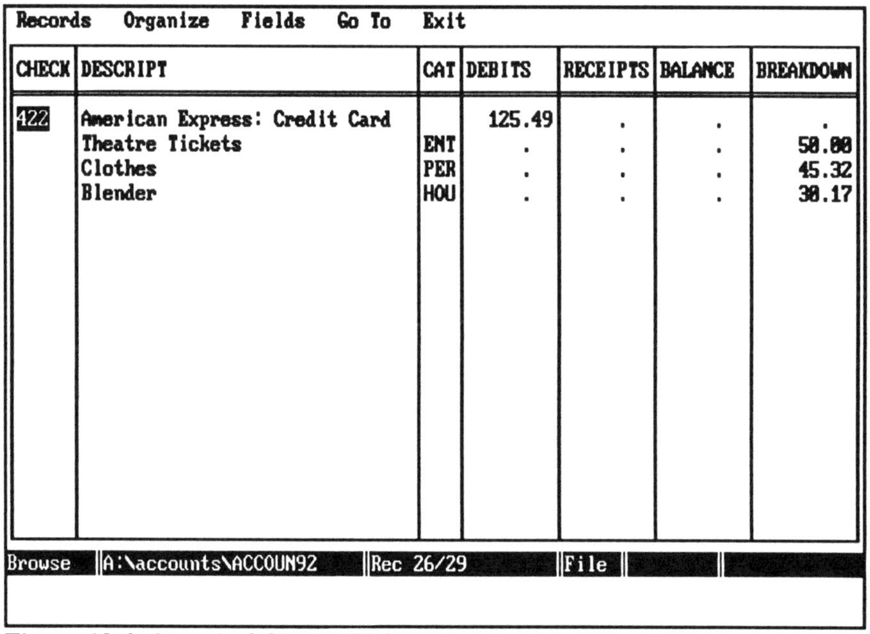

ACCOUNTS SYSTEM—MULTIPLE FILES

```
Records   Organize   Fields   Go To   Exit
CHECK DESCRIPT                         CAT  DEBITS  RECEIPTS  BALANCE  BREAKDOWN
 422  American Express: Credit Card         125.49     .         .         .
      Theatre Tickets                  ENT     .      .         .       50.00
      Clothes                          PER     .      .         .       45.32
      Blender                          HOU     .      .         .       30.17




Browse   A:\accounts\ACCOUN92    Rec 26/29    File
```

Figure 13.6 Spread of Check 422 into three budget categories

In the RECONCILED calculation the IIF(,,) statement:

**REPLACE RECONCILED WITH IIF(CASHED,;
OLDRECON + RECEIPTS - DEBITS, OLDRECON)**

guarantees the fact that only those records where CASHED is .T. is a new RECONCILED value computed. In cases where CASHED is .F., the RECONCILED balance takes on the same value as the RECONCILED balance of the previous record. The effect of this is to skip all those transactions that were not reflected in the bank statement.

In the BREAKDOWN field, the value of the DEBITS field is moved into it for every check that has *not* been spread. That this happens for only checks that have *not* been spread is guaranteed by the relation: **CAT<>" "** in the IIF(,,) function found in:

**REPLACE BREAKDOWN WITH IIF(CAT<>" " .AND. ;
DEBITS>0, DEBITS, BREAKDOWN)**

```
* REBALANC.PRG
* This balances both the Balance as well as the bank
* Reconciled checks.  It leaves the BREAKDOWN field
* with the spread of all the budget category amounts.
*
SELECT 1
USE &ACCOUNT
CLEAR
@ 12,20 SAY "Rebalancing Checkbook, Please Be Patient!"
STORE BALANCE TO OLDBALANCE
STORE RECONCILED TO OLDRECON
SKIP
DO WHILE .NOT. EOF()
   REPLACE BALANCE WITH OLDBALANCE + RECEIPTS - DEBITS
   REPLACE RECONCILED WITH IIF(CASHED, OLDRECON;
      + RECEIPTS - DEBITS, OLDRECON)
   REPLACE BREAKDOWN WITH IIF(CAT<>" " .AND. DEBITS>0,;
      DEBITS, BREAKDOWN)
   OLDBALANCE = BALANCE
   OLDRECON = RECONCILED
   SKIP
ENDDO
USE
RETURN
```

Listing 13.10 Program REBALANC.prg

Likewise, that this happens only for checks and not for deposits is guaranteed by the relation: **DEBITS>0** . If this is not the case, then whatever the old value of BREAKDOWN was, it is left with that value. Since a check that has been spread already has its spread amount in the BREAKDOWN field, there is no need for us to concern ourselves with the checks that *have* been spread.

Except for the BREAKDOWN and RECONCILED calculations, REBALANC.prg remains the same as BALANCE.prg. After running REBALANC.prg. Figure 13.7 shows how the new BALANCE and BREAKDOWN fields now appear. This BROWSE screen was created with the command:

ACCOUNTS SYSTEM—MULTIPLE FILES

```
. USE ACCOUN92
. BROWSE FIELD CHECK, DESCRIPT, CAT, DEBITS,
    RECEIPTS, BALANCE, BREAKDOWN
```

Notice that neither Check 422, which was spread, nor the deposits, were included in the BREAKDOWN field, but all the remaining items were included.

As for the RECONCILED field, Figure 13.8 shows the BROWSE:

```
. BROWSE FIELD CHECK, DESCRIPT, CAT, DEBITS,
    RECEIPTS, BALANCE, RECONCILED
```

Note here that none of the transactions made after Check 414 were cashed, as the RECONCILED amount remains constant from that point downward.

CHECK	DESCRIPT	CAT	DEBITS	RECEIPTS	BALANCE	BREAKDOWN
412	West Side Vets	PET	30.00	0.00	180.64	30.00
	Deposit: Travel Expense Reimb.	REI	0.00	38.25	218.89	0.00
413	Dr. Isaacs, M.D. (eye doct)	DOC	40.00	0.00	178.89	40.00
	Deposit: Salary	SAL	0.00	750.00	928.89	0.00
414	Cash: Gas & Tolls	CAR	34.65	0.00	894.24	34.65
415	Sullivan's: Dept. Store	GIF	25.66	0.00	868.58	25.66
416	Action Video	ENT	10.59	0.00	857.99	10.59
417	MBNA Payment Services:Cred. Car	HOU	100.00	0.00	757.99	100.00
418	Many Happy Returns: Tax Prep.	TAX	105.00	0.00	652.99	105.00
419	NYC Parking Violations Bur.	PER	35.00	0.00	617.99	35.00
420	Great American: Groceries	GRO	39.92	0.00	578.07	39.92
421	Trading Post: Maintenance items	MAI	28.47	0.00	549.60	28.47
422	American Express: Cred. Card		125.49	0.00	424.11	0.00
	Theatre Tickets	ENT	0.00	0.00	424.11	50.00
	Clothes	PER	0.00	0.00	424.11	45.32
	Blender	HOU	0.00	0.00	424.11	30.17

Browse | A:\accounts\ACCOUN92 | Rec 14/29 | File

Figure 13.7 BROWSE of BREAKDOWN field after running REBALANC.prg

472   ACCOUNTS SYSTEM—MULTIPLE FILES

Records	Organize	Fields	Go To	Exit				
CHECK	DESCRIPT			CAT	DEBITS	RECEIPTS	BALANCE	RECONCILE
412	West Side Vets			PET	30.00	0.00	180.64	338.76
	Deposit: Travel Expense Reimb.			REI	0.00	38.25	218.89	369.01
413	Dr. Isaacs, M.D. (eye doct)			DOC	40.00	0.00	178.89	329.01
	Deposit: Salary			SAL	0.00	750.00	928.89	1079.01
414	Cash: Gas & Tolls			CAR	34.65	0.00	894.24	1044.36
415	Sullivan's: Dept. Store			GIF	25.66	0.00	868.58	1044.36
416	Action Video			ENT	10.59	0.00	857.99	1044.36
417	MBNA Payment Services:Cred. Car			HOU	100.00	0.00	757.99	1044.36
418	Many Happy Returns: Tax Prep.			TAX	105.00	0.00	652.99	1044.36
419	NYC Parking Violations Bur.			PER	35.00	0.00	617.99	1044.36
420	Great American: Groceries			GRO	39.92	0.00	578.07	1044.36
421	Trading Post: Maintenance items			MAI	28.47	0.00	549.60	1044.36
422	American Express: Cred. Card				125.49	0.00	424.11	1044.36
	Theatre Tickets			ENT	0.00	0.00	424.11	1044.36
	Clothes			PER	0.00	0.00	424.11	1044.36
	Blender			HOU	0.00	0.00	424.11	1044.36
Browse	A:\accounts\ACCOUN92	Rec 14/29	File					

Figure 13.8 BROWSE of RECONCILED field after running REBALANC.prg

13.4.4 Design of RECONCIL.prg

This module is designed to BROWSE the ACCOUNTS database in order of check number and date. In this program when you are checking off all the checks that have been returned by the bank, you can find them quickly. Furthermore, a filter has been included so that the spread items do not appear. We reconcile only checks and deposits, not spreads—they are ignored.

The program, RECONCIL.prg, is shown in Listing 13.11.

The index, CHECKDAT, created as follows:

. INDEX ON CHECK+DTOS(DATE) FOR CHECK<>"   ";
.OR. DTOC(DATE)<>" / / " TAG CHECKDAT

insures the fact that any transaction having a check number (all checks) or any transaction having a date (deposits have dates as well as checks) will be included in our BROWSE. But the spread items that have neither check number nor date will not be included.

```
* RECONCIL.PRG
* This program puts entries in order of check number
* and date
*
USE &ACCOUNT ORDER CHECKDAT
BROW FIELD DATE, CHECK, DESCRIPT, CASHED, ;
   DEBITS, RECEIPTS, CAT
USE
RETURN
```

Listing 13.11 RECONCIL.prg used for checking off returned checks

While we're at it, we had better create the index CAT for this new database. Notice that we do *not* do an index "Unique" this time.

.INDEX ON UPPER(CAT) TAG CAT

Figure 13.9 shows the screen that appears when we run RECONCIL.prg. If we go and Freeze the CASHED field then it makes traversing the database and checking off all the returned checks and deposits very efficient.

13.5 Powerful Commands—The Design of SPREADIT.prg

We will now design the program that is at the heart of the ACCOUNTS system. SPREADIT.prg is a program that spreads our ACCOUNTS database into the various budget categories and then records them in the BUDGET database for future reference. (See Listing 13.12.)

DATE	CHECK	DESCRIPT	CASHED	DEBITS	RECEIPTS	CAT
01/01/92		Jan. 1 Balance	T	0.00	0.00	
01/05/92		Deposit: Salary	T	0.00	750.00	SAL
01/18/92		Deposit: Travel Expense Reimb.	T	0.00	38.25	REI
01/19/92		Deposit: Salary	T	0.00	750.00	SAL
01/09/92	401	Cash: January Allowance	T	100.00	0.00	PER
01/09/92	402	Sullivan Co. Cablevision	T	20.00	0.00	CAB
01/09/92	403	N.Y. Telephone: Dec. bill	T	50.00	0.00	TEL
01/12/92	404	Dr. John McIntyre, D.D.S.	T	75.00	0.00	DOC
01/13/92	405	Sierra Club: Donation	F	10.00	0.00	DON
01/14/92	406	Shoprite: Groceries	T	18.60	0.00	GRO
01/14/92	407	Farmer's Market: Groceries	T	4.20	0.00	GRO
01/14/92	408	Feed-n-things: Pet Food	T	8.50	0.00	PET
01/15/92	409	State Farm Mutual: Insurance	T	232.94	0.00	INS
01/15/92	410	Sherman's: auto repairs	T	10.00	0.00	CAR
01/16/92	411	NYSEG: Utilities	F	110.12	0.00	UTI
01/16/92	412	West Side Vets	F	30.00	0.00	PET
01/19/92	413	Dr. Isaacs, M.D. (eye doct)	T	40.00	0.00	DOC

| Browse | A:\accounts\ACCOUN92 | Rec 1/29 | File | | |

Figure 13.9 Opening Screen of RECONCIL.prg

SPREADIT.prg demonstrates the use of some commands that we have not seen before. The first of these is the TOTAL command.

13.5.1 Use of the TOTAL Command

After we have saved our screen and set the safety off, we place a message on the screen indicating what the computer is up to. Next we open our ACCOUNT database using the macro as usual and order the database in order of the CAT field.

Now what we want to do is to create a new database, which we will call SPREAD.DBF, which has one record per category type CAT. This one record will contain the sum total of each of the records having that particular value of CAT.

For example, in the ACCOUNT database, we have two records where the category is personal (i.e. CAT is "PER"). The

```
* SPREADIT.PRG
* This spreads all the various budget items into totals in
* each category.
SAVE SCREEN TO MAINSCREEN
SET SAFETY OFF
CLEAR
@ 12,20 SAY "Spreading Budget, Please Be Patient!"
* Make SPREAD.DBF a Totalled Version of ACCOUNTS database
USE &ACCOUNT ORDER CAT
TOTAL ON CAT TO SPREAD
USE
* Make Preparations to Relate BUDGET.DBF to SPREAD.DBF
SELECT 1
USE &BUDGET
REPLACE ALL INCOME WITH 0, SPENT WITH 0
SET ORDER TO CAT
SELECT 2
USE SPREAD
INDEX ON CAT TO CAT
SET RELATION TO CAT INTO &BUDGET
GOTO TOP
DO WHILE .NOT. EOF()
   SELECT 1
   IF FOUND()
      REPLACE SPENT WITH SPREAD->BREAKDOWN
      REPLACE INCOME WITH SPREAD->RECEIPTS
   ELSE
      CLEAR
      @ 12,20 SAY SPREAD->CAT + " Is Not Found In BUDGET!"
      WAIT
   ENDIF
   SELECT 2
   SKIP
ENDDO
CLOSE DATA
ERASE SPREAD.DBF
ERASE CAT.NDX
SET SAFETY ON
RESTORE SCREEN FROM MAINSCREEN
RETURN
```

Listing 13.12 Program SPREADIT.prg Introduces TOTAL & SET RELATION

476   ACCOUNTS SYSTEM—MULTIPLE FILES

first one has a DEBITS value of 100, while the second has a DEBITS value of 35. In our new database, SPREAD.DBF, there will be only one record where CAT is "PER", but the value of DEBITS in that record will be 135, the sum total of all the CAT = "PER" records in the database.

We can create this database using the single powerful command: **TOTAL**. The syntax of the command is: **TOTAL ON** *FieldName* **TO** *DataBase* . In this case *FieldName* is CAT and *DataBase* is SPREAD. Our command becomes: **TOTAL ON CAT TO SPREAD** . Now we have the database we want, one which has one unique record per CATegory and that unique record has the sum total of all the CATegories of that type.

The one rule that must be followed in using the TOTAL command is that the Accounts database must be indexed (or sorted) in the order of the field on which we want unique totals (i.e. CAT). It was for this reason that we opened it in ORDER of CAT.

13.5.2 Use of the **SET RELATION TO** Command

The **SET RELATION TO** command is one of the most powerful commands in the dBASE language. It allows two databases, ordered on a particular field, to be locked in step as we skip through one of them in a loop. The two requirements are that the two databases must both share at least one common field and they both must be indexed on that field.

Suppose we make the BUDGET database and SPREAD.DBF the two databases that we wish to "lockstep" together. The common field is CAT. If we open each database up in its own area, and put each in order of CAT, then we can use the **SET RELATION TO** command to relate the two to each other. Then if we step SPREAD.DBF through to the End-of-File, the budget database will also step itself through changing to a new value of CAT each time SPREAD.DBF changes to a new value of CAT. The syntax for our **SET RELATION TO** command is: **SET RELATION TO**

CommonFieldName **INTO** *OtherDataBase* . In this particular case, if we were currently in the work area of SPREAD.DBF, then the command would become: **SET RELATION TO CAT INTO &BUDGET** .

The sequence of commands that prepares and sets this relation is:

> **SELECT 1**
> **USE &BUDGET**
> **SET ORDER TO CAT**
> **SELECT 2**
> **USE SPREAD**
> **INDEX ON CAT TO CAT**
> **SET RELATION TO CAT INTO &BUDGET**

Looking at Listing 13.12, you'll notice that after opening the budget database, we did a REPLACE of all the INCOME and all the SPENT fields to the value of zero. This was done to insure the fact that if there are any CATegories in the budget database that are not included in SPREAD, that they will end up having a zero value.

Now we're ready for the loop. We plan to step SPREAD.DBF through every one of its unique records until we reach the End Of File of SPREAD.DBF. When we find a CAT in the budget database with a similar value (and we had better, or we didn't use proper codes), we will put the BREAKDOWN for that particular record into the SPENT field of the budget database. Likewise we will also update the INCOME field of the budget database with the value in the RECEIPTS field of SPREAD. If for any reason we do not find a CATegory in the budget database that we had in SPREAD, we broadcast the fact with a message to the screen calling attention to this error. Obviously, if we have used correct codes, this should never happen.

Notice that we have to refer to fields in the unselected database by using the full name (e.g. SPREAD->BREAKDOWN). Note also that we go back and forth between selected databases using the SELECT command.

After leaving the loop, we do a **CLOSE DATA** command. CLOSE DATA closes all the open databases in all the selected work areas. This instruction saves us from having to select each work area and then doing a USE in that work area. Finally we erase the database, SPREAD.DBF, and its associated index, CAT.NDX, which we no longer need. Next we turn the safety back on, and restore the screen, and we're done.

13.5.3 Design of BROWBUDG.prg

Now we want to browse the result of our work which we do with BROWBUDG.prg (see Listing 13.13).

The BROWSE of our budget database is shown in Figures 13.10 and 13.11. You will notice that budgeted amounts have been added to the fields BUDGETED and EXPECT_INC. Note that the list of categories begins with a BLANK item. If, by chance, we forget to place a category on any of our entries, then non-zero values will appear here in either the SPENT or INCOME fields. This is a good error detection device so we have included it.

Figure 13.12 shows the screen which occurs when we exit from the BROWSE screen. It gives the totals of the four memory variables: TOTBUDGET, TOTALSPENT, TOTEXPECT, and TOTINCOME which were generated by the CALCULATE command:

CALCULATE SUM(SPENT), SUM(BUDGETED),;
    SUM(INCOME),SUM(EXPECT_INC) TO ;
    TOTALSPENT, TOTBUDGET, TOTINCOME,;
    TOTEXPECT

```
* BROWBUDG.PRG
* This Browses the BUDGET Database as well as displaying
* the Totals.  SPREADIT.PRG should normally be run before
* executing this program.
*
SAVE SCREEN TO MAINSCREEN
USE &BUDGET
BROWSE
CALCULATE SUM(SPENT), SUM(BUDGETED), ;
    SUM(INCOME), SUM(EXPECT_INC) TO ;
    TOTALSPENT,TOTBUDGET, ;
    TOTINCOME, TOTEXPECT
@ 08,20 SAY "Total Anticipated Receipts Is: " + ;
    STR(TOTEXPECT,9,2)
@ 10,20 SAY "Total Received To Date Is: " + ;
    STR(TOTINCOME,9,2)
@ 14,20 SAY "Total Amount Budgeted Is: " + ;
    STR(TOTBUDGET,9,2)
@ 16,20 SAY "Total Amount Spent To Date Is: " + ;
    STR(TOTALSPENT,9,2)
@ 23,0
WAIT
USE
RESTORE SCREEN FROM MAINSCREEN
RETURN
```

Listing 13.13 BROWBUDG.prg, the BROWSE Program for BUDGET.DBF

CATEGORY	CAT	BUDGETED	SPENT	EXPECT_INC	INCOME
BLANK		.	0.00	.	0.00
CABLE TV	CAB	240.00	20.00	.	0.00
CAR	CAR	1000.00	44.65	.	0.00
DOCTORS	DOC	500.00	115.00	.	0.00
DONATIONS	DON	260.00	10.00	.	0.00
ENTERTAINMENT	ENT	300.00	60.59	.	0.00
GIFTS	GIF	300.00	25.66	.	0.00
GROCERIES	GRO	4000.00	62.72	.	0.00
HOUSEHOLD	HOU	500.00	130.17	.	0.00
INSURANCE	INS	500.00	232.94	.	0.00
INTEREST	INT	.	0.00	100.00	0.00
LOAN	LOA	3000.00	0.00	.	0.00
MAINTENANCE	MAI	1000.00	28.47	.	0.00
OTHER	OTH	400.00	0.00	.	0.00
PERSONAL	PER	2400.00	180.32	.	0.00
PET	PET	500.00	38.50	.	0.00
REIMBURSEMENTS	REI	.	0.00	400.00	38.25
SALARY	SAL	.	0.00	19500.00	1500.00

Figure 13.10 Opening Screen of BROWBUDG.prg

The benefit of this program should now be apparent. At the touch of a finger you can see just how you're doing with respect to your budget. And of course, at the end of the year, it makes the record keeping for doing your income taxes a simple task indeed.

13.6 Design of the SETUP Module

At the beginning of each new year, it is desirable to create a new accounts and a new budget database. It is for this reason that macros were used to hold the names of our two databases. The easiest way to create new databases is simply to copy the old ones and eliminate the unwanted data. The program, SETUP.prg, shown in Listing 13.14, shows how this might be done.

CATEGORY	CAT	BUDGETED	SPENT	EXPECT_INC	INCOME
SALARY	SAL	.	0.00	19500.00	1500.00
TAX	TAX	200.00	105.00	.	0.00
TELEPHONE	TEL	600.00	50.00	.	0.00
TRAVEL	TRA	500.00	0.00	.	0.00
UTILITIES	UTI	1000.00	110.12	.	0.00

Figure 13.11 The BROWSE of the second page of the BUDGET Database

After doing our usual SAVE SCREEN, we make a best guess as to what value NEWYEAR might have assuming that WHICHYEAR holds the value of our current year. We do this by adding one to WHICHYEAR. However, WHICHYEAR is not a numeric memory variable, hence we must first convert it to numeric. This is done by means of the **VAL()** function. **VAL**(*TextString*) gives the numeric value of whatever numbers may be present at the beginning of *TextString*. If there are no numbers, then it returns the value of zero.

Next we want to add one to this value. Finally, we want to convert the numeric value arrived at back to a string variable so that we can concatenate it to form our new file name. For this reason we take the **STR()** function of the resulting sum. Thus, if WHICHYEAR had a value of "92", then NEWYEAR will take on the value of "93". This is simply a default value. We will now display this preset value and give the user the option of changing it to the value that he or she desires.

```
          Total Anticipated Receipts Is:  20000.00

          Total Received To Date Is:   1538.25


          Total Amount Budgeted Is:  18000.00

          Total Amount Spent To Date Is:   1214.14
```

Press any key to continue...

Figure 13.12 Display of Totals calculated by BROWBUDG.prg

13.6.1 The Use of a "Do Until" Loop

In certain computer languages there is a loop type called the "Do Until" loop. The way this loop works is shown in Figure 13.13. No precondition is necessary in order to enter this loop. However, there is an exit condition that must be satisfied before execution is allowed to leave the loop. Hence the second two rules of the three rules of DO WHILE loops still apply to a "Do Until" loop:

2. Within the loop the *LoopCondition* must be able to be modified.

3. The *LoopCondition* must, at some point, be able to take on a value that allows the loop to be exited.

ACCOUNTS SYSTEM—MULTIPLE FILES

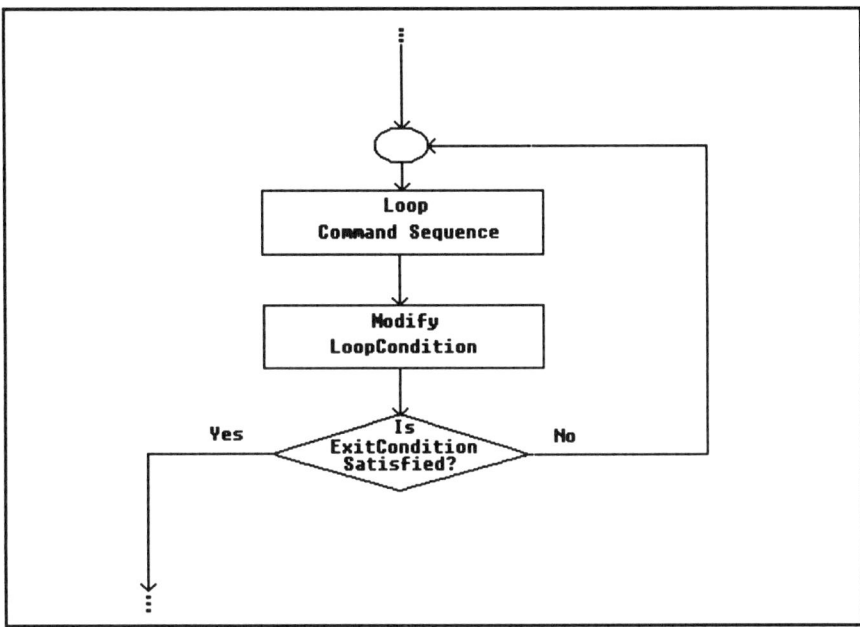

Figure 13.13 The "Do Until" Loop

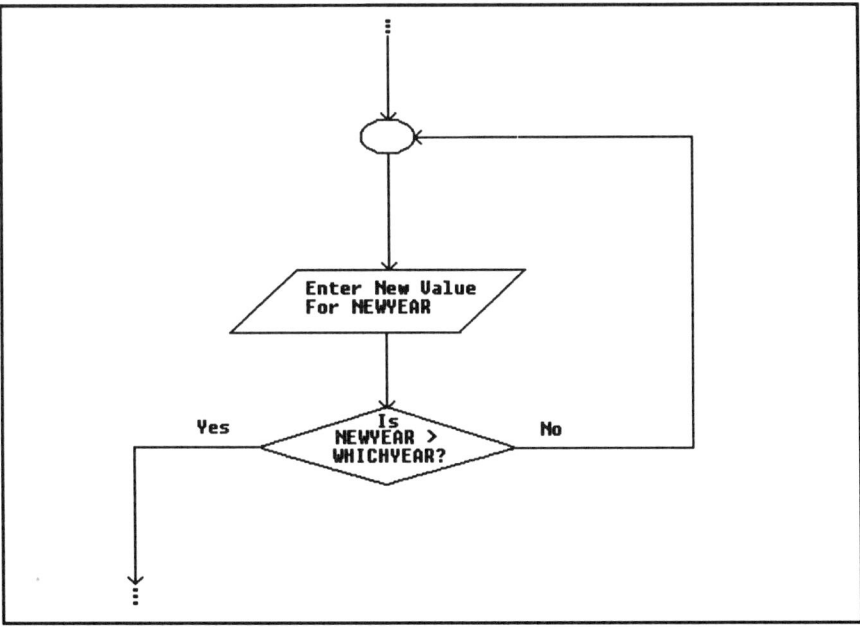

Figure 13.14 "Do Until" Loop contained in SETUP.prg

```
* SETUP.PRG
* This creates a new ACCOUNTS database and
* a new BUDGET
* database from the old existing versions.
SAVE SCREEN TO ACCOSCREEN
STORE STR(VAL(WHICHYEAR) + 1,2) TO NEWYEAR
CLEAR
DO WHILE .T.                  && Perform a Do Until Loop
   @ 12,17 SAY "Enter Account Year Desired: " GET NEWYEAR
   READ
   IF NEWYEAR>WHICHYEAR
      EXIT
   ENDIF
ENDDO
STORE "ACCOUN" + NEWYEAR TO NEWACCOUNT
STORE "BUDGET" + NEWYEAR TO NEWBUDGET
USE &ACCOUNT   && Create new Accounts DBF with one blank record
COPY STRUCTURE TO &NEWACCOUNT
USE &NEWACCOUNT
APPEND BLANK
INDEX ON UPPER(CAT) TAG CAT
INDEX ON CHECK + DTOS(DATE) FOR CHECK<>" " .OR. ;
           DTOC(DATE)<>" / / " TAG CHECKDAT
USE &BUDGET   && Create Budget with no SPENT and no INCOME
COPY TO &NEWBUDGET
USE &NEWBUDGET
REPLACE ALL SPENT WITH 0.0, INCOME WITH 0.0
INDEX ON UPPER(CAT) TAG CAT
* Edit and/or Add Categories in New Budget Database
STORE .T. TO EDITBUDGET
STORE .F. TO PACKIT
CLEAR
@ 12,17 SAY "Do You Want To Edit The New Budget Database: " ;
      GET EDITBUDGET
READ
IF EDITBUDGET
   BROWSE
   @ 12,22 SAY "Do You Want To Pack the New Budget: " ;
         GET PACKIT
   READ
   IF PACKIT
      PACK
   ENDIF
ENDIF
USE
RESTORE SCREEN FROM ACCOSCREEN
RETURN
```

Listing 13.14 Program SETUP.prg

ACCOUNTS SYSTEM—MULTIPLE FILES

This loop type does not explicitly exist in dBASE IV but may be easily created in the following way. If we begin our DO WHILE loop with the command, **DO WHILE .T.**, then there is nothing to stop us from entering the loop to begin with. The exit condition comes in the form of an **IF—ENDIF** selection statement. If the condition is satisfied, then the **EXIT** command is executed and the loop is exited. Figure 13.14 shows how the "Do Until" loop is implemented using these commands. In the particular case shown in the program SETUP.prg, the "Do Until" loop is as follows:

DO WHILE .T.
  @ 12,17 SAY "Enter Account Year Desired: "
    GET NEWYEAR
  READ
  IF NEWYEAR > WHICHYEAR
    EXIT
  ENDIF
ENDDO

The reason for using this loop is to make sure that the year that is chosen for our new databases is greater than the present year. We will accept any year greater than this year, but not this year or any earlier, as we do not want to copy on top of an already existing database. This "Do Until" loop guarantees that the only way we can exit from the loop is to choose some year greater than the current year.

The opening screen of SETUP.prg is shown in Figure 13.15.

Now we're ready to create our new accounts database. We do this by opening the old accounts database and then copying only its structure (no records) to our new database name given in **&NEWACCOUNT**. However, because this new database has zero records, we must add at least one blank record. If we don't do this, we will never be able to browse this database. It is for this reason that we append a blank record to the new ACCOUNTS database

486   ACCOUNTS SYSTEM—MULTIPLE FILES

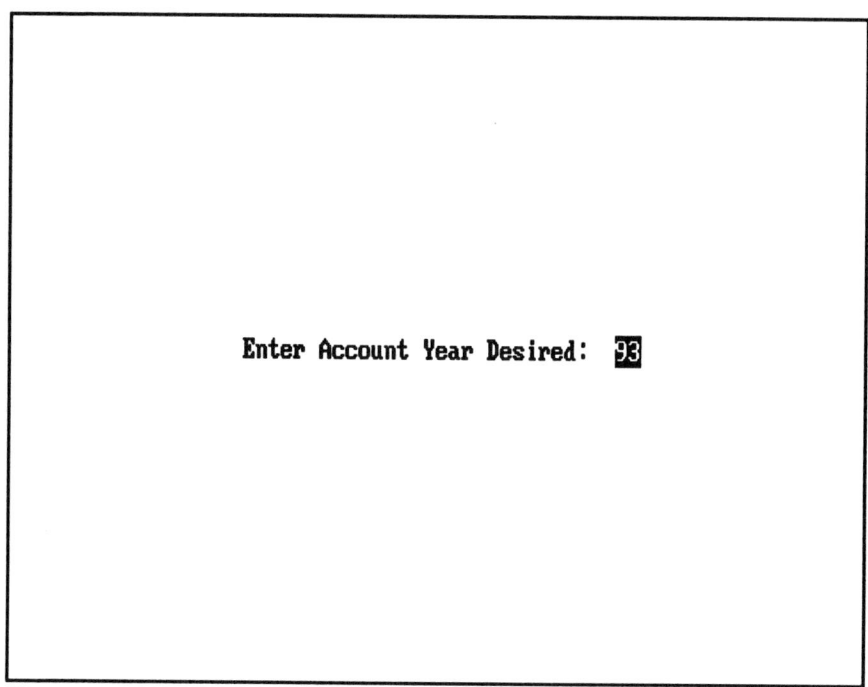

Figure 13.15 Opening screen of SETUP.prg

with the **APPEND BLANK** instruction. Finally, we create the two production index tags, CAT and CHECKDAT, that we need to order our new database.

Now we're ready to create the new budget database. In this case we copy the entire old budget database to the new one. This is because we will probably want to use the same budget categories, and even budget amounts that we used in the previous year.

However, we wish to start out with zero amount spent and zero income received. It is for that reason that we clear those two fields using the REPLACE command. Finally, we again create the production index tag CAT to order this database.

Next we ask the question, "Do You Want to Edit The New Budget Database?" (see Figure 13.16). If the answer is "Yes", then we browse the database giving us the opportunity to alter the values and append and delete records. We then check to see if the user wants to pack the database (see Figure 13.17). If the answer is affirmative, then we pack it. Finally we close the database and restore the screen.

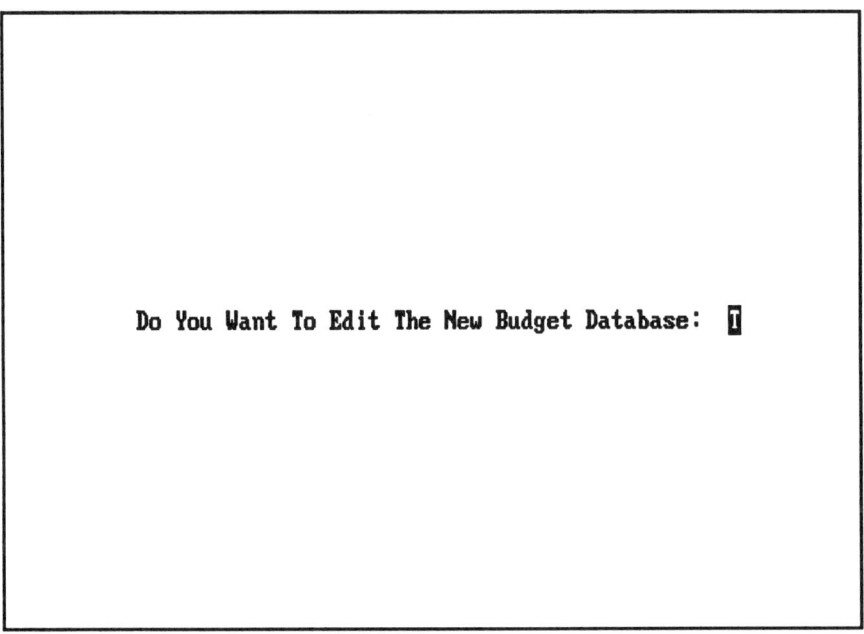

Figure 13.16 Second screen of SETUP.prg

13.6.2 The Design of CHANGEYR.prg

CHANGEYR.prg is a program which allows the user to change which particular accounts year that he or she may want to examine. This allows the user to save the ledgers and budgets for many years in the same directory. CHANGEYR.prg also gives the user the option of changing the default year stored in the memory file, YEAR.MEM. Listing 13.15 shows the program.

Note that once again we have a "Do Until" loop. The purpose of this loop is to insure the fact that we only choose a file name that actually exists in our current directory. This is accomplished by means of the **FILE()** function. If the argument of

```
                    Do You Want To Pack the New Budget:  ▮
```

Figure 13.17 Last Screen Displayed in SETUP.prg

FILE(*FileName*), *FileName*, does not exist, then **FILE()** returns the value of .F., otherwise it returns .T. . The loop is shown below and its flowchart is shown in Figure 13.18.

```
DO WHILE .T.
   @ 12,17 SAY "Enter Account Year Desired: " ;
      GET TRYYEAR
   READ
   ACCOUNT = "ACCOUN" + TRYYEAR + ".DBF"
   IF .NOT. FILE(ACCOUNT)
      @ 14,17 SAY ACCOUNT + " Does Not Exist. ;
         Try Another Year!"
      TRYYEAR = WHICHYEAR
   ELSE
      EXIT
   ENDIF
ENDDO
```

CASE STUDY
ACCOUNTS SYSTEM—MULTIPLE FILES

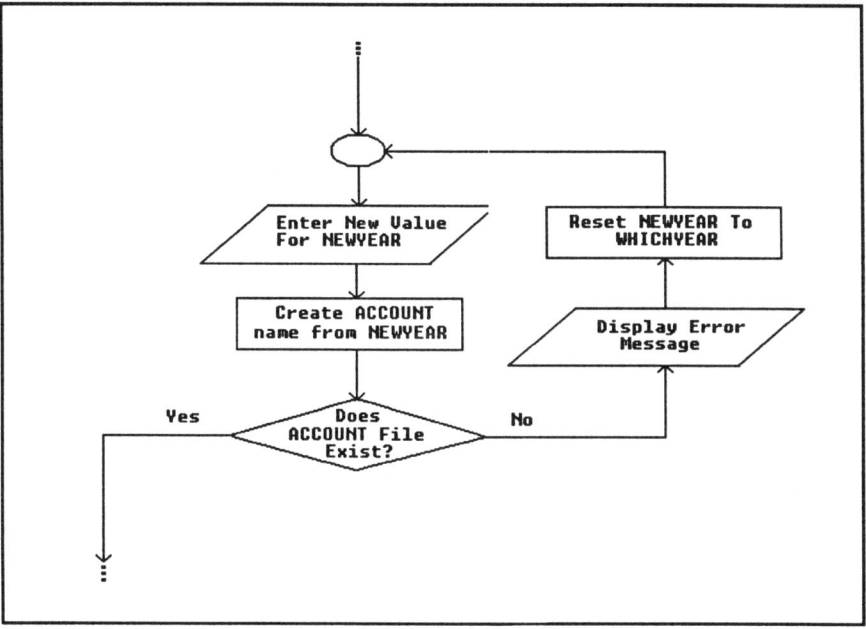

Figure 13.18 Flowchart of "Do Until" loop in CHANGEYR.prg

The ACCOUNT filename is put together by concatenating whatever year we enter for TRYYEAR (see Figure 13.19) with "ACCOUN" on the left and ".DBF" on the right. As long as we keep selecting years whose corresponding accounts do not exist, we will not be allowed to exit the loop, and we will get an appropriate error message. For example, were we to enter the year, "94", then we would get the error message shown in Figure 13.20. Note that we also try to help the user out by setting TRYYEAR to a year that we know exists, our tried and true WHICHYEAR. In our example shown in Figure 13.20, the year is set back to "92" which we all know exists. As soon as we select a year whose corresponding accounts file does exist (e.g. '93), we are allowed to exit.

Next we reassign our new updated NEWYEAR values to WHICHYEAR, ACCOUNT, and BUDGET. Then we ask the question, do you want to make this newly selected accounts year be the default year (i.e. shall we save it to our YEAR memory file?), as

```
* CHANGEYR.PRG
* This changes the Budget and Account Year Database
*
SAVE SCREEN TO ACCOSCREEN
STORE WHICHYEAR TO TRYYEAR
CLEAR
* Perform a Do Until Loop
DO WHILE .T.
  @ 12,17 SAY "Enter Account Year Desired: " GET TRYYEAR
  READ
  ACCOUNT = "ACCOUN" + TRYYEAR + ".DBF"
  IF .NOT. FILE(ACCOUNT)
    @ 14,17 SAY ACCOUNT + ;
            " Does Not Exist.  Try Another Year!"
    TRYYEAR = WHICHYEAR
  ELSE
    EXIT
  ENDIF
ENDDO
WHICHYEAR = TRYYEAR
ACCOUNT = "ACCOUN" + WHICHYEAR
BUDGET = "BUDGET" + WHICHYEAR
ANSWER = .F.
CLEAR
@ 12,20 SAY "Do You Want To Make " + WHICHYEAR + ;
        " The Default Year? "   GET ANSWER
READ
IF ANSWER
  THEYEAR = WHICHYEAR
  SET SAFETY OFF
  SAVE TO YEAR ALL LIKE THEYEAR
  SET SAFETY ON
ENDIF
RESTORE SCREEN FROM ACCOSCREEN
RETURN
```

Listing 13.15 The Program CHANGEYR.prg

ACCOUNTS SYSTEM—MULTIPLE FILES 491

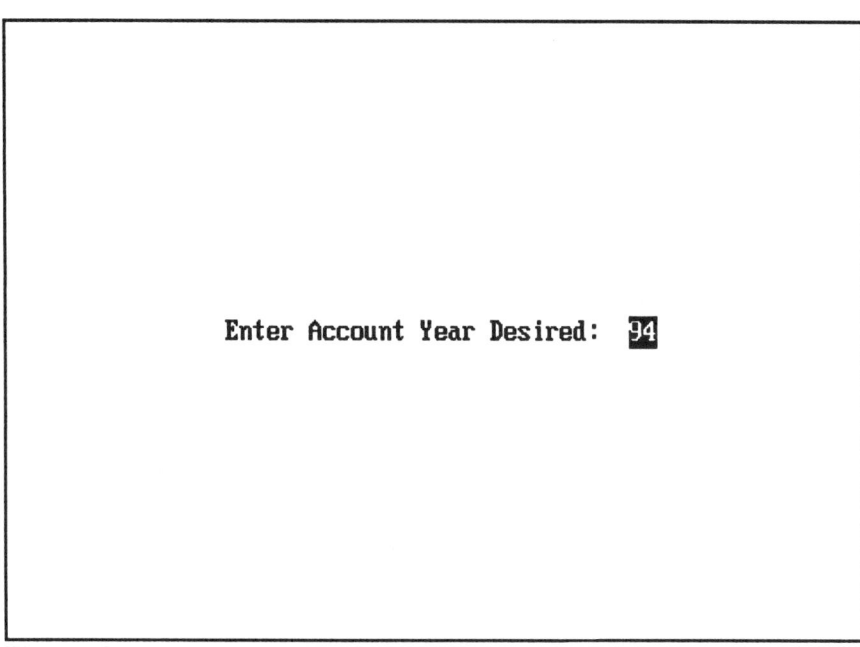

Figure 13.19 Opening Screen of CHANGEYR.prg

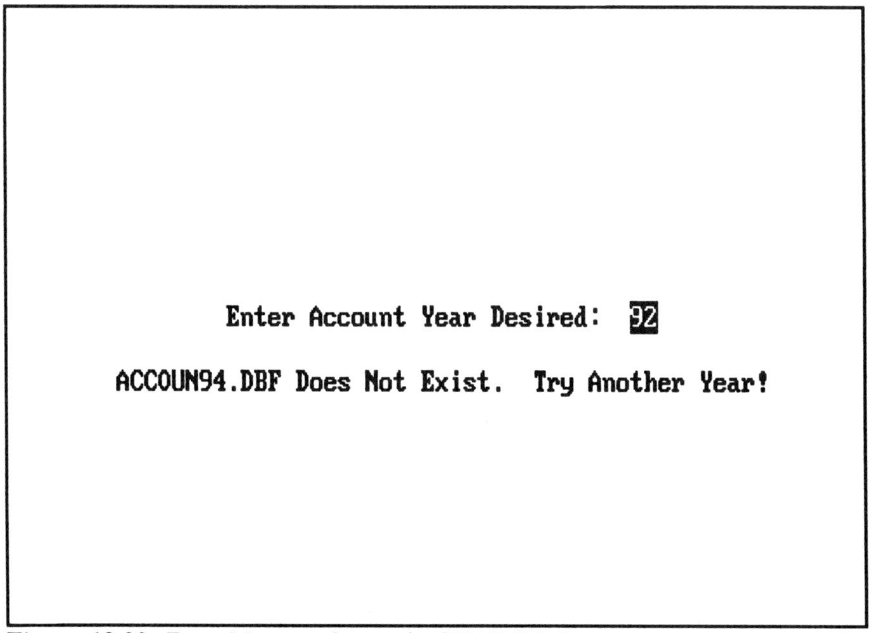

Figure 13.20 Error Message Screen in CHANGEYR.prg

shown in Figure 13.21. If the answer is yes, we save this new value to YEAR.MEM with the command: **SAVE TO** *MemoryFile* **ALL LIKE** *MemoryVariableExpression*, where YEAR.MEM is the *MemoryFile* and THEYEAR is the *MemoryVariableExpression*[45].

If we decide not to change the default year, then for the remainder of this particular session in the ACCOUNTS system, the NEWYEAR will be the ACCOUNTS year that we examine. However, the next time we run the system, the old year value contained in THEYEAR will again determine the ACCOUNTS year with which we work.

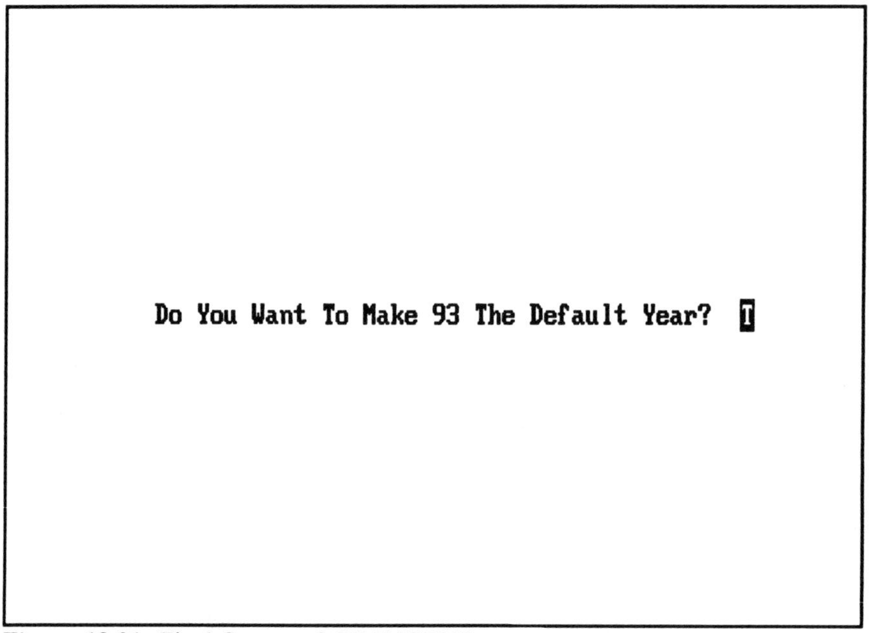

```
Do You Want To Make 93 The Default Year? ▮
```

Figure 13.21 Final Screen of CHANGEYR.prg

---

[45]The *MemoryVariableExpression* may be a wildcard expression as well as the name of a particular memory variable. In this way a wide range of selected memory variables may be saved while avoiding saving all the rest.

13.7 Use of FUNCTION and PICTURE in Design of SEARCAT.prg

We will now design the first of the search modules. These modules allow us to browse a selected portion of our ledger. The first of these will be SEARCAT.prg, the search module that does a selected browse of all transactions having to do with a particular category. The program is shown in Listing 13.16.

Since we must select a particular value for CAT, it would be good for us to be able to call CATHELP.prg, just as we did in BROWSIT.prg. For that reason, the program begins with: **ON KEY LABEL F1 DO CATHELP**. Next we ask the question as to what category we wish to filter on. This is shown in Figure 13.22.

Now that we've entered the value of CAT that we wish to limit our BROWSE to, we set our filter accordingly. If we're not at the end of the file (i.e. there are some records with that value of CAT in our database), then we browse them. Note that we do not include the BALANCE field in the browse as that field only is appropriate to the natural order of the database with no records missing. Figure 13.23 shows the browse when we have selected CAT="GRO".

After we're done with the browse, we calculate our totals for both the debits as well as the receipts. Then we display the results. Note the use of the **FUNCTION** and the **PICTURE** clauses. These two clauses give us great latitude in the way that we are able to display our data.

If we examine the totals output shown in Figure 13.24, we see that each number begins with a "$". This is controlled by the **FUNCTION "$"** clause. Note that the "Net Difference" also indicates whether the amount is a debit (DB) or a credit (CR). Figure 13.25 shows the browse of the case where we've chosen CAT="SAL" (Salary). Clearly the "Net Difference" should be positive in this case. Examining the resulting totals screen, shown in Figure 13.26, we see that the "Net Difference" is indeed a credit

```
* SEARCAT.PRG
* This does a category search on the database
*
ON KEY LABEL F1 DO CATHELP
USE &ACCOUNT
STORE [ ] TO WHICHCAT
CLEAR
@ 12,20 SAY "Enter Category to Be Searched: " GET WHICHCAT
READ
SET FILTER TO UPPER(CAT)=UPPER(WHICHCAT)
GOTO TOP
IF .NOT. EOF()
   BROW FIELD DATE, CHECK, DESCRIPT, BREAKDOWN, ;
      RECEIPTS, CASHED, CAT
ENDIF
CALCULATE SUM(DEBITS), SUM(RECEIPTS) TO;
      TOTDEBITS, TOTRECEIPT
CLEAR
@ 09,24 SAY "The Totals for Category " + WHICHCAT + " are:"
@ 11,24 SAY "Total Receipts = "
@ 11,41 SAY TOTRECEIPT FUNCTION "$" PICTURE "99,999.99"
@ 13,24 SAY "Total  Debits  = "
@ 13,41 SAY TOTDEBITS FUNCTION "$" PICTURE "99,999.99"
@ 15,24 SAY "Net Difference = "
@ 15,41 SAY TOTRECEIPT - TOTDEBITS FUNCTION "$CX" ;
                  PICTURE "99,999.99"
WAIT []
SET FILTER TO
USE
ON KEY LABEL F1
RETURN
```

Listing 13.16 Category Search Program: SEARCAT.prg

ACCOUNTS SYSTEM—MULTIPLE FILES

```
Enter Category to Be Searched: GRO
```

Figure 13.22 Opening Screen of SEARCAT.prg

DATE	CHECK	DESCRIPT	BREAKDOWN	RECEIPTS	CASHED	CAT
01/14/92	406	Shoprite: Groceries	18.60	0.00	T	GRO
01/14/92	407	Farmer's Market: Groceries	4.20	0.00	T	GRO
01/27/92	420	Great American: Groceries	39.92	0.00	F	GRO

Figure 13.23 Browse Screen resulting from choosing CAT="GRO"

(CR). This results from using the **FUNCTION "$CX"** clause (the **C** causes a "CR" to be displayed for a positive number, and the **X** causes a DB to be displayed for a negative number.) Table 13.1 gives a list of the format functions used in SAY instructions in dBASE IV.

The "99,999" template in the **PICTURE "99,999.99"** clause causes the numerical variable to be displayed using a comma if its value exceeds 999.99. **PICTURE** templates are used to format the data so that it appears just as you want it to. Table 13.2 shows the template symbols used in SAY instructions provided by dBASE IV.

The list of format functions and picture templates used for GET instructions, not only includes the functions and templates shown in Tables 13.1 and 13.2, but contains a few additional symbols[46].

The other two search modules, SEARDESC.prg and SEARCOUT.prg, contain no new concepts and so are left as exercises for the reader to create.

13.8 The Budget Report

Both LEDGREPO.prg and BUDGREPO.prg are very straightforward modules and are left up to the reader as exercises. The report form for LEDGREPO.prg, LEDGER.FRM, we already created in Chapter 4. The report form for BUDGREPO.prg should give an output that looks like that shown in Listing 13.17.

Note the formatting that is shown in Listing 13.17. There are commas and $ in the totals and also zero items are shown as blanks.

---

[46] A more complete list of the Format Functions and Picture Templates used with the GET instruction may be obtained from the DBASE IV LANGUAGE REFERENCE MANUAL or from such reference guides as: DBASE IV PROGRAMMER'S INSTANT REFERENCE, Alan Simpson, 2nd Edition, SYBEX, 1991.

ACCOUNTS SYSTEM—MULTIPLE FILES

```
The Totals for Category GRO are:

Total Receipts  =    $0.00

Total Debits    =    $62.72

Net Difference  =    $62.72 DB
```

Figure 13.24 The SEARCAT.PRG Totals for CAT="GRO"

DATE	CHECK	DESCRIPT	BREAKDOWN	RECEIPTS	CASHED	CAT
01/05/92		Deposit: Salary	0.00	750.00	T	SAL
01/19/92		Deposit: Salary	0.00	750.00	T	SAL

Figure 13.25 Browse Screen of SEARCAT for CAT="SAL"

Table 13.1 Format Functions used in SAY Instructions

Function	Description
!	Displays all letters in upper case
^	Displays numbers in scientific notation
$	Displays data in currency format
(	Encloses negative numbers in parentheses
B	Left-aligns text within a field
C	Displays CR(credit) after a positive number
D	The current SET DATE format for dates
E	European date format
I	Centers text within a field
J	Right-aligns text within a field
L	Displays leading zeroes
R	Inserts template characters into displayed data
Sn	Displays the left n characters of the data
X	Displays DB(debit) after a negative number
Z	Displays zero as a blank space

This was done by making use of the FUNCTION and PICTURE attributes in the "Display Attributes" screen of the report generator.

For example, the "Display Attributes" screen for the total of the BUDGETED field is shown in Figure 13.27. It is apparent that the PICTURE template has already been changed to "999,999.99" and that we're just about ready to select the picture function menu option. Striking the enter key, we get the picture function menu shown in Figure 13.28. Note that we have changed the default on "Currency" to "On". Accepting that selection by typing **Ctrl-End**, we return to the screen shown in Figure 13.29. This display attributes screen will give us the formatting for the AMOUNT BUDGETED total shown in Listing 13.17.

ACCOUNTS SYSTEM—MULTIPLE FILES

Table 13.2 Picture Template Symbols used in SAY Instructions

Template	Description
!	Converts letters to upper case
#	Allows only digits, blanks, & signs
$	Displays leading $'s in front of number
*	Displays asterisks in place of leading zeroes
.	Specifies decimal position
,	Displays if there are digits to left of comma
9	Allows only digits for character data Allows digits and signs for numeric data
other	Any other characters are added as template data

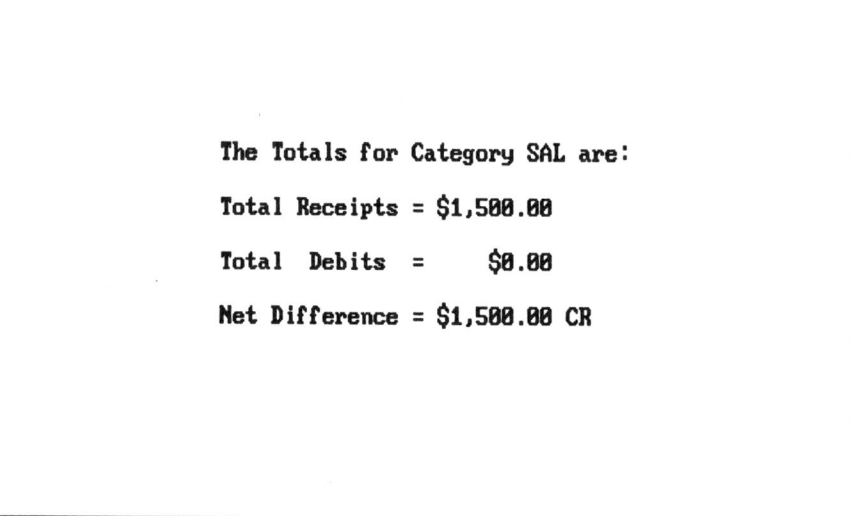

Figure 13.26 The Totals of SEARCAT.PRG for CAT="SAL"

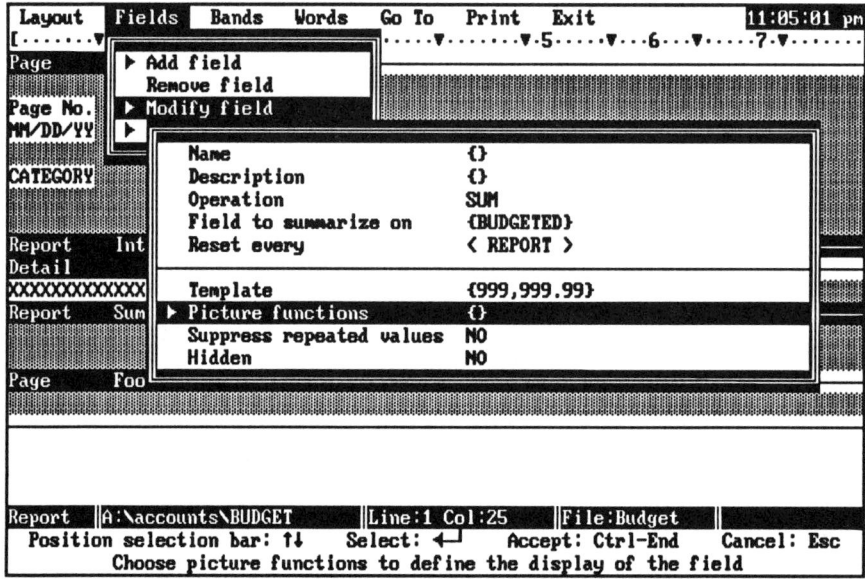

Figure 13.27 Display Attributes Screen For BUDGETED Total after changing the Picture Template to "999,999.99"

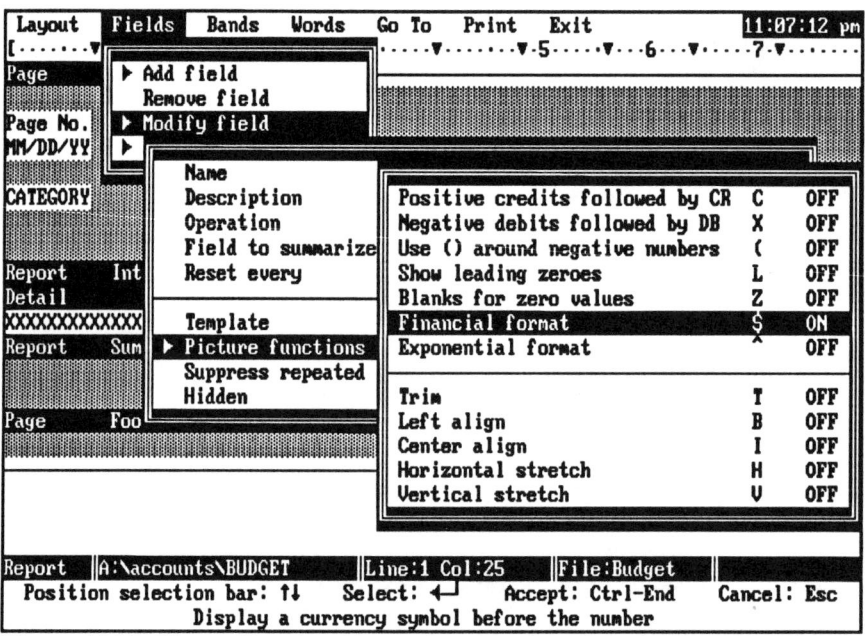

Figure 13.28 Picture Function Menu after changing Financial Format to **On**

ACCOUNTS SYSTEM—MULTIPLE FILES

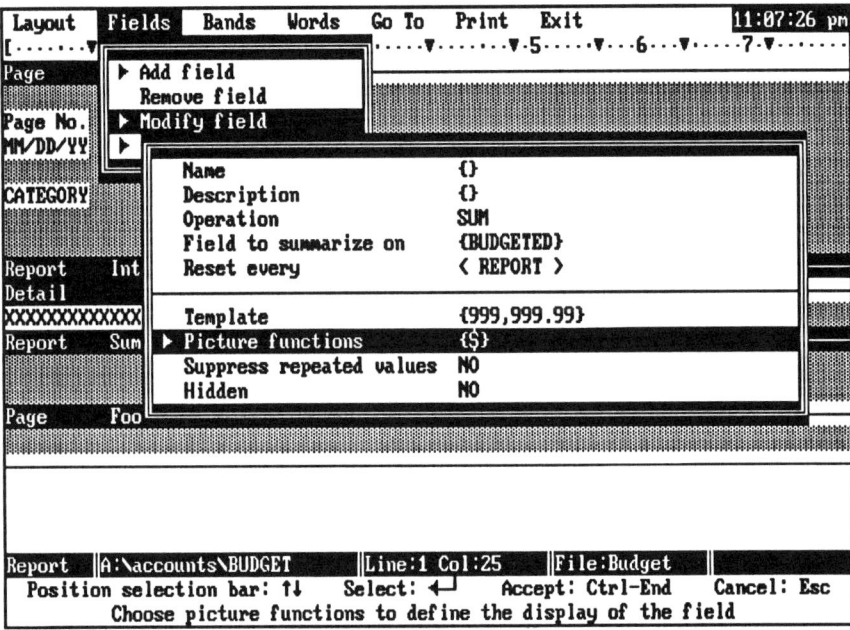

Figure 13.29 Final Display Attributes screen for BUDGETED Total

It is left as an exercise to the reader to reproduce the report shown in Listing 13.17 using these attributes.

This completes the design of the ACCOUNTS system.

13.9 Summary

In this chapter we have implemented a "Top Down" design of an ACCOUNTS system which uses two, or more, databases. We did this with an expanded version of our ACCOUNTS database along with a new BUDGET database that we designed. By using saved memory variables, we were able to select which year's ledger and budget we wish to access.

Stubs were introduced as a means of debugging our high level menus. The TOTAL command was introduced as a means of calculating the totals on each category in CAT. Using the SET

```
Page No.   1
05/09/91                              BUDGET REPORT

CATEGORY         CAT    AMOUNT       AMOUNT     EXPECTED    ACTUAL
                        BUDGETED     SPENT      INCOME      INCOME
BLANK
CABLE TV         CAB      240.00       20.00
CAR              CAR    1,000.00       44.65
DOCTORS          DOC      500.00      115.00
DONATIONS        DON      260.00       10.00
ENTERTAINMENT    ENT      300.00       60.59
GIFTS            GIF      300.00       25.66
GROCERIES        GRO    4,000.00       62.72
HOUSEHOLD        HOU      500.00      130.17
INSURANCE        INS      500.00      232.94
INTEREST         INT                              100.00
LOAN             LOA    3,000.00
MAINTENANCE      MAI    1,000.00       28.47
OTHER            OTH      400.00
PERSONAL         PER    2,400.00      180.32
PET              PET      500.00       38.50
REIMBURSEMENTS   REI                              400.00      38.25
SALARY           SAL                           19,500.00   1,500.00
TAX              TAX      200.00      105.00
TELEPHONE        TEL      600.00       50.00
TRAVEL           TRA      500.00
UTILITIES        UTI    1,800.00      110.12
         Totals:      $18,000.00   $1,214.14  $20,000.00  $1,538.25
```

Listing 13.17 Budget Report generated by BUDGET.FRM in BUDGREPO.prg

RELATION TO command, we were then able to drop all these totals into our BUDGET database very easily.

Next the concept of a "DO UNTIL" loop was presented. We implemented this loop by means of the instructions, DO WHILE .T., and EXIT.

The FILE() function was introduced as a means of determining whether or not a particular file exists in a directory.

Finally, the picture FUNCTION was introduced and the PICTURE template was examined in more detail in order to format our output in exactly the way we desired.

13.10 Review

In Chapter 12 we have presented the following new commands:

APPEND BLANK
CLOSE DATA
DO WHILE .T.
EXIT
SAVE TO *MemoryFile* ALL LIKE *MemVarExpression*
SELECT
SET RELATION TO
SKIP *n*
TOTAL

Add these instructions to your glossary of dBASE programming commands. In addition, add these new functions to your glossary of functions:

FILE()
VAL()

13.11 Laboratory Work

Go through all the steps outlined in this chapter. You will need to create the menu program, ACCOMENU.prg, in order to test the rest of the programs that are created in this chapter.

13.12 Exercises

1. Create the menu program: ACCOMENU.prg. The opening menu screen for this program appears in Figure 13.4. The system structure chart, which ACCOMENU.prg implements, is shown in Figure 13.2. In addition, you will need to write the CASE programs associated with this menu:

a) ACCOCASE.prg
b) BUDGCASE.prg
c) SET_CASE.prg
d) INQUCASE.prg
e) REPOCASE.prg

Hand these in.

2. Write the remaining inquiry programs, which are called by INQUCASE.prg (and hand these in):

   a) SEARDESC.prg does a browse of all the transactions having the DESCRIPTION entered.

   b) SEARCOUT.prg does a browse of all outstanding checks (those that have not been cashed).

3. Create the report form, BUDGET.FRM, which generates the output shown in Listing 13.17. Hand in an example of a report generated by this report form.

4. Write the report generating programs which are called by REPOCASE.prg (and hand them in):

   a) BUDGREPO.prg, which runs the BUDGET report form.

   b) LEDGREPO.prg, which runs the LEDGER report form.

5. Write the backup program, ACCOBACK.prg, which backs up the ACCOUNTS system on whatever backup medium that is relevant in your particular situation. Hand it in.

13.13 Term Project

Make an appointment with your instructor to demonstrate your system. Check over your system stepping through every module covering all possible input choices. (You can be reasonably confident that your instructor will ask you to demonstrate every facet of your system.) If there are parts to your system that have not been implemented, or whose implementation is not complete, or whose implementation has not been fully debugged, indicate this to the instructor at the very beginning of your project review session.

You might practice for this demonstration with your instructor by demonstrating your system to other students and eliciting their feedback.

CHAPTER 14

FUNCTIONS, ARRAYS & QUERIES

14.0   Topics Covered In Chapter 14

User-Defined Functions.

Arrays.

PUBLIC and PRIVATE memory variable declarations.

Inserting Memory Variables into a Screen Form.

Attaching Functions as a condition for accepting new values into a field in a Screen Form.

Creation of an automatically recalculating screen form.

Use of the Query Generator to create View Files.

Using Query Generator to create View files of Multiple Databases with Multiple Keys.

Use of the JOIN command.

Use of the UPDATE command.

14.1 User Defined Functions

In this chapter we'll be talking about some advanced topics that will not only increase the productivity of the user, but also give his/her work that professional touch.

We'll start by proposing an enhancement to be made to the budget system we developed in the preceding chapter. It would be nice if we were able to adjust our budget items on the screen and have the new totals appear before us instantaneously in much the same fashion as they would in a spreadsheet[47]. In this way we could quickly make both sides of our budget, income and expenditures, balance without having to change back and forth between screens. In order to accomplish this task, we need to introduce three new concepts: user-defined functions, arrays, and public and private memory variables.

14.1.1 Elements of User-Defined Functions

Let us begin by formally defining what a function is. A function is a process which operates on a particular argument or arguments that are sent to it and returns a value in response. A user-defined function is simply a function that has been defined by the user, rather than by dBASE.

User-defined functions not only make programming simpler, but they also can make certain operations possible that can be done no other way. In order to use a user defined function, it is first necessary to create a procedure file in which it can be imbedded. The reason for this is that a function must always be in memory so that when program operation comes across one, it knows exactly what to do without having to search the disk for it.

---

[47]Spreadsheets are another type of application program which allow you to mathematically interrelate different fields (cells) on a screen such that whenever changes are made to one item, all other affected items are instantaneously updated. Lotus 123 is an example of such an application.

FUNCTIONS, ARRAYS & QUERIES

If we look at the functions with which we have been dealing, we notice that a function always has parentheses following it [e.g. EOF(), CTOD("12/31/92")]. Within these parentheses go the arguments to the functions. There may be zero arguments [e.g. PAGENO()], or there might be three arguments [e.g. STR(TOTAL,8,2)], or anything in between. These arguments are referred to as parameters and are the values sent to the function to be operated on.

The format for a function is as follows:

FUNCTION *FunctionName*
PARAMETERS *Argument1, Argument2, ...*
   Command 1
   Command 2
   .
   .
   .
   Command N
RETURN *ValueReturned*

Let's look at an example of a commonly generated user defined function. There is no function in dBASE IV which will give you the normal full character date. Rather than go to all the trouble to which we went in order to generate the full date for our mailmerge letter, let's simply define a function which will generate it for us.

14.1.2 Function Example: CDATE()

We would like a date function that instead of yielding: **"12/31/92"** , for example, would yield: **Thursday, December 31, 1992.** To do this, we would create the following procedure file which we will call **FUNCTION.PRG**. (We could have given it any name we wanted.)

. **MODIFY COMMAND FUNCTION**

The Listing 14.1 shows that the function name, CDATE, is given immediately after the FUNCTION declaration statement. The single parameter is the date which is contained in the parentheses of CDATE(), when the function is called. The manipulations that we use to obtain the character day of the week, the numeric day of the week as a string of characters, the character month, and the year as a string of characters are the standard ones we have used in the past. We concatenate them all together, and we return this full date.

Turning the procedure file on, we can then produce the desired date format simply by using the standard print to screen command:

. SET PROCEDURE TO FUNCTION
. ? CDATE(CTOD("12/31/92"))
Thursday, December 31, 1992

Now we may use this newly defined function just as we use any other dBASE function, so long as the procedure file is active.

```
FUNCTION CDATE
PARAMETERS   TheDate
  SET TALK OFF
  STORE CDOW(TheDate) TO DayOfWeek
  STORE TRIM(STR(DAY(TheDate),2)) To TheDay
  STORE CMONTH(TheDate) TO TheMonth
  STORE STR(YEAR(TheDate),4) to TheYear
  STORE DayOfWeek + ", " + TheMonth + " " ;
     + TheDay + ", " + TheYear TO FullDate
RETURN FullDate
```

Listing 14.1 User-Defined Function: **CDATE()** contained in the Procedure file **FUNCTIONS.PRG**

14.2 Use of Arrays in dBASE

The easiest way to think of an array is to think of it as a database that is kept in memory as a series of memory variables rather than on the disk as a file. The reason that you would want such a thing is for two principle reasons: 1) Speed in accessibility; 2) Being able to access database data while you are locked to a particular record. It is this latter reason that brings up the need to introduce this topic here.

In an array, information is divided into rows and columns[48], just as in a Browse screen. Were you to copy a database into an array, each column would contain a different field, and each row would contain a different record. An array refers to the information contained within it through the use of subscripts. For example, were we to create an array called BUDARRAY, then we would refer to each of the elements in BUDARRAY through their row number and column number: **BUDARRAY**[*RowNumber, ColumnNumber*]. So if we wanted to refer to the information contained in row number 1 and column number 2, we might type:

. ? BUDARRAY[1,2]

Just as you create a database, you must **DECLARE** an array. This is because the computer must know how much memory to set aside for this quantity of data. The DECLARE statement has the syntax:

DECLARE *ArrayName* [*MaxNumberRows,*
 MaxNumberColumns]

Supposing BUDARRAY had 6 columns and 22 rows, the declaration statement would be:

. **DECLARE BUDGET[22,6]**

---

[48] If an array has but one column, then the column number can be omitted.

Our next step will be to copy the contents of the database, BUDGET.dbf to BUDARRAY. This is done with the **COPY TO ARRAY** command. The syntax for this command is: **COPY TO ARRAY** *ArrayName* . This copies the currently open database to the array whose name is **ArrayName**. In our case the steps would be:

. USE BUDGET
. DECLARE BUDARRAY[RECCOUNT(),6]
. COPY TO ARRAY BUDARRAY

Note that for the maximum number of records in our array, we used the function **RECCOUNT()** which will give the number of records in the currently open database. Since we're copying the entire database into an array, it is only natural that we would want to make our row specification subject to the current number of records in the database. Since there are six fields, and this doesn't change, we can fix the number of columns to a constant. The structure of BUDGET.dbf is shown in Listing 14.2.

```
Number of data records:        22
Date of last update   : 03/31/92
Field  Field Name  Type         Width     Dec     Index
    1  CATEGORY    Character       18                 N
    2  CAT         Character        3                 N
    3  BUDGETED    Numeric          8      2          N
    4  SPENT       Numeric          8      2          N
    5  EXPECT_INC  Numeric          8      2          N
    6  INCOME      Numeric          8      2          N
** Total **                        54
```

Listing 14.2 Structure of the Database BUDGET.dbf

If we did not wish to copy all the fields into the array, but simply those that we wish to utilize, then we would use the **FIELDS** option. In this case the syntax is: **COPY TO ARRAY** *ArrayName* **FIELDS** *Field1, Field2,..., FieldN*. Since the only fields that we really need are the four numeric fields, we will use this form of the command. Now our commands become:

. **USE BUDARRAY**
. **DECLARE BUDARRAY[RECCOUNT(),4]**
. **COPY TO ARRAY BUDARRAY FIELDS BUDGETED,;**
    SPENT, EXPECT_INC, INCOME
. **DISPLAY MEMORY**

Listing 14.3 shows how the data is stored in the database. The result of the last command (the first 10 rows of data) is shown in Listing 14.4. This shows how the values are stored in memory. Compare the two data storage formats.

CATEGORY	CAT	BUDGETED	SPENT	EXPECT_INC	INCOME
BLANK					
CABLE TV	CAB	240.00			
CAR	CAR	1000.00	44.65		
DOCTORS	DOC	500.00	115.00		
DONATIONS	DON	260.00	10.00		
ENTERTAINMENT	ENT	300.00	60.59		
GIFTS	GIF	300.00	25.66		
GROCERIES	GRO	4000.00	62.72		
HOUSEHOLD	HOU	500.00	138.17		
INSURANCE	INS	500.00	232.94		
INTEREST	INT			100.00	
LOAN	LOA	3000.00			
MAINTENANCE	MAI	1000.00	28.47		
OTHER	OTH	400.00			
PERSONAL	PER	2500.00	180.32		
PET	PET	500.00	38.50		
REIMBURSEMENTS	REI			400.00	38.25
SALARY	SAL			19500.00	1500.00
TAX	TAX	200.00	105.00		
TELEPHONE	TEL	600.00	50.00		
TRAVEL	TRA	500.00			
UTILITIES	UTI	1000.00	110.12		

Listing 14.3 Contents of database BUDGET.dbf

```
BUDARRAY    pub  A  [22, 4]
  [1, 1]    elem N         0     (0.000000000000000000)
  [1, 2]    elem N         0     (0.000000000000000000)
  [1, 3]    elem N         0     (0.000000000000000000)
  [1, 4]    elem N         0     (0.000000000000000000)
  [2, 1]    elem N       240     (240.000000000000000)
  [2, 2]    elem N         0     (0.000000000000000000)
  [2, 3]    elem N         0     (0.000000000000000000)
  [2, 4]    elem N         0     (0.000000000000000000)
  [3, 1]    elem N      1000     (1000.000000000000000)
  [3, 2]    elem N     44.65     (44.650000000000000)
  [3, 3]    elem N         0     (0.000000000000000000)
  [3, 4]    elem N         0     (0.000000000000000000)
  [4, 1]    elem N       500     (500.000000000000000)
  [4, 2]    elem N       115     (115.000000000000000)
  [4, 3]    elem N         0     (0.000000000000000000)
  [4, 4]    elem N         0     (0.000000000000000000)
  [5, 1]    elem N       260     (260.000000000000000)
  [5, 2]    elem N        10     (10.000000000000000)
  [5, 3]    elem N         0     (0.000000000000000000)
  [5, 4]    elem N         0     (0.000000000000000000)
  [6, 1]    elem N       300     (300.000000000000000)
  [6, 2]    elem N     60.59     (60.590000000000000)
  [6, 3]    elem N         0     (0.000000000000000000)
  [6, 4]    elem N         0     (0.000000000000000000)
  [7, 1]    elem N       300     (300.000000000000000)
  [7, 2]    elem N     25.66     (25.660000000000000)
  [7, 3]    elem N         0     (0.000000000000000000)
  [7, 4]    elem N         0     (0.000000000000000000)
  [8, 1]    elem N      4000     (4000.000000000000000)
  [8, 2]    elem N     62.72     (62.720000000000000)
  [8, 3]    elem N         0     (0.000000000000000000)
  [8, 4]    elem N         0     (0.000000000000000000)
  [9, 1]    elem N       500     (500.000000000000000)
  [9, 2]    elem N    138.17     (138.170000000000000)
  [9, 3]    elem N         0     (0.000000000000000000)
  [9, 4]    elem N         0     (0.000000000000000000)
 [10, 1]    elem N       500     (500.000000000000000)
 [10, 2]    elem N    232.94     (232.940000000000000)
 [10, 3]    elem N         0     (0.000000000000000000)
 [10, 4]    elem N         0     (0.000000000000000000)
```

Listing 14.4 First ten rows of the array BUDGET

FUNCTIONS, ARRAYS & QUERIES

As a last step, let's calculate the totals for each of our four numeric columns of data and store the results as memory variables. We will need these variables when we create our customized screen form.

```
. SUM BUDGETED, SPENT, EXPECT_INC, INCOME ;
    TO TOTALBUDG, TOTALSPENT, TOTALEXPEC,;
    TOTALINCOME
```

We'll want to put all these steps together in a program so that we can generate our array upon demand without having to remember all the details we just went through. In order to do this, we need to introduce one more new concept: PUBLIC memory variables.

14.3 PUBLIC & PRIVATE Memory Variables

You may have noticed that all the memory variables that we have created in the programs that we have written ceased to exist once the program execution was over. This is dBASE's way of tidying up and saving unused memory space. The problem that this presents to us is what if we use a program in which to create memory variables which will be used elsewhere (i.e. at the command line, or in another program).

The way to get around this problem is to declare the memory variables that we intend to create as **PUBLIC** memory variables. If they are PUBLIC, then they will continue to exist after the program is over.

In general undeclared memory variables defined within a program are said to be **PRIVATE** with respect to any program (or command line) which calls the program. Undeclared variables (those not declared as PUBLIC or PRIVATE) defined in a program are released when the program returns to the command line.

Let's see what happens when we define three memory variables: one a PUBLIC memory variable, one a PRIVATE memory variable, and one an undeclared memory variable, and then execution is transferred to another program. In Figure 14.1 we have a program B which is called by a program A (e.g. program A might be a menu program which calls program B among others). In addition, suppose program B calls some program C. Now suppose that we create three memory variables in program B: an undeclared memory variable, **Dog** (no declaration as to PUBLIC or PRIVATE); a PUBLIC memory variable, **Cat**; and a PRIVATE memory variable, **Mouse**. These memory variables will exist as long as program B is running. However, as soon as the execution returns to program A, what happens to them depends on how they were declared. The undeclared memory variable, **Dog**, will cease to exist. The PUBLIC memory variable, **Cat**, will continue to exist. The PRIVATE memory variable, **Mouse**, will of course cease to exist. The story is somewhat different in program C, which is called by program B. Here, both **Dog** and **Cat** exist. Only **Mouse** will cease to exist.

Cat, of course, will exist everywhere since it is PUBLIC, and **Mouse** will exist only in program B, since it is **PRIVATE** in program B. **Dog**, the undeclared memory variable, has a more interesting story. **Dog** is said to be PUBLIC for all programs called by program B, but is said to be PRIVATE for all programs calling program B (above program B in hierarchy).

The rule is: *undeclared memory variables are always assumed PUBLIC to those programs which are called by the program which created the memory variables, but are always assumed PRIVATE with respect to those programs which call the program which created the memory variables.*

The command line (dot prompt) is always considered to be the highest level from which programs are called. In the example shown in Figure 14.1, the command line is assumed to call program A. These rules can be circumvented by means of the PUBLIC and PRIVATE declaration commands. The syntax is: **PUBLIC** *Variable1, Variable2, ...* ; and **PRIVATE** *Variable1, Variable2, ...*

FUNCTIONS, ARRAYS & QUERIES

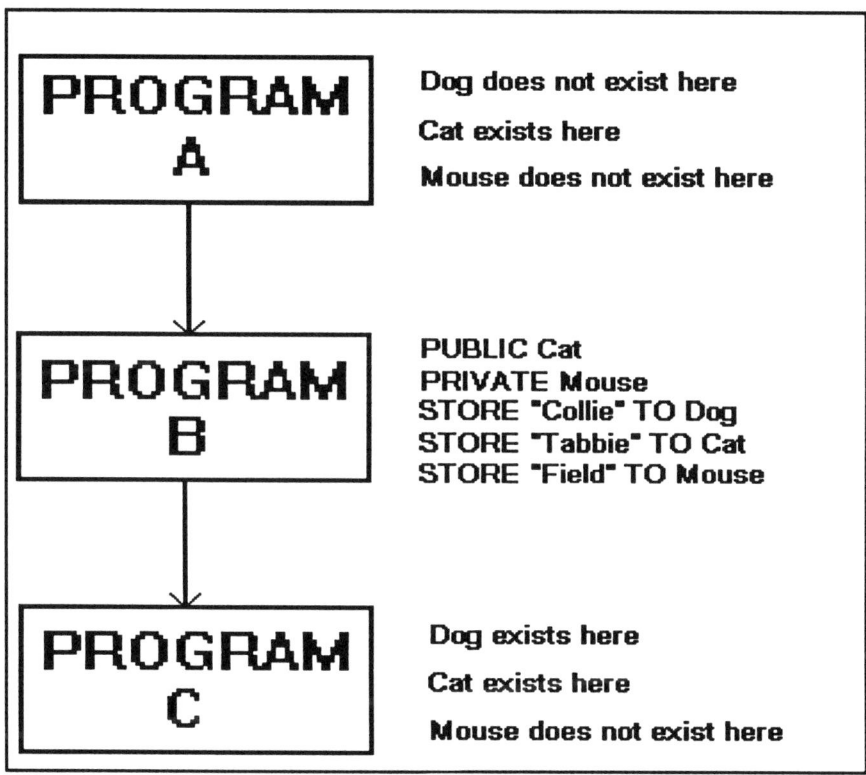

Figure 14.1 Effect of PUBLIC, PRIVATE and undeclared Memory Variables as we Move Between Programs

Listing 14.5 shows the program MAKEARRA.prg. This program circumvents the rule by declaring all our memory variables as being PUBLIC. Now they will persist once the program is over.

In the same way, we can always override the rule by declaring variables used in any program as PUBLIC or PRIVATE depending on how we want them to behave. Note that it is usually good practice to declare all memory variables either PUBLIC or PRIVATE depending on how far reaching you want them to be. Most of the time, memory variables should be PRIVATE so that if a variable of the same name is used in more than one place, it will not affect its use in any other place.

```
* MAKEARRA.PRG
* This creates the Array: BUDGET, plus the
* totals on each of the columns of the
* array.  The array and the Totals are
* created as PUBLIC memory variables so
* that they may be examined at the command
* line.  These values need to be
* preset so that the Screen, BUDGET.SCR
* can be generated.
*
PUBLIC BUDGET, TOTALBUDG, TOTALSPENT,;
   TOTALEXPEC, TOTALINCOM, DUMMY, BUDARRAY
BUDGET = "BUDGET92"
DUMMY = .T.
USE &BUDGET
DECLARE BUDARRAY[RECCOUNT(),4]
COPY TO ARRAY BUDARRAY FIELDS BUDGETED,;
   SPENT, EXPECT_INC, INCOME
SUM BUDGETED, SPENT, EXPECT_INC, INCOME ;
   TO TOTALBUDG, TOTALSPENT, TOTALEXPEC,;
   TOTALINCOM
GOTO TOP
RETURN
```

Listing 14.5 Program MAKEARRA.prg which creates the BUDGET array and its totals

Likewise, unless it is the intention of the user to have the memory variables available once program execution has returned to the command line, it is best to RELEASE all PUBLIC memory variables before leaving the program.

Now that we have this array data and the rest of the memory variables in memory, we are now ready to design our screen form which will allow us to play with our budget. This was a necessary step for us to take as our screen generator will not allow us to insert memory variables that have not been previously defined.

14.4 Inserting Memory Variables Into a Customized Screen Form

Using the standard methods that we devised in Chapter 6, we can create a format screen for BUDGET.

. CREATE SCREEN BUDGET

Figure 14.2 shows the customized screen after we have included all of the standard fields from our Budget database. We are now ready to add into our form the additional memory variables which contain the sum of the four columns. To do this, we select Fields Menu window as usual. But this time, instead of choosing the option, "Add Field", we choose the option, "Insert Memory Variable" as shown in Figure 14.3.

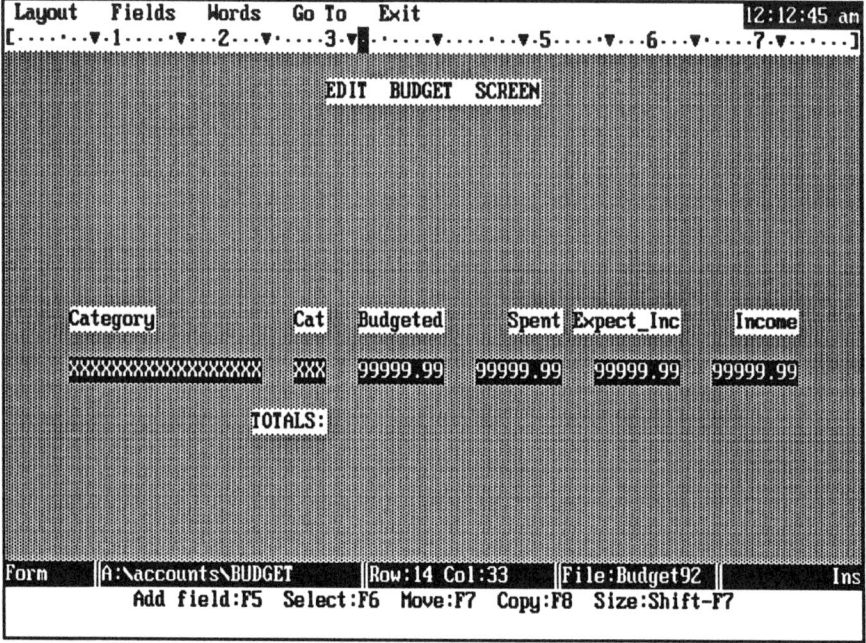

Figure 14.2 Screen Form for BUDGET after adding standard fields

520   FUNCTIONS, ARRAYS & QUERIES

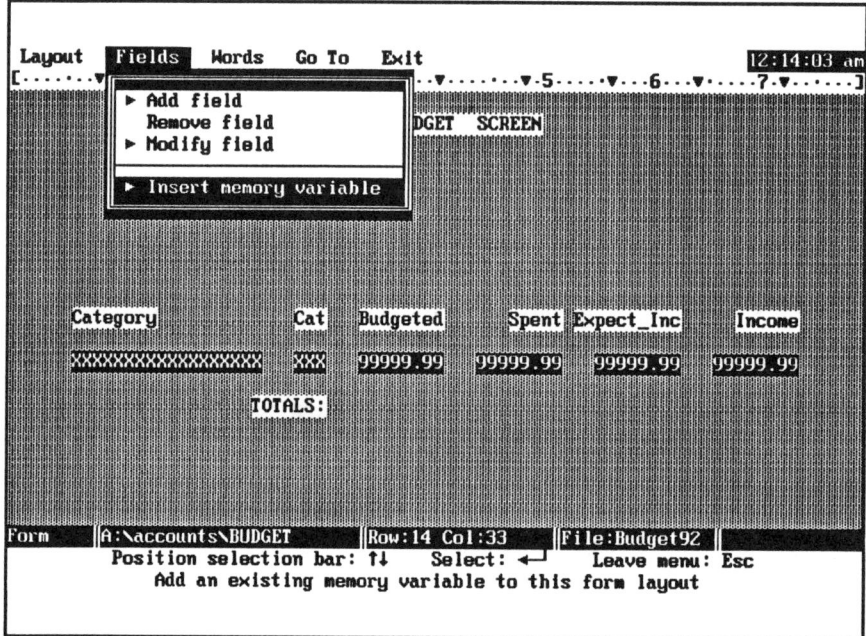

Figure 14.3 Selecting Menu Option "Insert Memory Variable"

Next we type in the name of the memory variable that we wish to insert, TOTALBUDG, as shown in Figure 14.4. Then we have to identify that the variable type is numeric as shown in Figure 14.5. The template then needs to be adjusted so that it is only 8 characters wide with two decimal places, as shown in Figure 14.6.

Finally, we need to set an edit option so that these particular memory variables may not be edited directly on the screen. The values that are shown will be the results of calculations that are made on the database (array) values. Figure 14.6 shows us selecting the "Edit Option", and Figure 14.7 shows us changing the "Editing Allowed" option from **YES** to **NO**. Having done this, we do two Ctrl-End keystrokes and return to the Screen shown in Figure 14.8.

Repeating this process for the other three total memory variables: TOTALSPENT, TOTALEXPEC, TOTALINCOM; we obtain the screen shown in Figure 14.9. We can now exit and save the screen, BUDGET.SCR. We are not quite done with it yet, but we first need to define a new user-defined function that we will use to update the screen while we are in the EDIT mode.

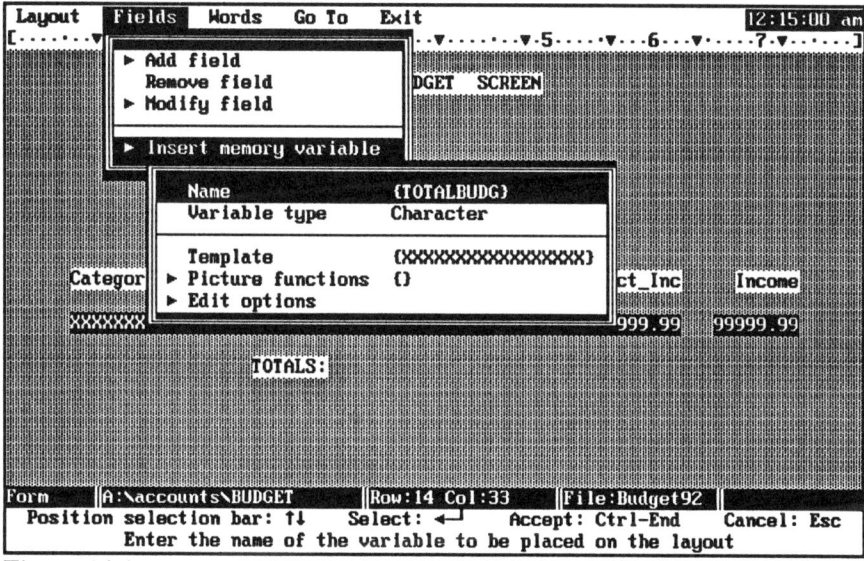

Figure 14.4 Inserting the Memory Variable TOTALBUDG

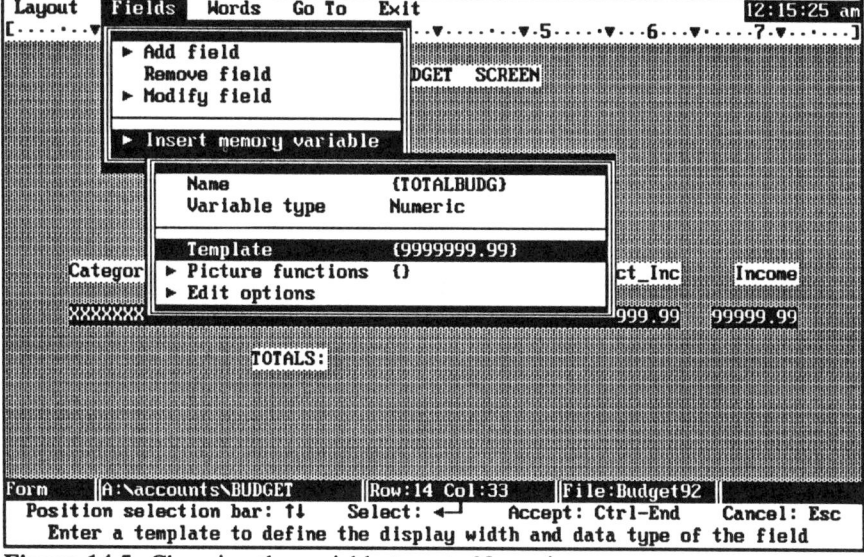

Figure 14.5 Changing the variable type to Numeric

522 FUNCTIONS, ARRAYS & QUERIES

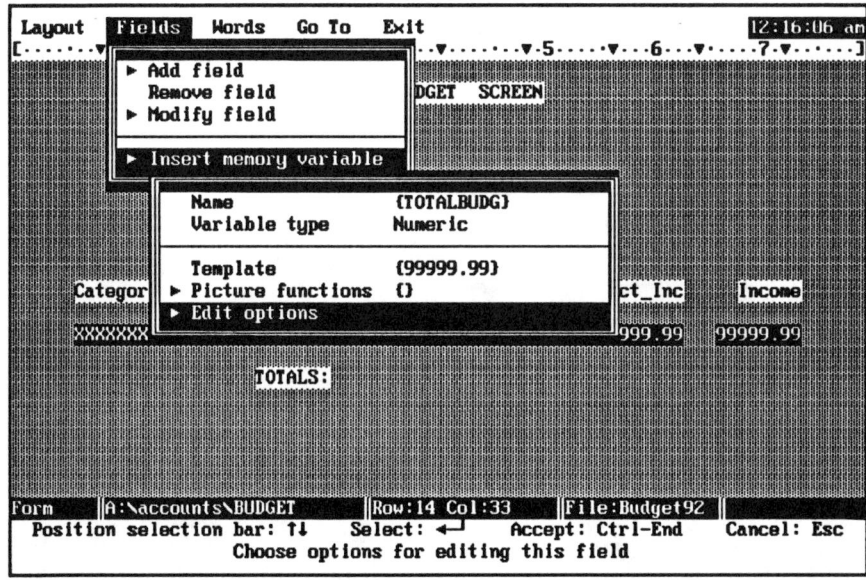

Figure 14.6 Choosing Edit Options on Menu

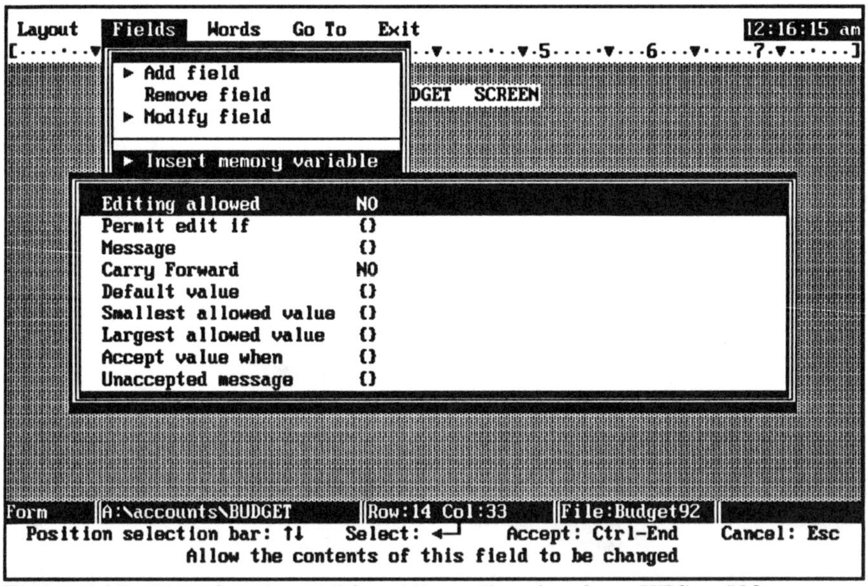

Figure 14.7 Changing the "Editing Allowed" option from **YES** to **NO**

FUNCTIONS, ARRAYS & QUERIES 523

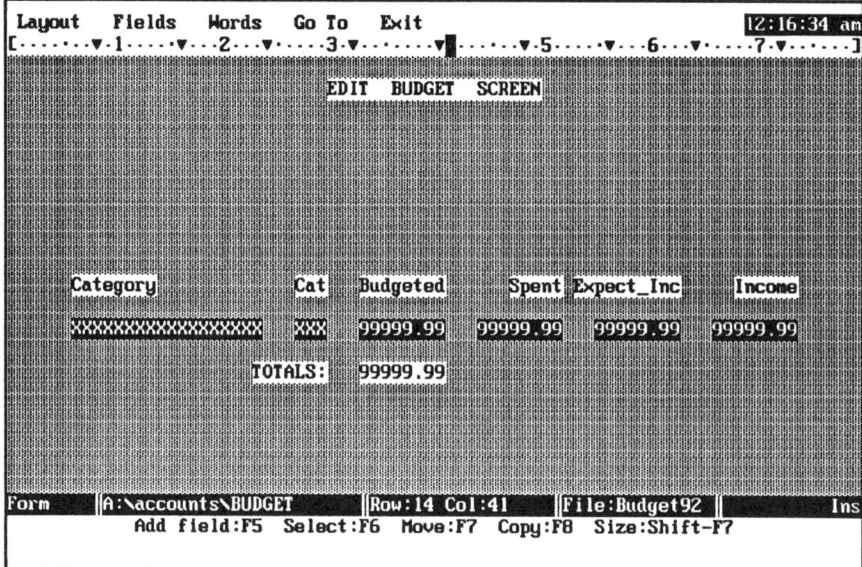

Figure 14.8 BUDGET screen with new Memory Variable, TOTALBUDG, Added

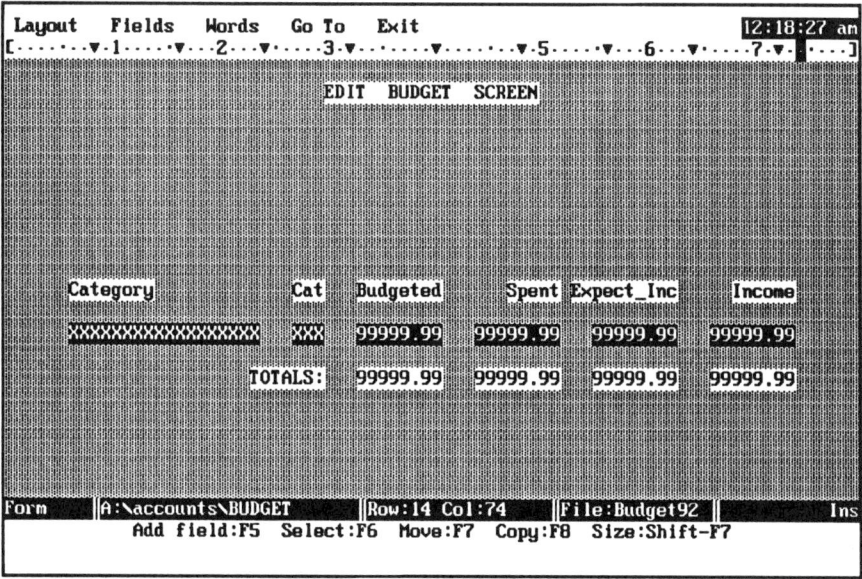

Figure 14.9 BUDGET Screen with four Memory Variable Totals Added

14.5 Design of the Re-Calculation Function: RETOTAL()

We will now design **RETOTAL(*amount*)**, which will recalculate the totals for BUDGETED, SPENT, EXPECT_INC, and INCOME each time any one of those fields is altered in any way. Listing 14.6 shows the program. The parameter to the function can be anything, as its value will be ignored. However, as something must be there, we have provided the dummy memory variable. The first step is to record the current value from the screen into the array at the current record number. In this way, any change made to the database from the keyboard will be immediately incorporated.

Next we preset all the totals to be zero in preparation for re-totaling. Then we start our counter at 1, and enter a loop which will sum for all the rows in the array (which is equivalent to all the records in our BUDGET database). Now we accumulate our totals for each of our four fields. Furthermore, we increment our row number each time we go through the loop until we've done all RECCOUNT() number of rows in the array.

When we have accumulated all our totals for the array, we leave the loop and very carefully display these new amounts on the screen in precisely the same locations that they were defined to be in the format file. Hence, each time a change is made, the result of it is immediately laid on top of whatever value might have been in the total row previously. This has the effect of updating our screen instantaneously. We end our function by returning the PROCEED value of .T.. This allows the screen to carry on with its display.

Let's save our function in a procedure file called **BUDGPROC.prg**. Now we need to attach our new function to each of the four fields in our BUDGET screen form.

14.5.1 Attaching a Function to a Screen Entry

We must begin by setting "on" our new procedure file:

. SET PROCEDURE TO BUDGPROC

```
FUNCTION RETOTAL
* Re-Totals all the BUDGETED, SPENT,
* EXPECT_INC, and INCOME fields contained in
* BUDARRAY, as field values are changed on
* the Format Screen BUDGET.
*
PARAMETERS DUMMY
*   This part of the program grabs the changes
*   from the screen and stores them in the
*   array so that the array is always up to date
*
    BUDARRAY[RECNO(),1] = BUDGETED
    BUDARRAY[RECNO(),2] = SPENT
    BUDARRAY[RECNO(),3] = EXPECT_INC
    BUDARRAY[RECNO(),4] = INCOME
*   This presets all our accumulated Totals
*   to zero
    TOTALBUDG  = 0
    TOTALSPENT = 0
    TOTALEXPEC = 0
    TOTALINCOM = 0
    ROW = 1       && Start with record number 1
*   Total for every record in the database BUDGET
    DO WHILE ROW <= RECCOUNT()
       TOTALBUDG  = BUDARRAY[ROW,1] + TOTALBUDG
       TOTALSPENT = BUDARRAY[ROW,2] + TOTALSPENT
       TOTALEXPEC = BUDARRAY[ROW,3] + TOTALEXPEC
       TOTALINCOM = BUDARRAY[ROW,4] + TOTALINCOM
       ROW = ROW + 1
    ENDDO
*   Now replace the values on the screen with
*   new Totals
    @ 10,33 SAY TOTALBUDG  PICTURE "99999.99"
    @ 10,44 SAY TOTALSPENT PICTURE "99999.99"
    @ 10,55 SAY TOTALEXPEC PICTURE "99999.99"
    @ 10,66 SAY TOTALINCOM PICTURE "99999.99"
*   Return a logical value of .T. to calling
*   program
    PROCEED = .T.
RETURN PROCEED
```

Listing 14.6 Function RETOTAL contained in Procedure FUNCPROC

526 FUNCTIONS, ARRAYS & QUERIES

Now we are ready to go back into our screen form, BUDGET, in order to make our final modification.

. MODIFY SCREEN BUDGET

Placing the cursor on the first numeric field, **BUDGETED**, we pull down the fields menu by striking Alt-F. This time we select: **Modify Existing Field**.

This time we move down to the "**Accept Value When**" option (see Figure 14.10), and we type in the name of the function that we want to use to control the values entered on the screen. Now each time we place a new value in that field, this function will take control and retotal all the totals and display the new results, before the value is accepted in the field.

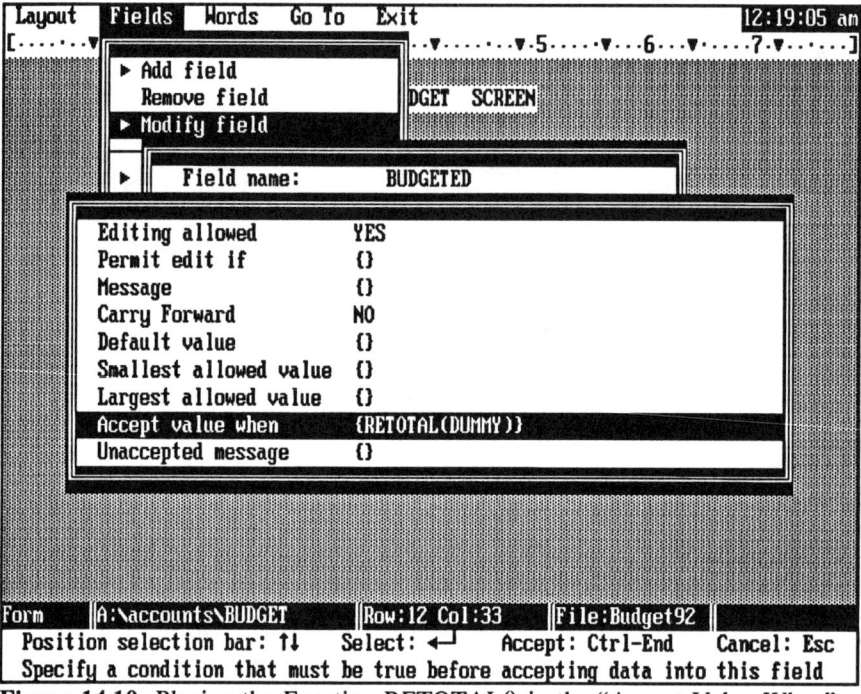

Figure 14.10 Placing the Function RETOTAL() in the "Accept Value When" entry

For example, let's now go into the edit mode and modify the first record in BUDGET. Figure 14.11 shows the record labeled BLANK. Note that our budget shows us currently making $20,000 this year but only spending $18,000. This means that we have $2,000 we can put in a savings account. Figure 14.12 shows where we have replaced the word "BLANK" with "SAVINGS" and have added a BUDGETED amount of $2,000 to this record. As soon as we touch the Enter key, note that the TOTALBUDG amount just below the $2,000 has immediately changed to $20,000. Our budget is now balanced.

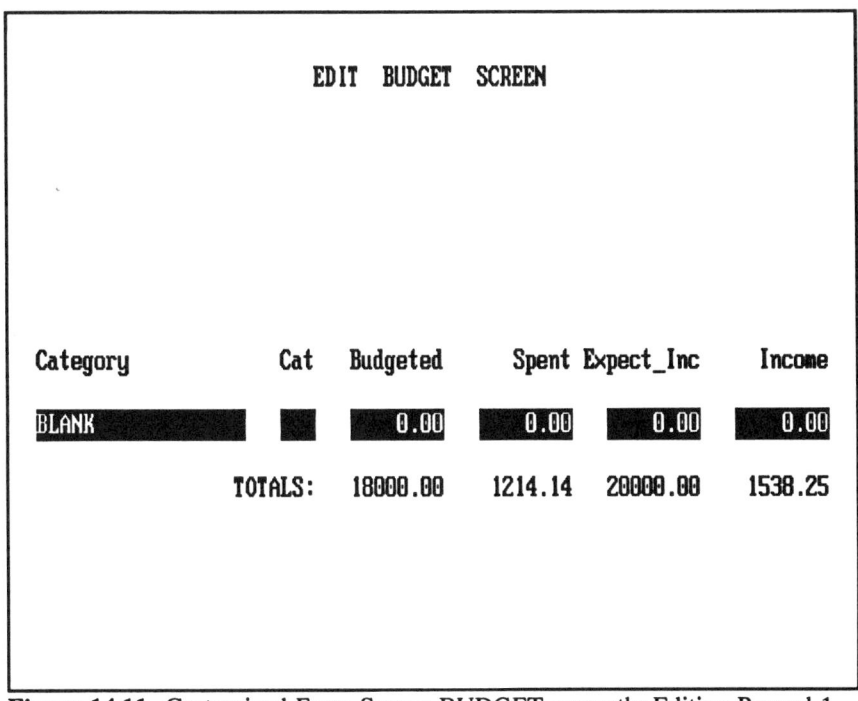

Figure 14.11 Customized Form Screen BUDGET currently Editing Record 1

528 FUNCTIONS, ARRAYS & QUERIES

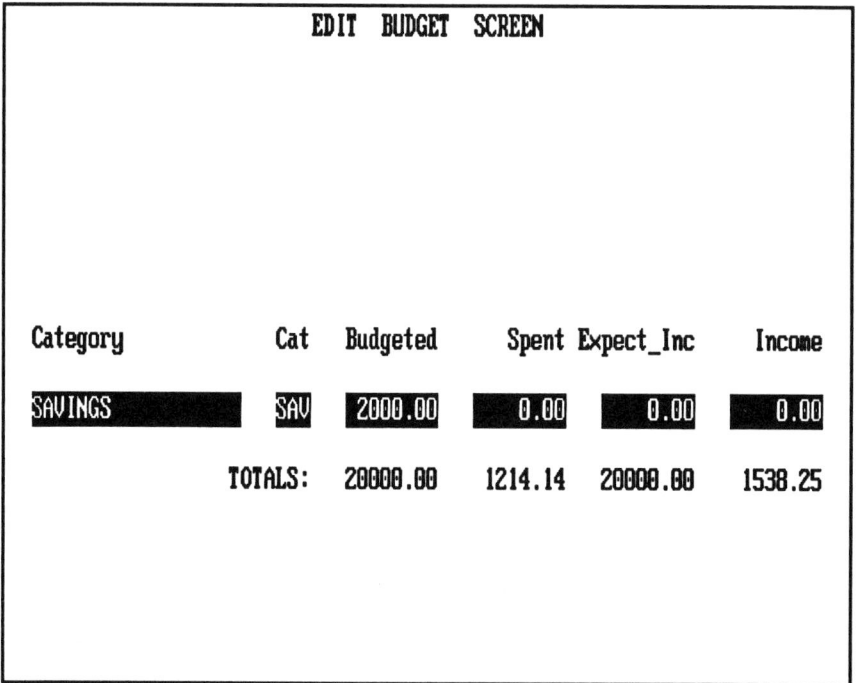

Figure 14.12 Changing the BUDGETED amount with an immediate recalculation of TOTALBUDG

14.5.2 The Program BUDGEDIT.prg

As a final act, let's combine MAKEARRA.prg with the opening of the procedure file and the format file as shown in Listing 14.7. The reason for doing this is that we want to be sure that the contents of the array, BUDARRAY, accurately reflect the current contents of the budget database. This final program, BUDGEDIT.prg, now handles all these details including opening and closing the procedure and format files.

14.6 Query Generator

One of the elements that is associated with a database is a query, which is a formalized means of extracting information from the database. Up till now we have been doing searches on our

FUNCTIONS, ARRAYS & QUERIES

```
* BUDGEDIT.PRG
* This regenerates the BUDGET Array
* from BUDGET.dbf
* and recalculates the totals in
* preparation for going into Edit.
* This prepares the screen of the
* BUDGET format file for the ability
* to retotal the four numeric fields
* each time they are altered.
*
USE &BUDGET
DECLARE BUDARRAY[RECCOUNT(),4]
COPY TO ARRAY BUDARRAY FIELDS ;
   BUDGETED, SPENT, EXPECT_INC,;
   INCOME
SUM BUDGETED, SPENT, EXPECT_INC, ;
   INCOME TO TOTALBUDG, TOTALSPENT, ;
   TOTALEXPEC, TOTALINCOM
GOTO TOP
SET PROCEDURE TO BUDGPROC
SET FORMAT TO BUDGET
EDIT
SET FORMAT TO
SET PROCEDURE TO
USE
RETURN
```

Listing 14.7 BUDGEDIT.prg which generates array, totals, opens Procedure and Format Files databases (e.g. COM_EVAL.prg and COM_GRAD.prg), and conditional reports in order to extract the information we sought. This gave us a very flexible way of getting information out of our database. However, there are two advantages that queries have over the searches that we have done:

1. Non-programmers can create **Queries By Example**[49] quite easily, and save them as files to be used again.

2. Queries can combine databases having a common key which effectively creates an entity that can be handled as though it were one single database.

It is this second property that interests us in the **Query Generator.** To this end we shall now create a **QUERY** file that will: 1) combine two databases in a one to one relationship; and 2) then combine three databases in a many to one relationship.

14.6.1 Creating a QUERY of Two Databases Linked Together on a Single Common Key

Let us start by creating a second database called **GRADES.DBF**, which has the structure shown in Listing 14.8. These GRADES represent the additional grades that have been acquired by our COMPCLAS students. Each of the students has been assigned an ID Number. As this is the key by which the students are identified, we have to add this field to the COMPCLAS database so that we can link the two databases together. The amended COMPCLAS database is shown in Listing 14.9.

---

[49] This is a topic that is handled in Appendix C for those who are interested in this application. For general programming applications, using the **SET FILTER TO ...** instruction is more efficient for the "initiated".

```
Field  Field Name   Type       Width   Dec   Index
    1  ID_NUMBER    Character      4               Y
    2  FINAL        Numeric        3               N
    3  MIDTERM      Numeric        3               N
    4  HOMEWORK1    Numeric        3               N
    5  HOMEWORK2    Numeric        3               N
    6  HOMEWORK3    Numeric        3               N
    7  HOMEWORK4    Numeric        3               N
    8  HOMEWORK5    Numeric        3               N
    9  HOMEWORK6    Numeric        3               N
   10  HOMEWORK7    Numeric        3               N
   11  HOMEWORK8    Numeric        3               N
   12  HOMEWORK9    Numeric        3               N
   13  HOMEWORK10   Numeric        3               N
   14  HOMEWORK11   Numeric        3               N
   15  HOMEWORK12   Numeric        3               N
   16  HOMEWORK13   Numeric        3               N
** Total **                       50
```

Listing 14.8 Structure of the database GRADES.dbf.

```
Field  Field Name   Type       Width   Dec   Index
    1  ID_NUMBER    Character      4               N
    2  FIRSTNAME    Character     15               N
    3  LASTNAME     Character     15               N
    4  TERM_PROJ    Logical        1               N
    5  EVALUATION   Date           8               N
    6  PROJ_GRADE   Numeric        3               N
    7  ADDRESS      Character     25               N
    8  CITY_ST_ZP   Character     25               N
    9  FINALGRADE   Character      1               N
   10  COMMENTS     Memo          10               N
** Total **                      108
```

Listing 14.9 Amended Structure of COMPCLAS.dbf to Include the field ID_NUMBER

532   FUNCTIONS, ARRAYS & QUERIES

Let us now create our query file. The syntax is: **CREATE QUERY** *QueryName*. Since this query will represent a one-to-one linking of two databases; we shall call it **SINGLE**.

. **CREATE QUERY SINGLE**

Figure 14.13 shows the resulting Query screen.

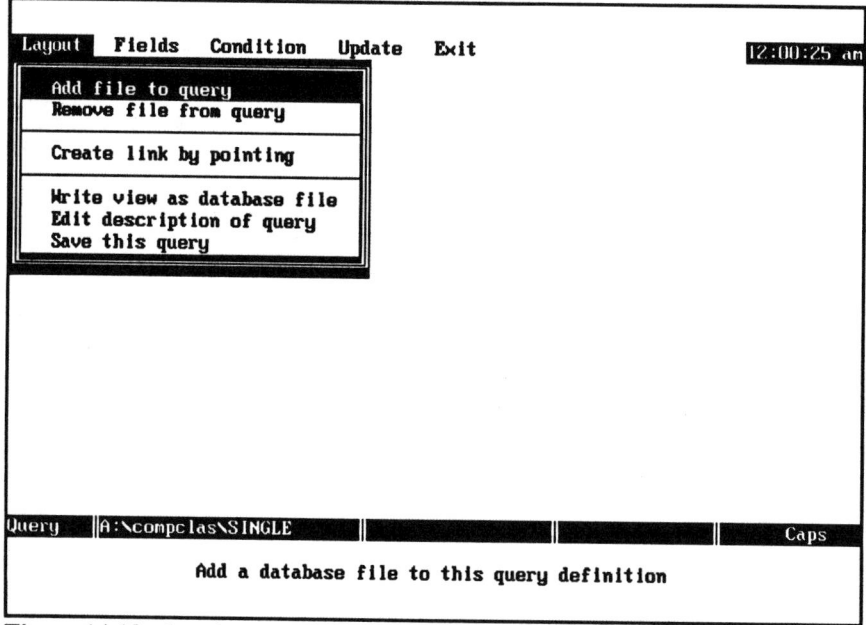

Figure 14.13 Opening Query Screen for SINGLE.QBE

Striking the Enter key on the "Add file to Query", we get the screen shown in Figure 14.14. Striking the Enter key once more gives us the screen shown in Figure 14.15.

Next we return to the "Layout" menu by depressing the Alt key and striking **L**. Figure 14.16 shows the result after having struck the Enter key on the "Add file to query" menu item, and selecting **GRADES.DBF** for our second database. Figure 14.17 shows the query SINGLE comprised of our two databases, **COMPCLAS.DBF** and **GRADES.DBF**. Now move the cursor into the ID_NUMBER field by striking the Tab key.

FUNCTIONS, ARRAYS & QUERIES 533

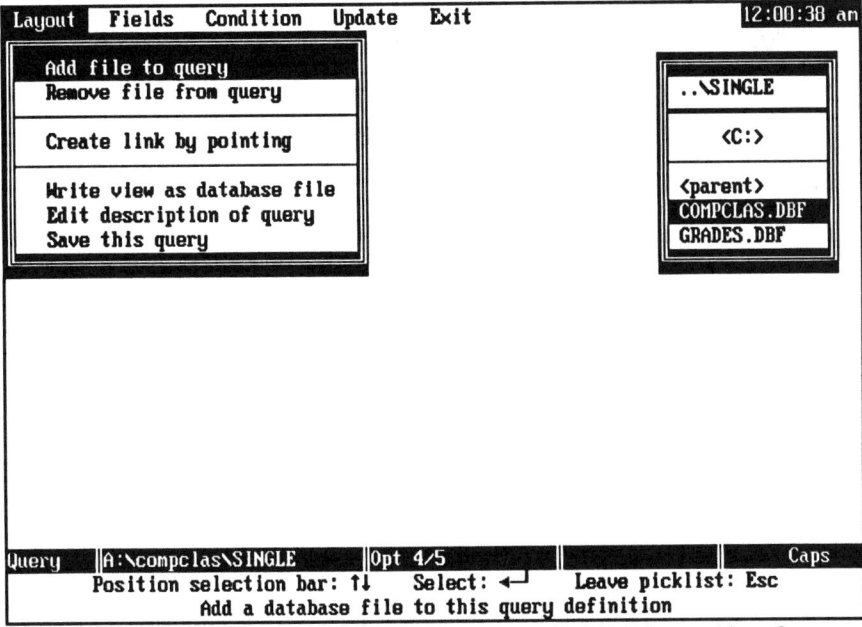

Figure 14.14 Selecting the first Database, COMPCLAS.dbf, to add to Query

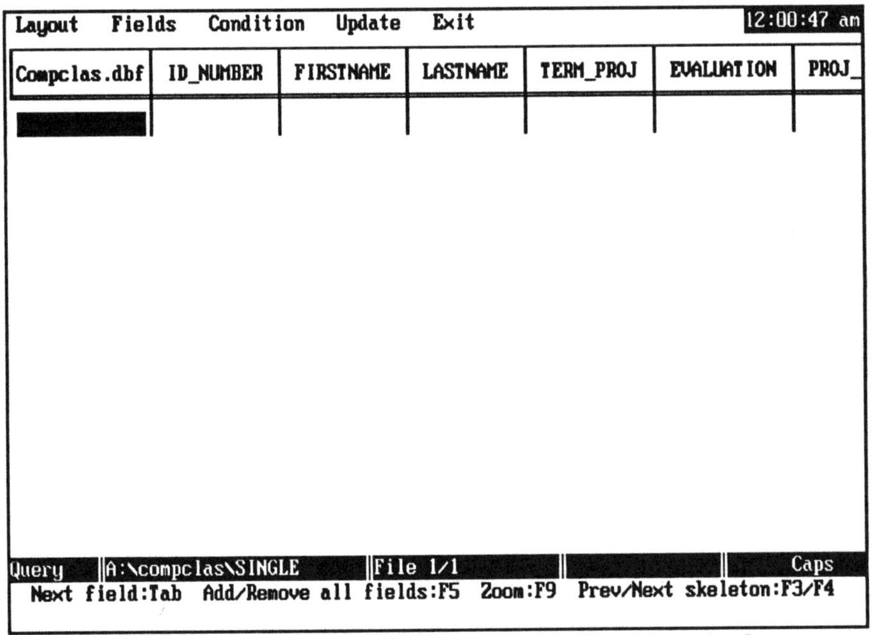

Figure 14.15 Query Screen after Adding COMPCLAS.DBF to the Query

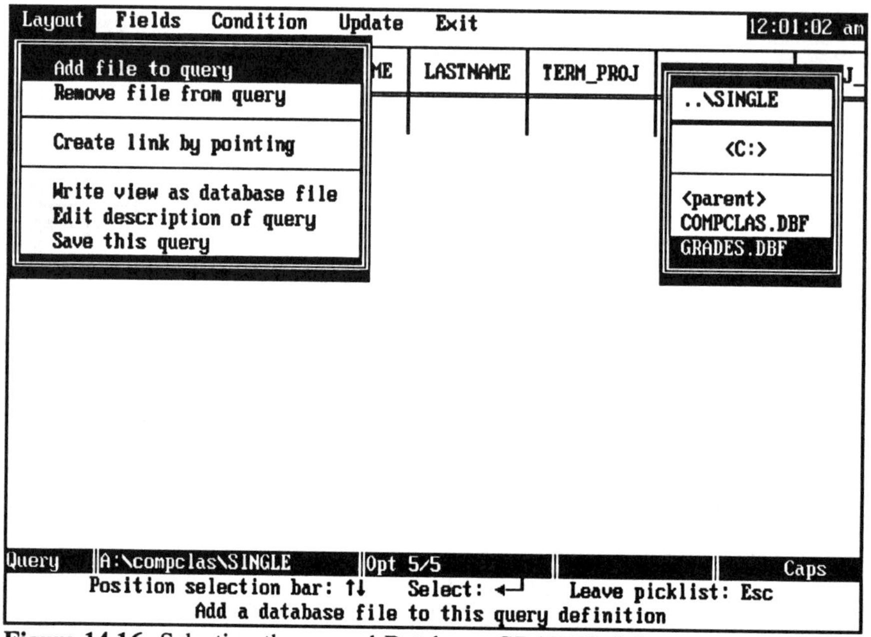

534 FUNCTIONS, ARRAYS & QUERIES

Figure 14.16 Selecting the second Database, GRADES.dbf, to add to Query

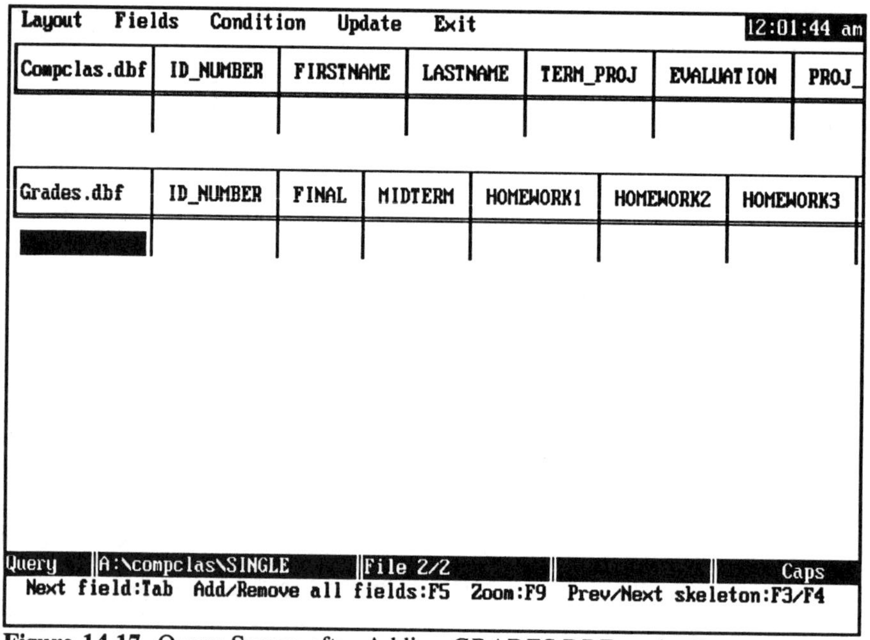

Figure 14.17 Query Screen after Adding GRADES.DBF to the Query

Figure 14.18 shows us having selected the menu "Layout", once more, in order to select the menu item: "Create Link By Pointing". Now hit the Enter key. You may move the cursor from one database to the next by striking the F3 key. Move to the ID_NUMBER field in the second database, and strike the Enter key once more. Figure 14.19 shows the result, a SINGLE link between the two databases labeled, LINK1.

We wish to be certain that when we create our view that we include indexes. This is done by striking ALT-F and putting the cursor down on the bottom menu option, "Include Indexes", and hitting the Enter key. The result of having done this is shown in Figure 14.20.

Now we're ready to create the view from our two linked databases. We do this by placing the cursor in the first field that we would like to add to the view. Then we access the "Fields" menu once more, and then select the "Add field to view" menu item as shown in Figure 14.20. The result of this action is shown in Figure 14.21, where the field, ID_NUMBER, has been selected to become the first field given to our view.

We repeat this process for all the rest of the fields that we would like to add to our view from both databases: Firstname; Lastname; Final; Midterm; Proj_Grade; Homework1;...Homework13. Thus we get the view shown in Figure 14.22. This, then, defines our query view file that we will use as though it were a single database.

Using our usual Alt-E keystroke pair to exit the query generator, we return to the dot prompt with the query file, **SINGLE.QBE**, acting as the entity carrying the relevant information in both the COMPCLAS as well as GRADES databases. We can now browse, edit, search, and make reports on this entity just as though it were a real database, not just a creation of the dBASE system. We shall do this with a browse as shown in Figure 14.23[50].

---

[50]It was not necessary to leave the QUERY mode in order to look at the Browse. This could have been done by simply striking the "F2" key.

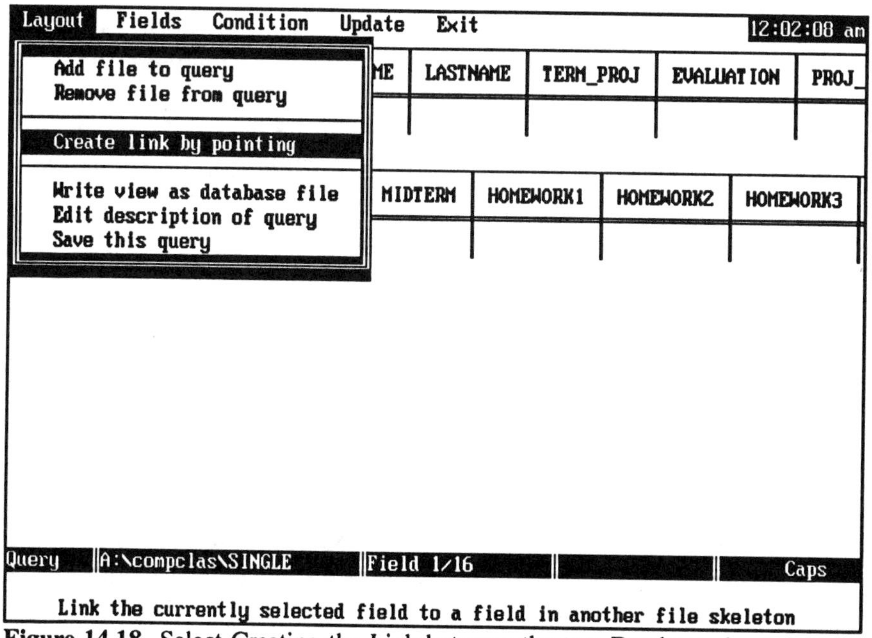

536 FUNCTIONS, ARRAYS & QUERIES

Figure 14.18 Select Creating the Link between the two Databases by Pointing

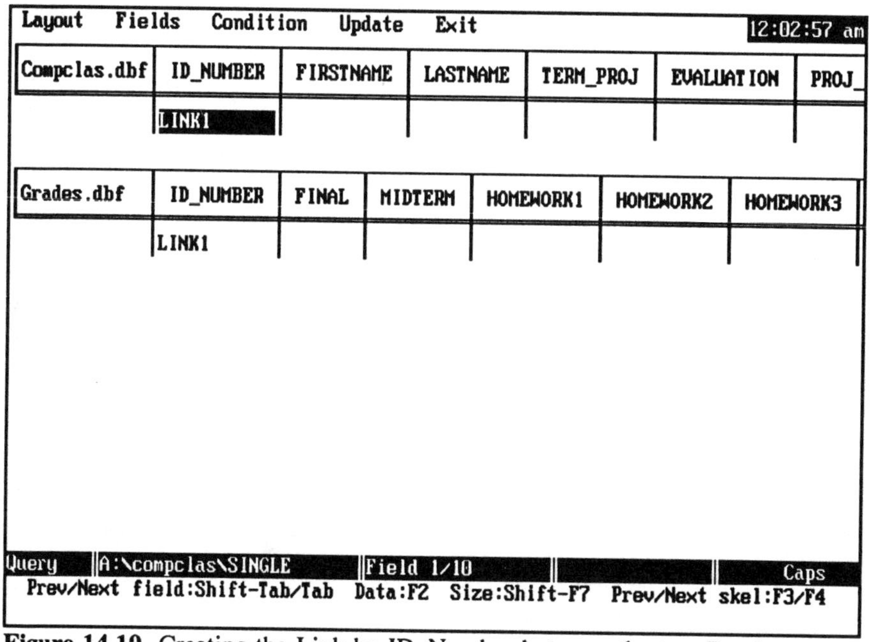

Figure 14.19 Creating the Link by ID_Number between the two Databases

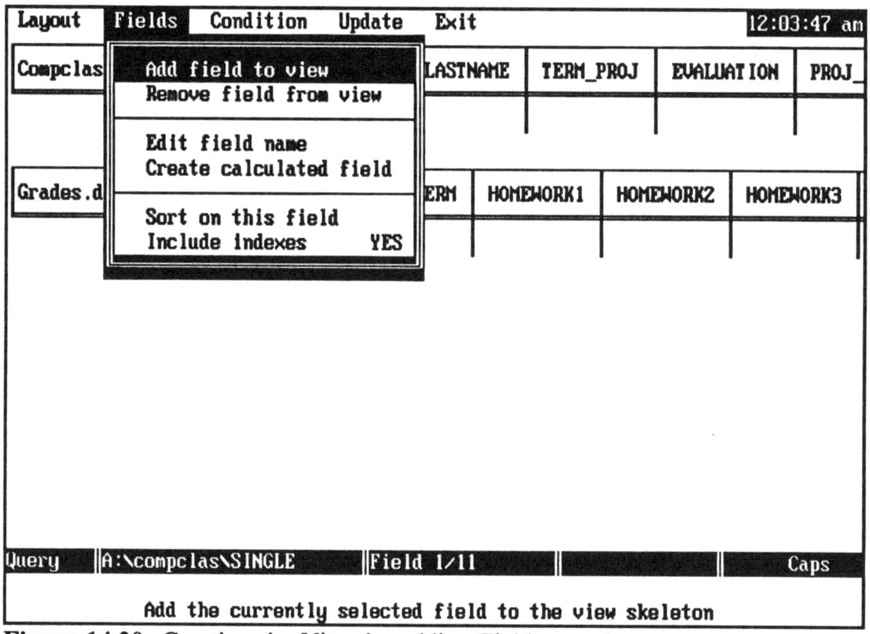

FUNCTIONS, ARRAYS & QUERIES 537

Figure 14.20 Creating the View by adding Fields, one by one

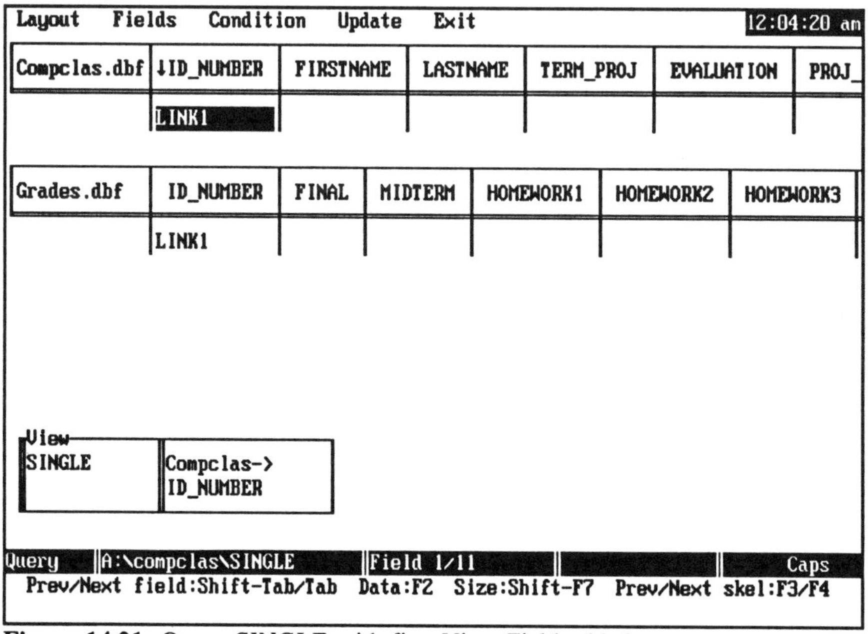

Figure 14.21 Query SINGLE with first View Field added

538   FUNCTIONS, ARRAYS & QUERIES

```
Layout   Fields   Condition   Update   Exit              12:10:23 am
┌─────────────┬───────────┬───────────┬──────────┬──────────┬──────────┬──────┐
│ Compclas.dbf│ ↓ID_NUMBER│ ↓FIRSTNAME│ ↓LASTNAME│ TERM_PROJ│ EVALUATION│↓PROJ│
├─────────────┼───────────┼───────────┼──────────┼──────────┼──────────┼──────┤
│             │ LINK1     │           │          │          │          │      │
└─────────────┴───────────┴───────────┴──────────┴──────────┴──────────┴──────┘

┌─────────────┬───────────┬─────────┬──────────┬───────────┬───────────┬───────────┐
│ Grades.dbf  │ ID_NUMBER │ ↓FINAL  │ ↓MIDTERM │ ↓HOMEWORK1│ ↓HOMEWORK2│ ↓HOMEWORK3│
├─────────────┼───────────┼─────────┼──────────┼───────────┼───────────┼───────────┤
│             │ LINK1     │         │          │           │           │           │
└─────────────┴───────────┴─────────┴──────────┴───────────┴───────────┴───────────┘

┌View──┬────────────┬────────────┬────────────┬──────────┐
│SINGLE│ Compclas-> │ Compclas-> │ Compclas-> │ Grades-> │
│      │ ID_NUMBER  │ FIRSTNAME  │ LASTNAME   │ FINAL    │
└──────┴────────────┴────────────┴────────────┴──────────┘
Query    A:\compclas\SINGLE      Field 1/19
         Remove from view:F5  Select:F6  Move:F7  Prev/Next skeleton:F3/F4
```

Figure 14.22 View of SINGLE Link Query with all desired fields added

```
Records   Organize   Fields   Go To   Exit
┌──────────┬──────────┬────────────┬──────┬───────┬──────────┬──────────┬──┐
│ID_NUMBER │FIRSTNAME │LASTNAME    │FINAL │MIDTERM│PROJ_GRADE│HOMEWORK1 │H │
├──────────┼──────────┼────────────┼──────┼───────┼──────────┼──────────┼──┤
│2001      │Derek     │Caruthers   │  84  │  79   │    0     │   95     │  │
│2002      │Matts     │Engleberg   │      │  60   │   62     │   80     │  │
│2003      │Nancy     │Hardwick    │  80  │  85   │    0     │   90     │  │
│2004      │Wendel    │Little      │      │  85   │   87     │   95     │  │
│2005      │Consuelo  │Naboa       │      │  90   │   89     │  100     │1 │
│2006      │Gladys    │Naboa       │      │  95   │   93     │  100     │1 │
│2007      │Jonathan  │Samuels     │      │  80   │   76     │   90     │  │
│2008      │Mary Beth │Swazey      │      │  50   │   52     │   80     │  │
│2009      │Jeremy    │Witherspoon │      │  80   │   82     │  100     │  │
│2010      │Mary      │Wong        │      │  80   │   85     │   95     │  │
└──────────┴──────────┴────────────┴──────┴───────┴──────────┴──────────┴──┘
Browse   A:\compclas\SINGLE      Rec 3/10        View  ReadOnly
```

Figure 14.23 A Browse of the Query File SINGLE, consisting of COMPCLAS linked with GRADES

FUNCTIONS, ARRAYS & QUERIES   539

Note that the only unusual thing about the query file, **SINGLE.QBE**, is that there is the comment "ReadOnly" written on the status bar. This means that we cannot write to either database in its present form. However, what we can do is to view it in any way that we like just as though **SINGLE.QBE** were its own database. In as much as we already know how to extract information from a database through our reports and searches, we have just received a powerful tool that takes us beyond the limitations of our single databases with which we have been working.

To close our query file we can type **CLOSE DATA**, just as we do with multiple databases. To open it again, anew, we need to type, **SET VIEW TO** *QueryFileName*. In this case it would be:

. **SET VIEW TO SINGLE**

14.6.2 Creating a QUERY of Multiple Databases Using Multiple Keys

Let's take the query view file one step further. Let us suppose that we have a video store where students come and rent videos. The first ten members to join this video rental store just happen to be our ten COMPCLAS students. We will call the database that they were all entered into, **MEMBERS.DBF** . The structure of MEMBERS.DBF is shown in Listing 14.10. The contents of the database is shown in the browse screen contained in Figure 14.24. Note the field in MEMBERS.dbf that is labeled SSN (Social Security Number). This field will be used as the account number for each of the members.

In addition, the video store keeps a list of all the videos that they have in stock. The structure of the database, **VIDEOS.DBF**, is shown in Listing 14.11. The contents of the database is shown in the Browse screen contained in Figure 14.25. Note that each Title in stock has its own code number. However, there may be more than one copy of each of these tapes depending upon their popularity. The field, NUMBERCOPY, indicates how many copies of each Title are in stock.

```
Structure for database: MEMBERS.DBF
Field    Field Name   Type         Width    Dec    Index
    1    LASTNAME     Character       15                N
    2    FIRSTNAME    Character       15                N
    3    SSN          Character        9                Y
    4    ADDRESS      Character       21                N
    5    CITY         Character       15                N
    6    ST           Character        2                N
    7    ZIP          Character        9                N
    8    PHONE        Character       15                N
    9    JOINED       Date             8                N
** Total **                          110
```

Listing 14.10 Structure of Database MEMBERS.dbf

LASTNAME	FIRSTNAME	SSN	ADDRESS	CITY
Caruthers	Derek	037926758	21 Spring Glen Road	Cooks Falls
Little	Wendel	039674322	1821 Cochecton Street	Jeffersonville
Naboa	Gladys	042976153	324 Catskill Terrace	Sundown
Swazey	Mary Beth	121897563	85 Cider Mill Lane	North Branch
Engleberg	Matts	123669867	2021 Mountain View	Mountaindale
Naboa	Consuelo	139650732	324 Catskill Terrace	Sundown
Hardwick	Nancy	142769867	512 Delaware Overlook	Callicoon
Witherspoon	Jeremy	165329971	821 Kiamesha Circle	Glen Spey
Samuels	Jonathan	221987521	96 Rainbow's End	Roscoe
Wong	Mary	331987456	321 Lakeside Ave.	Swan Lake

| Browse | C:\...video\MEMBERS | Rec 3/10 | File | Caps |

Figure 14.24 Contents of the Database MEMBERS.dbf

FUNCTIONS, ARRAYS & QUERIES 541

```
Records   Organize   Fields   Go To   Exit
CODE  TITLE                              RATING  LENGTH  TYPE             DISTRIBUTR
1329  BUTCH CASSIDY & SUNDANCE KID       PG-13   128     ACTION           TRI-STAR
2243  HANS CHRISTIAN ANDERSON            G       105     CHILDREN'S       MGM
2961  CASABLANCA                         PG-13   122     ADVENTURE        UNIVERSAL
3243  THE HOUND OF THE BASKERVILLES      PG      122     MYSTERY          COLUMBIA
3394  ABBOTT & COSTELLO IN HOLLYWOOD     PG-13   115     COMEDY           UNIVERSAL
4185  FRANKENSTEIN                       R       115     HORROR           UNIVERSAL
4392  FANTASIA                           G       90      ANIMATED         BUENA VISTA
4482  STAGECOACH                         PG      122     WESTERN          WARNER BROS
4498  MUSIC MAN                          G       122     MUSICAL          WARNER BROS
4589  THE SOUND OF MUSIC                 G       131     MUSICAL          20TH CENTURY
5439  GONE WITH THE WIND                 PG-13   188     DRAMA            MGM
5586  THE DAY THE EARTH STOOD STILL      PG      122     SCIENCE FICTION  RKO
7742  WIZARD OF OZ                       PG      118     CLASSICAL        MGM

Browse    C:\...video\VIDEOS        Rec 1/13       File                   Caps
```

Figure 14.25 Contents of the database VIDEOS.dbf

Finally, we have the file, **TAPESOUT.DBF**, which links the MEMBERS and the VIDEOS databases together. This file tells which member, by SSN, has rented which tape, by CODE and COPY. The structure of this database is shown in Listing 14.12. Its contents, showing who has rented what, is shown in Listing 14.13.

```
Structure for database: VIDEOS.DBF
Field   Field Name   Type        Width   Dec   Index
    1   CODE         Character     4             Y
    2   TITLE        Character    30             Y
    3   RATING       Character     5             N
    4   LENGTH       Numeric       3             N
    5   TYPE         Character    15             N
    6   DISTRIBUTR   Character    16             N
    7   RELEASDATE   Date          8             N
    8   NUMBERCOPY   Numeric       2             N
** Total **                       84
```

Listing 14.11 Contents of Database VIDEOS.dbf

```
Structure for database: TAPESOUT.DBF
Field  Field Name  Type        Width    Dec    Index
    1  SSN         Character       9                Y
    2  CODE        Character       4                Y
    3  COPY        Character       1                N
** Total **                       15
```

Listing 14.12 Structure of Database TAPESOUT.dbf

```
          SSN        CODE  COPY
          042976153  3394  A
          042976153  4498  A
          037926758  1329  A
          165329971  3243  A
          165329971  4392  A
          165329971  5586  A
          142769867  4498  B
          221987521  4482  A
          221987521  3394  B
          221987521  7742  A
          221987521  5439  A
          123669867  2243  A
          123669867  4392  B
          121897563  4105  A
          121897563  5439  B
          221987563  2961  A
          331987456  4498  C
```

Listing 14.13 Contents of TAPESOUT.dbf

The field, SSN, relates MEMBERS.dbf to TAPESOUT.dbf, and the field, CODE, relates TAPESOUT.dbf to VIDEOS.dbf. MEMBERS.dbf is indexed on SSN as well as on LASTNAME + FIRSTNAME, TAPESOUT.dbf is indexed on SSN and CODE, while VIDEOS.dbf is indexed on CODE and TITLE. Using the query generator we can create a view file that ties these three databases together and makes them appear as one read only file.

We can start by opening MEMBERS.dbf, and then creating the query file MULTIPLE.QBE:

. USE MEMBERS
. CREATE QUERY MULTIPLE

FUNCTIONS, ARRAYS & QUERIES

What we get when we enter the query generator is the same sort of screen that we first saw in Figure 14.15. Next, we choose the "Layout" menu by striking **Alt-L**, and we add the two databases: TAPESOUT.dbf, and VIDEOS.dbf to our query work area.

Next we choose the "Fields" menu by striking **Alt-F**, and we select the menu item "Include indexes", as shown in Figure 14.26. As the default value was **NO**, we changed this default to a **YES** by striking the Enter key. We do this for each of the three databases. The result is shown in Figure 14.27. The # sign indicates fields on which a respective database is indexed.

Now we need to link them together. Move the cursor to SSN in Members.dbf. Choosing the "Create link by pointing" menu item from the "Layout" menu as shown in Figure 14.18, we link SSN in MEMBERS.dbf with SSN in TAPESOUT.dbf. Likewise we link CODE in TAPESOUT.dbf with CODE in VIDEOS.dbf. The result is shown in Figure 14.28.

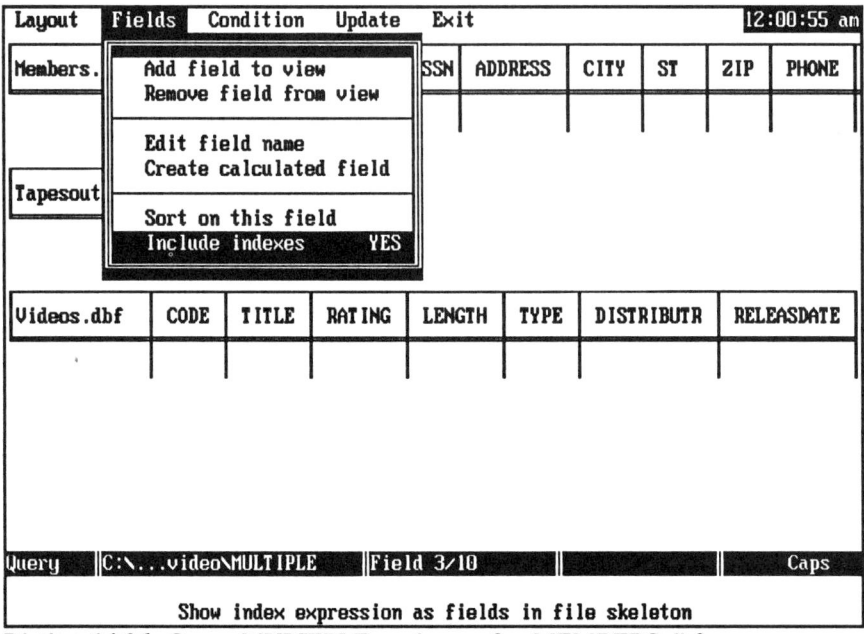

Listing 14.26 Query MULTIPLE made up of: MEMBERS.dbf, TAPESOUT.DBF, and VIDEOS.dbf

544   FUNCTIONS, ARRAYS & QUERIES

```
Layout   Fields   Condition   Update   Exit                12:03:07 am
┌───────────┬──────────┬──────────┬──────┬─────────┬──────┬────┬─────┬──────┐
│Members.dbf│ LASTNAME │ FIRSTNAME│# SSN │ ADDRESS │ CITY │ ST │ ZIP │PHONE │
├───────────┼──────────┼──────────┼──────┼─────────┼──────┼────┼─────┼──────┤
│           │          │          │      │         │      │    │     │      │
└───────────┴──────────┴──────────┴──────┴─────────┴──────┴────┴─────┴──────┘

┌────────────┬──────┬───────┬──────┐
│Tapesout.dbf│# SSN │# CODE │ COPY │
├────────────┼──────┼───────┼──────┤
│            │      │       │      │
└────────────┴──────┴───────┴──────┘

┌──────────┬───────┬───────┬────────┬────────┬──────┬──────────┬──────────┐
│Videos.dbf│# CODE │ TITLE │ RATING │ LENGTH │ TYPE │DISTRIBUTR│RELEASDATE│
├──────────┼───────┼───────┼────────┼────────┼──────┼──────────┼──────────┤
│          │▇▇▇▇▇▇▇│       │        │        │      │          │          │
└──────────┴───────┴───────┴────────┴────────┴──────┴──────────┴──────────┘

Query    C:\...video\MULTIPLE    Field 1/7                        Caps
   Prev/Next field:Shift-Tab/Tab  Data:F2  Size:Shift-F7  Prev/Next skel:F3/F4
```

Figure 14.27 The three databases making up our Query file with their Indices Included

```
Layout   Fields   Condition   Update   Exit                12:03:53 am
┌───────────┬──────────┬──────────┬──────┬─────────┬──────┬────┬─────┬──────┐
│Members.dbf│ LASTNAME │ FIRSTNAME│# SSN │ ADDRESS │ CITY │ ST │ ZIP │PHONE │
├───────────┼──────────┼──────────┼──────┼─────────┼──────┼────┼─────┼──────┤
│           │          │          │LINK1 │         │      │    │     │      │
└───────────┴──────────┴──────────┴──────┴─────────┴──────┴────┴─────┴──────┘

┌────────────┬──────┬───────┬──────┐
│Tapesout.dbf│# SSN │# CODE │ COPY │
├────────────┼──────┼───────┼──────┤
│            │LINK1 │ LINK2 │      │
└────────────┴──────┴───────┴──────┘

┌──────────┬───────┬───────┬────────┬────────┬──────┬──────────┬──────────┐
│Videos.dbf│# CODE │ TITLE │ RATING │ LENGTH │ TYPE │DISTRIBUTR│RELEASDATE│
├──────────┼───────┼───────┼────────┼────────┼──────┼──────────┼──────────┤
│          │ LINK2 │       │        │        │      │          │          │
└──────────┴───────┴───────┴────────┴────────┴──────┴──────────┴──────────┘

Query    C:\...video\MULTIPLE    Field 1/7                        Caps
   Prev/Next field:Shift-Tab/Tab  Data:F2  Size:Shift-F7  Prev/Next skel:F3/F4
```

Figure 14.28 Linking the three databases together with common key fields

Now we are ready to create our view. Selecting the "Add field to view" menu item from the "Fields" menu, as shown in Figure 14.20, we create our view which is shown at the bottom of Figure 14.29. The only field not shown here is the LASTNAME field from the MEMBERS.dbf database, which was the first field added to our view.

The only thing left to do is to indicate how we want our database ordered. Because we included indexes in our query, we now have access to the index field, "LASTNAME+FIRSTNAME", in the Members.dbf database. Since this is a more convenient ordering for our transactions than is the social security number, we have moved the cursor to this field. Figure 14.30 shows that the "Sort on this field" menu item has been selected from the "Fields" menu. Striking the Enter key immediately brings down the window shown in Figure 14.31. Choosing ascending ASCII[51], as indicated, and striking Enter, we get the screen shown in Figure 14.32.

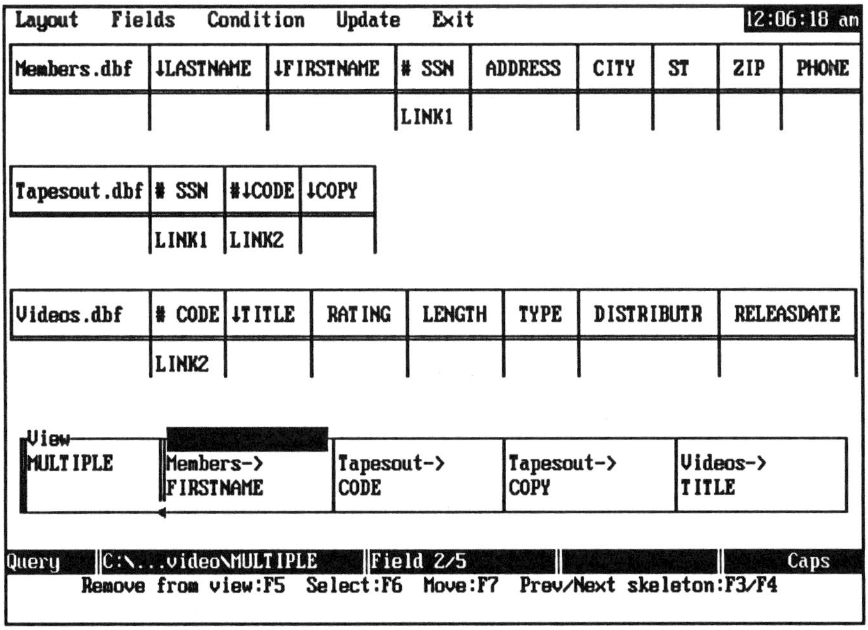

Figure 14.29 Query MULTIPLE.QBE with View selected

---

[51]We had no choice but to choose Ascending ASCII as the order must agree with the order in which the index was ordered.

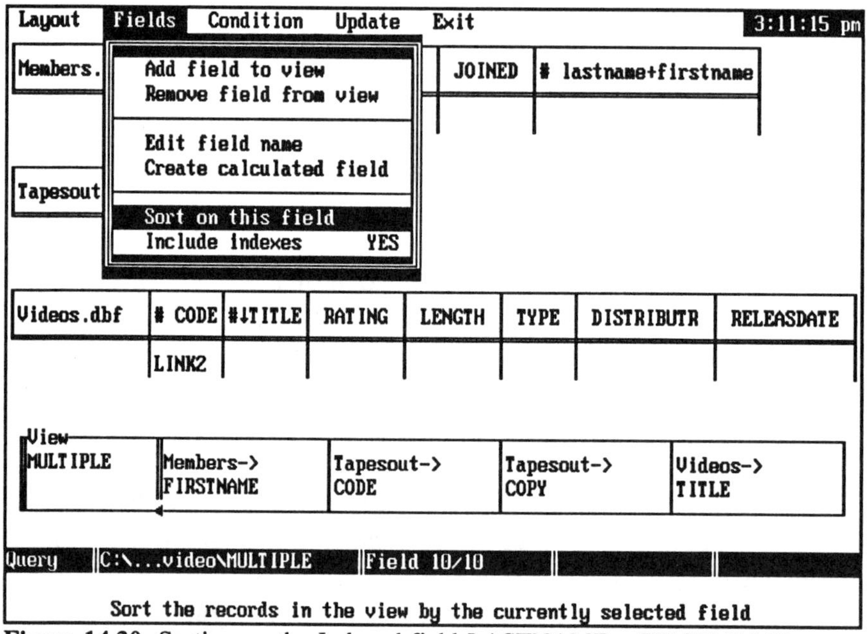

546   FUNCTIONS, ARRAYS & QUERIES

Figure 14.30 Sorting on the Indexed field LASTNAME + FIRSTNAME

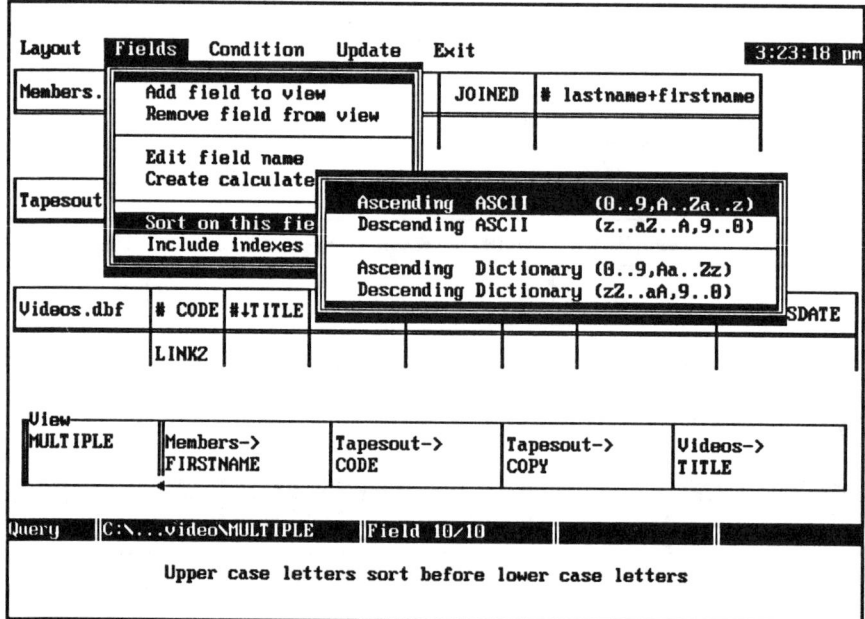

Figure 14.31 Choosing Ascending ASCII Order in LASTNAME+FIRSTNAME for MULTIPLE.QBE

FUNCTIONS, ARRAYS & QUERIES

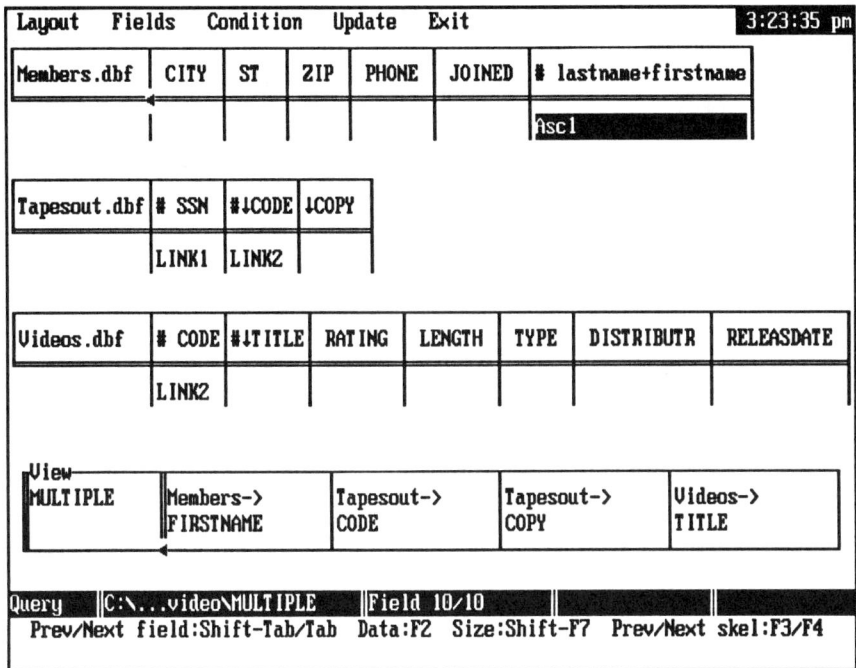

Figure 14.32 LASTNAME+FIRSTNAME chosen to be the Sorting Field for MULTIPLE.QBE

Saving our query file, and browsing the result, we get the screen shown in Figure 14.33. We can now see what videos each of the members are taking in order of the member's last and first names. To change the order so that we can see at a glance how many videos of each title are checked out, we need to go back into the query generator, and choose the CODE or TITLE field as the field on which to sort. Since it would be nice to have an alphabetical listing by title, we will choose the TITLE field. The result is shown in Figure 14.34 where the "Asc2" is now down in the TITLE field box. (The original "Asc1" up in the SSN field box was erased by means of the space bar.)

Browsing the result of this form of the query, we get the result shown in Figure 14.35. The screen is now organized by title.

548 FUNCTIONS, ARRAYS & QUERIES

Records	Organize	Fields	Go To	Exit	
LASTNAME	FIRSTNAME	CODE	COPY	TITLE	
Caruthers	Derek	1329	A	BUTCH CASSIDY & SUNDANCE KID
Engleberg	Matts	2243	A	HANS CHRISTIAN ANDERSON
Engleberg	Matts	4392	B	FANTASIA
Hardwick	Nancy	4498	B	MUSIC MAN
Naboa	Gladys	3394	A	ABBOTT & COSTELLO IN HOLLYWOOD
Naboa	Gladys	4498	A	MUSIC MAN
Samuels	Jonathan	4482	A	STAGECOACH
Samuels	Jonathan	3394	B	ABBOTT & COSTELLO IN HOLLYWOOD
Samuels	Jonathan	7742	A	WIZARD OF OZ
Samuels	Jonathan	5439	A	GONE WITH THE WIND
Swazey	Mary Beth	4185	A	FRANKENSTEIN
Swazey	Mary Beth	5439	B	GONE WITH THE WIND
Swazey	Mary Beth	2961	A	CASABLANCA
Witherspoon	Jeremy	3243	A	THE HOUND OF THE BASKERVILLES
Witherspoon	Jeremy	4392	A	FANTASIA
Witherspoon	Jeremy	5586	A	THE DAY THE EARTH STOOD STILL
Wong	Mary	4498	C	MUSIC MAN

Browse C:\...video\MULTIPLE   Rec 3/10   View ReadOnly

Figure 14.33 Browse of Query MULTIPLE.QBE in order of LASTNAME+FIRSTNAME

Layout	Fields	Condition	Update	Exit			3:17:33 p
Members.dbf	CITY	ST	ZIP	PHONE	JOINED	# lastname+firstname
	←						

Tapesout.dbf	# SSN	#↓CODE	↓COPY				
	LINK1	LINK2					

Videos.dbf	# CODE	#↓TITLE	RATING	LENGTH	TYPE	DISTRIBUTR	RELEASDATE
	LINK2	asc2					

View MULTIPLE	Members-> FIRSTNAME	Tapesout-> CODE	Tapesout-> COPY	Videos-> TITLE

Query C:\...video\MULTIPLE   Field 2/7
Prev/Next field:Shift-Tab/Tab Data:F2 Size:Shift-F7 Prev/Next skel:F3/F4

Figure 14.34 Query MULTIPLE.QBE ordered by TITLE

Records	Organize	Fields	Go To	Exit	
LASTNAME	FIRSTNAME	CODE	COPY	TITLE	
Naboa	Gladys	3394	A	ABBOTT & COSTELLO IN HOLLYWOOD	
Samuels	Jonathan	3394	B	ABBOTT & COSTELLO IN HOLLYWOOD	
Caruthers	Derek	1329	A	BUTCH CASSIDY & SUNDANCE KID	
Swazey	Mary Beth	2961	A	CASABLANCA	
Witherspoon	Jeremy	4392	A	FANTASIA	
Engleberg	Matts	4392	B	FANTASIA	
Swazey	Mary Beth	4185	A	FRANKENSTEIN	
Samuels	Jonathan	5439	A	GONE WITH THE WIND	
Swazey	Mary Beth	5439	B	GONE WITH THE WIND	
Engleberg	Matts	2243	A	HANS CHRISTIAN ANDERSON	
Naboa	Gladys	4498	A	MUSIC MAN	
Hardwick	Nancy	4498	B	MUSIC MAN	
Wong	Mary	4498	C	MUSIC MAN	
Samuels	Jonathan	4482	A	STAGECOACH	
Witherspoon	Jeremy	5586	A	THE DAY THE EARTH STOOD STILL	
Witherspoon	Jeremy	3243	A	THE HOUND OF THE BASKERVILLES	
Samuels	Jonathan	7742	A	WIZARD OF OZ	
Browse	C:\...video\MULTIPLE	Rec 6/13		View	ReadOnly

Figure 14.35 Browse of MULTIPLE.QBE ordered on TITLE

The one requirement here is that the key fields used uniquely refer to one record each in the two databases, MEMBERS.dbf and VIDEOS.dbf. By using the unique social security number of each member, and giving each video a unique code number, we have guaranteed this result. The uniqueness in Code number did not need to extend to the linking database TAPESOUT.dbf. The uniqueness of the tape was guaranteed by the fact that each tape having the same CODE had a different COPY letter.

This has given us an idea of the power of the query view file. This ability to link several databases together to form one virtually composite file is at the heart of the relational database concept.

14.6.3 Creating a Composite Database

Suppose that for some reason we really want to create a composite database and not be left with just a view file which vanishes the moment that we close it with **CLOSE DATA**. This can be simply done once the view file is created and active. Were we to go to the dot prompt after creating the query shown in Figure 14.34, and perform a COPY TO ... command, we would generate this new database. For example:

. **COPY TO COMPOSIT**
. **USE COMPOSIT**
. **BROWSE**

executed after exiting from the browse of Figure 14.35, gives the result shown in Figure 14.36. Now we have a real database that we can alter, add records to, delete records from, etc. However, we should exercise care here. Just because we make some changes in COMPOSIT.dbf, doesn't mean that these changes have filtered back down to the original MEMBERS, VIDEOS, and TAPESOUT databases from which this database was generated.

LASTNAME	FIRSTNAME	CODE	COPY	TITLE
Naboa	Gladys	3394	A	ABBOTT & COSTELLO IN HOLLYWOOD
Samuels	Jonathan	3394	B	ABBOTT & COSTELLO IN HOLLYWOOD
Caruthers	Derek	1329	A	BUTCH CASSIDY & SUNDANCE KID
Swazey	Mary Beth	2961	A	CASABLANCA
Witherspoon	Jeremy	4392	A	FANTASIA
Engleberg	Matts	4392	B	FANTASIA
Swazey	Mary Beth	4105	A	FRANKENSTEIN
Samuels	Jonathan	5439	A	GONE WITH THE WIND
Swazey	Mary Beth	5439	B	GONE WITH THE WIND
Engleberg	Matts	2243	A	HANS CHRISTIAN ANDERSON
Naboa	Gladys	4498	A	MUSIC MAN
Hardwick	Nancy	4498	B	MUSIC MAN
Wong	Mary	4498	C	MUSIC MAN
Samuels	Jonathan	4482	A	STAGECOACH
Witherspoon	Jeremy	5586	A	THE DAY THE EARTH STOOD STILL
Witherspoon	Jeremy	3243	A	THE HOUND OF THE BASKERVILLES
Samuels	Jonathan	7742	A	WIZARD OF OZ

Figure 14.36 Creating COMPOSIT.dbf from MULTIPLE.QBE by using COPY command

FUNCTIONS, ARRAYS & QUERIES

One needs to get real clear as to which the master database is. The whole concept of a database is that all the information resides in one place, not in many, and that any changes made to the data are reflected everywhere automatically. It is for this reason that the query view file has its appeal. Changes are still made to the original MEMBERS, TAPESOUT and VIDEOS databases which remain the masters.

If, on the other hand, you intend to make the COMPOSIT database the master database, and not use MEMBERS and VIDEOS again, then that is fine. However, if this was your intention from the beginning, then there is a far easier way of creating the COMPOSIT database than going to all the trouble of making a query view file. This is done by means of the JOIN command.

14.7 Use of the JOIN Command

The simplest syntax for this powerful command is as follows: **JOIN WITH** *SecondDatabase* **TO** *NewDatabase* **FOR** *FirstDatabaseKey(s) = SecondDatabaseKey(s)*. We define which database is the first and second by opening one database in selected area 1, and the other in selected area 2. The crucial element is that both databases have identical keys, although it is not necessary that the keys have the same field names.

Let us combine COMPCLAS.dbf and GRADES.dbf, as we did to generate SINGLE.QBE. The steps to do this would be as follows:

```
. SELECT 1
. USE GRADES ORDER ID_NUMBER
. SELECT 2
. USE COMPCLAS ORDER ID_NUMBER
. JOIN WITH GRADES TO NEWFILE FOR;
    ID_NUMBER=GRADES->ID_NUMBER;
    FIELD ID_NUMBER, FIRSTNAME;
    LASTNAME,GRADES->FINAL,;
    GRADES->MIDTERM, PROJ_GRADE
```

552   FUNCTIONS, ARRAYS & QUERIES

Note that we added a **FIELD** clause to the **JOIN** command in order to specify exactly what the fields in the result should be. We also made sure both files were in the same order on the same key in different work areas before proceeding. If we open and browse our result:

. USE NEWFILE
. BROWSE

we get the result shown in Figure 14.37.

To produce the COMPOSIT database would require us to use the JOIN command twice, first to JOIN MEMBERS.dbf with TAPESOUT.dbf to create a TEMP.dbf, and then a JOIN of TEMP.dbf with VIDEOS.dbf to produce the final result. Listing 14.14 shows us a short program, called **VIDEOMEM.prg**, that will do this for us. The result of executing **DO VIDEOMEM**, is identical to that shown in Figure 14.36.

ID_NUMBER	FIRSTNAME	LASTNAME	FINAL	MIDTERM	PROJ_GRADE
2001	Derek	Caruthers	84	79	8
2002	Matts	Engleberg		68	62
2003	Nancy	Hardwick	88	85	8
2004	Wendel	Little		85	87
2005	Consuelo	Naboa		90	89
2006	Gladys	Naboa		95	93
2007	Jonathan	Samuels		88	76
2008	Mary Beth	Swazey		50	52
2009	Jeremy	Witherspoon		88	82
2010	Mary	Wong		88	85

Figure 14.37 Using JOIN command with COMPCLAS.dbf & GRADES.dbf to create NEWFILE.dbf

```
* VIDEOMEM.prg
* Using the JOIN command to combine the three
* databases MEMBERS.dbf, TAPESOUT.dbf, and
* VIDEOS.dbf.
*
SET STATUS OFF
SET SAFETY OFF
* Do First Join
SELECT 1
USE MEMBERS ORDER SSN
SELECT 2
USE TAPESOUT
INDEX ON SSN TAG SSN
JOIN WITH MEMBERS TO TEMP FOR ;
    SSN=MEMBERS->SSN ;
    FIELD MEMBERS->FIRST, MEMBERS->LAST,;
        CODE, COPY
CLOSE DATA
* Do Second Join
SELECT 1
USE TEMP
INDEX ON CODE TO CODE
SELECT 2
USE VIDEOS
INDEX ON CODE TAG CODE
JOIN WITH TEMP TO COMPOSIT;
    FOR CODE=TEMP->CODE;
    FIELD TEMP->FIRST, TEMP->LAST, TEMP->COPY,;
        CODE, DESCRIPTION
CLOSE DATA
ERASE TEMP.DBF
ERASE CODE.NDX
* Display Result
USE COMPOSIT
INDEX ON TITLE TAG TITLE
BROWSE
USE
SET SAFETY ON
SET STATUS ON
RETURN
```

Listing 14.14 Joining MEMBERS.dbf, TAPESOUT.dbf, and VIDEOS.dbf to form COMPOSIT.dbf

554 FUNCTIONS, ARRAYS & QUERIES

The JOIN command thus gives us a direct way of combining two or more databases on a common key to form a third database. I leave it to the reader to decide which of these procedures is simpler.

14.8 Use of the UPDATE Command

There are times when we are away from our Master database, and yet we have collected data in a file that we would like to use to update our Master database. For example, although I keep my master COMPCLAS database at school, I often grade homework at home. Rather than wait till I get back to school the next day to enter the data, I input the data into a short update file, which I then use to update my master file at school[52].

Listing 14.15 shows the structure of a file called NEWGRADE.dbf which I plan to use to update my GRADES file. Listing 14.16 shows the latest grades that I have entered into this file for the computer class.

```
Structure for database: NEWGRADE.DBF
Field  Field Name  Type        Width   Dec   Index
    1  ID_NUMBER   Character       4             N
    2  HOMEWORK11  Numeric         3             N
** Total **                        8
```

Listing 14.15 Structure of the Update File: NEWGRADE.dbf

---

[52]A word of caution. There is a great temptation to keep a copy of the same database in two different places and then simply copy the more recently updated version from one location over the older version at the other location. Such a scheme sounds like it might work, but inevitably data will be lost using this procedure. Either you will accidently copy an older version onto a newer version, or you will find yourself updating both databases with different information and you will find yourself in the dilemma of sharing the new information between the two databases. Using the update procedure outlined in this section is a far more secure way to handle updating your database.

```
ID NUMBER      HOMEWORK11
  Z001            85
  Z002            75
  Z003            70
  Z004            90
  Z005            90
  Z006            95
  Z007            80
  Z008            60
  Z009            85
  Z010            90
```

Listing 14.16 Contents of the update file: NEWGRADE.dbf

Now we are ready to demonstrate the use of the **UPDATE** command. The syntax is: **UPDATE ON** *KeyField* **FROM** *UpdateFile* **REPLACE** *Field1* **WITH** *UpdateFile->Field1*, *Field2* **WITH** *UpdateFile->Field2*, ... **RANDOM**. The requirement is that the master database (GRADES.dbf in this example) be in *KeyField* ascending order. If the *UpdateFile* is in *KeyField* ascending order also, then the key word, **RANDOM**, can be omitted, and execution will proceed more quickly. For example, in the case of GRADES.dbf and NEWGRADE.dbf, the following commands would have to be executed.

. **SELECT 1**
. **USE NEWGRADE**
. **SELECT 2**
. **USE GRADES ORDER ID_NUMBER**
. **UPDATE ON ID_NUMBER FROM NEWGRADE;**
  REPLACE HOMEWORK11 WITH;
  NEWGRADE->HOMEWORK11 RANDOM
. **BROWSE FIELD ID_NUMBER, HOMEWORK11**

Figure 14.38 shows the result of the browse of the updated GRADES database.

14.8.1 Design of an Updating Program for the COMPCLAS System

As a final program design, we will create a program that will take whatever update we have for the GRADES database and will add the grades for that particular field to the GRADES database.

```
┌─────────────────────────────────────────────────────────────┐
│ Records  Organize  Fields  Go To  Exit                      │
├──────────┬──────────────────────────────────────────────────┤
│ID_NUMBER │HOMEWORK11                                        │
├──────────┼──────────────────────────────────────────────────┤
│ 2001     │                                               85 │
│ 2002     │                                               75 │
│ 2003     │                                               78 │
│ 2004     │                                               90 │
│ 2005     │                                               90 │
│ 2006     │                                               95 │
│ 2007     │                                               80 │
│ 2008     │                                               60 │
│ 2009     │                                               85 │
│ 2010     │                                               90 │
│          │                                                  │
├──────────┴──────────────────────────────────────────────────┤
│Browse  C:\...update\GRADES    Rec 3/10    File       Caps   │
└─────────────────────────────────────────────────────────────┘
```

Figure 14.38 A BROWSE FIELD ID_NUMBER, HOMEWORK11 of GRADES.dbf after the Update

The only thing different in this program is the creation of a macro which allows us to enter any field we like as the field that we wish to update. The program is called UPGRADE.prg and is shown in Listing 14.17. We do use two new functions in this program, **LTRIM()** and **RTRIM()**. The RTRIM() function (Right Trim) is identical to the TRIM() function which we have used up to now. The LTRIM() function removes all leading blanks which might have been typed in by accident. The result of executing this program is identical to the results shown in Figure 14.38.

As a final note, there does exist an update query (not to be confused with the UPDATE command) which you design in much the same way as you design a query. It allows you to do in the query mode what you do in a program or from the dot prompt with the REPLACE command. As such, it offers no particular advantage to the programmer.

```
* UPGRADE.PRG
* This program Updates GRADES.dbf from the file
* NEWGRADES.dbf by means of the UPDATE command.
*
STORE SPACE(10) TO WHICHFIELD
CLEAR
@ 12,20 SAY "Enter Name Of Field To Be Updated: " ;
    GET WHICHFIELD
READ
STORE LTRIM(RTRIM(WHICHFIELD)) TO WHICHFIELD
ARGUMENT = WHICHFIELD + " WITH NEWGRADE->" + WHICHFIELD
SELECT 1
USE NEWGRADE
GOTO TOP
SELECT 2
USE GRADES ORDER ID_NUMBER
UPDATE ON ID_NUMBER FROM NEWGRADE REPLACE &ARGUMENT;
    RANDOM
GOTO TOP
BROW FIELD ID_NUMBER, &WHICHFIELD
CLOSE DATA
RETURN
```

Listing 14.17 UPGRADE.prg which updates GRADES.dbf from the update file NEWGRADE.dbf

14.9 Summary

In this chapter we have examined a number of advanced features of dBASE IV. We started out with an introduction to user-defined functions. Then we introduced the concept of arrays. Next, public and private memory variable declarations were introduced. We then saw how we could insert memory variables into a screen form, and how we could attach functions as a condition for accepting new values into the Screen Form.

Familiarizing ourselves with these tools allowed us to design a screen that updated each time we changed any values on the screen in much the same way that a spreadsheet does.

Next we introduced ourselves to the query file and what its capabilities were. We limited our examination of the Query Generator to its ability to tie multiple databases together. This application of the query file gives us the illusion of having two or more separate databases, linked by common keys, behaving as a single database. We saw that we could easily generate a composite database from the query file by simply doing a copy, or we could do this within a program or from the dot prompt using the JOIN command.

Finally, we presented the UPDATE command which allows us to update one master database from another updating database.

14.10 Review

In Chapter 14 we have presented the following new commands:

    COPY TO ARRAY
    CREATE QUERY
    DECLARE
    FUNCTION
    JOIN
    PRIVATE
    PUBLIC
    UPDATE

Add these to your glossary of dBASE commands. In addition, the following Functions were introduced:

    LTRIM()
    RECCOUNT()
    RTRIM()

14.11 Laboratory Work

Go through all the steps outlined in this chapter. Using arrays, and user-defined functions, create the automatically recalculating screen shown in Figure 14.11.

Familiarize yourself with the use of queries for the purpose of linking two or more databases together. Create the query for the three databases linked together as shown in Figure 14.35. Using the JOIN instruction, link the three databases together to form one composite database.

Using the program, UPGRADE.prg, update the GRADES database as shown in Figure 14.38.

14.12 Exercises

1. Using the database, GRADES.dbf, create an automatically recalculating screen that will recalculate the average of an individual's grades each time a particular grade for that student has been entered, and display that on the screen. You may assume that all grades are weighted equally for this purpose.

2. Add to the previous problem the capability of computing the overall average of *all* the students' grades, and displaying this on the screen each time a particular student's grade is changed. (Hint: you will need to use arrays in order to do this.)

3. Let us suppose that all the students in COMPCLAS.dbf also take other courses at the college. The courses available are shown in the database COURDESC.dbf whose structure and contents is shown in Listings 14.18 and 14.19. If we use the structure shown in Listing 14.9 for COMPCLAS.dbf then we associate the course taken by the student with the student via his/her ID_NUMBER and the COURSNUMB as shown in the database ZNUMCOUR.dbf. The structure and contents for ZNUMCOUR are given in Listings 14.20 and 14.21. Link these three databases together so that you may create the Query whose Browse is shown in Figure 14.39. Call your Query COURSES.QBE.

FUNCTIONS, ARRAYS & QUERIES

FIRSTNAME	LASTNAME	COURSENUMB	DESCRIPT	UNIT
Matts	Engleberg	BUS14011	ACCOUNTING I	4
Mary Beth	Swazey	BUS14011	ACCOUNTING I	4
Derek	Caruthers	CPT12001	PRINCIPLES OF DATA PROCESSING	3
Matts	Engleberg	CPT12001	PRINCIPLES OF DATA PROCESSING	3
Nancy	Hardwick	CPT12001	PRINCIPLES OF DATA PROCESSING	3
Wendel	Little	CPT12001	PRINCIPLES OF DATA PROCESSING	3
Consuelo	Naboa	CPT12001	PRINCIPLES OF DATA PROCESSING	3
Gladys	Naboa	CPT12001	PRINCIPLES OF DATA PROCESSING	3
Jonathan	Samuels	CPT12001	PRINCIPLES OF DATA PROCESSING	3
Mary Beth	Swazey	CPT12001	PRINCIPLES OF DATA PROCESSING	3
Mary	Wong	CPT12001	PRINCIPLES OF DATA PROCESSING	3
Jeremy	Witherspoon	CPT12001	PRINCIPLES OF DATA PROCESSING	3
Matts	Engleberg	ENG1000A	ENGLISH COMPOSITION	3
Consuelo	Naboa	MAT10001	COLLEGE MATH	3
Consuelo	Naboa	SBS13002	WESTERN CIVILIZATION	3
Jeremy	Witherspoon	SBS13002	WESTERN CIVILIZATION	3
Consuelo	Naboa	SCI11001	BIOLOGY I	4
Mary	Wong	SCI11001	BIOLOGY I	4

Figure 14.39 Browse of Query COURSES.QBE

```
Structure for database: COURDESC.DBF
  Field  Field Name  Type        Width   Dec   Index
      1  COURSENUMB  Character       8          N
      2  DESCRIPT    Character      30          N
      3  UNITS       Numeric         1          N
** Total **                         40
```

Listing 14.18 Structure of COURDESC.dbf

```
COURSENUMB  DESCRIPT                        UNITS
CPT12001    PRINCIPLES OF DATA PROCESSING     3
BUS14011    ACCOUNTING I                      4
ENG1000A    ENGLISH COMPOSITION               3
SCI11001    BIOLOGY I                         4
MAT10001    COLLEGE MATH                      3
SBS13002    WESTERN CIVILIZATION              3
```

Listing 14.19 Contents of COURDESC.dbf

```
Structure for database: ZNUMCOUR.DBF
Field  Field Name  Type       Width   Dec   Index
    1  ID_NUMBER   Character      4           N
    2  COURSENUMB  Character      8           N
** Total **                      13
```

Listing 14.20 Structure of ZNUMCOUR.dbf which links COMPCLAS.dbf to COURDESC.dbf

```
ID_NUMBER  COURSENUMB
Z001       CPT12001
Z002       CPT12001
Z002       BUS14011
Z002       ENG1000A
Z003       CPT12001
Z004       CPT12001
Z005       CPT12001
Z005       SBS13002
Z005       MAT10001
Z005       SCI11001
Z006       CPT12001
Z007       CPT12001
Z008       CPT12001
Z008       BUS14011
Z009       CPT12001
Z009       SBS13002
Z010       CPT12001
Z010       SCI11001
```

Listing 14.21 Contents of database ZNUMCOUR.dbf

4. Join the three databases, of the previous problem, together to form a new database by the name of COURSES.dbf. Use the JOIN command in a program similar to that given in VIDEOMEM.prg. Call your program COURJOIN.prg.

5. Rewrite the UPGRADE.prg program such that the UPDATE command can be executed without resorting to the RANDOM keyword.

14.13 Term Project

Present your project to the rest of the class. Outline what your system does, what the databases are that you use. Show the system structure chart of your system. Step through your menu showing the class what each part of your system does. Be prepared to answer any questions that the class may have about your project.

APPENDIX A

SETTING UP THE PROPER PATHWAYS AND DIRECTORIES

A.1 Accessing an Already Installed Copy of dBASE IV on Your Hard Drive

If you already have dBASE IV installed on your hard drive and would like to use it, chances are that the directory in which dBASE IV exists is already on the pathway. Put your diskette into drive **A:** and change your default disk drive to **A:** by typing **A:** at the **C>** prompt.

C> A:
A>

Now type **DBASE** at the **A>** prompt.

A> DBASE

If it automatically goes into dBASE IV, then that's fine, there's nothing more left to be done. If it does not, then you need to change the pathway to include the directory in which dBASE IV exists. The "pathway" is where DOS searches for the command when it doesn't find the file it is looking for in the current directory. Since dBASE doesn't exist in the data directory on drive **A:** , we need to be certain that the directory in which dBASE exists is included in the pathway.

If you type:

A> DIR C:

you'll see the root directory of the hard disk drive. Chances are you will see the dBASE IV directory listed there. Probable names for it are: **\DBASE, \DBASE4,** or **\DBASEIV**. Whatever name it has, that's the name that you want to include in the pathway.

Since it does not hurt to include directories in your pathway which are not there, here is a pathway which should work most of the time:

PATH = C:\;C:\DOS;C:\DBASE;C:\DBASE4;C:\DBASEIV

Having executed this command, it now tells the system, that in addition to searching the current directory for any command entered, also check the root directory of the **C:** drive as well as the **\DOS** directory, as well as the dBASE directory regardless of the spelling under which it may appear. Now you should be able to type: **DBASE** at the **A>** prompt and have the system go into dBASE IV.

A> DBASE

These last two steps must be repeated each time you go into dBASE unless you alter the **AUTOEXEC.BAT** file on drive **C:** (or put one in if one does not already exist). Any **AUTOEXEC.BAT** file should include a pathway command similar to the one shown above which includes the directory containing dBASE IV.

A.2 Creating An AUTOEXEC.BAT file that Establishes the Proper Pathway

An **AUTOEXEC.BAT** file may be produced by first returning to the root directory of drive **C:** . This is done by typing:

A> C:
C> CD \

Now that you are in the root directory of drive **C:** , type **DIR** to be sure that no **AUTOEXEC.BAT** file already exists. If none exists, then type:

C> COPY CON:AUTOEXEC.BAT
PATH = C:\;C:\DOS;C:\DBASE;C:\DBASE4;C:\DBASEIV
PROMPT = pg

APPENDIX A

Now strike the **F6** key followed by the **Enter** key and your **AUTOEXEC.BAT** file is created.

If an **AUTOEXEC.BAT** file does exist, then it should be modified by making sure that the PATH command contained in the AUTOEXEC.BAT file has all the pathways included above. If it does not, these pathways should be added to whatever pathways already exist. (Note that the PROMPT command has also been included. The purpose of this command is to let the DOS prompt tell us what drive and directory we are in at any time.)

The most straightforward way of modifying an already existing AUTOEXEC.BAT file is by typing out whatever is currently in it, and then re-entering it with the modifications given above. One may type out the contents of the AUTOEXEC.BAT file by typing:

```
C> TYPE AUTOEXEC.BAT
XXXXXXXXXXXXXXXXXXXXXXXXXX
PATH = XXXXXXXXXXXXXXXXXXXX
XXXXXXXXXXXXXXXXXXXXXXXXXXX
XXXXXXXXXXXXXXXXXXXXXXXXXXX
```

The X's represent whatever is already contained in the file AUTOEXEC.BAT. Note that we assume that some PATH statement already exists. Now simply type:

```
C>  COPY CON: AUTOEXEC.BAT
XXXXXXXXXXXXXXX
PATH=XXXXXXXXXX;C:\DBASE;C:\DBASE4;C:\DBASEIV
XXXXXXXXXXXXXXX
XXXXXXXXXXXXXXX
PROMPT = $p$g
```

The X's represent whatever was in the original AUTOEXEC.BAT file plus the **C:\DBASE;C:\DBASE4;C:\DBASEIV** pathways to the PATH command and the **PROMPT = pg** command. Now strike the **F6** key followed by the **Enter** key, and your new **AUTOEXEC.BAT** file is created.

A.3 Creating a CONFIG.SYS file that Establishes the Proper System Config

Finally, you should check to be sure that you have a **CONFIG.SYS** file. This is a file that initially configures your computer so that it may be able to perform in the most optimal way with the software that you use.

Once more, type **DIR**, at the DOS prompt, to be sure that no **CONFIG.SYS** file already exists. If none exists, then type:

```
C> COPY CON: CONFIG.SYS
   FILES = 99
   BUFFERS = 15
```

Now strike the **F6** key followed by the **Enter** key, and your new **CONFIG.SYS** file is created.

If the CONFIG.SYS file already exists, then use the method you used with the AUTOEXEC.BAT file above to modify your CONFIG.SYS.

The **FILES=99** command allows dBASE to have as many as ninety nine files open simultaneously. This is a minimum number and can be increased. Likewise the **BUFFERS=15** is also a minimum number. Each Buffer represents 528 bytes of memory. This allows memory to be set aside to hold data from the disk so that everytime a new character is needed from a file the operation does not have to go back to the disk for it. This speeds up operation significantly.

In order to make use of your **AUTOEXEC.BAT** and your **CONFIG.SYS** files, however, you must reboot (depress the keys marked: **Ctrl**, **Alt**, and **Del** simultaneously). Having done this, you may now go to any directory or drive that you choose, and execute **DBASE** and the system should go into dBASE IV with the current drive and directory being the default drive and directory.

APPENDIX A

A.4 Creating the Proper Directories

Put your diskette into drive **A:** and change your default disk drive to **A:** by typing **A:** at the **C>** prompt.

C:\> **A:**
A:\>

We will now create the four directories that we will need in the course of this textbook: **COMPCLAS, ACCOUNTS, MAILIST,** and **PROJECT**. This is done by means of the Make Directory command. Typing the following at the DOS prompt:

A:\> **MD \COMPCLAS**
A:\> **MD \ACCOUNTS**
A:\> **MD \MAILIST**
A:\> **MD \PROJECT**

We have now created the four directories in which we will be doing all the work that we do in this text.

APPENDIX B

FREE FORM REPORTS

B.1 The Free Form Report

So far we have made: 1) a columnar report which gave us one record per row; 2) a mailmerge report which gave us one record per page; 3) a label form report which gave us a multiple line printout of each record with no regard to page breaks. The final report, which completes the set, is the free form report which gives us a multiple line printout of each record with normal page formatting (including page breaks).

Quite often we want to print out more information from each record in our database than will fit onto one line. In such cases, the columnar report will no longer suffice, and we have to move to a free form report.

Our COMPCLAS database is now a case in point. Suppose we want to print out the contents of every field of each record. With a record containing field widths totalling 102 characters, all this information will not fit on a standard 80 column page printout[53].

The Report Form Generator has a remaining quick layout item called the "Form Layout". Let's go into the Report Form Generator calling our new report form: FREEFORM.FRM.

. CREATE REPORT FREEFORM

Now let us immediately choose the "Layout" menu option pressing **Alt-L** and then select the "Form Layout" menu item as

---

[53]Of course if we used a wide carriage printer, or if we used compressed print we could make it all fit. However, if the database is large enough, none of these techniques will work.

shown in Figure B.1. The result is shown in Figure B.2. Notice that rather than one row per record, as in the columnar report, there is one row per field. In this manner, a record of virtually any size can be printed out.

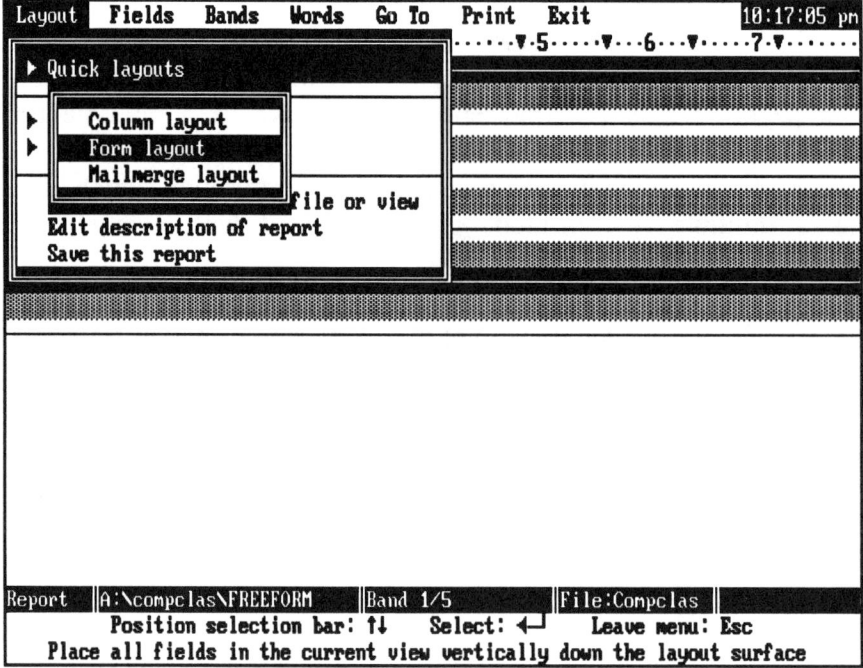

Figure B.1 Selecting "Form layout" in the Report Form Generator

We could accept this particular layout as is. However, it tends to bunch all the information on the left side of the paper, thus wasting space and paper. We can compress this a bit by putting two fields per line. We could have done this from scratch in much the same way as we built the columnar report, but it is also quite easy to move all the existing fields into the spaces where you want them to be.

Let's begin by moving the LASTNAME field over to column 52. We do this in the standard way we learned in Chapter 4 (Press the keys: **F6**; Enter; **F7**, move cursor to desired position; Enter). Similarly, the Field Name can also be moved (using the **F6** key and

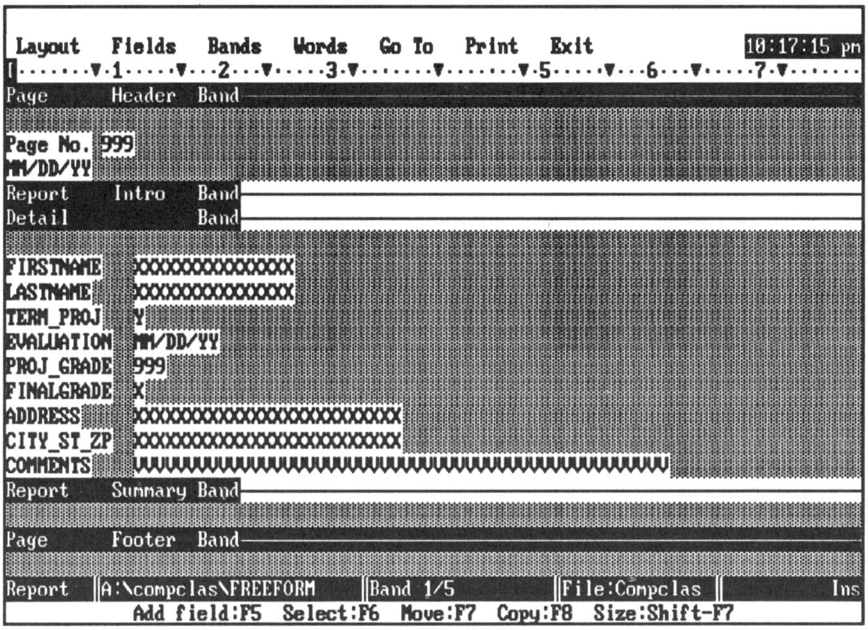

APPENDIX B 571

Figure B.2 The "Form layout" created by Report Form Generator

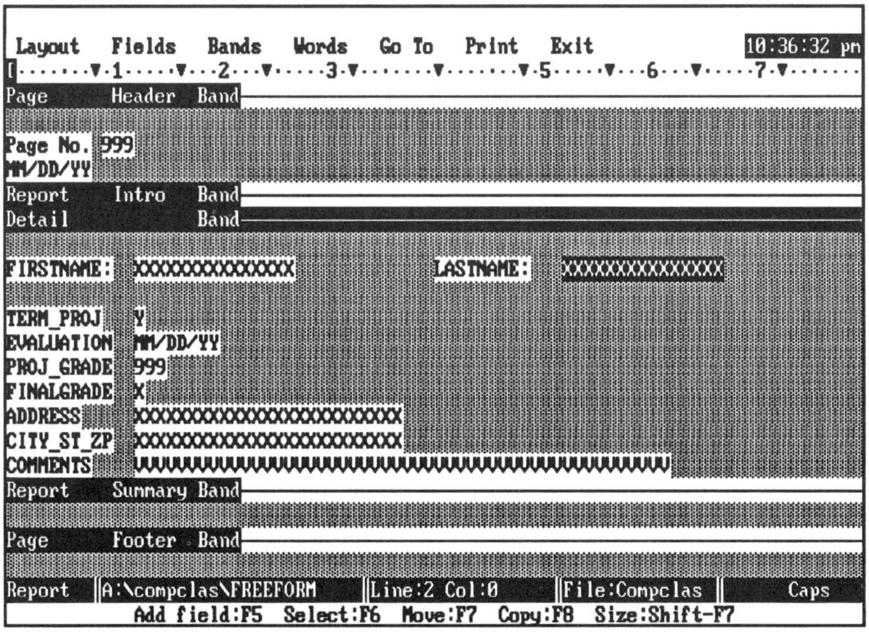

Figure B.3 Moving LASTNAME field to new position at column 52

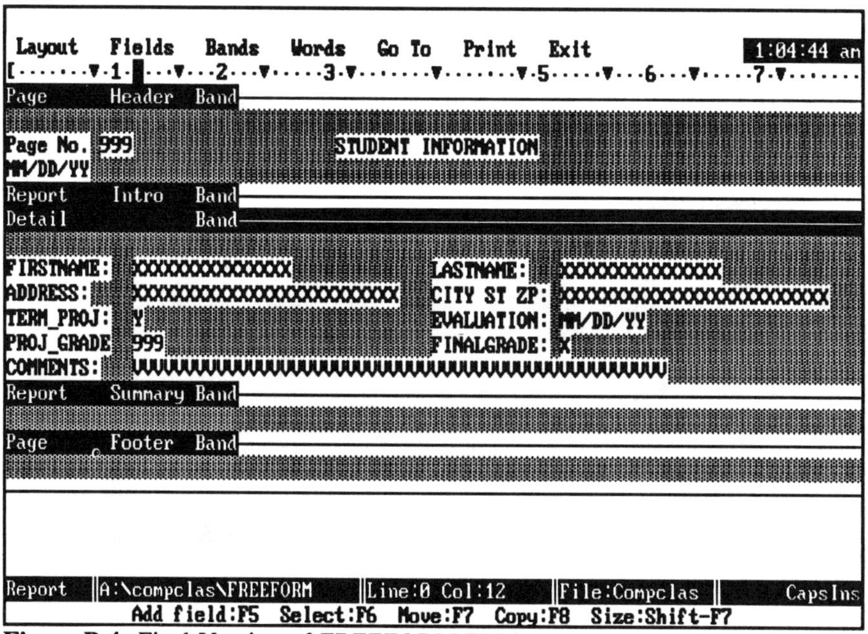

Figure B.4 Final Version of FREEFORM.FRM

the arrow key to extend the selection for the entire field name; Enter; **F7,** move cursor to desired position; Enter). Moving the field name from the old position to the new, we get the screen shown in Figure B.3.

In the same way, we can move the ADDRESS, CITY_ST_ZP fields to the next line, the TERM_PROJ and EVALUATION fields to the next line, and the PROJ_GRADE and FINALGRADE fields to the following line. Extra lines can be deleted with the **Ctrl-Y** keystroke pair. New lines can be inserted with the **Ctrl-N** keystroke pair. The result of doing all this moving is shown in Figure B.4. Note that we have added a title to the report form thus completing FREEFORM.FRM. Executing the command:

. REPORT FORM FREEFORM TO PRINT

produces the report which is shown in Listings B.1a and B.1b.

Notice that the COMMENT line at the bottom of the report form uses a series of **V**'s in its template to indicate where the text

```
Page No.   1                    STUDENT INFORMATION
03/03/91

FIRSTNAME:  Gladys                  LASTNAME:   Naboa
ADDRESS:    324 Catskill Terrace    CITY ST ZP: Sundown, NY  12782
TERM_PROJ:  Y                       EVALUATION: 12/15/92
PROJ_GRADE  93                      FINALGRADE:
COMMENTS:   Gladys does superior work.  She seems to be very
            highly motivated.

FIRSTNAME:  Consuelo                LASTNAME:   Naboa
ADDRESS:    324 Catskill Terrace    CITY ST ZP: Sundown, NY  12782
TERM_PROJ:  Y                       EVALUATION: 12/16/92
PROJ_GRADE  89                      FINALGRADE:
COMMENTS:   Consuelo would have had a clear "A" on her Term
            Project, but she misspelled 6 words.  She should
            consult her dictionary more.

FIRSTNAME:  Derek                   LASTNAME:   Caruthers
ADDRESS:    21 Spring Glen Road     CITY ST ZP: Cooks Falls, NY  12728
TERM_PROJ:  N                       EVALUATION:   /  /
PROJ_GRADE  0                       FINALGRADE:
COMMENTS:   Derek elected to take the Final instead.

FIRSTNAME:  Wendel                  LASTNAME:   Little
ADDRESS:    1021 Cochecton Street   CITY ST ZP: Jeffersonville, NY 12748
TERM_PROJ:  Y                       EVALUATION: 12/17/92
PROJ_GRADE  87                      FINALGRADE:
COMMENTS:

FIRSTNAME:  Jeremy                  LASTNAME:   Witherspoon
ADDRESS:    821 Kiamesha Circle     CITY ST ZP: Glen Spey, NY  12737
TERM_PROJ:  Y                       EVALUATION: 12/19/92
PROJ_GRADE  82                      FINALGRADE:
COMMENTS:   Jeremy is bright, but he's just a little sloppy in
            his work.  If he would take more time to be
            precise, he would do "A" work.

FIRSTNAME:  Nancy                   LASTNAME:   Hardwick
ADDRESS:    512 Delaware Overlook   CITY ST ZP: Callicoon, NY  12723
TERM_PROJ:  N                       EVALUATION:   /  /
PROJ_GRADE  0                       FINALGRADE:
COMMENTS:   Nancy elected to take the Final.
```

Listing B.1a First page of COMPCLAS report generated by FREEFORM.FRM

data will go, rather than **X**'s. This is to indicate that the field width is limited to a width shown on the screen. Any characters beyond this limit will be wrapped around to the line immediately below that line and will continue on until the field contents are exhausted.

As you can see examining the report output, the Memo field contents does indeed wrap itself according to the template width formed by the **V**'s. Note that for records where there is something entered in the Memo field that there is sometimes a two space gap between adjacent records (and sometimes not), whereas there is only a one space gap between records in which there is nothing in the Memo field. This seems to be simply an anomaly of dBASE IV.

```
Page No.   2                    STUDENT INFORMATION
03/03/91


FIRSTNAME:  Jonathan                    LASTNAME:    Samuels
ADDRESS:    96 Rainbow's End            CITY ST ZP:  Roscoe, NY   12776
TERM_PROJ:  Y                           EVALUATION:  12/14/92
PROJ_GRADE  76                          FINALGRADE:
COMMENTS:

FIRSTNAME:  Matts                       LASTNAME:    Engleberg
ADDRESS:    2021 Mountain View          CITY ST ZP:  Mountaindale, NY  12758
TERM_PROJ:  Y                           EVALUATION:  12/13/92
PROJ_GRADE  62                          FINALGRADE:
COMMENTS:

FIRSTNAME:  Mary Beth                   LASTNAME:    Swazey
ADDRESS:    85 Cider Mill Lane          CITY ST ZP:  North Branch, NY  12766
TERM_PROJ:  Y                           EVALUATION:  12/14/92
PROJ_GRADE  52                          FINALGRADE:
COMMENTS:    Mary Beth clearly did not put any effort into her
             project.  Her attendance has been very spotty
             also.

FIRSTNAME:  Mary                        LASTNAME:    Wong
ADDRESS:    321 Lakeside Avenue         CITY ST ZP:  Swan Lake, NY  12783
TERM_PROJ:  N                           EVALUATION:  12/20/92
PROJ_GRADE  85                          FINALGRADE:
COMMENTS:
```

Listing B.1b Second Page of COMPCLAS report generated by FREEFORM.FRM

What we've seen is that we can have flexibility in creating whatever form of report that we would like using the report form generator.

APPENDIX C

QUERY BY EXAMPLE

C.1 Creation of Simple Queries

The query by example file allows you to make queries that will create whatever search conditions that you might want. Its chief advantage is that the user does not have to know how to program in dBASE IV. All the user has to do is to follow the steps outlined in Appendix C and a query can be easily generated.

Supposing we wish to create some queries on the database COMPCLAS. We will begin by opening the database COMPCLAS.dbf and then going into the query generator:

. USE COMPCLAS
. CREATE QUERY COMPCLAS

Note that we have given the query the name **COMPCLAS.QBE** (the extensions of queries by example is **.QBE**). Figure C.1 shows the screen that results.

Now suppose that we wish to create a query view file that only selects records of those people having a last name of "Naboa". This is done by simply typing "Naboa" in the box labeled "LASTNAME" as shown in Figure C.2. Striking the "F2" key, we immediately go into the BROWSE mode and we find that we have the records displayed of only the "Naboa" sisters (See Figure C.3).

If you wish to have a query view file that selects only those students who turned in Term Projects, then we need to put a **.T.** in the TERM_PROJ field box, as shown in Figure C.4. Striking the "F2" key and going into Browse mode, we see the records of only those students who actually turned in their term project (See Figure C.5)

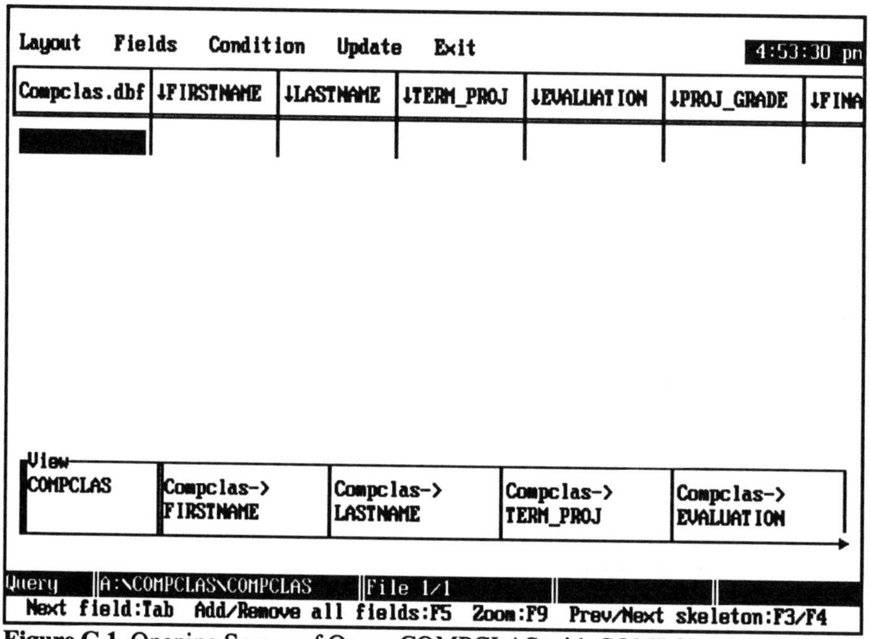

Figure C.1 Opening Screen of Query COMPCLAS with COMPCLAS.dbf already opened

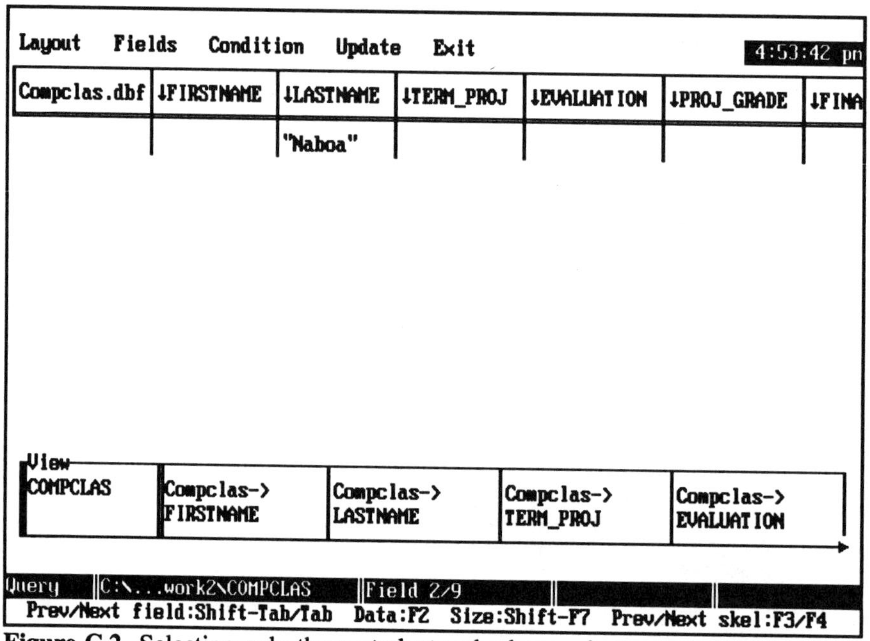

Figure C.2 Selecting only those students who have a last name of "Naboa"

APPENDIX C

```
┌─────────────────────────────────────────────────────────────────────┐
│ Records   Organize   Fields   Go To   Exit                          │
├──────────┬──────────┬─────────┬──────────┬──────────┬──────────┬────┤
│FIRSTNAME │LASTNAME  │TERM_PROJ│EVALUATION│PROJ_GRADE│FINALGRADE│ADD │
├──────────┼──────────┼─────────┼──────────┼──────────┼──────────┼────┤
│ Gladys   │ Naboa    │ T       │ 12/15/92 │    93    │          │    │
│ Consuelo │ Naboa    │ T       │ 12/16/92 │    89    │          │    │
│                                                                     │
└─────────────────────────────────────────────────────────────────────┘
 Browse  A:\COMPCLAS\COMPCLAS   Rec 1/10       View
```

Figure C.3 Browse of Records selected by Query where "Naboa" was stipulated for the "LASTNAME"

```
┌─────────────────────────────────────────────────────────────────────┐
│ Layout   Fields   Condition   Update   Exit           4:54:45 pm    │
├────────────┬─────────┬─────────┬─────────┬──────────┬──────────┬────┤
│Compclas.dbf│↓FIRSTNAME│↓LASTNAME│↓TERM_PROJ│↓EVALUATION│↓PROJ_GRADE│↓FINA│
├────────────┼─────────┼─────────┼─────────┼──────────┼──────────┼────┤
│            │         │         │   .T.   │          │          │    │
│                                                                     │
│ ┌View──────────                                                     │
│ │COMPCLAS    │Compclas->│Compclas->│Compclas->│Compclas->│         │
│ │            │FIRSTNAME │LASTNAME  │TERM_PROJ │EVALUATION│         │
└─────────────────────────────────────────────────────────────────────┘
 Query  A:\COMPCLAS\COMPCLAS   Field 3/9
  Prev/Next field:Shift-Tab/Tab  Data:F2  Size:Shift-F7  Prev/Next skel:F3/F4
```

Figure C.4 Selecting only those students who turned in Term Projects

Records	Organize	Fields	Go To	Exit		
FIRSTNAME	LASTNAME	TERM_PROJ	EVALUATION	PROJ_GRADE	FINALGRADE	ADD
Gladys	Naboa	T	12/15/92	93		
Consuelo	Naboa	T	12/16/92	89		
Wendel	Little	T	12/17/92	87		
Jeremy	Witherspoon	T	12/19/92	82		
Jonathan	Samuels	T	12/14/92	76		
Matts	Engleberg	T	12/13/92	62		
Mary Beth	Swazey	T	12/14/92	52		
Mary	Wong	T	12/28/92	85		

Browse A:\COMPCLAS\COMPCLAS Rec 1/10 View

Figure C.5 Browse of Query View File that was created by placing .T. in the TERM_PROJ box

If we want to query all those people who have an evaluation date of "12/14/92", then we insert that date (in braces) in the EVALUATION field box as shown in Figure C.6. The resulting Browse is shown in Figure C.7

Finally, if we are interested in all those people who got passing grades on their Term Project (PROJ_GRADE >= 60), we simply put the expression: **>=60** into the PROJ_GRADE box as shown in Figure C.8. The resulting browse of the query is shown in Figure C.9.

APPENDIX C

```
Layout   Fields   Condition   Update   Exit                          4:55:43 pm
┌─────────────┬──────────┬──────────┬──────────┬──────────┬──────────┬──────┐
│Compclas.dbf │↓FIRSTNAME│↓LASTNAME │↓TERM_PROJ│↓EVALUATION│↓PROJ_GRADE│↓FINA│
├─────────────┼──────────┼──────────┼──────────┼──────────┼──────────┼──────┤
│             │          │          │          │{12/14/92}│          │      │
│             │          │          │          │          │          │      │
└─────────────┴──────────┴──────────┴──────────┴──────────┴──────────┴──────┘

┌View─────────┬──────────┬──────────┬──────────┬──────────┐
│COMPCLAS     │Compclas->│Compclas->│Compclas->│Compclas->│
│             │FIRSTNAME │LASTNAME  │TERM_PROJ │EVALUATION│
└─────────────┴──────────┴──────────┴──────────┴──────────┘

Query   A:\COMPCLAS\COMPCLAS     Field 4/9
Prev/Next field:Shift-Tab/Tab  Data:F2  Size:Shift-F7  Prev/Next skel:F3/F4
```

Figure C.6 Selecting those records with an Evaluation Date of "12/14/92"

```
Records   Organize   Fields   Go To   Exit
┌──────────┬──────────┬──────────┬──────────┬──────────┬──────────┬───┐
│FIRSTNAME │LASTNAME  │TERM_PROJ │EVALUATION│PROJ_GRADE│FINALGRADE│ADD│
├──────────┼──────────┼──────────┼──────────┼──────────┼──────────┼───┤
│Jonathan  │Samuels   │T         │12/14/92  │    76    │          │   │
│Mary Beth │Swazey    │T         │12/14/92  │    52    │          │   │
└──────────┴──────────┴──────────┴──────────┴──────────┴──────────┴───┘

Browse   A:\COMPCLAS\COMPCLAS     Rec 7/10      View
```

Figure C.7 Browse of Query for those people having an Evaluation Date of "12/14/92"

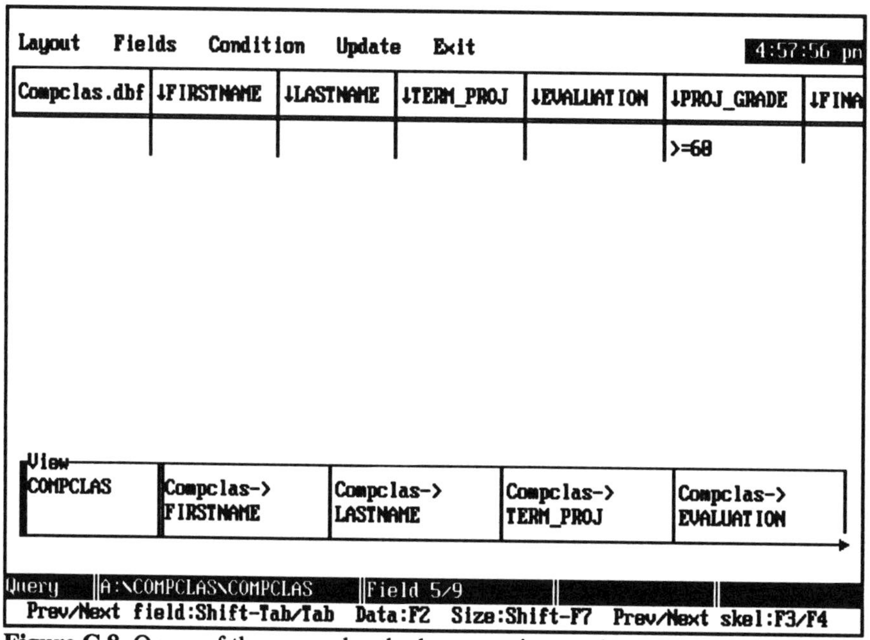

580 APPENDIX C

Layout	Fields	Condition	Update	Exit		4:57:56 pm
Compclas.dbf	↓FIRSTNAME	↓LASTNAME	↓TERM_PROJ	↓EVALUATION	↓PROJ_GRADE	↓FINA
					>=68	

View—
| COMPCLAS | Compclas-> FIRSTNAME | Compclas-> LASTNAME | Compclas-> TERM_PROJ | Compclas-> EVALUATION |

Query ‖ A:\COMPCLAS\COMPCLAS ‖ Field 5/9
Prev/Next field:Shift-Tab/Tab   Data:F2   Size:Shift-F7   Prev/Next skel:F3/F4

Figure C.8 Query of those people who have passing marks on their Term Projects

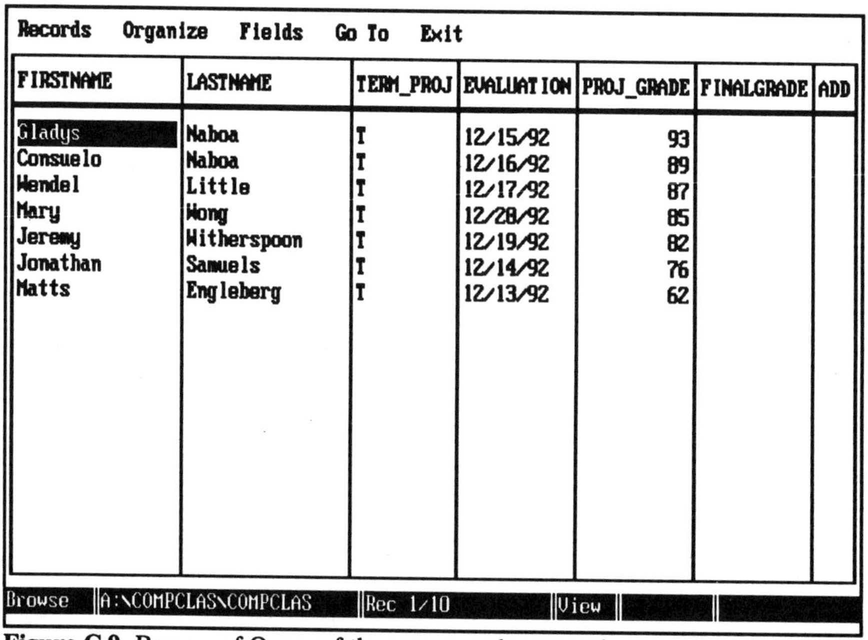

Records	Organize	Fields	Go To	Exit		
FIRSTNAME	LASTNAME	TERM_PROJ	EVALUATION	PROJ_GRADE	FINALGRADE	ADD
Gladys	Naboa	T	12/15/92	93		
Consuelo	Naboa	T	12/16/92	89		
Wendel	Little	T	12/17/92	87		
Mary	Wong	T	12/28/92	85		
Jeremy	Witherspoon	T	12/19/92	82		
Jonathan	Samuels	T	12/14/92	76		
Matts	Engleberg	T	12/13/92	62		

Browse ‖ A:\COMPCLAS\COMPCLAS ‖ Rec 1/10 ‖ View

Figure C.9 Browse of Query of those persons have passing grades on their Term Project

C.2 Queries With More Than One Condition in an AND Relationship

Let us now look at the case where we have several conditions that we would like to "AND" together. Suppose we were interested in all those people with passing grades less than 91 and who had Evaluation dates of between "12/18/92" and "12/20/92". The way we would enter this in a query is shown in Figure C.10. Note that the range of grades >=60 and grades <91 are simply separated by a comma. The same is true for the range of dates.

The rule is: Multiple conditions in the same field, to be ANDed, are separated by commas. Multiple conditions with different fields, to be ANDed, are listed on the same line. In this example, the only two people meeting all four criteria are shown in Figure C.11.

C.3 Queries With More Than One Condition in an OR Relationship

Supposing we would like to create multiple conditions for including records in our query where any record satisfying any one of the criteria is included. This is an inclusive OR condition. This type of query comes in two varieties: 1) those whose inclusive OR conditions are all contained in the same field; and 2) those whose inclusive OR conditions are contained within separate fields. Let's consider the first case first:

C.3.1 Queries With Inclusive OR Conditions Existing in the Same Field

Specifically, suppose we are interested in seeing those people who have either of the two evaluation dates "12/13/92" or "12/20/92". The way this is done is shown in Figure C.12.

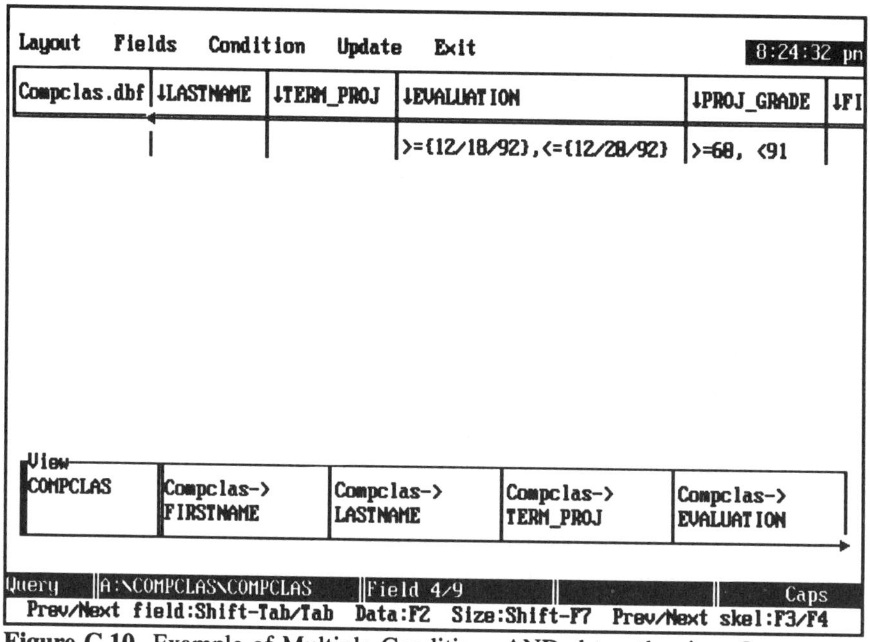

582   APPENDIX C

```
Layout   Fields   Condition   Update   Exit                        8:24:32 pm
Compclas.dbf  ↓LASTNAME  ↓TERM_PROJ  ↓EVALUATION              ↓PROJ_GRADE  ↓FI
                                     >={12/18/92},<={12/28/92}  >=68, <91


  ┌View────
  │COMPCLAS    Compclas->      Compclas->      Compclas->      Compclas->
              FIRSTNAME       LASTNAME        TERM_PROJ       EVALUATION

Query    A:\COMPCLAS\COMPCLAS   Field 4/9                              Caps
      Prev/Next field:Shift-Tab/Tab  Data:F2  Size:Shift-F7  Prev/Next skel:F3/F4
```

Figure C.10   Example of Multiple Conditions ANDed together in a Query

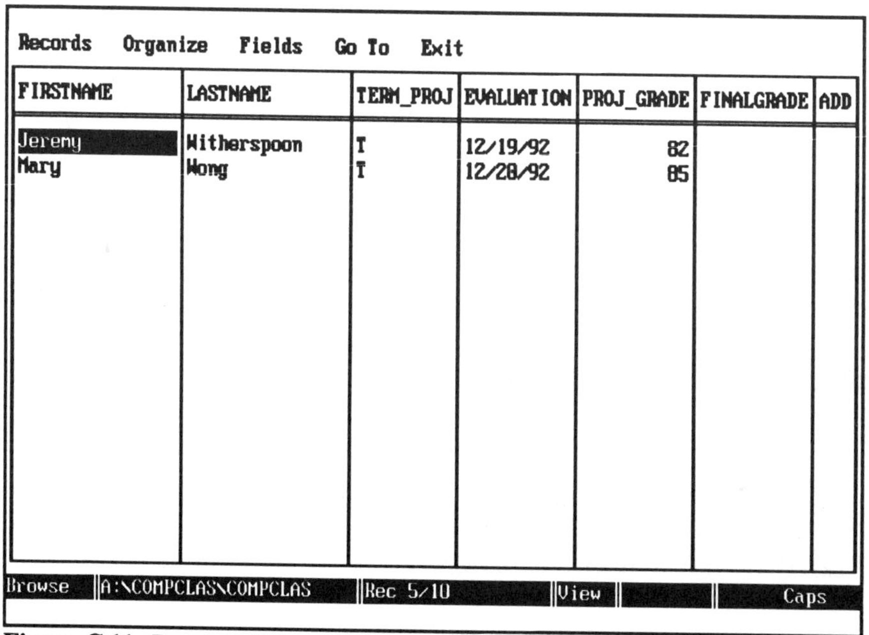

```
Records   Organize   Fields   Go To   Exit
FIRSTNAME    LASTNAME      TERM_PROJ  EVALUATION  PROJ_GRADE  FINALGRADE  ADD
Jeremy       Witherspoon   T          12/19/92    82
Mary         Wong          T          12/28/92    85




Browse   A:\COMPCLAS\COMPCLAS   Rec 5/10          View                    Caps
```

Figure C.11   Browse of Query with Multiple Conditions ANDed Together

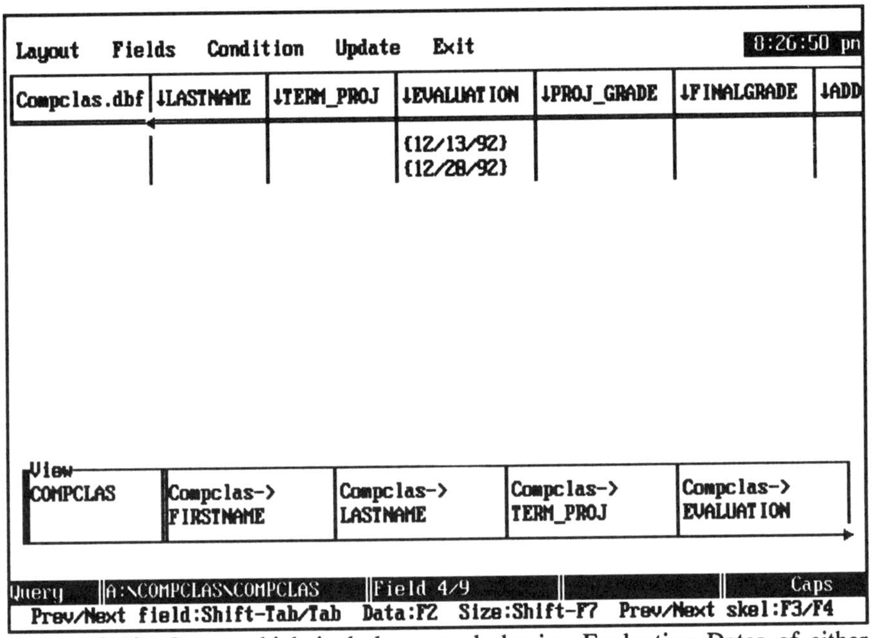

```
 Layout    Fields   Condition   Update   Exit                    8:26:50 pm
┌────────────┬──────────┬───────────┬────────────┬────────────┬────────────┬─────
│Compclas.dbf│↓LASTNAME │↓TERM_PROJ │↓EVALUATION │↓PROJ_GRADE │↓FINALGRADE │↓ADD
│            │          │           │{12/13/92}  │            │            │
│            │          │           │{12/28/92}  │            │            │
```

┌View─────────┬─────────────┬─────────────┬─────────────┬─────────────┐
│COMPCLAS   │Compclas->   │Compclas->   │Compclas->   │Compclas->   │
│   │FIRSTNAME   │LASTNAME   │TERM_PROJ   │EVALUATION   │
└─────────────┴─────────────┴─────────────┴─────────────┴─────────────┘

 Query   A:\COMPCLAS\COMPCLAS   Field 4/9   Caps
  Prev/Next field:Shift-Tab/Tab Data:F2 Size:Shift-F7 Prev/Next skel:F3/F4

Figure C.12 Query which includes records having Evaluation Dates of either "12/13/92" OR "12/20/92"

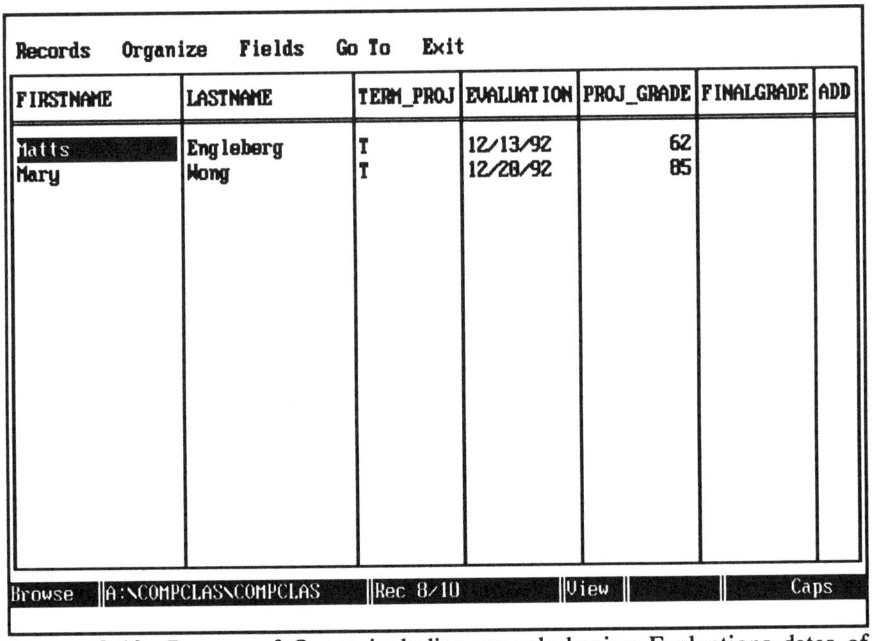

 Records   Organize   Fields   Go To   Exit
┌───────────┬───────────┬──────────┬───────────┬───────────┬───────────┬─────┐
│FIRSTNAME │LASTNAME   │TERM_PROJ │EVALUATION │PROJ_GRADE │FINALGRADE │ADD │
├───────────┼───────────┼──────────┼───────────┼───────────┼───────────┼─────┤
│Matts   │Engleberg │T   │12/13/92   │   62   │   │   │
│Mary   │Wong   │T   │12/28/92   │   85   │   │   │
└───────────┴───────────┴──────────┴───────────┴───────────┴───────────┴─────┘

 Browse   A:\COMPCLAS\COMPCLAS   Rec 8/10   View   Caps

Figure C.13 Browse of Query including records having Evaluations dates of "12/13/92" OR "12/20/92"

Note that simply by striking the down arrow key we may add as many inclusive OR conditions as we like. The browse of this query is shown in Figure C.13.

C.3.2 Queries With Inclusive OR Conditions Existing in Different Fields

The principle here is the same as the first case, ORed conditions are placed on separate lines. The only difference is the field box in which they are placed is different. For example, supposing we were interested in those people who had an evaluation date of "12/13/92", OR who had a PROJ_GRADE greater than 90. Figure C.14 shows how we create this ORed condition. Figure C.15 shows the browse of the result.

The underlying principle is that ORed conditions are placed on separate lines while ANDed conditions are placed on the same line (and are separated by commas if the ANDed conditions exist within the same field).

APPENDIX C 585

```
 Layout   Fields   Condition   Update   Exit            8:33:10 pm
┌─────────────┬──────────┬──────────┬───────────┬──────────┬───────────┬─────┐
│Compclas.dbf │↓LASTNAME │↓TERM_PROJ│↓EVALUATION│↓PROJ_GRADE│↓FINALGRADE│↓ADD│
│             │          │          │{12/13/92} │           │           │    │
│             │          │          │           │>90        │           │    │
│             │          │          │           │           │           │    │
│                                                                            │
│ ┌View──────────────────────────────────────────────────────────────────┐   │
│ │COMPCLAS │Compclas->│Compclas-> │Compclas-> │Compclas->              │   │
│ │         │FIRSTNAME │LASTNAME   │TERM_PROJ  │EVALUATION              │   │
└─┴─────────┴──────────┴───────────┴───────────┴────────────────────────┴───┘
 Query    A:\COMPCLAS\COMPCLAS    Field 5/9                         Caps
 Prev/Next field:Shift-Tab/Tab  Data:F2  Size:Shift-F7  Prev/Next skel:F3/F4
```

Figure C.14 Query of those people who have an Evaluation date of "12/13/92" OR who have a grade >90

```
 Records   Organize   Fields   Go To   Exit
┌───────────┬──────────┬──────────┬──────────┬──────────┬──────────┬─────┐
│FIRSTNAME  │LASTNAME  │TERM_PROJ │EVALUATION│PROJ_GRADE│FINALGRADE│ADD  │
├───────────┼──────────┼──────────┼──────────┼──────────┼──────────┼─────┤
│Gladys     │Naboa     │T         │12/15/92  │    93    │          │     │
│Matts      │Engleberg │T         │12/13/92  │    62    │          │     │
│           │          │          │          │          │          │     │
└───────────┴──────────┴──────────┴──────────┴──────────┴──────────┴─────┘
 Browse    A:\COMPCLAS\COMPCLAS   Rec 1/10      View            Caps
```

Figure C.15 Browse of Query of those people having an Evaluation date of "12/13/92" OR a grade >90

INDEX

A

@, 239, 240
ACCEPT, 279
ACTIVATE, 340
ACTIVATE MENU, 253
ACTIVATE WINDOW, 347
Alt, 13
ANSI, 265
APPEND, 15
APPEND BLANK, 487
Argument, 87, 394
Arguments, 509
Arrays, 511
ASCII, 440
ASSIST, 8
AUTOEXEC.BAT, 564
AVERAGE, 172
AVG(), 173, 181

B

Band
  Detail, 107
  Group, 133
  Group intro, 134
  Group summary, 134
  Page Footer, 107
  Page Header, 107
  Report Intro, 107
  Report Summary, 107
BAR(), 346
Boilerplate, 194
Bottom Up, 452
BROWSE, 19, 50
  FIELD, 52
  Freeze, 58
  Lock, 56
BUFFERS, 566

C

CD, 7
CDOW(), 199
CLEAR, 230
Clipper, 432
CLOSE DATA, 479
CNT(), 173
Columnar, 104
Command File, 226
Compile, 105, 219, 227, 229
Concatenation, 83
CONFIG.DB, 374
CONFIG.SYS, 566
Connector, 265
Contents list, 428
Control center, 8
COPY, 390
COPY FILE, 141
COPY TO ARRAY, 512
COUNT, 168
CREATE, 10
CREATE LABEL, 184
CREATE QUERY, 532
CREATE REPORT, 106
CREATE SCREEN, 206
CTOD(), 164

D

DATADICT.DOC, 442
DBASE II, 432
DBASE III, 432
DBF, 105
DBMS, 73
DBSETUP.EXE, 380
DBT, 105
DEACTIVATE MENU, 252, 253
DEBUG, 404

Decision, 265
DECLARE, 511
DEFINE BAR, 340
DEFINE MENU, 250
DEFINE PAD, 251
DEFINE POPUP, 340
DEFINE WINDOW, 347
DELETE, 41
Descending, 76, 91, 98
DIR, 78
DISKCOPY, 389
DISPLAY ALL, 39
Display Attributes, 116
DISPLAY MEMORY, 233, 281
DISPLAY STRUCTURE, 281
DO CASE, 273
Do Until Loop, 483
DO WHILE, 297
DO WHILE .T., 486
DOS, 6
DTOC(), 167
DTOS(), 87

E

EDIT, 18
ENDSCAN, 321
ENDTEXT, 421
EOF(), 244, 305
ERASE, 79
Error
　runtime, 404, 411
　syntax, 404
EXCLUSIVE, xxi, 375, 377, 386
EXIT, 486
Extension
　.DBO, 229
　.FMO, 219
　.FMT, 219
　.LBG, 184
　.LBL, 184
　.LBO, 184
　.MDX, 83
　.NDX, 80

　.PRG, 229
　.QBE, 530, 532, 575
　.SCR, 219

F

Field
　Calculated, 141, 199
　Character, 10
　Date, 10
　Floating point, 10
　Logical, 10
　Memo, 10
　Numeric, 10
　Predefined, 120, 196
FILE(), 488
FILES, 566
FIND, 176
Flow Charts, 264
FOR, 99
FOR clause, 158
Format File, 219
FOUND(), 316
Foxplus, 432
FoxPro, 432
Free form, 104
Function, 87, 494, 508

G

GET, 241

H

Hidden 144

I

IIF(,,), 89
IIF(), 244
INDEX, 73, 79, 81

INDEX

INPUT, 265, 278
INSERT, 47
INSERT BEFORE, 48

J

JOIN, 551

L

Label Form Generator, 184
LEN(), 422
LIKE(,), 166
Line
  Navigation, 36
  Status, 36
LINENO(), 405
LIST, 26
LOCATE, 174, 243
LOCATE WHILE, 315
Logical Operator, 158
Loop, 263
LTRIM(), 556

M

Machine language, 229
Macro, 394, 464
Mailmerge, 104, 194
MAX(), 173
MD, 567
Memory File, 459
Memory Variables
  System, 233
  User Defined, 232
Menu, 13
MESSAGE, 251
MIN(), 173
MODIFY COMMAND, 226
MODIFY LABEL, 190

MODIFY REPORT, 118
MODIFY SCREEN, 213
MODIFY STRUCTURE, 36

N

Narrative of System Function, 428
Natural order, 94
Norton Editor, 379

O

Object Code, 360
ON KEY LABEL, 419, 423
ON PAD, 340
ON SELECTION PAD, 251
Output, 265

P

PACK, 46, 230
Parameters, 509
Pathway, 563
PICTURE, 241, 494
PRIVATE, 515
PROCEDURE, 354
Procedure file, 508
Process, 264
Program, 229
Program listing, 428
Program Structure Chart, 351, 456
Program Structure Diagram, 427
PROGRAM(), 409
Programming
  Structured, 262
PROMPT, 565
Prototyping, 336
Pseudo Compiler, 360
PUBLIC, 515

Q

Queries By Example, 530
Query, 528, 530
Query By Example, 575
Query Generator, 528, 530
Query Update, 556
QUIT, 28

R

READ, 241
RECALL, 45
RECCOUNT(), 512
Reconcile, 468
Reconciliation, 457
Record Selection, 158
Relational Operator, 158
RELEASE, 282
RELEASE ALL, 282
REPLACE, 282
Report, 104
  Free Form, 569
  Mailmerge, 194
  Columnar, 104
REPORT FORM, 118, 202
Report Form Generator, 104
RESTORE, 281
RESTORE SCREEN, 346
RETURN, 253
Root directory, 7
RTRIM(), 556
RUN, 391
RUNTIME, 360

S

SAVE, 281
SAVE SCREEN, 346
SAY, 239
SCAN, 321
SCAN FOR, 328
Search
  Backward, 65
  Forward, 65
SEEK, 176
SELECT, 465, 479
Selecting Records, 158
Selection, 263
SET, 368
SET COLOR TO, 373
SET CONFIRM ON, 368
SET CONSOLE OFF, 387
SET CONSOLE ON, 387
SET DIRECTORY TO, 123
SET FILTER, 162
SET FORMAT, 219
SET PROCEDURE TO, 354, 359
SET RELATION TO, 477
SET TRAP ON, 411
Simple sequence, 262
SKIP, 305
SKIP n, 465
SORT, 73
Source Code, 229, 360
SPACE(), 243
Spread, 469
STD(), 173
STORE, 232
Structure
  Iteration, 263, 296
  Loop, 296
  Selection, 263
Stubs, 461
Subtotal, 133
SUM, 170
SUM(), 173
Switches, 368
System Structure Chart, 452
System Structure Diagram, 428, 441
Systems Design
  Bottom Up, 336
  Top Down, 336

T

TAG, 85
Template, 104, 116
TEXT, 421
Top Down, 452
TOTAL, 475
TREE.DOC, 441
TRIM(), 246
TYPE, 248

U

UNIQUE, 98
UPDATE, 554
UPPER(), 246
USE, 17
USE...ORDER..., 309
User friendly, 337
User Instruction Guide, 429
User-Defined Functions, 508

V

VAL(), 482
VAR(), 173

W

WAIT, 230, 280, 320
Wildcard, 166
Window, 13, 241
  ACTIVATE, 347
  DEFINE, 347
WINDOW(), 422
Word Perfect, 391
Word processing, 195
WordStar, 376